BRITAIN'S BIRDS

An identification guide to the birds of Great Britain and Ireland

Rob Hume, Robert Still, Andy Swash, Hugh Harrop and David Tipling

Consultant: Chris Batty

WILDGuides

PRINCETON
press.princeton.edu

Published by Princeton University Press,
41 William Street, Princeton, New Jersey 08540
In the United Kingdom: Princeton University Press, 6 Oxford Street,
Woodstock, Oxfordshire OX20 1TR
press.princeton.edu

Requests for permission to reproduce material from this work should be sent to
Permissions, Princeton University Press

First published 2016
2nd Edition 2020

Copyright © 2016, 2020 Princeton University Press

Copyright in the photographs remains with the individual photographers.

All rights reserved. No part of this publication may be reproduced, stored in a retrieval system, or transmitted, in any form or by any means, electronic, mechanical, photocopying, recording, or otherwise, without the prior permission of the publishers.

British Library Cataloging-in-Publication Data is available

Library of Congress Control Number 2020930980
ISBN 978-0-691-19979-5

Production and design by **WILD**Guides Ltd., Old Basing, Hampshire UK.
Printed in Italy

Published under license from RSPB Sales Ltd. to raise awareness of the Royal Society for the Protection of Birds (Charity registration England and Wales no 207076, Scotland SC037654). For all items sold Princeton University Press will donate a minimum of 40 pence to RSPB Sales Ltd, the trading subsidiary of the RSPB. All subsequent sellers of this book are not commercial participators for the purpose of Part II of the Charities Act 1992.
www.rspb.org.uk

10 9 8 7 6 5 4 3 2 1

Contents

Introduction	4
The parts of a bird	5
How to use this book	6
The species accounts	8
The types of bird	10
Wildfowl (swans, geese, ducks)	16
Waterbirds (cormorants, divers, grebes and pelicans)	76
Seabirds (Gannet, Fulmar, shearwaters, petrels)	93
Auks (puffins, guillemots, Razorbill, murrelets)	106
Gulls and terns	120
Skuas	174
Waders (plovers, sandpipers, curlews, godwits, snipe and related species)	183
Crakes and rails (includes Moorhen, coots, gallinules)	246
Large waterside birds (herons, bitterns, egrets, Spoonbill, cranes, storks, ibis)	255
'Gamebirds' (partridges, grouse, pheasants and Quail)	271
Bustards	280
Pigeons and doves	282
Sandgrouse	284
Owls and nightjars	291
Birds of prey (eagles, kites, Osprey, buzzards, harriers, hawks, falcons and related species)	302
Kingfishers, cuckoos, Hoopoe, bee-eaters, Roller and parrots	336
Woodpeckers	343
Aerial feeders (swifts, swallows, martins)	348
Larks, pipits and wagtails	357
Dipper, Wren, accentors, oriole, starlings and waxwings	378
Thrushes, chats and wheatears	388
Flycatchers	417
Warblers, cisticola and crests	422
Shrikes	458
Tits, nuthatches and 'creepers'	465
Corvids (crows, Jay, Magpie, Nutcracker)	478
Sparrows and finches	488
Buntings	510
Vagrant landbirds from North America	524
Birds of uncertain origin and escapes/introductions	538
British & Irish Lists, status and legislation	540
Acknowledgements and photo credits	557
Identification and beyond	566
Index	568

Introduction

This complete, authoritative photographic guide to the wild birds of Britain and Ireland has been fully revised and updated since the first edition in 2016. The opportunity to add more pictures and to improve on some of those used before has been enjoyable and exciting. More than 800 new images have been used. Together with improved reproduction techniques and valuable advice generously given by many people, this has resulted in a substantial advance.

The book now covers all 631 species accepted onto the British and Irish lists up to the end of 2019 and details all the plumages likely to be seen in the region. It also covers one species recorded during 2019 that has not yet been officially added to the Irish list, 15 that are still under review, and four that were clearly one of two or three near-identical species, but not specifically identified. Another 13 species are illustrated. These have been introduced, or escaped from captivity, and have bred in the wild and may become established, or may lead to confusion with regular species.

While many people have helped in various ways, special mention must be made of the contribution made by Chris Batty, who has spent countless hours examining thousands of photographs and verifying the identification, age and sex of the birds shown.

It is these photographs that make this book stand out. While a substantial number were taken by the authors (Harrop, Tipling and Swash), bird photographers worldwide have enthusiastically offered images to help fill the inevitable gaps. Most photographs were taken in Britain or Ireland and include images of many individual rarities that have occurred. Each image is specifically credited to the photographer in the acknowledgements section on *pages 557–565*. A special mention must go to the staff at the Agami Picture Library in the Netherlands. Without their invaluable and enthusiastic assistance, the book could not have been produced.

Each regularly occurring species has a map, adapted from base maps kindly supplied by BirdLife International, the international authority on the status of wild birds. Our treatment of species and subspecies follows the British Ornithologists' Union (BOU) and Irish Rare Birds Committee (IRBC) (which follow the International Ornithological Congress (IOC) recommendations), but other authorities, such as BirdLife International, treat some differently (*e.g.* Hooded and Carrion Crows). This book illustrates and describes all of the forms; whether species or subspecies is of no consequence for their identification. The scientific names used are those on the BOU/IRBC/IOC lists, but where some are still not universally accepted or not well known to birdwatchers, earlier, more familiar, names are shown in brackets.

Up-to-date population estimates for regular breeding, wintering and migrant birds, and the number of records of rarities in Britain and in Ireland, are summarized. For the increasing number of species that are of conservation concern, information is included on their status based on current knowledge and assessments up to June 2019.

All species on the British or Irish lists are listed in taxonomic (scientific) order according to the BOU/IRBC/IOC. Uniquely, this list summarizes the conservation status and relevant conservation legislation relating to each species (see *pages 540–567*) and has been verified by experts at Biocensus ecological consultants and the RSPB.

Recent studies and events reinforce the need to take action to conserve birds and habitats worldwide. This book is intended to help people identify what they see, but if it also brings more people to appreciate birds, and so to understand the need to ensure their survival in a fast-changing world, it will have been worth the effort.

The parts of a bird

These annotated images show the basic, essential terms used throughout this book (other terms specific to a particular group are covered in the relevant introductory section).

Wingbars: The term 'wingbar' is used to describe any obvious 'bar' along the spread wing. This is typically formed of contrasting tips to the wing coverts and/or pale bases to the flight feathers. On some species such as **Blue Tit** (*right*) this bar is obvious on the closed wing, in others, such as **Sanderling** (*below*), it is barely discernible or not visible – particularly any pale bases to the flight feathers. Note that the term 'bar' usually refers to a 'crosswise' pattern or line, whereas 'streak' means a 'lengthwise' mark along the wing.

SANDERLING
- covert tips barely discernible
- pale bases to flight feathers
- covert tips
- covert tips (visible on closed wing)

BLUE TIT
- stripe over eye (supercilium)
- eyestripe
- cap
- wingbar

UPPERWING
- rump
- back
- uppertail coverts
- midwing: greater coverts
- innerwing: wing coverts and secondaries
- forewing: lesser and median coverts
- SECONDARIES
- PRIMARIES
- primary coverts
- hindwing: secondaries and inner primaries
- outerwing: primary coverts and primaries
- wingtip: outer primaries

UNDERWING
- flight feathers
- PRIMARIES
- SECONDARIES
- 'wingpit' (axillaries)
- trailing edge

FIELDFARE

- wingtip (closed)
- rump
- uppertail coverts
- tail
- flank
- thigh
- wing coverts: greater, median, lesser
- back
- 'shoulder'
- neck
- nape
- crown
- eyering
- forehead
- lore
- upper mandible
- bill
- throat
- chin
- 'moustache'
- cheek
- alula
- belly
- breast

INTRODUCTION
How to use this book

The book will help birdwatchers, whatever their level of experience and expertise, to identify the birds they see, using a simple step-by-step approach, comprehensive descriptions, essential comparisons and an unparalleled set of photographs.

First, search the gallery of thumbnail images. Decide roughly what bird you are looking at – perhaps a duck, a gull, a woodpecker, or a small songbird. Then turn to the relevant section where possibilities can be narrowed down using the introductions to broad groups of birds. These briefly outline the species within each section, and subdivide them to focus more closely onto the right bird (and to highlight others that might need to be excluded).

Alternatively, especially with more experience, simply scan through the book to find the most likely group, or to pinpoint the bird that looks like the best fit. The book's 3,500+ photographs provide an incomparable set of images of British and Irish birds. They enable detailed comparisons of birds in similar poses and similar lighting and to scale. Browsing the pages will be a rewarding experience – but it is all too easy to go wrong. Bear in mind that colours can be affected by many factors, such as bright sunlight, dull conditions, or reflections from water or foliage. Close-up pictures showing such great detail also require careful interpretation. More distant birds (such as ducks on a lake on a dull day) show broader 'patterns'. Occasionally, look at the pictures with half-closed eyes, reducing colour and detail to more of a tonal pattern.

Given a likely answer to your identification problem, check all the material on the pages – is the bird in the right location, in the right habitat, at the right season? Is there a commoner, or more likely, alternative? One feature might seem just right, but is it overruled by others – the tail colour, the wingbar, the bird's size, or the shape of its bill? A single feature is never as reliable as an overall assessment. Mistakes are easily made by jumping to a wrong conclusion without checking all available facts, or looking carefully at all the bird's features.

Checking the texts and pictures against the bird as you watch is invaluable, but you may not have time: concentrate on the bird while you can. Taking photographs is helpful but may reduce the time you spend actually watching and enjoying the bird. Making notes and sketches ensures you look at the bird closely and systematically (you cannot note down the colour of the legs or bill, or undertail coverts, without looking at them first!), helps to build up an overall assessment of what it looks like, how it behaves and how it calls or sings, and, importantly, embeds this in your memory far more than pressing a camera shutter button.

Many behavioural features are best learned by experience: for example, a small flock of black birds flying closely together may be Starlings, but not Blackbirds, which fly solitarily. A pair of finches flying side-by-side may be Bullfinches, or Goldfinches, but will be less likely to be Chaffinches. A flock of small birds flying fast and close together may be finches or sparrows, but not wagtails or pipits, which fly in much looser groups. Many species have distinctive behaviours or movements, such as wing and tail flicks, not all of which can be described in the space available.

The book is arranged to allow close comparison of similar species. It begins with water birds (those that swim habitually) and moves via seabirds (from Gannet through shearwaters, petrels and auks to gulls and terns) to waterside birds, including those conventionally termed 'waders' (or shorebirds), followed by herons and egrets and 'crakes and rails'. Following these are the grouse and partridges, pigeons, owls and birds of prey, a mixed group including kingfishers, cuckoos and woodpeckers, then the large and varied grouping known as Passerines, or 'perching birds'.

A note on ageing

This book uses a traditional terminology for the age of birds, rather than a 'calendar year' system, which may be less informative. If, for example, a young bird hatches in June, it will grow its first feathers – *juvenile* plumage – ready for its first flight. Much of this plumage is quickly replaced, usually all of the head and body feathers but with many of the wing and tail feathers retained. This is now '*1st-winter*' plumage, which may last from August to March. There follows another moult, usually into a '*1st-summer*' stage, which may be easily recognizable or only subtly different from an adult. An autumn moult, at just over one year old, produces a fully adult plumage or a further intermediate stage, '2nd-winter'. Thus, in its first calendar year, a bird may be in juvenile or 1st-winter plumage; in its second calendar year, it may be 1st-winter, 1st-summer or 2nd-winter (hence the calendar year does not indicate the bird's appearance unless the date and stage of moult are known). The book has many pictures captioned '1st-winter' and '1st-summer', which may seem unnecessarily confusing. While wishing simply to show 'breeding' (or summer) and 'non-breeding' (winter) plumages, photographs reveal such detail that other plumage stages can often be identified, which have been labelled as accurately as possible. Most small birds have a short lifespan, high mortality and a high 'turnover', so in any breeding population in summer, a substantial proportion will be one-year old ('1st-summer' birds). These are labelled as '1st-summer' rather than 'Adult', with minor differences described. For example, you may see male Blackbirds breeding in their first-summer, essentially looking like adults but with browner wings than older individuals.

Note that some species, especially gulls, take two, three or four years to become fully mature: these are indicated by a 'roundel' symbol (*e.g.* ③) with the number of years indicated.

The book has been designed with identification in mind, by grouping together similar-looking birds for ease of comparison and highlighting key features. It is structured to help you put a name to a bird by taking the minimum number of steps combined with careful observation.

The identification process

1 When you first see an unfamiliar bird, look carefully and try to note all the points relevant to an identification: if you can write them down, all the better. Now go to **The types of bird** (*pages 10–15*), a gallery that shows the range of birds found in Great Britain and Ireland. Glance through the relevant images and look for the one that most closely matches your bird, to get to the relevant group.

2 The page reference from your chosen image will take you to a **group introduction** or **species account**. For larger groupings, the introduction may refer you to a sub-group and, if needed, further subdivisions, gradually reducing the options before referring you to a handful of possibilities.

3 By now you should be in the part of the book that matches your bird. Details in the accounts should enable you to put a name to the species you are looking at.

If something is not right then:

a) refer back to the introductory section for that species group, where information on commonly confused groups/species can be found.

b) consider the possibility of an exotic 'escape' or a rare bird. In the case of rare birds that look similar to more common species a page reference is given on a species accounts page.

INTRODUCTION

The species accounts

The species accounts are divided into 30 broad sections. Each has an introduction summarizing the number of species recorded and their features common to the group. A few species have been introduced (*e.g.* Canada Goose, Pheasant, Little Owl). Casual 'escapes' from collections cannot be predicted but some have 'escaped' from captivity and have bred 'in the wild'. Brief details are included of those that might become established, such as Black Swan. The categories are listed and explained on *p. 538*. Technical jargon is avoided and everyday terms are used in the book, but a few specialist terms do help – for example 'pale tips to the greater coverts' is more precise than 'spots on the wing'. Sometimes judging relative lengths of tail, wingtip and tertials, for example, must be attempted – so knowing such feather groups is interesting, informative and invaluable (see *page 5*). Such terms are explained in a group introduction where they are of particular relevance. As far as possible each species account is presented in a consistent manner, as explained below.

Using the accounts

A combination of factors is more likely to give an accurate identification than one or two features. Study the photographs, read the descriptions, but also check the status and habitat preferences. You may find that, for example, a 'yellow' wagtail is likely to be a Grey Wagtail at certain times of year; or that the brown owl in an Irish wood is probably a Long-eared, not a Tawny Owl. Any bird could occur almost anywhere, but overwhelmingly often the bird you see will be in the right place, in its proper habitat, at the right time of year.

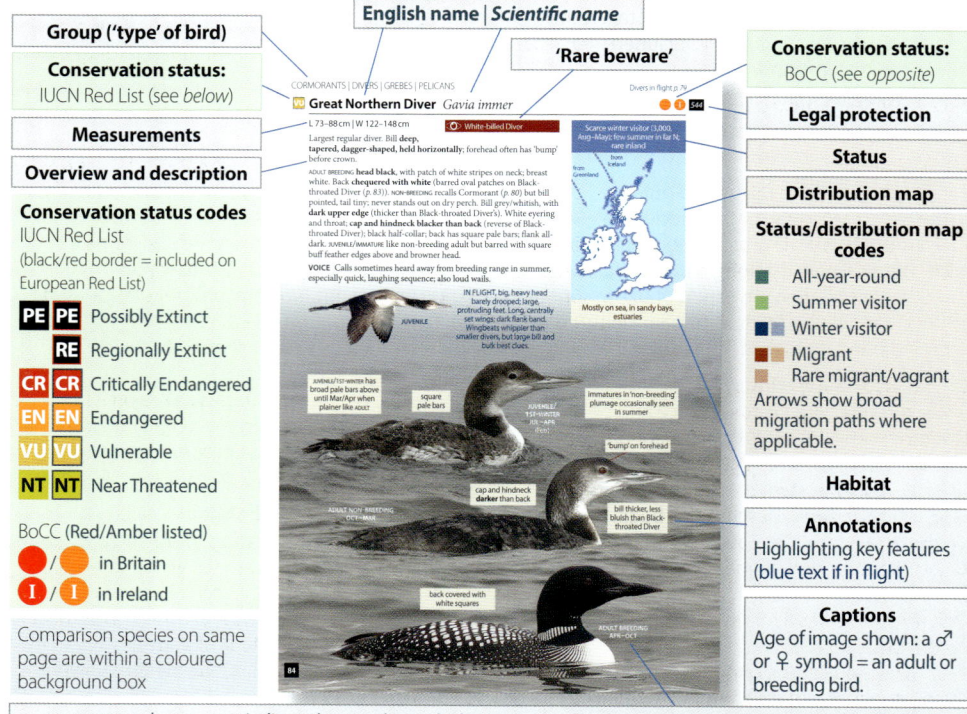

Group ('type' of bird)

Conservation status: IUCN Red List (see *below*)

Measurements

Overview and description

Conservation status codes
IUCN Red List
(black/red border = included on European Red List)

- **PE** / **PE** Possibly Extinct
- **RE** Regionally Extinct
- **CR** / **CR** Critically Endangered
- **EN** / **EN** Endangered
- **VU** / **VU** Vulnerable
- **NT** / **NT** Near Threatened

BoCC (Red/Amber listed)
- ● / ● in Britain
- Ⓘ / Ⓘ in Ireland

Comparison species on same page are within a coloured background box

English name | *Scientific name*

'Rare beware'

Conservation status: BoCC (see *opposite*)

Legal protection

Status

Distribution map

Status/distribution map codes
- ■ All-year-round
- ■ Summer visitor
- ■ ■ Winter visitor
- ■ ■ Migrant
- ■ Rare migrant/vagrant

Arrows show broad migration paths where applicable.

Habitat

Annotations
Highlighting key features (blue text if in flight)

Captions
Age of image shown: a ♂ or ♀ symbol = an adult or breeding bird.

DATE RANGES, such as SEP–MAR, indicate the months in which a particular plumage may be seen (no range means all-year). [Dates] in square brackets indicate the month when photo was taken (for transitional plumages and where helpful).

👁 'Rare beware'

The 'rare beware' or 'go to' symbol indicates other species that are very similar or may be mistaken in some circumstances, and similar rare species that should be checked.

THE SPECIES ACCOUNTS

English and scientific names
Each species has a common **English name** and *scientific name* (in *italics*). Different font sizes are used to distinguish regular, scarce and rare species.
- English names vary between authorities. This book generally uses those names recommended by the British Ornithologists' Union Records Committee (BOURC) and adopted for the Irish List, as these are best known to most people. Other English names are shown (in brackets) if thay are in frequent usage.
- The scientific name consists of two words – the first refers to the genus, which classifies those species that are closely related, the second refers to the species. The combination of these two words is unique to a species and applicable worldwide. A species can be variable in appearance and voice across its range and often these variations are classified as subspecies. These are identified using a third word and are covered in the relevant species accounts. In some cases where scientific names have changed as a result of recent taxonomic research the former name is included in brackets to prevent confusion.

NB a ◆ symbol after a name indicates that the species has only been recorded in Ireland.

Measurements
The length (bill-tip to tail-tip laid out on a flat surface) and wingspan of the species are given as a range, (with male and female separate if appropriate). NB A very long bill or tail feathers, can give a misleading indication of size in some cases; and a slim bird that is the same length as a rounded one may look much 'smaller' in reality.

Overview and description
A summary of general appearance and behaviour leads into detailed notes on different plumages (where relevant) according to age, sex and time of year. Important or diagnostic points are highlighted in **bold**. Descriptions begin with MALE, where appropriate qualified with ADULT and/or BREEDING (summer) plumage, followed by NON-BREEDING, then FEMALE, and immature birds:
- JUVENILE indicates a bird with feathers grown for its first flight.
- 1ST-WINTER indicates a bird that has undertaken its 1st-winter partial moult. Subsequent age definitions vary according to species, some being almost indistinguishable from older individuals when just one year old, while others take several years to mature.

The term 'ADULT' on its own may be taken to mean that sexes look alike; similarly, BREEDING/NON-BREEDING plumages will be the same unless specified. Where helpful, a description of the bird IN FLIGHT follows, as well as **VOICE**, giving an approximation of calls and/or song. While vocalizations can be essential, writing them in words is difficult – they serve as useful *aide mémoires* if you have heard the bird already, or give a indication of what to expect.

Conservation status, legal protection and Irish records
- Species or subspecies on the Red or Amber list, as a Bird of Conservation Concern (**BoCC**) in Britain or Ireland (see *p. 541*), are indicated by an appropriate colour-coded dot.
- Species listed by the International Union for Conservation of Nature (IUCN) as Threatened or Near Threatened, globally or in Europe, and that are on the **IUCN Red List** (see *p. 542*) have a colour-coded square. Squares with a black border indicate the European Red List status.
- Species afforded **legal protection** are indicated by a black square with a number referring to the page on which information regarding that species can be found.

Status
The **Status** box indicates how common (or otherwise) the species is in Britain and Ireland, with an estimate of the population, and the time of year it is generally seen. Birds referred to as 'migrants' travel to and from Britain and Ireland, or pass through or close by, on an annual cycle.
- **Rare migrant:** >1,000 records in total, or usually >100 recorded each year.
- **Very rare migrant:** >300 records, or >50 recorded each year.
- **Vagrant** describes a species that is off its usual migration route. The area of origin for these species is given. Numbers of records are given in close approximations (*e.g.* <5, <25, <50, <100).

Distribution map and habitat
Maps for all regular breeding, wintering and migrant species show summer, winter or all-year-round distribution, and typical migration routes where relevant. A box below the map gives most likely **habitats** in which to find a species. For rare migrants and vagrants this information is given in their **status** box.

Area modifiers are as follows: C = Central, E = East, N = North, NE = North-east, NW = North-west, S = South, SE = South-east, SW = South-west, W = West. Note that 'N Europe' includes Scandinavia.

INTRODUCTION
The types of bird

This gallery of thumbnail images of typical birds from each group should allow you to go quickly to the relevant introductory section, main sub-section or specific page when trying to identify a bird.

WILDFOWL (*page 16*)

Swans *pages 19–22*

Geese *pages 23–35*

Shelduck *pages 34–35*

Ducks (dabbling) *pages 38–45*

Ducks (diving) *pages 46–53*

SAWBILL

Ducks (sea) *pages 54–59*

WATERBIRDS (*page 76*)

Cormorants *pages 80–81*

Divers *pages 82–85*

Grebes *pages 86–90*

THE TYPES OF BIRD

LARGE WATERSIDE BIRDS (*page 255*)

Herons, Bitterns
pages 260–267

Egrets
pages 262–264

Spoonbills, Ibises
pages 259, 266

Cranes, Storks
pages 258, 265

BITTERN

IBIS

STORK

SEABIRDS (*page 93*)

Auks
pages 106–112

Gannet
page 97

Shearwaters/ Petrels
pages 98–103

👁 RARE SEABIRDS

See *pages 114–119* for other very rare seabirds that are different in form from those shown here.

Storm Petrels
pages 104–105

GULLS and TERNS (*page 120*)

Gulls (larger)
pages 124–142

Gulls (smaller)
pages 143–150

Terns
pages 160–173

SKUAS (*page 174*)

Skuas
pages 176–182

INTRODUCTION

WADERS (page 183)

Snipes
pages 222–224

Plovers (smaller)
pages 193–196

Plovers (larger)
pages 197–199

Stone-curlew
page 189

Sandpipers
pages 213–215

Small sandpipers / 'peeps'
pages 200–209

'Shanks'
pages 210–212

Godwits / Curlews
pages 216–219

Avocet and **Stilt**
pages 192 and *193*

Oystercatcher and **Turnstone**
pages 190 and *191*

Phalaropes
pages 220–221

OTHER WADERS
See *pages 226–228* for pratincoles and coursers

CRAKES and RAILS (page 246)

Moorhen / Coots
pages 248–249

Rails
page 250

Crakes
page 251

Corncrake
page 247

12

THE TYPES OF BIRD

BIRDS OF PREY (Raptors) (*page 302*) and CUCKOO (*page 338*)

Eagles *pages 304–305*

Kites *page 414*

Osprey *page 310*

Harriers *pages 315–318*

Buzzards *pages 311–313*

Hawks *pages 324–325*

Falcons *pages 326–329*

Cuckoos *page 338*

OWLS and NIGHTJARS (*page 291*)

Owls *pages 292–299*

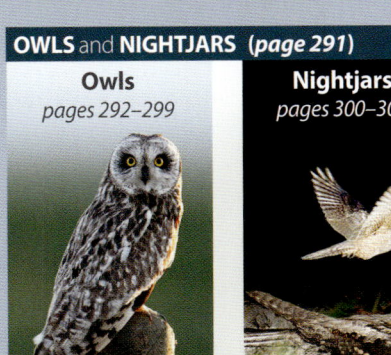

Nightjars *pages 300–301*

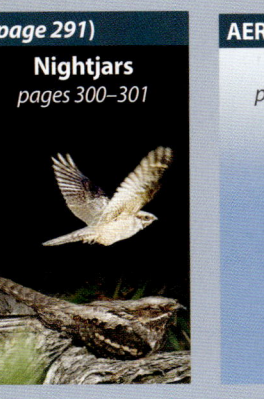

AERIAL FEEDERS (*page 348*)

Swifts *pages 349–351*

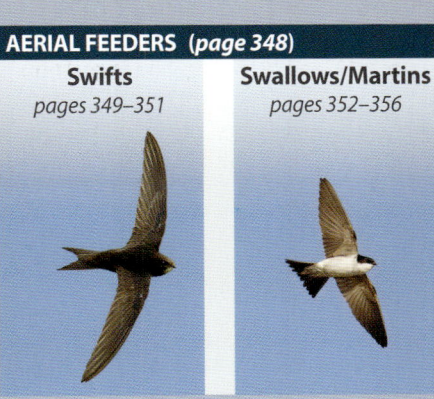

Swallows/Martins *pages 352–356*

'GAMEBIRDS' Pheasants | Partridges | Grouse | Quail (*page 291*)

Pheasants *pages 278*

Grouse *pages 274–277*

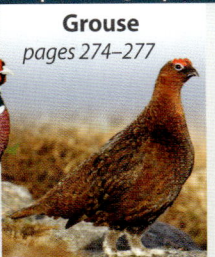

Partridges *pages 272–273*

Bustards

Bustards *pages 280–281*
ALL LARGER THAN PHEASANT

INTRODUCTION

'HIGHER LANDBIRDS' (page 336)

Kingfishers *page 337*

Parakeets *page 342*

PIGEONS and DOVES (page 282)

Doves *pages 288–290*

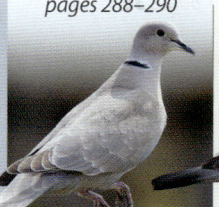

Pigeons *pages 284–287*

Bee-eaters *page 340*

Roller *page 341*

WOODPECKERS (page 343)

Woodpeckers *pages 345–347*

Wryneck *page 344*

Hoopoe *page 339*

👁 SANDGROUSE

1 species: extremely unlikely vagrant, related to pigeons – *page 284*.

👁 AMERICAN LANDBIRDS

See *page 524* for vagrant landbirds from America. All of these are either from, or bear a close enough resemblance to, groups shown here. Using this initial guide and subsequent pointers should enable you to find these species.

PASSERINES

Oriole *page 378, 383*

PASSERINES (page references in *bold* indicate introductory sections)

Jay pages **478**, 480

Crows pages **478**–487

Magpie pages **478**, 481

Shrikes pages **458**–464

THE TYPES OF BIRD

PASSERINES (page references in *bold* indicate introductory sections)

Larks
pages **357**–363

Pipits
pages **357**, 364–371

Wagtails
pages **357**, 372–377

Dipper
page **378**–379

Wren
pages **378**, 381–382

Accentors
page **378**, 380

Starlings
pages **378**, 384–385

Thrushes
pages **388**–399

Nuthatches
pages **465**, 474

'Creepers'
pages **465**, 475

Waxwings
pages **378**, 386

Chats/Wheatears
pages **388**, 400–416

Warblers ('reed')
pages **422**–429

Warblers (other)
pages **422**, 430–438

Crests
pages **422**, 424–425

Flycatchers
pages **417**–421

Tits
pages **465**–473

Sparrows
pages **488**, 490–491

Finches
pages **488**, 492–507

Buntings
pages **510**–523

15

WILDFOWL

SWAN/GOOSE ID head pattern | bill + leg colour | upperwing/underwing pattern | call

Water or waterside birds, some freely using both water and dry land habitats nearby, often feeding on land and resting or roosting on water, safe from predators.
3 swans: 1 resident, 2 widespread but local winter visitors (1 breeds in small numbers); 1 'escape'.
14 geese + several distinct subspecies: 2 introduced residents that breed, 1 native breeder that is also widely introduced and a winter visitor; 5 regular winter visitors; 6 rare; also some 'escapes'.
2 shelducks: only 1 regular.
41 ducks: 20 frequent, others rare or irregular; 15 breed (2 introduced); 1 summer visitor, others mostly increase in abundance autumn–spring; several escapes likely.

Swans (pp. 19–22) large, white; swim, upend, walk and feed on open ground, but lack agility. Fly straight, powerfully. Mute Swan all year, widespread; two 'wild swans' mostly November to March at a few regular sites.

MUTE SWAN

MUTE SWAN

Swan ageing/sexing
Swan sexes alike except male heavier, and in Mute Swan larger 'knob' on bill. Juveniles dull, become whiter during first year; dull bill gradually gains adult colours.

MUTE SWAN

Geese (pp. 23–35) introduced Canada and Greylag Geese all year; wild, migratory geese spend the winter mostly in the north, East Anglia and Ireland. Large, sociable, water/waterside birds, obvious 'farmyard' goose shape; may form big flocks (most at traditional sites), dramatic and vocal in flight. Sexes alike; juveniles differ slightly until spring.

'Grey geese' are grey-brown: check bill/ leg colours, wing patterns, subtleties of shape, head-body contrasts. Juveniles less neatly barred.

Other geese are black and white on head, neck and breast: check patterns. Juveniles duller, less neat.

Shelducks (pp. 34–35) intermediate between ducks and geese; walk freely on mud or dry land but always close to water. Sexes almost alike; juveniles differ in plumage.

CANADA GOOSE

GREYLAG GOOSE

SHELDUCK

INTRODUCTION

DUCK ID   BREEDING MALES: overall pattern and shape
FEMALES/JUVENILES: size/shape | bill + leg colours | upperwing pattern | belly colour

Ducks (pp. 36–75) can be divided into dabbling (or surface-feeding) ducks (pp. 38–45), diving ducks (pp. 46–53) and 'sea' ducks (pp. 54–59). Males are brightest in winter, when easily identified; females, juveniles and males in summer more difficult. Check bill and leg colours, wing pattern and colour and, on females, presence or absence of white belly. Upperwing may have long central stripe, or a patch of colour and bars on hindwing ('speculum'). Records of rarer birds are bedevilled by escapes from collections (see pp. 60–62), and confusing hybrids (see p. 63).

GARGANEY ♂ — speculum, upperwing
SHOVELER ♀ — underwing, belly

DABBLING (SURFACE-FEEDING) DUCKS swim with slightly raised tail on open water or amongst flooded vegetation, or paddle in muddy shallows; some feed on land, often at night. Flight fast, agile, with quick take off from water or land.

GADWALL ♂

Some feed by upending

MALLARD ♂ + ♀

RED-BREASTED MERGANSER ♀

'Sawbills' (Red-breasted Merganser, Goosander, Smew) elongated, with long, serrated bill.

TUFTED DUCK ♂

GOLDENEYE ♀

DIVING DUCKS rounder-backed, tail low, and dive from the surface while swimming. Some drift in flocks by day, others are dispersed when feeding, in flocks when asleep. Some stand at the water's edge, others can barely walk. Flight low, straight, fast but less agile than surface-feeders, with pattering run at take off; settle onto water, not dry ground. Some diving ducks (such as eiders and scoters) are essentially marine, occasional on inland waters, often ones and twos amongst commoner species. This group is termed **'sea' ducks** for convenience.

POSSIBLE CONFUSION GROUPS   Coots, grebes, divers, auks, cormorants and gulls all swim. **Coots** are round-backed, short-tailed; **grebes** round-bodied, almost tailless; **divers** long-bodied, short-tailed, dagger-billed; **auks** squat, dumpy, small-winged; **cormorants** longer-tailed, hook-billed; **gulls** square-tailed, long-winged.

GULL pp. 120–159
AUK pp. 106–113
COOT p. 249
DIVER pp. 82–85
CORMORANT pp. 80–81
MERGANSER (duck) p. 52
GREBE pp. 86–90

Wildfowl in flight

▶ IN FLIGHT: SWANS *p. 22* | GEESE *p. 23* | DUCKS *p. 36*

Swans in pairs, family groups or small, shapeless flocks or 'V'-formations; **geese** typically in flocks, often large numbers; in straight lines, 'V'-formations or shapeless masses; **ducks** are seen singly, in pairs, small groups or flocks (particularly 'sea' ducks and Wigeon).

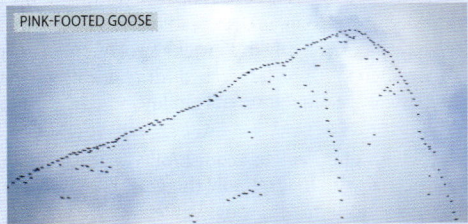

PINK-FOOTED GOOSE

PINK-FOOTED GOOSE

BEWICK'S SWAN

SHOVELER

Moult sequence in ducks (Mallard)

Juvenile from fledging until autumn; look much like adult females.

NB **1ST-WINTER** (first breeding plumage from SEP–APR) and **1ST-SUMMER** (first non-breeding plumage from MAY–AUG) birds generally very similar to adults, the differences being mainly in feather wear and fringe colours that indicate retained juvenile feathers.

ADULT ♂ BREEDING
OCT–MAY

JUVENILE
JUL–SEP
[Aug]

1st moult
JUVENILE → 1ST-WINTER
JUL–SEP: males start to develop adult colours.

2nd moult
1ST-WINTER → 1ST-SUMMER
DEC–APR: protracted full body moult.

3rd moult   1ST-SUMMER → ADULT BREEDING
AUG–NOV: full body moult, timing as adult, brings the bird into breeding condition; thereafter following the **adult yearly (4th/5th+) moult cycle**.

4th moult   ADULT BREEDING → ADULT NON-BREEDING ('ECLIPSE')
MAY–JUL (♂); JUL–AUG (♀): includes wing feathers, birds flightless JUN/JUL

5th+ moult   ADULT NON-BREEDING → ADULT BREEDING   AUG–NOV.

DEC

SEP

MAR

'ECLIPSE'

ADULT ♀
ALL YEAR

JUN

ADULT ♂ NON-BREEDING ('ECLIPSE')
JUN–SEP

♀♀ look the same year-round; ♂♂ in 'eclipse' similar to ♀♀, but become increasingly easy to tell apart by late winter.

Swans in flight *p. 22*

SWANS

Mute Swan *Cygnus olor*

L 140–160 cm | W 200–240 cm

Huge and white; the familiar swan of park lakes and riversides. Neck often in sinuous 'S'-curve, can be raised straight, thin or thick and ruffled. Bill and long, flattish head typically down-tilted (generally held more horizontally in Bewick's and Whooper Swans (*pp. 20–21*)). Wings often more-or-less arched (dramatically in threat). **Tail slim, pointed, angled up** (shorter, held low, squarer, less tapered in Bewick's/Whooper Swans).

ADULT white, often stained reddish/olive on head and neck; **bill uniquely orange-red with black 'knob' (biggest on old males) and tip.** JUVENILE dull grey-coffee-brown, wings whiter. 1ST-WINTER increasingly patched white with age (Bewick's/Whooper Swans paler, drabber); bill grey with black tip, no 'knob'. Legs grey-black. IN FLIGHT, told by head/bill shape/colour and rhythmic, **whooping wing noise**.

VOICE Calls frequently, mostly quiet grunts, hisses and reedy, weak or squeaky trumpeting.

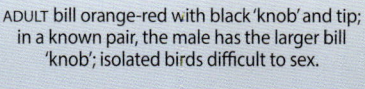

Common and widespread resident; introduced (historically) (74,000; 6,000 breeding pairs)

Sheltered sea coasts to inland waters, wetlands, grassy fields

JUVENILE/1ST-WINTER black face; bill grey with black tip

ADULT bill orange-red with black 'knob' and tip; in a known pair, the male has the larger bill 'knob'; isolated birds difficult to sex.

1ST-WINTER JUN–APR

ADULT ♂

ADULT ♀

So-called 'Polish' form all-white in downy stage, immature white with pale legs.

wings arched to assert dominance, normally held lower (see *p. 16*)

down-tilted head

pointed tail

ADULT ♂

WILDFOWL

Swans in flight *p. 22*

Bewick's Swan *Cygnus columbianus*

L 115–130 cm | W 170–195 cm   👁 Trumpeter Swan (*p. 62*)

Smallest swan, still large, but size of isolated birds difficult to judge. Generally shy and wild, usually in flocks.

ADULT white, sometimes stained on head; bill long, wide, slightly concave on top with **rounded yellow patch** short of nostril (pattern unique to individuals). JUVENILE **plainer, greyer** than Mute Swan (*p. 19*), whiter with age; **bill pattern like adult**, black and pale cream/grey, often pink, even raspberry red; base becomes yellower over winter. Legs black (rarely brown or yellowish). Long, heavy bill typically horizontal, on shapely, rounded head. Neck can appear thick or thin and sinuous – feeds with neck looped in 'S'-shape. Tail shorter, held lower than Mute Swan.

VOICE Yapping, **honking, whooping notes**, less bugling than Whooper Swan; usually single or double notes (Whooper Swan often three or four). In flight, wings lack hum of Mute Swan.

Scarce and local winter visitor; numerous at a few traditional sites (7,000, mostly Nov–Mar)

from Arctic NE Russia

Freshwater, marshes, wet and ploughed fields

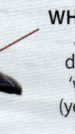

WHOOPER SWAN
all ages have diagnostic pale 'wedge' on bill (yellow in adults)

BEWICK'S SWAN
yellow on bill is rounded patch; extent variable (may join across top or form isolated patches)

'WHISTLING SWAN'
ssp. *columbianus*

Vagrant from N America: <10 records (5 Ireland), Dec–Mar. Bill black with small yellow spot on facial skin, but size variable; overlaps with dark Bewick's Swans (ssp. *bewickii*) so some individuals difficult to judge.

ADULT

short square tail

SWANS

Whooper Swan *Cygnus cygnus*

543

L 140–160 cm | W 205–235 cm 👁 Trumpeter Swan *(p. 62)*

Scarce and local winter visitor, numerous at a few traditional areas (11,000, mostly Nov–Mar); rare breeder (20 pairs)

from Iceland

Large, angular, wild swan. Only slightly smaller than Mute Swan (*p. 19*) but most similar to smaller Bewick's Swan. Large, **wedge-shaped head and bill** on long, upright neck when alert; **bill typically held more horizontal** than Mute Swan (neck curved when relaxed).

ADULT white (stained dark in summer). Yellow on bill forms **long triangle** either side, joining across base. Bill has a longer, flatter profile (less concave) than Bewick's Swan. JUVENILE like Bewick's Swan, less brown than Mute Swan. Bill has adult pattern, **pointed 'wedge' of whitish** or cream with dark pink/grey tip, slowly becoming pale yellow as winter progresses.

VOICE Like Bewick's Swan but more **bugling or clanging**, deep, nasal, often three/four notes (Bewick's Swan usually one/two). Flock chorus noisy, confused and varied. In flight, wings do not give musical throb of Mute Swan.

Freshwater, wet fields, marshes, occasionally on coasts

At a distance the longer, more upright necks of **Whooper Swans** (six birds in the background) are distinctive compared to the shorter, more sinuous necks of **Bewick's Swans** (two birds in left foreground).

Although smaller than in Whooper Swan, the bill of **Bewick's Swan** can appear surprisingly long and heavy when seen close up

JUVENILES OCT–MAR

(dark bill)   (pale bill)

BEWICK'S SWAN

no black on face (compare with Mute Swan)

diagnostic pale 'wedge'

WHOOPER SWAN

ADULT

short square tail

21

WILDFOWL

Swans in flight

Direct flight powerful, straight, in shapeless groups (Whooper Swans often in 'V' or wavy line). Head/neck outstretched, tail short. Descend with wings stiffly arched, body angled, legs lowered before splashing down on water or landing on the ground with a short run.

MUTE SWAN

ADULT swans have all-white upperwings.

IMMATURE **Mute Swan** has strongest contrast: dark coverts/pale hindwing.

MUTE SWAN

BEWICK'S SWAN

MUTE SWAN (p. 19)

huge; head/bill best visual features but loud humming throb of wingbeats distinctive

IMMATURE **Whooper** and **Bewick's Swans** upperwing relatively uniform.

BEWICK'S SWAN (p. 20)

smaller than Whooper Swan, with shorter neck – but hard to judge

WHOOPER SWAN (p. 21)

huge, rangy, with fine-pointed head

SWANS and GEESE IN FLIGHT

Geese in flight

White-fronted Goose
Quick, agile, in lines/'V's. Adult **belly distinctively marked** (but beware, as juvenile is unmarked). Sharp, bright, laughing calls with yodelling 'catch'.

Pink-footed Goose
In long lines, 'V's or masses. Head and neck short and dark. Nasal, bubbly, deep chorus interspersed with high "*wink-wink*."

Bean Geese:
Taiga long-necked, long-winged; **Tundra** less so. Nasal, deep double- or triple-note calls.

Greylag Goose
In lines, 'V's or a shapeless mass. Head large, chunky and pale. Coarse, clattering, cackling chorus.

underwing paler than on Bean Goose

darkest underwing

palest underwing

JUVENILE

GREYLAG GOOSE (p. 29)

BEAN GEESE (p. 30)

PINK-FOOTED GOOSE (p. 31)

WHITE-FRONTED GOOSE (p. 32)

upperwing dark, mid-grey towards tip

upperwing pale bluish-grey contrasting with dark trailing edge

upperwing largely mid- or pale blue-grey

upperwing mid-grey on outer part

Very distinctive black-and-white wings in the white form most often seen in Britain/Ireland.

BARNACLE GOOSE (p. 28)

white forehead

white 'collar'

BRENT GOOSE (p. 26)

SNOW GOOSE (p. 33)

grey, patterned

grey, plain

grey-brown

CANADA GOOSE (p. 24)

white chin

Barnacle Goose
Neat, narrow-winged, pale greyish, upperwing mid-grey with blackish edge; black neck and breast. Sharp, barking, yappy calls.

Brent Goose
Dumpy, dark, thick-necked. Obvious white stern and tail. Short, deep, rolled, rumbling calls.

Canada Goose
Very large and long-necked. Big white stern against black tail. Upperwing dark brown, breast very pale; black neck. Deep, honking calls.

WILDFOWL | Geese in flight *p. 23*

Canada Goose *Branta canadensis*

L 80–105 cm | W 155–180 cm

Very large, long-necked, striking goose; dramatic in large flocks.

Browner than other geese, barred paler, with **white breast**. **Unique black 'stocking' on neck, white 'chinstrap'**. (Barnacle Goose (*p. 28*) has black over breast, more white on face.) **Black bill and legs**, big white stern. JUVENILE very like adult but duller, less sharply patterned (feather edges on upperparts rounder).

VOICE Loud, deep, full honks, including double "*ar-hunk.*"

There are many subspecies of Canada Geese, recently split into two species, Canada Goose and Cackling Goose, each with a number of subspecies, which may occur in Britain and Ireland as natural vagrants. **Beware, however, that these forms also turn up as 'escapes'.** Additionally, there is overlap in size and plumage detail such that the groups are best treated as a cline. The basic differences between Canada and Cacking Geese are summarized *below*; the differences between the subspecies recorded in Britain and/or Ireland are detailed *opposite*.

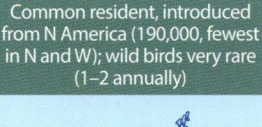

Common resident, introduced from N America (190,000, fewest in N and W); wild birds very rare (1–2 annually)

Mostly lowland lakes, gravel pits, grassy river valleys, some estuaries

IN FLIGHT, huge, even against Greylag Geese (*p. 29*), dark, long-necked, black tail obvious.

Canada Geese typically fly as a close flock

CANADA GOOSE: less inclined forehead, longer bill, long-necked

large-bodied

CACKLING GOOSE: steep forehead, stubby bill, short-necked

small-bodied

NB Canada Goose ssp. *parvipes* is intermediate in form and plumage

'ATLANTIC' CANADA GOOSE
ssp. *canadensis*

black neck

white 'chinstrap'

GEESE

Canada Geese subspecies

The resident, naturalized population is known as 'Atlantic' Canada Goose (ssp. *canadensis*). Vagrants from N America are very rare (Oct–Mar) and are generally the smaller forms that differ in their head and bill characters: note carefully the extent of pale/white on base of neck and breast, as well as size and structure. However, these features are variable and overlap between subspecies and sexes (males average 5% larger than females).

'TODD'S' CANADA ssp. *interior*
Similar in size to 'Atlantic' but generally has a darker, browner back that meets the slimmer black neck; breast averages darker.

VAGRANT CANADA GEESE ssp. *parvipes*
Small forms, e.g. in so-called ssp. '*parvipes*' (not recorded), vary: some very like Cackling Goose, others very similar to ssp. *interior* or ssp. *canadensis*. Isolated individuals may not be identifiable.

'ATLANTIC' CANADA ssp. *canadensis*
Large, averages palest, black neck separated from brown back with clear white.

'RICHARDSON'S CACKLING GOOSE'
ssp. *hutchinsii*

Cackling Goose *Branta hutchinsii*
(Lesser Canada Goose)
L 55–110 cm | W 150 cm

Very like small Canada Goose, but has steep forehead, stubby bill and shorter neck. Ssp. *hutchinsii* is the most likely vagrant.

Vagrant from N America: most Oct–Mar, probably annual Britain and Ireland, mostly with Barnacle Geese in N and W.

'TAVERNER'S CACKLING GOOSE' ssp. *taverneri* [not illustrated]
As 'Richardsons' but averages larger and darker, with a more rounded head (similar to paler-breasted Canada Goose ssp. *parvipes*, with which it may intergrade). 40–75% have dark stripe under chin.

'RICHARDSON'S CACKLING GOOSE' ssp. *hutchinsii*
Pale breast, often with a golden wash; 5–10% have dark stripe under chin.

'RIDGWAY'S CACKLING GOOSE' ssp. *minima*
Smallest, with small bill, short neck and relatively long legs. Variable, but typically darkish brown with purplish sheen on breast.

WILDFOWL Geese in flight *p. 23*

Brent Goose *Branta bernicla*

L 55–62 cm | W 105–117 cm ssp. *hrota* 543

Small goose (length of Mallard (*p. 40*) but looks bigger), swims and upends in saltmarsh creeks, even around seaweedy rocks, grazes on fields, parks.

Generally **very dark with white back end**. Three subspecies occur – 'dark-bellied', 'pale-bellied' and Black Brant (see *opposite* for last two). 'Dark-bellied' ssp. *bernicla* dark brown-grey. **Black head, neck, breast** contrast sharply against browner belly (depending on angle and light). Small **white patch** high on side of neck. Plain greyish back, **big white stern**. Flank barred pale; **dark on belly extends between legs**.
JUVENILE has pale bars on wings, no neck patch until midwinter.

VOICE Deep, rolling croaks, "*grr-r-unk*," with conversational character; loud, quick, even chorus from big flock.

Locally numerous winter visitor ('dark-bellied' 100,000 (most in NE, SE, S); 'pale-bellied' 41,500 (38,000 of which in Ireland)), most Oct–Mar. 'Black Brant' rare but annual vagrant (10–15/year)

'Pale-bellied' from Canadian Arctic
'Dark-bellied' from Eurasian Arctic

IN FLIGHT, long-winged, heavy, thickset, dark goose with extended black head, neck and breast; bold white stern.

flies in irregular flocks, but small groups form lines and 'V's

Coasts, saltmarshes, muddy creeks, grassy pastures, arable

'DARK-BELLIED' BRENT GOOSE
ssp. *bernicla*

white patch on side of neck

striking white rear-end   dark behind legs   subtle contrast between breast and belly

ADULT

GEESE

VU **Red-breasted Goose** 543
NT *Branta ruficollis*
L 54–60 cm | W 110–125 cm

IN FLIGHT, easily overlooked in Brent Goose flocks; white wingbars, white belly.

Striking, but 'disappears' surprisingly easily in large flocks of other geese. Basically black-and-white with **bold panels of deep rust-red** on head and neck; black lower breast contrasting with white belly/vent and **broad white flank stripe**.

ADULT

Vagrant from Asia: <100 records (1 Ireland), Oct–Mar. Occasional 'escapes'. Usually with Brent or White-fronted Geese (*p. 32*). Marshes, pasture.

'PALE-BELLIED' BRENT GOOSE (ssp. *hrota*)
Palest on body; contrast between **black breast and pale belly**; flank whitish with greyer bars, a few darker ones at rear. Pale belly, no black between legs.

'GREY-BELLIED' BRENT GOOSE (taxonomic status uncertain [*not illustrated*]) – Rare, variable, between sspp. *hrota* and *nigricans* (perhaps hybrid); like *hrota* with darker, brownish-grey belly barely extending between legs, diffuse paler flank and darker back; broader white neck patches may just meet on front.

'BLACK BRANT' (ssp. *nigricans*)
Vagrant from N America/E Siberia: 300 records (<50 Ireland), Oct–Mar; complicated by intergrades/hybrids.
Neck patches typically **broad and bold, meet in front**; back darker; belly darker, head slightly larger than 'dark-bellied' Brent Goose; **shining white flank patch**, broken by bars on lower edge, two or three dark bars at rear. Black on belly extends behind legs.

'PALE-BELLIED' BRENT GOOSE
ssp. *hrota* ADULT

'BLACK BRANT'
ssp. *nigricans* ADULT

neck patches large; meet on front

strong contrast between breast and belly

prominent white flank

pale behind legs

dark behind legs

JUVENILE OCT–MAR
'PALE-BELLIED'

'DARK-BELLIED'
JUVENILE OCT–MAR

pale behind legs

dark behind legs

27

WILDFOWL Geese in flight *p. 23*

Barnacle Goose *Branta leucopsis*   543

L 58–70 cm | W 120–142 cm   ◉ Emperor Goose (*p. 62*)

Small, clean, immaculate goose, **lacking any brown**.
At long range, bright pale grey with sharp vertical divide against black front. Black neck widens into **black 'breastplate'**, contrasting with white belly. Large **white/yellowish face patch** surrounds black eyeline. Bill short, deep, stubby; bill and legs black. ADULT back neatly barred. JUVENILE duller than adult, barring on back less regular.

VOICE Barking calls, vary in pitch "*kaw*;" yapping flock chorus.

Very locally numerous winter visitor (94,000, including 40,000 Islay, 33,000 Solway, 5,500 Ireland), Oct–Apr; local introduced resident (3,000)

from Greenland
from Svalbard

Estuaries, coastal meadows, saltmarsh; lakes, gravel pits

Barnacle Goose skeins generally form long lines.

IN FLIGHT, upperwing mid-grey or pale steely-slate, underwing boldly contrasted (like Greylag Goose).

ADULT
blackish back and black rump contrast with pale wings

white extends onto forehead

black 'breastplate'

ADULT

Greylag Goose *Anser anser*

L 74–84 cm | W 149–168 cm

Obvious 'farmyard goose' form. Introduced flocks approachable; winter migrants wilder. Large, big-headed, heavily built; **pale brown** with **large, pale orange bill** (paler at tip). **Legs pale pink** (some pale to bright orange, at least in introduced flocks). Low winter light gives strongly contrasted buff/brown effect, **breast pale**; prominent white rear-end. Some have white near bill or black spots on belly, but not like smaller, small-billed White-fronted Goose (*p. 32*). (Juvenile White-fronted Goose lacks white or black markings but has smaller bill, orange legs and darker wings.) ADULT has neat bars above; JUVENILE more rounded, irregular pale feather edges.

VOICE Noisy; clattering, clanging or cackling chorus from flock – "*kya-gaa-gaa*" or "*ang-ang-ank*."

Locally common resident, many introduced populations (46,000 pairs, 225,000 in winter). Wild immigrants mostly Scotland (85,000, Oct–Mar); native breeder (3,200 pairs, most Scottish islands)

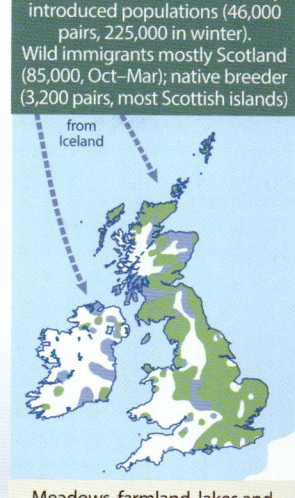

Meadows, farmland, lakes and gravel pits

IN FLIGHT, **underwing strikingly contrasted** (like Barnacle Goose). **Pale blue-grey upperwing** much paler than Pink-footed Goose (*p. 31*). Dull white uppertail, with mid-grey central band.

ADULT

Greylag skeins can be lines, 'V's, or shapeless.

Greylag Geese on water look large and bulky; they sit either tall or squat with head held upright and tail raised to reveal a white stern (see *p. 16*).

ADULT

WILDFOWL

Geese in flight *p. 23*

Bean Geese

Two very similar species (sometimes treated as subspecies); overlap between the two makes some isolated individuals difficult to identify but the key feature is the shape and patterning of the bill. Large, dark brown; similar to Pink-footed Goose but with a longer head/bill profile.

ADULT head and neck dark brown; back brown with sharply defined whitish bars; breast pale buffish, flank brown, closely barred whitish, not contrasting with back (flank darker than back on Pink-footed Goose). **Legs orange**. JUVENILE has dark back with crescentic whitish feather edges, giving 'scaly' effect.

VOICE Calls lower than White-fronted (*p. 32*) and Pink-footed Geese, less harsh or clattering than Greylag Goose (*p. 29*): deep "*ung-ung*," "*hank-unk*" or "*yak-ak-ak*."

from Arctic NE Russia

Rough, rushy fields, wet pastures, arable land

IN FLIGHT, dark overall, upperwing dark brown; tail dark with narrow white 'U'-shape at base.

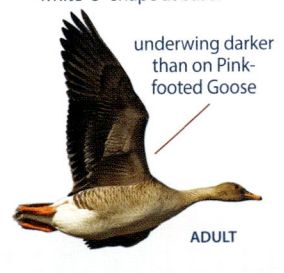

underwing darker than on Pink-footed Goose

ADULT

| Rare winter visitor (400, most at a few sites in Scotland and East Anglia); <250 records Ireland; most Oct–Apr. | Rare winter visitor (300, erratic, most E England); <50 records Ireland; most Oct–Apr. |

Taiga Bean Goose
Anser fabalis 543

L 66–89 cm | W 140 cm–174 cm

Head and **relatively long neck** dark brown; **little contrast** with upper breast. Bill long, lower edge straight; largely orange with small black marks around base and tip.

Tundra Bean Goose
Anser serrirostris 543

L 65–88 cm | W 140 cm–174 cm

Head and **relatively short neck** rich dark brown, **generally contrasting** with upper breast (similar to Pink-footed Goose). Bill thick, lower edge bulging; black with narrow orange band near tip.

JUVENILE/1ST-WINTER (SEP–MAR) have 'scaly' back feathers

TAIGA BEAN GOOSE

dark brown head (both species)

TUNDRA BEAN GOOSE

brown back

ADULT

ADULT

flank 'thumbprint' same tone as back

Pink-footed Goose *Anser brachyrhynchus*

L 64–76 cm | W 137–161 cm

Familiar goose form; small bill and head and barred grey back give neat appearance. Often in large, crowded flocks.

ADULT has **round, dark head, short neck**; **short, dark bill** with narrow pink band; **contrasted pale buff breast**. Back dusky blue-grey, less brown than bean geese. Legs dull **pink** to darker purple-pink. Upperwing has extensive grey, darker than on Greylag Goose (*p. 29*); broad white tail tip. JUVENILE drabber, browner than adult, but dark bill rules out young White-fronted Goose (*p. 32*). Needs care to separate small-billed Tundra Bean Goose within Pink-footed Goose flocks.

VOICE Deep, nasal, gabbling chorus from flock, with frequent distinctive, high, sharp "*wink-wink*" interspersed.

Locally abundant winter visitor: (360,000, Sep–Apr) from Iceland

Fields, coastal marshes, lakes

IN FLIGHT, uniformly paler back/upperwing, greyer back, darker flank than bean geese; pink legs usually distinct (orange on bean geese).

Pink-footed Goose skeins can be lines, 'V's or shapeless, but tend to be more 'clumped' and changing in form than Greylag Goose skeins.

underwing paler than on bean geese

ADULT

PINK-FOOTED
variable pink band on small black bill

TUNDRA BEAN
bulging; open 'grin'
shorter, thicker bill than Taiga Bean's; black with narrow orange band

TAIGA BEAN
straight
long, largely orange bill

NB The shape and amount of colour on the bill varies between individuals in Pink-footed, Taiga Bean and Tundra Bean Geese.

very dark, rounded head

greyish back

ADULT

lacks white flank stripe

JUVENILE OCT–MAR

flank 'thumbprint' darker than back

WILDFOWL

Geese in flight *p. 23*

White-fronted Goose *Anser albifrons*

543

ssp. *flavirostris*

L 64–78 cm | W 130–160 cm   ◉ Lesser White-fronted Goose

Boldly marked lively, agile goose (easily leaps into flight); two distinct subspecies.

ADULT **European ssp.** *albifrons* mid-brown; buff neck and breast; long **white stripe** along flank. **White forehead 'blaze'** with straight, vertical edge in side view. Belly has variable **black bars** and blotches, occasionally solid. Bill pale **pink**; legs rich orange. **Greenland ssp.** *flavirostris* darker, 'oily' brown, black belly bars often more extensive. Bill **orange** with paler tip (hard to judge orange/pink in poor light). Upperwing dark; subtle grey less obvious than on Pink-footed Goose (p. 31). JUVENILE lacks white face, flank stripe and black belly bars: puzzling if alone, best told by leg/bill colour and dark wings with little grey. Develops white forehead by Feb.

VOICE High, laughing, yodelling with a catch in the middle: "*kyu-yu*" or "*lyo-lyok.*" Flock chorus high, yapping/yodelling.

Scarce and local winter visitor (Oct–Mar) (European ssp. *albifrons* in S, rare (2,000, most traditional sites abandoned; <200 records Ireland); Greenland ssp. *flavirostris* in N and W (22,000, incl. 9,000 Ireland))

from Greenland

from Arctic NE Russia

Estuaries, pastures; Greenland ssp. also islands, rushy fields, moors

ADULT

IN FLIGHT, ADULT plain greyish underwings, distinct black barring on belly; JUVENILE plain beneath except white vent; orange legs help if discernible.

JUVENILE

bill orange with pale tip

'GREENLAND' WHITE-FRONTED GOOSE ssp. *flavirostris*

ADULT

dark markings on belly often more extensive than on ssp. *albifrons*

'EUROPEAN' WHITE-FRONTED GOOSE ssp. *albifrons*

ADULT

JUVENILE OCT–JAN

juveniles lack white on face and dark barring on belly, and white flank stripe is faint

GEESE

Snow Goose
Anser (Chen) caerulescens
L 65–75 cm | W 133–156 cm

Chunky goose: ADULT **pure white** (commonest form) with **black wingtips** (grey patch on leading edge); bill and feet red-pink. Dark form **white head, dark blue-grey body**, paler wings. JUVENILE/IMMATURE pale brownish; dark eyeline, dark bill, grey legs.

Very rare migrant from N America: <10 per year (>100 records Ireland), most Oct–Mar. Released/escaped birds (180 Britain) widespread (even breeding). Marshes, pasture.

⊙ Ross's Goose, Emperor Goose (p.62). Beware hybrids involving Barnacle (p.28) and other geese, often with white heads and dark legs

ADULT
ADULT white form
1ST-WINTER white form
ADULT dark form

Lesser White-fronted Goose *Anser erythropus* 543
VU / **EN**
L 56–66 cm | W 115–135 cm

Like small, neat White-fronted Goose but less barred above, less black beneath, chunkier head, shorter neck and smaller bill. ADULT **white on forehead that curves back above eye**. **Bill bright pink**. **Yellow eyering** obvious even at distance (weak on White-fronted Goose). JUVENILE lacks white on forehead but has **yellow eyering**. Small bill has **pale nail** (dark on young White-fronted Goose). Hard to find, especially juveniles: search flocks for white forehead 'blaze' (adult), long wingtip and fast feeding action, then confirm with eyering/bill features.

Vagrant from N Europe: <150 records (<5 Ireland), Oct–Mar. With White-fronted Geese or bean geese (p.30). Pasture.

white 'blaze' on forehead — white curves back above eye
ADULTS
no eyering — yellow eyering
WHITE-FRONTED — LESSER W-F
JUVENILES
dark nail — pale nail

'EUROPEAN' WHITE-FRONTED GOOSE
ssp. *albifrons*
ADULT
LESSER WHITE-FRONTED GOOSE
ADULT

Shelduck *Tadorna tadorna*

L 55–65 cm | W 100–120 cm

Fairly common and widespread resident (15,000 pairs, much reduced by autumn); common in winter (61,000)

to/from North Sea + S Baltic

Coastal marshes, lagoons, estuaries, inland gravel pits, wet meadows

Big, heavy, long-legged duck, at home on dry ground, mud or water. Striking adults unmistakable; juvenile puzzling but unlike any other bird.

ADULT strikingly **bright white**. Glossy green-black head, **long black bands** along back, **orange-brown band** around front of body. **Bill vivid red**, MALE'S with big basal 'knob'. FEMALE has whitish face/cheek marks. Legs clear pink. JUVENILE has long-legged, short-billed, big-bodied look of adult, but is gangly. **Largely white**; brownish bands along back, dark brown back of head and neck (white around eye and lower face). **Pinkish bill, greyish legs**. Vaguely like Egyptian Goose.

VOICE Wings whistle in flight; calls variable, whistling notes and deep rhythmic "*ga-ga-ga-ga-ga*."

IN FLIGHT, deep-chested, heavy; broad dark trailing edge and black tips to white wing.

JUVENILE JUN–OCT

GEESE

Egyptian Goose *Alopochen aegyptiaca*

Local resident, introduced from Africa (3,500, increasing, mostly in East Anglia and S England)

Parks, lakes, reservoirs

L 63–73 cm | W 110–120 cm

Medium-sized, upright goose; long-legged but relatively short-necked.

Pale overall; olive-brown back, greyer or **rufous** towards rear, pale breast. Pale crown, **dark neck ring and 'mask'**. Bill small, pink and black; legs rather long, red-pink. JUVENILE no 'mask'.

VOICE Monotonous, repetitive, rhythmic bark or babble in alarm, various hissing and gagging notes.

ADULT

IN FLIGHT, white forewing remarkably striking.

grey type has pale head and weaker 'mask'

ADULT

JUVENILE JUN–FEB

Juvenile plumage similar to adult, but more drab; lacks clear head pattern.

Ruddy Shelduck 543
Tadorna ferruginea
L 58–70 cm | W 110–135 cm

Obvious shelduck shape/size with long-legged gait. Rich **orange-brown** with **pale head**; black bill and legs. MALE has black neck ring; FEMALE whiter face.

NB Other similar-looking shelducks occasionally wander free from collections.

Vagrant from Asia: most Jul–Oct. UK birds perhaps escapes. Estuaries.

IN FLIGHT, big **white patch at front of black wing**, above and below (beware Egyptian Goose); black rump/tail.

♂

♀

35

WILDFOWL

Regularly occurring ducks in flight

RED-BREASTED MERGANSER (p. 52)

GOOSANDER (p. 53)

SHELDUCK (p. 34)

MALLARD (p. 40)

GADWALL (p. 42)

SHOVELER (p. 41)

PINTAIL (p. 43)

TEAL (p. 44)

POCHARD (p. 47)

GARGANEY (p. 45)

POCHARD (p. 47)

GARGANEY (p. 45)

TEAL (p. 44)

WIGEON (p. 39)

WIGEON (p. 39)

BLUE-WINGED TEAL (p. 67)   Annual North American vagrants

AMERICAN WIGEON (p. 64)

36

DUCKS IN FLIGHT

SMEW (p. 51)

GOLDENEYE (p. 50)

SURF SCOTER (p. 74)

LONG-TAILED DUCK (p. 54)

VELVET SCOTER (p. 56)

COMMON SCOTER (p. 57)

KING EIDER (p. 72)

See also Ring-necked Duck (p. 69) and Lesser Scaup (p. 68).

1ST-WINTER

EIDER (p. 58)

SCAUP (p. 49)

1ST-WINTER

TUFTED DUCK (p. 48)

FERRUGINOUS DUCK (p. 69)

WILDFOWL

Identifying female-type dabbling ducks

Female dabbling or surface-feeding ducks can look very similar. **On birds flying overhead**, take note of underwing patterns, underwing/body contrast. **On standing birds** check overall shape, bill size and colour, head shape, belly colour and leg length.

SHOVELER (p. 41) — UNDERWING white, BELLY brown
MALLARD (p. 40) — UNDERWING white, BELLY brown
GADWALL (p. 42) — UNDERWING white, BELLY white
GARGANEY (p. 45) — UNDERWING white with black leading edge
TEAL (p. 44) — UNDERWING white with speckled leading edge
WIGEON — UNDERWING grey
PINTAIL (p. 43) — UNDERWING dark, BELLY white

WHITE-BELLIED

WIGEON
- white line
- grey
- grey with black tip
- sharp contrast

TEAL (p. 44)
30% smaller than other dabbling ducks shown
- green (if visible)

GARGANEY (p. 45)
- well-marked 'stripy' face
- all-dark

PINTAIL (p. 43)
- dark (if visible)
- grey
- grey
- blended

GADWALL (p. 42)
- white (if visible)
- clear orange sides
- pale orange
- sharp contrast

BROWN-BELLIED

SHOVELER (p. 41)
- green (if visible)
- orange; spatulate
- orange

MALLARD (p. 40)
- blue (if visible)
- diffuse orange and brown
- orange

Ducks in flight *p. 36*

DABBLING DUCKS

Wigeon *Mareca (Anas) penelope*

L 43–50 cm | W 72–85 cm

American Wigeon (*p. 64*)
Falcated Duck (♀) (*p. 65*)

Locally common winter visitor (470,000, most Sep–Mar); rare breeder (400 pairs) in far N

from Iceland
from Scandinavia
from Siberia

Estuaries, lakes, wet meadows

Short-legged, **short-billed** duck; noisy flocks graze on land or swim, rising as one when disturbed. Smaller than Mallard (*p. 40*), bigger than Teal (*p. 44*). **Grey legs and black-tipped grey bill** are always an instant clue.

MALE blue-grey; **black-and-white rear-end**. Head **red-brown with pale forehead**; body slightly paler (Teal darker overall). Pink breast, striking on sleeping birds. **White forewing** may show (thinner line on Teal). 1ST-WINTER MALE lacks white on wing; 'ECLIPSE' MALE like female but **redder**; **white wing patch**. Colourful/patchy intermediates in autumn (grey legs/bill helpful clues). FEMALE/JUVENILE barred/spotted, not streaked like Mallard/Gadwall/Pintail, grey-brown to **tawny**; greyer head with variable smudge behind eye. **White belly**, plain flank.

VOICE Distinctive: MALE gives an explosive whistle, "*whe-ooo*" or "*whew!*;" FEMALE low growl, "*ra-kraa*." Chatty flock chorus.

IN FLIGHT, fast; tapered, swept-back wings; short, pointed tail. ADULT FEMALE hindwing dull green; JUVENILE hindwing brown.

FEMALE grey forewing; dark hindwing; lacks white

♀ / 1ST-WINTER

♂

MALE striking white forewing (grey in 1ST-WINTER)

'ECLIPSE' and 1ST-WINTER MALES have some grey feathers on back

short grey bill with black tip

'ECLIPSE' ♂
MAY–OCT [Sep]

BREEDING MALE has distinctive head pattern and black-and-white rear-end

♂ NOV–APR

crisp white fringes to wing coverts and very fresh feather edges indicate ADULT FEMALE

♀ [Dec]

Browner, barred type, showing individual variation. Tertials lost through early moult. Some feather edges old and worn.

1ST-SUMMER ♀
[Mar]

WILDFOWL　　　　　　　　　　　　　　　　　　　　　　　　　　　　Ducks in flight *p. 36*

Mallard *Anas platyrhynchos*

L 50–60 cm | W 81–95 cm　　　　　Black Duck (*p. 65*)　　　　543

Familiar, wild or semi-tame duck. Surface-feeding, upends and sometimes dives; frequent on dry land. Various 'throwbacks' to escaped domestic forms quite frequent; 'wild' form described here.

MALE pale, with lengthwise brown bands; black-and-white rear-end. Head **green** (blue/purple gloss) above white ring. **Bill yellow**; **legs bright orange**. 'ECLIPSE' MALE like rusty female, with **yellow bill**, green-black cap and eyestripe, mottled rufous breast. FEMALE dull **yellow-brown, streaked blackish**; brown 'V'-shapes on flank; nearly **white tail** useful feature at long range. Head more-or-less striped; bill brown, marked with orange/yellowish. **Legs bright orange.** JUVENILE like skinny female with blacker crown and streaked (less spotted) breast.

VOICE Quiet quack, nasal whistles from MALE. Loud, short quack and long, coarse, descending series from FEMALE.

IN FLIGHT, large, long-necked, long-winged; wingbeats mostly below body level. **Dark blue hindwing** with two parallel **white lines**. FEMALE has dark belly and white underwings (*see p. 38*).

dark band between two white lines

Common and widespread resident (100,000 pairs) and winter visitor (650,000)

from N and W Europe

Watery places from coast to high moors, town parks

'ECLIPSE' MALE loses strong colours and pattern, may look greyish or more rusty; head greyer than female's, bill remains yellow

'ECLIPSE' ♂ JUN–SEP (Jul)

curly tail

♂ OCT–MAY

orange legs

white tail

Domestic forms and descendants introduce variations, such as white breast, into wild population.

40

Comparison of females p.38

DABBLING DUCKS

Shoveler *Spatula (Anas) clypeata*

L 44–52 cm | W 73–82 cm

Blue-winged Teal (p.67)

543

Big, large-headed duck with **long, heavy bill**. Feeds/rests in water or at water's edge, not wandering far over drier land. Long body, shoulders low in water; head low, well forward. Upends, showing markedly long wingtips. On land, more 'tear drop' shape, tapered to high tail, than deep-bellied Mallard.

MALE head greenish-black (blacker than Mallard); **eye yellow**, bill black, **breast white**. Flank red-brown, **black-and-white rear-end**. 'ECLIPSE'/ JUVENILE MALE like female but often redder; greyish head with striking but variable **upright whitish crescent** on face. Yellow eye on adult, dark on juvenile. FEMALE pale, streaked; **dark belly**, **orange legs** (like Mallard). JUVENILE more finely marked.

VOICE Calls weak, MALE a nasal "*too-took*," FEMALE a quiet, hoarse quack. Taking flight, wings make loud whoosh.

IN FLIGHT, MALE **forewing pale blue**; **no white line at rear**; FEMALE white underwing/dark belly, like Mallard (Gadwall and Wigeon have white belly) (see p.38).

Scarce breeder (1,000 pairs) and fairly common winter visitor (18,000, most Aug–Apr)

from Iceland

from N and W Europe

To S Europe

Lakes, reservoirs, saltmarshes, coastal lagoons

no white trailing edge

grey forewing ♀

blue forewing ♂

'ECLIPSE' MALE gradually develops white crescent on face, which becomes more striking in autumn

'ECLIPSE' ♂ APR–SEP [Sep]

white foreparts/dark reddish flank unique

♂ SEP–APR

orange legs

♀

41

WILDFOWL

Ducks in flight *p. 36*

Gadwall *Mareca (Anas) strepera*

543

L 46–56 cm | W 78–90 cm

Large dabbling duck; much like Mallard (*p. 40*) but squarer head, steep forehead, slim bill; long-bodied. Square **white patch** on innerwing: triangle or diamond on swimming bird; smaller on juvenile.

MALE grey with **black rear-end** (no white). Head buffish; back streaked black with pale feather edges; tertials may create pale patch. Face pale, almost silvery Aug–Oct; **black bill** looks 'stuck-on'. 'ECLIPSE' MALE like female, bill orange on sides, but sharper contrast between grey head and brown breast; blacker rump; retains chestnut and black on wing. FEMALE **like Mallard**, but **belly white** (obvious in flight). Head paler, greyer or buff; tail dull. Well-defined orange side to bill; **legs orange-yellow**. JUVENILE has mottled belly and finely streaked breast (less spotted than female).

VOICE Quiet quacks, frequent nasal "*nhek-nhek*" from MALE; very vocal in displays from Aug onwards.

IN FLIGHT, upperwing looks dark with obvious white square on hindwing close to body; FEMALE slim, narrow-winged, with white belly (*see p. 38*).

Widespread resident (1,200 pairs) and winter visitor (25,000, mostly Oct–Mar)

from Iceland

from W Europe

Watery places from coast to high moors, town parks

white wing patch

'ECLIPSE' ♂ APR–SEP [Apr]   more solid blackish feather centres than Mallard

orange side to bill

white on wing often hidden

black bill

black stern

♂ OCT–APR

Comparison of females *p. 38*

DABBLING DUCKS

Pintail *Anas acuta*

543

L 51–62 cm | W 79–87 cm

Large surface-feeding/grazing duck, like Mallard (*p. 40*) but more elegant; longer neck but body quite deep and heavy.

MALE lead-grey with **white breast** (not so brilliant as Shoveler's (*p. 41*) and often stained); head dark with **white stripe**. Stern black, with yellow-buff patch (white on Wigeon (*p. 39*)). **Legs grey**; **bill bluish with black stripe**. Long tail spike easy to see even at long range (Long-tailed Duck (*p. 54*) is only other duck with tail spike, but plumage very different). 'ECLIPSE' MALE can be puzzling: very pale, blurry buffish with soft bars and streaks and dark chequering above, becoming patchy grey; plain gingery head against long, blue-sided, black bill. FEMALE much like Mallard but finely marked with lacy loops and streaks; head **plainer buffy-brown**. **Bill grey**; **legs grey** (never orange).

VOICE MALE whistles; FEMALE gives short, low quacks.

IN FLIGHT, distinctive, with long white line along trailing edge. Long wings, long tail, slim neck fairly obvious.

Widespread but localized winter visitor (29,000, mostly Sep–Apr) and rare breeder (20 pairs)

from Iceland
from Arctic Russia
from Scandinavia and NW Europe

Mainly estuaries, but also inland floods, wet meadows, lakes

white trailing edge ♀

♂

'ECLIPSE' ♂ JUL–OCT [Oct]

becomes very pale on neck and body in autumn

plain head

♀ slim grey bill

white neck stripe

♂ NOV–JUN

buff flank patch

WILDFOWL   Ducks in flight *p. 36*

Teal *Anas crecca*

L 34–38 cm | W 53–59 cm   👁 Rare teal (pp. 66–67)

Small, agile dabbling duck; groups in flight recall waders with twists and turns; near-vertical when taking off. Often on muddy watersides, hidden in weeds, or flooded willows; upland moors in summer.

MALE compact; often looks dark (but bright in low winter sun). **Dark grey** with **white stripe** along body and black-edged, **mustard-yellow triangle** on stern. Head dark; glossy green panel, edged buff, behind eye. **Bill black**, slim; **legs black**. 'ECLIPSE' MALE/FEMALE coarsely mottled (less streaky than Mallard (*p. 40*) or Gadwall (*p. 42*)). **Whitish streak beside tail**. JUVENILE like female but more finely streaked.

VOICE Often heard from 'invisible' birds on marsh or reservoir: MALE gives a high, sharp, ringing whistle, "*crree*" (may not bring 'duck' to mind); FEMALE has low, gruff, nasal quack.

Scarce breeder (2,100 pairs) and common and widespread winter visitor (210,000, mostly Oct–Mar)

from Iceland
from N and W Europe
from Siberia

IN FLIGHT, **central wingbar broader than hindwing line**; **flashy grass-green** between stripes rules out Garganey.

broad midwing stripe; flash of green

Moors, waterside thickets; in winter lakes, pits, estuaries

'ECLIPSE' ♂ MAY–OCT [Oct]

dark, with pale triangle at rear

dabbles in shallow water/wet mud (Wigeon graze on drier grass)

'ECLIPSE'/JUVENILE MALE like female, often with dark cap and pale face; any grey vermiculations indicate that it is a male.

white streak near tail

horizontal white stripe

♂ OCT–APR

pale triangle

Comparison of females *p. 38*

DABBLING DUCKS

Garganey *Spatula (Anas) querquedula*

L 37–41 cm | W 59–67 cm

Rare teal (pp. 66–67)

Rare summer visitor (<100 pairs breed), scarce migrant (most Mar/Apr and Aug/Sep)

Small dabbling duck, slightly larger than Teal. Spring males distinctive; females and immature males harder to identify.

MALE head and breast warm brown; **white crescent over eye**; pale, drooping feathers over wing. FEMALE/JUVENILE like Teal but with larger, paler, more obvious flank spots; dark cap, stripe through eye and band across cheek; long whitish stripe over eye (thin in middle) and whitish upper cheek line; clear **white spot by bill**. 'ECLIPSE' MALE like darkish female with stronger head markings and white chin. In autumn, pick out by head pattern and dark olive speculum (brilliant green on Teal).

VOICE Infrequent: spring MALE gives a curious dry rattle; FEMALE a nasal "*ga ga ga*" and weak quack.

IN FLIGHT, MALE forewing pale blue; FEMALE milky-grey spilling onto outerwing (dark on Teal). Garganey has **equal parallel white stripes** (unequal on Teal; see Mallard (*p. 40*)). Contrasted blackish edge to forewing beneath.

1 via Iberia
2 via Italy
To sub-Saharan Africa

Freshwater habitat, wet meadows

dull dark band between two white lines

NOTE: 'ECLIPSE' MALE (MAY–SEP) similar to JUVENILE but underparts unstreaked white.

JUVENILE JUN–OCT [Sep]

Spring birds often favour tall, flooded vegetation.

pale streak near tail very weak or absent

broad pale stripe slightly broken over eye

dark eyestripe

dark stripe across cheek

drooped back feathers

WILDFOWL — Ducks in flight p. 36

Red-crested Pochard *Netta rufina*

L 53–57 cm | W 85–90 cm

Big, bulky, large-headed duck; generally a surface-feeder.

MALE colourful, **fuzzy orange crown**, sharply defined black neck and breast; body pale brown and white; bill long, **pink-red**. 'ECLIPSE' MALE browner; **bill red**, head two-tone with dark cap/pale brown cheeks. FEMALE dusty pale brown; large head brown with darker eye patch, **lower half pale buff-white**; bill grey with pink patch near tip (female Common Scoter (*p. 57*) similar but darker with dark bill and all-dark wings in flight).

VOICE Quiet and insignificant, but squeaky "sneeze" in display.

Rare Eurasian vagrant and scarce introduced breeder in Cotswolds (300 pairs), occasionally elsewhere; number of truly wild birds hard to determine.

Reedy lakes, pits and reservoirs

white edge to forewing

IN FLIGHT, **broad white band** along full length of wing.

white wingbar (rules out scoters)

like high-crowned Common Scoter with pale bill band

JUVENILE ♂ JUN–OCT [Oct]

'ECLIPSE' MALE (MAY–SEP) looks similar to juvenile male but eye bright and bill all-red

'fuzzy' crown

red eye and bill

white flank obvious at long range

♂ OCT–MAR

DIVING DUCKS

Pochard *Aythya ferina*

VU
VU

544

L 42–49 cm | W 67–75 cm

Redhead, Canvasback (p. 71), Ring-necked Duck (♀) (p. 69)

Scarce breeder (600 pairs); fairly common and widespread winter visitor (38,000, mostly Aug–Apr)

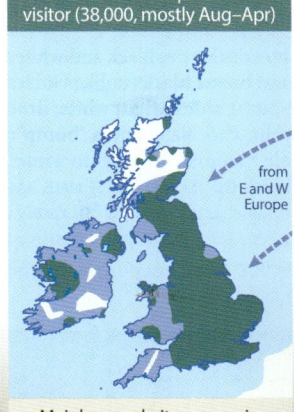

Medium-sized diving duck, often rests by day with smaller, more active Tufted Ducks (p. 48). Sleek, rather round-bodied; round-headed with a **sloping forehead**.

MALE pale grey, **dark at both ends**; head rich red-brown, bright in good light, eye red; pale blue-grey band across dark bill. 'ECLIPSE' MALE like female with redder head, red eye. FEMALE **greyish, diffusely mottled brownish**, with darker brown breast and stern; head pale brown, with **whitish eyering and around bill and throat**, pale line curls over cheek; long, grey bill with pale central band. JUVENILE browner than female, with darker cap and paler cheek; whitish beside bill and on chin can be puzzling (see female Ring-necked Duck (p. 69)).

VOICE Infrequent: MALE gives nasal "*wha-oo*" in display; FEMALE a purring growl.

from E and W Europe

IN FLIGHT, broad, pale grey panel along spread wing; lack of white safely rules out Tufted Duck and Scaup (p. 49).

Mainly gravel pits, reservoirs (winter); breeds on reedy lakes

all plumages have a deep-based, tapered bill with a pale band

rather pale, pattern obscure

'ECLIPSE' ♂
MAY–SEP [Aug]

♀

♀

Brown (worn) ADULT FEMALES and brownish JUVENILES are usually inseparable.

pale body with dark head/neck and rear-end

♂ SEP–MAY

Tufted Duck *Aythya fuligula*

L 40–47 cm | W 65–72 cm

Medium-sized round-headed diving duck with **tuft on head**.

👁 Lesser Scaup (*p. 68*), Ring-necked Duck (*p. 69*), Ferruginous Duck (*p. 69*)

MALE distinctive black and white (bright purple gloss on cheek). **Head and breast black** (unlike Goldeneye (*p. 50*)), back black (unlike Scaup), **sides bright white**; droopy 'tuft', yellow eyes. FEMALE dark, plain-chocolate brown, **'bump' or slight tuft on back of head** (rules out Scaup); flank paler in winter, belly white. Bill slim, grey, with **broad black tip**. FEMALE/'ECLIPSE' MALE/JUVENILE may have white facial marks, often sharply defined but rarely as extensive as on Scaup. Often whitish under tail (less bright/extensive than rare Ferruginous Duck (*p. 69*)).

VOICE Loud, rough growling notes; bubbling whistles from displaying males.

Fairly common and widespread breeder (16,000 pairs) and winter visitor (110,000, most Sep–Apr)

from Iceland

from N and W Europe

IN FLIGHT, long white wingbar (grey on Pochard (*p. 47*)).

Lakes, reservoirs, pits, rivers, occasionally on the sea

Flocks of Tufted Ducks, common on inland waters, are worth checking for unusual species.

'ECLIPSE' MALE (MAY–SEP) looks similar to 1st-winter male

1ST-WINTER ♂ OCT–MAR [Mar]

some FEMALES can have 'Scaup-like' white patches above the bill; the hint of tuft is always the 'give-away' feature

♀

♂ SEP–MAY

DIVING DUCKS

VU Scaup *Aythya marila*

L 42–51 cm | W 71–80 cm

Lesser Scaup (p. 68), Ring-necked Duck (p. 69)

Medium-sized diving duck, similar to Tufted Duck and Pochard (p. 47): combines pattern of both with Pochard's shape/size; strong, leaping dive. Broader beam and wider bill than Tufted Duck and larger, rounded head with **no trace of a 'tuft'**.

MALE **pale in middle, black both ends**, flank **white**; grey back excludes Tufted Duck. FEMALE paler ginger-brown than Tufted Duck, greyer back (like Pochard); forehead steep; **small black spot at tip of broad bill** (wide band on Tufted Duck). **White 'blaze' on face** higher over bill than any Tufted Duck; pale **ear patch**, especially Mar–Sep. JUVENILE needs care, especially inland – **larger**, broader than Tufted Duck with **rounded head** and wider bill. White face diffuse, but pale **ear patch** is good clue.

Scarce and declining winter visitor, mostly on N, NW and NE coasts (5,000, Sep –Apr)

from Iceland

from N Europe

Offshore, estuaries, occasional inland

IN FLIGHT (see also p. 68), white wingbar excludes Pochard.

white wingbar ♀

♂

Flocks at sea are highly unlikely to be Tufted Ducks or Pochards; Scaup is typically a marine duck, but very localized.

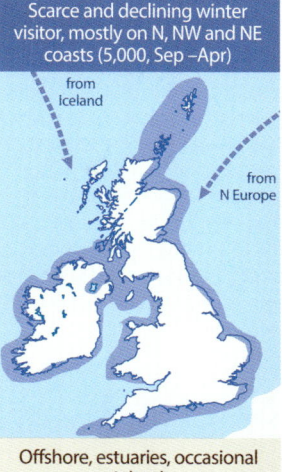

all have domed forehead; smooth, curved nape

1ST-WINTER ♂
OCT–MAR [Feb]

JUVENILE bill has smudgy triangular dark tip unlike adult, but less sharp band than Tufted Duck

'ECLIPSE' MALE (MAY–SEP) looks similar to 1st-winter male

white ear patch in summer

♀ MAR–SEP

♀ SEP–MAR

black head, white flank rules out Pochard; grey back rules out Tufted Duck

♂ SEP–JUN

49

WILDFOWL

Ducks in flight p. 36

Goldeneye *Bucephalus clangula*

L 40–48 cm | W 62–77 cm

Barrow's Goldeneye (p. 73)

Rounded duck, dives feverishly; elusive, but groups sleep with head back, long tail raised, or display actively (males throw their head back and call). MALE **white below** (brighter than Goosander (p. 53)); black back, green-black head with **white face spot**. Bill black, eye yellow, legs orange. FEMALE **dark**, **grey**, **round-backed**. Dark head with low, round nape; **triangular bill**; white collar; white in wing (often hidden). Bill grey with orange band; eye yellow or white, legs orange. JUVENILE like female but neck darker; male develops white body and face patch during winter.

VOICE Rarely heard. When displaying, MALE makes ratchety, clock-winding "*nhair-nhairr*" sounds; FEMALE deep growls. Wings (especially adult males') whistle loudly in fast flight, often heard before birds are seen.

Fairly common and widespread winter visitor (27,000, Sep–Apr); rare breeder in far N (<200 pairs)

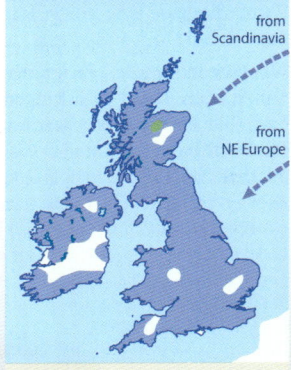

from Scandinavia

from NE Europe

Sea coasts, lakes and reservoirs, even small, cold upland pools; nests in holes in trees, nestboxes

IN FLIGHT, MALE innerwing largely white, outerwing black; FEMALE innerwing white crossed by two dark bars, belly white; JUVENILE like female but only one dark bar.

1ST-SUMMER ♂ MAR–OCT

'1ST-WINTER' ♂ NOV–MAR [Feb]

'ECLIPSE' and 1ST-YEAR MALES have variable white face patch below the eye (sometimes lacking).

very dark, peaked head

grey body

short triangular bill ♀

round white face spot

contrasting black-and-white body

♀ can look all-dark at distance, or with varying amounts of white visible on the wing; pattern may resemble Velvet Scoter (p. 56) – which has a less rounded body and a flatter head.

♂ OCT–JUN

DIVING DUCKS: SAWBILLS

Smew *Mergellus albellus* 544

L 38–44 | W 56–69 cm

Lively, alert, small-headed diving duck; often elusive (frequently under flooded waterside bushes or in reeds).

MALE **predominantly white** with pale grey flank and **black eye patch**. Close up, black nape beneath white crest; black back and grey rear-end (white much more 'up front' than Goldeneye and Goosander (*p. 53*)); two fine black lines on side of breast. Crest can be raised and pushed forward extravagantly. FEMALE lead grey with **red-brown head, lower third white**; blacker around eye. Steep forehead and small grey bill echo male's shape; crest splayed upwards against wind. Smaller and shorter-billed than Goosander, more extensive white on face (like winter male Ruddy Duck (*p. 60*) but white on wings). JUVENILE like female but head redder without dark area around eye; males develop white during the winter.

IN FLIGHT, MALE **piebald**, white around breast; FEMALE wings white in front, white lines across back; JUVENILE like female but less white.

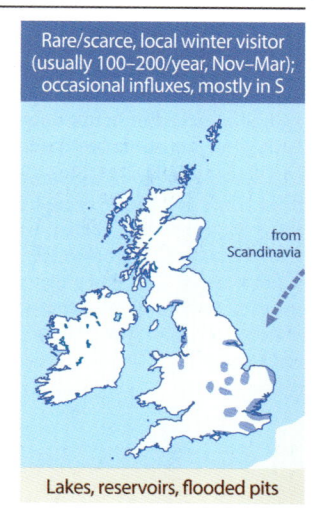

Rare/scarce, local winter visitor (usually 100–200/year, Nov–Mar); occasional influxes, mostly in S

from Scandinavia

Lakes, reservoirs, flooded pits

Smew may be seen in display shortly before migrating north in Mar.

♀ white forewing
white underside
♂

like ♀ but without dark around eye

1ST-WINTER
OCT–MAY [Feb]

lead-grey body

white patch
♀

body white with black marks

♂ OCT–MAY

WILDFOWL

Ducks in flight *p. 36*

NT Red-breasted Merganser *Mergus serrator*

544

L 52–58 cm | W 67–82 cm

⊙ Hooded Merganser (*p. 70*)

Extravagant diving duck. May stand at water's edge showing heavy white belly (often stained orange) and vivid orange legs. Nests on ground (Goosander in tree holes) and more marine than Goosander, often pairs, sometimes scores/hundreds.

MALE **green-black** head with **long, wispy crest** and **red eye**. **White band** above **grey flank**; **orange-brown breast** with black sides; white collar. Bill bright red, slender. 'ECLIPSE' MALE like female with white forewing. FEMALE drab brownish-grey; dull pale breast **blends** into **orange-brown** neck and gingery head and throat. Thin, double-pointed crest. Bill slim, slightly upswept (hint of a smile), pale red. JUVENILE like female; young male develops adult plumage through 1ST-WINTER.

VOICE Insignificant, deep growl.

IN FLIGHT, innerwing white, crossed by black bars (MALE) or black line (FEMALE) (usually clear white on Goosander).

Scarce and local breeder (2,800 pairs), mostly on coast in N and NW; widespread but uncommon and local in winter (9,000)

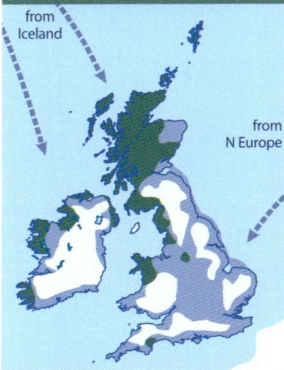

from Iceland

from N Europe

Breeds near coast, estuaries; in winter mostly on sea

'ECLIPSE' ♂
MAY–OCT
[Oct]

Males moult in summer, acquiring subdued 'eclipse' plumage; look like females, but show extensive white in wings.

long, slim profile

spiky, pale head

slim bill; nostrils closer to eye than to bill tip

brown head fades into pale body

♀

♂ at distance looks dark with long white streak

red eye
slim bill
white collar above dark breast

♂ NOV–MAY

DIVING DUCKS: SAWBILLS

Goosander *Mergus merganser*

L 58–68 cm | W 78–94 cm

Hooded Merganser (p. 70)

Conspicuous large, long-bodied, long-billed diving duck (Red-breasted Merganser only likely confusion, but see Great Crested Grebe (p. 86)). Frequently stands at water's edge, heavy-bodied, rather horizontal stance, revealing bright red legs.

MALE large **green-black** head with bulbous forehead, **drooped, rounded crest** and **dark eye**. White/pale salmon-pink (some intense pink, others pure white or yellowish in evening light); black back. Bill thick-based, strongly hooked, deep plum-red. 'ECLIPSE' MALE like female with bigger white wing patch. FEMALE pale, clean grey; pale breast **sharply divided** from red-brown head and upper neck. Well-defined **white chin patch**. Rounded, drooping crest (paler, more ragged in summer), raised in 'anvil' shape in courtship. Bill long, red. JUVENILE like female with white stripe from bill to eye, duller bill, less white on wing; young male develops white underparts through 1ST-WINTER.

VOICE   Croaking flight note.

IN FLIGHT, long, heavy, head outstretched (fast, direct); innerwing white, outerwing black.

Scarce and local breeder in SW, Wales and N (3,500 pairs); more common and widespread in winter (12,000)

from N Scandinavia

from NE Europe

Breeds near rivers; winter mostly bigger lakes, reservoirs, rivers

'ECLIPSE' ♂ JUL–OCT [Oct]

'ECLIPSE' MALE Goosanders are less distinctive but still look big, heavy and thick-billed compared to Red-breasted Mergansers.

deep-based bill; nostrils halfway between eye and bill tip

neat white chin

sharp contrast between head and body ♀

dark eye

deep, dark bill

white breast

♂ NOV–JUL

WILDFOWL Ducks in flight *p. 36*

Long-tailed Duck *Clangula hyemalis*

VU VU ● I 544

L ♂ 49–62 cm (incl. tail 10–15 cm); ♀ 39–47 cm | W 65–82 cm

Small 'sea' duck. Complex plumages often puzzling, but recognizable character: auk-like (*p. 106*), thickset, squat, sometimes humped at rear with tail down; large, rounded head with **short, deep, triangular bill**.
MALE long, whippy tail feathers (see Pintail *p. 43*, but no real confusion: Long-tailed Duck does not stand on mud or grass). WINTER MALE **white with dark brown bands**, broad breast-band, grey flank; two-tone dark patch on side of head; bill dark with pink band. SUMMER MALE darker, streaked rusty-buff and black, head and breast very dark; pale face patch, white eyering. WINTER FEMALE dark above, pale below; white head with dark cap and **dark smudge on cheek**; bill grey. SUMMER FEMALE darker, more extensive dark cap and cheek marking, finer whitish line back from eye and white neck patch. JUVENILE (sometimes solitary, sometimes inland) like female, but face greyer with **whitish around eye** and more extensive **dark cheek** – often identified by elimination (nothing else fits): dumpy shape, triangular bill, frequent diving with **wingtips splayed**.
VOICE Male gives frequent, nasal, yodelling "*ar-ar-ardl-ow;*" quiet "*gag*" notes.

Scarce and local winter visitor, mainly to N and E coasts (11,000, Aug–May; declining)

from N Europe

Offshore, sandy bays; occasional inland

JUVENILE JUN–SEP

dark ♀

light ♀

♂ [Oct]

head patterns variable but males can always be told by the pink band on the bill

♀ NOV–APR

♂ NOV–APR

'SEA' DUCKS

♂ WINTER

♀ WINTER

IN FLIGHT, wings very dark, rump **dark with white sides**, recalling Guillemot (*p. 108*).

long, straggling flocks fly low over sea, often with Common Scoters (*p. 57*)

white stripe tapers behind eye

white collar

white spectacle

grey face

white flank

♀ MAY–JUN

♂ MAY–JUN

WILDFOWL　　　　　　　　　　　　　　　　　　　　　　　　　　　　　　Ducks in flight p. 36

Velvet Scoter *Melanitta fusca*

VU
VU
L 51–58 cm | W 79–97 cm

Rare scoters (p. 74–75), Harlequin Duck (♀) (p. 74)

Scarce and declining winter visitor (3,000, most autumn-winter), mostly to NE coast

Large, bulky 'sea' duck, associates with Common Scoter. Angular, wedge-shaped head recalls Eider (p. 58) but bill slimmer; tail short. Distinctive **white hindwing panel in flight** but tends to be hidden at rest (thin line at best, hard to see at long range), so watch scoter flocks to catch frequent wing-flapping, when Velvet Scoters' white marks flash brightly.

ADULT MALE **black**, with white 'tick' under eye; bill has curved yellow side 'panel' and black top; legs red (blackish on Common Scoter). FEMALE very dark brown with hint of pale spot near bill and pale cheek, or typically whiter cheek spot and pale patch near bill (see female Scaup p. 49); bill deep-based, tapering (slightly upwards) to slender tip; legs reddish. JUVENILE like female with well-marked face and whiter belly.

from Scandinavia

Offshore, bays; rare inland

IN FLIGHT, shows prominent **white hindwing panel**.

JUVENILE JUN–SEP

light belly

♀ dark belly

♂

A suspected Velvet Scoter may eventually flap its wings and reveal its white wing patches.

two white patches on head

♀

1ST-SUMMER ♂ APR–OCT [May]

'ECLIPSE' MALE duller, brownish-black JUN–SEP

curved yellow patch on bill

white wing patch (does not always show when swimming)

♂ OCT–JUN

'SEA' DUCKS

Common Scoter *Melanitta nigra*

544

L 44–54 cm | W 70–84 cm

Black Scoter (p. 75)

Large 'sea' duck, with heavy body but long, pointed tail, slender neck, elegant shape; blackish legs. On sea in long, ragged groups, showing on rising swell; often raises head and tail. Sits up from water with lowered head, to flap wings.

ADULT MALE **black**; bill wedge-shaped with yellow patch on top, in front of **basal bulge**. **Pale grey** under wingtips shows when flapped on water, more obvious in flight. IMMATURE MALE brown at first, gaining black in blotches. FEMALE dark, obscurely barred, with **blackish-brown cap**, **dusky-buff cheek**, darker near bill/below eye and on throat (darker than female Red-crested Pochard (p. 46) and male Ruddy Duck (p. 60)). Worn, ragged pale buff patches on back Jul–Aug. JUVENILE like female with whitish belly.

VOICE Whistled, piping notes and growling note from FEMALE.

Common passage migrant and winter visitor (100,000); rare breeder in N Scotland and NW Ireland (<100 pairs, declining)

from Iceland

from N Europe and W Siberia

Nests near moorland lakes; winters at sea, mostly in big sandy bays or well offshore; rare late summer migrant inland

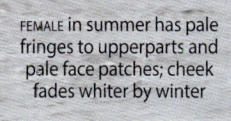

IN FLIGHT, lacks white but outerwing paler, as if slightly translucent over dark sea.

FEMALE in summer has pale fringes to upperparts and pale face patches; cheek fades whiter by winter

Scoter flocks trail across the waves, birds at rear following rise and fall of leaders in 'roller coaster' effect; look for white wing patches revealing Velvet Scoters (at least eight here!)

♀ MAY–OCT [Jun]

♀ OCT–APR [Jan]

'ECLIPSE' MALE duller, brownish-black JUN–SEP

♂ OCT–JUN

Slim, pointed tail (often raised clear of water).

WILDFOWL   Ducks in flight *p. 36*

NT **Eider** *Somateria mollissima*   ● ssp. *mollissima*   ● ssp. *faeroeensis*   **I**   **544**
VU

L 60–70 cm | W 95–105 cm   👁 King Eider (*p. 72*),   Locally common breeder (26,000
                                Steller's Eider (♀) (*p. 73*)   pairs); more common and
Big, long, heavy 'sea' duck.   widespread in winter (60,000)
Wedge-shaped head, short, often cocked, tail. No common duck
much like it, but immature/summer males can confuse.
MALE black and white, with salmon-pink breast (fades paler/yellower);
white back and flank spot; black body; sea-green patch on nape. **Long
white 'wedge'** beside long grey bill. 'ECLIPSE' MALE **piebald**, with blacker
face, browner breast, darker back. Pale greenish-grey bill blends into
pale line over eye and cheek. 1ST-YEAR MALE rather similar or very dark
with whiter breast, mottled above. (Beware domesticated Mallard
types (black/brown with white breast (*p. 60*)) – look for obvious head/
bill details.) FEMALE rich brown, **barred** not streaked; dark at distance,
rufous close up; striking crosswise barring over flank, chequered/
barred back. Pale **brown 'wedge'** beside bill, which has pale 'blob'-tip.

VOICE Passionate cooing "*aa-ooh*" from MALE and guttural
"*gak-ak-ak-ak-ak*" from FEMALE.

Sea coasts and islands; rare inland

IN FLIGHT, MALE white in front/on top, black behind/
beneath; FEMALE hindwing dark, with or without
double white line (like Mallard (*p. 40*));
JUVENILE plainer, greyer brown.

1ST-YEAR ♂
[Apr]

♀

♂

FEMALES show considerable
variation in overall colour:
rufous, sandy or greyish

♀

Winter FEMALE is darker than
summer; females in Shetland (ssp.
faeroeensis) are darker and more
finely barred than southern ones
(ssp. *mollissima*); all become darker
with wear (pale edges reduced).

♀

'SEA' DUCKS

♂ of **northern ssp.** *borealis* from Arctic N Atlantic (records to date not proven: ring recovery required to prove provenance) has orange-yellow bill and small white tuft on back.

♂ of **Nearctic ssp.** *dresseri* from Atlantic N America (1 record: Ireland, Apr) has longer, rounded facial lobe; small white tuft on back; green line under eye.

BRITISH/IRISH ssp.
mollissima/faeroeensis

NORTHERN ssp. *borealis*

NORTHERN ssp. *borealis*

NEARCTIC ssp. *dresseri*

♂ JUL–SEP

1ST-YEAR ♂ [Apr]

♂ OCT–JUN

59

WILDFOWL

Introductions, escapes and hybrids

Wildfowl escaping from collections can appear almost anywhere, and the excitement of seeing a 'rare' duck or goose may therefore be reduced by the chance of its being an escapee. Some species are now established as regular breeding birds in the wild. Also beware frequent hybrids (especially Canada × Greylag Goose), which produce obviously different plumages. Shown on *pages 60–63* are some of the more frequently encountered escapes and hybrids – some are similar to naturally occurring (wild) species and may therefore lead to confusion.

Mallard (domesticated) *Anas platyrhynchos*
L 50–60 cm | W 81–95 cm
Many varieties: may be white with yellow bill (so-called 'Aylesbury' Duck), dark brown, beige with dark brown head (vague pattern of male Mallard (*p. 40*)) or black-brown with a white breast.

Canada × Greylag Goose hybrid
L 80–100 cm | W 150–180 cm
Typically very large, brown, with variable dark grey and white patterning on head and neck; bill and legs pinkish, orange or blackish.

'Stifftails' Two broadly similar diving ducks that habitually raise their tail high above the water; males have a striking blue bill.

Introduced resident; formerly widespread, progressively being eradicated (<20 remain)

Reed-fringed lakes and ponds

Ruddy Duck *Oxyura jamaicensis*

L 35–43 cm | W 50–55 cm

Small, round-backed, large-headed duck; long, stiff tail often flat on water – inconspicuous until raised.

MALE bright coppery-red with bold black cap, nape and neck **enclosing white face**; bill blue. WINTER MALE dull, dark, with black cap and **stark white face**; bill dark grey. FEMALE/JUVENILE grey-brown; dark cap to below eye; **cheek pale**, crossed by smudgy dark band; bill grey. Confusion possible with Smew (*p. 51*), larger female Common Scoter (*p. 57*), and much bigger, paler Red-crested Pochard (*p. 46*).

VOICE MALE has low croak in display.

EN **White-headed Duck** *Oxyura leucocephala*   544
EN 43–48 cm | W 55–65 cm
Like Ruddy Duck; bill **bulges at base**.
MALE pale rusty-brown, **head white**, small black cap, collar; no white under tail. IMMATURE blackish head.
FEMALE grey bill; black crown; bold dark band across whitish cheeks; body finely barred.

IN FLIGHT, low, fast, direct; wings and rump plain dark brown.

NON-BREEDING ♂
SEP–APR

dark bill
(in winter)

♀/JUVENILE

face pattern less bold than White-headed Duck; bill does not bulge at base

♀

dark cap

♂ APR–SEP

Rare (escapees but **possible vagrant** from S Europe). Lakes, reservoirs

bold face pattern; bill bulges at base

♀

white head

♂

60

DABBLING DUCKS

Mandarin *Aix galericulata*

L 41–49 cm | W 65–75 cm

Small and unobtrusive duck, often in/near trees.

MALE unmistakable: dark, with **broad white band over eye** beneath long, rusty crest overlying back; lower face a broad golden-buff fan; **unique upright 'orange peel' 'sails'**. FEMALE very dark, breast finely streaked white, **flank boldly spotted**; blunt, thick crest above fine **white 'spectacle'**; white throat; small grey bill.

VOICE High, squeaky whistle in flight.

Long-established introduction from Asia: scarce (3,000 breeding pairs), mostly in the south; rare wanderer elsewhere

IN FLIGHT, small, fast, direct; upperwing dark with thin white trailing edge.

Wooded lakes, rivers, park ponds; nests in holes in trees

'ECLIPSE' MALE (APR–SEP) like FEMALE but bill red with pale tip (dark tip on Wood Duck).

straight

pale bill tip

spotted flank

thicker patch behind eye — curved

black bill tip

distinctive 'sails'

♂ OCT–JUN

Wood Duck *Aix sponsa*
47–54 cm | W 66–73 cm

MALE multicoloured like Mandarin but lacks 'sails'. FEMALE like Mandarin but has **thicker white patch behind eye**, buffier flank spots.

Rare (escapees but **possible vagrant** from N America). Wooded lakes, rivers

WILDFOWL

Black Swan *Cygnus atratus*
L 110–140 cm | WS 160–200 cm
Black with white in wings (obvious in flight); bill red.

Rare (introduced from Australia), has bred. Lakes, rivers, estuaries, meadows.

Trumpeter Swan *Cygnus buccinator*
L 150–180 cm | W 230–260 cm
Like **Whooper Swan** (p. 21) but **bill black**.

Rare (introduced from N America), has bred. Lakes, meadows.

Bar-headed Goose *Anser indicus*
L 71–76 cm | WS 140–160 cm
ID Pale grey with **white head crossed by two black bars on nape**; **bill and legs orange**.

Uncommon (introduced from Asia), has bred. Lakes, reservoirs.

Emperor Goose *Anser (Chen) canagicus* NT
L 68–89 cm | W 120 cm
Blue- or bronze-grey with **dark bars**; **head and hindneck white**; **legs orange**.

Rare (introduced from N America), has bred. Lakes, meadows.

Ross's Goose *Anser (Chen) rossii*
L 53–66 cm | W 115–130 cm
Like small white Snow Goose (p. 33) with more rounded head and **small, grey-based bill**.

Rare (escapees but **possible vagrant** from N America), has bred. Lakes, meadows.

Muscovy Duck (domesticated)
Cairina moschata
L 66–84 cm | WS 120–140 cm
Large; generally **glossy black** and white (but many varieties including white, brown and black) with red bill, **knobbly or warty** at base.

Fairly common (introduced from America), has bred. Lakes, reservoirs.

Cinnamon Teal *Spatula cyanoptera*
L 35–45 cm | WS 55–60 cm
MALE **rufous brown** with black bill and **red eye**. FEMALE like Blue-winged Teal (p. 67) but pale loral spot less distinct and bill wider at tip. IN FLIGHT, blue forewing.

Uncommon (introduced from N America), has bred. Lakes, reservoirs.

Marbled Duck
Marmaronetta angustirostris
L 39–42 cm | WS 55–60 cm
Small, pale, mottled, Teal-like (p. 44); sexes similar. Dull sandy-brown with darker back and more-or-less obvious **dark 'mask'**; dark bill. Flank spotted pale buff, not streaked. IN FLIGHT, whitish hindwing, dark beyond angle of wing; white underwing.

Rare (escapees but **possible vagrant** from S Europe), has bred. Lakes, reservoirs.

INTRODUCED WILDFOWL | HYBRID DUCKS

Hybrid ducks

Ducks interbreed more than most birds, mainly in captivity. Resulting hybrids differ according to which parent is male, and female progeny are generally less noticeable than males. They usually show obviously mixed features, but may look remarkably like a third species. Many combinations occur: this sample shows both subtle and obvious results. Hybrid possibilities must always be borne in mind when identifying rare wildfowl, especially Ferruginous Duck (p. 69), Redhead (p. 71) and Lesser Scaup (p. 68).

Mallard × Pintail
Male combines colours and shapes of both parents (pp. 40 & 43) but clearly differs from either.

Shoveler × Gadwall
Body largely like male Gadwall (p. 42) but peculiar head pattern incorporates Shoveler (p. 41) green.

Wigeon × American Wigeon
Intermediate, or closer to one parent (pp. 39 & 64); pale head with dark band, grey body frequent.

Tufted Duck × Pochard
Like dark Scaup (p. 49) with a tuft, or Lesser Scaup (p. 68) with a uniform back; larger black bill tip.

Tufted Duck × Ferruginous Duck
Like Ferruginous Duck (p. 69) but with a duller eye and a tuft; or Tufted Duck (p. 48) with a dark flank.

Pochard × Ferruginous Duck
Like Ferruginous Duck (p. 69) but often reddish eye, greyer body, white under tail reduced.

Tufted Duck × Ring-necked Duck
Like Ring-necked Duck (p. 69) but with a tuft on the nape; grey flank lacks white peak at front.

Scaup × Tufted Duck
Both sexes like Scaup (p. 49) or Lesser Scaup (p. 68) but with more black on bill tip; small 'tuft'.

RARE WILDFOWL

Rare dabbling ducks

American Wigeon
Mareca (Anas) americana
L 48–56 cm | W 76–89 cm

Distinctive 'wigeon' form and pattern. MALE told from Wigeon (*p. 39*) by **white forehead and crown** above **dark head band**; body pale purplish/pinkish. FEMALE/IMMATURE/'ECLIPSE' MALE difficult to pick out and identify (see *below*).

IN FLIGHT, bold white forewing on MALE, whitish forewing bar on FEMALE; dull, dark speculum (see *below*).

Vagrant from N America: >500 records (<200 Ireland), 10–15 per year, most Sep–Mar. Freshwater, estuaries.

♂ NOV–APR

Identification of female wigeons

IN FLIGHT, axillaries ('wing pit') entirely white on American Wigeon (greyer on Wigeon). FEMALE whitish upperwing bar broad on American Wigeon (narrow on Wigeon). A good strategy is to wait patiently for a swimming bird to flap its wings.

broad bar

narrow bar

white

greyish

American Wigeon generally slightly more contrast between greyer head and more orangey body than female Wigeon, and hint (or more) of male's dark head band/pale forehead (but some Wigeon very similar).

AMERICAN WIGEON

WIGEON

Wigeon usually warmer brown with variable hint of an 'eyepatch'.

RARE DABBLING DUCKS

Black Duck *Anas rubripes*
L 53–61 cm | W 85–96 cm

Like female Mallard (*p. 40*) but darker (although beware some domesticated types) with contrasting paler head/neck, **pale bill** and orange legs. MALE **bill yellowish**. FEMALE **bill greenish**.

IN FLIGHT, underwing white; hindwing patch purplish-blue with **no white lines**.

two white lines — MALLARD

white underwing — BLACK DUCK

Vagrant from N America: <75 records (<25 Ireland), Oct–Mar; some long-stayers. Freshwater.

dark edges to tail (white on Mallard)

Long-staying individuals have bred with Mallard, producing confusing hybrids with intermediate characters.

Falcated Duck
Mareca (Anas) falcata
L 46–53 cm | WS 70–75 cm

MALE grey body; head dark, glossed green, with **bulky, drooping nape**; white throat; **domed/drooping feathers over buff stern**. FEMALE like brown Wigeon (*p. 39*) with longer grey bill. **Greyish head**; breast and flank tawny with black 'V's.

IN FLIGHT, upperwing and underwing pale grey (darker on FEMALE) with very dark hindwing band broadly edged white.

Vagrant from Asia: 1 record (Britain), Aug–Apr (plus occasional escapes). Freshwater.

Falcated Duck is perhaps most likely to associate with Wigeon.

♂ OCT–MAY

65

RARE WILDFOWL

Rare dabbling ducks (teal)

Females and juveniles of the rare teal are similar to Teal (p. 44) and Garganey (p. 45). The wing and head patterns are important features for identification.

green patch; midwing bar broadest

grey patch; two whitish bars

blue forewing

dark hindwing, white line at rear

TEAL **GARGANEY** **BLUE-WINGED TEAL** **BAIKAL TEAL**

pale spot absent or subtle at best

pale spot; cheek band

white spot against plain cheek; heavy bill

dark-bordered white spot; cheek plain

Green-winged Teal
Anas carolinensis

L 34–38 cm | W 53–59 cm

MALE very similar to Teal (p. 44) but **vertical white band beside breast**; lacks horizontal white line and pale buff edge to green head band. FEMALE near-identical to Teal but may have stronger facial stripes and pale spot by bill.

Vagrant from N America: 20–60 per year, most Sep–Mar. Freshwater.

IN FLIGHT, greyish, with black/green speculum and buff midwing bar.

TEAL — midwing bar white

midwing bar largely buff (note 'green' patch may flash blue)

'ECLIPSE' ♂ MAY–OCT [Oct]

♀ has same buff midwing bar but browner forewing

tuft on hindneck longer than on Teal (minute on ♀)

♂ OCT–APR

vertical white band

66

RARE DABBLING DUCKS (TEAL)

Blue-winged Teal
Spatula (Anas) discors
L 37–41 cm | W 58 cm

MALE distinctive: **white face crescent**; tawny flank, spotted black; white patch near black stern. OTHER PLUMAGES difficult: look for **broken pale line over eye**, white eyering, **white spot against bill** in front of **plain cheek**, white throat, relatively heavy blackish bill and **yellowish legs**.

Vagrant from N America: <300 records (<150 Ireland), most Sep–Mar. Freshwater.

👁 Cinnamon Teal (♀) (p. 62)

IN FLIGHT, bold pale blue forewing with white rear edge; blackish speculum.

slightly spatulate bill

white crescent

♂ OCT–APR

Baikal Teal
Sibirionetta (Anas) formosa
L 39–43 cm | W 55–60 cm

MALE unmistakable: **black/white/buff/green patterned** head. OTHER PLUMAGES like Teal (p. 44) and Garganey (p. 45) with **dark-bordered whitish face spot** and slight pale streak beside tail.

Vagrant from Asia: <10 records (1 Ireland), Nov–Apr. Occasional escapes. Freshwater, estuaries.

IN FLIGHT, rather uniform above; dark speculum with buff front edge; white trailing edge.

♂ OCT–APR

67

RARE WILDFOWL

Rare diving ducks

Regular scrutiny of wildfowl flocks might eventually result in the discovery of a rare bird. Lesser Scaup, Ring-necked Duck and Ferruginous Duck all tend to be found associating loosely with Tufted Ducks and Pochards on inland waters. Rare 'sea' ducks such as Surf Scoter and King Eider become mixed with close relatives, and finding them is a challenge.

Lesser Scaup *Aythya affinis*
L 38–45 cm | W 60–65 cm

Vagrant from N America: <200 records (<50 Ireland), most Oct–Mar. Usually with diving duck flocks; a few long-stayers. Freshwater.

Small 'scaup'. MALE like Scaup (*p. 49*) with coarsely barred grey back, white flank, **small bump/'tuft' on back of head**. FEMALE like small, dark Scaup with tiny tuft on head, greyer back and less black on bill tip than Tufted Duck (*p. 48*). Beware hybrids (*p. 63*).

IN FLIGHT, white **wingbar only on innerwing**.

♂ SEP–JUN

♀

Identification of scaups

FEMALES

LESSER SCAUP — peak at back of crown; small black nail on bill

SCAUP — rounder head higher on forehead; small black nail on bill

TUFTED DUCK — tuft on nape; white face small or obscure; broad, dark bill tip

SCAUP ♂ — head 'peaks' at front; outer part of wingbar white

LESSER SCAUP ♂ — head 'peaks' at rear; outer part of wingbar greyish

68

RARE DIVING DUCKS

Ring-necked Duck
Aythya collaris
L 37–46 cm | W 65–70 cm

Vagrant from N America: 20–30 per year (>300 records Ireland), most Sep–Mar. With Pochard/Tufted Duck flocks. Freshwater.

MALE like smart Tufted Duck (p. 48) with high-peaked head (no tuft) and grey (not white) flank outlined in white and with **white front peak**; white ring on bill. FEMALE like Tufted Duck but whitish around bill extends to throat; eyering and 'spectacle' line; banded bill like male (see Pochard (p. 47) and Redhead (p. 71); also beware hybrids (p. 63).

IN FLIGHT, **broad grey wingbar**; white leading edge to wing on MALE. White belly shows well.

grey wingbar

TUFTED DUCK
white wingbar

subtly distinctive head pattern

pale band on bill

♂ SEP–JUN

grey flank with white 'spur' at front

♀

NT Ferruginous Duck
Aythya nyroca
L 38–42 cm | W 60–67 cm

Vagrant from E Europe: <500 records, <10 per year (<200 Ireland), most Sep–Apr, declining. Freshwater.

544

Small, smart diving duck, like sleek, bright female Tufted Duck (p. 48) with slender bill.

MALE glossy mahogany-brown with dark back; **white under tail** edged black. **Eye white**. Bill grey with soft pale band. FEMALE browner with dark eye. Smooth, peaked head shape (higher than Pochard (p. 47)). **Upperparts always unmarked**: grey bars indicate hybrid (p. 63). Female Tufted Duck may show white under tail but rarely so sharply defined or bright. JUVENILE as female but all-grey bill, dark cap/paler rear cheek, dark eye, duller/faintly spotted white under tail.

IN FLIGHT, **broad white wingbar**; white leading edge to wing on MALE. White belly prominent.

♂ white belly patch

♂ broad white wingbar

head shape can vary, from quite flat-crowned to a distinctive high peak

white eye

dark eye

dark collar (hard to see)

♂ ♀

69

RARE WILDFOWL

Very rare diving ducks from North America

Hooded Merganser
Lophodytes cucullatus
L 42–50 cm | W 75–80 cm

MALE unmistakable: black head with **fan-like**, black-edged, white crest; white breast, tawny flank, **black bill**. FEMALE/IMMATURE grey-brown, dull greyish bill, dusky face blending into wide, fanned, tawny crest.

Vagrant from N America: <20 records (<10 Ireland), Oct–Mar. Lakes, reservoirs.

IN FLIGHT, pale upperwing with black and white midwing bar edged black; MALE also has small whitish forewing patch.

'fuzzy' crest, dark face

♀

♂ SEP–JUN

Bufflehead
Bucephala albeola
L 32–39 cm | W 55–60 cm

Tiny. MALE white with black back; head dark, iridescent, with **broad white band** behind eye and around nape. FEMALE brown, with small white panel behind eye.

Vagrant from N America: <30 records (plus escapes) (<5 Ireland), Oct–Mar.

IN FLIGHT, white stripe beside dark back; broad, diagonal white wingbar.

like Goldeneye (p. 50) with white cheek

♀

big white nape

♂ SEP–JUN

70

RARE DIVING DUCKS

Redhead *Aythya americana*
L 44–51 cm | W 65–70 cm

Like large, dark Pochard (*p. 47*) with rounder head, **steep forehead/bulging forecrown** and cocked tail when resting. MALE has **golden eye**, pale grey bill with broad black tip beyond diffuse pale band. FEMALE has dark cap, plain, pale face, more uniform body than Pochard, whiter under tail.

IN FLIGHT, upperwing grey with broad paler grey hindwing band extending to tip and thin dark trailing edge; head rounded against paler bill.

dark cap

both sexes have a steep forecrown

golden eye

♂ SEP–JUN

Vagrant from N America: <10 records (1 Ireland), most autumn–winter.

POCHARD has a sloping forehead like **Canvasback** but both sexes have pale areas on the bill – like **Redhead**, but that species has a steep forehead and males have a golden eye.

POCHARD

Canvasback *Aythya valisineria*
L 49–56 cm | W 70–80 cm

Like large, long Pochard (*p. 47*) with **long, all-black bill** sloping up towards high crown. MALE very pale grey with dark face; black of breast angled against grey back and flank (straight in Pochard). FEMALE greyer than Pochard.

N American vagrant: <15 records (Britain), winter.

IN FLIGHT, upperwing grey with broad paler grey hindwing band extending to tip and thin dark trailing edge; head slopes into long, dark bill.

both sexes have a long, sweeping black bill

♂ SEP–JUN

71

RARE WILDFOWL

Rare 'sea' ducks | Eiders and goldeneye

King Eider *Somateria spectabilis*
L 55–63 cm | W 87–100 cm

Rare associate of Eider (*p. 58*) flocks; male immediately obvious (although beware odd Eider plumages) but female difficult. MALE blacker than Eider with deeper salmon-pink breast; **head bluer**, with **red bill** and bulging **orange frontal shield**. 1ST-YEAR MALE like same-age Eider but **bill reddish** and **frontal shield yellow**. FEMALE rusty, neatly marked with bars and chevrons. Close up, look for tiny **'sails'** on back, 'smiling' dark gape line, shorter facial 'wedge' against **smaller bill with dark tip** (pale tip on Eider).

IN FLIGHT, WINTER MALE like Eider but less white on upperparts; bill colour best clue; FEMALE as Eider (head shape only real difference).

Vagrant from Arctic: <300 records (<35 Ireland), average 5 per year plus returnees, all months. Invariably with Eider flocks on coast.

EIDER

KING EIDER

STELLER'S EIDER

To identify FEMALE eiders, concentrate on the head shape, bill profile and shape of the gape.

1ST-YEAR ♂ [Mar]

1ST-YEAR ♂ [May]

bill colours developing

hint of a tuft

pale, plain head

curved gape line

♀

unique head and bill unmistakable

♂ OCT–JUN

RARE 'SEA' DUCKS

NT Barrow's Goldeneye
Bucephala islandica
L 44–54 cm | W 77–83 cm

Very like Goldeneye (p. 50).

MALE has more black above and bold **kidney-shaped** white face patch on heavier head. FEMALE larger than Goldeneye with **more bushy nape**, rounder crown and shorter bill.

IN FLIGHT, MALE upperwing black, with thin black bar separating narrow white forewing patch from broad white hindwing; FEMALE has little white on forewing.

little white on forewing

extensive white on forewing

dark bar splits white

no dark bar

more bushy nape, smaller bill and 'rounder' crown than Goldeneye

GOLDENEYE

rounded face patch

kidney-shaped face patch

white spots

black 'spur'

Vagrant from Iceland/Nearctic: <5 records (1 Ireland), Oct–Apr. Coasts, freshwater.

VU Steller's Eider
Polysticta stelleri
L 42–48 cm | W 68–77 cm

Very small eider. MALE unmistakable: pale yellow-buff with black back and stern; head **greyish-white** with black neck ring and **dark nape spot**. 'ECLIPSE' MALE like female but with white forewing. FEMALE/IMMATURE dark brown, faintly barred; bill thick, plain grey, without 'lobes' of Eider (p. 58); spike-like tail.

IN FLIGHT, MALE distinct bold pattern; FEMALE dark with two white lines on hindwing (recalling Mallard (p. 40)) and white flash on underwing.

white wingbars may show when swimming

MALE 'ECLIPSE' (MAY–SEP) like FEMALE but with white forewing.

♂ SEP–JUN

Vagrant from Arctic: <35 records (Britain), Sep–Mar. Coasts.

73

RARE WILDFOWL

Rare 'sea' ducks | Harlequin Duck and Scoters

Surf Scoter *Melanitta perspicillata*
L 45–56 cm | W 75–85 cm

Big, bulky scoter; dives with open wings (like Velvet Scoter (*p. 56*); Common Scoter (*p. 57*) more often with wings closed). MALE bulky-headed, **black** with big **white nape patch** and forehead triangle. Bill swollen, boldly patched black, white and orange. FEMALE like Velvet Scoter with double facial spots, sometimes hint of nape patch; bill more **deeply triangular** with hint of darker basal patch. **Wings all-dark**, so check head to find one, then check wings to rule out Velvet Scoter.

IN FLIGHT, dark overall except paler flight feathers on underwing (striking when lit by low sun).

neck patch most obvious feature at long range

Bill colour and white patches develop during first year.

FEMALE may lack pale nape patch: plain wing unlike Velvet Scoter, requiring patience until bird flaps or flies.

Vagrant from N America: <750 records, 15–20 per year (<300 records Ireland), all months. In scoter flocks. Coasts.

Harlequin Duck *Histrionicus histrionicus*
L 38–43 cm | W 65–68 cm

Small, round, small-billed 'sea' duck. MALE blue-grey with **white patches**, rusty flank. OTHER PLUMAGES scoter-like, dark brown with smudgy pale face patch and bright **white ear spot**; all-dark wing.

IN FLIGHT, round-bodied; ♀ dark overall; ♂ dark with white stripe beside back and white breast stripes.

Vagrant from N America/Iceland: <20 records (Britain), Oct–Apr. Coasts.

RARE 'SEA' DUCKS

'White-winged' Scoters Two very similar species typically found at sea associating with other scoters. Both have white wing patches and, as such, resemble Velvet Scoter (*p. 56*). Good views of the head and bill details are required for identification. Females in particular exhibit subtle differences.

Vagrant from N America: <5 records (Britain), Oct.

White-winged Scoter *Melanitta deglandi*
L 50–57 cm | W 78–95 cm

MALE has **high forehead**, **peaked crown** and **angular 'step' on bill**; bill black with a **yellowish ridge** and **short pinkish-red side streak towards tip** (see *below*); white eye patch sweeps upwards. Flank dark brown. FEMALE/1ST-WINTER (not recorded) steep forehead, but bill heavy-based.

Vagrant from Asia: 1 record (Ireland), Feb–Apr.

Stejneger's (Siberian) Scoter ◆
Melanitta stejnegeri
L 50–57 cm | WS 78–95 cm

MALE has **low, smooth crown** and **angled/hooked 'knob' on bill** (small on IMMATURES); bill black with a **pink-red ridge** and **short yellow side streak towards tip** (see *below*); short white eye patch hooks upwards. Flank black. FEMALE/1ST-WINTER (not recorded) like White-winged Scoter but forehead subtly flatter.

Black Scoter *Melanitta americana*
NT
L 44–54 cm | W 70–85 cm

Very like Common Scoter (*p. 57*), with which it is generally found. MALE has big, wide, **domed yellow patch** at base of bill. FEMALE has hooked tip and typically some yellow streaks on the bill.

Vagrant from N America: <50 records (1 Ireland), Sep–Apr. Coasts.

CORMORANTS | DIVERS | GREBES | PELICANS

WATERBIRDS (cormorants, divers, grebes and pelicans)

Highly specialized waterbirds, unable to walk on land properly; divers slide onto waterside nests, grebes occasionally stand upright at the water's edge, cormorants often stand out on ground or perch. All swim and dive under from surface, reappearing far away, so often hard to follow.

3 cormorants: 1 widespread, 1 marine, 1 vagrant.

5 divers: 2 breed locally but are widespread in winter, 1 other regular, 1 rare migrant, 1 vagrant.

6 grebes: 2 breed commonly, 2 are rare and restricted, scarce but more widespread in winter, 1 regular but declining migrant, 1 vagrant.

1 pelican: a single vagrant record (see *p. 92*) (plus one of uncertain provenance (see *p. 539*)).

CORMORANT ID face pattern | crest shape | bill size | underparts colour | habitat

Cormorants (*pp. 78, 80–81*) are long-bodied, long-tailed, hook-billed waterbirds with webbed feet (all four toes webbed); swim low with head up and tail flat on water and always dive from surface. Fly well, Cormorant occasionally soaring high, or gliding down (often several in unison) to settle with precision. Shag more strictly marine, braving roughest surf on rocky coasts. Cormorant equally at home inland and on large rivers, often in treetop roosts and breeding colonies, locally regular on overhead power lines. Both often perch with their wings widely spread.

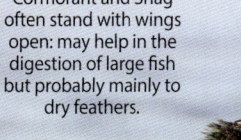

Ageing/sexing
Sexes alike; juveniles browner than adults, gaining full colours after two–three years.

CORMORANT

Cormorant and Shag often stand with wings open: may help in the digestion of large fish but probably mainly to dry feathers.

CORMORANT

SHAG

SHAG

When diving, Cormorant rolls forwards in the water; Shag more often with a forwards leap.

POSSIBLE CONFUSION GROUPS
Diving ducks (such as Red-breasted Merganser) small and slim; **grebes** much smaller, pointed bill tip; **auks** squat, dumpy, small-winged; **divers**, range from Mallard to Cormorant in size, have pointed bill, slimmer head/neck profile, short tail.

MERGANSER (duck) *p. 52*

GREBE *pp. 86–90*

AUK *pp. 106–113*

DIVER *pp. 82–85*

CORMORANT *pp. 80–81*

INTRODUCTION

DIVER ID
BREEDING PLUMAGE – distinctive: head colour | throat pattern/colour | back pattern
NON-BREEDING PLUMAGE – all much alike: size | bill shape | head/neck /flank patterns
IN FLIGHT – can be difficult: neck shape | size | wingbeats

Divers (pp. 79, 82–85) are long-bodied, short-tailed waterbirds with a dagger-like bill and webbed feet. Two species breed on Scottish lochs (Red-throated Divers fly, giving quacking calls, to feed at sea; Black-throated Divers stay on large lochs with islands). All divers are more widespread from autumn to spring (Black-throated Diver scarcest of the regular three; White-billed Diver a rare migrant and Pacific Diver a vagrant). Red-throated Diver is locally numerous but like all divers usually in ones and twos. All are scarce inland but might linger on a large reservoir.

Ageing/sexing
Sexes alike; breeding and non-breeding plumages differ; juveniles resemble non-breeding adult but are separable at close range by detailed head pattern and shape of pale feather edging/ barring on back.

RED-THROATED DIVER

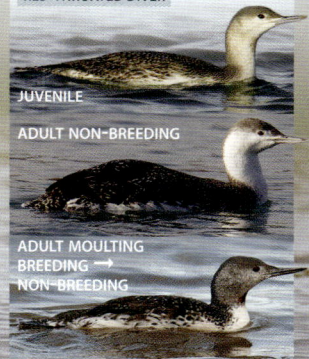

JUVENILE
ADULT NON-BREEDING
ADULT MOULTING BREEDING → NON-BREEDING

Divers submerge from the surface, with a smooth, low, forward roll.

ADULT BREEDING
ADULT BREEDING
RED-THROATED DIVER

GREBE ID
BREEDING PLUMAGE – distinctive: size | bill shape | head pattern | neck colour
NON-BREEDING PLUMAGE: – size | bill shape | head pattern
Beware 'intermediate' plumages in autumn and spring

Grebes (p. 78, 86–90) are rather rounded, very short-tailed waterbirds with a pointed bill and unwebbed feet, but broad, flat lobes on the toes. Smaller than divers and take off with a run and land with breast-first splash. Largest is Great Crested Grebe, widespread on lakes and large rivers, and often on the sea; in flight, long and slim with trailing feet, white in wing rules out divers. Little Grebe smallest, common on lakes and rivers, scarce on the sea. Others much scarcer: Slavonian Grebe (rare breeder in Scotland, rare on coasts in winter), Black-necked Grebe (rare breeder, scarce or rare on lakes and coasts in winter) and larger Red-necked Grebe (declining and rare, autumn and winter).

Ageing/sexing
Sexes alike; breeding and non-breeding plumages differ; juveniles distinctive but 1st-winter like non-breeding adult, separable by smudgy head/neck patterns with hint of breeding colour.

GREAT CRESTED GREBE

JUVENILE
ADULT NON-BREEDING

ADULT NON-BREEDING
Flight infrequent, low, fast, lacking manoeuvrability.

Grebes swim buoyantly and dive frequently.

ADULT BREEDING
GREAT CRESTED GREBE

CORMORANTS | DIVERS | GREBES | PELICANS

Cormorants, divers and grebes in flight

Cormorants have broad, rounded wings and a long, broad tail. Divers have long, narrow wings, trailing feet and a direct, powerful flight action. Grebes look weak fliers, low over the water, head stretched out and feet trailing, with quick beats.

CORMORANT (p. 80) in flight, head extended, neck kinked; long, broad tail and wings (geese have shorter tails (see p. 23)), lengthy glides. May fly high over water (Shag low) or land, often in synchronized groups; can soar high up. Wings hunched/bowed, often in long glide, rolling to lose height.

ADULT MAR–JUN

JUVENILE

SHAG

IMMATURE

CORMORANT

ADULT MAR–JUN

ADULT JAN–JUN

ADULT

SHAG (p. 81) in flight like Cormorant but quicker action; usually low over sea, going round headlands/islands rather than over them. Deeper rear body, straighter neck.

NON-BREEDING GREBES IN FLIGHT

ADULT AUG–MAR

ADULT AUG–MAR

ADULT AUG–MAR

GREAT CRESTED GREBE
Long, thin neck, big trailing feet; large white wing patches.

LITTLE GREBE [N/I]
Little or no white on dull brown wing.

BLACK-NECKED GREBE
Long, slim wings with broad white rear edge.

SLAVONIAN GREBE
Rounded wings, white rear edge and 'shoulder'.

RED-NECKED GREBE [N/I]
Much less white than Great Crested Grebe, stockier shape.

Non-breeding grebes

GREAT CRESTED GREBE (p. 86)
long **pinkish bill**; distinct dark cap; **white above eye**; head shape **slightly 'horned'**; white cheeks and dark on hindneck narrow

RED-NECKED GREBE (p. 87)
long **yellow bill**; dark cap merges into dull white cheek below eye; **dark on hindneck broad**, smudging onto foreneck

BLACK-NECKED GREBE (p. 88)
short, slightly upturned bill; **steep forehead**; dark cap usually merges into white cheek creating 'comma' shape

SLAVONIAN GREBE (p. 89)
short, straightish bill; shallow forehead; dark cap usually very distinct from **white cheeks**

LITTLE GREBE (p. 90)
dull, buff and brown; darker, round cap

CORMORANTS, DIVERS and GREBES IN FLIGHT | NON-BREEDING PLUMAGES

RED-THROATED DIVER APR–NOV
typically drop-necked profile

BLACK-THROATED DIVER FEB–OCT
straight, 'tube' neck

WHITE-BILLED DIVER APR–OCT

GREAT NORTHERN DIVER APR–OCT

RED-THROATED DIVER AUG–MAR

BLACK-THROATED DIVER OCT–MAR

PACIFIC DIVER OCT–MAR
not safely identifiable in flight

GREAT NORTHERN DIVER OCT–MAR
very big; long wings

WHITE-BILLED DIVER OCT–MAR
very big; very heavy head/bill

Non-breeding divers

WHITE-BILLED DIVER (p. 85)
pale head, pale bill typically uptilted, may be held horizontally

GREAT NORTHERN DIVER (p. 84)
dark cap broken by white around eye; cap/hindneck **darker than/same tone as** back; no white flank patch

RED-THROATED DIVER (p. 82)
'button' eye in pale face; **cap/hindneck much paler and narrower** than other divers

BLACK-THROATED DIVER (p. 83)
dark cap to eye level; **cap/hindneck paler than back; white flank patch** (compare with Pacific Diver p. 91)

79

CORMORANTS | DIVERS | GREBES | PELICANS   Cormorants in flight *p. 78*

Cormorant *Phalacrocorax carbo*

sspp. *carbo* and *sinensis*

L 77–94 cm | W 121–149 cm

Double-crested Cormorant (p. 92)

Common resident (14,000 pairs, plus 5,000 pairs Ireland) and winter visitor (41,000 Britain).

Very large, distinctive waterbird. Long bill barely tapers towards thick tip; **broad wings**; **long, rounded tail**. **Stands upright**, often with **spread wings**, or more horizontal in odd, contorted poses. Swims low, **bill uptilted**; rolls into dive (Shag 'leaps'); often singly or in pairs, occasionally scores in 'feeding frenzies'.

ADULT BREEDING **blackish**, with **white chin** and **white thigh**; variable whitish crown and neck plumes (continental and many S/E English birds white-headed in spring). NON-BREEDING blackish, with yellow around bill, whitish throat. JUVENILE black-brown, **whiter beneath** by winter; whitish chin, yellow face; later darker, or with dark breast, whiter belly. OLDER IMMATURES mottled black, with orange-yellow facial patch, pale bill, whitish face (Shag has less yellow, darker below eye).

VOICE Calls low, deep, guttural or cooing notes.

from N and W Europe

Subspecies *carbo* and *sinensis* ('Continental') may be difficult to assign to subspecies; *sinensis* whiter head (dark crest) earlier in spring. Check bare skin behind gape: *carbo* angle 38°–72°; *sinensis* 65°–110°, so 'square' shape (around 90°), with white patch parallel-sided, less fan-shaped, indicates *sinensis*.

ssp. *sinensis*

ssp. *carbo*

Coasts, inland waters

ADULT BREEDING
flattish belly

ADULT NON-BREEDING

IN FLIGHT, flocks fly in long lines, 'V'-shapes, often gliding; may soar high up. Neck extended, often kinked; long, broad tail; flattish belly.

relatively long, thick neck and long tail

ADULT BREEDING
birds from SE England and the continent may have white head in spring

ADULT NON-BREEDING
JUN–MAR

ADULT BREEDING
JAN–JUN

IMMATURE
variable but extensive white breast/front

CORMORANTS

Shag *Phalacrocorax aristotelis*

L 68–78 cm | W 95–110 cm

◉ Double-crested Cormorant (p. 92)

Locally common resident (27,000 pairs breed, 110,000 in winter). Coasts; rare inland.

Similar to Cormorant, but smaller, with **slimmer bill**, more rounded head, **steeper forehead** and thinner neck. Often stands with **spread wings**, typically held at a straighter angle than Cormorant. Often swims in breaking waves. Frequently large, loose **flocks on sea**: from long range a line of round heads on thin, upright, stick-like necks. Often dives with **upward leap** (Cormorant rolls forward).
ADULT BREEDING dark green-black, except **bright yellow gape** and chin (no white); **forward-curled crest** unique. NON-BREEDING lacks crest.
JUVENILE dark brown; **whitish chin spot** and eyering. IMMATURE develops paler underparts but little white except on vent; no strong contrast. Legs pale, sometimes yellowish. Often has worn, pale panel on wing.

VOICE Grunts and cackling alarm at nest.

IN FLIGHT, like Cormorant but quicker; usually low over sea, not high up or over land (flies around headlands). Neck extended but relatively short, less kinked; wings set farther back; deep belly.

Sea coasts (breeds on cliffs); rarely reservoirs/large rivers

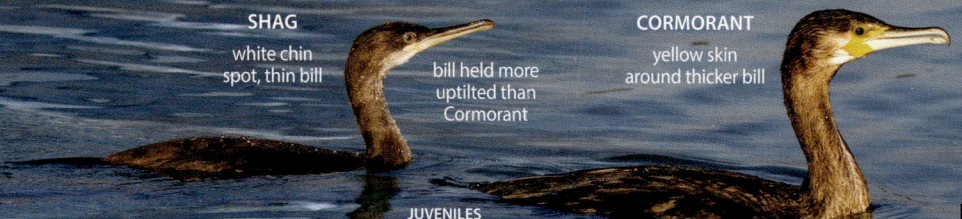

ADULT BREEDING
deep belly
relatively short neck and tail, neck narrow in middle

JUVENILE
CORMORANT

white chin spot

JUVENILE
OCT–AUG
[Jan]

brown breast

ADULT BREEDING
MAR–JUN

ADULT NON-BREEDING
JUN–MAR

SHAG
white chin spot, thin bill

bill held more uptilted than Cormorant

CORMORANT
yellow skin around thicker bill

JUVENILES

CORMORANTS | DIVERS | GREBES | PELICANS Divers in flight *p. 79*

Red-throated Diver *Gavia stellata*

L 55–67 cm | W 91–110 cm

Smallest diver, but overlaps in size with Black-throated Diver. On water, **neck upright, straight** (less sinuous than Black-throated Diver), **head and bill uptilted**, bill tapered to **straight upper edge**.
ADULT BREEDING **dark**, with **white breast**; head/neck grey, with fine lines on side and nape; red throat forms **narrow dark patch**, widest at bottom. Bill black; eye dark red. NON-BREEDING back grey, flecked white; flank whiter, mottled (sometimes forms rear patch as on Black-throated Diver). Breast and foreneck white; narrow dark cap and hindneck surround **bare white face with dark 'button' eye**. JUVENILE/IMMATURE similar to non-breeding adult but browner on foreneck and cheek.

VOICE Loud quacking "*kwuk kwuk kwuk*" in flight in summer; summer calls include wailing "*eeaaooow*" and remarkable fast, rhythmic duetting between pairs.

IN FLIGHT, elongated, **narrow-winged**: long wings dark above, white beneath, narrow dark flank line; head/**bill slightly drooped**, smallish feet trailed. Distinctive head-bobbing in synchrony with quick, deep wingbeats.

Scarce and local breeder Scotland (1,300 pairs); winters at coast (17,000, Sep–Mar); rare inland

from Iceland
from Svalbard
from Scandinavia

Breeds on lakes, feeds at nearest coast; winters at sea, bays, estuaries

ADULT BREEDING

typical 'drop-necked' flight profile

no black-and-white pattern on back

ADULT BREEDING APR–NOV

palest diver on head/neck, with extensive white

ADULT NON-BREEDING AUG–MAR

sloping forehead; white mark in front of eye

JUVENILE/1ST-WINTER has grey streaks on head, lost from Feb, when white-faced like ADULT

pale-speckled back

pale almost to back of neck

JUVENILE/ 1ST-WINTER JUL–FEB [Nov]

Non-breeding divers *p. 79* DIVERS

Black-throated Diver *Gavia arctica* 544

L 63–75 cm | W 100–122 cm   **Pacific Diver (*p. 91*)**

Medium-sized diver. Bill **dagger-shaped, held horizontally** (compare Red-throated Diver). In summer, head and neck appear inflated, especially in display. From rear, body narrow, neck narrower than **bulbous head** (body wider, neck more uniformly thick on Great Northern Diver (*p. 84*)).

ADULT BREEDING immaculate: grey head, blacker throat; **broad black throat patch** offset by black-and-white-stripes on foreneck and breast. Back black with **oval patches of white bars**. NON-BREEDING dark brown and white (vaguely like huge Guillemot (*p. 108*)). Grey-brown nape **slightly paler than back** (reverse of Great Northern Diver); dark cap extends to eye. Front edge of dark hindneck extends as faint, forward point. **White rear flank patch.** JUVENILE/IMMATURE like non-breeding adult but browner; rounded buff feather edges above and paler, greyer head.

VOICE Calls loud wailing scream/squeal and loud, rising, whistling series in summer.

IN FLIGHT, long, straight: **neck thick, hardly drooped**; large feet trail.

Rare and local breeder N Scotland (200 pairs); scarce UK coast in winter (500); rare inland

from Scandinavia

Breeds on large lakes with islands; winters offshore

ADULT BREEDING

typical straight-necked flight profile

ADULT BREEDING FEB–OCT

back with oval patches of white bars

cap and hindneck **paler than back**

ADULT NON-BREEDING OCT–MAR

well-defined white cheek and front half of neck

white patch

JUVENILE/1ST-WINTER has pale scale-like fringes above until Feb/Mar, when plainer like ADULT

rounded pale edges

JUVENILE/ 1ST-WINTER JUL–MAR [Dec]

CORMORANTS | DIVERS | GREBES | PELICANS   Divers in flight *p. 79*

VU Great Northern Diver *Gavia immer* 544

L 73–88 cm | W 122–148 cm   ◉ White-billed Diver

Largest regular diver. Bill **deep, tapered, dagger-shaped, held horizontally**; forehead often has 'bump' before crown.

ADULT BREEDING **head black**, with patch of white stripes on neck; breast white. Back **chequered with white** (barred oval patches on Black-throated Diver (*p. 83*)). NON-BREEDING recalls Cormorant (*p. 80*) but bill pointed, tail tiny; never stands out on dry perch. Bill grey/whitish, with **dark upper edge** (thicker than Black-throated Diver's). White eyering and throat; **cap and hindneck blacker than back** (reverse of Black-throated Diver); black half-collar; back has square pale bars; flank all-dark. JUVENILE/IMMATURE like non-breeding adult but barred with square buff feather edges above and browner head.

VOICE Calls sometimes heard away from breeding range in summer, especially quick, laughing sequence; also loud wails.

Scarce winter visitor (3,000, Aug–May); few summer in far N; rare inland

from Greenland / from Iceland

Mostly on sea, in sandy bays, estuaries

JUVENILE

IN FLIGHT, big, heavy head barely drooped; large, protruding feet. Long, centrally set wings; dark flank band. Wingbeats whippier than smaller divers, but large bill and bulk best clues.

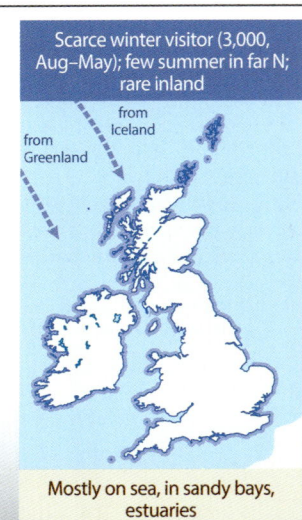

JUVENILE/1ST-WINTER has broad pale bars above until Mar/Apr when plainer like ADULT

square pale bars

JUVENILE/ 1ST-WINTER JUL–APR [Feb]

immatures in 'non-breeding' plumage occasionally seen in summer

'bump' on forehead

cap and hindneck **as dark as** back

ADULT NON-BREEDING OCT–MAR

bill thicker, less bluish than Black-throated Diver

back covered with white squares

ADULT BREEDING APR–OCT

Non-breeding divers p. 79 — DIVERS

NT White-billed Diver *Gavia adamsii* 544
VU L 77–90 cm | W 135–150 cm

Massive diver, like Great Northern Diver, but bill deeper, lower edge more sharply angled to pointed tip (Great Northern Diver's less extreme). Feathers extend to middle of nostril or beyond (only reach base to middle of nostril on Great Northern Diver). **Head and bill raised** (like huge Red-throated Diver (*p. 82*)). ADULT BREEDING bill **pale yellow/ivory** against black head. NON-BREEDING/IMMATURE **top of bill dark only at base; tip all-pale**. Diffuse pale patches on rear cheek around dark cheek mark; narrow dark band on hindneck.

IN FLIGHT, large, heavy-headed, thick-necked, with obvious large feet; pale neck with dark band can be obvious but much variation.

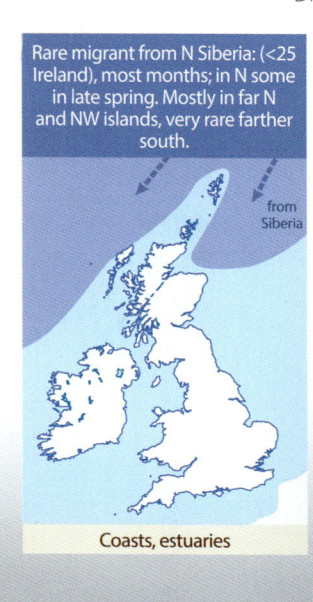

Rare migrant from N Siberia: (<25 Ireland), most months; in N some in late spring. Mostly in far N and NW islands, very rare farther south.

from Siberia

Coasts, estuaries

1ST-WINTER → 1ST-SUMMER [May]

1ST-SUMMER MAR–OCT [Jul]

top of the bill with dark base and pale tip

In non-breeding plumage, some Great Northern Divers have a very pale bill, but the less 'upturned' shape and dark ridge and tip should distinguish them from White-billed Diver.

JUVENILE
GREAT NORTHERN DIVER

2ND-WINTER OCT–MAR [Dec]

ADULT BREEDING APR–OCT

CORMORANTS | DIVERS | GREBES | PELICANS   Non-breeding grebes *p.78*

Great Crested Grebe *Podiceps cristatus*

L 46–51 cm | W 59–73 cm

Largest grebe (but size often hard to judge). Neck silvery-white: slim but broad-based, withdrawn into shoulders or bolt upright (giving impression of distant 'L'-shape on water). Bill slim, dagger-like, pink or pinkish. Dives frequently from surface. Often in sizeable flocks in winter. Rarely on land; cannot walk.

ADULT BREEDING black crest; broad, rounded, **chestnut ruff** (spread in display); **white** face, foreneck and breast. NON-BREEDING **white neck** (lacks ruff); narrow black cap, **white line over eye** and black line from bill to eye (black cap extends to eye on Red-necked Grebe). JUVENILE nondescript pale fawn with whiter breast; black-and-white stripes on head at first.

IN FLIGHT, white patches at front and rear of narrow wings. Fast, direct; neck outstretched; legs and feet drooped. Settles breast-first, feet trailing.

VOICE Summer calls loud, croaking or nasal. Chicks' persistent loud, whistling "*pli-pli-pli*" a common wetland sound in summer.

Widespread but local breeding resident (4,600 pairs, 19,000 in winter)

from N and W Europe

Lakes, reservoirs; sea coasts outside the breeding season

JUVENILE MAY–AUG

white patch on forewing extends back (all plumages)

ADULT NON-BREEDING

some are less bright on cheek

[Dec]

[Jan]

ADULT NON-BREEDING AUG–MAR

thin black cap; white above eye

bill pink

cheek bright white

ADULT BREEDING MAR–JUL

Red-necked Grebe *Podiceps grisegena*

L 40–46 cm | W 55–60 cm

Large, rather stocky grebe, similar to larger Great Crested Grebe and smaller Slavonian Grebe (*p. 89*). Bill heavy (slight drooped effect) with variable **yellow base**; **neck relatively thick**; eye dark or yellow, not red. Often dives with slight 'leap' (Great Crested Grebe has smooth dive). Often solitary, or one or two with other grebes.

ADULT BREEDING black cap with short tuft at back. Grey face edged white; **rusty-orange neck and breast** (lacks white breast of Great Crested Grebe). Bill **yellow-and-black**. Eye black. NON-BREEDING **black cap extends to eye**. Cheeks smudgy grey or duller white than Great Crested Grebe or Slavonian Grebe (but can be tricky); white 'hook' on ear coverts. **Foreneck greyish** or rusty buff, breast whitest. JUVENILE bill paler, face striped at first. 1ST-WINTER eye yellow.

IN FLIGHT, like Great Crested Grebe but less white on innerwing.

N American/NE Asian ssp. *holboellii* (vagrant: 1 record (Britain), Sep) larger, with bigger bill than regularly occurring ssp. *grisegena*.

Rare and declining autumn/winter visitor mostly NE/E (50 per year, mostly Sep–Mar); rare inland

from W Europe

Mainly along sea coasts, harbours; rarely reservoirs

JUVENILE MAY–AUG

dark cap extends below eye (unlike Great Crested Grebe); cheeks dull white (Great Crested and Slavonian Grebes bright white)

ADULT BREEDING

white patch on forewing only (all plumages)

NON-BREEDING SEP–FEB

bill yellow

Autumn adults and juveniles, in 'in between' plumages, more-or-less rusty on neck; juveniles retain some black-and-white striping on head.

ADULT BREEDING MAR–SEP

CORMORANTS | DIVERS | GREBES | PELICANS Non-breeding grebes p.78

Black-necked Grebe *Podiceps nigricollis*

545

L 28–34 cm | W 45–50 cm

Small grebe with **faintly upturned**, all-dark bill, high crown and red eye; much like Slavonian Grebe, with marked seasonal changes. Buoyant on water, between long dives.

ADULT BREEDING **mostly black**, with coppery-red flank, **peaked crown** and **drooping** golden-yellow 'fan' behind eye (acquires yellow 'fans', and dark head in Feb/Mar, while breast and flank still white). NON-BREEDING black, white and grey; similar to Slavonian Grebe but steeper forehead, high crown peaked in middle; **black cap extends below eye**. Contrast between dark crown and pale cheek can be sharp, but typically cheek dusky with whiter 'hook' at rear; **broad dark nape**, grey foreneck (silky white on Slavonian Grebe, but see bigger Red-necked Grebe (p. 87)). Flank and stern whitish, streaked grey. Cherry-red eyes catch sun at remarkably long range. JUVENILE striped on head; in winter loses stripes but retains orange-buff wash over face/neck.

IN FLIGHT, white hindwing line extends to outer half but no 'shoulder' spot as on Slavonian Grebe.

VOICE Weak trills and rising whistles; silent in winter.

Rare, local, erratic breeder (50 pairs), scarce migrant and winter visitor (130 birds per year)

from S Scandinavia and E Europe

Breeds on freshwater lakes, winters on coast and a few lakes/reservoirs

JUVENILE
JUN–AUG
striped face

TRANSITIONAL BETWEEN BREEDING/NON-BREEDING
FEB–MAY, AUG–SEP [Feb]

high crown, more black on face

'fuzzy' blend between cap and cheek

dark bill
slightly upturned

NON-BREEDING
SEP–APR

NON-BREEDING
no shoulder spot
extensive white hindwing patch

ADULT BREEDING
APR–OCT

GREBES

VU **Slavonian Grebe** *Podiceps auritus* 545
NT
L 31–38 cm | W 46–55 cm

Smallish grebe with small, **straight, pale-tipped** dark bill (bigger and yellow-based on Red-necked Grebe (*p. 87*)), rather rounded crown and red eye; marked seasonal changes in plumage: easily identified in summer, more difficult in winter.

ADULT BREEDING underparts and **neck deep rusty-red**; head black with broad, flat or raised 'wedge' of golden-yellow behind eye. NON-BREEDING black, white and grey; similar to Black-necked Grebe but relatively low crown; black cap peaks at rear and extends to bottom of eye, **sharply defined** against white cheeks that **almost meet on nape**. Whitish mark in front of cherry-red eye. Bill grey; dark band, whiter tip useful in good light, even at long range. JUVENILE striped on head; stripes lost during winter leaving dusky marks on face, resembling Black-necked Grebe.

IN FLIGHT, white hindwing patch, restricted to inner half; usually small whitish 'shoulder' spot.

VOICE Rather insignificant whinnies in summer.

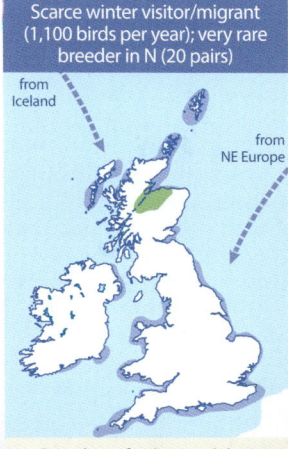

Scarce winter visitor/migrant (1,100 birds per year); very rare breeder in N (20 pairs)

from Iceland
from NE Europe

Breeds on freshwater lakes, winters around coast (harbours, estuaries)

striped head
JUVENILE
JUN–AUG

TRANSITIONAL BETWEEN
BREEDING/NON-BREEDING
FEB–MAY, AUG–SEP [Sep]

sharp contrast
between cap and cheek

restricted white hindwing patch
shoulder spot
NON-BREEDING

flatter crown, more white on face

pale area on lores
note pink line from bill to eye
bill straight, **pale tip**
NON-BREEDING
JUL–MAR

ADULT BREEDING
MAR–JUL

89

CORMORANTS | DIVERS | GREBES | PELICANS   Non-breeding grebes *p. 78*

Little Grebe *Tachybaptus ruficollis*

L 23–29 cm | W 40–45 cm   Pied-billed Grebe

Smallest, brownest, roundest and most dumpy grebe, with cork-like buoyancy. Often sits at the water's edge, occasionally stands upright on short legs. Compare with Black-necked Grebe (*p. 88*); non-breeding adult/juvenile head pattern can be contrasty, but brown/buff not black/white as other small grebes.

ADULT BREEDING **very dark**, with blackish cap, back and breast; **chestnut-red face**; pale yellow spot at base of short bill. Flank feathers spread to reveal rich orange-buff. NON-BREEDING paler, browner, more contrast between dark back and buff flank, and between dark cap and pale cheek/whitish throat (less black-and-white than other small grebes (*pp. 88–89*)). Pale bill with **whitish basal spot**. JUVENILE dark face and cap, striped cheek; short, stout bill unlike other small grebes.

IN FLIGHT, wings dull dark brown; longer necked and with trailing dark feet when skittering across water.

VOICE Loud, sudden whinnying, descending trill is a characteristic waterside sound in summer. Various short, thin, puzzling whistles from juveniles. Short pipes and trills in autumn/winter.

Widespread and locally common resident (7,500 breeding pairs) and winter visitor (16,000 UK)

Breeds on lakes and rivers; winters on coast and lakes

JUVENILE MAY–AUG

JUVENILE (MOULTING) JUL–OCT

often shows strong contrast on head, but brown/buff, not black/white

NON-BREEDING SEP–MAR

ADULT BREEDING APR–SEP

RARE DIVERS AND GREBES

Pacific Diver *Gavia pacifica*
L 60–63 cm | W 109–122 cm

Vagrant from N America: <30 records (<5 Ireland), Nov–May. Coastal waters.

All plumages as Black-throated Diver (*p. 83*) but lack white rear flank patch. Head more rounded, with steeper forehead above smaller bill. Shows slight dark 'chinstrap' and dark vent band in winter.

ADULT BREEDING MAR–SEP

no obvious flank patch

chinstrap

ADULT NON-BREEDING OCT–MAR

BLACK-THROATED DIVER

white rear flank patch

ADULT OCT–MAR

no chinstrap

Pied-billed Grebe *Podilymbus podiceps*
L 31–38 cm | W 45–62 cm

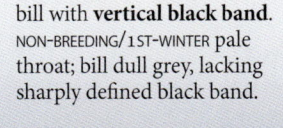

Vagrant from N America: <50 records (<20 Ireland), most months. Freshwater.

Smallish grebe with large 'frog-like' head and deep, almost triangular, arched bill. Dark brown, with darker crown and whitish stern. ADULT BREEDING white eyering; black throat; white bill with **vertical black band**. NON-BREEDING/1ST-WINTER pale throat; bill dull grey, lacking sharply defined black band.

1ST-WINTER SEP–MAR

ADULT BREEDING MAR–SEP

RARE CORMORANTS | PELICAN

Double-crested Cormorant
Phalacrocorax auritus
L 70–90 cm | W 95–130 cm

Very like Cormorant (*p. 80*) and difficult to identify in immature/winter plumages. Size and bill shape between Cormorant and Shag (*p. 81*); rather long tail has 12 feathers (as does Shag; Cormorant has 14). ADULT orange facial skin with **no white**. IMMATURE **orange face**; breast paler than belly (reverse of Cormorant); lower mandible yellow.

Vagrant from N America: <5 records (1 Britain, Dec; 1 Ireland, Nov–Jan). Freshwater.

small patch of yellow skin

feathered

IMMATURE CORMORANT

JUVENILE SHAG

ADULT

bare orange patch broad and rounded beneath chin; no white on face

orange skin in front of eye

lower mandible yellow

IMMATURE

Dalmatian Pelican
Pelecanus crispus
L 160–180 cm | W 290–345 cm

Massive waterbird with very long bill, short legs. ADULT grey-white; short, curly crest; legs grey; eye pale in pink/yellow skin; bill pouch pinkish-yellow (orange in spring). JUVENILE/1ST-YEAR pale grey-brown; bill pouch pink/yellowish. IN FLIGHT, upperwing dull black, grey and whitish; underwing grey with whitish central band. (Great White Pelican (*p. 539*) (occasional escape) has more clearly defined white forewing/black outerwing and hindwing above and below.)

Vagrant from E Europe: 1 record (Britain), May–Nov. Open water.

Great White Pelican (*p. 539*)

ADULT

ADULT

ADULT

SEABIRDS

Seabirds include Gannet, shearwaters, petrels, storm petrels and auks, which are covered in this section, as well as some ducks, cormorants, divers, grebes, gulls, terns, skuas and phalaropes (specialized sea-going waders), which are treated in separate sections. Some of these are much more strictly marine than others, but those introduced here are all true seabirds, only rarely driven inland by gales. Sexes are alike; juveniles differ slightly or scarcely at all from adults in most species, although several age groups are identifiable in Gannet.

17 shearwaters, petrels and storm petrels (plus 3 identified only to species pair/group): 4 breed and are widespread, 4 regular migrants (2 from Southern Hemisphere), others rare or extremely rare vagrants.

3 gannets and boobies: 1 very local breeder but ranges widely around coasts, others extremely rare.

9 auks: 4 breed; 1 regular autumn/winter migrant; 4 extremely rare vagrants.

Other species
As well as the groups covered in this section and the others mentioned above, almost anything can be seen flying over the sea, from migrant swallows to birds of prey: so not every bird you see over the waves will necessarily be a 'seabird'.

Rare seabirds
2 albatrosses; 2 frigatebirds; 1 tropicbird; 2 boobies; 3 petrels plus 1 difficult species group; 3 storm petrels plus 2 difficult species pairs/groups

True seabirds roam widely over the oceans and inevitably some travel far from their normal geographical range. The chance of seeing a rare seabird is very small, but always there. The main problem in identifying them is often that they fly by once and disappear, never to be seen again.

Watching seabirds
Seabirds may be seen from the coast, especially from headlands or at their summer breeding colonies, or from vessels at sea. Coastal 'seawatching' is a specialist pastime: weather conditions greatly influence the likelihood of success. In autumn (Aug–Nov) seabirds move south and many are brought close inshore by strong winds and rain (reducing visibility). Some favoured seawatching sites are on headlands at the end of a large bay. Winds force birds into the bay, but they must then exit close inshore past the headland. Similar conditions may take seabirds far inland. A few appear in bizarre locations (*e.g.* a Manx Shearwater grounded in a garden, or a Puffin by a roadside) but most have an uncanny ability to find large lakes and reservoirs, where a skua, petrel or Little Auk might appear during or after the storm. Certain species, such as Leach's Petrel, Little Auk, Kittiwake, Arctic Skua, are relatively regular inland while others, such as Sooty Shearwater, Fulmar, Guillemot and Razorbill, are truly exceptional.

Storm petrels can be seen from headlands, though far more likely from ships/long-distance ferries. Search constantly with binoculars for birds flying low over the waves.

A group of Manx Shearwaters off Ireland in August

SEABIRDS

Gannets and boobies (*pp. 96–97, 118*) are big, long-winged and easily seen from a great distance over the sea. Gannets are seen at times from most British and Irish shorelines. They fly effortlessly in gales and dive to feed from a height, or go in at an acute angle (not from the surface). Gannet breeds in a few large colonies, mostly on islands, but is widespread offshore; extremely rare inland.

Gannet: ageing/sexing
Sexes alike. Juveniles (early autumn) very dark; in next year most become paler with whiter belly; over subsequent years, variable rate of progress through chequered stages to adulthood.

Auks (see also *p. 106*)
Auks (*pp. 106–113*) are heavy-bodied, slender-winged, short-legged seabirds (smaller than most ducks), that breed on cliffs or rocky islets. Puffin can stand upright, whereas others rest on flexed legs and cannot walk; all can be easily watched at breeding sites by day. In breeding plumages they are more distinct, but non-breeding plumages (when head/bill differences are reduced) present greater identification difficulties, especially at long range when swimming or flying over the sea.

Possible confusion: resting 'tubenoses'
Shearwaters and especially Fulmar will rest on the sea, where they may initially be thought to be gulls – apart from the 'tubenose' that is diagnostic of the group, the closed wings of shearwaters and petrels are generally barely longer than their tail.

tubular nostril

GANNET

PUFFIN

GREAT BLACK-BACKED GULL IMMATURE

Gulls fairly bowed wings; round tail; relaxed flight

See also terns (*p. 120*)

IMMATURE

GANNET

JUVENILE/1ST-YEAR

GREAT SKUA

GREAT BLACK-BACKED GULL

INTRODUCTION

SHEARWATER ID size and shape | upperpart colour | underpart colour | head pattern
SMALL PETREL ID rump pattern | upper/underwing pattern | tail shape | wing shape

Shearwaters, petrels and storm petrels ('tubenoses')

A group of 145 species worldwide with tubular nostrils on top of the bill that enable them to locate oily food by scent and to excrete excess salt. They range from giant albatrosses to tiny storm petrels.

Of the **petrels** (pp. 98, 116–118), only the Fulmar is widespread in Britain and Ireland, easy to see by day at cliff-ledge nests, and the most gull-like due to its grey-and-white plumage. Three other petrels, plus three usually identifiable only to a group of near-identical species, are all very rare.

Shearwaters (pp. 99–103) are slender-winged and usually seen flying low over the sea. Manx Shearwater breeds around Britain and Ireland, only coming to land at night to visit nesting burrows, but is seen frequently from coasts or from ships. Other shearwaters are rare and mainly seen late summer to early autumn as they pass through the region's waters: Balearic Shearwater is a threatened Mediterranean species that feeds in the English Channel in late summer; Sooty Shearwater (most frequent) and Great Shearwater breed in the southern hemisphere, passing through in early autumn (austral spring) at the northern end of their migration loop; and Cory's Shearwater is a visitor from the Macaronesian islands.

Storm petrels (pp. 104–105, 118–119) are smaller seabirds. Two are regular, others rare, best sought on boat trips or from exposed headlands. Leach's Petrel breeds on remote islands and is generally scarce at sea, but regularly seen close inshore during autumn gales. Storm Petrel breeds more widely and likewise comes to land only at night, but is generally less frequent from southern coasts.

DISTANT SHEARWATERS

Fulmar (petrel) – good baseline for comparison/ generally most familiar: big head/broad tail

LARGE: Cory's and **Great Shearwaters** – slim-winged, relaxed action

MEDIUM: Sooty Shearwater – dark, slim-winged, heavy-bellied

SMALL: Manx and **Balearic Shearwaters** – narrow wings, fast action

LARGE — CORY'S SHEARWATER
FULMAR (baseline)
MEDIUM — SOOTY SHEARWATER
SMALL — MANX SHEARWATER

Fulmar white head/grey tail; stiff wings; flap-and-glide

Storm petrels tiny, dark; erratic flight

Shearwaters small head; thin bill; narrow, stiff wings; 'shearing' or flap-and-glide

Auks heavy-bodied, narrow-winged; direct flight with whirring wingbeats

FULMAR | STORM PETREL | MANX SHEARWATER | GUILLEMOT (AUK)

95

SEABIRDS

Gannets moult wing feathers semi-continuously and three generations of feathers may be seen at once: moult may even be asymmetrical. Individuals develop at different rates, so plumages are very variable and ageing difficult.

JUVENILE/1ST-YEAR (fledging to following April or May)
A few one-year-olds as dark as juveniles, even in July.

brown

no dark feathers

ADULT

trailing edge all white

ADULT (4–5 years+)
Almost half at the end of their 4th year already look adult; very few retain dark spots after their 5th year.

TYPICAL 1-YEAR-OLD
Some remain this dark well into second year.

white

dark feathers on back

3RD-YEAR
Typically has a few dark secondaries (not all black) and one or two dark tail feathers, some small black marks on back/scapulars.

LATE 1ST-YEAR OR 2ND-YEAR
Some 2nd-years more boldly chequered with white.

trailing edge and scapulars with dark marks

Less advanced 3rd-years have 'piano key' hindwing, variable black-and-white patches on back, black tail feathers; more advanced individuals, close to adult.

Gannet *Morus bassanus*

L 85–97 cm | W 170–192 cm

Albatrosses (p. 114), Brown & Red-footed Boobies (p. 118)

Big, elegant, dramatic seabird with heavy head, dagger-like bill, slim, pointed tail and long wings. Best northern hemisphere substitute for albatross when shearing/banking in strong wind.

ADULT **gleaming white** with **black wingtips**: easy to identify even at great range. Head golden-buff or yellowish. Bill dagger-like. JUVENILE dark; copious white spots give grizzled greyish look. 2ND–3RD YEARS **chequered with black and white patches**: striking two- to three-year-old birds piebald with yellow head. Near-adults have dark feathers on trailing edge, dark central tail, otherwise like adult.

IN FLIGHT, flies steadily, singly or in lines, well above sea, or glides close to waves, with slow rolling effect; periodically circles and **plunge-dives**. Flight is controlled even in gale: long glides, steep banks; head/neck extended, held higher and looking longer than **spiky tail**. Immature gulls (especially Great Black-backed Gull (p. 134)) may confuse, but wings more bowed, head and tail short, different flight action.

VOICE Calls at colony have strange, repetitive, mechanical effect in constant guttural chorus.

Locally abundant resident (260,000 pairs, including 33,000 in Ireland (breeds Jan–Oct), plus many non-breeders); common summer/autumn migrant; thinly spread around coast all year

At sea/offshore; breeds at scattered colonies, most on islands

splashes from plunge-diving Gannets can be visible at a great distance

Gannets swim high in the water, big and white, pointed at both ends: ADULT like a distant swan unexpectedly at sea (for JUVENILE on water – see p. 94).

A Gannet will periodically circle and then plunge vertically, entering the water with a splash. Closer to the surface, it may slip in at an angle, with little or no splash.

SEABIRDS

Fulmar *Fulmarus glacialis*

L 43–52 cm | W 101–117 cm

Gull-like petrel; **cannot stand** or walk, sitting or shuffling at best. Evocative seabird, around coastal cliffs during much of year. On cliffs or grassy slopes, scattered white 'blobs' on broad ledges. On sea, swims **high in water**, head and tail up, leaning forward.

Sexes alike; no seasonal changes. Pale **grey and white**. Grey upperwing, dusky tips (**no black**), whitish patch beyond joint. Plain **grey rump and tail** (unlike any gull). Head white or yellowish-white, **dark eye patch**; bill stubby. Underwing white with **dark rim** (less marked on northern birds – *see inset*).

IN FLIGHT, wings rather stiff, with slightly whippy beats, held quite straight (angled in glides on clifftop air currents). Masterful glides over sea in strong winds; heavy in flat calm.

VOICE Tuneless, loud, throaty, choking, cackling notes from ledge.

ssp. *glacialis* see p. 541

Breeding pairs are more loosely scattered than most cliff-nesting seabirds.

Locally common breeder (540,000 pairs, including 39,000 in Ireland, Nov–Aug); present all year, widely offshore

Offshore/at sea; breeds on coastal cliffs (few inland in N)

no black on wingtip

pale patch

thickset; long, straight wings

Scarce northern birds darker overall, smoky brownish-grey with pale wing patches more striking.

swims high, tail up

SHEARWATERS

NT **Sooty Shearwater** *Ardenna (Puffinus) griseus* **I** 545

L 40–50 cm | W 93–106 cm

👁 Balearic Shearwater (p. 103); possibly other seabirds – see pp. 94–95

Large, **dark** smoky-brown shearwater, most likely to be seen out to sea; uniform blackish on water at a distance, with head up, long wingtips held high.

IN FLIGHT, angular, dynamic but heavy-bodied; flexible, almost whippy beats of long, pointed, **narrow wings**, held straight, slightly bowed or slightly angled, with faintly paler hindwing and largely **pale underwing** that gives silvery-whitish flash in good light. Beware others in silhouette and especially dark Balearic Shearwater (*p. 103*) (which is smaller with shorter, blunter wings, shorter tail and faster flight action) and dark skuas (*pp. 174–182*).

Scarce but regular migrant Jul–Sep (few thousands per year)

from/to S Atlantic

Offshore/at sea, off headlands

Heavy-bellied, narrow winged. In stronger wind, few flaps low down between long, high, curving glides, belly to wind.

all-dark above

stout body

pale underwing band

in calm winds, flies low; 3–7 quick, stiff-winged flaps between glides of 3–5 seconds

pale underwing band

sexes and age groups look alike, as other shearwaters

SEABIRDS

GREAT SHEARWATER

white above tail

blackish cap and bill

dark marks on underwing

pale head and bill

CORY'S SHEARWATER

all-white underwing

more distinct 'W' effect across wings than Cory's Shearwater

two dark spots

SCOPOLI'S SHEARWATER

single dark spot

white along inner webs of primaries

SHEARWATERS

Great Shearwater
Ardenna (Puffinus) gravis
L 43–51 cm | W 105–122 cm

At sea/offshore

Rare summer migrant (50–100 per year, most in SW, sporadically hundreds or thousands)

Large shearwater: usually far out at sea. Need to exclude Fulmar (*p. 98*), Cory's Shearwater and smaller, faded Manx Shearwater (*p. 103*) (on which white rump sides can give illusion of white patch at base of tail) for safe identification. Dark brown and white, **sharply defined dark brown cap** (appears blackish at distance). Bill slim, **black**. White patch at base of tail more obvious than on almost all Cory's Shearwaters; beneath, dark belly/'wingpit' patches may be visible – best way to rule out Cory's Shearwater. Moulting birds in autumn show ragged whitish midwing.

IN FLIGHT, wingbeats stiffer, quicker than Cory's Shearwater (recalls Fulmar) but equally variable.

from/to S Atlantic

Cory's Shearwater
Calonectris borealis
L 50–56 cm | W 118–126 cm

At sea/offshore

Rare/scarce (erratic) migrant in late summer/autumn, most in SW (usually few, occasionally 100s)

Large (size of Lesser Black-backed Gull (*p. 132*)), heavy-bodied shearwater with relaxed flight action. Brown and white. Pale back/darker wing; slight dark band across innerwing, but only 'shoulder' clearly pale. Tail narrow (unlike gulls), with whitish marks above base. **Head dull**, more-or-less hooded, or dark-faced; **bill thick, pale yellow** (obvious against dark water). Underside clean white. Underwing white with thin black trailing edge; white rounded against broad dark tip, tip sometimes streaked paler.

IN FLIGHT, lethargic in calm air, with 2–4 slow, even, shallow downbeats (often seemingly turning on lowered wingtip, sometimes dipped into water as banks) and glides on **bowed wings**. Wind induces more active flight, in gale **high, towering climbs**. Juvenile Gannet (*p. 97*) is bigger, with longer, sharper bill and tail.

from/to Macaronesia

Scopoli's Shearwater *Calonectris diomedea*
L 44–49 cm | W 117–135 cm

Vagrant from Mediterranean: <5 records (Britain), Jul–Aug. At sea.

Like Cory's Shearwater but more distinct 'W' effect across more extensively pale upperwing; underwing white, with thin brownish trailing edge, white of underwing rather square against white-streaked dark primaries. **Single dark spot on white primary coverts** beneath wing (two on Cory's Shearwater) may show on photographs. Pale bill less obvious; face often darker.

IN FLIGHT, like Cory's Shearwater but occasional bursts of 5–7 flaps between glides.

GREAT SHEARWATER

CORY'S SHEARWATER

SEABIRDS

Balearic Shearwaters sometimes associate with Manx flocks.

Shearwaters dive for food and sit on the sea in rafts. Manx Shearwaters are often offshore near breeding colonies in the evening.

feet protrude

little/no foot projection

blackish upperside

dark flank

BALEARIC

white flank mark

white 'hook' behind cheek

MANX

uniformly brown above

heavy build

BALEARIC SHEARWATER

dark vent

dark mark

clean flank

white vent

thick bill, bulging tip

dull underparts

diagonal band to dark patch on hindwing

dark bar above white flank typical

white belly

MANX SHEARWATER

brown vent

feet protrude

slim bill

clean white underparts

faint pale 'hook'

hindwing often silvery

tiny bill

clean white below

white over eye

MACARONESIAN (BAROLO) SHEARWATER

YELKOUAN SHEARWATER

102

SHEARWATERS

Manx Shearwater 545
Puffinus puffinus

L 30–35 cm | W 71–83 cm

By far the commonest shearwater. Smallish, slim, with tapered body and stiff-winged flight.

Blackish (fades browner), **white below**. Dark cap, white lower face; white flank rounded beside rump.

IN FLIGHT, narrow wings and long body give dark cross-shape, low over water: **alternates black and white** as bird banks over. Wingbeats **quick, flicked, between glides** – in wind, almost all glides, with higher, banking turns on wingtip. On migration, groups/long, thin lines; in summer, near colonies (visited at night), evening gatherings offshore, often settling on water.

VOICE Chorus of guttural croaks, laughing notes and deep cooing calls at colony at night.

Offshore/at sea; breeds on offshore islands in N and W (300,000–370,000 pairs, including 37,000 in Ireland)

Locally abundant breeder; common migrant around coast

to Atlantic coast of South America

CR Balearic Shearwater
CR *Puffinus mauretanicus* 545

L 34–39 cm | W 78–90 cm

Highly threatened Mediterranean equivalent of Manx Shearwater; migrates to feed in Biscay/English Channel in Jul–Sep. Like **thickset, brown** Manx Shearwater, **dusky brownish beneath**, dark under tail; bill grey.

IN FLIGHT, fast, with quick wingbeats, looks a little dumpier than Manx Shearwater with heavy belly, shorter tail and **projecting toes**. Sooty Shearwater (*p. 99*) is bigger, with longer, slender, angled wings.

Offshore/at sea

Rare: summer/autumn migrant; non-breeding summer visitor in S

from/to Mediterranean

VU Yelkouan Shearwater 545
Puffinus yelkouan

L 30–35 cm | W 70–84 cm

Small shearwater; slender form, appearance more like Manx than drabber Balearic Shearwater, but plumage features variable. Dark bar above flank, dark diagonal band on underwing, dark vent and blurred neck sides helpful.

Vagrant from Mediterranean: 1 record (Britain), Jul. Offshore.

Macaronesian (Barolo) Shearwater
Puffinus baroli

L 25–30 cm | W 58–67 cm

Small, squat shearwater. Black and white; black cap above eye, leaving **white, disk-like face**. Smaller, shorter-winged than Manx Shearwater; may show whitish bar across rear wing, or silvery hindwing.

IN FLIGHT, clearly a shearwater (but see Razorbill (*p. 109*)), but **more wingbeats, shorter glides** but slower progress than Manx; bowed wings may resemble Common Sandpiper (*p. 215*). May settle briefly with raised wings.

VOICE Higher than Manx Shearwater: penetrating, rhythmic "*pi-pi-pi-poo, pi-poo.*"

Vagrant from Atlantic islands: <100 records (25 Ireland), May–Sep. Offshore; occasionally in Manx Shearwater colonies.

MANX SHEARWATER

BALEARIC SHEARWATER

103

SEABIRDS

👁 Rare Storm Petrels (*p. 117*)

STORM PETRELS

pale upperwing band

dusky underwing

forked tail

LEACH'S PETREL

white bar

square/ round tail

square tail; projecting toes

plain upperwing

pale upperwing band

STORM PETREL

WILSON'S PETREL

STORM PETREL

white bar

dark underwing

WILSON'S PETREL

yellow webs

104

STORM PETRELS

Leach's Petrel *Oceanodroma leucorhoa*

L 18–21 cm | W 43–48 cm

Offshore/at sea, storm-blown inland; breeds at a few colonies in far N and W, May–Sep (48,000 pairs)

Scarce and very local summer visitor; scarce autumn migrant

Small, long-winged storm petrel with white rump. Breeding sites more far-flung than those of Storm Petrel, but more likely inland or blown inshore after autumn gale. Most likely to be seen IN FLIGHT. Larger than Storm Petrel. Sooty brown; **paler band across innerwing** reaches front edge (brightest, greyest on JUVENILES). **White rump** relatively small (rarely absent), often broken by central dark band (sometimes just a small notch). Upperwing band often obvious; **underwing all-dark**. **Wings long, pushed forward and angled**; tail forked or notched (hard to see); tail shape/rump patterns very variable. Flight erratic, with sudden turns or rising twists. When feeding, stalls or hangs into wind, foot-patters; in gales may patter along beach.

VOICE Visits nesting burrow at night, when gives a long, high-pitched purring, punctuated by higher double note.

Storm Petrel *Hydrobates pelagicus*

L 15–16 cm | W 37–41 cm

At sea/offshore; breeds on islands in N and W, May–Sep (100,000 pairs in Ireland, 26,000 in UK)

Locally common summer visitor; scarce migrant; very few in winter

Tiny, delicate, martin-like seabird with white rump. Most likely to be seen IN FLIGHT. Smoky brown-black, except **bold white rump** wrapping around each side. Weak, fine pale wingbar above (on JUVENILE) and broad **white band along underwing** (key feature). Wings curve back, like broad House Martin (*p. 352*) with rounder tips; tail **broad and rounded**. Easy, smooth, rolling, swooping, twirling action depending on circumstance; often seen from ships, flying over or beside wake or more directly alongside. More easily seen than Leach's Petrel, May–Aug, from headlands, offshore near breeding sites and from boats/ferries.

VOICE Visits nesting burrow at night, when gives prolonged, slightly squeaky, rolling purr, punctuated by short, deeper note.

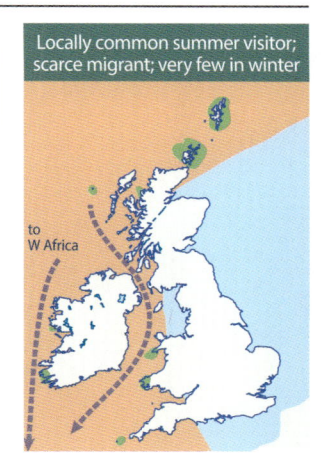

Wilson's Petrel *Oceanites oceanicus*

L 16–18·5 cm | W 38–42 cm

Rare migrant from Southern Oceans: >1,500 records (including >500 Ireland), 30–50 per year, Jul–Oct. Mostly in the SW. Offshore/at sea.

Small storm petrel with white rump. Only likely to be seen IN FLIGHT. Larger than Storm Petrel. Mixes characters of Storm and Leach's Petrels, with **square** or concave tail (slightly 'dished' so raised sides give concave effect), **broad grey upperwing band** not quite reaching leading edge (does so on Leach's Petrel); **all-dark underwing** and extensive **wrap-around white rump**. Long legs trail beyond tail (can be withdrawn, so beware); broad, paddle-shaped wings, smoothly rounded on leading edge, tapering back to point in direct flight; trailing edge straighter than on Leach's Petrel. Flight Swallow-like (*p. 353*) and low; when feeding, bounces, skips with wings raised. Variation in size influences flight action. **Yellow webs between toes**, usually show best in photographs and unlikely to be seen well in the field.

AUKS

9 species: 4 breed; 1 regular autumn/winter migrant; 4 very or extremely rare vagrants.

AUK ID bill shape and colour | head pattern | underwing

NOTE: Great Auk *Pinguinus impennis* [*not illustrated*] which was once regularly recorded from St Kilda and Orkney (last recorded in about 1840) is now extinct.

Strictly seabirds, associated with cliffs and islands in summer, but out at sea at other times, auks are heavy-bodied and short-legged, often seen in flight low over the sea or swimming. In flight they look heavy, small-winged, with a fast, whirring action: high speed but little agility. On water, they sit low but are buoyant, and dive under from the surface.

Black Guillemots like small rocky islands and boulder-strewn shores, Guillemots prefer flat-topped offshore stacks and long narrow ledges on sheer cliffs. Razorbills share the cliffs but nest in small cavities. Puffins burrow into soft earth higher up or nest inside cavities in scree slopes. While the others squat upright, settled on the length of their legs, Puffins stand properly on their webbed feet and walk quite well. Little Auks are just autumn/winter migrants, flying fast offshore or swimming, sometimes exhausted, close inshore.

Auk ageing/moult

Juvenile Guillemots and Razorbills leave the cliff ledges half-grown, with an adult; they look like adults by the following spring. Adults are flightless for 6–7 weeks in the autumn while they moult. Young Puffins leave the burrow at night, alone, and young Black Guillemots also go to sea unaccompanied.

PUFFIN

Puffins may nest in huge colonies, but even there tend to be widely scattered and not seen in such large, dense groups as breeding Guillemots (*below*).

GUILLEMOTS

Auks in flight

Auks passing far offshore, low over the sea, often in strong winds, are difficult. Look for overall colour, underwing and rump patterns, and try to estimate size.

NB dark feathers in white suggest 1ST-SUMMER bird

AUKS IN FLIGHT

BLACK GUILLEMOT (p. 111) BREEDING

PUFFIN (p. 110) BREEDING

LITTLE AUK (p. 112) BREEDING

GUILLEMOT — streaked flanks, dark, BREEDING; short tail; feet project, BREEDING

RAZORBILL — white underwing and flanks, BREEDING

BRÜNNICH'S GUILLEMOT — white underwing and flanks, BREEDING

RAZORBILL BREEDING — short tail; feet project

BRÜNNICH'S GUILLEMOT BREEDING — white along bill

GUILLEMOT (p. 108) BREEDING — long tail; feet same length

RAZORBILL (p. 109) BREEDING — white across bill

BRÜNNICH'S GUILLEMOT BREEDING

GUILLEMOT NON-BREEDING

RAZORBILL NON-BREEDING

BRÜNNICH'S GUILLEMOT (p. 113) NON-BREEDING — no white behind eye

LITTLE AUK (p. 112) NON-BREEDING

BLACK GUILLEMOT (p. 111) NON-BREEDING

AUKS　　　　　　　　　　　　　　　　　　　　　　　　　　　　　　　　　　Auks in flight p. 107

NT Guillemot *Uria aalge*

L 38–46 cm | W 61–73 cm

Brünnich's Guillemot, Rare murrelets (p. 113)

Ssp. *aalge* breeding in N Britain is darker than ssp. *albionis* breeding in Ireland and S Britain.

Locally abundant breeding resident (1.3 million birds); rare inshore in winter

Cliff-breeding seabird, nesting on open ledges. On land, upright, legs set far back near **short, square tail**; **bill pointed**. On sea, long and low, short neck upright with head/bill held horizontally. Dives frequently, opening wings slightly as does so.

ADULT BREEDING **dark brown** to blackish above; white upper breast rounded against dark foreneck. Short white bar on closed wing (forms trailing edge in flight). **Rump dark with narrow white sides** (Long-tailed Duck (p. 54) and Razorbill have wider white sides). A few (with increasing frequency northwards) show white line behind eye ('bridled'). NON-BREEDING/JUVENILE/IMMATURE dark on crown/nape, white face/cheek; **dark line bisects white rear cheek**.

VOICE Calls on cliffs long, whirring notes; at sea, young bird calls with loud, musical whistle, "*plee-u*," puzzling at first.

On/off rocky coasts/cliffs in summer, offshore in winter

IN FLIGHT, tapered both ends, fat in middle; narrow, mid-set wings, **fast, rather whirring action** over sea (not high except when visiting cliff).

JUVENILE/1ST-WINTER (juvenile initially identifiable by small size and call, but after Sep not safely distinguished from non-breeding adult)

ADULT BREEDING

Guillemot colonies on flat rocks or high, sheer cliffs are noisy, busy places in summer.

black — ADULT NON-BREEDING AUG–MAR

pointed bill

white — ADULT BREEDING DEC–AUG 'BRIDLED'

short tail

NON-BREEDING AUG–MAR

marked flank

ADULT BREEDING DEC–AUG ssp. *aalge*

AUKS

NT # Razorbill *Alca torda*
NT

except ssp. *torda* | I

L 38–43 cm | W 60–69 cm

👁 **Brünnich's Guillemot** (p. 113)
Ssp. breeding in Britain and Ireland is *islandica*; **northern ssp. *torda*,** a winter migrant, is generally larger but overlap makes recognition impossible at times.

Cliff-breeding seabird, nests in cavities/crevices, less often on open ledges. Shape like Guillemot but more bull-necked, **tail pointed, bill blunt**. More often in estuaries/deep bays than Guillemot. Dives often, opening wings slightly as does so.

ADULT BREEDING **black and white**, white upper breast pointed against dark foreneck; bill **blade-shaped**, less pointed than Guillemot, black with **white cross-band** and **line to eye**. NON-BREEDING/JUVENILE/IMMATURE bill blunt; all-dark on young bird; crown black; white blob behind eye but less obvious line across cheek than Guillemot. Squat, head sunk low, if tired/inshore.

VOICE Calls at nest guttural, growling "*goarrr*," harder, less whirring/musical than Guillemot.

Locally common breeding resident (164,000 birds); scarce inshore in winter

On/off rocky coasts/cliffs in summer, offshore in winter

IN FLIGHT, difficult to tell from Guillemot unless bill shape visible: a little shorter, dumpier (see Little Auk (p. 112)), cleaner white under wing. **Parallel white rump sides** (see Long-tailed Duck (p. 54)).

ADULT BREEDING

thick bill

JUVENILE/1ST-WINTER
JUL–MAR

Razorbills tend to be scattered more thinly amongst Guillemots in mixed colonies.

ADULT NON-BREEDING
AUG–MAR

white

ADULT BREEDING
FEB–AUG

long, pointed tail often raised when swimming

109

AUKS   Auks in flight p. 107

VU
EN
Puffin *Fratercula arctica*   549

L 28–34 cm | W 50–60 cm   👁 Tufted Puffin (p. 113)

Small, upright auk, standing/waddling on toes (Guillemot (p. 108) and Razorbill (p. 109) rest on lower part of leg). Adult distinctive, juvenile potentially confusing. Often on same cliffs as Razorbill and Guillemot, but nests in cavities or burrows into earth or detritus slopes amongst lush vegetation, often on offshore islands.

ADULT BREEDING black and white, but large, round head and bright bill unique. **Pale grey disk on face; triangular red, yellow and grey bill; orange legs**. NON-BREEDING more tricky, especially when flying at long range: face much darker; bill smaller and much duller and darker, but still obvious deep shield-shape, not pointed like Guillemot or so shallow as Razorbill. JUVENILE has even smaller bill: see Little Auk (p. 112), but face dark, cheeks dusky, upperwing plain black.

VOICE Low, hard cooing and "*arrk arrk*" notes.

Locally common summer resident (580,000 pairs Britain, 20,000 pairs Ireland); rare inshore in winter

Cliffs, islands; at sea in winter

IN FLIGHT, **dark underwing**, lack of white trailing edge on top; dark breast-band; dark rear flank. Fast, whirring wingbeats

ADULT BREEDING FEB–OCT

ADULT BREEDING

Puffin colonies may be associated with other auks or in quite different places on clifftop slopes or small grassy islands.

JUVENILE JUL–DEC

face becomes dusky and bill smaller and duller after breeding

ADULT NON-BREEDING SEP–MAR

ADULT BREEDING FEB–OCT

AUKS

Black Guillemot *Cepphus grylle*

L 32–38 cm | W 49–58 cm

Small, slim-billed auk, unlike Guillemot (*p. 108*) in behaviour: pairs favour rocky islets, piers, offshore rocks, boulders, harbours and sheltered Scottish sea lochs, not on ledges of sheer cliffs.

ADULT BREEDING smoky black with **oval white wing patch**, striking at very long range. Underwing mostly white. Inside bill and **legs bright red**. NON-BREEDING head and body smudgy white, back barred grey-black; wing black with large, unmarked, white patch. Bill tapered to point, like small Guillemot, but **legs red**. JUVENILE dark, barred black and white on flank, browner on head; wing patch barred blackish. 1ST-WINTER like non-breeding adult, but black spots/bars reduce clarity of white upperwing patch. Could potentially be confused with non-breeding grebes (see *p. 78*).

VOICE High, shrill whistle.

Widespread but uncommon resident in N, W (38,000 pairs); rare in S in winter

Rocky shores, islands, sheltered inshore waters

ADULT BREEDING

IN FLIGHT, low, whirring, big oval white patch on upperwing and white underwing obvious, especially in summer.

ADULT NON-BREEDING

ADULT BREEDING
FEB–AUG

Black Guillemots nest as isolated pairs or small groups around rocky islets, or at the foot of larger cliffs.

JUVENILE → 1ST-WINTER
JUL–MAY [Dec]

ADULT
NON-BREEDING
AUG–MAR

ADULT BREEDING
FEB–AUG

111

Little Auk *Alle alle*

L 19–21 cm | W 34–38 cm

Rare murrelets

Rare/scarce autumn/winter visitor to N, E; rare in S/W and inland after gales (100s–low 1,000s)
from Arctic

Tiny, thickset, short-billed auk (see Puffin (*p. 110*) and Black Guillemot (*p. 111*)). Most likely in late autumn during/after gales. Tired/storm-blown bird swims with head hunched, wings slightly drooped and **flicked open as it dives**.

ADULT BREEDING (rare in Britain) black, white belly; fine white streaks on closed wing. Short, stout bill and large head give frog-like effect but healthy, alert bird can be quite slim-necked. NON-BREEDING/1ST-WINTER sharply contrasted black-and-white, with **bold black hood extending around eye**, **white collar**; **white streaks on wing** (rules out Puffin).

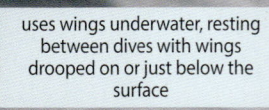

IN FLIGHT, small, dumpy, with slender wings (sometimes look surprisingly long, as bird or group twists and banks, like a small wader). Fast, whirring wingbeats: see Puffin, which also has slim wings with dark underside and fast beats – Little Auk has quicker whirr of more swept-back wings and thin white trailing edge. Size of Starling (*p. 384*); even rarely caught up in Starling flocks.

NON-BREEDING/1ST-WINTER

BREEDING

Offshore/at sea; rarely inland waters

JUVENILE/1ST-WINTER
RAZORBILL
(size comparison)

NON-BREEDING/1ST-WINTER
LITTLE AUK

BREEDING MAR–AUG

Little Auks in breeding plumage have very rarely been recorded in Britain in colonies of other auks.

uses wings underwater, resting between dives with wings drooped on or just below the surface

healthy, alert birds hold their head up

NON-BREEDING/1ST-WINTER OCT–MAR

exhausted birds often droop wings, head hunched down

Ssp. *alle* (Greenland, Iceland E to N W Siberia) frequent; also ssp. *polaris* (Franz Josef Land) recorded, based on longer wing.

NON-BREEDING/1ST-WINTER OCT–MAR

Rare auks

Brünnich's Guillemot
Uria lomvia
L 40–44 cm | W 64–75 cm

Like Guillemot (*p. 108*) but blacker and **bill thicker** (but pointed, unlike Razorbill (*p. 109*)). ADULT BREEDING **white streak along cutting edges of bill** to gape; white breast extends to a point up front of dark neck (as Razorbill). NON-BREEDING/1ST-WINTER difficult: peaked dark head with **no white on rear cheek** or behind eye (cap extends to well below eye, leaving small white face). Flank **unmarked white**. May have chinstrap effect. IN FLIGHT, deeper, rounder, less tapered body than Guillemot, and 'wingpits' lack dark marks.

GUILLEMOT (winter) — white
RAZORBILL (winter) — white
NON-BREEDING AUG–MAR — dark; white along bill; unmarked flank
ADULT BREEDING DEC–AUG

Vagrant from Arctic/Iceland: <50 records (1 Ireland), Oct–Jan, extremely rare in summer. Coast.

Tufted Puffin
Fratercula cirrhata
L 36–41 cm | W 60–63 cm

Like Puffin (*p. 110*) but black with red bill, white face, yellowish crest.

Vagrant from N Pacific: 1 record (Britain), Sep. Coast.

ADULT BREEDING

Ancient Murrelet
Synthliboramphus antiquus
L 27 cm | W 45–48 cm

Tiny, short-billed, grey-backed auk; head black with white lower cheek and neck; pale bill.

Vagrant from N Pacific: 1 record (Britain), May (for 2 years). Coast.

ADULT BREEDING

NT Long-billed Murrelet
Brachyramphus perdix
L 25 cm | W 45 cm

Like tiny Guillemot (*p. 108*) with pointed bill; dark crown to below eye; whitish patch beside back.

Vagrant from E Asia/N Pacific: 1 record (Britain), Nov. Coast.

1ST-WINTER

RARE AUKS

113

/ RARE SEABIRDS

Rare seabirds | Albatrosses and frigatebirds

Watching seabirds from headlands, especially during strong winds, can be exciting. Rare birds may appear almost anywhere but are, naturally, unpredictable: a 'once in a lifetime' rarity may suddenly appear and be gone within minutes, never to be seen again.
A disciplined assessment of all features – size, shape, flight action, plumage patterns – has to be attempted if possible!

GANNET (p. 97)
TO SCALE

Black-browed Albatross
Thalassarche melanophris
L 80–95 cm | W 200–235 cm

Only likely flying over sea. Bigger than Gannet (p. 97); stout-billed, round-headed, **square-tailed** (like giant Fulmar (p. 98)); very long, slender wings. White with black back/upperwings and **dusky tail** (check immature Gannet, adult Great Black-backed Gull (p. 134)). Underwing crucial: **broad white band** between **narrow black trailing edge** and **broader black leading edge**. Bill yellow/orange. Black eyebrow. IMMATURES darker bill tip, greyish collar, dusky underwing masking pattern.

Vagrant from Southern Oceans: <50 records (<15 Ireland), most months. Offshore/islands.

dark tail-band (unlike Great Black-backed Gull)
ADULT
broad black leading edge to underwing

Dark tail may be 'lost' against dark water, creating an odd tailless effect.

BLACK-BROWED ALBATROSS

IMMATURE

extent of white on underwing increases with age

dark tip to yellowish bill

ADULT

EN Atlantic Yellow-nosed Albatross
Thalassarche chlororhynchos
L 90 cm | W 200–210 cm

Shape and actions as Black-browed Albatross: look for **black bill with a yellow stripe along ridge** and **narrow black margins to white underwing**.

Vagrant from Southern Oceans: 1 record (Britain), Jun–Jul (on coast/inland). Usually at sea.

blackish bill

narrow black leading edge to underwing

ADULT

ATLANTIC YELLOW-NOSED ALBATROSS

ALBATROSSES | FRIGATEBIRDS

> IN FLIGHT, frigatebirds fly with **angled wings** and can soar to a great height over the sea or nearby land; chase other birds/flying fish over waves.

Magnificent Frigatebird
Fregata magnificens
L 90–114 cm | W 215–245 cm

Huge, long-winged seabird with **long, forked tail** (closes into single spike) and long, hooked bill. ADULT MALE **black**, glossed green on head and tail, **purple on back**, with **red throat sac**. Bill grey, legs black. ADULT FEMALE upperwing brown with pale forewing band; head, neck, underwing and belly black; **breast white**. JUVENILE brown above with paler forewing band; head, breast and belly white, with angular dark flank patch or incomplete brown breast-band; underwing all-dark. Bill whitish. IMMATURE underside more extensively white, extending slightly onto underwing (confusingly like juvenile Ascension Frigatebird but lacks breast-band); rear flank dark.

> Vagrant from America: <10 records (<5 Ireland), Jun–Dec. Most on coast but has been storm-driven inland.

VU Ascension Frigatebird
Fregata aquila
L 85–105 cm | W 205–230 cm

Shape and actions very similar to Magnificent Frigatebird, adult males practically indistinguishable at sea. ADULT MALE black, **glossed green above**, with **red throat sac**. ADULT FEMALE typically all-dark except paler brown breast, but some have white breast patch. JUVENILE brown, with paler forewing band; head white; brown neck and **broad** breast-band; triangular **white belly, extending into point on underwing**. Bill pale grey. IMMATURE breast-band may be broken.

> Vagrant from South Atlantic: <5 records (Britain), Jul. On coast.

ADULT ♀

sooty brown-black

ADULT ♂

MAGNIFICENT FRIGATEBIRD

IMMATURE

whitish head and breast

black underwing

JUVENILE

JUVENILE

white belly patch extends onto underwing

ASCENSION FRIGATEBIRD

whitish head; dark breast

JUVENILE

Rare seabirds | Petrels and tropicbirds

It seems that almost any seabird might appear almost anywhere on the coast, far from its normal range, with recent records of unexpected species such as boobies and tropicbirds. Older 'Soft-plumaged Petrel' records in British and Irish waters are no longer identifiable, since the 'species' has been split into four: **Soft-plumaged Petrel** *Pterodroma mollis* (Southern Oceans), **Fea's Petrel** *P. feae* (Cape Verde), **Desertas Petrel** *P. deserta* (Desertas Islands, Madeira) and **Zino's Petrel** *P. madeira* (Madeira, <100 pairs). UK/Irish records are best referred to as Fea's/Desertas Petrels.

FULMAR (p. 98) TO SCALE

big, stout, pale-headed

EN Zino's Petrel 545
Pterodroma madeira
L 30–35 cm | W 80–90 cm

NT Fea's Petrel
Pterodroma feae

VU Desertas Petrel
Pterodroma deserta
L 33–36 cm | W 86–94 cm (both)

Manx Shearwater-sized (*p. 103*); sweeping glides on long, angled wings. **Grey and white** with subtle dark 'W' across upperwings, **plain grey rump/tail**, dusky breast side, **dark eye patch** and stubby black bill. Greyer underwing, less contrasting tail pattern than other *Pterodroma* petrels in the region. **Zino's Petrel** is smallest, slimmest, with most white on underwing and slimmest bill; **Fea's Petrel** usually has darkest underwing (but all three overlap) and stout bill; **Desertas Petrel** has deepest bill. Only extreme examples likely to be identifiable at sea.

Vagrant from Atlantic islands: <150 records (> 120 Ireland), Aug–Sep. At sea.

dusky above
dark around eye
FEA'S PETREL
ZINO'S PETREL
DESERTAS PETREL

DESERTAS PETREL
ZINO'S PETREL

State of primary moult can be a useful clue if 'gaps' are visible: Zino's Petrel moults Aug–Dec, Fea's Petrel Mar–Aug, Desertas Petrel Oct–Apr.

Fea's/Desertas Petrels have thick, heavy bill; Zino's Petrel has a slender bill.

LARGE PETRELS | TROPICBIRDS

Red-billed Tropicbird
Phaethon aethereus

L 45–50 cm (plus streamers of 46–56 cm) | W 100–115 cm

Like large, stocky tern (*pp. 144–152*) with **thick red bill**, very long, flexible, central tail spike. White upperwings with dark bars; **black on wingtips**.

Vagrant from tropical seas: <10 records (1 Ireland), Mar–Sep. At sea.

RED-BILLED TROPICBIRD
ADULT
black outerwing 'wedge'
white plumage

Bermuda Petrel ◆
Pterodroma cahow

L 35–38 cm | W 85–92 cm

Stocky, thick-billed, long-winged petrel; dark above, white below. Blurred **blackish 'mask' surrounded by grey**, white throat and collar; diffuse grey 'hood' effect; white crescent above base of tail **very thin or absent**. Underwing white with thin black trailing edge and broader black leading edge tapering back towards body.

Vagrant from W Atlantic: 1 record (Ireland, 195 miles off W coast), May. At sea.

dark stripe on underwing
white crescent above tail
dark nape
BERMUDA PETREL

Black-capped Petrel
Pterodroma hasitata

L 40 cm | W 98–105 cm

Only likely to be seen in flight, out to sea. Large petrel with white forehead, **black cap/nape** above full **white collar**; **white rump**; underwing white with black diagonal bar and trailing edge.

Vagrant from Caribbean: <5 records (Britain), Dec, Mar/Apr (corpses). At sea.

black cap/white collar
black stripe on underwing
black tail/white rump
BLACK-CAPPED PETREL

117

Rare seabirds | Boobies and smaller petrels

Red-footed Booby *Sula sula*
L 70cm | W 100cm

Like small Gannet (*p. 97*). Two main forms: white with black flight feathers (and sometimes tail) and dark brown (some with whiter rump, tail, belly). JUVENILE brown; head and underparts paler; bill bluish, facial skin pink; legs red.

> Vagrant from tropical Atlantic: 1 record (Britain), Sep. Coast.

Brown Booby *Sula leucogaster*
L 67–74 cm | WS 132–150 cm

Like small Gannet (*p. 97*). ADULT brown; belly and underwing white; bill pink, chin and legs yellow. JUVENILE brown; breast darker than belly (unlike Red-footed Booby); bill/face grey. 1ST-SUMMER like juvenile but belly white, mottled with brown. 2ND-SUMMER like adult but flank mottled with brown.

> Vagrant from Cape Verde: <5 records (1 Ireland), Aug–Sep. Coast.

Bulwer's Petrel ◆
Bulweria bulwerii
L 26–28 cm | W 67 cm

Dark-brown, shearwater-like (*p. 103*) petrel with long, slightly angled, pointed wings and tapered tail without fork. Paler band across upperwing can be striking. IN FLIGHT, buoyant, rolling, wavering action low over waves, wings pressed well forward.

> Vagrant from Atlantic islands: 1 record (Ireland), Aug. At sea.

EN White-faced Storm Petrel 544
Pelagodroma marina
L 20 cm | W 41–44 cm

Grey, black and white storm petrel with **white underside**, **dark cap and 'mask'** and **broad, paddle-shaped wings**.

> Vagrant from Atlantic islands: 1 historical record (Britain), Jan 1897.

BOOBIES | SMALLER PETRELS

Madeiran Storm Petrel 545
Oceanodroma castro

NT Cape Verde Storm Petrel
Oceanodroma jabejabe

VU Monteiro's Storm Petrel
VU *Oceanodroma monteiroi*
L 18–21 cm | W 43–49 cm

Like Leach's Petrel (*p. 105*); tail less notched, **white rump narrow, 'U'-shaped**; feet do not project beyond tail. Upperwing bands short of front edge; less elegant feeding actions than Leach's Petrel – head-up, wings fanned, tail spread.

NT Swinhoe's Petrel
Oceanodroma monorhis
L 18–21 cm | W 45–48 cm

Dark-brown storm petrel; size, shape as Leach's Petrel (*p. 105*); **white outer primary shafts**. Most trapped ashore, identified by biometrics/DNA testing. At sea, hard to separate from other dark-rumped petrels, including rare dark-rumped Leach's Petrel.

Vagrant from NW Pacific: <10 records (<5 Ireland), Jul–Aug. All but one tape-lured and trapped; other unidentified *Oceanodroma* petrels recorded spring, summer, autumn.

Black-bellied Storm Petrel
Fregetta tropica

White-bellied Storm Petrel
Fregetta grallaria
L 20 cm | W 46 cm

Small storm petrels with dashing, shearing flight. **White rump joins white underparts and underwing**. Black (or smudgy) belly stripe indicates Black-bellied Storm Petrel; white belly could be either species. Black-bellied Storm Petrel has more extensive hood than White-bellied Storm Petrel.

Vagrant from S Atlantic: 1 record (Britain), Sep (not identified to species).

Madeiran, Cape Verde and Monteiro's Storm Petrels are now treated as separate species, based on breeding seasons, moult and detailed morphological differences; identification in the field not yet possible.

Vagrant from Atlantic islands: <5 records not specifically identified (1 Ireland), Jul–Sep. At sea.

MADEIRAN STORM PETREL (GROUP)
- square tail
- short pale upperwing band
- dark underwing

SWINHOE'S PETREL
- rump dark
- forked tail
- pale primary marks

LEACH'S PETREL
- rump usually pale
- forked tail
- long pale upperwing band
- pale primary marks absent

BLACK-BELLIED STORM PETREL
- plain upperwing
- white breast with or without dark stripe

A species pair that can be near-impossible to identify: the only British record is undoubtedly one or the other, but it was not possible to determine which.

GULLS and TERNS

Water/waterside birds, web-footed, long-winged, rather short-legged; only gulls agile on foot. Sexes alike, but breeding, non-breeding and several sequential immature plumages differ.
26 gulls (plus several distinct subspecies): 7 breed; 19 migrants/winter visitors/vagrants – 6 regular, 13 rare/vagrant.
19 terns: 5 breed; 14 summer/passage migrants or vagrants – 1 regular, 13 rare/vagrant.

> **GULL ID** time of year | size | leg length | bill shape | bill and leg colour | back colour | head pattern | detailed wing/wingtip pattern | age and the effects of moult

Gulls (pp. 122–159)

Some are adaptable and opportunistic; gulls of some kind are likely almost anywhere, ranging over all kinds of open countryside, even onto high peaks in summer. Common species – Black-headed, Common, Lesser Black-backed, Herring and Great Black-backed Gulls – are associated with shores of mud, sand and rocks, harbours, playing fields, meadows, car parks and increasingly town centres, and watery places inland, including reservoirs on which thousands gather to roost, flying in long lines or 'V'-shapes (most flocks of large birds flying in lines or 'V's will be gulls).

Eight have dark hoods in breeding plumage, others are white-headed from January to August. In non-breeding plumage, 'hooded' gulls lose most of the head colour, while white-headed ones become streaky-headed. Breeding plumage can be acquired in mid-winter and lost by June or July. Smaller 'hooded' species generally breed on marshes; larger white-headed gulls tend to nest on cliffs and islands, increasingly on roofs.

Kittiwakes are marine, breeding on coastal cliffs, and ledges (not roofs or chimneys) on seaside buildings; flocks rest on beaches in summer.

Gull ageing/sexing

Sexes look alike but male gulls have a larger head and bill than females (and in some different body lengths affect the wingtip projection beyond the tail). There is a progression from juvenile to adult through intermediate plumages that become increasingly easy to identify. Smaller species may become mature within two years, larger ones in four or five years (see *pp. 122–123* for details of moult progression); the years to maturity for each species is shown with *e.g.* ③.

Possible confusion species
Immature gulls could be confused with skuas (*p. 174*).

> **TERN ID** size / structure | bill shape / colour | head pattern

Terns (pp. 160–173)

Most are long-tailed, grey-and-white, black-capped '**sea terns**' or shorter-tailed, duskier '**marsh terns**'. **Sea terns** dive from the air for food and are most common on the coast; some are migrants at inland waters. Common Terns also breed inland (where they feed more by dipping, diving less frequently). **Marsh terns** include Black Tern, a frequent migrant, and two rarities, all dip-feeders, flying into the wind and picking from the surface, rarely properly diving.

'MARSH TERNS': short bill, broad wings, notched tail

BLACK TERN

COMMON TERN
Bill to tail length: 31–35 cm
Weight: 110–140 g

'SEA TERNS': long bill, narrow wings, deep tail fork

COMMON TERN

Tern ageing/sexing

Sexes look alike; breeding, non-breeding and juvenile plumages differ; fully mature in two to three years. Ageing after juvenile can be difficult or impossible due to a complex moult strategy that has individuals in overlapping plumage types.

INTRODUCTION

HERRING GULL
JUVENILE MOULTING INTO 1ST-WINTER

- uppertail coverts
- tail
- rump
- tail-band
- lower back
- back
- nape
- crown
- scapulars
- lesser coverts
- median coverts
- greater coverts
- tertials (slide forward underneath scapulars as wing is straightened)
- secondaries (if darker than coverts, they form a hindwing band)
- alula
- primary coverts
- primaries (10)
- P1, P2, P3, P4, P5, P6, P7, P8, P9, P10

HERRING GULL
BREEDING

Primaries are moulted in sequence, P1 to P10; these numbers help describe patterns with precision

trailing edge

Notch on trailing edge shows where innermost primaries (P1 and P2) have been shed, at the onset of moult. (NB only one primary (P1) shed on left wing.)

- P3, P4, P5, P6, P7, P8, P9, P10
- 'mirror'
- primary tip

wingtip projection
A: beyond tertials
B: beyond tail

- primaries
- tertials
- scapulars
- A
- B
- tail
- vent/undertail coverts
- greater coverts
- median coverts
- lesser coverts
- nape
- crown
- back

HERRING GULL
JUVENILE MOULTING INTO 1ST-WINTER

BLACK-HEADED GULL

ADULT NON-BREEDING
- ear covert spot

ADULT BREEDING
- hood
- eye-crescents

GULLS AND TERNS: RELATIVE SIZES

Bill to tail lengths show relative sizes but underestimate differences in the 'bulk' of gulls. A Lesser Black-backed Gull is only a few centimetres shorter than a Great Black-backed Gull, but side-by-side the Lesser Black-backed Gull may seem barely 'half as big' as the Great Black-backed Gull, and may indeed weigh only half as much.

GREAT BLACK-BACKED GULL
Bill to tail length: 70 cm
Weight: 1,800 g

LITTLE TERN
Bill to tail length: 25 cm
Weight: 50 g

BLACK-HEADED GULL
Bill to tail length: 40 cm
Weight: 200–300 g

GULLS and TERNS

Moult sequence in gulls

Like other birds, gulls renew their feathers in a regular sequence of moults, producing distinct plumages. Because they are big and strongly patterned, the process is easily appreciated; it is summarized here for a gull that takes four or five years to reach maturity (Herring Gull) and one that takes two years (Black-headed Gull).

2ND-WINTER SEP–MAR [Jan]

pale eye

dark eye

JUVENILE JUN–AUG [Aug]

1ST-WINTER SEP–APR [Jan]

1ST-SUMMER MAR–OCT [Jun]

Bill colour changes progressively with age.

JUVENILE/1ST-YEAR primary feathers have pointed tips; tail feathers are rounded. All later stages have rounded primary tips and squarer tail feathers. On large, pale-eyed gulls, juveniles have dark eyes; becoming paler in the second year.

Herring Gull

1ST CALENDAR YEAR | 2ND CALENDAR YEAR | 3RD CALENDAR YEAR

Jun Jul Aug Sep Oct Nov Dec Jan Feb Mar Apr May Jun Jul Aug Sep Oct Nov Dec Jan Feb Mar Apr May Jun Jul A

JUVENILE | 1ST-WINTER | 2ND-WINTER
1ST-SUMMER | 2ND-SUMMER

1st moult
JUVENILE → 1ST-WINTER
Head and body feathers replaced.

1ST-WINTER → 1ST-SUMMER
Few or no feathers moulted, but brown/black areas fade to paler brown/buff.

2nd moult
1ST-SUMMER → 2ND-WINTER
Prolonged complete moult of head, body, tail and wing feathers.

3rd moult
2ND-WINTER → 2ND-SUMMER
Partial moult of head and body feathers only.

Black-headed Gull

1ST CALENDAR YEAR | 2ND CALENDAR YEAR | 3RD

Jun Jul Aug Sep Oct Nov Dec Jan Feb Mar Apr May Jun Jul Aug Sep Oct Nov Dec Jan

JUVENILE | 1ST-WINTER | 2ND-WINTER (ADULT)
1ST-SUMMER

FLEDGLING: MAY–JUN
in nest, fledging into juvenile plumage.

1st moult
JUVENILE → 1ST-WINTER
New head and body feathers replace juvenile brown.

2nd moult
1ST-WINTER → 1ST-SUMMER
Gains variable hood, wing and tail markings fade, feathers up to a year old.

3rd moult
1ST-SUMMER → 2ND-WINTER (ADULT)
White head with dark spot; bright red bill and legs; wing feathers new.

JUVENILE JUN–AUG

1ST-WINTER JUL–APR

1ST-SUMMER APR–SEP

MOULT

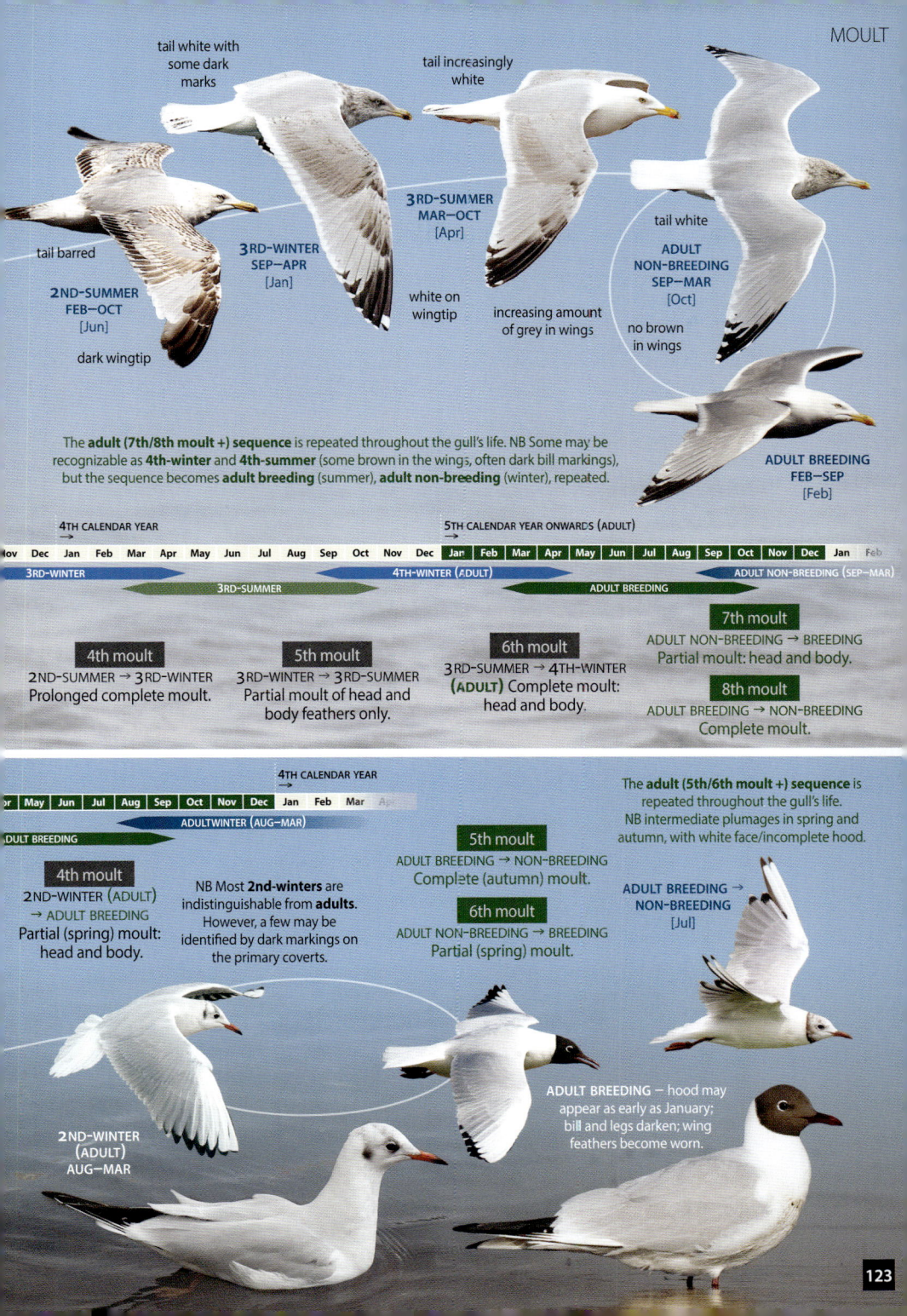

tail white with some dark marks

tail increasingly white

3RD-SUMMER MAR–OCT [Apr]

tail white

ADULT NON-BREEDING SEP–MAR [Oct]

3RD-WINTER SEP–APR [Jan]

white on wingtip

increasing amount of grey in wings

no brown in wings

tail barred

2ND-SUMMER FEB–OCT [Jun]

dark wingtip

The **adult (7th/8th moult +) sequence** is repeated throughout the gull's life. NB Some may be recognizable as **4th-winter** and **4th-summer** (some brown in the wings, often dark bill markings), but the sequence becomes **adult breeding** (summer), **adult non-breeding** (winter), repeated.

ADULT BREEDING FEB–SEP [Feb]

4TH CALENDAR YEAR

Nov	Dec	Jan	Feb	Mar	Apr	May	Jun	Jul	Aug	Sep	Oct	Nov	Dec

3RD-WINTER → 3RD-SUMMER → 4TH-WINTER (ADULT)

5TH CALENDAR YEAR ONWARDS (ADULT)

Jan	Feb	Mar	Apr	May	Jun	Jul	Aug	Sep	Oct	Nov	Dec	Jan	Feb

ADULT BREEDING → ADULT NON-BREEDING (SEP–MAR)

4th moult
2ND-SUMMER → 3RD-WINTER
Prolonged complete moult.

5th moult
3RD-WINTER → 3RD-SUMMER
Partial moult of head and body feathers only.

6th moult
3RD-SUMMER → 4TH-WINTER (ADULT) Complete moult: head and body.

7th moult
ADULT NON-BREEDING → BREEDING
Partial moult: head and body.

8th moult
ADULT BREEDING → NON-BREEDING
Complete moult.

4TH CALENDAR YEAR

Apr	May	Jun	Jul	Aug	Sep	Oct	Nov	Dec	Jan	Feb	Mar	Apr

ADULT BREEDING → ADULT WINTER (AUG–MAR)

4th moult
2ND-WINTER (ADULT) → ADULT BREEDING
Partial (spring) moult: head and body.

NB Most **2nd-winters** are indistinguishable from **adults**. However, a few may be identified by dark markings on the primary coverts.

5th moult
ADULT BREEDING → NON-BREEDING
Complete (autumn) moult.

6th moult
ADULT NON-BREEDING → BREEDING
Partial (spring) moult.

The **adult (5th/6th moult +) sequence** is repeated throughout the gull's life. NB intermediate plumages in spring and autumn, with white face/incomplete hood.

ADULT BREEDING → NON-BREEDING [Jul]

2ND-WINTER (ADULT) AUG–MAR

ADULT BREEDING — hood may appear as early as January; bill and legs darken; wing feathers become worn.

123

GULLS and TERNS

Larger gulls | Introduction

Large gulls are either **'dark-winged'** or **'white-winged'**. 'White-winged' gulls include difficult species and subspecies: they are treated together in the following pages.

Adult gulls interact in spring, when each species must look and sound unique: hence they are then easiest for us to identify. Immatures, having no 'need' to look different, are more difficult to identify. Most gulls vary in detail but critical features remain consistent: amongst thousands of Black-headed Gulls only one or two paler ones may stand out. But Herring and Lesser Black-backed Gulls vary widely between extremes of shade and size, and young Herring Gulls' feather patterns vary greatly, too. Concentrate on the important things: primary, tertial and tail patterns, and structure. Young Herring Gulls' pale inner primaries and young Lesser Black-backed Gulls' all-dark primaries will separate them, while endless variations in detail simply confuse. For some rare gulls, however, differences in detail must be grasped. As large gulls mature, adult back colour, wingtip patterns, bill colour and leg colour come into play, making identification more straightforward.

Leucism and hybrids

Melanin darkens and strengthens feathers: black rarely changes, but white feather tips wear off. Rare individuals with reduced pigment – leucistic – look very pale. White Common Gulls suggest Ivory Gulls, pale Herring Gulls look like Glaucous Gulls, but they don't quite 'fit'. Details such as 'shadows' of darker wingtips and tail-bands remove confusion. Gulls occasionally hybridize, especially where one species is extending its range – hybrid pairs may persist, or disappear as the population increases. Some hybrid gulls defy identification.

3RD-WINTER

3RD-WINTER

HERRING GULL (p. 130)

GLAUCOUS GULL (p. 140)

GREAT BLACK-BACKED GULL (p. 134)

GLAUCOUS GULL (p. 140)

1ST-WINTER

1ST-WINTER

2ND-WINTER

HERRING GULL (p. 130)

A young Glaucous Gull flying in to a reservoir roost is strikingly pale, but settled amongst thousands of birds may take some finding. Look for the pale wingtip. Glaucous Gulls are intermediate in size between Great Black-backed Gulls and Herring Gulls (northern Herring Gulls can be as large). Iceland Gulls are closer to the smaller end of the Herring Gull range.

Glaucous and Iceland Gulls have different 'expressions', but such subtleties are hard to describe.

1ST-WINTER (FADED JUVENILE)

GLAUCOUS GULL (p. 140)

ICELAND GULL (p. 141)

1ST-WINTER (FADED JUVENILE)

LARGER GULLS

Larger gulls | 'Dark-winged' regular adults

Adult gulls flying over may be identifiable at long range by their underwings:

Herring Gull has pale grey under flight feathers, black on wingtips;

Lesser Black-backed Gull has darker grey band under flight feathers;

Great Black-backed Gull is blacker beneath with broader white trailing edge extending to tip.

The pattern of the primaries is important for distinguishing Herring, Yellow-legged and Caspian Gulls – see p. 138

LESSER BLACK-BACKED GULL (p. 132)

GREAT BLACK-BACKED GULL (p. 134)

CASPIAN GULL (p. 137)

HERRING GULL (p. 130)

YELLOW-LEGGED GULL (p. 136)

YELLOW-LEGGED GULL (p. 136)

NB: American Herring Gull (p. 158) is more difficult when adult than in immature plumages.

HERRING GULL (p. 130)

ssp. *argentatus* is darker than ssp. *argenteus* with more white in the primaries – see p. 131

CASPIAN GULL (p. 137)

ssp. *graellsii*

GREAT BLACK-BACKED GULL (p. 134)

NB: Slaty-backed Gull (p. 156) has bright pink legs.

LESSER BLACK-BACKED GULL (p. 132)

ssp. *intermedius*

NB: ssp. *fuscus* is even blacker

125

GULLS and TERNS

Larger gulls | Juveniles/1st-winters
Look carefully at size, wingtip pattern and contrasts, tail-band and tail/rump contrasts, bill shape and colour.

LESSER BLACK-BACKED GULL (p. 132)
- contrasting covert band
- all dark flight feathers
- less heavy bill

black tail-band
- little/no contrast
- heavier bill
- pale inner primaries

YELLOW-LEGGED GULL (p. 136)

CASPIAN GULL (p. 137)
- white head
- 'striped' primaries

AMERICAN HERRING GULL (p. 158)
- black tail

- no covert band
- palest inner primaries

HERRING GULL (p. 130)
- weak tail-band

GREAT BLACK-BACKED GULL (p. 134)
- huge size; pale spots on inner primary tips

'Thayer's Gull' (p. 142)
- dusky hindwing and wingtip
- small head and bill

'Kumlien's Gull' (p. 142)
- dusky wingtip streaks

ICELAND GULL (p. 141)
- pale wings

GLAUCOUS GULL (p. 140)
- large head and bill
- pale wings

LARGER GULLS

LESSER BLACK-BACKED GULL (p. 132)
'wavy' pale edges and pale tip

YELLOW-LEGGED GULL (p. 136)
straight pale edges near tip only

'HERRING' TYPES
note structure; head shape; tertial pattern

CASPIAN GULL (p. 137)
U-shaped pale tip

longer legs than Herring Gull

AMERICAN HERRING GULL (p. 158)
variable pale 'notches' on edges

darker and larger than Herring Gull

'HERRING' GROUP

HERRING GULL (p. 130)

'Thayer's Gull' (p. 142)

VERY DARK

'Kumlien's Gull' (p. 142)

GREAT BLACK-BACKED GULL (p. 134)

extent of markings on the primaries grades from Iceland to 'Thayer's Gulls

BROWN MARKS

ICELAND GULL (p. 141)

WHITE/IVORY

'ICELAND' GROUP

SLATY-BACKED GULL (p. 156)
dark wingtip

'WHITE-WINGED' TYPES
note size and primary pattern; head, bill, legs

GLAUCOUS GULL (p. 140)

GLAUCOUS-WINGED GULL (p. 156)
pale wingtip

'bubblegum' pink legs

127

GULLS and TERNS

Larger gulls | regularly occurring 'dark-winged' 2nd-years

Adult colours begin to develop, but look for upperwing patterns, back/innerwing contrast

dark mottled back

GREAT BLACK-BACKED GULL (p. 134)

white head, dark collar

CASPIAN GULL (p. 137)

head shape and bill shape important

two birds showing variability

YELLOW-LEGGED GULL (p. 136)

dark back

LESSER BLACK-BACKED GULL (p. 132)

uniformly dark primaries

HERRING GULL (p. 130)

small dark eye in pear-shaped head

often shows pale upper tertials

long wingtip

long slim bill

back darker than Herring/Caspian Gull

bill often dark

long, dull legs

long wingtip

HERRING GULL (p. 130)

CASPIAN GULL (p. 137)

YELLOW-LEGGED GULL (p. 136)

dull legs

thick bill

bright pink legs

LESSER BLACK-BACKED GULL (p. 132)

GREAT BLACK-BACKED GULL (p. 134)

Larger gulls | regularly occurring 'dark-winged' 3rd-years

'DARK-WINGED' GULLS

Further progress towards adult patterns, identification becomes clearer but precise ageing difficult

GREAT BLACK-BACKED GULL (p. 134) — darkest back

pale grey back

CASPIAN GULL (p. 137)

wingtip pattern, head shape and bill shape important

long grey 'tongues' penetrate black

pale grey back

YELLOW-LEGGED GULL (p. 136)

palest grey back

HERRING GULL (p. 130)

mid-dark grey back

LESSER BLACK-BACKED GULL (p. 132)

2ND-SUMMER → 3RD-WINTER [Oct] (two outer primaries still to be replaced)

well-defined black wingtip

long wingtip

dark eye

long slim bill

dark eye

dark bill band frequent

YELLOW-LEGGED GULL (p. 136)

long wingtip

HERRING GULL (p. 130)

palest back

long legs

CASPIAN GULL (p. 137)

yellow legs

pink legs

LESSER BLACK-BACKED GULL (p. 132)

dark grey back

yellowish legs

blackest back

heaviest bill

GREAT BLACK-BACKED GULL (p. 134)

pinkish legs

129

GULLS and TERNS — Herring Gull moult sequence p. 122 | Larger gull comparisons by ages pp. 125–129

NT Herring Gull *Larus argentatus*

except ssp. *argentatus* | I | 548

L 54–60 cm | W 123–148 cm

Common large, pale-backed gull. ADULT **pale grey** above; wingtip black with white spots. **Eye cream** with yellow/orange ring; **bill yellow with red spot, legs pink**. ADULT BREEDING head and body white. ADULT NON-BREEDING head heavily streaked. JUVENILE/1ST-WINTER grey-brown, fading paler; tertials have **pale tips and 'notches'**. Bill and eye dark. Plumage bleached paler by May. 2ND-WINTER bill has pale base and tip; eye pale. 3RD-WINTER **pale grey** back; bill yellow with dark marks, reddish spot.

Yellow-legged Gull (p. 136) Caspian Gull (p. 137), American Herring Gull (p. 158), Vega Gull (p. 159), 'Thayer's Gull' (p. 142)

IN FLIGHT, ADULT wingtip black, two white 'mirrors' (or full white tip on outer feather). **Pale grey** beneath flight feathers. JUVENILE/1ST-WINTER **striking pale inner primary patch**. 2ND/3RD-YEARS become grey on back; **pale inner primaries**.

VOICE Yelping, barking notes, strident "*kyow*," soft "*gag-ag-gag*;" loud, trumpeting display call, higher pitched than Lesser Black-backed Gull (p. 132), "*kyyaa-kya-kya-ka-ka-ka-kya-kya-kyau*."

Common and widespread (140,000 pairs, including 6,000 in Ireland; 730,000 in winter)

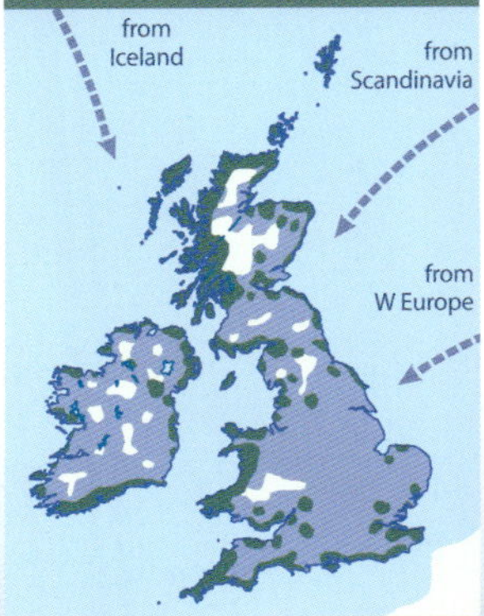

from Iceland
from Scandinavia
from W Europe

Cliffs, shores, coastal towns, lakes, reservoirs, fields, tips

JUVENILE | 2ND-WINTER | 3RD-WINTER | ADULT BREEDING

increasingly pale grey above with age

JUVENILE/1ST-WINTER pale inner primaries unlike Lesser Black-backed Gull, but see Great Black-backed Gull (p. 134).

black wingtips, one or two white 'mirrors', white tips, which wear off in summer. Underwing pale grey

British/Irish ssp. *argenteus* ADULT NON-BREEDING JUL–MAR

head variably streaked dark, bill may have dark marks

white spots on wingtip wear off by May/Jun

British/Irish ssp. *argenteus* ADULT BREEDING FEB–SEP

pink legs

NOTE: some adults from the Baltic have yellow legs – see Yellow-legged Gull (p. 136)

'DARK-WINGED' GULLS

ssp. argenteus

ssp. argentatus

Northern ssp. *argentatus* (frequent N/central Britain in winter) larger, darker and with less black/more white in wingtip, especially beneath, than British/Irish ssp. *argenteus*.

extreme 'Arctic' examples are like Glaucous × Herring Gull hybrids, but too dark, or like 'Thayer's Gull' (p. 142) but too big; dull bill

Northern ssp. *argentatus* ADULT NON-BREEDING JUL–MAR

British/Irish ssp. *argenteus* ADULT NON-BREEDING JUL–MAR

ssp. *argenteus* paler grey than ssp. *argentatus*; drab head autumn–winter

Remember: even the palest gull can look dark against bright water, or a white cloud.

2ND/3RD-YEARS develop adult plumage features at different rates, so ageing is difficult

3RD-WINTER AUG–MAR

bill colour and pattern from first- to third-year is highly variable

2ND-WINTER AUG–MAR

JUVENILE JUN–AUG

JUVENILES vary from darker to paler individuals. All become paler and more contrasted as plumage is worn and bleached by 1ST-WINTER

JUVENILE/1ST-WINTER paler than Lesser Black-backed Gull; **wider pale tips and 'notches' on tertials**, but very variable

1ST-WINTER AUG–MAR

131

GULLS and TERNS Larger gull comparisons by ages pp. 125–129

Lesser Black-backed Gull *Larus fuscus*

except ssp. *intermedius* **I**

L 48–56 cm | W 117–134 cm

Yellow-legged Gull (p. 136), Caspian Gull (p. 137), Slaty-backed Gull (p. 156)

Common large, dark-backed gull. ADULT BREEDING **dark grey** above, otherwise white except black-and-white wingtip; **legs bright yellow**. Eye cream with red ring. ADULT NON-BREEDING head/breast grey-brown; legs dull yellow. JUVENILE/1ST-WINTER pale buff, heavily mottled grey/brown; tertials with **narrow pale fringes**; greater coverts wear to dark brown. 2ND/3RD-YEARS increasingly grey above: 2ND-WINTER dark dull brown above, but bright white head and underparts by 3RD-SUMMER.

IN FLIGHT, ADULT grey upperwing, white trailing edge narrows towards black wingtip; small white 'mirrors'. **Dark grey** beneath flight feathers. JUVENILE/1ST-WINTER **primaries all-dark; dark midwing band**. 2ND-WINTER dark grey 'saddle' between brown wings.

VOICE Deep, throaty "*kyow*" and squealing notes; long, laughing calls deeper than Herring Gull (p. 130) (often heard from migrants inland).

Two subspecies regular: **British/Irish *graellsii*** and **darker *intermedius*** (breeds NW Europe, not always easily identifiable). Ssp. *fuscus* (Baltic Gull) recorded but rare: blackest, slimmest.

Locally common summer visitor; breeds in colonies in N and W (110,000 pairs, including 5,000 in Ireland); widespread migrant, winter visitor (130,000)

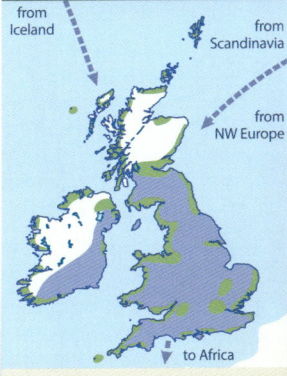

from Iceland
from Scandinavia
from NW Europe
to Africa

Coasts, reservoirs, fields, tips, roofs

2ND-WINTER

3RD-WINTER increasingly **dark grey on back** with age

ADULT BREEDING

1ST-SUMMER MAR–SEP [Apr]

JUVENILE/1ST-YEAR primaries all-dark, dark trailing edge and second dark band across coverts (Herring Gull has pale inner primaries, no covert band; Yellow-legged Gull intermediate)

black wingtip contrasts with rest of wing (unlike Great Black-backed Gull)

ssp. *graellsii* ADULT BREEDING FEB–AUG

ssp. *graellsii* ADULT NON-BREEDING JUL–MAR

wingtip spots wear off by May–Jun

ADULT from autumn to late winter variably streaked on head and breast, some very dark, others remain largely whitish; some have dark bill-tip marks

'DARK-WINGED' GULLS

Lesser Black-backed Gull subspecies

Two subspecies regular: British/Irish **graellsii** and darker **intermedius** (breeds NW Europe, not always easily identifiable). **Ssp. fuscus** (Baltic Gull) recorded but rare: blackest, slimmest.

ssp. *intermedius* [Oct]

Ssp. *intermedius* (regular S Britain in winter) can be as black as Great Black-backed Gull; whiter head than ssp. *graellsii* in winter, but not all are identifiable. Both these sspp. **moult all flight feathers May–Nov** (with only the outer 1 or 2 primaries still growing by Oct).

ssp. *fuscus* [Nov]

OUTER PRIMARIES OCT–NOV
in moult   not in moult

'BALTIC GULL' ssp. *fuscus* (Baltic, migrates S and E; rare in Britain and Ireland) has relatively long wings, small head, slender bill and short legs; adult black above, no contrast with wingtip; almost white head in winter. After first winter, *fuscus* replaces only 1–4 innermost primaries in Oct–Nov, the rest after migration.

ssp. *graellsii*
ADULT NON-BREEDING

ssp. *intermedius*
ADULT NON-BREEDING

wingtip spots
complete Oct–May

wingtip spots
irregular due to moult

wingtip spots
worn off

ssp. *fuscus*
ADULT
[May]

readily told from Herring Gull once the dark grey back starts to develop

3RD-WINTER
AUG–MAR

2ND-WINTER
AUG–MAR

JUVENILE/1ST-WINTER tertials blackish, **narrow pale tips** (pale 'notches' on Herring Gull). Gains whiter head, dark around eye like Yellow-legged Gull (p. 136), blackish bill

JUVENILE
JUN–AUG

GULLS and TERNS • Larger gull comparisons by ages pp. 125–129

Great Black-backed Gull *Larus marinus*

④ L 61–74 cm | W 144–166 cm • Slaty-backed Gull (p. 156)

Largest, most predatory gull; **massive bill**, especially on MALE. ADULT BREEDING **black** above, white below. Legs **pale pinkish**/whitish. ADULT NON-BREEDING **head remains mostly white**. JUVENILE/1ST-WINTER **heavy, black bill**; whitish head; **boldly chequered** black, brown and buff above. 2ND/3RD-YEARS increasingly black above.

IN FLIGHT, long wings; steady beats; soars well. ADULT back and wings black, broad white trailing edge right to black tip; large white 'mirror'. JUVENILE/1ST-WINTER like pale juvenile Herring Gull (p. 130) but pale inner primaries less contrasted and upperside boldly chequered. 2ND/3RD-YEARS increasingly patched with black.

VOICE Deep, loud, distinctive, barking "*huh-huh-huh*;" long, deep, choking "*hou-oow-o, how- how-ow-ow-ow o o o.*"

Locally common resident breeder (19,000 pairs, including 2,000 in Ireland); commoner, more widespread in winter (76,000)

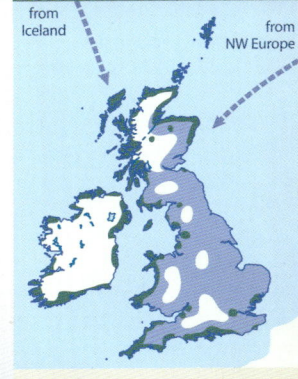

from Iceland • from NW Europe

Coasts, reservoirs, tips

JUVENILE/1ST WINTER upperside like pale juvenile Herring Gull; pale spots near tips of inner primaries

increasingly **blacker above** and whiter on head with age

1ST-WINTER • 2ND-WINTER • 3RD-WINTER

white trailing edge continues towards tip (narrower on Lesser Black-backed Gull (p. 132))

ADULT — no contrast between black wingtip and rest of wing (unlike Lesser Black-backed Gull)

4TH-WINTER JUL–MAR

head faintly spotted brown, Sep–Feb

white wingtip spots reduced by wear Feb–Sep

ADULT

'DARK-WINGED' GULLS

black/white contrast obvious; size and structure important

**3RD-WINTER
JUL–MAR**

blackish chequering above

big bill, especially on males – head/bill most obvious features

**2ND-WINTER
JUL–MAR**

JUVENILE/1ST-YEAR enormous; **heavy, black bill**, whiter head than Herring or Lesser Black-backed Gulls, **boldly chequered** above, whiter belly

**1ST-WINTER
JUL–MAR**

135

Yellow-legged Gull *Larus michahellis*

L 52–58 cm | W 120–140 cm

Compare: Herring Gull (p. 130), Caspian Gull

Scarce, most late summer/autumn/early winter (low 100s); very rare breeder (1–4 pairs)

from S Europe

Reservoirs, coasts, fields, tips

Large, grey-backed gull. ADULT BREEDING head white, upperparts **darker** grey than Herring Gull (p. 130), **paler** than Lesser Black-backed Gull (p. 132); wingtip black-and-white. Bill rich yellow with red spot. **Legs yellow**; eye yellow with red ring. ADULT NON-BREEDING head slightly streaked Jul–Sep, otherwise white (Herring/Lesser Black-backed Gulls streaked until Jan/Feb). JUVENILE grey-brown; more ginger-brown by 1ST-WINTER; head whiter with slight 'mask' and greyish 'shawl'. **Tertials dark with thin pale tips** (plus pale fringes on some birds). Later ageing unreliable, but 2ND-WINTER gains grey above. 3RD-YEAR blotched brown on grey, white below; bill blackish to bright yellow with black band.

IN FLIGHT, ADULT extensive black on wingtip; large white 'mirror' or tip on outer primary (see p. 138). 1ST-WINTER faint pale inner primary patch; thick black tail-band. 2ND/3RD-YEARS increasingly grey on back.

VOICE Deep barking notes; laughing *"kyowww oww yow ow-ow-ow…."*

1ST-WINTER SEP–MAR

2ND-WINTER SEP–MAR

3RD-WINTER SEP–MAR

ADULT

ADULT WINTER

'AZOREAN' or 'ATLANTIC GULL'
ssp. *atlantis* (vagrant; <10 records (<5 Ireland), Jul–Dec)
ADULT NON-BREEDING has defined dark, streaked hood reaching below gape, but very variable and overlaps with regular ssp. *michahellis*.

ADULTS look like this from late autumn to late summer: white-headed and dark-backed compared with typical non-breeding Herring Gull; males, especially, have bulbous head and thick bill

ADULT BREEDING OCT–JUL

Immature and in-flight identification *p. 138*

'DARK-WINGED' GULLS

Caspian Gull *Larus cachinnans*

549

L 55–60 cm | W 138–147 cm

👁 Herring Gull *(p. 130)*, Yellow-legged Gull

Large, pale-backed gull; high, broad shoulders slope down to long wingtip; legs long, slender. MALE long, parallel-edged bill; sloping forehead. FEMALE shorter bill and legs. ADULT back pale grey; wingtip black-and-white; head white all year. Eye yellow or dark, with red ring. Bill greenish-yellow with dull red spot, often dark band. Legs yellowish or pinkish-grey. JUVENILE dark brown, heavily streaked. 1ST-WINTER; white/grey/brown/black effect: head and underparts whitish, back pale greyish, wings brown, tertials/wingtip blackish. Tertial tips make white crescent. Bill and eye dark. 2ND-WINTER back grey, plain or with dark streaks/'anchor' shapes; darker 'shawl'. 3RD YEAR back/wing plain grey.

IN FLIGHT, ADULT black on outer 6/7 primaries, **indented by pale grey 'fingers'** (see *p. 138*). 1ST-WINTER black tail-band of even width; black hindwing band; outer primaries 'striped' blackish. 2ND-WINTER greyer above; clear-cut black tail-band. 3RD-WINTER like adult with darker primary coverts, less white in wingtip, a few dark tail markings.

VOICE Low-pitched barks and yelling notes, similar to Lesser Black-backed Gull *(p. 132)*.

Rare but increasing winter visitor, 300–400 per year; juveniles/1st-year birds from Aug; scattered). Vagrant Ireland (<15 records).

from C Europe

Beaches, inland lakes, tips

1ST-WINTER SEP–MAR

2ND-WINTER SEP–MAR

3RD-WINTER SEP–MAR

outer primary pattern of a grey/black border with whitish indented patches or 'fingers' may be striking

ADULT [Nov]

pale underwing, as if reflecting light from water or snow beneath

ADULT [Nov]

dark eye often distinct, set well forward

NOTE: pattern may sometimes be evident beneath far wingtip.

legs dull pinkish or yellowish

NOTE: black bill spot/band often shown by both sub-adult Herring and Yellow-legged Gulls

GULLS and TERNS

Yellow-legged and Caspian Gull Identification

Adults: Primaries are numbered according to the sequence in which they are moulted: innermost is P1, outermost P10. Details of patterns are needed to identify some of the rarest gulls.

YELLOW-LEGGED GULL
no paler patches
P5, P6, P7, P8, P9, P10

Like Herring Gull, often more black: more solid black on P5 and P6 feathers; some have complete white tip to outer feather (P10).

HERRING GULL ssp. *argenteus*
small pale grey patches
P5, P6, P7, P8, P9, P10

Large 'mirror' on outer feather (P10), sometimes joins tip; smaller 'mirror' on next; less black on P5 and P6; grey/black border with little paler grey.

CASPIAN GULL
whitish patches
P5, P6, P7, P8, P9, P10

Large white tip (joining 'mirror') on outer feather (P10) typical of westernmost breeding birds; large 'mirror' on P9 feather; more black on P5 and P6 feathers; grey/black border indented by whitish patches.

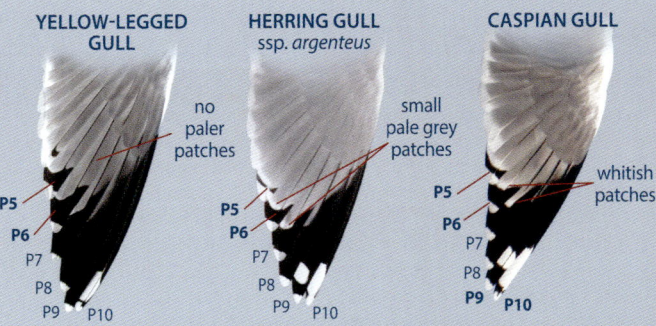

---

tail-band more solid than Herring, narrower than Lesser Black-backed

HERRING GULL

underwing paler

underwing more contrasting than Herring

CASPIAN GULL

YELLOW-LEGGED GULL

back greyish

back mottled brown

inner primaries darker than Herring, more 'striped'

inner primaries almost same tone as outer

head more rounded and usually not as pale as Caspian or Yellow-legged Gulls

upper tertials often replaced by new, pale grey feathers

CASPIAN GULL

HERRING GULL

YELLOW-LEGGED GULL

1st-winters
Look for head shape, bill shape, head/back/wing contrasts (see also *pp. 126–127*).

1ST-WINTER TERTIAL PATTERNS

HERRING GULL

'oak-leaf' pattern: scalloped pale edges

CASPIAN GULL

no straight pale edges; pale 'U'-shape on tip

YELLOW-LEGGED GULL

straight pale edges near tip

'White-winged' gulls in flight

'WHITE-WINGED' GULLS

ICELAND GULL ssp. *thayeri* ('Thayer's Gull') (p. 142)

JUVENILE/1ST-WINTER

ADULT NON-BREEDING

2ND-WINTER

3RD-WINTER

JUVENILE/1ST-WINTER

ICELAND GULL ssp. *kumlieni* ('Kumlien's Gull') (p. 142)

ADULT NON-BREEDING

3RD-WINTER

JUVENILE/1ST-WINTER

ICELAND GULL ssp. *glaucoides* (p. 141–142)

2ND-WINTER

ADULT NON-BREEDING

GLAUCOUS GULL (p. 140)

2ND-WINTER

3RD-WINTER

ADULT NON-BREEDING

JUVENILE/1ST-WINTER

1ST-WINTER

ADULT NON-BREEDING

GLAUCOUS-WINGED GULL (p. 156)

139

GULLS and TERNS
White-winged gulls in flight *p. 139*

Glaucous Gull *Larus hyperboreus*

④ L 63–68 cm | W 138–158 cm   ◯▶ Glaucous-winged Gull (*p. 156*)

Rare winter visitor (300–500 birds, most Oct–Apr; occasional long-stayers) from Greenland and Arctic Canada

'White-winged' gull, larger than Herring Gull (*p. 130*); **no black on wings**. 'Heavier' than Iceland Gull; bill and legs relatively **long**; **wingtip projects less** beyond tail. Head shape and expression can be distinctive but require care: long bill/head profile gives 'mean' look, when alert, but head rounded when relaxed. ADULT very pale grey above, **wingtip white**; head white (streaked brown Aug–Mar). On water, tertials/wingtip create long white triangle. Bill bright yellow, red spot; legs pale pink. JUVENILE coffee-brown, barred; **wingtip paler buff**. Bill pink with **sharply defined black tip**. Fades paler into 1st-winter, some darker below than on back. 1st-summer blotched white. 2nd-year similar but paler eye and dark band/pale tip to bill. 3rd-year patched pale grey above.

IN FLIGHT (see *p. 139*), heavy, long-winged. ADULT pale grey; **white wingtip**. 1st- and 2nd-years striking sandy-buff, wings fading to long, pointed **paler tips**; tail barred but has no dark band.

VOICE Infrequent yelping notes in winter: high, thin "*kee-ooow*."

Harbours, coasts, reservoirs, tips

Juvenile plumage fades to 1st-winter, and fades further by first-summer, when a small pale tip begins to develop on the bill.

JUVENILE/1ST-WINTER JUN–MAR

considerable variation

JUVENILE/1ST-WINTER DARK

JUVENILE/1ST-WINTER

2ND-WINTER SEP–MAR

wingtip can look long and pointed

JUVENILE/1ST-WINTER PALE

3RD-SUMMER FEB–SEP

ADULT NON-BREEDING SEP–MAR

'WHITE-WINGED' GULLS

Iceland Gull *Larus glaucoides*

④ L 52–60 cm | W 123–139 cm

'White-winged' gull, size as Herring Gull (*p. 130*). Dense feathering and relatively short legs give dumpy impression. **Long wingtip** most evident and often upswept when swimming, **projects well beyond tail**, especially on first-year birds; may droop beside tail when standing. Bill **relatively short**, **forehead steep**, **crown domed**; very little 'chin' when swimming. ADULT pale grey above, head and body white (head streaked brown Aug–Mar); **wingtip white**. Bill greenish-yellow with dark red spot; legs dusky pink. JUVENILE coffee-brown, barred; **wingtip paler buff**; black bill tip **extends as point into dull base**. Fades paler into 1ST-WINTER. Some 1ST-SUMMER birds almost white. 2ND-WINTER shows a little grey above; bill has pale tip and dark band. 3RD-YEAR patched pale grey above, may be whitish overall with grey 'saddle'.

IN FLIGHT (see *p. 139*), wings broad-based, taper to narrower tip than Glaucous Gull; more pot-bellied. ADULT very pale; **white wingtip**. JUVENILE/1ST-WINTER/2ND-WINTER pale buff with paler wingtip, no dark hindwing or tail-band.

VOICE Chattering calls and high, squealing "*kwee-ooo*."

Rare winter visitor (200–500 birds; Nov–Apr)
from Greenland and Arctic Canada

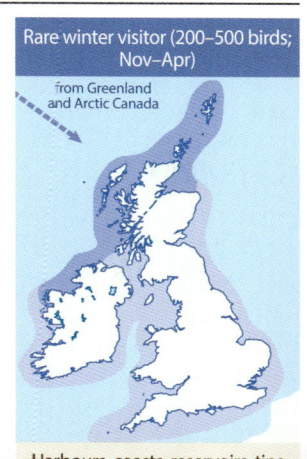

Harbours, coasts, reservoirs, tips

'KUMLIEN'S GULL'
ADULT NON-BREEDING
(well-marked)

'THAYER'S GULL'
ADULT NON-BREEDING

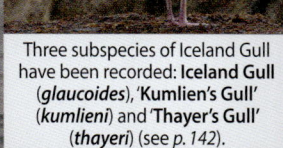

Three subspecies of Iceland Gull have been recorded: **Iceland Gull** (*glaucoides*), 'Kumlien's Gull' (*kumlieni*) and 'Thayer's Gull' (*thayeri*) (see *p. 142*).

JUVENILE/1ST-WINTER
JUN–MAR

bulging tertials variable, but often more obvious on Iceland Gull than Glaucous Gull

2ND-WINTER
SEP–MAR

3RD-WINTER
SEP–MAR

ADULT NON-BREEDING
SEP–MAR

GULLS and TERNS

See pp. 126–127 for comparison with other large gulls

Iceland Gull complex

Includes three subspecies, which are difficult to separate where characters intergrade.
ssp. *glaucoides* – **Iceland Gull** (see p. 141)
ssp. *kumlieni* – **'Kumlien's Gull'**
ssp. *thayeri* – **'Thayer's Gull'** (sometimes treated as a full species)

'Kumlien's Gull' – ssp. *kumlieni*
Rare winter visitor from NE Canada. Coasts. ADULT **white spots on grey wingtip**; **grey streaks** on spread primaries. Wingtip varies from almost white to almost as dark as 'Thayer's Gull'; 'average' birds distinctive. IMMATURES range from Iceland-type to darker with streaked wingtip, darker band on wing coverts and slight brown tail-band: more like pale immature 'Thayer's Gull', or hybrids.

'Thayer's Gull' – ssp. *thayeri*
Vagrant from Arctic N America: <50 records (<10 Ireland), Jan–Mar, Dec. Coasts. Between Herring Gull (p. 130) and Iceland Gull ssp. *glaucoides* in size and structure. ADULT like Herring Gull but with **smaller, duller bill, darker eye**, steeper forehead and deeper pink legs. **Slightly darker back** than Iceland Gull. JUVENILE/1ST-WINTER wingtip brown; upperparts more uniform than Herring Gull; tertials brown with mottled pale tips; rump/undertail broadly barred; bill like juvenile Iceland Gull but darker base. 2ND-WINTER wingtip dark brown; broad, crescentic pale feather tips. 3RD-WINTER like adult but brown tail-band. IN FLIGHT, white streaks or spots inside blackish wingtip (darkest 'Kumlien's Gull' similar but most have smaller, greyer marks).

ADULT NON-BREEDING

ADULT NON-BREEDING

'Kumlien's Gull' considerable variation

ADULT NON-BREEDING

ADULT NON-BREEDING

ICELAND GULL

'Thayer's Gull'

HERRING GULL

JUVENILE/1ST-WINTER

JUVENILE/1ST-WINTER

JUVENILE/1ST-WINTER

1ST-WINTER

palest extreme

considerable variation

typical 'Kumlien's Gull'

JUVENILE/1ST-WINTER

'Kumlien's Gull'

much like Herring Gull; Iceland Gull-like shape may catch the eye

JUVENILE/1ST-WINTER

'Thayer's Gull'

'Kumlien's Gull'

pale individual

closed wingtip like Herring Gull ('Kumlien's Gull' grey-and-white)

ADULT NON-BREEDING

'Thayer's Gull' ADULT NON-BREEDING

Regular small and medium-sized gulls in non-breeding plumage

SMALLER GULLS

👁 Rare smaller gulls (pp. 151–155)

1ST-WINTER

BLACK-HEADED GULL (p. 146)

1ST-WINTER

2ND-WINTER

ADULT NON-BREEDING

ADULT NON-BREEDING

ADULT NON-BREEDING

MEDITERRANEAN GULL (p. 147)

grey

COMMON GULL (p. 144)

grey-brown

2ND-WINTER

1ST-WINTER

JUVENILE

ADULT NON-BREEDING

ADULT NON-BREEDING

KITTIWAKE (p. 148)

JUVENILE

SABINE'S GULL (p. 149)

JUVENILE

1ST-SUMMER

JUVENILE

1ST-WINTER

ADULT NON-BREEDING

LITTLE GULL (p. 150)

1ST-WINTER

143

GULLS and TERNS   Smaller gulls in flight p. 143

Common Gull *Larus canus*

(3) L 40–46 cm | W 100–115 cm   ⬤ Ring-billed Gull (p. 154)

Medium-sized gull (between Black-headed Gull (p. 146) and Herring Gull (p. 130)). ADULT **darker** grey above than British/Irish Herring Gull (ssp. *argenteus*), with **bolder white patch** between grey back and black wingtip; **eye dark**; bill yellow, **no red spot**. **White wingtip spots** rule out Kittiwake (p. 148). **Legs green**. ADULT BREEDING head white. ADULT NON-BREEDING head streaked (sometimes has a dusky hood); bill dull, often with dark band. JUVENILE upperparts brown with neat pale fringes; flank and undertail white with variable brown bars. 1ST-WINTER back plain grey (some retain brown juvenile feathers); wings brown with buff feather edges. 1ST-SUMMER grey back darker than faded wing. 2ND-YEAR like dull adult with more brown-black on wingtip.

IN FLIGHT, ADULT wingtip black with large white spots (largest on P9 and P10) and extensive black underneath. 1ST-WINTER outerwing blackish, innerwing browner; tail white with clear-cut black tail-band. 2ND-YEAR smaller white spots in more extensive brown-black wingtip than adult.

VOICE Calls typically high-pitched and squealing, "*keeea*," "*klee-u*" and long, laughing, wailing "*ke-ke-ke-kleee-a kleee-a.*"

Locally common summer visitor (50,000 pairs, including 1,600 pairs Ireland), migrant; common winter visitor (700,000)

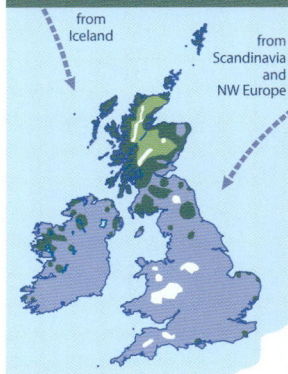

from Iceland
from Scandinavia and NW Europe

Breeds moors, lakes; in winter, grassy fields, shores, reservoirs

ADULT NON-BREEDING

Larger **Russian ssp. *heinei*** possibly regular in winter: darker back, paler eye, more extensive black in wingtip than **regular ssp. *canus*.**

dark band on bill variable

ADULT NON-BREEDING AUG–MAR

dark eye

bold white patch

yellow bill (no red spot)

wingtip spots wear off by Apr–May

yellow-green legs

ADULT BREEDING FEB–JUL

Round head, dark eye and slender bill give different, 'gentler', expression than Herring Gull.

SMALLER GULLS

- well-defined tail-band — **JUVENILE**
- neat tail-band / hindwing band — **1ST-WINTER**
- NB: outer primaries still growing — **2ND-WINTER**
- large white 'mirrors' — **ADULT BREEDING**

- wingtip dull black — **2ND-WINTER AUG–MAR**
- dark bill tip or band
- neat round head, slim bill
- grey back — **1ST-WINTER AUG–MAR**
- neat wing covert pattern
- by 1ST-SUMMER, grey back darker than bleached wings (see Mediterranean Gull (p.147))
- **JUVENILE JUN–AUG**

145

GULLS and TERNS · Black-headed Gull moult sequence p. 122 | Smaller gulls in flight p. 143

Black-headed Gull *Chroicocephalus (Larus) ridibundus*

L 35–39 cm | W 86–99 cm

Rare 'hooded' (p. 152–153), Slender-billed (p. 155) Gulls

Small, vocal 'white' gull with **white triangle** on outerwing and **dark underwing**. Light, buoyant, on pointed, angled wings; soars, hawks insects. ADULT BREEDING **dark brown hood**, fades paler (**white face** during spring and summer moults); **plum-red legs and bill**; long **black wingtip** with **white stripe** along lower edge. ADULT NON-BREEDING head white with **black ear-spot**; red legs and bill. JUVENILE dark tawny-brown on neck, back and wing. 1ST-WINTER white head and neck, dark ear-spot; back grey; brown in wing. 1ST-SUMMER patchy or full hood; brown wing markings fade paler.

IN FLIGHT, **long white triangle** (blaze) on outerwing; black primary tips; underwing **grey-black**, outermost feather **white**. JUVENILE/1ST-YEAR black streaks on white blaze (on some, black sufficiently extensive to isolate white spots towards tip); dark diagonal band across innerwing; dark tail-band; underwing pale grey, **white stripe** on leading edge.

VOICE Calls strident, shouted, screaming or grating: "*krree-arr*," "*karr*," and abrupt "*kek*" or "*kekek*."

Locally common (170,000 pairs, including 40,000 pairs Ireland); abundant and widespread winter visitor (2.2 million birds)

from Iceland
from Scandinavia NW and E Europe
to W Africa

Almost anywhere, breeds from coasts to uplands

1ST-WINTER — black streaks on white forewing — distinct white stripe on leading edge

ADULT BREEDING

ADULT NON-BREEDING

JUVENILE JUN–JUL — patchy, blotchy brown

ADULT NON-BREEDING JUL–MAR

1ST-SUMMER MAR–SEP

1ST-WINTER SEP–MAR

wingtip black with white streak on lower edge

♂ has longer body (tail reaches closer to wingtip) than ♀

ADULT BREEDING JAN–JUL

SMALLER GULLS

Mediterranean Gull *Ichthyaetus (Larus) melanocephalus*

548

(3) L 37–40 cm | W 94–102 cm

Small, very pale gull with a thick, blunt bill and rounded head. ADULT BREEDING **wingtip white**; **hood black** with bold white eye-crescents and **contrasting red bill**. ADULT NON-BREEDING head white with **blackish smudge** through eye and grey nape; bill and legs red or blackish. JUVENILE brown, with buff feather edges above; breast buff-brown; bill black. 1ST-YEAR back **pale** grey, underparts white; **grey smudge** behind eye; white eye-crescents; bill blackish (or orange/red at base); wingtip blackish. 2ND-YEAR like adult but **black marks on grey wingtip**.

IN FLIGHT, ADULT **wingtip** and **underwing white**. 1ST-WINTER like 1st-winter Common Gull (p. 144) with blacker hindwing band; midwing and back **very pale grey**; primaries blackish with white streaks when spread. 1ST-SUMMER dark areas fade browner. 2ND-YEAR **uniform pale grey** upperwing except **black streaks** on wingtip; white underwing.

VOICE Distinctive loud, nasal "*yaa-uh*" or "*ee-ow*."

Scarce summer visitor (600 pairs, including 5–10 pairs Ireland), migrant, winter visitor (1,800 birds); increasing

from Europe

Mostly coastal, nearby pools, fields, marshes

1ST-WINTER

ADULT BREEDING

white streaks, unlike Common Gull

2ND-WINTER JUL–APR

JUVENILE JUN–AUG

ADULT NON-BREEDING

ADULT NON-BREEDING → BREEDING [Mar]

ADULT BREEDING FEB–JUL

blackish bill, legs; brownish head, breast; scalloped back

1ST-WINTER SEP–MAR

ADULT NON-BREEDING JUN–MAR

♂ has longer body (tail reaches closer to wingtip) than ♀

GULLS and TERNS   Smaller gulls in flight *p. 143*

VU Kittiwake *Rissa tridactyla*

③ L 37–42 cm | W 93–105 cm

Small marine gull with a rounded head, slim wings and short tail. **Legs short, blackish** (brown on some). Stands but does not walk or forage on the ground. ADULT BREEDING bill yellow (**no red spot**); **eye black**. ADULT NON-BREEDING dingy **grey nape**, dark **cheek-spot**. JUVENILE **black bill**; **dark band along wing**; **black collar**. Gradual change through 1ST-WINTER (loses collar) to 1ST-SUMMER (when wing bands are faded and fragmented). 2ND YEAR looks like adult, or has dusky 'winter' head in summer, often with black marks on bill.

IN FLIGHT, wings slender and tapered; **steeply banking flight** in strong wind. ADULT **triangular black wingtip**; outerwing paler than innerwing; **underwing white with black tip**. JUVENILE black collar; **black 'W' across wings** broken by grey back; underwing white (dusky underwing band on Sabine's Gull). 1ST-WINTER/1ST-SUMMER loses collar and dark 'W' fades by May/Jun; hindwing white. 2ND YEAR like adult but black streaks on primary coverts and outer primaries.

VOICE Loud, wailing, nasal, rhythmic *"kitti-a waike"* (sometimes from migrants inland in spring); long, high, whining notes around colony.

Locally common (416,000 pairs, including 50,000 in Ireland), migrant; scarce winter visitor; rare inland (occasional passage flocks)

Mainly pelagic OCT–FEB

Breeds on cliffs, coastal buildings (ledges); beaches, offshore

JUVENILE

black 'W' across wings

1ST-SUMMER MAY–AUG

black collar (faded by 1ST-WINTER)

1ST-WINTER NOV–APR

prominent black wingtips as if 'dipped in ink'

ADULT NON-BREEDING

ADULT BREEDING

2ND-WINTER NOV–APR

black streaks

JUVENILE JUN–JAN

sharply defined black collar

ADULT NON-BREEDING AUG–MAR

yellow bill (no red spot)

ADULT BREEDING FEB–OCT

SMALLER GULLS

Sabine's Gull *Xema sabini*

② L 30–36 cm | W 80–87 cm

Small gull, usually seen in flight, showing striking **black, grey, white triangles** on wing (compare with Kittiwake and Little Gull (*p. 150*)). On water, dark, slim, tapered; closed tail (especially juvenile) forked, spread tail sharply triangular. Head dove-like; bill fairly short and thick. Picks from surface while swimming. ADULT BREEDING **hood lead-grey** bordered black; bill black with **yellow tip**; wingtip black with large **round white tips to primaries** (smaller with wear). ADULT NON-BREEDING blackish nape band. JUVENILE/1ST-WINTER crown, breast sides and back grey-brown with 'scaly' buff edges; wingtip and tail-band black.

IN FLIGHT, Quick, agile: broad, angled wings give great manoeuvrability; shearing flight in gales. **Triple-triangle wing** pattern at all ages (immature Kittiwake has black band and dull trailing edge, drabber in 1st-summer). **Dusky band on underwing** (unlike Kittiwake). Intermediate plumages with dark nape/neck/breast patches occur, but **wing pattern remains the same**.

VOICE Insignificant sharp "*kik*."

Rare coastal migrant (100–150, rarely up to 600 per year), very rare inland; mostly autumn but occasional spring/summer.

from Arctic Canada and Siberia

At sea; rarely storm-blown inland

clear white triangle

dusky underwing band

1ST-SUMMER [Jun]

ADULT BREEDING

ADULT NON-BREEDING [Oct]

NOTE: primary tips worn away

JUVENILE

Sabine's Gull has a complete moult in early–mid-winter followed by a partial one (head/body) in spring, more like some terns and skuas than most gulls.

JUVENILE JUN–JAN

ADULT NON-BREEDING AUG–MAR

ADULT BREEDING FEB–OCT

white primary tips can wear away

149

GULLS and TERNS Smaller gulls in flight *p. 143*

NT Little Gull *Hydrocoloeus (Larus) minutus*

2 L 24–28 cm | W 62–69 cm Ross's Gull

Tiny gull; feeds buoyantly (like Black Tern (*p. 166*)), dipping to water. ADULT BREEDING pale grey and white with **black hood** (no white eye-crescents); **wingtip white**; bill dark, legs red. ADULT NON-BREEDING grey cap, black ear-spot; legs pink. JUVENILE barred black/buff above; hindneck and side of breast blackish. 1ST-YEAR back pale grey; head/neck like adult, full or patchy hood Mar–Aug. 2ND YEAR like adult but black marks on wingtip.

IN FLIGHT, sometimes high, erratic, but mostly low over water. ADULT upperwing pale grey with **white trailing edge and wingtip**; underwing **blackish with white rim**. JUVENILE dusky hindneck and breast sides (thin collar on Kittiwake (*p. 148*)); **blackish 'W'** across wings and lower back. 1ST-YEAR grey back and rump; blackish 'W' fades browner Mar–Aug; dark streaks on hindwing (whiter on 1st-year Kittiwake); outer primaries striped black and white. 2ND YEAR as adult but black streaks on wingtip, underwing mottled grey/black.

VOICE Calls insignificant "*kik*," "*kek*."

Scarce migrant, mostly autumn/early winter (small numbers but 100s in few favoured places).

from E Europe

Offshore, coastal lagoons; scarce on inland waters

1ST-WINTER

2ND-WINTER SEP–MAR

ADULT NON-BREEDING

ADULT BREEDING

JUVENILE JUN–AUG

1ST-WINTER SEP–MAR

no white eye-crescents; no red on bill

ADULT NON-BREEDING AUG–MAR

black under far wingtip often shows

ADULT BREEDING FEB–JUL

very short legs

RARE ARCTIC GULLS

EN Ross's Gull *Rhodostethia rosea*
L 29–32 cm | W 73–80 cm

Dove-like; long wings; **tail wedge-shaped or pointed**. ADULT BREEDING pale pink and grey, **black ring** outlines same hood shape as Black-headed Gull (p. 146). **Upperwing pale, broad white trailing edge**; underwing grey with white rear edge. ADULT NON-BREEDING, nape grey; tiny ear-spot. 1ST-WINTER dark 'W' across upperwings resembles same-age Little Gull and Kittiwake (p. 148) but **dark trailing edge to outerwing behind long 'finger' of white**; grey underwing band.

ADULT BREEDING MAR–AUG

1ST-WINTER

easily overlooked as Little Gull

ADULT NON-BREEDING

1ST-WINTER SEP–MAR

1ST-SUMMER gains black neck ring

round head, short dark bill

ADULT NON-BREEDING AUG–MAR

short legs

Vagrant from Arctic: <200 records (<25 Ireland), all months, most Nov–Feb. Coasts.

NT Ivory Gull *Pagophila eburnea*
L 41–47 cm | W 100–113 cm

Size of Common Gull (p. 144); pigeon-like, with short legs and long wings. ADULT **wholly white** except black eye and legs, and **grey bill with yellow tip**. JUVENILE (persists through first winter) white with **scattered blackish spots** and **grey face**. Legs black (rules out albinistic Common Gull, but not albinistic Kittiwake (p. 148)).

Note: white individuals of other gulls occasionally appear, so bill and leg colours vital to confirm identification.

JUVENILE

ADULT

ADULT

long, broad wingtip

some birds more heavily spotted on wings

JUVENILE SEP–MAR

Vagrant from Arctic: <200 records (<20 Ireland), all months, most Nov–Feb. Coasts.

RARE GULLS

Rare 'hooded' gulls from North America

Three gulls from North America are exciting finds, most likely in flocks of common smaller gulls, including at lake or reservoir roosts. Bonaparte's Gull resembles a dainty Black-headed Gull (p. 146); Laughing and Franklin's Gulls are black-hooded like Mediterranean Gull (p. 147) but much darker grey above.

Laughing Gull *Leucophaeus (Larus) atricilla*

② L 36–41 cm | W 98–110 cm

Small–medium-sized gull; **slate-grey above**. ADULT BREEDING **hood black**; white eye-crescents do not meet behind eye (unlike in Franklin's Gull); **bill and legs red**. ADULT NON-BREEDING head white with grey cheek and nape. 1ST-WINTER wing blotched brown; **breast-band and flank grey**; bill blackish; legs dark grey. 2ND YEAR like adult but flank and wingtip browner. IN FLIGHT, ADULT upperwing mid-grey with white trailing edge, grey contrasts with **extensive black wingtip triangle**; small white tips wear off by Aug. 1ST-WINTER back grey; innerwing brown with grey midwing band, outerwing blackish; black tail-band and grey sides accentuate white rump.

2ND-SUMMER MAR–SEP

ADULT NON-BREEDING

1ST-WINTER

white eye-crescents

dingy on breast (unlike Franklin's Gull)

long, heavy, black bill

1ST-SUMMER MAR–SEP

white eye-crescents do not meet behind eye

ADULT BREEDING FEB–JUL

1ST-WINTER AUG–MAR

ADULT NON-BREEDING JUL–MAR

<250 records (<50 Ireland), all months. Most on coast; beaches, lakes.

AMERICAN HOODED

Bonaparte's Gull
Chroicocephalus (Larus) philadelphia

L 31–34 cm | W 79–84 cm

Like small Black-headed Gull (p. 146) with **white underwing, black bill** and **pink legs**. ADULT BREEDING **hood black**, with thin white eye-crescents. ADULT NON-BREEDING head white with black ear-spot. 1ST YEAR upperwing like Black-headed Gull, but inner primary coverts paler, outer ones edged dark; **blacker diagonal bar and trailing edge**; underwing **white with** long, dark trailing edge.

small head and bill, like Little Gull (p. 150)

ADULT BREEDING MAR–SEP

grey nape may be conspicuous

ADULT NON-BREEDING AUG–MAR

ADULT NON-BREEDING

BLACK-HEADED GULL

1ST-WINTER

1ST-WINTER SEP–MAR

<300 records (<100 Ireland), all months, most autumn. Coasts, inland waters.

Franklin's Gull *Leucophaeus (Larus) pipixcan*

L 32–36 cm | W 81–93 cm

Small gull; **slate-grey above**. ADULT BREEDING **hood black**; thick white eye-crescents **meet behind eye** (unlike in Laughing Gull). ADULT NON-BREEDING/ 1ST YEAR/ 2ND YEAR **dark half-hood**; white face and eye-crescents. IN FLIGHT, ADULT upperwing mid-grey; white trailing edge **curves forward** inside small **black-and-white wingtip**; underwing white with black tip (resembling Kittiwake (p. 148)); grey centre to tail. 1ST-WINTER hindwing, outerwing and tail-band blackish. 2ND YEAR more black/less white on wingtip than adult but mottled white band between black and grey (unlike Laughing Gull).

2ND-YEAR birds difficult to tell from adults

1ST-SUMMER MAR–SEP [Apr]

<100 records (<20 Ireland), most May–Aug, Nov–Jan. Most coastal; beaches, lakes.

ADULT BREEDING MAR–SEP

1ST-WINTER

white breast

thick white eye-crescents meet behind eye

ADULT NON-BREEDING AUG–MAR

in winter, all ages, dusky hood remains prominent

2ND-WINTER/ ADULT NON-BREEDING difficult; adults often show more white in wingtip

1ST-WINTER SEP–MAR

153

RARE GULLS

Ring-billed Gull *Larus delawarensis*
③ L 41–49 cm | W 112–124 cm

Vagrant from N America: 10–15 per year, all months, most Oct–Mar. Estuaries, lakes.

Like Common Gull (*p. 144*) but slightly larger, longer-legged and **paler on back**, with **smaller white patch** on more rounded tertials. ADULT BREEDING **eye yellow** with dark ring; **bill thick, yellow** with **black band** and paler tip (can appear dark-tipped at distance). ADULT NON-BREEDING head streaked, nape more spotted than Common Gull. 1ST-WINTER back pale; bill thick, pink (yellow by Mar) with black tip. 2ND YEAR as adult but smaller white wingtip spots; dark marks on tertials on some. IN FLIGHT, ADULT **very pale**; like Common Gull, wings broader but sharper-tipped, with more black and one or two **smaller** 'mirrors'. 1ST-WINTER like Common Gull but wingtip and trailing edge **blacker**, midwing and inner primaries **very pale**, tail-band less clear-cut. 2ND YEAR like adult but more black on wingtip, one small white 'mirror'; blackish marks on hindwing and tail (rare on Common Gull).

small 'mirrors'

ADULT NON-BREEDING

RING-BILLED GULL

COMMON GULL

pale midwing panel

dark

1ST-WINTER

nape spotted, less streaked than Common Gull

bill ring looks like dark tip at moderate range

ADULT NON-BREEDING AUG–MAR

ADULT BREEDING FEB–JUL

ADULT NON-BREEDING

ADULT BREEDING

2ND-YEAR and ADULT paler than Common Gull; less white between grey back and black wingtip

2ND-WINTER AUG–MAR

2ND-WINTER

COMMON GULL

1ST-WINTER AUG–MAR

1ST-WINTER

154

MEDIUM/SMALL

Great Black-headed (Pallas's) Gull
Ichthyaetus (Larus) ichthyaetus

③ L 58–67 cm | W 146–162 cm

Large gull with **long head/bill profile** and **white eye-crescents**. ADULT pale grey and white with black wingtip; **legs yellow**; bill long, yellow with black/red band. BREEDING **black hood**. NON-BREEDING head white with **dusky 'mask'**. IN FLIGHT, ADULT **white wingtip with black band**. 1ST-WINTER grey back, wing brown with darker flight feathers; black tail-band. 2ND-WINTER tail-band reduced, black wingtip and primary coverts, small white 'mirror'.

Vagrant from Middle East: 1 historical record (Britain, adult, May 1859). On coast.

ADULT NON-BREEDING AUG–MAR

1ST-WINTER

dusky 'mask' in winter; black hood in summer

dark 'mask', white eye-crescents

pink bill, well-defined black tip

pale grey with dark mottles

1ST-WINTER SEP–MAR

ADULT BREEDING MAR–JUL

Slender-billed Gull *Chroicocephalus (Larus) genei*

② L 37–42 cm | W 90–102 cm   548

Pattern as Black-headed Gull (p. 146), but **pale-headed**: bulkier on water; longer-legged. Long neck, forward-leaning pose. Forehead slopes into long, straight, pointed bill. ADULT BREEDING **head pure white**; body flushed pink; **bill dark red to blackish**; legs red. ADULT NON-BREEDING grey ear-spot. 1ST-YEAR bill and legs pale orange; weak brown markings on innerwing, dark hindwing band, thin black tail-band.

Vagrant from SE Europe: <10 records (Britain), May–Jun. S and E coasts. Shallow lagoons.

ADULT BREEDING

1ST-WINTER AUG–MAR

long bill

dusky ear spot

black tail-band

plain head

pale eye (often hard to see)

ADULT BREEDING MAR–JUL

pink flush

ginger-brown markings on spread wing

1ST-SUMMER MAR–AUG

long bill and legs pale orange

RARE GULLS

Slaty-backed Gull
Larus schistisagus
L 55–68 cm | W 135–160 cm

Two forms: PALE (upperparts dark grey) and DARK (upperparts blackish). ADULT much like Lesser Black-backed Gull (*p. 132*) but **legs bright pink**, bill thick. 1ST-WINTER (not recorded) **thin dark centres to tertials, pale fringes to brown primaries**; tail solidly dark brown; bill dull with black tip.
IN FLIGHT, see *opposite*.

Vagrant from coastal E Siberia, N Japan: <5 records (1 Britain), Jan–Feb. Coasts, tips.

ADULT NON-BREEDING DARK FORM SEP–MAR

1ST-WINTER SEP–MAR

3RD-WINTER PALE FORM SEP–MAR

bright pink legs at all ages

Glaucous-winged Gull
Larus glaucescens
L 60–66 cm | W 137–150 cm

Identification complicated by Glaucous Gull (*p. 140*) × Herring Gull (*p. 130*) hybrids (in Iceland). ADULT (not recorded) looks like heavy-, drooping-billed Glaucous Gull with **dark eye, white tips and 'mirror' on grey primaries**. In winter, **'scaly' grey marks on head and breast** (straighter bill, paler eye, brown head streaks on hybrids). Short legs dark pink. 1ST-WINTER like greyish, drab, uniform Glaucous Gull with head and neck finely barred/'scaly', darker wingtip/tail above, same shade as back (paler than back on Glaucous Gull), but bright, pale flight feathers below; bill all-black at first. (Similar 1st-winter 'Thayer's Gull' (*p. 142*) has smaller head/bill, larger eye, darker wingtip.) 2ND-WINTER (not recorded) paler than 1st-winter, bill blackish with pink base. 3RD-WINTER more like adult with black band on bill.
IN FLIGHT, see *opposite*.

Vagrant from N America: <10 records (1 Ireland), Dec–Apr. Coasts, pools, tips.

ADULT NON-BREEDING AUG–MAR

1ST-WINTER AUG–MAR

2ND-WINTER AUG–MAR

LARGE

GLAUCOUS GULL — darker than Glaucous
1ST-WINTER
2ND-WINTER
two white 'mirrors' and white tips on black wingtip
single 'mirror'
white spots between pale grey and dark grey tips, large white 'mirror'
middle primaries have **white spot between grey base and black subterminal band**, above and below
GLAUCOUS-WINGED GULL
ADULT NON-BREEDING
broad white tertial tips/trailing edge
LESSER BLACK-BACKED GULL
ADULT PALE FORM
SLATY-BACKED GULL

Audouin's Gull 548
Ichthyaetus (Larus) audouinii
L 44–52 cm | W 117–128 cm

Medium–large, slim-winged, pale gull; **legs grey**; **eye dark**. ADULT upperparts pale grey, underparts paler grey; head white all year. Bill **red with black band**. White spots on black wingtip (wear off by Aug). JUVENILE (not recorded) brown, with neat buff fringes to upperpart feathers; bill pink-grey with black tip. **Tertials have narrow pale edges.** 1ST-YEAR grey back; dark 'mask'; base of bill red by 1ST-SUMMER. 2ND-YEAR pale grey with blackish wingtip and tail-band.
IN FLIGHT, ADULT wingtip black with small white 'mirror'; underwing white with **bold black triangle at tip**. JUVENILE dark brown, with white rump, black hindwing band and tail-band; underwing dark with white central band.

Vagrant from Iberia: <10 records (Britain), May–Aug. S and E coasts. Beaches.

2ND-WINTER
2ND-SUMMER MAR–SEP
ADULT
dark underwing with whitish central band
1ST-SUMMER MAR–SEP
JUVENILE JUN–SEP
pale, plain head with white eye-crescents; black-tipped grey bill
2ND-WINTER SEP–MAR
bright white head against greyer body; dark eye and bill
ADULT FEB–SEP

157

RARE GULLS

'Herring' Gulls

Circling the globe south of the Arctic 'Herring Gulls' have evolved into several species, but subspecies/species and lines of division remain controversial. Recent occurrences suggest almost any of these can appear in Britain and Ireland, but identification of some remains contentious.

American Herring Gull *Larus smithsonianus*

(4) L 60–66 cm | W 120–155 cm

Vagrant from N America: <120 records, mostly (<100) Ireland, most months, some long-stayers. Coastal, beaches.

Extremely similar to Herring Gull (p. 130): large, heavily built. ADULT like dark Herring Gull (ssp. *argentatus*) with darker head streaks or 'mask' often extending onto breast sides; bill colour and extent of dark band variable on both species. 1ST-WINTER generally darker than same-age Herring Gull, with dark band on greater coverts; **dark brown belly**; **blackish tail**; heavily **barred rump/undertail**; usually plain, dark neck and breast sides.

IN FLIGHT (see *opposite*), dark underwing coverts contrast with pale flight feathers. 2ND-WINTER dark beneath and on rump/tail but very variable, and rate of development to adult varies.

ADULT NON-BREEDING

4TH-WINTER OR ADULT NON-BREEDING AUG–MAR

HERRING GULL

4TH-WINTER AUG–MAR

2ND-WINTER AUG–MAR

JUVENILE Herring Gull has paler greater coverts and a paler, more streaked neck, breast and underparts. Ssp. *argenteus* smaller than American Herring Gull.

HERRING GULL

1ST-WINTER AUG–MAR

'HERRING-TYPE'

3RD-WINTER more blackish marks on outerwing and tail than Herring Gull (even 4TH-WINTER often has isolated black spots)

3RD-WINTER
AMERICAN HERRING GULL

3RD-WINTER
HERRING GULL

VEGA GULL
ADULT NON-BREEDING

pattern of black/white on Vega Gull highly variable but most have black from P4 or P5 outwards, and pale spots between grey base and black tip on middle feathers

more solidly blackish tail, finely marked only at edges

darker greater covert band

darker neck/breast

1ST-WINTER

darker bars on rump

1ST-WINTER

HERRING GULL ssp. *argenteus*

P3 P4 P5 P6 P7 P8 P9 P10

VEGA GULL

P3 P4 P5 P6 P7 P8 P9 P10

Vega Gull *Larus vegae* ◆
L 55–65 cm | W 125–160 cm

East Asian counterpart of Herring Gull (p. 130) and American Herring Gull (of which it is sometimes considered a subspecies). Slender, 'gentle-looking' gull with high crown/nape, rather short bill and darkish eye. ADULT back darker than British/Irish Herring Gull (ssp. *argenteus*). Legs dull, pale pinkish, rarely yellowish. Bill pale, greenish-yellow; most (60–70%) have no black on bill and most (90%) have red spot reaching cutting edge (on others, red restricted to smaller patch). Still moulting outer primaries in Jan/Feb (Herring Gull moult complete by Dec/Jan).

Vagrant from E Asia: 1 record (Ireland), Jan. Coastal.

HERRING GULL

ADULT JUL–MAR

ADULT NON-BREEDING Herring Gulls variable, but vast majority have a pale iris; often some black on bill

dark spots

broad white tertial tips

ADULT NON-BREEDING JUL–MAR

159

GULLS and TERNS

Regularly occurring terns in flight (adults in breeding plumage)

LITTLE TERN

SANDWICH TERN (p. 165)

GULL-BILLED TERN (p. 169)

COMMON TERN (p. 162)

ARCTIC TERN (p. 163)

ROSEATE TERN (p. 164)

WHISKERED TERN (p. 168)

BLACK TERN (p. 166)

CASPIAN TERN (p. 168)

WHITE-WINGED BLACK TERN (p. 167)

TERNS IN FLIGHT

Little Tern *Sternula (Sterna) albifrons*

L 21–25 cm | W 41–47 cm

Least Tern

Small, pale tern with long, tapered wings; closed tail forms a long 'spike'. ADULT pale grey and pure white; black cap/eyestripe and **white forehead** (all year). **Bill yellow** with black tip; legs yellow to orange. Closed wingtip long, with black lower edge. JUVENILE barred blackish above, dusky on crown, buff on breast; legs dull to bright yellowish.

IN FLIGHT, fast, direct; quick, regular, sweeping beats of swept-back wings. When feeding, more erratic, with **frequent fast hovers** before splashing headlong dives into water (a real 'smack', not a dip). ADULT **outer primaries blackish**, rump and tail white. JUVENILE blunter-winged; back tinged buff-brown; forewing, hindwing band and outerwing dark.

VOICE Quick, rasping "*kreet*" and fast, rhythmic "*kiereet kiereet*."

Scarce/rare summer visitor, Apr–Sep (2,000 pairs, including 200 in Ireland)

to W Africa

Sandy/shingle coasts; rare inland

hovering

ADULT

JUVENILE

forewing dark, hindwing pale: quick flight action unlike Black Tern (*p. 166*)

ADULT

white rump

JUVENILE JUN–OCT

ADULT APR–SEP

Least Tern

Sternula (Sterna) antillarum

L 55–65 cm | W 125–160 cm

North American counterpart of Little Tern (of which sometimes treated as a subspecies). ADULT may be identifiable by **grey rump** (white on Little Tern) and chirping, squeaky call-notes.

Vagrant from N America: 1 record (Britain), Jun–Jul (returning bird for ten consecutive years). Coasts.

ADULT

grey rump

ADULT APR–SEP

GULLS and TERNS　　　　　　　　　　　　　　　　　　　　　　　　　　　Terns in flight *p. 160*

Common Tern *Sterna hirundo*

L 34–37 cm | W 70–80 cm

Roseate (p. 164), Forster's (p. 169), Whiskered (p. 168) Terns

Locally common summer visitor, Apr–Oct (14,500 pairs, including 4,000 in Ireland), migrant

Medium-sized, pale tern; very like Arctic Tern but **longer legs and bill**. ADULT BREEDING pale grey above, greyish-white below, black cap; long tail streamers. Bill **scarlet with black tip**; legs red. ADULT NON-BREEDING from Jul/Aug, forehead and underparts white; bill and legs blackish. JUVENILE forehead buff, cap black; back buff-brown; blackish forewing. Underparts white. Bill **orange** with dark tip. 1ST-SUMMER see *below*.

IN FLIGHT, different profile from Arctic Tern: longer flatter bill/head/neck, shorter tail, longer innerwing. Hovers before confident plunge; inland, dips to surface like Black Tern (p. 166). See *annotations below*.

VOICE Calls sharp "*kit*," squabbling "*kit-it-it-it*," long-drawn, nasal "*kierri-kierri*."

from/to Scandinavia

from/to W Africa

Coasts, islands, inland lakes, rivers

spring adult has dark streak on 5th/6th primary; in summer, grey 'bloom' wears off old outer feathers, creating dark outerwing; newer inner primaries remain pale (no such contrast on Arctic Tern)

broad dark trailing edge against restricted translucent patch

ADULT BREEDING

flattish head and longish neck

browner than juvenile Arctic Tern; underwing as adult

rump pale grey

JUVENILE [Aug]

blackish forewing, pale midwing, grey hindwing bar

2ND-SUMMER (presumed) APR–AUG [Aug]
In 2nd-summer, most are like adult breeding

1ST-SUMMER (rare in Britain/Ireland) (not illustrated) may be aged APR–JUL by blackish shoulder bar, hindwing band and outer primaries.

white forehead, black bill

back browner, forehead faintly browner and bill paler than juvenile Arctic Tern

JUVENILE JUN–OCT [Sep]

usually strong black 'shoulder' bar

bill scarlet with black tip (slightly longer, weightier, less 'spiky' than Arctic Tern's)

relatively short tail

pale inner primaries contrast with darker wingtip

relatively long legs

ADULT BREEDING APR–SEP

Arctic Tern *Sterna paradisaea*

L 33–39 cm | W 66–77 cm

👁 Roseate Tern (p. 164), Whiskered Tern (p. 168)

Medium-sized, pale tern; very like Common Tern but bill shorter, **legs very short**. ADULT BREEDING pale grey above and below, quite contrasted white cheek and throat; very long tail streamers. Bill **all deep red**. ADULT NON-BREEDING from Sep/Oct, white forehead (Jul/Aug on Common Tern); bill blackish. JUVENILE forehead white, buff tinge quickly fades; back scaled grey, white and blackish. Bill all-black or dark red at base. 1ST-SUMMER see *below*.

IN FLIGHT, short bill, round head, 'neckless' shape, deep breast, short innerwing, outerwing long and tapered. Relaxed, elastic beats. Hovers, half-dives/hovers again before plunge. See *annotations below*.

VOICE Calls like Common Tern, more piping/ringing, more emphasis on last rather than first syllable.

Locally common summer visitor, Apr–Oct (55,000 pairs, including 3,500 Ireland; declining), migrant from/to Arctic Canada, Iceland and Greenland · from/to Arctic · from/to S Africa and S oceans

Coasts, islands, offshore; scarce inland

primaries all moulted in winter – all feathers the same age with no contrast, unlike on Common Tern

thin dark trailing edge
translucent primaries and secondaries
long tail streamers
ADULT BREEDING
roundish head and shortish neck

greyer than juvenile Common Tern; underwing as adult
rump white
JUVENILE [Aug]
diffuse dark forewing blends back to white hindwing

1ST-SUMMER APR–AUG [Aug] very similar to non-breeding adult

JUVENILE (fresh) [Aug]
red bill base on fresh juvenile soon becomes darker

back greyer than juvenile Common Tern

'spiky' bill
JUVENILE (faded) JUN–OCT [Aug]

relatively long tail
closed wingtip all silvery, no contrast
relatively short legs
ADULT BREEDING APR–SEP

GULLS and TERNS

Terns in flight p. 160

Roseate Tern *Sterna dougallii*

L 33–36 cm | W 67–76 cm

Common Tern (p. 162), Arctic Tern (p. 163), Forster's Tern (p. 169)

Rare summer visitor, Apr–Oct (850 pairs, including 750 in Ireland); rare migrant

Resembles Common Tern (p. 162) but **very pale**. ADULT BREEDING pale grey above; underparts white, flushed pink (pink may persist in autumn). Black cap curves down hindneck. Blackish stripe along closed wingtip. Tail very long. Bill long, slim: **black with small red base** Apr–May, half or more red by Aug. ADULT NON-BREEDING white forehead from Sep/Oct. JUVENILE forehead **dark buff-grey**; back scaled blackish; bill and legs **blackish**.

IN FLIGHT, round head, long bill, long tail. ADULT very pale; front edge to outerwing increasingly blackish by Jun/Jul. JUVENILE back spotted blackish, upperwing pale with dark hindwing band. Rather stiff, quick, fast beats; often dives from straight flight without hovering.

VOICE Calls include distinct double "*chivik.*"

to W Africa

Islands, coasts; very rare inland

blackish streaks on outerwing like Sandwich or Common Tern, unlike Arctic Tern

underwing has dusky streaks, but no blackish trailing edge; translucent patch (like Common Tern)

ADULT BREEDING
[Sep]
[Jul]

JUVENILE

similar to a very young Sandwich Tern: scaled blackish above; cap, bill and legs dark

JUVENILE (more advanced) [Aug]

JUVENILE JUN–OCT [Aug]

angle on lower mandible one-third distance from base to tip (half to two-thirds on Common Tern)

ADULT BREEDING [Aug]

ADULT BREEDING [Jul]

ADULT BREEDING [May]

bill changes from black in breeding birds to black with bright red base by Jun–Aug, but blackish from Sep

Sandwich Tern *Thalasseus (Sterna) sandvicensis*

L 37–43 cm | W 85–97 cm

Gull-billed Tern (p. 169), Cabot's Tern (p. 173)

Large, **very pale** tern, **white below**; short tail; **spiky crest**. Bill and legs long, black. ADULT BREEDING **black cap**, forehead white by Jun; **black bill with pale (yellow) tip**. JUVENILE blackish 'mask'; short black-brown bars/arrows above.

IN FLIGHT, long, angular wings, short-tail; powerful action, high-dives with big splash. ADULT upperwing whitish, outer primaries dark by Apr/May, blackish by Aug/Sep. Underwing white, inner primaries translucent, outer ones with black tips. JUVENILE upperwing mottled brownish, with darker wingtips and hindwing band; tail short with blackish 'corners' to shallow fork.

VOICE Highly distinctive, loud, rhythmic, abrupt, short, tearing "*kierr-ik, ki-rink*" or "*ko-yok.*" Young: high, whining "*srreee-i.*"

Locally common summer visitor, Mar–Oct (14,000 pairs, including 3,700 in Ireland); a few winter

to W Africa

Sandy coasts, lagoons; scarce inland

wingtip blackish by late summer; pale after autumn moult; forehead white from Jun/Jul

ADULT NON-BREEDING

JUVENILE

slight darker 'W' across upperwings; dark corners to short tail. Trails behind adult, calling to be fed

dusky cap (becomes blacker 'mask'/white forehead)

grey with dark scaly patterning above

blackish bill

black cap, ragged crest

JUVENILE JUN–DEC [Sep]

blackish legs

yellow-tipped black bill

ADULT NON-BREEDING JUL–FEB

ADULT BREEDING MAR–JUL

GULLS and TERNS Terns in flight *p. 160*

Black Tern *Chlidonias niger*

L 22–26 cm | W 56–62 cm

White-winged Black Tern, Whiskered Tern (p. 168)

Smaller than Common Tern (*p. 162*) with **shallow tail fork** and short black bill. Often perches on buoys, posts, rafts, *etc*. See juvenile Little Tern (*p. 161*). ADULT BREEDING dark grey, **smoky black** below, **white under tail**; pale underwing. In Aug–Sep, mottled as black is lost. Legs black. ADULT NON-BREEDING **black cap** extending down onto cheek and nape; white half-ring around eye; mid-grey upperparts, pale grey rump; white underparts with **dusky patch beside breast**. Legs dull reddish. JUVENILE barred brown back, dark front and rear edges on innerwing; a few are paler above, some darker with paler rump. **Dark breast patch**.

IN FLIGHT, buoyant, flies into wind, dips to surface (but Common Tern also does so over inland waters); flocks may fly high and circle.

VOICE Call insignificant, slightly squeaky, "*ki-ki-ki*" or "*kyeh*."

Scarce spring and autumn migrant (100s/low 1,000s: Apr–Oct).

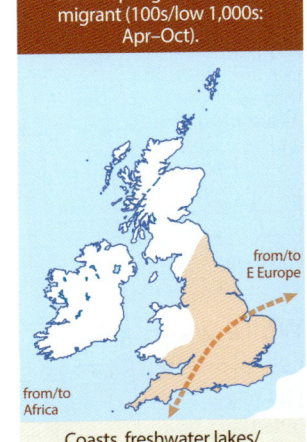

from/to E Europe
from/to Africa

Coasts, freshwater lakes/reservoirs

N American ssp. *surinamensis* (vagrant, <10 records (<5 Ireland): Aug–Sep)
BREEDING jet-black on head/breast; JUVENILE crown grey, cheek black; grey flank.

'AMERICAN' BLACK TERN ssp. *surinamensis*

'EUROPEAN' BLACK TERN ssp. *niger*

JUVENILE

grey flank

white flank

JUVENILE

ADULT BREEDING

ADULT BREEDING → NON-BREEDING JUL–OCT [Sep]

ADULT NON-BREEDING SEP–FEB

pale back

JUVENILE JUN–OCT

short legs

dusky breast patch

ADULT BREEDING APR–AUG

MARSH TERNS

Juvenile 'marsh' tern identification

Non-breeding, juvenile and 1st-winter 'marsh' terns are more difficult than breeding adults. All are white beneath and on the underwing. Check the precise head pattern, the side of the breast and the contrast between back, wings and rump.

- **BLACK TERN**: grey rump; dusky patch; darkish wings barely contrast with back
- **WHITE-WINGED BLACK TERN**: white rump; pale grey wings contrast with back
- **WHISKERED TERN**: grey rump; pale grey wings contrast with back

White-winged Black Tern *Chlidonias leucopterus*
L 20–24 cm | W 50–56 cm

Like Black Tern but a little **dumpier, longer-legged** and **shorter-billed**. ADULT BREEDING silvery grey above with **white forewings, black below** (patched white from Jul); **white tail**, Bill black, **legs red**. ADULT NON-BREEDING paler than Black Tern with almost white rump; **no dark patch beside breast**; crown streaked, isolated **dark cheek spot**. JUVENILE (the most likely plumage in autumn) like young Black Tern but **no breast patch**; back more **solidly dark brown**, wings pale grey, creating **dark-saddled effect**; **rump white**.

IN FLIGHT, fractionally heavier than Black Tern, with straighter wings and less airy, floating action.

Very rare migrant from E Europe: 1,000 records, about 20–25 per year, Apr–Oct, most early autumn; > 100 records, Ireland. Inland and on coasts, mostly in S Britain but widely scattered. Marshes, lakes, coast. Winters in Africa.

- JUVENILE
- ADULT BREEDING → NON-BREEDING JUL–OCT [Sep]
- ADULT NON-BREEDING SEP–FEB [Feb]
- ADULT BREEDING
- JUVENILE JUN–OCT — darker back, paler wings than Black Tern; unmarked breast; long legs
- ADULT BREEDING MAR–AUG

RARE TERNS

Terns in flight *p. 160* | Juvenile 'marsh' terns in flight *p. 167*

Whiskered Tern
Chlidonias hybrida 549
L 24–28 cm | W 57–63 cm

Like robust Black Tern (*p. 166*) with long bill and legs. ADULT BREEDING black cap; upperparts pale grey. **Broad white cheek** and throat; **underparts blackish-grey** with white vent. Bill and legs dark red. ADULT NON-BREEDING/JUVENILE white below; no breast patch; bill reddish at base; white crown **streaked black**, cheek white.

IN FLIGHT, broader-winged than Black Tern. JUVENILE back barred brown; wings paler with grey hindwing band but no blackish 'shoulder'. Rump grey. Tail has white sides, dark tip.

> Very rare migrant from S Europe: <250 records, 4–5 per year (<25 records Ireland), Apr–Oct. Lakes, marshes, lagoons. Winters in Africa.

ADULT BREEDING
ADULT NON-BREEDING
JUVENILE → 1ST-WINTER JUN–NOV [Nov]
ADULT BREEDING MAR–AUG
ADULT NON-BREEDING AUG–MAR

Caspian Tern
Hydroprogne caspia 549
L 48–55 cm | W 96–111 cm

Size of large gull with **gull-like** proportions. Bill large, **dagger-like**, red with dark at tip. Legs black. ADULT BREEDING pale grey and white with **black cap**; bill **deep red**. ADULT NON-BREEDING/1ST-YEAR cap dark, finely streaked white; bill red. JUVENILE like non-breeding adult but barred blackish above; bill orange-red.

IN FLIGHT, **pointed, angled wings**; **black under tip**. JUVENILE dark hindwing band and wingtip; grey tail.

👁 **Large 'orange-billed' terns** (*p. 170*)

> Very rare migrant from W Europe: <500 records, about 5 per year (vagrant Ireland, <15 records), Apr–Oct. Coasts, lakes. Winters in Africa.

ADULT BREEDING
1ST-WINTER SEP–MAR [Feb]
ADULT NON-BREEDING AUG–MAR
ADULT BREEDING MAR–AUG

168

RARE TERNS

Gull-billed Tern
Gelochelidon nilotica   549
L 35–42 cm | W 76–86 cm

Resembles Sandwich Tern (*p. 165*) but head rounded. Feeds over dry ground/marshland. ADULT BREEDING black cap but no crest; legs black. **Bill stout, all-black** (but see juvenile Sandwich Tern). ADULT NON-BREEDING/1ST-WINTER **black patch through eye** (see Forster's Tern). IN FLIGHT, **rump and tail pale grey**. Dark outer/pale inner primary contrast like Sandwich/Common (*p. 162*) Terns; fresh primaries have **dark trailing edge**. 1ST-WINTER very pale; weak dark eye patch; rump whitish, tail pale grey.

> Forster's Tern (non-breeding)
>
> Very rare migrant from S Europe: <400 records, about 3 per year (<25 records Ireland), May–Sep. Has bred once. Lagoons, marshes/wet meadows. Winters in Africa.

Forster's Tern *Sterna forsteri*
L 33–36 cm | W 64–70 cm

Much like Common Tern (*p. 162*); more obvious in winter (terns being rare at that time of year, and plumage more distinctive, but see Sandwich Tern (*p. 165*) and Gull-billed Tern). ADULT BREEDING bill red with extensive black tip; legs red; tail grey with white edge; upperwing pale grey, paler towards tip; **underparts white**. ADULT NON-BREEDING bill black; **upperwing frosty white**; solid **black 'mask'** behind eye. 1ST-YEAR like non-breeding adult but has weak dark tips to primaries and coverts.

> Vagrant from N America: >100 records (<40 in Ireland), Jan–Mar, Aug–Dec. Coasts, estuaries.

Rare terns | Large 'orange-billed' terns

Large, 'orange-' or 'red-billed', black-legged terns present a challenge when seen in isolation. A good size comparison is vital. Check the precise pattern of the forehead/crown/crest area and the bill colour (including darker or paler tip etc.) and assess the relative length and thickness of the bill. Rump/tail colour is important but difficult to judge in bright sunlight.

CASPIAN TERN
TO SCALE

Royal Tern
Thalasseus maximus
(*Sterna maxima*)
L 42–49 cm | W 86–92 cm

Large, elegant, well-proportioned tern (see Caspian (*p. 168*), Lesser Crested and Elegant Terns). Bigger than Sandwich Tern (*p. 165*), nearer Common Gull (*p. 144*) in size (vital to assess size). Long, dagger-like bill **more slender than Caspian Tern's**. ADULT BREEDING black cap, short crest. Bill **orange-red**; legs black. Upperwing similar to Common Tern (*p. 162*) (outer primaries wear to black). ADULT NON-BREEDING **white forehead and crown above dark eye** on ssp. *maximus* (Caspian Tern has dark forehead).

Vagrant from America/Africa: <10 records (<5 Ireland), Mar–Dec. Coasts.

West African Crested Tern
Thalasseus albididorsalis
L 42–49 cm | W 86–92 cm

Very similar to Royal Tern (previously treated as a ssp.), but bill slimmer, more yellow-orange, less red. NON-BREEDING forehead white, crown streaked over eye.

One suspected but not yet accepted: adult (Ireland/Wales, Jun). Coasts

thin black line on underwing (extensively black on Caspian Tern)

ROYAL TERN
ADULT BREEDING

rump/tail white

ADULT BREEDING

WEST AFRICAN CRESTED TERN
ADULT NON-BREEDING
JUL–MAR

WEST AFRICAN CRESTED TERN

white extends behind eye in winter, unlike Caspian Tern

ROYAL TERN
ADULT NON-BREEDING
JUL–MAR

ROYAL TERN
ADULT BREEDING
MAR–AUG

RARE TERNS

Elegant Tern
Thalasseus (Sterna) elegans
L 43 cm | W 76–81 cm

Black-capped, black-legged tern, size/shape as Sandwich Tern (p. 165) but see Lesser Crested Tern; long, slender orange bill with redder base and paler **drooped tip**. Rump and short tail almost white. ADULT long, narrow, shaggy, drooped crest; From Jul, forehead white, **broad black 'mask' encloses eye**.

Vagrant from N America: <15 records (<10 Ireland), May–Jul. Coasts.

rump/tail look white
ADULT BREEDING
ADULT NON-BREEDING JUL–MAR
long, drooped crest in summer
ADULT BREEDING MAR–AUG

Lesser Crested Tern
Thalasseus (Sterna) bengalensis
L 33–40 cm | W 76–82 cm

Size of Sandwich Tern (p. 165), smaller than Royal Tern; **size/structure** judgment imperative for identification. Broader-winged than Sandwich and Elegant Terns, less extreme angularity; flies with bill held more horizontally. Bill tapered to finer tip than Royal Tern. ADULT BREEDING upperparts **darker than Sandwich Tern** and Royal Tern. Bill **bright orange**, or deep orange with paler tip (paler, less red, than Royal Tern, less slender than Elegant Tern). IN FLIGHT, **rump and tail pale grey** (hard to see in strong light). Fresh primaries (Sep–Mar) very pale, silvery; outer ones become dark with wear.

Vagrant from Africa: <20 records (1 Ireland), May–Aug. Has bred (mixed pair with Sandwich Tern). Coasts.

rump/tail very pale grey
ADULT
extensive white crown in winter
ADULT NON-BREEDING AUG–MAR
short crest in summer
ADULT BREEDING MAR–AUG

RARE TERNS

Bridled Tern
Onychoprion anaethetus
L 37–42 cm | W 65–72 cm

Large, slender tern, dark above, white below; pattern like Sooty Tern with more clearly **contrasted jet-black cap against grey-brown back**. ADULT upperparts **grey-brown**; cap black; **white forehead extends back over eye** in side view, a **striking 'V'** from in front. IN FLIGHT, dark above, white below, with dark trailing edge to underwing (Sooty Tern has broader, blacker trailing edge and tip). Worn birds brownish with dark trailing edge/paler coverts on upperwing. In strong light, underside can look dark in shade, or reflect blue/green from the sea. Long, forked tail has blackish centre and thin white sides.

Vagrant from tropical seas: <50 records (Britain), Apr–Oct. Coasts, reservoirs.

ADULT

underside of primaries show white 'wedge'

long white line over and beyond eye

ADULT

Sooty Tern
Onychoprion fuscatus
L 42–45 cm | W 72–80 cm

Large, long, slim, elegant, dark-backed tern, pattern like Bridled Tern but more uniformly blackish above. ADULT black, sooty-grey and white. Upperparts blackish, fading browner/greyish; **cap jet black**, **white forehead extends only to eye** (deep/broad white 'blob', blunt over eye in side view). **Bill long and black**. IN FLIGHT, dark above, white below, with blackish trailing edge and wingtip on underwing (Bridled Tern has greyer trailing edge and tip). Long, forked tail has blackish centre and **long white sides** (less striking on Bridled Tern).

Vagrant from tropical seas: <30 records (<5 Ireland), Apr–Sep. Coasts.

ADULT

underside of primaries all-dark

NOTE: NON-BREEDING ADULT has fine whitish feather edges above.

short white line to eye

ADULT

RARE TERNS

Aleutian Tern
Onychoprion aleuticus
L 32–34 cm | W 75–80 cm

Medium–small tern, grey above, white below, like small, pale Bridled Tern with spiky **black bill**; short **black legs**. ADULT BREEDING neat **white forehead** extends back to just over eye; black eyestripe; white cheek and throat; pale grey underparts. ADULT NON-BREEDING (not recorded) white between eye and bill. IN FLIGHT, underwing pale with broad **dark trailing edge to secondaries** and outer primaries, broken in centre. Rump and long, forked tail white.

Vagrant from N Pacific coasts: 1 record (Britain), May. Coasts.

Labels: ADULT BREEDING; black trailing edge to innerwing beneath; short white line to eye like Bridled Tern; ADULT BREEDING MAR–AUG

Cabot's Tern
Thalasseus acuflavidus
(*Sterna acuflavida*)
L 37–40 cm | W 85–95 cm

Very similar to Sandwich Tern (p. 165) with a slightly shorter, thicker bill, thinner white fringes on inner webs of outer primaries and more sharply defined black nape/white crown Jul–Nov (speckled border on Sandwich Tern). IN FLIGHT, as Sandwich Tern but white tips to primaries narrower or absent (may be visible on photographs).

Ssp. *acuflavidus* (one record, Britain) has black bill with yellow tip (dark/dull yellowish tinge on juvenile); ssp. *eurygnathus* (**Cayenne Tern**) (one, unconfirmed, Britain) has a dull yellow to orange bill and sometimes yellowish on legs. NB both sometimes treated as sspp. of Sandwich Tern.

Vagrant from N America: 1 record (Britain), Nov (American-ringed 1st-winter bird found dead in a wood inland). Usually coastal.

Labels: white tips narrow/absent; broader white tips to **fresh** outer primaries; SANDWICH TERN ADULT BREEDING; CABOT'S TERN ADULT BREEDING; SANDWICH TERN; speckled; ADULT NON-BREEDING MAR–JUL; ADULT BREEDING JUL–FEB; more solid black; ADULT NON-BREEDING AUG–MAR; bill slightly thicker than Sandwich Tern's; ADULT BREEDING MAR–AUG

173

SKUAS

SKUA ID size | tail shape | underparts pattern | rump/vent barring | underwing pattern

Island- or moorland-breeding seabirds that feed at sea and spend the winter far south of Britain and Ireland. They breed in the north, and in spring and autumn may be seen widely from coasts, especially headlands. Inland records are mostly linked to autumn gales.
4 regular species: 2 breed; plus at least one vagrant not yet identified to species level.

Skuas fly low over the sea, with a relaxed yet purposeful action, and pursue terns and gulls (Great Skua even chases Gannet) to force them to disgorge food. On their breeding grounds, all are predatory on mammals and birds. Their dark silhouettes and tightly turning, twisting pursuits identify them as skuas at great range, but closer views are needed to separate species. Adults have distinctive tail projections but immatures can be difficult to identify.

Arctic and **Pomarine Skuas** have dark and pale forms (and 'intermediates'), and distinct 1st-winter plumages (second-year birds tend to remain farther south all year), all with a pale outerwing 'flash'. **Long-tailed Skua**, a rare migrant, passes by a few remote north-western headlands (and may even cross overland) in larger numbers in spring; adults very rarely show a fully dark plumage, but 1st-winter birds are variable.

Great Skua is larger than the others, and has no pale-bellied forms, being dark, more-or-less streaked, with bold white wing patches. It is big enough to tackle almost any seabird. Increasing numbers may hasten declines in Arctic Skua, already affected by declines in smaller seabirds.

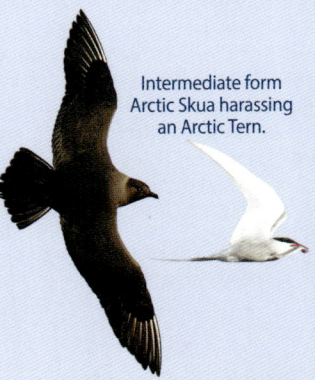

Intermediate form Arctic Skua harassing an Arctic Tern.

Possible confusion species
A skua's smooth or barred appearance and lack of a white rump rules out most immature gulls

Ageing and moult sequence in skuas

The timing and extent of moult in skuas explain some of the variations in winter and immature plumages, mostly rare in British and Irish waters. The moult sequence over the time to maturity (3–5 years) is shown here. Juvenile Pomarine Skuas, for example, quickly moult their body feathers, then the wings and tail from February to July, unlike adults. A complete moult follows from the following July; subsequent moults are patchy in winter and spring, so immature birds in summer have variable amounts of winter plumage retained before the next complete moult in summer and autumn. Bleached old feathers alongside dark new ones create bizarre patterns. The steadily increasing tail projection is the best indication of age in smaller skuas.

POMARINE SKUA PALE FORMS

JUVENILE JUL–OCT [Oct]

1ST-SUMMER (2ND CALENDAR YEAR) NOV–JUN [May]

KEY: W = wing; T = tail; HB = head and body

INTRODUCTION

Skua forms (in flight – see p. 182)

Arctic and Pomarine Skuas have recognizable forms (or morphs): pale and dark (the term 'phase' is best avoided, as individuals do not change from one form to another). However, these interbreed freely and produce a more-or-less continuous gradation between extremes ('intermediate' birds). Juveniles also show differences but they are generally much less clear-cut. Juvenile Long-tailed Skuas have various forms, but adults are more constant.

Arctic Skua forms, left to right: pale, intermediate and dark

Pomarine Skuas migrating past North Uist: flocks often pass headlands in the far north-west and along English Channel coasts at the end of April/early May

2ND-SUMMER
(3RD CALENDAR YEAR)
JUL–APR
[Aug]

Years 2–(5) Immature moults are often not completed, further increasing the confusing array of plumages that may be encountered – most immature birds have shorter central tail feathers than adults.

ADULT BREEDING
APR–JUN
[May]

ADULT NON-BREEDING
JUL–APR
[Oct]

Adults moult their whole plumage from August (or July in failed breeders) to December, and some head and body feathers again between February and April.

Immature plumage moult cycle repeated until breeding maturity is reached within 3–5 years.

immature plumages
IMMATURE MOULT

| W |
| T |
| HB |

| Oct | Nov | Dec | Jan | Feb | Mar | Apr | May | Jun | Jul | Aug | Sep | Oct | Nov | Dec | Jan | Feb | Mar | Apr |

3RD
↓
5TH
CALENDAR
YEAR

FIRST FULL PRE-BREEDING MOULT

failed and non-breeders may start in July

HB
T
W

POST-BREEDING MOULT
PRE-BREEDING MOULT
adult plumage moult cycle repeated

SKUAS   Comparison of adult skuas p. 182

Arctic Skua *Stercorarius parasiticus*

L 38–41 cm (plus up to 7 cm tail projection) | W 107–125 cm

Small, slim skua (size of Kittiwake (*p. 148*)) with flat belly, small head, slim bill (Pomarine Skua deep-bellied, larger head and bill). ADULT dark olive-brown above; black cap; underparts white to dark brown. JUVENILE **rusty-brown**, barred paler; neck usually **pale buffish**; primary tips pale. Bill blue-grey with small black tip.

IN FLIGHT, relaxed, direct. Individuals (or groups of 2–5) will approach terns or Kittiwakes low down from behind, often resulting in a twisting chase as the target evades the pursuing skua. ADULT thin, **pointed tail projection**; white 'flash' on outerwing. PALE FORM variable breast-band and **white underparts**. DARK FORM all-brown. JUVENILE short, pointed tail projection (difficult to see). **Wavy** pale bars under tail **contrast with darker belly**. Below, broad whitish patch towards tip; pale mark on primary coverts weak.

VOICE In diving display flights, loud, nasal "*waaa-ooh*" or "*mee-ah!*"

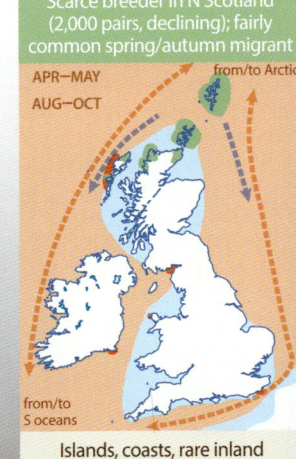

Scarce breeder in N Scotland (2,000 pairs, declining); fairly common spring/autumn migrant

APR–MAY
AUG–OCT
from/to Arctic
from/to S oceans

Islands, coasts, rare inland

ADULT BREEDING PALE FORM

adults are aggressive to intruders, including people, at colonies

JUVENILE JUL–NOV
see p. 180

ADULT BREEDING DARK FORM

ADULT BREEDING INTERMEDIATE

Mixed form pairs are frequent and, as a result, gradations between the forms are recognizable at any age.

ADULT BREEDING PALE FORM

Identification of juvenile skuas pp. 180–181

SKUAS

Pomarine Skua *Stercorarius pomarinus*

L 38–57 cm (plus up to 10 cm tail projection) | W 110–138 cm

Bulky skua (size of Common Gull (*p. 144*)) with broad wings, deep body, thick bill (Arctic Skua slimmer, smaller head and bill). ADULT dark brown above; black cap; underparts white, often dark breast-band and barred flank. DARK FORM all-dark brown. JUVENILE **dull brown** to blackish; neck dark; primary tips dark. Bill buff to bluish with black tip.

IN FLIGHT, heavy, gull-like; flocks low over sea in spring. Individuals (or groups of 2–3) dive at Kittiwakes/terns from height; also rest on sea before chasing larger gulls, low down from behind. ADULT **long, broad, 'spoon'-like tail projections** ('spoons' may break off). **White 'flash'** on outerwing. JUVENILE short, rounded tail projection (rarely visible). Typically dark (Arctic Skua paler); straight pale bars on belly, vent and undertail coverts. Broad white patch under primaries, plus **pale crescent on primary coverts**.

Widespread, generally scarce spring and autumn/early winter migrant (100s–low 1,000s a year)

↑ APR–MAY from/to Siberia
↓ AUG–NOV

from/to W Africa and mid-Atlantic · APR–MAY

Coasts, offshore; very rare inland

ADULT BREEDING PALE FORM

'spoon'-like tail projections

JUVENILE AUG–NOV *see p. 180*

ADULT BREEDING DARK FORM

ADULT PALE FORM [Dec]

ADULT BREEDING PALE FORM [Jun]

177

Long-tailed Skua *Stercorarius longicaudus*

L 35–43 cm (plus up to 15 cm tail projection) | W 102–117 cm

Small (size of Black-headed Gull (*p. 146*)), slim skua; deep-chested, but 'petite' head and bill. ADULT greyish-brown above, black cap, breast white, belly dark greyish; DARK FORM all-dark, extremely rare. Very long tail projection. JUVENILE greyish, often **pale on head and belly**, some very dark. Slim bill has extensive black tip.

IN FLIGHT, tern-like. ADULT like pale Arctic Skua, **greyer with blackish flight feathers**; two white shaft streaks on outer primaries (white 'flash' on upperwing very thin). White breast **merges into dusky belly**. **Underwing all-dark** (pale primary patch on Arctic Skua). Tail projection very long, flexible (beware longest Arctic Skuas). JUVENILE tail slim, projection slender, blunt. 1ST-YEAR tail projection needle-points.

Rare spring and autumn migrant on coasts; rarely flocks (10s/low 100s) in spring in NW

MAY–JUN
AUG–SEP

from/to Arctic

from/to S oceans

Coasts, offshore; very rare inland

ADULT BREEDING

ADULT BREEDING DARK FORM

JUVENILE AUG–OCT
see p. 180

some have darker belly with white on breast, but dark form very rare

ADULT BREEDING MAR–OCT

Identification of juvenile skuas pp. 180–181

SKUAS

Great Skua (Bonxie) *Stercorarius (Catharacta) skua*

L 50–58 cm | W 125–140 cm

Largest, heaviest, most gull-like, predatory skua. Warm brown, streaked buff, with **broad white 'flash'** on outerwing. Many show dark cap/pale face. Aggressive to people at its colonies. Displays on ground with raised wings.

IN FLIGHT, over sea often flies low and direct but may also soar high. Fast, twisting pursuit of birds as large as Gannet (*p. 97*); may dive on seabird and kill it with bill. **Broad-based wings**, tapered to point ADULT **broad, crescentic white 'flash'** on dark wing. JUVENILE/1ST-WINTER dark, barred buff above, uniform rufous below; wing 'flashes' smaller, especially above.

VOICE Short barking calls at colony.

Local breeder N Scotland (9,600 pairs), Ireland (<50 pairs); widespread spring and autumn/early winter migrant

↑ APR–MAY   from/to Norway
↓ AUG–NOV

from/to N and M Atlantic

Islands, coasts; rare inland

Even at long range, white wing patches more striking than those of smaller skuas.

ADULT

South Polar Skua
Stercorarius maccormicki

Vagrant from South Atlantic: <5 records (Britain), Oct, Feb. Coast.

DNA analysis initially suggested British records involved Brown Skua *S. antarcticus*, but now considered most likely to be South Polar Skua; hybrids also possible. Very like Great Skua but more compact, with thinner bill, more uniform, greyer upperparts and paler neck and underparts, which may bleach to pale buff.

JUVENILE JUL–NOV

ADULT

SKUAS

Identification of juvenile skuas

LONG-TAILED SKUA (p. 178)

- primary tips dark, or fine pale edges
- PALE
- small; varies from pale greyish to very dark
- bill short, stubby
- DARK

ARCTIC SKUA (p. 176)

- varies from buff bars on brown to very dark
- PALE
- bill slim, dull grey, black tip
- 'INTERMEDIATE'
- neat, pale primary tips

POMARINE SKUA (p. 177)

- primary tips dark, or fine pale tips
- 'INTERMEDIATE'
- bill thick, pale base, dark tip (like Arctic Skua), visible at longer range
- varies from buff bars on brown, to very dark with rufous bars or solidly blackish

GREAT SKUA (p. 179)

- ochre streaks on neck and wing coverts
- largest, most streaked, but dark individuals much like dark Pomarine Skua

Adult skuas in fresh plumage have plumage patterns, tail projections and size differences that easily distinguish them. Juveniles and 1st-winter birds are much harder: although size, shape and actions may make them seem distinctive at a distance, birds seen more closely often provoke controversy. It might seem unlikely that a Pomarine Skua could be confused with a Great Skua, for example, but a very dark bird sitting on a beach can be surprisingly difficult. That in itself might help rule out the smaller Arctic Skua: but flying Arctic/Pomarine Skua juveniles, especially in poor viewing conditions, may often be left unidentified even by experienced observers.

LONG-TAILED SKUA
(p. 178)
small primary flash
white flash on darkest birds
generally greyer than Arctic Skua
pale-barred rump
barred
tail rather long and slender, with bunt central projection
PALE/'INTERMEDIATE'
whitish
'INTERMEDIATE'/DARK
central tail feathers typically rounded but can be pointed or thin
paler birds: blackish
rump not paler than nape
ARCTIC SKUA
(p. 176)
PALE
DARK
short tail point
white flash on upperwing
most are rufous-brown; yellower/rusty head, underside. Palest have paler neck; broad pale bars under tail; dark rump
may show second crescent but not as strong as on Pomarine
'INTERMEDIATE'
short, blunt, or no tail point
POMARINE SKUA
(p. 177)
whitish primary patch plus second crescent on underwing primary coverts
pale crescent on wing coverts can be striking
palest are barred buff across rump, under tail; barred underwing
PALE
PALE
'INTERMEDIATE'
resembles dark Pomarine Skua but lacks pale barring on rump and vent
tail short: square or wedge-shaped; central feathers barely protruding
GREAT SKUA
(p. 179)
large white wing patches

SKUAS

Adult skuas in flight

ARCTIC SKUA (p. 176)

POMARINE SKUA (p. 177)

LONG-TAILED SKUA (p. 178)

PALE

PALE

PALE

PALE

PALE

'INTERMEDIATE'

DARK

DARK

GREAT SKUA (p. 179)

WADERS

WADER GROUP ID size | leg length + colour | bill length + shape

78 species recorded: 18 breed regularly, 6 rare or irregular breeders; 7 mostly autumn–spring visitors, 5 spring–autumn visitors and 5 passage migrants; more than 40 are very rare migrants / vagrants.

Waders are birds that, with few exceptions, feed on or near the water's edge, at least for part of the year. Other species do so, too: herons, crakes, gulls, wagtails, even finches and buntings.

Identifying waders (see p. 184)

All waders **walk**: they do not hop. A long, fine bill used for probing soft mud should identify a 'wader', but they have many bill shapes. Most birds wading into shallows and picking from water will be waders (except for herons, Spoonbill, crakes/rails and some gulls). Bill shapes and leg lengths, together with flight patterns, are invaluable in deciding which 'group' a wader belongs to. Within each group, identification of a species relies on plumage details, with many species having identifiable breeding and non-breeding plumages, as well as intermediate stages. Juvenile waders, especially, tend to have well-demarcated feather groups and feathers are often neatly marked, so learning these feather tracts is well worthwhile.

Most are sociable, others solitary: if you see a large flock of small waders, they will not be, for example, Common or Green Sandpipers, or phalaropes. Some breed in territories, defended from others, but flock as soon as the breeding season is over.

Mixed feeding flocks (Lapwings, Golden Plovers, Black-tailed Godwits, Dunlins and Redshank above) fly up together but tend to separate out quite quickly.

The majority are long-distance migrants. Many waders (even of species that breed here or come in winter) 'pass through' in spring, coming from farther south, stopping briefly and dashing on northwards – usually later than might be supposed as their destination, the Arctic tundra, remains frozen until early summer. They return in 'autumn', earlier than might be expected: adults that have finished breeding or failed to breed might return in July/August, whereas juveniles often come in a second wave in August/September.

Breeding colours may be seen on migrants before they leave in spring and again, now faded or patchy as they moult, in autumn.

Wader ageing/sexing

Some waders, such as **Sanderling** (shown), have a range of plumages; others look the same year-round.

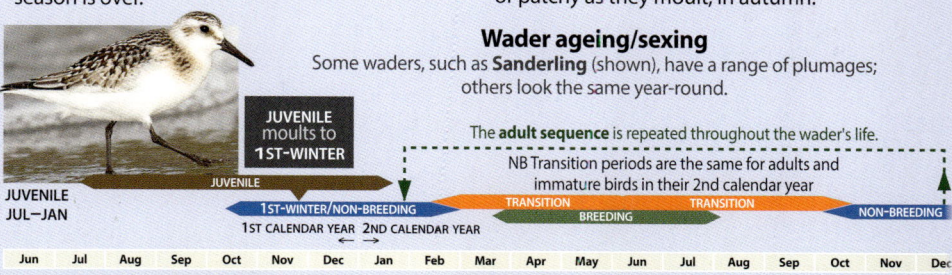

JUVENILE moults to 1ST-WINTER

The **adult sequence** is repeated throughout the wader's life.

NB Transition periods are the same for adults and immature birds in their 2nd calendar year

JUVENILE JUL–JAN

JUVENILE | 1ST-WINTER/NON-BREEDING | TRANSITION | BREEDING | TRANSITION | NON-BREEDING

1ST CALENDAR YEAR | 2ND CALENDAR YEAR

Jun Jul Aug Sep Oct Nov Dec Jan Feb Mar Apr May Jun Jul Aug Sep Oct Nov Dec

1ST-WINTER / NON-BREEDING OCT–FEB

Transition FEB–MAY
1ST-WINTER → 1ST-SUMMER / NON-BREEDING → BREEDING

ADULT BREEDING MAR–AUG
(dark, rufous type)

Transition JUN–SEP
1ST-SUMMER → NON-BREEDING / BREEDING → NON-BREEDING

WADERS

Wader identification

Bill length and shape
Focus on the relative length and overall shape of the bill.

LONG, EVENLY DOWNCURVED
Curlews and whimbrels

CURLEW

LONG, STRAIGHT, TAPERED
Godwits, sandpipers (larger), snipe, Woodcock, phalaropes

BLACK-TAILED GODWIT

LONG, SLIM, SLIGHTLY UPCURVED
Godwits, sandpipers

GREENSHANK

LONG, SLIGHTLY DOWNCURVED
Sandpipers

CURLEW SANDPIPER

SHORT, STOUT, POINTED
Plovers, Turnstone

GREY PLOVER

Plumage features
Look for obvious rump, wing and tail patterns in flight.

CURLEW SANDPIPER
- wingbar
- rump
- *bold white rump; dark tail*

GREENSHANK
- *tail barred; rump white, merging with back to form a white 'triangle'*

LITTLE RINGED PLOVER
- *tail dark; rump dark with white sides*

COMMON SANDPIPER
- *the relationship between wingtip and tail tip is used in identification for some species*
- fringe (edge of feather)
- eyering
- scapulars
- tertials
- tail
- wingtip
- primaries
- vent
- coverts
- LESSER, MEDIAN, GREATER
- *the length of the leg above the 'knee' can be useful for identification*
- 'knee' – actually the equivalent of an ankle

The types of wader

Waders, such as **Stone-curlew** (*p. 189*), **Oystercatcher** (*p. 190*), **Avocet** (*p. 192*) and the rare **Black-winged Stilt** (*p. 193*) and vagrant **Cream-coloured Courser** (*p. 228*) are unlike anything else and easy to identify. **Pratincoles** (vagrants, *pp. 226–227*) and the rest of the waders are distinctive as types but are often more difficult to identify to species. In these groups, sexes look alike and seasonal differences are slight.

Pratincole

| Stone-curlew | Oystercatcher | Avocet | Stilt | Courser |

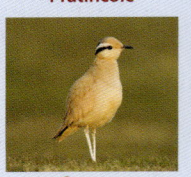

INTRODUCTION

Plovers – including 'ringed' and 'golden' types, and lapwings (pp. 193–199). Stocky waders with a short, stubby, bill. Characteristic run–stop action, tilting to pick from the surface.

Turnstone (p. 191) – small but distinctive black-and-white wader of rocky coasts, with a short, wedge-shaped bill.

GOLDEN PLOVER   RINGED PLOVER   TURNSTONE

Sandpipers (pp. 200–215) – small to medium-sized waders of mudflats and watersides that can be divided into distinct groups (examples of each shown here). The smallest sandpipers and stints are referred to as 'peeps'. Scarcer species sometimes with similar common ones, such as Little Stints amongst Dunlins. Some breed, most are passage migrants and many winter.

With the exception of curlews and snipe, waders on this page have seasonal differences, obvious or slight, and some differ between male and female.

SMALL SANDPIPERS / 'PEEPS'   'SHANKS'   SANDPIPERS   ♂ and ♀ differ in size

DUNLIN   REDSHANK   GREEN SANDPIPER   RUFF (juvenile)

Godwits (pp. 216–217) – larger than 'shanks', long-legged and long-billed: pattern on spread wings key to identification. Black-tailed Godwits favour muddy creeks or marshy places; a few breed. Bar-tailed Godwits mostly on open estuaries; breed in the Arctic.

Curlews and **whimbrels** (pp. 218–219) – big, gull-like: spangled brown, with long, downcurved bill. Curlews present year-round and have evocative calls. Whimbrels mostly spring and autumn migrants, a few breeding in far north.

BAR-TAILED GODWIT   CURLEW

Snipes and **Woodcock** (pp. 222–224) – brown, with striped head. Snipe has a remarkably long bill; Jack Snipe's shorter. Woodcocks feed at night in open fields but mostly seen flying over woods at dusk in summer, or flushed from woodland floor in winter.

Phalaropes (pp. 220–221) – feed while swimming. Grey Phalaropes occasionally inland after autumn gales, or close inshore in rough weather, very rare in spring. Red-necked Phalaropes scarcer but a few breed in far north.

♂ and ♀ look different

SNIPE   RED-NECKED PHALAROPE ♂

WADERS

Waders in flight 1/2

Whimbrel

Curlew

WHIMBREL
(p. 219)

CURLEW
(p. 218)

Black-tailed Godwit

Bar-tailed Godwit

BLACK-TAILED GODWIT
(p. 217)

BAR-TAILED GODWIT
(p. 216)

REDSHANK
(p. 210)

SPOTTED REDSHANK
(p. 211)

GREENSHANK
(p. 212)

See also yellowlegs *(p. 244)*

WADERS IN FLIGHT

TURNSTONE (p. 191)

GREY PHALAROPE (p. 221)

RED-NECKED PHALAROPE (p. 220)

see also p. 188

see also p. 188

RINGED PLOVER (p. 194)

CURLEW SANDPIPER (p. 205)

See also rare 'peeps' (p. 234)

DUNLIN (p. 202)

LITTLE STINT (p. 207)

SANDERLING (p. 200)

PURPLE SANDPIPER (p. 204)

TEMMINCK'S STINT (p. 206)

KNOT (p. 201)

WOOD SANDPIPER (p. 213)

RUFF (p. 208)

WOODCOCK (p. 224)

GREEN SANDPIPER (p. 214)

See also Great Snipe (p. 241)

SNIPE (p. 222)

JACK SNIPE (p. 223)

COMMON SANDPIPER (p. 215)

See also Spotted Sandpiper (p. 242)

187

WADERS
Waders in flight 2/2

BLACK-WINGED STILT (p. 193)

AVOCET (p. 192)

OYSTERCATCHER (p. 190)

NON-BREEDING

LAPWING (p. 197)

TURNSTONE (p. 191)

NON-BREEDING

see also p. 187

BREEDING

GREY PLOVER (p. 199)

JUVENILE

BREEDING (moulting)

1ST-WINTER

See also American and Pacific Golden Plovers (p. 230).

BREEDING (moulting)

JUVENILES

GOLDEN PLOVER (p. 198)

JUVENILE

RINGED PLOVER (p. 194)

DOTTEREL (p. 196)

JUVENILE

see also p. 188

BREEDING

BREEDING

BREEDING

LITTLE RINGED PLOVER (p. 195)

KENTISH PLOVER (p. 193)

BREEDING

IN FLIGHT | STONE-CURLEW

Stone-curlew *Burhinus oedicnemus*

L 38–45 cm | W 76–88 cm

Large, pale, long-tailed wader of dry ground. Remains still for long periods, standing upright, resting on lower leg or sitting down, but has long-striding, hesitant walk or forward-leaning run. Secretive, but active and noisy towards dusk. Loose flocks gather on stony ground or around gravel pits before migration.

Pale face created by **yellow bill base**, **white forehead** and **white stripe** across cheek and over eye; large **yellow eye** less striking unless close up. Pale yellow legs 'disappear' against background. **Pale horizontal band** along closed wing, with dark line above and below on ADULT: lower line blackish on MALE; browner, with fine dark streaks, on FEMALE. JUVENILE has broader buff band without black outline.

VOICE Calls at dusk: loud, Oystercatcher-like (*p. 190*) pipes and sharp "*ki-vi-vi*," and Curlew-like (*p. 218*) whistles.

Rare summer migrant (400–475 pairs, Mar–Sep); (<50 records Ireland)

to S Europe and N Africa

Downland, stony areas, sparse crops, heaths, grassland

IN FLIGHT, white bands and spots on mostly blackish wing; plain rump/tail. Wings stiff, bowed; white beneath.

ADULT

JUVENILE

white stripes on head more obvious at distance than pale eye

ADULT ♂

ADULT ♀

yellow legs

lower border to pale band across wing black on ♂, browner on ♀

WADERS

Waders in flight p. 188

NT
VU
Oystercatcher *Haematopus ostralegus*
L 39–44 cm | W 72–83 cm

Unmistakable large **black-and-white** wader with **orange bill** and rather short **pink legs**; strident calls. Classic sight and sound of estuaries, sandy or shingle beaches, quiet lochsides and upland fields; on coast, often in huge flocks. Favours mudflats and mussel scarps, but found in all kinds of waterside habitats and damp fields.

ADULT BREEDING entirely black head; **vivid orange** bill; eye bright red. ADULT NON-BREEDING/1ST-WINTER broad white frontal collar; back brownish; bill darker at tip. JUVENILE back brownish with buff fringes; white collar weak or absent; bill dark grey with pinkish base; legs greyish.

VOICE Shrill, piping, penetrating notes, such as "*peep*," "*k-peep*," "*kip-kip-kip*" and fast, bubbling, ecstatic piping from small groups with open bills pointing down.

Common resident, migrant, most in N (113,000 pairs breed); common winter visitor (340,000)

from Iceland
from Norway

to S Europe

Breeds on coasts, upland meadows, occasionally gravel pits; winter estuaries, rocky, sandy, shingle shores

IN FLIGHT, **triangular white rump and long, broad white wingbar** creates 'dazzle' effect.

1ST-WINTER SEP–MAR

ADULT NON-BREEDING

ADULT NON-BREEDING AUG–MAY

bill tip pointed or chisel-shaped

white 'collar' outside breeding season

vivid orange bill

ADULT BREEDING DEC–SEP

Turnstone *Arenaria interpres*

L 21–24 cm | W 43–49 cm

Small, stocky, long-bodied, low-slung wader. Mixes with Dunlin (p. 202), Sanderling (p. 200) and Purple Sandpiper (p. 204). Busy but inconspicuous flocks (on weed/rocks/strandline). As name suggests, actually does turn stones or heaves over piles of seaweed.

Blackish breast, white belly, **bright orange legs**, thick, strong bill tapers to point. Pattern obvious, seasonal changes marked. ADULT BREEDING **black-and-white head**, **bright rusty-ginger** and black above. ADULT NON-BREEDING black breast-band, pale breast side; bright white underparts; dark, dull back. JUVENILE neater 'V'-shaped buff fringes above, paler cheek than non-breeding adult. 1ST-WINTER as juvenile with head like non-breeding adult.

VOICE Short, fast, clipped, rather low-pitched, or strung into quick chattering trills if flushed – "*kew*," "*tuk-a-tuk*."

IN FLIGHT, chequered: white back and 'shoulder' bands, wingbar and tail base conspicuous against dark background.

Locally common, widespread winter visitor (50,000, Aug–May); scarce migrant inland

from Canada and Greenland — from Russia
from/to Morocco — from/to W Africa

Estuaries, sandy/stony beaches, rocky shores, piers/groynes

ADULT BREEDING
ADULT NON-BREEDING
JUVENILE

ADULT ♂ BREEDING has a more defined black-and-white head and less streaking in chestnut on back than ADULT ♀ BREEDING, but these features are unreliable for identification unless the pair is seen together.

ADULT ♀ BREEDING APR–SEP
1ST-WINTER JUL–MAY
ADULT ♂ BREEDING APR–SEP
ADULT NON-BREEDING SEP–MAY

WADERS

Waders in flight *p. 188*

Avocet *Recurvirostra avosetta*

L 42–46 cm | W 67–77 cm

Scarce summer migrant (1,900 pairs, mainly E England, few inland and in NW), very locally common winter visitor (7,500, most in SW); (<200 records Ireland)

Distinctive large, **black-and-white** wader: unique fine, black **upcurved bill** enough to identify it at close range; at a distance, can be 'lost' in gull flocks on shiny mudflats. Feeds in shallow water with regular sideswipes of bill; swims frequently, feeding with tail held high.

ADULT bright white; curved **black bands** around white oval patch on closed wing; black cap to below eye and back of neck. Long **grey legs**. JUVENILE like adult but mottled brown over white areas of upper back, and black areas duller. 1ST-WINTER like adult but some pale fringes on black of crown and wing coverts; wingtip faded browner.

VOICE Calls ringing, piping, *"klute"* or *"krup krup krup."*

Coastal lagoons, shallow lakes, estuaries

IN FLIGHT, strikingly white with black wingtips and forewing bar.

ADULT

white oval outlined in black

ADULT

upcurved bill

1ST-WINTER
SEP–MAR

AVOCET | STILT | PLOVERS

Black-winged Stilt
Himantopus himantopus
L 33–36 cm | W 60 cm   547

Elegant **black-and-white** wader with long wings, slender body, fine, needle-like bill and **long legs**.
ADULT **pink-red legs**. MALE green-glossed black above (FEMALE browner), white below; head variably white, dusky black or grey. JUVENILE/1ST-WINTER duller and paler with yellow/orange legs.
VOICE Frenetic, tern-like calls near nest, "*kyik kyik kyik*;" migrants usually silent.

♂ and ♀ head patterns vary: ♂ more extreme (blackest, whitest), ♀ more dusky, but head darker than ♂'s in many pairs.

Rare migrant from S Europe: <600 records (<100 Ireland), all months, most May–Jun; rarely breeds. Favours coastal lagoons.

IN FLIGHT, **underwing black** against white body; long **white 'V'** up back. Legs trail far beyond tail (feet often crossed). JUVENILE broad **whitish trailing edge** to wing.

ADULT

ADULT

JUVENILE / 1ST-WINTER
JUL–MAR

Kentish Plover
Charadrius alexandrinus
L 15–17 cm | W 31–32 cm   547

Small, pale 'ringed' plover with **incomplete breast-band**, all-black bill and **dark legs**. Round head, rounded body and short, tapered rear-end, thin legs set well back. Runs on beach like Sanderling (*p. 200*). MALE BREEDING **rufous cap, forehead band**, eyestripe and **breast patch black**. MALE NON-BREEDING cheek and breast patch brown. FEMALE like non-breeding male, but more cinnamon-buff on cheek and nape Mar–Jul. JUVENILE buff feather-edges above, breast patch pale brown; **legs grey to black**.
VOICE Unlike other 'ringed' plovers: short, hard "*pwit*" or "*bip*" or metallic "*tip*".

See juvenile Little Ringed and Ringed Plovers (*pp. 194–195*); check leg colour (NB a few Kentish Plover have yellowish legs).

Very rare migrant from Europe: 10–15 per year (<20 records Ireland), most Mar–Jun. Sandy shores, pools, sandy 'waste' ground. Winters in S Europe/ NW Africa.

IN FLIGHT, white wingbar and broad **white sides** to tail.

♂ BREEDING   NON-BREEDING

♂ BREEDING
MAR–JUL

white 'collar'

♀ BREEDING
MAR–JUL

dark bill

incomplete breast-band

dark legs

ADULT
NON-BREEDING
JUL–MAR

WADERS

Waders in flight p. 188

Ringed Plover *Charadrius hiaticula*

L 17–19.5 cm | W 35–41 cm

Semipalmated Plover (p. 232)
Rare *Charadrius* plovers (pp. 232–233)

● except ssp. *tundrae*

Commonest brown, white and black 'ringed' plover; often by freshwater, but most numerous on coast. Short bill. Typical plover run-stop-tilt-stand action. Mixes with Dunlin (p. 202) and other waders. Heavier, dumpier than Little Ringed Plover, with shorter rear-end but longer, deeper belly.

ADULT BREEDING brown above, white below; broad **black head bands and breast 'ring'** (boldest on MALE), Bill bright **orange** with contrasting black tip. **Legs bright orange.** ADULT NON-BREEDING/1ST-WINTER black cheek and breast-band blurred brown. JUVENILE duller, 'ring' reduced to brownish side patches but sharply defined white forehead and white stripe over eye (unlike Little Ringed Plover); legs dull yellow-ochre.

VOICE Loud, musical, soft "*too-ee*" or "*ploo-eep*." Alarm note shorter pipe. Song quick, rhythmic sequence of "*too looee*" notes, usually in low, waving, straight-winged flight.

Common resident (5,300 pairs), migrant (30,000), winter visitor (37,000); inland mostly Mar–Oct

ssp. *psammodromus* from Greenland via Iceland
ssp. *tundrae* from Russia
↑APR
↓AUG/SEP
MAY↑
AUG/OCT↓
from Baltic
to W Africa
to W Africa to France and Spain

Sand/shingle, muddy estuaries, inland lake shores

IN FLIGHT, all ages reveal **long white wingbar**; black 'blob' near tip of wedge-shaped tail.

ADULT ♂ BREEDING

JUVENILE
white wingbar

JUVENILE MAY–OCT
rounded edge to cheek
whitish forehead and stripe over eye

ADULT NON-BREEDING AUG–MAR
black-tipped orange bill

ADULT ♀ BREEDING SEP–FEB
females' markings more subdued than males'
British/Irish ssp. *hiaticula*

Subspecies *tundrae* (breeds N Eurasia) and *psammodromus* (breeds Canada, Iceland, Faeroes) are passage migrants, wintering in Africa, probably inseparable; both are slightly smaller and darker than **British/Irish breeding ssp. *hiaticula*** and have a more marked adult non-breeding plumage, with brown 'rings'.

ssp. *tundrae* ADULT ♂ BREEDING

ADULT ♂ BREEDING SEP–FEB

yellow/orange legs

194

PLOVERS

Little Ringed Plover *Charadrius dubius*

L 15·5–18 cm | W 32–35 cm

Rare *Charadrius* plovers (pp. 232–233)

Small, brown, white and black 'ringed' plover, standing/running on freshwater margins and rough stony/sandy waste. Similar to Ringed Plover but smaller, with rounder body and long, **tapered rear-end**.

ADULT BREEDING brown above, white below; broad **black head bands and breast 'ring'** (boldest on MALE). Close up, **yellow ring around eye** easy to see. Small bill dark with dull pale base; legs dull, pinkish. ADULT NON-BREEDING black patterning duller. JUVENILE pale eyering sometimes visible; **upper half of head brownish**, forehead diffusely buff, extending over eye (whiter stripe over eye on Ringed Plover); angular dark cheek marking (rounder on Ringed Plover); legs dull ochre.

VOICE Good clue to presence and identity – short, abrupt, "*tew*" or "*te-u*" with downward, not upward, inflection. Song hard, rolling "*cree-a cree-a*" in low, bat-like display flight.

Scarce summer migrant (1,200 breeding pairs, Mar–Oct); (<200 records Ireland)

to Africa

Gravel pits, waste ground, shingle reservoir edges, coastal pools

IN FLIGHT, **plain upperwing** (only finest of pale lines, no white wingbar).

ADULT ♂

RINGED PLOVER JUVENILE
- distinct white stripe
- usually rounded

JUVENILE MAY–OCT
- indistinct paler area
- 'angular' edge to cheek
- brownish top half of head

ADULT ♀ BREEDING FEB–OCT
- yellow ring around eye
- black bill

ADULT ♂ BREEDING FEB–OCT
- pale pinkish/yellowish legs

WADERS

Dotterel *Charadrius (Eudromias) morinellus*

L 20·5–24 cm | W 57–64 cm

Sociable Lapwing (p. 229)

Typical small plover shape; unique multicoloured, partridge-like colours in summer. Upright, long-legged and slender when alert, rounded when relaxed. Often confiding.

ADULT BREEDING pale at distance, FEMALE darker, more richly coloured than MALE. **Blackish cap** and contrasting **broad white stripe** over eye forms **striking white 'V'** from rear. Narrow white crescentic breast-band; **black belly** (often most obvious on FEMALE). **Yellowish legs** often 'lost' against background or in long grass/crops. ADULT NON-BREEDING underparts white. JUVENILE pale; dark cap, **buff-white stripe** over eye; weak, pale breast-band; belly peachy-buff. Buff fringes to dark feathers above. **Legs yellow-ochre** (unlike Golden Plover (*p. 198*), Grey Plover (*p. 199*), or sand plover types (*p. 233*)).

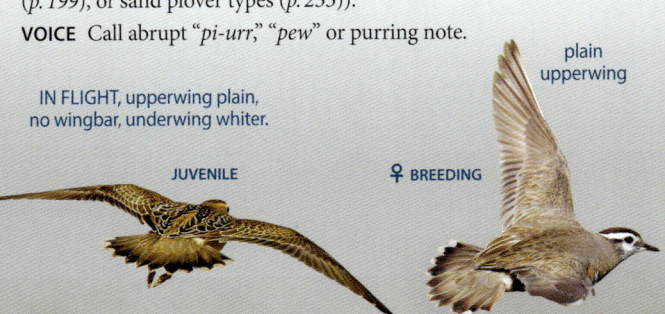

VOICE Call abrupt "*pi-urr*," "*pew*" or purring note.

Rare and very local summer migrant (500–700 breeding males, Apr–Oct); (<400 records Ireland)

Breeds northern plateaux; on migration inland fields and hills/moors (small groups) in spring, mostly coastal (singles) in autumn

IN FLIGHT, upperwing plain, no wingbar, underwing whiter.

JUVENILE

♀ BREEDING — plain upperwing

Small groups ('trips') of spring migrants can 'disappear' against the background: dark belly patches may show best.

ADULT ♀ BREEDING — prominent white stripe, white crescent, bright, strongly contrasting, dark belly

ADULT ♂ BREEDING — dull, weakly contrasting, white stripe

JUVENILE JUL–OCT

PLOVERS

Lapwing *Vanellus vanellus*

547

L 28–31 cm | W 82–87 cm

Social, mostly dry land wader. Flocks (Jun onwards) form lines or irregular masses. Slower flight than other waders, gulls, pigeons and Jackdaws, but tumbling display flight (Mar–Jun) distinctive.

Green above; **black breast**, **white underparts** (looks 'black-and-white' at long range). Slender, **upswept black crest**. Back rich green; emerald, violet and blue on 'shoulder'; dull **orange under tail**; legs purple-red. MALE BREEDING glossy green above, violet on 'shoulder'; all-black breast-band, throat, forehead and face; white cheek. FEMALE BREEDING olive-green above, little violet; breast-band, forehead and face brown-black mixed with white. ADULT NON-BREEDING buffish face and throat, buff feather edges on back and wing coverts. JUVENILE has short crest, broad buff tips to feathers above. 1ST-WINTER buff edges to wing coverts wear off; black breast-band narrow. 1ST/2ND-SUMMER crest shorter than adult male.

VOICE Calls include creaky, nasal "*pee-wit*," "*wheet*" and emphatic, strong, shrill "*pwee-y-weet*." Song wheezy, rasping in tumbling flight; ripping, throbbing wing noise.

Locally common (150,000 pairs, declining); many more autumn/winter (640,000), declining

from N, E and W Europe

Saltmarshes, wet meadows, ploughed fields, moors, lakesides

IN FLIGHT, broadly rounded wing, **black outer half**, black-and-white beneath. MALE has more rounded wing with wider, purer white tips on outer three primaries than FEMALE.

JUVENILE APR–SEP

Juvenile has short crest and broad buff feather edges on crown and upperparts.

ADULT ♂

ADULT ♀

crest 2× head length suggests adult male

crest = head length suggests female/1st-year, but much overlap

violet on 'shoulder' and glossy scapulars

ADULT NON-BREEDING (probably ♀) OCT–FEB [Oct]

less violet on 'shoulder', duller green than ♂

ADULT ♂ BREEDING FEB–AUG

WADERS Waders in flight *p. 188*

Golden Plover *Pluvialis apricaria*

L 25–28 cm | W 53–59 cm

○ American/Pacific Golden Plovers (*p. 230*)

Scarce and local breeder (23,000 pairs); common migrant and winter visitor (400,000 Britain, 150,000 Ireland)

Rather dainty, round-bodied, small-headed plover, **smaller-billed** than Grey Plover. Often scattered across fields, running and tilting forwards. Frequently mixed with Lapwing (*p. 197*), separating out in flight; large flocks form long, fast-moving lines over pastures or cereal fields, sometimes estuaries.

ADULT BREEDING brown, spangled black, cream and **yellow** above; **broad white band** around **black face, foreneck and breast** (British/Irish breeders have narrow black foreneck mottled white; northern breeders (spring flocks), black foreneck **wide, broadly edged white**).

VOICE Call a loud, piping, mournful whistle, "*peeuw*;" rhythmic song given in flight over moors, repeated "*poo-peeee-oo*."

from Iceland
from Scandinavia

IN FLIGHT whitish wingbar; **rump and tail dark; white underwing** and belly.

dark rump
JUVENILE
white underwing
ADULT BREEDING

Moors, upland grassland; winter widespread, mostly traditional areas, meadows, fields, saltmarsh

JUVENILE JUN–OCT [Oct]
yellow and black spots

1ST-WINTER AUG–MAR [Oct]
yellow and whitish spots

ADULT NON-BREEDING SEP–MAR [Nov]

both with marked belly
white belly

JUVENILE spangled yellow and black, breast and flank more barred, less streaked. 1ST-WINTER has pale spots bleached to off-white, yellow on new feathers. ADULT NON-BREEDING spangled yellow and grey, with white belly; looks **yellowish-brown** with little contrast.

ADULT ♀ BREEDING (southern) FEB–AUG
yellow spangling on upperparts

ADULT ♀ BREEDING (northern) or ADULT ♂ BREEDING (southern) FEB–AUG

ADULT ♂ BREEDING (northern) FEB–AUG

PLOVERS

Grey Plover *Pluvialis squatarola* 547

L 26–29 cm | W 56–63 cm

American/Pacific Golden Plovers (p. 230)

Stout-bodied 'estuarine' plover; like Golden Plover but has a larger head and heavier bill; easily missed amongst other waders on mudflats but short bill is distinctive. Widely scattered (territorial) when feeding on mud but roosts in tight flocks.

ADULT BREEDING silver-grey, spangled black above; **broad white band** around **black face and foreneck ends as patch beside breast; solid black belly** (Golden Plover has white flank stripe), vent white. Moulting birds (Mar–May/Jul–Sep) are piebald and eye-catching. ADULT NON-BREEDING/1ST-WINTER drab: mottled pale buff-grey above, dull whitish below (can look dark in dull light but pale close up). JUVENILE brownish-grey, with yellow buff spots above (more like Golden Plover).

VOICE Frequent estuary sound, relaxed, plaintive whistle, trisyllabic with downslur in middle: "*tee-yoo-eee*."

Locally common winter visitor (44,000) and migrant (peak 70,000, Apr)

from Siberia

from/to W and S Africa

Estuaries, coastal pools; rare inland

IN FLIGHT white wingbar stronger than Golden Plover's; **white rump** and uniquely **black 'wingpits'**.

JUVENILE

white rump

black 'wingpits'

ADULT BREEDING MAR–JUL

1ST-WINTER similar to ADULT NON-BREEDING but with some retained boldly spotted juvenile wing coverts/tertials

JUVENILE JUN–OCT

Late spring/early autumn migrants may show breeding plumage (MAR–SEP) – note size next to Bar-tailed Godwit (p. 216).

ADULT NON-BREEDING → BREEDING MAR–MAY [May]

ADULT NON-BREEDING SEP–MAR [Oct]

199

WADERS Waders in flight *p. 186*

Sanderling *Calidris alba*

L 18–21 cm | W 35–39 cm   Rare 'peeps' *(p. 234)*

Locally common migrant, winter visitor (18,000, Jul–May); scarce inland (mostly May)

from Greenland

from Siberia

Small sandpiper; typically at water's edge on smooth sand, also mudflats (migrants (May), briefly inland). Runs beside waves on sandy beaches, also picks while walking on mud (less standing/probing than Dunlin *(p. 202)*). In winter mixed flocks at roost, **purer grey** Sanderlings stand out.

Compared with Dunlin and Little Stint *(p. 207)*, larger, with straight, rather stout black bill; **black legs** (feet **lack hind toe**). ADULT BREEDING head, back and breast marbled rusty-brown and cream; underparts pure white. ADULT NON-BREEDING pearl **grey above, white below**. JUVENILE grey, spangled with complex **black spots** above; **blackish 'shoulder'**; neck/side of breast bright buff, rest of underparts **unmarked bright white**. 1ST-WINTER like non-breeding adult but retains juvenile coverts.

VOICE Short, hard "*plit*" or "*twik*," lacking any 'musical' quality.

Sandy or muddy coasts

IN FLIGHT, **dark wing** with **broad white wingbar**; **dark rump with white sides**.

1ST-WINTER OCT–MAR

JUVENILES AND MOULTING ADULTS [Aug]

bright, 'clean' grey and white

dark spangles above

unmarked (all plumages)

JUVENILE JUL–OCT

ADULT NON BREEDING AUG–MAR

no hind toe

pale fringes wear off to reveal brighter colours: some individuals silvery with black/rufous spots; most darker, rufous and black

ADULT BREEDING MAR–AUG [May]

ADULT BREEDING MAR–AUG [Jun]

SMALL SANDPIPERS

Knot *Calidris canutus*

L 23–26 cm | W 45–54 cm

Great Knot (p. 239)

Medium-sized (bigger than Dunlin (p. 202)), dumpy, highly social sandpiper; tends to feed **slowly** and shoulder-to-shoulder, even small groups. Most in large flocks on a few estuaries, some on rocky shores.

Rather **short, thick, straight**, black bill; short, **dull grey-green legs**. ADULT BREEDING back marbled black/brown; underparts bright **pale orange-red**; faded orange by Jul/Aug. ADULT NON-BREEDING **drab, grey**, paler beneath (Dunlin and Redshank (p. 210) much browner). JUVENILE greyish above with fine buff/white feather edges (**lacy effect**); underparts **pale peach** with fine grey streaks. 1ST-WINTER like non-breeding adult but some juvenile coverts retained.

VOICE Obscure, soft "*whet*" or "*nut*," as unmusical rapid chorus from jostling flocks at roost.

IN FLIGHT, white wingbar, **pale grey rump**. Co-ordinated, tight, rolling flocks, often aerobatic, using vast amount of airspace, flashing white/smoky grey at distance.

Locally common winter visitor, migrant (330,000 in autumn/winter, Jul–May); scarce inland

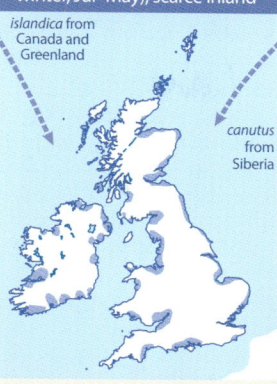

islandica from Canada and Greenland

canutus from Siberia

Feeds on coastal mudflats; roosts in flocks on lagoons, spits

Ssp. *canutus* breeds Siberia, migrant; ssp. *islandica* breeds Canada, Greenland, winters, fractionally shorter-billed and paler beneath in summer.

NOTE: ADULT NON-BREEDING and 1ST-WINTER very similar but 1ST-WINTER retains some JUVENILE wing coverts, which have a subterminal dark band; ADULT's wing coverts are all plain.

grey rump

JUVENILE

1ST-WINTER AUG–MAR [Feb]

drab grey

greenish legs

JUVENILE JUL–OCT

pale grey, flushed orange below

ADULT BREEDING FEB–SEP

pale orange head and underparts

WADERS | Waders in flight *p. 186*

Dunlin *Calidris alpina*

L 17–21 cm | W 32–36 cm

Rare 'peeps' (pp. 234–237)

except ssp. *arctica* | **I**

Benchmark for scarcer sandpipers; usually commonest Starling-sized (*p. 384*) wader, on coast or inland. Small (smaller than Knot (*p. 201*)), round-shouldered, forward-leaning; picks more than probes between quick runs. Roosts in packed groups, with other small waders.

Medium to long, slightly downcurved, '**droop-tipped**' black bill; rather short, blackish legs. ADULT BREEDING red-brown, streaked black above; **black belly patch**. ADULT NON-BREEDING mouse-brown above, white below. On sparkling mud, looks dark, with white belly; in direct sun, paler, browner (Sanderling (*p. 200*) purer grey). JUVENILE bright buff, plain-headed; long, **cream lines on back** (see Little Stint) by Sep increasingly mixed with new greyer feathers; **dusky streaks on flank** (unlike Little Stint and Curlew Sandpiper (*p. 205*)). 1ST-WINTER like non-breeding adult but some juvenile coverts retained.

VOICE Call thin, scratchy/'reedy', vibrant "*trreee*." Song, often from spring flocks, develops into vibrant 'referee's whistle' which runs down – "*shrree-ruee-ruee-we-we-we-wee wee.*"

Three subspecies: ssp. *schinzii* (breeds Britain, Ireland; common migrant); ssp. *alpina* (breeds Scandinavia, Siberia; migrant, winter); ssp. *arctica* (breeds Greenland, Spitsbergen; scarce migrant).

Scarce and local breeder (9,000 pairs, Jun–Jul); locally common migrant, winter visitor (360,000, Aug–May), declining; frequent inland spring/autumn

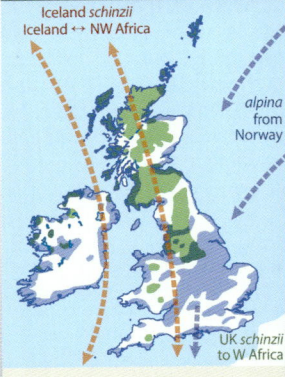

Iceland *schinzii*
Iceland ↔ NW Africa

alpina from Norway

UK *schinzii* to W Africa

Breeds moors/hills/northern islands; at other times all kinds of watersides, especially estuaries, muddy reservoir edges

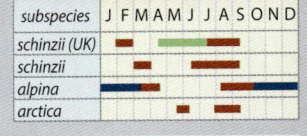

UK and Ireland Dunlin migration

subspecies	J	F	M	A	M	J	J	A	S	O	N	D
schinzii (UK)				—	—	—	—					
schinzii					—	—		—	—			
alpina	—	—	—	—	—			—	—	—	—	—
arctica					—	—		—	—			

Ssp. *schinzii* small, bill variable (♂ 23–36 mm); breeding bird (Mar–Apr onwards) has large black feather centres on back, yellowish-red/cinnamon fringes; rufous scapulars, often a few old, winter feathers; breast streaks quite dense, some blotches; solid black belly.

1ST-WINTER SEP–APR [Dec]

'droop-tipped' bill

white underparts, streaked breast-band

black legs

Breeding ♂ has whitish hindneck

Breeding ♀ browner hindneck, less contrast with crown and back

ssp. *schinzii* ADULT ♀ BREEDING MAR–SEP [Jun]

black belly patch

ssp. *schinzii* ADULT ♂ BREEDING MAR–SEP [Jun]

SMALL SANDPIPERS

white rump with dark central line

white wingbar

JUVENILES

IN FLIGHT, fast-flying flocks aerobatic, flash dark and white as they rise, fall and turn.

♀♀ longer-billed than ♂♂; N European/Siberian *alpina* longest-billed subspecies but much overlap

JUVENILES

creamy line along scapulars

dusky streaks on flank

JUVENILE JUN–OCT

Dunlin subspecies in Britain and Ireland: *schinzii*, *arctica* and *alpina*

Identifying the three subspecies that occur is not straightforward: plumage differences are not always obvious, and vary with state of moult and wear. Breeding plumage is gained by incomplete head/body moult in spring; new feathers have broad, pale fringes that wear thinner and darker, giving variation in individual appearance, but subspecies often distinctive in May and June. Females are larger and longer-billed than males and measurements overlap between subspecies, so size/structure not wholly reliable. 1st-summer birds may also be intermediate between adult breeding and non-breeding, with grey intermixed above and less solid black patch below.

ssp. *arctica*
ADULT ♂ BREEDING
MAR–SEP [Jun]

Ssp. *alpina* largest, longest-billed (27–36 mm); breeding plumage (later than others, Apr–May onwards) wider pale grey feather edges on back, wearing away to reveal deeper rusty-red.

Ssp. *arctica* distinctly 'small' (recalls Little Stint (p. 207)); bill averages shorter (♂ 23–29 mm; ♀ 27–32 mm) than ssp. *schinzii*; breeding (Mar–Apr onwards) paler; back feathers with larger black centres and narrower, yellower fringes; some grey feathers in mantle and scapulars; some scapulars narrowly fringed buffy-yellow; breast streaks thinner, no blotches, on whiter background; pale feather fringes on black belly.

ssp. *alpina*
ADULT ♀ BREEDING
MAR–SEP [Jun]

WADERS

Purple Sandpiper *Calidris maritima*

L 19–22 cm | W 37–42 cm   ⊙ Great Knot (*p. 239*)

Small, dumpy, dark sandpiper with white belly; often on wave-washed rocks with Turnstones (*p. 191*). Looks dull at distance, exquisitely patterned close up. Short, **pale** legs; thick-based, slightly downcurved bill **orange at base**.

ADULT BREEDING (rare in Britain/Ireland) chequered black and rufous above; white, finely streaked black below; dull greenish-yellow legs. Migrants in Aug–Sep often retain some rufous. ADULT NON-BREEDING **dark grey-brown** above, with pale feather fringes; **head plain** except for white eyering and chin; whitish, mottled grey below; **orange-yellow** legs. JUVENILE more heavily mottled black on back, with distinct crescentic white fringes on wing coverts. 1ST-WINTER back plainer, white fringes to wing coverts retained.

VOICE Call weak, sharp "*quit*" or "*quit-it*".

IN FLIGHT, stocky but fast, direct (or leaping over breaking wave); dark with white wingbar; **broad black rump** with white sides.

Scarce winter visitor (25,000, Aug–Apr), rare inland; very rare breeder in far N highlands

from Greenland   from Norway

Rocky coasts, piers, groynes – not on wide, muddy shores

ADULT NON-BREEDING

JUVENILE AUG–SEP [Aug]

orange-yellow base to bill

paler fringes to coverts than adult

1ST-WINTER SEP–MAR

orange-yellow legs

plain head

ADULT NON-BREEDING AUG–MAR

ADULT BREEDING MAY–AUG

darker legs

SMALL SANDPIPERS

Curlew Sandpiper *Calidris ferruginea*

L 19–22 cm | W 37–42 cm

Rare 'peeps' (pp. 234–237)

Small, elegant sandpiper, most numerous in autumn: adults Jul/Aug, juveniles later, often with Dunlins (p. 202) and Little Stints (p. 207). **Call** draws attention; **white rump** obvious in mixed flock. Like tall, long-necked Dunlin with longer, **smoothly downcurved bill** and longer legs (often hidden as wades deeply, bill tilted down).

ADULT BREEDING broad white feather fringes wear off to reveal **coppery-red**; white eyering and chin; white rump mottled blackish. During moult in Jul–Aug, retains **faded red patches** on dull white. ADULT NON-BREEDING pale grey above, white below. JUVENILE grey-brown above with crescentic buff feather edges; pale stripe over eye; **peachy-buff** on breast, **flank and belly plain white**. 1ST-WINTER (Sep–Mar) like non-breeding adult but some juvenile coverts retained.

VOICE Rich trill "*chirrup*" distinctive amongst thin Dunlin notes.

Scarce but widespread migrant; rare winter/spring (about 740 per year, most Aug–Oct)

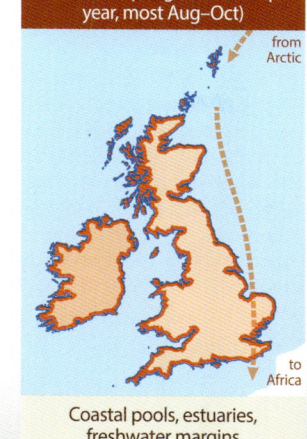

from Arctic

to Africa

Coastal pools, estuaries, freshwater margins

white rump

JUVENILE

IN FLIGHT, broad **white rump** catches eye in fast-flying mixed flock (with *e.g.* Dunlin)

cap diffusely streaked; stripe over eye shorter, less contrasting

DUNLIN 1ST-WINTER (long-billed)

juveniles look 'cleaner', fresher than Dunlin

back and wings 'scaled'

streaked cap over long, white eyestripe

dark markings

JUVENILE JUL–OCT

peachy wash (often very obvious)

no markings

ADULT BREEDING [Jun]

ADULT BREEDING → NON-BREEDING [Jul]

WADERS   Waders in flight *p. 186*

Temminck's Stint *Calidris temminckii*

L 13·5–15 cm | W 30–35 cm   👁 Rare 'peeps' *(pp. 234–237)*

Scarce/rare migrant (100–150 per year: most May; very rare breeder). Vagrant Ireland (<50 records)

Very small; important to separate from Little Stint and Dunlin *(p. 202)*, best told by **pale legs**. See Common Sandpiper *(p. 215)* (much bigger). Creeps secretively along freshwater margins (mostly spring migrants (May) in twos and threes or single juveniles in autumn).

Elongated, **long-winged**; **dull upperparts** and **greyish breast-band** with paler centre and white underparts give Common Sandpiper-like impression. Bill faintly downcurved. ADULT BREEDING olive-brown above with irregular **blackish blotching** (weakly edged rufous). Breast finely marked, forming narrow band. ADULT NON-BREEDING plain brown above, white below with grey-brown breast-band. JUVENILE/1ST-WINTER pale brown above with thin, **crescentic, brown-and-cream** feather fringes, almost plain head with weak pale line behind eye, dull breast-band and white underparts.

VOICE Call distinctive: dry, rippled trill "*si-si-si-si-si.*"

Pools, reservoir edges

IN FLIGHT, white wingbar; **white sides of rump extend onto outer tail feathers** (best seen as bird takes off). Tends to go up and fly far away when disturbed, but often calls.

ADULT BREEDING [Jun]

[Apr]

white outer tail feathers

ADULT NON-BREEDING SEP–MAR [Nov]

JUVENILE JUL–OCT [Aug]

long wings

distinct breast-band

pale yellowish legs

ADULT BREEDING APR–AUG [May]

dark blotches

ADULT BREEDING APR–AUG [Apr]

pale ochre/greenish legs

Little Stint *Calidris minuta*

L 14–15.5 cm | W 28–31 cm

Rare 'peeps' (pp. 234–237)

Very small; compare with larger Dunlin (*p. 202*) and Sanderling (*p. 200*) and much scarcer, pale-legged Temminck's Stint. **Bill short, straight**; **legs black**. Always **white beneath**, with buffy patch on side of breast but no dark streaks on flank or belly. Dainty, quick-moving, thin-legged (often half-crouched); most in autumn (especially juveniles, Aug–Oct).

Rounded; impression more like small Dunlin than Temminck's Stint. ADULT BREEDING (uncommon) black-and-rufous above, white below. ADULT NON-BREEDING grey with dark grey spots above, white below. JUVENILE/1ST-WINTER thin pale lines along upperparts form white 'V' seen from rear. Upperparts spotted rufous and black (by Sep–Oct, black spots more isolated as rufous fades and grey-buff feathers appear). Streaked cap (dark centre, rufous sides) above whitish line, **forked** above eye.

VOICE Call distinctive: short, hard "*tip*," sometimes tripled.

Widespread but scarce migrant (around 750 per year, most Jul–Oct); a few in winter/spring

from Arctic

to Africa

Coastal pools, watersides inland

IN FLIGHT, Dunlin-like pattern: white wingbar and rump sides; grey tail (Temminck's Stint has white tail sides).

JUVENILE — grey outer tail feathers

JUVENILE

JUVENILE (rufous individual) JUL–OCT

JUVENILE — White lines along scapulars form 'V' seen from rear.

JUVENILE (greyish individual) JUL–OCT

no palmations between toes (a feature of some similar rare 'peeps')

ADULT NON-BREEDING AUG–MAR — black legs

white edges to feathers obscure pattern but wear away by summer

ADULT BREEDING (advanced individual) APR–AUG [Jun]

bright, clean white beneath

ADULT BREEDING APR–AUG [Jun]

'PEEPS'

207

WADERS   Waders in flight p. 186

Ruff *Calidris (Philomachus) pugnax*

L ♂ 29–32 cm | W 54–60 cm
♀ 22–26 cm | W 46–49 cm

👁 Buff-breasted (*p. 240*),
Pectoral (*p. 238*) Sandpipers

Very rare/irregular breeder (<10 nests); fairly common migrant (low 1,000s), scarce winter (800)

Medium-sized wader (♂ larger than ♀); non-breeding birds rather like Redshank (*p. 210*), but more elongated and longer legged. Small head with short, **slightly downcurved bill**; **legs pale** ochre or greenish (red on NON-BREEDING MALES). Thin white wingbar in flight; calls insignificant.

ADULT MALE BREEDING (rare in Britain/Ireland) extravagantly **patterned chestnut or blackish**, with flamboyant broad black/rufous/white ruff and flowing crest. Most often seen in intermediate stages with **white or rufous on head and breast**, but no full ruff. FEMALE/MALE NON-BREEDING grey-brown above with black spots and bars; **plain head** with variable amount of white on face or chin developing on older birds; plain **buff breast**. JUVENILE dark above with well-defined **pale buff fringes** ('scaly' effect); **plain olive-buff** underparts; black bill.

VOICE Usually silent; low quacking notes.

from/to Scandinavia and Russia

from/to Africa

Wet meadows, freshwater margins, estuaries/creeks

JUVENILES

♂   ♀

Sexing a non-breeding individual can be difficult in the absence of a size comparison. The differences between the Redshank-sized ♀ and the noticeably larger ♂ can be seen in these two juveniles.

JUVENILE
JUL–OCT [Aug]

unbarred tertials

'clean' buff underparts

ADULT NON-BREEDING
JUL–FEB [Aug]
(sized as ♀)

♂ NON-BREEDING
JUL–FEB [Oct]

ADULT NON-BREEDING bare part colours vary considerably; leg colour can be greyish, ochre, orange or red; bill colour ranges from all-dark to dark with a reddish or orange base.

SMALL SANDPIPERS

IN FLIGHT, thin white wingbar, white rump sides form almost or complete 'V' from above. Large-winged; flight rather slow, relaxed.

Moulting males are seen more frequently than 'fully ruffed' individuals.

JUVENILE ♀

Some breeding males lack a ruff.

[Mar]

[Apr]

[Apr]

ADULT

Some, probably older, individuals have white around the base of the bill.

[May]

ADULT ♂♂ PRE-BREEDING MAR–MAY

ADULT (sized as ♀)

[Mar]

[Apr]

Striking white-headed 'satellite' males on fringes of display ground attract females' attention.

ADULT ♂ BREEDING MAY–JUN (different colour forms)

209

WADERS

Waders in flight *p. 186*

Redshank *Tringa totanus*

L 24–27 cm | W 47–53 cm

Lesser Yellowlegs (*p. 244*), Terek Sandpiper (*p. 242*)

Locally common resident (39,000 pairs, declining), migrant, winter visitor (125,000)

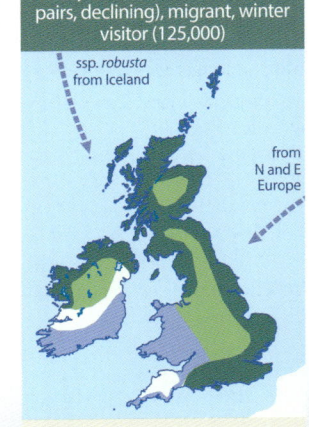

ssp. *robusta* from Iceland

from N and E Europe

Medium-sized, **brown**, estuary/saltmarsh/poolside wader. Slim, straight bill with **red at base** and **bright orange-red legs** rule out all but Spotted Redshank and non-breeding Ruff (*p. 208*). Silhouette on mud dumpier than Spotted Redshank or Greenshank (*p. 212*), taller than Knot (*p. 201*); singly or in small groups; roosts in jostling flocks. Noisy, active, often bobs head.

ADULT BREEDING brown, **spotted/barred blackish**. ADULT NON-BREEDING plainer brown with white belly; white eyering. JUVENILE brown, with feather fringes on back and wings distinctly spotted dark brown and buff; pale **yellow-orange legs**. 1ST-WINTER like non-breeding adult but some pale spotted juvenile coverts and tertials retained.

VOICE Bright, musical "*teu*" or sad "*teu-hu*;" 'bouncy' "*teu-huhu*," quicker, less even than Greenshank. Frenetic "*pit-u-pit-u-pit-u*" when flushed, "*kyip*" in alarm; rhythmic, musical "*t'leeo-t'leeo-t'leeo*" song.

IN FLIGHT, **white triangle** up back, **broad white hindwing** instantly obvious. Quick to take flight. Often settles with wings raised, flashing white underside.

ADULT BREEDING
white triangle up back
white hindwing

Estuaries, marshes, wetlands, river valleys

Birds from Iceland, ssp. *robusta*, are larger than **resident/mainland European ssp. *totanus***, but size overlaps and any identification is unreliable.

ADULT BREEDING MAR–OCT

Breeding birds are notoriously nervous if approached, and often perch on posts, calling loudly.

NB some juveniles have yellowish legs and could be mistaken for Lesser Yellowlegs (*p. 244*).

pale feather edges

JUVENILE JUN–SEP
pale legs

weak head pattern; indistinct white line above eye

ADULT NON-BREEDING JUL–MAR
plainer body than in breeding plumage

whole bill base red

vivid red legs

ADULT BREEDING MAR–OCT

'SHANKS'

Spotted Redshank *Tringa erythropus*

548

L 29–33 cm | W 61–67 cm

👁 **Wilson's Phalarope (juvenile)** (p. 226)

Medium–large wader; like slim-billed, long-legged, deep-bodied Redshank with **longer, fine-tipped bill** and longer legs. Wades deeply, runs/darts, upends, swims.

ADULT BREEDING blackish, with broad white fringes, Apr–May, that wear away leaving solid **black** by May–Jun; by Jul–Aug, patchy black, grey and white; legs blackish or dark red. ADULT NON-BREEDING **pale grey** above (no hint of brown), whiter below; **white line above eye** (widest in front, unlike Redshank or Greenshank (p. 212)); legs **bright red**. JUVENILE grey-brown, with **brownish bars** below; legs orange-red. 1ST-WINTER like non-breeding adult but some juvenile coverts retained.

VOICE Distinctive call invaluable clue: sharp, clearly enunciated "*tchew-it!*"

Scarce migrant (about 420 per year); a few present almost all year on coastal lagoons

from/to Sweden and Finland

from/to S Europe and Africa

Shallow fresh, brackish or salt water coastal habitats

IN FLIGHT wings plain; narrow **white 'wedge' or oval on back** (see Greenshank). Wings arched; long-body but pot-bellied, short-winged effect. Legs extend well beyond tail tip (but sometimes held forward out of sight).

NON-BREEDING

long, white oval patch on back

rather plain wings

legs extend well beyond tail

ADULT NON-BREEDING → BREEDING

[Apr]

With non-breeding and breeding plumages so different, transitional stages are highly variable.

black head and underparts

ADULT BREEDING MAR–MAY

distinct white line, widest in front of eye

red on lower edge of bill only

ADULT NON-BREEDING JUL–MAR

long, bright red legs

long, slightly droop-tipped bill

JUVENILE JUN–SEP

brownish barring on flank

211

WADERS   Waders in flight *p. 186*

Greenshank *Tringa nebularia*

L 30–34 cm | W 55–62 cm

👁 Marsh Sandpiper (*p. 243*), Greater Yellowlegs (*p. 244*)

Rare and local breeder in far N (1,100 pairs); scarce migrant (1,000s), winter visitor (1,000)

Medium–large, long, elegant, greyish wader with long, **slightly upturned**, grey-based bill and **greenish** legs (colour blends in with background, unlike other 'shanks' where vivid red legs stand out). Often by freshwater, coastal lagoons and creeks, less frequently on open mudflats; breeds on remote bogs. **Bigger, greyer** than Redshank (*p. 210*); see Spotted Redshank (*p. 211*), which may also look pale and greyish. Feeds sedately, sometimes with fast runs and occasionally wading deeply, but generally less quick/agile than Spotted Redshank.

ADULT BREEDING streaked/spotted blackish and grey; **yellow-green** legs. ADULT NON-BREEDING greyer, whitish streaks concentrated on hindneck; **white-faced**, dark eye; white wing covert fringes complete; grey-green legs. JUVENILE pale wing covert fringes broken at tip; pale greenish legs. 1ST-WINTER like non-breeding adult but some juvenile coverts retained.

VOICE Loud, **distinct**, frequent estuary sound: ringing, powerful "*tyew-tyew-tyew*" on same note (compare with Redshank).

from Scandinavia

Breeds on peat bogs, extensive damp forest clearings; winters lakes, reservoirs, estuaries

JUVENILE → 1ST-WINTER [Sep]

no wingbar

IN FLIGHT, all-**dark wings**; **long white triangle up back**.

BREEDING MAR–JUL

blackish streaks

yellow-green legs

bill upcurved, pale at base

white feather fringes 'broken' at tip

white feather fringes continuous

JUVENILE JUN–NOV

ADULT NON-BREEDING AUG–MAR

bright white beneath

pale yellowish legs

'SHANKS' | SANDPIPERS

Wood Sandpiper *Tringa glareola*

L 18·5–21 cm | W 35–39 cm

Lesser Yellowlegs (*p. 244*), Wilson's Phalarope (*p. 226*)

Small, rounded sandpiper with slender neck and wingtip; brown-and-white. Bill fine; **legs long, yellowish**. **Long pale stripe extends from bill to well behind eye** (only from eye to bill on darker-backed Green Sandpiper (*p. 214*)). Bobs head, 'pumps' rear-end up and down rather less than Green Sandpiper; may stretch head/neck more upright.

ADULT BREEDING back brown, strongly chequered white. NON-BREEDING (rare Britain and Ireland) has small buff spots above. JUVENILE back mid-brown with **bold pale spots** (Green Sandpiper is darker, with smaller spots); breast streaked brown but no well-defined breast-band.

VOICE Call **thin, high, quick** "*chiff-iff-iff*" on even pitch (without Green Sandpiper's down-up rhythm), usually in flight. Song rhythmic, slurred trill "*trulu-chulu-chulu-chulu.*"

IN FLIGHT, rises high and fast; **square white rump** against **brown wings** and back shows less contrast than Green Sandpiper but **tail more barred**; feet project beyond tail. Underwing **dusky grey-buff**.

Very rare breeder (20 pairs) in N. Scarce autumn, rare spring migrant; (low 100s per year, most Jul–Sep)

from/to Scandinavia and Russia

from/to sub-Saharan Africa

Freshwater or brackish marshes, lagoons and shallow pools

ADULT BREEDING

no wingbar

scattered dark spots and pale spangling on back

ADULT BREEDING
MAR–AUG

broad pale stripe over eye

JUVENILE
JUN–SEP

chequered back

yellowish legs

yellow legs

WADERS
Waders in flight *p. 186*

Green Sandpiper *Tringa ochropus*

L 20–24 cm | W 39–44 cm   👁 Solitary Sandpiper (*p. 243*)

Widespread, scarce autumn migrant, fewer in spring; small numbers winter (low 100s / year)

Small, slender sandpiper; long wings equal to tail; **very dark** above, strongly **contrasted white** beneath (no white 'hook' in front of 'shoulder', obvious on smaller, paler Common Sandpiper). Bill straight (longer, heavier than Common Sandpiper's, thicker than Wood Sandpiper's (*p. 213*); **legs dull greenish**. **Short white line** from bill to top of eye (extends behind eye on Wood Sandpiper). Bobs head and 'pumps' rear-end up and down.

ADULT BREEDING **back black-brown**, spotted white; breast-band greyish, streaked darker. ADULT NON-BREEDING less strongly spotted above. JUVENILE clearly spotted buffish above (but not so chequered as Wood Sandpiper). 1ST-WINTER hard to distinguish from non-breeding adult but has some spotted juvenile wing coverts.

VOICE Rich, fluty, yodelling "*tluee-wee-wee*" call in flight. Song sharp, rising-falling, thin "*whip-i-too, whip-i-too, whip-i-too.*"

from/to Scandinavia

All kinds of water bodies

IN FLIGHT, **square white rump** striking; few dark bands on tail: **'black and white'** as it gets up and goes, like big House Martin (*p. 352*). White belly, **blackish underwings**, unlike any other common wader.

square white rump

very dark underwings

dark wings, no wingbar

ADULT NON-BREEDING

white stripe only reaches eye

finely speckled

ADULT NON-BREEDING AUG–MAR

WOOD — JUVENILE

GREEN — ADULT BREEDING APR–AUG

COMMON — JUVENILE

Comparison of Wood, Green and Common Sandpipers

white eyering

JUVENILE JUN–SEP

small buff spots above

bright white beneath

SANDPIPERS

Common Sandpiper *Actitis hypoleucos*

L 18–20·5 cm | W 32–35 cm   Spotted Sandpiper (p. 242)

Small, slim, rather elongated sandpiper, tail extending **well beyond wingtip**; plain sandy-olive-brown above (colour as Ringed Plover (p. 194)), eye-catching **white below**; breast sides dusky with **white 'hook'** in front of 'shoulder'. Bill straight, pale at base; legs inconspicuous greenish-ochre. Pale stripe over eye, pale eyering. Creeps forward, bobbing head; **'pumps' rear-end up and down**.

ADULT BREEDING upperparts brown with dark streaks and bars. ADULT NON-BREEDING plainer above. JUVENILE **close double-bars** of blackish-brown and cream across wing; pale 'notches' on tertials and tail side. 1ST-WINTER hard to distinguish from adult but has some closely barred juvenile wing coverts.

VOICE Distinctive call: loud, ringing "*swee-wee-wee-wee*" with slight melancholy fall in pitch and volume. Song varies this into fast rhythmic trills and runs.

IN FLIGHT, **white wingbar**; white sides to tail, rounded, dark 'blob' tip. **Flies low**; 'flicked' or fluttering, beats of **stiff, arched wings**.

Locally common summer migrant (24,000 pairs breed, Apr–Oct), rare in winter

from/to Scandinavia
to Africa
from/to Africa

Nests by rivers, lakes, mostly in upland N and W Britain and Ireland; on migration by freshwater; creeks, rocks on coast

ADULT BREEDING
white wingbar
white on underwings
dark tail and centre to rump

In summer often heard before seen; typically perched on rocks in midstream.

ADULT NON-BREEDING AUG–MAR

ADULT NON-BREEDING has a weaker head pattern and a plain back; barring on wing coverts becomes uneven with wear.

ADULT BREEDING MAR–AUG
dark bars/arrowheads above; single dark bar on wing coverts
long tail

pale stripe over eye
JUVENILE JUN–SEP
white 'hook'

Neat bars on wing coverts: double dark bands indicate JUVENILE.

WADERS

Waders in flight *p. 186*

NT Bar-tailed Godwit *Limosa lapponica*

54

L 33–41 cm | W 62–72 cm

Large **very long-billed** wader with medium-length, blackish legs, **short above joint**. Bill tapered and **slightly upcurved**; pink-based (blackish in breeding birds) (Black-tailed Godwit's bill straighter, mostly orange or pink). Flocks feed well-spaced on open mud, less often in narrow, hidden creeks than Black-tailed Godwit, and far less frequently inland.

ADULT MALE BREEDING (fades by Jul) **bright coppery-red extending under tail**; little or no white, **no dark flank bars** (unlike Black-tailed Godwit). ADULT FEMALE BREEDING paler orange. ADULT NON-BREEDING grey-brown above and on breast, with fine **dark streaks**; white below with sparse brown barring on flank. JUVENILE dark **brown upperparts heavily streaked**; buff breast; pale 'notches' on tertials. (More like Whimbrel (*p. 219*) or Curlew (*p. 218*) at long range.) 1ST-WINTER like non-breeding adult but retains some juvenile coverts with pale spots on fringes.

VOICE Nasal, wickering "*ki-wee ki-wee*" or "*ik-ik-ik*."

Locally common winter visitor (43,000, Aug–Apr; declining), migrant; rare inland

from Siberia

Muddy/sandy estuaries

IN FLIGHT dull upperwing, pale inner/dark outer half; long **white triangle up back**, barred tail. Fast, twisting, acrobatic descents to roost or new feeding area.

no wingbar

white triangle up back

JUVENILES

dark cap

JUVENILE JUN–OCT

streaked back and wings

ADULT NON-BREEDING SEP–MAY

ADULT ♂ BREEDING FEB–AUG

ADULT ♀ BREEDING FEB–AUG

legs shorter above 'knee' than Black-tailed Godwit

GODWITS

NT
VU
Black-tailed Godwit *Limosa limosa*

● ssp. *limosa*   ● ssp. *islandica*   **I**   547

L 37–42 cm | W 63–74 cm   👁 Hudsonian Godwit (p. 228)

Large, **long-billed** wader with **long, black legs, long above joint**. Bill **straight, mostly orange or pink** (Bar-tailed Godwit's slightly upcurved and pink-based, but dark in breeding birds). Often excitable groups; when feeding, bill pointed down to toes, probed deeply, in mud or shallow water. Frequent inland.

ADULT MALE BREEDING **coppery-red**; flank white with **black bars**. ADULT FEMALE BREEDING as male but pale orange. ADULT NON-BREEDING **plain grey-brown** above and on breast, white below. JUVENILE dark brown upperparts with **rusty fringes**; **orange-buff** neck and breast. 1ST-WINTER like non-breeding adult with some pale-fringed juvenile coverts.

VOICE Quick, nasal notes; mechanical/metallic bickering when feeding.

IN FLIGHT, broad **white wingbar** (longer, narrower than Oystercatcher's (p. 190)); **white underwing with black edges**; **square white rump**, black tail. Flight fast, with deep beats of bowed wings; narrow head extended, legs trail, but can look rather small; flocks manoeuvre tightly.

Very rare and local breeder (50–60 pairs); locally common winter visitor (50,000, mostly E, S and SW)

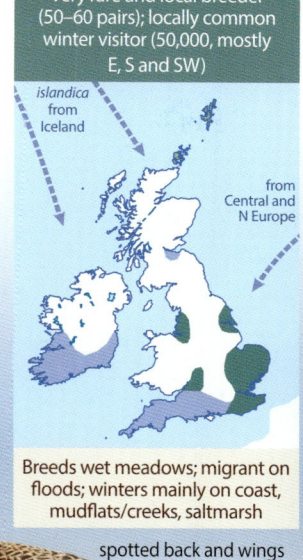

islandica from Iceland

from Central and N Europe

Breeds wet meadows; migrant on floods; winters mainly on coast, mudflats/creeks, saltmarsh

square white rump; black tail

white wingbar

ssp. *islandica* JUVENILES

rusty wash

spotted back and wings

ssp. *islandica* JUVENILE JUL–NOV

ADULT NON-BREEDING JUN–MAR

plain back and wings

ssp. *limosa* JUVENILE JUL–NOV

ssp. *limosa*

JUVENILE of ssp. *islandica* has stronger, more extensive rusty wash; darker back and wings and more boldly marked tertials than ssp. *limosa*.

Two subspecies: ssp. *islandica* (breeds Iceland) – shorter bill and legs; brighter and darker; more extensive chestnut head, neck and breast than ssp. *limosa* (breeds rest of Europe but rare in Britain) – paler, more diffuse red Feb–Jul.

BREEDING FEB–JUL

Icelandic ssp. *islandica* ADULT ♂

'European' ssp. *limosa* ADULT ♂

'European' ssp. *limosa* ADULT ♀ FEB–JUL

WADERS   Waders in flight *p. 186*

NT **Curlew** *Numenius arquata*
VU
L 48–57 cm | W 89–106 cm

Scarce resident (66,000 pairs, 100 pairs Ireland, declining rapidly); common winter visitor (150,000)

Largest estuary (and moorland) wader. Brown, streaked, with **long, smoothly downcurved** bill. Larger and paler than similar Whimbrel, with weaker head pattern. Feeds singly or spread out in loose flocks, with rather slow action (compared with Whimbrel and godwits) but roosts in tighter groups.

ADULT mid- or buffy-brown, with **plain head** (slightly paler over eye and darker cap, but without Whimbrel's obvious stripes). Sexes look similar but MALE's bill relatively short and less strongly curved compared with FEMALE's very long bill (but overlap). Bill black-brown during breeding season, otherwise pink-based. JUVENILE spotted buff on upperparts.

VOICE Coarse or barking "*whaup*" notes; loud "*vi-vi-vi*" of alarm; clear, fluty "*cur-lee*" and "*cue-cue-cue*." Song loud, mournful, accelerating into mesmeric bubbling trill, often heard on estuaries but most ecstatic on breeding moors.

from Scandinavia

Breeds moors, river valleys; winters mostly on coast, estuaries, saltmarshes, meadows

Flocks on migration form lines or 'V's, reminiscent of gulls.

IN FLIGHT, like Whimbrel/Bar-tailed Godwit: dark outerwing, pale innerwing, **white 'V' up back**; long bill usually obvious.

plain crown (sometimes with faint stripe)

ADULT ♂

bill smoothly curved

♂ has shorter bill than ♀

plain face with 'isolated' dark eye

JUVENILE [Aug]

brighter, buffier than Whimbrel

ADULT ♀

JUVENILE JUN–OCT [Sep]

218

CURLEWS

Whimbrel *Numenius phaeopus*

L 37–45 cm | W 78–88 cm

👁 Little Whimbrel (p. 240)

Large, brown, streaked wader with long, **downcurved** bill. Smaller and darker than similar Curlew, with stronger head pattern. Slightly shorter **bill more 'angled' towards tip** (less smoothly curved than Curlew). Larger than godwits. Flocks migrate in spring, sometimes inland, otherwise mostly small, scattered groups on coasts.

ADULT (sexes alike) brown, with dark streaks (greyer than Curlew); dark crown with **pale central stripe**; dark eyestripe and broad **pale stripe over eye**. Pale spots on upperparts wear off, creating 'notched' feather edges and darker appearance by Jul. Bill black when breeding, but pink base from Jul. JUVENILE fresh upperpart feathers have bright buff fringes.

VOICE Call diagnostic: quick, even repetition of short whistle in rippling trill "*pipipipipipip*." Song long whistles developing into even, sad trill.

Two subspecies recorded: ssp. *phaeopus* (breeds N Europe and W Russia) and ssp. *islandicus* (breeds Iceland, Faeroes, Scotland) are both regular in Britain/Ireland and only distinguishable on basis of breeding range).

Rare breeder N isles (400 pairs); widespread but scarce migrant (3,000), rare winter (30–50)

from/to Iceland
from/to Scandinavia and Russia
from/to W Africa

Damp meadows, saltmarshes, estuaries

IN FLIGHT, dark wings, inner half paler; dark tail; **white triangle on rump/lower back**. Darker, deeper-chested, chunkier; quicker flight action than Curlew.

obvious pale crown stripe

broad pale stripe over and dark line through eye

bill shorter than Curlew's and distinctly angled towards tip

ADULT

colder brown than Curlew

ADULT

JUVENILE — dark rump

JUVENILE

Hudsonian Whimbrel
Numenius hudsonicus

L 37–45 cm | W 78–88 cm

As Whimbrel, but brighter, stronger buff; head stripes rich dark brown and white; **back and rump all-dark**.

Vagrant from N America: <20 records (<5 Ireland), Oct–Apr. Estuaries, saltmarshes.

WADERS

Red-necked Phalarope *Phalaropus lobatus*

L 17–19 cm | W 30–34 cm

👁 Wilson's Phalarope (p. 226)

Waders in flight *p. 186*

🔴 **I** 54

Very rare summer breeder in N Isles (20–25 males); rare migrant (<100 per year)

Small, rather elongated wader, usually seen swimming. Rotund; high shoulders taper to pointed wingtip/tail, held clear of water when swimming (sometimes 'spins' on water when feeding). **Bill needle-like**, all-black. Smaller than Grey Phalarope, with finer bill.

ADULT BREEDING **dark grey** with **buff stripes above**, **grey breast**, **white chin/throat** and **rufous on neck** (brightest on FEMALE). ADULT NON-BREEDING pale grey above with **white lines down back**, white below; black cap and 'mask', which tends to **turn down at rear**. JUVENILE **blackish** with long buff lines above at first (darker than juvenile Grey Phalarope), developing grey/white/blackish stripes as moults into 1ST-WINTER (Grey Phalarope increasingly has round grey patches in black); pale pinkish on neck (quickly fades white); white below; legs black.

VOICE Short, sharp "*kwit*;" MALE gives 'warbling' notes and FEMALE a repeated "*wewewewewe*" when breeding.

to tropical Atlantic/ E Pacific

Breeds on marshy pools; offshore

ADULT ♀ BREEDING

JUVENILE

1ST-WINTER AUG–APR

'mask' tends to turn down at rear

white lines on back

IN FLIGHT, very dark wings with white wingbar; non-breeding adults/juveniles very similar to Grey Phalarope and not safely identifiable at distance.

ADULT ♂ APR–AUG

dark grey breast

fine, all-black bill

black and buff stripes on back

JUVENILE JUN–OCT

ADULT ♀ APR–AUG

PHALAROPES

Grey Phalarope *Phalaropus fulicarius*

L 20–22 cm | W 36–41 cm

👁 **Wilson's Phalarope** (p. 226)

Small, rather elongated wader, usually seen swimming buoyantly at sea, leaping over breaking waves; sometimes wades at water's edge. Rotund; high shoulders taper to pointed wingtip/tail, held clear of water when swimming. Bill relatively thick and broad (compared with Red-necked Phalarope), but not always easy to judge. Does not breed in Britain/Ireland but commonest phalarope; in autumn/early winter after storms, most phalaropes seen will be Grey Phalaropes.

ADULT BREEDING (very rare) orange-red, back streaked black and buff; head black with broad **white cheek** (FEMALE brightest); bill **orange** with black tip. ADULT NON-BREEDING/1ST-WINTER pale grey above; white below; black cap and 'mask', which tends to **rise at rear**; faint **pale area at bill base** JUVENILE **black-brown** above, increasingly **blotched** grey; buff/apricot on foreneck (quickly fades white); legs tinged ochre.

VOICE Short "*pit*."

Rare but regular autumn migrant (400–600 per year); very rare in spring, winter

to tropical Atlantic

Mostly coastal, most near shore after gales

JUVENILE →
1ST-WINTER [Oct]

Juvenile phalaropes compared

'mask' tends to droop at rear — 'needle' bill — **RED-NECKED**

relatively thick bill — 'mask' tends to rise at rear — **GREY** JUVENILE → 1ST-WINTER [Sep]

ADULT ♂ APR–AUG

ADULT ♀ APR–AUG

JUVENILE →
1ST-WINTER
[Oct]

IN FLIGHT, dark wings with white wingbar, like long-winged, pot-bellied Sanderling (p. 200).

'mask' tends to rise at rear

JUVENILE →
1ST-WINTER
[Oct]

SANDERLING
ADULT/1ST-WINTER
Sanderling in flight very similar but has narrower dark centre to rump/tail and lacks dark 'mask'.

faint pale base to bill

1ST-WINTER
AUG–APR
[Oct]

JUVENILE →
1ST-WINTER
JUL–APR [Sep]

221

WADERS

Waders in flight *p. 186*

Snipe *Gallinago gallinago*

L 23–28 cm | W 39–45 cm

👁 Great Snipe (*p. 241*), Wison's Snipe (*p. 241*)

Medium-sized, dark, short-legged wader with **very long bill** (angled down, even in flight). In or near tall vegetation on wet mud, but small groups may feed on more open mud beside freshwater. Typically flies off in rolling zigzag, **with noisy calls**.

Dark brown with buff lines above; head striped black and buff, crown black with **pale central stripe**; flank **barred** dark brown. Age, sex and seasonal differences insignificant, but JUVENILE has narrow pale wing covert fringes until Oct/Nov. 1ST-WINTER like adult but a few old, faded juvenile wing coverts retained.

VOICE Loud, harsh "*skaarch*;" rhythmic "*chip-per chip-per*," often from post or wire, mainly Mar–Jun; harsh "*chip*." Vibrant, buzzing "*h'h'hhhhhhh'h*" made by tail feathers in switchback display flight.

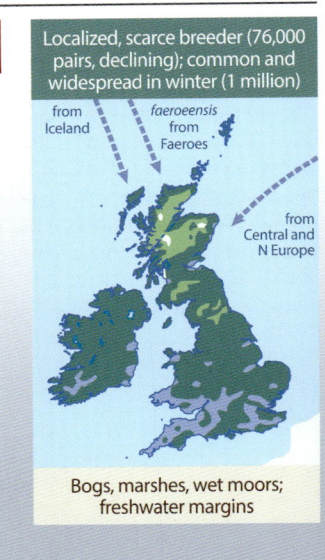

Localized, scarce breeder (76,000 pairs, declining); common and widespread in winter (1 million)

from Iceland / *faeroeensis* from Faeroes / from Central and N Europe

Bogs, marshes, wet moors; freshwater margins

IN FLIGHT, **white trailing edge** to dark wing; rufous on tail. If flushed, flies high. Settles with tail fanned, revealing **white tip**.

outer tail feathers spread in diving display flight

ADULT

white trailing edge

JUVENILE ssp. *gallinago*

JUVENILE ssp. *faeroeensis*

Snipe from Iceland, Shetland, Orkney and the Faeroes are ssp. *faeroeensis* (shown above right), but only Faeroese birds are really distinct: redder overall, with narrower white stripes. The subspecies breeding in the rest of Britain and Ireland is *gallinago*.

pale central stripe

extremely long bill

broad flank bars

ADULT

SNIPE

Jack Snipe *Lymnocryptes minimus*

L 18–20 cm | W 33–36 cm

Small, dark, cryptically plumaged wader; **bill not excessively long**. Feeds inconspicuously with distinctive **'bouncy' action**. Very hard to see unless almost trodden on, when flies up quickly, often circling briefly before dropping again. Usually silent when flushed but can give a quiet croak (Snipe flies off high; calling loudly).

Two **long, golden-buff stripes** down each side of body beside green-glossed, blackish band. Head shows **dark central crown** (pale line on Snipe) and two pale stripes over eye; flank **streaked** (not barred as on Snipe). Age, sex and seasonal differences insignificant.

VOICE Song in display flight (very rare in Britain) a low, muffled, almost liquid, rhythmic "*cu-tal-puc, cu-tal-puc, cu-tal-puc…*" (like a galloping horse).

IN FLIGHT, wings quite long, rather straight, dark, with weak pale trailing edge; dark, pointed tail. More useful is the noticeably more 'normal' bill, not the extreme length of Snipe's.

Local winter visitor (100,000, Oct–Mar)

from Scandinavia and Russia

Wet grassy marshes, reedbeds

weaker trailing edge than Snipe

dark crown without prominent pale central stripe

prominent pale central crown stripe

JACK SNIPE   **SNIPE**

Typically very well hidden on the ground, long stripes down the back and along the sides mimicking grass stems; much smaller than Snipe (right) with no pale stripe down the centre of dark crown.

dark crown   long pale stripes along body

bill not remarkably long

223

WADERS

Woodcock *Scolopax rusticola*

L 33–38 cm | W 55–65 cm

👁 Great Snipe (p. 241)

Rather like large Snipe (p. 222) but more barrel-shaped and with different habitat preference and behaviour. Not often encountered: usually flushed within woodland (flying off fast and straight, without calling) or seen **flying over at dusk**; feeds at night in damp fields and ditches.

Large, rusty-brown, ground-dwelling wader with a **long, straight bill**. Pale, peaked forehead and **black bands across crown and rear of head**. Upperparts with cryptic 'dead-leaf' patterning, underparts closely barred. Sex, age and seasonal differences insignificant.

VOICE Alternate sharp, whistled "*tsiwik!*" and low, croaking grunt, "*rorrk-rorrk*" during display flight at dusk.

IN FLIGHT, **rufous on rump and tail**. Wings long, broad-based with no marked pattern. Rises fast, twisting, with whoosh of wings. Flies over trees in display (roding), **calling distinctively**, pot-bellied, quick, flickering action seemingly superimposed on slower beats. Head up, thick bill angled down; feet often slightly lowered.

Scarce resident (78,000 pairs; declining), widespread winter visitor (about 1 million, Britain & Ireland)

from N and W Europe

Woodland, adjacent pasture, ditches

rufous rump and tail

broad wing base

barred underside

black bands across head

'leaf-litter' pattern

'Roding' display flight usually detected by calls, then silhouette above trees: same route repeated.

Rare waders

Waders the world over fall into more-or-less the same groups as those seen in Britain and Ireland. Most rare waders have an obvious affinity with commoner ones, but some have a different character that is unlike that of more familiar birds.

With most, an essential first step is to decide what age it is or at least what plumage it is in – adult breeding or non-breeding, or juvenile (in autumn). Try to fit it into one of the groups in the following table – is it a 'shank', a 'peep', a godwit, or maybe a snipe? Look at the common birds within that group. Does your 'mystery bird' fit any of those? If not, then look at the rare options and try to work through the book to the best available possibilities. Figuring out what the bird is **not** is as important as trying to decide what it is.

Vagrant waders	
Some 42 species of wader have been recorded in Britain and/or Ireland as vagrants from Europe, North America or Asia. All are listed in taxonomic order below, with any relevant common comparison species in square brackets.	
Lapwings	Sociable Lapwing (p. 229), White-tailed Lapwing (p. 229)
Pluvialis plovers	[**Golden Plover** p. 198] Pacific Golden Plover (p. 230), American Golden Plover (p. 230)
Charadrius plovers	['**ringed' plovers pp. 193–195**] Semipalmated Plover (p. 232), Killdeer (p. 231), Lesser Sand Plover (p. 233), Greater Sand Plover (p. 233), Caspian Plover (p. 233)
Upland Sandpiper	Upland Sandpiper (p. 240)
Curlews & godwits	[**Curlew, Whimbrel pp. 218–219**] Little Whimbrel (p. 240), Eskimo Curlew (p. 240), [**godwits pp. 216–217**] Hudsonian Godwit (p. 228)
Calidris sandpipers/ 'peeps'	[**Knot p. 201; Dunlin p. 202; Curlew Sandpiper p. 205; Little Stint p. 207; Temminck's Stint p. 206**] Great Knot (p. 239), Broad-billed Sandpiper (p. 236), Sharp-tailed Sandpiper (p. 238), Stilt Sandpiper (p. 239), Long-toed Stint (p. 236), Red-necked Stint (p. 235), Baird's Sandpiper (p. 237), Least Sandpiper (p. 236), White-rumped Sandpiper (p. 237), Buff-breasted Sandpiper (p. 240), Pectoral Sandpiper (p. 238), Semipalmated Sandpiper (p. 235), Western Sandpiper (p. 235)
Dowitchers	Long-billed Dowitcher (p. 245), Short-billed Dowitcher (p. 245)
Snipe	[**Snipe p. 222**] Great Snipe (p. 241), Wilson's Snipe (p. 241)
Phalaropes	[**phalaropes pp. 220–221**] Wilson's Phalarope (p. 226)
Terek Sandpiper	Terek Sandpiper (p. 242)
Actitis sandpipers	[**Common Sandpiper p. 215**] Spotted Sandpiper (p. 242)
Tringa sandpipers	[**Green Sandpiper p. 214**] Solitary Sandpiper (p. 243), Grey-tailed Tattler (p. 243), ['**shanks' pp. 210–212**] Lesser Yellowlegs (p. 244), Marsh Sandpiper (p. 243), Greater Yellowlegs (p. 244)
Coursers	Cream-coloured Courser (p. 228)
Pratincoles	Collared Pratincole (p. 227), Black-winged Pratincole (p. 227), Oriental Pratincole (p. 227)

Greenshank (centre) with rare Marsh Sandpiper and Lesser Yellowlegs

Marsh Sandpiper: from SE Europe, a rare vagrant, looks like a small, dainty Greenshank.

Lesser Yellowlegs: from N America, typically an autumn vagrant, often long-staying.

RARE WADERS

Wilson's Phalarope
Phalaropus tricolor
L 22–24 cm | W 40–42 cm

Distinctive large phalarope with **long, fine, black bill**. Unlikely to be confused, but see other phalaropes (*pp. 220–221*), Wood Sandpiper (*p. 213*) and Lesser Yellowlegs (*p. 244*); non-breeding Spotted Redshank (*p. 211*) can also raise false hopes when swimming! On water, low, long-bodied with upright head/neck. On land, slightly awkward **forward-leaning** unbalanced look.

ADULT BREEDING unmistakable; black band through eye widening into **rufous neck stripe** (FEMALE brighter than MALE). Legs black. NON-BREEDING/1ST-YEAR pale grey above, white below. JUVENILE dark-centred, buff-edged feathers above; darkish cap and hint of dark band through eye but no black 'mask' like smaller phalaropes; otherwise **very white**. **Legs yellow**.

VOICE Flight call "*chu*."

Vagrant from N America: <350 records (<100 Ireland), May–Nov, most Aug–Oct, declining. Freshwater, coastal lagoons.

NON-BREEDING

ADULT ♀ BREEDING

IN FLIGHT, **wings dark, plain; rump white, square or 'U'-shaped**.

ADULT ♂ BREEDING MAR–AUG

ADULT ♀ BREEDING MAR–AUG

dark feathers on grey back

JUVENILE → 1ST-WINTER JUL–DEC [Aug]

NON-BREEDING

1ST-YEAR/NON-BREEDING as JUVENILE but back and wing coverts plain grey.

Pratincoles

Short-billed, short-legged, very long-winged; rest on open ground (rounded shape, or more elongated if alert) and feed in the air (like a brown tern with long, forked tail). ADULT BREEDING sandy-brown above, pale below with white belly; blacker wingtip. Buff throat outlined in black; red base to bill. ADULT NON-BREEDING throat less well defined; pale fringes above. JUVENILE (all species) dark spots/creamy scaling above; speckled breast. For all ages, structure and wing coloration best identification features.

COLLARED PRATINCOLE

ADULT NON-BREEDING

Pratincoles in breeding plumage are difficult on the ground, easier in flight; non-breeding (and moulting) individuals and juveniles are difficult.

Pratincoles – summary of key features of breeding adults			
	Black-winged	**Collared**	**Oriental**
TAIL/WINGTIP	**tail shorter**	**tail longer**	**tail much shorter**
BILL BASE	smaller red mark	larger red mark	
NOSTRIL	elongate/oval; length 2–3½ × width	slit; length 2½–4 × width	oval; length <2 × width
UNDERWING	**all-black**	rusty red in good light	
UPPERWING	**dark**, little contrast with dark flight feathers	pale, with **contrasting dark flight feathers**	darker than Collared
TRAILING EDGE	**dark**; faintly translucent at most	**white, usually obvious**	white very narrow or absent

PHALAROPES | PRATINCOLES

underwing black — BLACK-WINGED PRATINCOLE

underwing rusty-red — COLLARED PRATINCOLE — **white trailing edge** — contrasting flight feathers

underwing rusty-red — **short tail** — ORIENTAL PRATINCOLE

Black-winged Pratincole
Glareola nordmanni
L 24–28 cm | W 60–70 cm

Red area at bill base very restricted; tail falls short of wingtip.

Vagrant from Asia: <50 records, (<5 Ireland), Apr–Nov, most Aug. Scattered. Open areas.

long oval

ADULT BREEDING MAR–AUG

Collared Pratincole
Glareola pratincola
L 24–28 cm | W 60–70 cm

Red area at bill base; tail longer than wingtip (**beware tails that are broken or not fully grown**).

Vagrant from S Europe: <100 records, (<5 Ireland), Apr–Nov, most May–Jun. Scattered. Marshes.

slit

tail longer than wingtip

red base to bill

ADULT BREEDING MAR–AUG

Oriental Pratincole
Glareola maldivarum
L 23–27 cm | W 55–65 cm

Much like Collared Pratincole but **tail shorter** and wing darker above. Belly buff, less shining white; tail much shorter than wingtip.

Vagrant from Asia: <10 records (Britain), May–Sep. E, SE coasts. Marshes.

oval

ADULT BREEDING MAR–AUG

227

RARE WADERS

Hudsonian Godwit
Limosa haemastica
L 37–42 cm | W 67–79 cm

Similar to, but slightly smaller than, Black-tailed Godwit (*p. 217*) with finer bill. ADULT BREEDING greyish head, bold buff/white marbling on blackish back and dark red underparts. FEMALE paler and more barred below than MALE. ADULT NON-BREEDING plain grey-brown above, paler below; bold buff stripe in front of eye. JUVENILE (not recorded) mottled grey-brown above, head and underparts plain grey-buff. IN FLIGHT, **blackish underwing**, white wingbar much less prominent than on Black-tailed Godwit.

VOICE Descending "*tow-wit*."

Vagrant from N America: <5 records (<5 Ireland), Apr–Sep. Marshes.

BLACK-TAILED GODWIT
white underwing

1ST-SUMMER ♂
black underwing

ADULT ♀ BREEDING
MAR–AUG

1ST-SUMMER ♂
JUL–OCT [Sep]

NT Cream-coloured Courser 548
Cursorius cursor
L 24–27 cm | W 51–57 cm

Small, rounded, upright, with plover-like actions. Pale tawny-buff with long, whitish legs and faintly downcurved black bill. ADULT curved black and white stripes behind eye. JUVENILE/ 1ST-WINTER head pattern less well defined.

VOICE Abrupt, low "*kwit*" or "*krip*."

Vagrant from N Africa/Middle East: <50 records (most old), (1 Ireland), all months, most Sep–Dec. Short grassland.

JUVENILE
JUL–AUG

IN FLIGHT, **outerwing black** above, and whole of **underwing black**.

'clean' head stripes

ADULT

'dull' head pattern

JUVENILE →
1ST-WINTER
AUG–OCT [Oct]

JUVENILE more barred above

long pale legs

GODWITS | COURSERS | LAPWINGS

Sociable Lapwing
(Sociable Plover)
Vanellus gregarius
L 27–30 cm | W 65–70 cm

Typically with Lapwings (*p. 197*); similar form but narrower wingtips in flight. ADULT BREEDING (not recorded) grey-brown, washed mauve/purplish; dark red/**black belly**; **black cap** and **eyestripe**, white over eye. Bill and legs black. ADULT NON-BREEDING dull with whiter belly. Narrow black cap and eyestripe, **broad buff-white stripe** over eye. 1ST-WINTER duller, with pale fringes and dark spots on breast.

VOICE Harsh "*kereck*."

> Vagrant from Asia: <50 records (most old, declining) (<5 Ireland), most months, mainly Sep–Dec. Scattered. Marshes, pastures.

IN FLIGHT, **outerwing black**, innerwing brown with **broad white hindwing**; black patch on tail.

ADULT BREEDING MAR–AUG

1ST-WINTER SEP–MAR

dark cap, broad white stripe over eye

ADULT NON-BREEDING AUG–MAR

White-tailed Lapwing
(White-tailed Plover)
Vanellus leucurus
L 26–29 cm | W 75–85 cm

Unmistakable tall, upstanding wader, smaller than Lapwing (*p. 197*): **long yellow legs**, black bill and **plain, round head**. JUVENILE (not recorded) spotted black on sandy-buff back.

VOICE Nasal "*pi-er-it*" in flight.

> Vagrant from E Europe: <15 records (Britain), May–Jul. Freshwater margins.

IN FLIGHT, black wingtip, **broad white midwing band; rump and tail pure white**. Long yellow legs trail.

ADULT

plain head

ADULT

purplish-brown 'breastplate' in summer

black and white bands along closed wing

vivid yellow legs

229

RARE WADERS

Rare 'golden' plovers

Two rare golden plovers associate with Golden Plovers and can be difficult to identify. American Golden Plover much more likely than Pacific Golden Plover. Both have dusky underwing (white on Golden Plover). Some differences in plumage but best identified by structure and voice (see table *opposite*).

Golden Plover
p. 198

American Golden Plover
Pluvialis dominica
L 24–27 cm | W 55–60 cm

Vagrant from N America: <750 records, 10–30 per year (<350 records Ireland), most May–Oct. Widespread. Marshes, pasture.

Pacific Golden Plover
Pluvialis fulva
L 21–25 cm | W 50–55 cm

Vagrant from Asia: <100 records (<20 records Ireland), most months, mainly May–Nov. Widespread. Coastal lagoons.

ADULT BREEDING FEB–AUG

ADULT BREEDING FEB–AUG

ADULT BREEDING FEB–AUG

ADULT BREEDING
UPPERPARTS: finely patterned;
FLANK: white;
UNDERTAIL: mottled black/white

ADULT BREEDING
UPPERPARTS: coarsely patterned;
FLANK: little or no white;
UNDERTAIL: black

ADULT BREEDING
UPPERPARTS: coarsely patterned;
FLANK: narrow band of white;
UNDERTAIL: mottled black/white – a few like American Golden Plover

JUVENILE / 1ST-WINTER yellow-brown overall; cap indistinct on bland yellow-buff head.

JUVENILE / 1ST-WINTER greyish overall; dark cap; prominent white stripe over eye; dark in front of eye.

JUVENILE / 1ST-WINTER yellow-brown overall (as Golden Plover); dark cap; yellowish stripe over eye; pale in front of eye.

both species smaller, slimmer and longer-legged than Golden Plover

JUVENILE JUN–MAR

JUVENILE JUN–OCT

1ST-WINTER AUG–MAR

tips of tertials well short of tail tip

tips of tertials well short of tail tip

tip of tertials close to tail tip

dark

pale

wingtip ± tail

wingtip projects well beyond tail

wingtip projects slightly beyond tail

PLOVERS

Non-breeding 'golden' plovers in flight

all have dark rump and tail

GOLDEN — underwing white; feet do not project

AMERICAN GOLDEN — underwing dusky; feet barely project

PACIFIC GOLDEN — underwing dusky; feet strongly project

Identification of 'golden' plovers – summary of key features			
	Golden Plover	American Golden Plover	Pacific Golden Plover
Underwing	**Largely white**	**Dusky grey-brown**	
Size/legs	Largest; legs relatively short	Slightly smaller than Golden Plover; legs long	Smallest, slim; legs long; in flight feet project beyond tail
Wingtip projection	Equals tail tip or just longer	Clearly longer than tail	Slightly longer than tail
Tertial tips	Well short of tail tip	Short of tail tip	Close to tail tip
Primary tips	3–4 visible	4–5 visible	3 visible
Voice	*"tooee"* or *"peooo"*	Double *"clu-eet"*	Definite *"tchoo-it"*

Killdeer *Charadrius vociferus*
L 23·5–26 cm | W 59–63 cm

Like large, long-tailed 'ringed' plover, brown above, white below, but with **double breast-band**. Favours grassy places, sandy shores.

VOICE Call long, rising *"klu-ee,"* resembles Grey Plover (*p. 199*) but slightly thinner or higher, less trisyllabic.

Vagrant from N America: <100 records (<25 Ireland), Sep–May, most Nov–Apr. Scattered. Coasts, lakesides.

IN FLIGHT, blackish wings with long, broad white wingbar and **bright rufous rump** blending in to long, dark tail.

1ST-WINTER

1ST-WINTER
AUG–MAR

double breast-band

231

RARE WADERS

Rare *Charadrius* plovers

Caspian Plover and especially the sand plover pair can be difficult to identify, and Kentish Plover (p. 193) should also be borne in mind: a combination of size, head and bill shape and proportions, and presence or absence of a white collar helps, while features such as leg colour and call can be useful for some individuals. If possible, build up a complete assessment over a long period of observation.

Identification of rare *Charadrius* plovers – summary of key features						
	Bill and head	**Legs**	**Adult breeding**	**Non-breeding**	**In flight**	**Voice**
Ringed Plover (p. 194) 18–20 cm	BILL blunt, **two-tone**; HEAD round	Short; **orange**	**Black and white** breast-bands	White collar. Blackish breast ring	White wingbar	Whistled "*too-lee*"
Kentish Plover (p. 193) 15–17 cm	BILL small, black; HEAD small, round	Grey to **black**	Small dark 'mask' and breast marks	White collar. Small dark breast marks	White wingbar; **white tail sides**	Short "*pwit*"
Greater Sand Plover 22–25 cm	BILL **long, tapered**; black, 'nail' ≥ ½ bill length; HEAD big, bulky, angular	Longest; **yellow-green** to greenish-grey	Black 'mask', white throat, chestnut breast	Grey-brown head, distinct breast patches. No white collar	Broadest white wingbar; toes may project	Trill or shorter note
Lesser Sand Plover 19–21 cm	BILL **Shortish, blunt**, black, 'nail' < ½ bill length; HEAD rounded	Greenish-grey to **blackish**	Black 'mask', white throat, chestnut breast and flank	Grey-brown head, distinct breast patches. No white collar	White wingbar; feet do not project	"*chitik*"
Caspian Plover 18–20 cm	BILL long, fine, black; HEAD small, neat	Long; brownish/ greenish	White over eye and throat, **rufous breast-band**	Poorly defined breast-band. No white collar	Short, narrow white wingbar; dark tail	Loud "*tyup*"

Semipalmated Plover
Charadrius semipalmatus
L 16–17·5 cm | W 31–32 cm

Very like Ringed Plover (p. 194): small size and **call** may draw attention. Front toes have small webs (one tiny web on Ringed Plover). Rounder head and **short, stubby bill** different from Ringed Plover on some, others less distinct. ADULT BREEDING weaker whitish stripe over black cheek and thinner black breast-band than Ringed Plover. On ADULT NON-BREEDING (head/breast-bands dark brown) and JUVENILE / 1ST-YEAR (head and breast-bands mid-brown), **white throat extends above point of gape** (solid dark on Ringed Plover).

VOICE Vaguely Spotted Redshank-like (p. 211), rising "*chewee*."

Vagrant from N America:
<10 records (<5 Ireland),
Mar–Nov. Scattered. Mudflats.

'Ringed' plover calls at-a-glance	
Little Ringed Plover p. 195	abrupt down-inflected "*tew*" or "*te-u*"
Ringed Plover (p. 194)	"*too-ee*" or "*ploo-eep*"
Semipalmated Plover	rising "*chewee*"

IN FLIGHT, white wingbar.
ADULT BREEDING
prominent stripe
narrow yellow eyering
weak whitish stripe
ADULT ♂ BREEDING
RINGED PLOVER
broad
JUVENILE
dark
ADULT ♂ BREEDING MAR–AUG
narrow breast-band
white
JUVENILE JUN–AUG

SMALLER PLOVERS

See table *opposite* for summary of key features.

Greater Sand Plover
Charadrius leschenaultii
L 22–25 cm | W 53–60 cm

ADULT ♂ BREEDING MAR–AUG

Vagrant from Asia: <20 records (1 Ireland), Apr–Dec. Scattered. Coasts, reservoirs.

ADULT NON-BREEDING/1ST-WINTER

ADULT NON-BREEDING AUG–MAR

Western ssp. *columbinus* has smallest bill, close to Lesser Sand Plover

legs usually green, long and strong

bill 'heavy': 'nail' ≥ ½ total bill length

'nail'

Lesser Sand Plover
Charadrius mongolus
L 19–21 cm | W 45–58 cm

ADULT ♂ BREEDING MAR–AUG

white — 'mongolus' group
dark — 'atrifrons' group

Vagrant from Asia: <10 records (1 Ireland), May–Aug. Scattered. Coasts.

ADULT NON-BREEDING/1ST-WINTER

ADULT NON-BREEDING AUG–MAR

NB the 'nail' is the slightly bulging frontal portion of the upper mandible

legs variable in colour; distinctive when blackish

bill 'neat': 'nail' < ½ total bill length

'nail'

Caspian Plover
Charadrius asiaticus
L 18–20 cm | W 55–61 cm

ADULT ♂ BREEDING MAR–AUG

Vagrant from Asia: <10 records (Britain), May, Jul. Scattered. Coasts.

JUVENILE/1ST-WINTER

1ST-WINTER AUG–MAR

bill distinctly pointed

legs brown-green, rather long

Rare waders: 'Peeps'

'Peeps' is a useful American collective term for the smallest sandpipers and stints. The five rare 'peeps' can be separated into two groups:

Pale-legged (p. 236): two species; leg colour as Temminck's Stint but plumage more like Little Stint. Great care needs to be taken to distinguish the rare species from one another.

Dark-legged: three species which must be separated with care from Little Stint and each other. Semipalmated Sandpiper is most frequent, Western Sandpiper very rare and Red-necked Stint extremely unlikely. Look for bill shape, webbing between toes, scapular patterns, head patterns. Most are juveniles in late autumn; greyer non-breeding adults are even more difficult, structure and call being the most important identification features.

See **Temminck's Stint** (p. 206), **Little Stint** (p. 207)

Temminck's Stint differs from other pale-legged 'peeps' in that it lacks a 'V' on the back, has an **unstreaked buff-brown breast** and has **white sides to the tail**.

Little Stint has unwebbed toes; Semipalmated (inset) and Western Sandpipers have tiny webs.

Identification of juvenile dark-legged 'peeps' – summary of key features

	Little Stint (p. 207)	Red-necked Stint	Semipalmated Sandpiper	Western Sandpiper
Voice	"*stit-tit*"	"*kreet*"	Rolled "*tchrrp*"	Thin "*jeet*"
Toes	Unwebbed		Tiny webs	
Bill	Straight; fine tip	Straight; thick tip	Straight; 'blob' tip	Faintly curved; longer, finer tip than Semipalmated
Crown	dark centre, streaked sides	evenly streaked		
Eyestripe + cheek	EYESTRIPE: **forked** CHEEK: diffuse streaks	EYESTRIPE: rarely forked CHEEK: diffuse streaks	EYESTRIPE: unforked, bright CHEEK: **dark patch**	EYESTRIPE: unforked, strong, white CHEEK: diffuse streaks
Tertials	Blackish, edged rufous	Grey, edged off-white	Grey, edged buff	Grey-brown, edged whitish/buff
Primary project'n	**long**	medium	short	**very short**
Scapulars	CENTRES: dark, round EDGES: rufous-and-white	CENTRES: upper rows dark, round; lower rows pale; dark anchor shapes at tip	CENTRES: dark; blunt anchor shapes EDGES: **'scaly', whitish**	CENTRES: blackish; pointed anchor shapes EDGES: **bright rufous**
Breast	Buff-white, sides pale, few streaks	Grey-buff, extensive fine streaks	White or buff, sides greyer; streaked	Orange-buff wash, sides streaked
Back	White 'V'	Obscure 'V'	Obscure/no 'V'	Obscure 'V'

'PEEPS'

IN FLIGHT, all the rare dark-legged 'peeps' have a dark-centred rump and a thin white wingbar.

JUVENILE pale 'V' **LITTLE STINT**

JUVENILE **WESTERN SANDPIPER**

JUVENILE **SEMIPALMATED SANDPIPER**

JUVENILE **RED-NECKED STINT**

ADULT NON-BREEDING

DARK-LEGGED 'PEEPS'

See table opposite for summary of key features.

Western Sandpiper *Calidris mauri*
L 14–17 cm | W 27–29 cm

Vagrant from N America: <20 records (<10 Ireland), Jul–Nov. Freshwater, estuaries.

- evenly streaked cap
- rufous fringes
- JUVENILE AUG–OCT
- long, fine-tipped bill
- tiny web

Semipalmated Sandpiper
Calidris pusilla
L 13–15 cm | W 27–29 cm

ADULT [May] | ADULT [Dec]

Vagrant from N America: <350 records (<200 Ireland), most Sep–Oct. Freshwater, estuaries.

- evenly streaked cap
- JUVENILE AUG–OCT
- 'blob'-tipped bill
- tiny web

Red-necked Stint *Calidris ruficollis*
L 13–16 cm | W 28–30 cm

ADULT BREEDING [May]

Vagrant from Asia: <20 records (<5 Ireland), Jul–Sep. Marshes.

- call useful
- short bill
- elongated body, short legs
- JUVENILE AUG–OCT
- long wings but projection beyond tail short

235

RARE WADERS

PALE-LEGGED 'PEEPS'

Both rare pale-legged species have a pale 'V' on the back and grey sides to the tail.

Long-toed Stint *Calidris subminuta*
L 14–15·5 cm | W 27–29 cm

VOICE rippled *"chrrup"*; FORM **long-necked, tapered**; LEGS: long; TOES: long; HEAD PATTERN: CROWN rufous; STRIPE OVER EYE forked, falls short of bill; BETWEEN EYE AND BILL broken dark line; CHEEK PATCH isolated; BREAST greyish, streaks mostly on sides.

Vagrant from Asia (<5 records (1 Ireland): Jun, Aug; scattered). Marshes

Least Sandpiper *Calidris minutilla*
L 13–14·5 cm | W 27–28 cm

VOICE *"kreeet"*; FORM **chunky, squat**; LEGS: short; TOES: short; HEAD PATTERN: CROWN streaked rufous and black; STRIPE OVER EYE unforked, joins over bill BETWEEN EYE AND BILL: unbroken dark line; CHEEK PATCH reaches eye; BREAST streaked buff band.

Vagrant from N America: <60 records (<15 Ireland), Feb, May, Jul–Nov. Scattered. Waterside habitats.

Broad-billed Sandpiper
Calidris falcinellus
L 15–18 cm | W 34–37 cm

Small, short-legged, size between Dunlin (*p. 202*) and Little Stint (*p. 207*); often looks distinctively dark. Bill **thick at base, downward curve at tip**. Dark eyestripe; **white band above eye forks** in narrow 'V'. Head pattern weaker in winter; at other times well marked. ADULT BREEDING buff-white fringes on upperparts wear off to reveal dark brown with rufous edges; hint of pale 'V'. Breast streaked, belly white. Legs dark olive-grey. NON-BREEDING plainer, greyish; head pattern remains characteristic, but weaker. JUVENILE bright, striped black, rufous and cream above, flank mottled orange-buff. Legs yellowish or greenish.

VOICE Dry, upward buzz or trill, *"brrree-et"*.

Vagrant from N Europe: <300 records (<25 Ireland), Apr–Oct, most spring on E coast. Freshwater, estuaries.

JUVENILE AUG–OCT — long legs — elongated

ADULT [May]
ADULT [Nov]
JUVENILE
JUVENILE AUG–OCT — short legs — squat

IN FLIGHT, dark; very thin whitish wingbar blending into paler outerwing; broad, blackish rump with narrow white sides.

JUVENILE
strong head pattern
JUVENILE JUL–OCT
bill slightly kinked at tip
very dark above
dark streaks, white belly
ADULT BREEDING MAR–JUL
grey above
head pattern rather weak
1ST-WINTER AUG–MAR
NON-BREEDING ADULT has paler, more uniform covert

'PEEPS'/SANDPIPERS

White-rumped Sandpiper *Calidris fuscicollis*
L 16–18 cm | W 38–40 cm

Like long, sleek, short-legged, short-billed Dunlin (p. 202); legs black. ADULT NON-BREEDING greyish; scattered black-centred feathers above. JUVENILE colour/pattern resemble Little Stint (p. 207): white 'V' on back and stripe over eye; breast streaked, belly white (lacks dark marks and golden/buff of juvenile Dunlin).

IN FLIGHT, **white crescent across base of tail** (unlike 'peeps'); see Curlew Sandpiper (p. 205).

VOICE Call sharp, thin "*tjeet*."

Vagrant from N America: <500 records (<375 Ireland), 10–20 per year, most Aug–Oct. Freshwater, estuaries.

JUVENILE

JUVENILE

CURLEW SANDPIPER

grey replaces black-centred feathers after breeding

round, pale feather edges above

pale base

JUVENILE JUL–OCT

ADULT [Sep]

flank streaked

wings very long; extend beyond tail

DUNLIN

wings and tail ± equal

Baird's Sandpiper *Calidris bairdii*
L 14–17 cm | W 40–43 cm

Long, low, short-legged; similar to White-rumped Sandpiper but longer-winged. ADULT NON-BREEDING dull greyish-brown with a few black spots above. JUVENILE buffy (White-rumped Sandpiper greyer, but see also juvenile Dunlin (p. 202)); upperparts brownish with buff-white fringes (no white 'V'); streaked buff breast-band; white beneath.

VOICE Call purring "*prreet*."

IN FLIGHT, Dunlin-like; **dark-centred rump** rules out White-rumped Sandpiper.

dark flank marks

JUVENILE

JUVENILE

JUVENILE JUL–OCT

Vagrant from N America: <500 records (<200 Ireland), about 6 per year, all months, most Jul–Nov. Freshwater, estuaries.

broad pale 'scaly' edges above

bold dark spots above

ADULT [Jun]

flank plain

very short legs

wings very long; extend beyond tail

RARE WADERS

Pectoral Sandpiper *Calidris melanotos*
L 19–23 cm | W 43–47 cm

Usually larger than Dunlin (*p. 202*), smaller than Ruff (*p. 208*). **Streaked breast-band** against white belly. Legs **yellow-ochre** to greenish-yellow. Creeps or squats in wet vegetation, muddy areas or edges of reedbeds. Bill thick, medium-length, **faintly downcurved**, like Ruff, but pale at base. ADULT dull brownish above. JUVENILE rusty cap; brown above with **cream fringes** and **pale 'V'** (like juvenile Ruff); grey-buff, streaked brown, **ending sharply against white belly** (breast-band most distinctive seen head-on).

VOICE Call trilled "*krrrt*."

DUNLIN — obvious / faint
ADULT BREEDING

IN FLIGHT, dark-centred rump; thin white wingbar.

stout bill, slightly decurved; pale base

ADULT BREEDING MAR–AUG

pale 'V' on back

streaked breast against white belly

NON-BREEDING breast-band less boldly streaked

JUVENILE JUL–OCT

clean white belly below breast-band

yellowish legs

Vagrant from N America: 50–175 per year, Apr–Dec, most Jul–Nov. Scattered. Marshes.

Sharp-tailed Sandpiper
Calidris acuminata
L 17–21 cm | W 36–43 cm

Like Pectoral Sandpiper, pale-legged, but with **rufous cap**. ADULT BREEDING **orange-buff breast-band**; black spots extend into dark 'V'-shapes on flank and **dark streaks under tail**. ADULT NON-BREEDING/JUVENILE pale **buff to bright orange-buff** on breast, whiter in centre; dark streaks only on side and throat. **Rufous cap**.

VOICE High, short notes repeated, "*shilip-sheep-sheep-ip*."

Vagrant from Asia: <50 records (<10 Ireland), Jan, Apr, most Jul–Nov. Freshwater.

IN FLIGHT dark-centred rump; thin white wingbar.

rufous cap ADULT
spotted

bright rufous cap

JUVENILE JUL–OCT

breast streaks diffuse; no breast-band

ADULT BREEDING MAR–AUG

SANDPIPERS

Great Knot
Calidris tenuirostris
L 24–27 cm | W 58 cm

Like Knot (*p. 201*) with **longer, weightier bill**, smaller head and longer wings. ADULT BREEDING upperparts blackish with rusty-brown patches; **breast black**; rest of underparts **white, heavily spotted black**. ADULT NON-BREEDING dull, drab, greyish, more **spotted on breast** than Knot. JUVENILE dull grey, like Knot, but blackish spots above and darker grey-brown breast-band and flank spots.

VOICE Generally silent.

Vagrant from Asia: <10 records (1 Ireland), Jun–Oct. Estuaries.

IN FLIGHT, thin white wingbar, blackish 'wrist' patch and wingtips and **dark tail band** contrasting with **whitish rump**.

ADULT BREEDING

ADULT NON-BREEDING

breast-band may be streaked/spotted dark

ADULT NON-BREEDING AUG–MAR

JUVENILE JUL–OCT

ADULT BREEDING MAR–AUG

Stilt Sandpiper
Calidris himantopus
L 18–23 cm | W 38–47 cm

Like large Curlew Sandpiper (*p. 205*) or small dowitcher (*p. 245*) with **longer, greenish-yellow legs** and **thicker, slightly droop-tipped bill**. Long neck withdrawn or extended up and forward, bill angled down. ADULT BREEDING **underparts barred**; rufous cap and cheek patch. ADULT NON-BREEDING grey-and-white with dark grey-brown cap; soft grey flank streaks. JUVENILE brighter, pale fringes above ('scaly' effect).

VOICE Low, single "*whu*."

Vagrant from N America: <50 records (<20 Ireland), Apr–Nov, most Aug–Sep. Freshwater.

IN FLIGHT, weak wingbar; white rump.

JUVENILE

ADULT BREEDING MAR–AUG

rufous cheek

barred below

faintly downcurved bill

JUVENILE JUL–OCT

long pale legs

RARE WADERS

NT Buff-breasted Sandpiper
Calidris subruficollis
L 18–20 cm | W 43–47 cm

Like small (Dunlin-sized (*p. 202*)), rounded juvenile Ruff (*p. 208*): bright, clear buff; **small round head**; short dark bill; **mustard-yellow legs**. ADULT buffy-brown face, pale eyering; black-centred, buff-fringed feathers above; buff underparts with neat black spotting on breast sides. JUVENILE paler than adult with whitish fringes above.

> Vagrant from N America: 10–60/year (<500 records, Ireland), May–Jun, most Aug–Oct. Mainly grassland.

IN FLIGHT, long, pointed wings, plain above; **rump dark without white sides. Dark-edged white underwing** obvious.

ADULT

rather plain head

bright scaling above

ADULT

JUVENILE JUL–OCT

Nearly all British/Irish records are JUVENILES in autumn.

Upland Sandpiper
Bartramia longicauda
L 28–32 cm | W 50–55 cm

Small, pale wader with small head, long body, **longish tail, short, fine, yellow-based bill** and medium–short **yellow legs**. Black-brown cap with narrow pale central stripe visible when seen head-on; neatly marked cream feather edges and 'notches' on tertial fringes.

VOICE Usually silent.

> Vagrant from N America: <70 records (<15 Ireland), Apr–Dec, most Sep–Oct. Mostly on coast. Grassland.

IN FLIGHT, dark wing and rump.

ADULT

small head

JUVENILE JUL–OCT

bright yellow legs

Long, tapered shape; long tail (extends beyond wingtip)

Little Whimbrel
Numenius minutus
L 29–32 cm | W 57–63 cm

Like small, pale Whimbrel (*p. 219*) with paler face and shorter bill.

VOICE Flight call recalls Whimbrel but higher and thinner: a rising "*quip quip quip.*"

> Vagrant from Asia: <5 records (Britain), Aug–Sep. Grassland.

IN FLIGHT, **dark rump**.

ADULT

ADULT

> **PE** Eskimo Curlew *Numenius borealis* from N America [*not illustrated*] has been recorded as a vagrant (<5 historical records Britain, 1 Ireland; last 1887), but is now possibly extinct.

SNIPE | GRASSLAND WADERS

NT Great Snipe
Gallinago media
L 26–30 cm | W 43–50 cm

Large snipe; bill a little shorter and thicker than Snipe's (*p. 222*). Difficult to find, see and identify; migrants often in drier areas than Snipe (but tired Snipe can appear anywhere). ADULT coarsely marked: 'marbled' effect, with 'loopy' **white tips to wing coverts**. Long, crescentic **bars across flank and under belly** (compare with Snipe). JUVENILE stripes above and bars below all narrower than on adult.

VOICE Short insignificant "*brad*" and rush of wings on rising.

Very rare migrant/vagrant from N Europe: <800 records (<25 Ireland), mainly Sep–Nov, few Mar–Apr. Widespread, most N and E coasts. Marshes, rushy ground.

IN FLIGHT, **blackish midwing panel, edged white** each side, extending to leading edge around primary coverts; weak white trailing edge. Head/neck held quite straight. Spreads tail to reveal large triangular **white corners** (slightly less white on juvenile).

white-edged dark panel — no white edge
SNIPE
barred — white

JUVENILE JUL–OCT
white tips to wing coverts

SNIPE TAIL FEATHERS

SNIPE	GREAT SNIPE
SNIPE 14 (12–18) feathers, narrow white tips	GREAT SNIPE 16 (14–18) feathers, **outer four white** (adult), **white with dark bars** (juvenile)

SNIPE vs. WILSON'S SNIPE
Outer tail feather with:
2–3 dark bars = **Snipe**;
4+ bars = **Wilson's Snipe**/a few Snipe

Wilson's Snipe
Gallinago delicata
L 23–28 cm | W 41–44 cm

Very like Snipe (*p. 222*); ideally requires close views/photographs of raised wing and tail to assess fine details (see insets).

VOICE Calls "*scaipe*" when flushed.

Vagrant from N America: <15 records (1 Ireland), Sep–Nov. Coastal marshes.

SNIPE
1ST-WINTER AUG–MAR

SNIPE — mostly white — slightly broader
AXILLARIES: **dark < white**

WILSON'S SNIPE — extensive black barring — slightly narrower
AXILLARIES: **dark ≥ white**

Compared to **Snipe**, **Wilson's Snipe** has thicker dark bars on axillaries, a darker, more extensively barred underwing, and a slightly narrower white trailing edge.

1ST-WINTER AUG–MAR

RARE WADERS

Spotted Sandpiper
Actitis macularius
L 18–20 cm | W 37–40 cm

Very like Common Sandpiper (p. 215) – see table for structure and plumage differences. Behaviourally, Spotted Sandpiper typically adopts a more crouched posture, creeping on flexed legs and bobbing the head and tail more than Common Sandpiper.

Vagrant from N America: <250 records (50 Ireland), 4–5 per year, mostly Sep–Mar. Freshwater, coasts.

Spotted / Common Sandpipers – comparison of key features		
	Common Sandpiper (p. 215)	**Spotted Sandpiper**
Structure	Attenuated body, long tail	Rounded body, **short tail**
Voice	Spotted Sandpiper can be similar to Common Sandpiper but less ringing; often gives a sharp, short, whistled "*peet*" or "*pit-wit*," which Common Sandpiper does not.	
Legs	Greenish to brownish-yellow	**yellow** to **pale yellowish**
Breeding	UNDERPARTS: plain	UNDERPARTS: **spotted**
Non-breeding	**Best identified on structure/call**: Spotted Sandpiper typically has a bolder eyestripe, greyer/plainer breast and unmarked tertial edges (hard to see)	
Juvenile	TERTIALS: edges with pale spots GREATER COVERTS: all barred BILL: usually all-dark	TERTIALS: **edges plain** GREATER COVERTS: barring **on tips** BILL: grey-pink with dark tip

ADULT BREEDING MAR–AUG — weak wingbar on innerwing; dark secondaries with white trailing edge create 'speculum' effect — less white in tail than Common Sandpiper

strong wingbar on innerwing — BREEDING

COMMON SANDPIPER — JUVENILE — long tail — darkish bill — greenish legs — pale spots on edges — TERTIALS

BREEDING ADULTS are unmistakably (albeit variably) spotted black beneath.

JUVENILE → 1ST-WINTER JUL–OCT [Oct] — short tail — bolder eyestripe — pale bill — greyer/plainer breast sides — yellow legs — plain edges — TERTIALS

Terek Sandpiper
Xenus cinereus
L 22–25 cm | W 32–35 cm

548

Like large, greyish Common Sandpiper (p. 215) with hunched neck and **long upcurved bill**. Short, **orange-yellow legs**. ADULT BREEDING grey-brown, dark band beside back. ADULT NON-BREEDING plainer, paler, greyer, bright white below. JUVENILE greyish above with paler fringes.

VOICE Fluty "*dududududu*."

Vagrant from Asia: <100 records (<10 Ireland), Apr–Nov, rare winter. Freshwater, estuaries.

IN FLIGHT, grey rump, broad **white trailing edge to wing** behind black stripe; see Redshank (p. 210).

ADULT BREEDING

JUVENILE JUL–OCT

ADULT BREEDING MAR–AUG

SPOTTED / TEREK | TRINGA

Marsh Sandpiper
Tringa stagnatilis
L 22–25 cm | W 55–59 cm

Like small, delicately built Greenshank (p. 212); clearly slighter overall, with long, slender legs (approaching stilt-like effect) and **fine, straight, dark bill**. Important to compare size with other waders. ADULT BREEDING clearly spotted black on buff. ADULT NON-BREEDING dark cap, white stripe over eye, less streaked/spotted. JUVENILE has broad buff fringes on upperpart feathers.

VOICE Call important for identification: "*kyew*" or "*kyu-kyu-kyu*," higher, quicker, weaker than Greenshank.

Vagrant from Asia: <150 records (<10 Ireland), Apr–Dec, mostly Apr–Aug. Widespread.

Solitary Sandpiper
Tringa solitaria
L 18–21 cm | W 50 cm

Like smallish, delicate Green Sandpiper (p. 214) with **bolder white eyering**, more tapered rear-end.

VOICE High-pitched "*peet-weet-weet*."

Vagrant from N America: <50 records (<10 Ireland), May–Nov, mostly Aug–Oct. Freshwater/brackish marshes.

Grey-tailed Tattler
Tringa brevipes
L 23–27 cm | W 51 cm

Medium-sized, slender, elongated grey wader, most like Redshank (p. 210) in shape, with colours of non-breeding Knot (p. 201); dark bill, **yellow legs**. Whitish line over eye and **thick black eyestripe**, both widest in front of eye.

VOICE Piping, melancholy "*tweet-weet*."

Vagrant from Asia: <5 records (Britain), Oct–Dec. Estuaries.

---

fine, straight, dark bill

GREENSHANK
thick-based, upturned, two-toned bill
1ST-WINTER

ADULT NON-BREEDING

IN FLIGHT, pattern like Greenshank with **dark wings**, even longer **thin white triangle** up back; toes project farther beyond tail.

needle-fine bill

plain above

pale fringes

ADULT NON-BREEDING
AUG–MAR

black chequers

streaks and spots on breast
ADULT BREEDING
MAR–AUG

long, greenish legs

JUVENILE →
1ST-WINTER
JUL–MAR
[Sep]

ADULT NON-BREEDING

GREEN SANDPIPER
eyering less distinct
JUVENILE

IN FLIGHT, plain wings; **grey rump and tail**.

1ST-WINTER
AUG–MAR

JUVENILE
JUL–OCT

IN FLIGHT, plain wings, **dark rump**.

JUVENILE
AUG–OCT

NON-BREEDING
AUG–MAR

RARE WADERS

See Redshank (p. 210), Greenshank (p. 212), Wood Sandpiper (p. 213)

Rare American waders: Yellowlegs

The two yellowlegs are difficult to separate: both are told from Redshank by the **plain, dark upperwing** and from Greenshank by the **square white rump**; both have clearly **yellow legs** (Redshank sometimes yellowish-orange, Greenshank often yellowish-green). Wood Sandpiper is smaller, with a bolder head pattern and shorter wings (wingtips project beyond tail to variable extent in both yellowlegs). Adult yellowlegs in breeding plumage are easier to identify than non-breeding adults and juveniles (most likely in Britain and Ireland). Size comparison with nearby waders, bill shape and colour, and calls are essential features for safe identification.

Calls at-a-glance	
Redshank (p. 210)	Ringing "*tyew yew-yew,*" fading away
Greenshank (p. 212)	Loud, even-pitched "*teuw-teuw-teuw*"
Lesser Yellowlegs	1–4 squeaky notes, "*teu deu*" or "*tchew*"
Greater Yellowlegs	As Greenshank: loud, quick "*tyu-tyu-tyu*"

REDSHANK   **LESSER YELLOWLEGS**   **GREATER YELLOWLEGS**   **GREENSHANK**

Vagrant from N America: <500 records (<200 Ireland), most Aug–Dec. Widespread. Freshwater, estuaries.

Vagrant from N America: <50 records (<20 Ireland), most Apr–Nov. Widespread. Freshwater, estuaries.

Lesser Yellowlegs *Tringa flavipes*
L 23–25 cm | W 65–67 cm

Bill rather **short**, fine, straight, **all-dark** (JUVENILE base yellowish). Wingtip may extend well beyond tail. ADULT BREEDING grey-brown, spangled buff-white above; breast streaked; belly white. NON-BREEDING plainer and greyer. JUVENILE breast streaks blurred and diffuse.

ADULT BREEDING MAR–AUG   bill slightly longer than head

flank scarcely marked

Greater Yellowlegs *Tringa melanoleuca*
L 29–33 cm | W 65–70 cm

Bill rather **long** (longer than head), slightly **upturned**, thicker base **pale grey**. Wingtip usually extends just beyond tail. ADULT BREEDING upperparts spotted, flank barred. JUVENILE/NON-BREEDING fine, distinct black-brown streaks on breast; underparts white.

BREEDING MAR–AUG   bill longer than head

flank strongly barred

1ST-WINTER AUG–MAR

wingtip projection beyond tail variable, usually short

JUVENILE JUL–OCT

wingtip projection beyond tail variable, may be long

BEHAVIOUR picks food from surface, rarely wades deeply.

BEHAVIOUR submerges head and bill when feeding, often wades belly deep.

YELLOWLEGS | DOWITCHERS

Rare American waders: Dowitchers

Dowitchers are like an over-sized Knot (p. 201), with a long, Snipe-like (p. 222) bill and longer greenish legs. Both the rare Long-billed Dowitcher (**LBD**) and very rare Short-billed Dowitcher (**SBD**) have a strong head pattern and, **IN FLIGHT**, a dark upperwing with a whitish trailing edge and a **long white triangle** or oval on the lower back/rump. They are extremely difficult to separate: bill length varies with age and sex, with much overlap; tail pattern (relative width of black and white bars) also overlaps; they are best distinguished by a suite of features including the flight call.

Dowitcher calls

LBD – sharp, abrupt "*ip*," "*eeep*," "*peep*" and bubbly notes

SBD – short, quick, 2–4 even-pitched calls: "*sdeu-du-du*," "*chuchu-do-do*"

Long-billed Dowitcher
Limnodromus scolopaceus
L 27–30 cm | W 48–50 cm

Vagrant from N America: <400 records (<150 Ireland), most Sep–Oct, few Apr–May. Mostly coastal. Freshwater, saltmarsh.

TAIL BARS: **black > white**

SCAPULARS: neat, rusty fringes/'notches'

TERTIALS: plain dark grey with narrow, pale/rusty fringes

JUVENILE JUL–OCT

Short-billed Dowitcher
Limnodromus griseus
L 25–29 cm | W 48–50 cm

Vagrant from N America: <10 records (<5 Ireland), Mar–Nov. Coast. Freshwater, estuaries.

TAIL BARS: **black < white**

SCAPULARS: irregular markings

TERTIALS: dark with rufous bars/blotches; rufous/buff fringes

JUVENILE JUL–OCT

JUVENILES: TERTIAL + SCAPULAR: **pattern and colour**

ADULT BREEDING MAR–AUG

COVERTS short, square buff tips

BREAST SIDE rufous with **dark spots**

UNDERPARTS **rufous**

ADULT BREEDING MAR–AUG

COVERTS long, curved buff edges

BREAST SIDE rufous with **dark bars**

UNDERPARTS **whitish**

ADULT BREEDING: UNDERPARTS: **colour** | BREAST SIDE: **shape of markings**

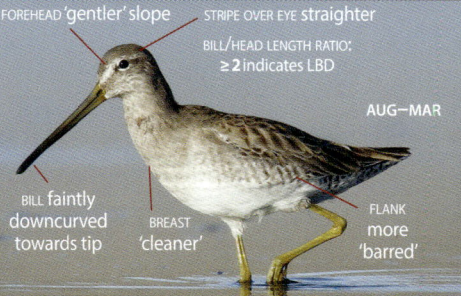

FOREHEAD 'gentler' slope STRIPE OVER EYE straighter

BILL/HEAD LENGTH RATIO: ≥ **2** indicates LBD

AUG–MAR

BILL faintly downcurved towards tip

BREAST 'cleaner'

FLANK more 'barred'

FOREHEAD steeper slope STRIPE OVER EYE more arched

BILL/HEAD LENGTH RATIO: ≈ **1·5** indicates SBD

AUG–MAR

BILL ± thicker, usually more downcurved

BREAST 'dirtier'

FLANK more 'chevroned'

NON-BREEDING: Plumages near-identical – best identified by call and a suite of comparative features as shown above, although these are variable and individuals may have mixed features; as such, they are only indicative of species.

CRAKES and RAILS

CRAKE and RAIL ID   form | bill shape/colour | leg colour | undertail and flank patterns

Long-toed, short-billed, mostly waterside or water birds, often secretive, quick to run for cover (less likely to fly).
12 species: 5 breed, of which only 3 are widespread; 7 rare vagrants.

Coot and **Moorhen** are familiar water or waterside birds, **Water Rail** is widespread but far less well known. Other crakes, including summer visiting **Corncrake**, which breeds in northern Scotland and Ireland, are rare and difficult to see.

Coot (*p. 249*) is like a blackish duck with a white bill and bare facial shield (juvenile also has white on the face and neck). Social, noisy, quarrelsome at times, either on open water or grazing on short grass. Winter flocks can be large, recalling wildfowl. Low-tailed, round-backed, and often dives underwater; surface-feeding ducks often associate with Coots.

Moorhen (*p. 248*) (a 'gallinule') less often out on open water, more likely in ones and twos, but sometimes up to 50 or so in loose groups on open ground, frequently in ditches and reedy channels or along riversides – even up in waterside bushes. Diagnostic white flank stripe; swims with cocked tail (revealing big patch of white each side) and bobbing head, much less round-backed than Coot.

Water Rail (*p. 250*) generally keeps out of sight in dense waterside vegetation, but comes out into the open beside ditches and muddy spots, even on woodland pools under trees, or in icy weather: look for the long, slim bill.

Corncrake is very secretive and usually only a voice from deep within a hay crop: the loud, ratchet-like double call is unmistakable, but seeing the bird is difficult and requires much patience.

Crake ageing/sexing

Sexes similar, except in some crakes. Juveniles are usually distinguishable but become increasingly like adults by their first winter, with duller bill colours.

COOT

MOORHEN

Moorhens and Coots habitually swim, but look rather different on land: Coots upright, Moorhens often more crouched.

WATER RAIL

SPOTTED CRAKE

Rare crakes are difficult to detect in their densely vegetated habitats, and are often best located by their characteristic songs at night.

Corncrake *Crex crex*

L 27–30 cm | W 42–53 cm

Fairly small, secretive crake with short bill. Heard more often than seen, usually from hay crop or patches of irises and/or nettles, often beside fences/stone walls.

ADULT pale yellowish-brown, streaked blackish; **flank barred rufous and grey**; **spread wing rufous**. Face and breast **bluish-grey** (greyest on MALE), overall greyer or rusty according to angle of view. JUVENILE like adult but narrower pale fringes above; sides of head, foreneck and breast buff-brown, less grey; legs grey.

VOICE Unique, rhythmic, dry, rasping double "*crairk-crairk*," with open bill, head thrown upwards; calls at any time, but especially after dark (sounds like a loud, hard rattle at close range).

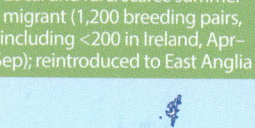

Local and rare/scarce summer migrant (1,200 breeding pairs, including <200 in Ireland, Apr–Sep); reintroduced to East Anglia

Hay fields, iris and nettle beds

IN FLIGHT, low, quick; quite slender but rounded rufous wings; head outstretched, legs trailing.

MALE may stand upright, especially if singing, sometimes on a on rock or wall, but more typically hidden in dense vegetation, such as an iris bed.

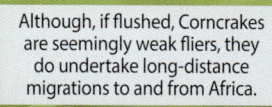

Although, if flushed, Corncrakes are seemingly weak fliers, they do undertake long-distance migrations to and from Africa.

ADULT

black streaks above; rusty wing patch

ADULT

CRAKES and RAILS

Moorhen *Gallinula chloropus*

L 30–38 cm | W 55–60 cm

👁 Purple Gallinule, Allen's Gallinule (*p. 254*)

Medium-sized dark, rounded 'rail' that moves with a creeping, springy action on longish legs and toes with head held low and well forward; **bobs head** rhythmically when swimming, tail raised. Typically in water/waterside habitats, scuttling off if disturbed (half run/half flight) but often feeds on open grass, sometimes in loose groups (not flocks as Coot), occasionally in bushes.

Sexes alike. ADULT very dark: back brown, head and underparts blue-grey; long **white patch under tail** and **white flank stripe**. Unique **red-and-yellow bill**. Legs green with red 'garter'. JUVENILE paler brown with whitish throat; similar white flank stripe and patch under tail. Bill dull olive-brown. By Nov, like adult with dark bill.

VOICE Varied, typically bubbling, explosive "*kurrt;*" also abrupt "*ki-yek*" and "*krek-krek-krek*" call (often in flight at night).

Common resident, particularly in the lowlands (240,000 pairs; 320,000 in winter)

All kinds of waterside habitats

Often runs across water surface on long, slender toes.

IN FLIGHT, low, brief, with wings lifted high on upbeat, legs dangling; not usually seen in higher, full flight by day (migrates at night).

ADULT

Equally likely to be well-hidden in dense, wet vegetation.

JUVENILE
MAY–OCT

white beside tail

white streaks on flank

red facial shield

wingtips/tail raised

ADULT

big white patch under tail

248

MOORHEN | COOT

Coot *Fulica atra*

NT

L 36–39 cm | W 70–80 cm

👁 **American Coot** (p.252)

Common resident (25,000 pairs), migrant, winter visitor (190,000 on larger waters/coasts)

Large, rounded, greyish-black, social 'rail'; rather duck-like on water. More strictly a water bird than Moorhen, but feeds on adjacent grassy places. Black at distance: when swimming, **back rounded, high at rear**, but tail low. Dives frequently. May be puzzling in unexpected places, *e.g.* occasionally on sea. Flocks may number hundreds (Moorhens few, more scattered). Less agile than Moorhen; stands more upright, body more rounded, on thicker legs set well back.

Sexes alike. ADULT all slaty-black, blackest on head; **white facial shield and bill** striking at great range. Legs grey. JUVENILE grey-black, **dull white lower face and breast** (like non-breeding grebes (*pp. 86–89*)).

VOICE Loud, sudden "*kowk!*" and various sharp, metallic notes. Young have feeble but far-carrying whistles.

from NE Europe

Often runs across water on flat, broadly lobed toes.

IN FLIGHT, heavy, clumsy, lacks manoeuvrability; broad wing has pale trailing edge. Disturbed flocks may circle over lake, some birds often 'collapsing' onto nearby land.

Lakes, pools, reservoirs, rivers, marshes, coastal waters

ADULT

Typically looks heavy and clumsy, with rounded, small-headed shape on land.

white face and breast

JUVENILE MAY–OCT

big white facial shield

wingtips/tail held low

ADULT

no white under tail

CRAKES and RAILS

Water Rail *Rallus aquaticus*

L 23–26 cm | W 38–45 cm

Small, round, long-billed rail; compressed and slender end-on, creeps through dense reeds and waterside vegetation. Usually heard more than seen; secretive walk and scuttling run, or short, fast flight to cover. Sometimes more in the open during cold weather/towards dusk.

Sexes alike. ADULT appears dark unless close up or in bright light. Back brown, streaked black; sides of head and **breast slate-grey**; throat unmarked grey. At close range, flank **barred black-and-white**; white-tipped **buff patch under short, raised tail**. **Bill long, red-based**; legs pink. JUVENILE breast, chin, stripe over eye buff or whitish, head mostly brown; bill mostly blackish with orange-pink at base. 1ST-WINTER like adult but some have buff streaks on face, whitish or buff throat; juvenile wing feathers very worn by Feb/Mar.

VOICE Piglet squeals, moaning and repeated loud, short, Blackbird-like "*kip;*" song an accelerating series of short notes, often at night.

Scarce resident (1,100 pairs); fairly common winter visitor (10,000+)

from N and E Europe

Watersides, dense sedge/reed/fen, riverside thickets, woodland ponds, wet ditches

IN FLIGHT, quite small, narrow wings, slender head/bill outstretched and legs dangling; white mark under leading edge of wing (may also be visible in open-winged run to cover).

1ST-WINTER SEP–MAR

JUVENILE JUN–DEC

ADULT

ADULT

rounded profile with pointed tail and long, spike-like bill

Spotted Crake *Porzana porzana*

CRAKES and RAILS

546

L 19–22·5 cm | W 37–42 cm

👁 Sora (*p. 253*), other rare crakes (*pp. 252–253*)

Small, squat, rounded, dark grey-brown, **short-billed** crake, combining overall impression of Water Rail with short bill of Moorhen (*p. 248*) but smaller and harder to see than either. Typically secretive in its wetland habitat but not necessarily shy: patience may be rewarded if a bird walks onto open mud.

Sexes alike. ADULT breast spotted white, flank barred. Prominent buff patch under tail. Bill short, straight, stout, **red at base**. **Legs green** (pink on Water Rail). JUVENILE/1ST-WINTER like adult but generally duller; bill dark with yellowish base until Feb.

VOICE Sings at night, a sharp, upslurred whistle ending in 'whiplash' or dripping effect, repeated endlessly.

IN FLIGHT, white leading edge to wing catches eye in brief whirring rise from waterside cover before bird 'collapses' out of sight.

Rare, erratic summer visitor (25 breeding pairs) and autumn migrant (25–50 per year); declining

Wetlands, coastal pools

JUVENILE JUN–SEP

Round body, large feet and plumage pattern indicate a rail or crake.

1ST-WINTER SEP–MAR

dull bill

white spots on brown breast

ADULT

rounded profile; short bill

wavy bars on flank

bright bill

white spots on grey breast

RARE CRAKES

American Coot
Fulica americana
L 34–43 cm | W 58–71 cm

Very similar to Coot (*p. 249*). Greyish-black with **white undertail coverts**; white bill has **dark band** near tip and purple patch on small 'shield'; black face **rounded** against bill (Coot has dark undertail coverts, all-white bill and a sharp black point between the bill and facial shield).

Vagrant from N America: <20 records (<5 Ireland), Nov–Apr. Scattered. Wetlands.

COOT — sharp black point

no obvious facial shield, rounded face against bill

dark band on bill

white under tail

Rare crakes

Little Crake
Porzana (Zapornia) parva
L 17–19 cm | W 34–39 cm

546

Very small (sparrow-sized) crake of reedbeds/fen and open water in ditches and pools. Has sharply defined patterns close up, but looks 'dull and dark' in a brief glimpse. **Primary projection (beyond tertials) rather long**. Pale crescentic streak on upper edge of tertials beside often **cocked tail**. **Short bill** green with **red base**; **legs green**. MALE upperparts brown with dark stripes and a few small white marks; underparts **blue-slate**. FEMALE pale buff-brown, streaked black on back. JUVENILE flank barred; white spots on back; little red on bill.

Vagrant from E Europe: >100 records (<5 Ireland, historical), autumn and spring, most Mar–May. Scattered. Marshes.

long wings and tail

minute red gape

JUVENILE JUN–DEC

ADULT ♀

bright buff beneath

both sexes with red on bill

ADULT ♂

clean grey beneath

CRAKES | COOTS

Baillon's Crake
Porzana (Zapornia) pusilla
L 16–18 cm | W 33–37 cm
546

Very small (sparrow-sized), rounded crake; on mud or in waterside vegetation. Dark, but detailed patterning distinctive close up. **Primary projection (beyond tertials) short.** No pale crescent on tertials. **Bill green (no red).** ADULT sexes alike (but FEMALE may have white zigzag bars on scapulars): back brown, with black streaks and narrow **white lines and spots**; underparts grey, **rear flank barred black-and-white**. Eye bright red. Legs pinkish to dull greenish. JUVENILE brown, with pale spots/streaks; bill dull yellow-green; legs pinkish/ochre.

VOICE Spring call at night, a low, dry rattle, 1–2 seconds.

> Vagrant from E Europe: <100 records (<5 Ireland), all months, most Jun–Aug. Scattered; has bred. Marshes.

Labels on images: short wings; JUVENILE JUN–DEC; no red on bill; barred flank; ADULT; green bill

Sora (Rail) *Porzana carolina*
L 18–21 cm | W 35–40 cm

Very similar to Spotted Crake (*p. 251*). At all ages, tertials (cloaking closed wingtips) **plain brown with darker centre** (Spotted Crake tertials have broad buff upper edge and several wavy white lines across). Sexes alike. ADULT **brown above, grey below, flank barred white; bill yellow** (no red); **black face/throat patch** extensive, sharply defined and extended into short bib (smaller, duller, more blurred or absent on Spotted Crake). JUVENILE/1ST-WINTER has almost **plain grey-brown breast** (Spotted Crake has white spots), **brownish crown with thin black central streak** (evenly streaked black on Spotted Crake).

> Vagrant from N America: <30 records (<5 Ireland), Aug–Apr. Scattered, most near coast. Marshes.

Labels on images: SPOTTED CRAKE; tertials plain, no barring; tertials barred; ADULT; dusky/blackish face; 1ST-WINTER SEP–MAR

Rare gallinules

Allen's Gallinule
Porphyrio alleni
L 22–25 cm | W 48–52 cm

Sexes alike. ADULT (not recorded) like small, green-backed, violet-breasted Moorhen (p. 248) with red legs and dark red bill with bluish frontal shield. JUVENILE greenish-brown with buff feather edges (wear off) and **buff undertail coverts** (white on Purple Gallinule); **bill and legs reddish-brown**; attains adult-like plumage during first year.

Vagrant from N Africa: <5 records (Britain) (immatures), Jan–Mar. Scattered. Marshes.

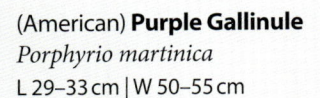

(American) Purple Gallinule
Porphyrio martinica
L 29–33 cm | W 50–55 cm

Sexes alike. ADULT (not recorded) like green-backed, blue-bodied Moorhen (p. 248) with yellow legs and red-and-yellow bill with blue frontal shield. JUVENILE buffy-tan with greenish back; plain white undertail coverts, without central dark band of Moorhen (buff on Allen's Gallinule); bill dull with dull blue frontal shield; legs yellowish; attains adult-like plumage in first winter.

Vagrant from N America: <5 records (1 Ireland) (immatures), Apr/May, Nov, Jan, Feb. Scattered. Marshes.

Western Swamphen
(Purple Gallinule)
Porphyrio porphyrio
L 38–50 cm | WS 90–100 cm

Like giant bluish Moorhen (p. 248) with bright blue face and throat; white patch beneath tail; big red bill and facial shield; legs and long toes red. Sexes alike.

Vagrant from S Europe: 1 record (Britain), Jul–Jan. Marshes/wetland.

LARGE WATERSIDE BIRDS

TYPE ID size | bill size, shape and colour | flight shape, especially neck / underside pattern

All are water or waterside birds, some conspicuous, others extremely skulking.
8 herons: one widespread, two rare migrants, others vagrants.
4 bitterns: one scarce, one rare migrant, two vagrants.
4 egrets: one widespread, two colonizing, others vagrants.
1 spoonbill: migrant and winter visitor to SW England; rare breeder E England
2 cranes: 1 localized breeder and scarce migrant, one extreme vagrant (also escapes).
2 storks: both rare migrants.
1 ibis: rare migrant, increasing.

Herons (pp. 260, 266–270), **bitterns** (pp. 261, 267, 270), **egrets** (pp. 262–264) Very large to fairly small with a dagger-like bill. Herons grey/brown/buff wings; bitterns predominantly brown; egrets white. In flight, wings arched, neck curled back.

Spoonbill (p. 259) Large, white, with unique spatulate bill. In flight, wings slightly arched, neck straight.

Cranes (pp. 258, 270) Very large, upright with relatively small head and bill; 'bush' of drooping feathers over tail. In flight, wings flat, neck straight.

Storks (p. 265) Very large, black-and-white with heavy, dagger-like, red bill. In flight, wings flat, neck straight.

Ibis (p. 266) Glossy Ibis, large, very dark, with decurved bill. In flight, long and skinny with rounded wings, straight neck.

Waterbird ageing/sexing

Sexes similar (except Little Bittern). Juveniles generally duller than adults but in some species (*e.g.* Bittern) not obvious. Larger species (*e.g.* Grey Heron) have intermediate immature stages.

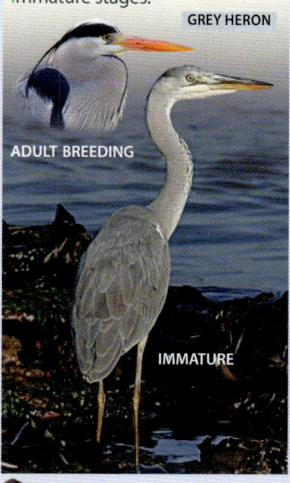

GREY HERON
ADULT BREEDING
IMMATURE

GLOSSY IBIS | LITTLE EGRET | SPOONBILL | WHITE STORK | CRANE | GREY HERON | BITTERN

NB Great White Egret is the same size as Grey Heron

Groups of Little Egrets have become widespread and frequent in recent decades.

LARGE WATERSIDE BIRDS

Large waterside birds in flight

HERONS AND EGRETS
(pp. 260–270)
Neck curled back; large bill

STORKS
(p. 265)
Neck outstretched; large bill

CRANES
(pp. 258, 270)
Neck outstretched; small bill

GLOSSY IBIS
(p. 266)
ADULT

LITTLE BITTERN
(p. 267)
ADULT ♀
ADULT ♂

NIGHT-HERON
(p. 267)
JUVENILE
ADULT
ADULT

BITTERN
(p. 261)

GREY HERON
(p. 260)
ADULT

PURPLE HERON
(p. 266)
JUVENILE
ADULT

LARGE WATERSIDE BIRDS IN FLIGHT

WHITE STORK — ADULT

CRANE — ADULT

CRANE (p. 258) — ADULT

BLACK STORK (p. 265) — ADULT

WHITE STORK (p. 265) — ADULT

GREAT WHITE EGRET (p. 263) — ADULT

SPOONBILL (p. 259) — JUVENILE / ADULT

LITTLE EGRET (p. 262) — ADULT

CATTLE EGRET (p. 264) — ADULT

SQUACCO HERON (p. 268) — ADULT

257

LARGE WATERSIDE BIRDS • Large waterside birds in flight *p.256*

Crane *Grus grus*

L 96–119 cm | W 180–222 cm   Sandhill Crane (*p.270*)

Rare and local resident, mostly E and S Britain, reintroduced SW (50 pairs); erratic migrant; (<250 records Ireland)

Huge, upstanding waterside bird, mainly associated with marshy wetlands but sometimes on drier ground. Flies with **legs and head outstretched**, on **flat wings** (unlike any heron).

ADULT pale grey (back often stained brown); **black-tipped 'bustle'** (tertials overlap wingtips and tail). Black face and throat, **white nape**, red crown. JUVENILE/IMMATURE has plain grey-brown head.

VOICE Loud, ringing or jarring "*krroo.*"

IN FLIGHT, wingtips, trailing edge smoky black (Grey Heron (*p.260*) pattern). Heavy-bellied; thick foreparts taper into outstretched neck; wings broad, straight, tips upcurved. Migrant flocks (very rare in Britain) form long chevrons or 'V's.

Marshes, open meadows, floods

ADULT

ADULT

JUVENILE JUL–MAR

Spoonbill *Platalea leucorodia*

L 80–93 cm | W 120–135 cm

Large, white waterside bird; wades more actively than herons, heavier and thicker-legged than more elegant egrets. Stands in shallows (or on tree), head tucked back when sleeping; feeds by marching slowly with long strides, **open bill swept from side to side** through water. Colonial breeder, sometimes in small groups outside breeding season.

ADULT **white**, with yellow chin and yellow-buff breast. Spiky white **crest**, drooped, raised or blown aside in wind. Legs black. Bill unique in Europe: long, black, with broad, **rounded, flat, yellow tip**. JUVENILE drab white, with **black spots on wingtip**; bill pink. 1ST-YEAR bill dark with pink underside.

VOICE Silent.

IN FLIGHT vaguely swan-like (but much smaller, with quicker wing action); neck outstretched, long legs trail; wingbeats faster, stiffer than egrets.

Scarce spring/autumn migrant, rare breeder (<25 pairs, recently established); (<300 records Ireland). Winter visitor (40–50) on S and E coasts; rare inland. Lakes, marshes, estuaries

Lagoons, estuaries, lakes

JUVENILE — black wingtips

ADULT

On 1ST-WINTER, bill blackish without yellow tip, but pale beneath.

JUVENILE JUL–MAR

ADULT

yellow-buff on neck and bushy crest most obvious Mar–Jul

LARGE WATERSIDE BIRDS   Large waterside birds in flight p.256

Grey Heron *Ardea cinerea*

L 84–102 cm | W 155–175 cm

👁 Purple Heron (p. 266), Great Blue Heron (p. 269)

Common resident, occasional migrant (14,000 pairs in Britain and Ireland, >60,000 winter)

Large, pale **grey**, long-legged, **long-necked** heron; usually at waterside, often wading in shallow water but can also be seen on drier ground or in trees. Bill dagger-like; neck withdrawn into shoulders or extended, forward-leaning or with 'double bend' allowing sudden lunge.

ADULT pale grey; blackish 'shoulder'/flank; **white head** with **black band above eye** to thin crest; neck may be faintly pinkish with black spots on front. Bill yellow; legs yellow-brown. ADULT BREEDING (Feb–May) has orange/pink-red bill and pale plumes on back. JUVENILE/1ST-WINTER head grey, dark streaks on neck.

VOICE Loud, harsh or more trumpeting "*fraank!*" and "*shraaah.*" At nest, rhythmic bill clattering, croaks, grunts and challenging screams.

All kinds of watersides. Breeds mainly in treetop colonies

ADULT BREEDING

IN FLIGHT, flight feathers smoky grey-black, forewing pale; white patch on leading edge. **Neck withdrawn** (may briefly be stretched out), legs trailed. Wings very broad, **strongly arched**. Capable of high soaring, and steep, twisting descents to nest, usually in treetop.

black crown stripes

pale neck

bill brighter, neck flushed pinkish-grey, in spring

ADULT BREEDING FEB–MAY

no trace of brown

dull head and bill

ADULT NON-BREEDING APR–FEB

grey neck

JUVENILE JUN–MAR

legs greyish

HERON | BITTERN

Bittern *Botaurus stellaris*

L 69–81 cm | W 100–130 cm

👁 American Bittern (p. 270)

Large, **brown**, heron-like; remarkably **cryptic** in reedbeds, where hard to see as creeps through dense vegetation, occasionally visible in thin patches or crossing open ditch. Walks in low crouch with springy action; shimmers body from side to side. Stands still for long periods, bill often raised skywards.

Sexes and ages look similar. **Yellowish tawny-brown**, marked with black/brown all over (just like winter reedbed); some more rufous, others more yellowish. Black cap and streak from bill; long dark stripes down foreneck. Legs green.

VOICE Spring call of male unmistakable 'boom' – loud, very deep, "*ah-whump!*"

IN FLIGHT, wings broad, arched; pale band on coverts. Head hunched back in thick 'wedge'.

Scarce and local breeder (200 males) and winter visitor (800); (<250 records Ireland, Oct–Mar).

from N and C Europe

Extensive reedbeds; smaller marshy areas in winter

legs and huge feet light green

Often senses/searches for fish with bill tip immersed; may squat or raise neck remarkably high. Severely affected by icing, as unable to feed, so forced to move elsewhere during very hard weather.

LARGE WATERSIDE BIRDS

Little Egret *Egretta garzetta*

L 55–65 cm | W 88–106 cm

Cattle Egret (p.264), Little Blue Heron (p.269), Snowy Egret (p.269)

Increasing resident, wanderer; spreading inland and to N following colonization (900 pairs breed; 4,800 in winter)

Medium-sized, all-white egret with slim bill, tapered face and throat. Stands still for long spells, wading and watching, or leaps and runs, stirs feet to attract fish. Often perches in tree.

ADULT BREEDING white; **two long plumes** from nape; long, wispy, undivided plumes shroud tail and wingtip. Facial skin becomes brighter yellow with variable blue/mauve patches/stripes. Legs black with **yellow feet** (can be covered in mud). ADULT NON-BREEDING bill dull with greenish/yellowish base; legs greenish with yellow feet, yellow extending up to joint on back of leg. JUVENILE lacks plumes, has greyish or yellowish base to bill, greenish legs.

VOICE Call short, deep croak; croaks and growls at nest.

IN FLIGHT, neck coiled back onto deep breast; wings long, quite broad; legs trailed, with yellow feet usually obvious; quite quick, springy wingbeats.

ADULT NON-BREEDING

from Europe

Coastal pools, estuaries, lakes, riversides

JUVENILE [Jan]

legs greenish, yellowish on feet extending up to 'knee', becoming blacker by Mar

bill greyer than adult's, often yellowish at base of lower mandible

JUVENILE JUN–MAR [Sep]

facial colour varies from pink/blue to yellowish in spring

head plumes reduced, back plumes untidy

two long plumes from nape

ADULT NON-BREEDING MAY–FEB

ADULT BREEDING FEB–JUL

legs blackish, feet yellow

EGRETS

Great White Egret *Ardea alba*

545

L 85–105 cm | W 140–170 cm

Large, all-white egret; size of Grey Heron (*p. 260*) with similar sedate actions; often perches in tree.

ADULT BREEDING **long cloak of fine, wispy plumes** on back, widely spread in display (no head plumes as on Little Egret); bill black, facial skin yellow or pale green. Legs black, with yellow or red above joint. ADULT NON-BREEDING/IMMATURE no plumes; bill typically **bright yellow** (best clue by far); legs and **feet dark**, often **yellowish above 'knee' joint**.

VOICE Dry croak.

IN FLIGHT, neck withdrawn onto deep breast; wings long, broad, distinctly bowed; legs long, trailing, all-dark. Rather heavy flight action (slower wingbeats than Little Egret; size and action more like Grey Heron).

Scarce migrant/winter visitor from W Europe: 100–150 per year; very rare breeder (<10 pairs, increasing); (<125 records Ireland)

from Europe

Marshes, wet meadows, floods, lakesides

flight silhouette as Little Egret, but 50% larger

ADULT NON-BREEDING

black bill

variable facial colour and long, wispy back plumes

ADULT BREEDING
FEB–JUN

yellow bill

ADULT NON-BREEDING
MAY–FEB

legs variable but feet always dark

263

RARE LARGE WATERSIDE BIRDS

Egrets compared

Egrets are stark white, with long legs and a long, curved or angular neck. Try to compare size with Grey Heron (*p. 260*) or other waterside birds (Great White Egret is as tall as Grey Heron, Little Egret smaller but often hard to judge in isolation and in flight). Look for bill, leg and foot colours and check bill/head/chin shapes and proportions.

GREAT WHITE EGRET

LITTLE EGRET

CATTLE EGRET

Cattle Egret *Bubulcus ibis*

L 42–52 cm | W 82–95 cm

Squacco Heron (*p. 268*)

Scarce migrant from S Europe: up to 200 per year (<400 records Ireland), most Oct–Mar; has bred. Lakes, marshes, meadows.

Small **white** egret marked with **buff** in summer. Feeds among cattle on muddy/grassy fields (although beware that Little Egrets (*p. 262*) will also feed around cattle!). Rather rounded (Little Egret a little slimmer, more elegant); **bill shortish, dagger-shaped** and always **pale**; legs relatively short, pale; feet brownish. Head rounded with 'baggy' throat beneath bill base (smoothly tapered on Little Egret).

ADULT BREEDING white, with **rich buff crown**, breast patch and back plumes. **Bill yellow**; bill and facial skin variably red Feb–Jul. Legs pale yellowish-brown. ADULT NON-BREEDING/IMMATURE all-white; bill yellow, legs dusky **greyish-brown**.

VOICE Coarse croaks.

IN FLIGHT, rather quick wing action and short neck/bill and short legs, but easily overlooked as Little Egret at distance.

ADULT NON-BREEDING

ADULT BREEDING

from Europe

Coastal pools, estuaries, lakes, riversides

rich buff patches

yellow bill

ADULT NON-BREEDING / IMMATURE
MAY–FEB

ADULT BREEDING
MAR–JUL

dark legs

pale legs

Large waterside birds in flight *p. 256*

EGRETS | STORKS

White Stork *Ciconia ciconia* 545
L 95–110 cm | W 180–218 cm

Huge; **white** or dirty white with **black wingtip**; long-legged; long-necked, with long, heavy, dagger-like bill. Feeds with slow, striding walk. ADULT **bill bright red**; **legs red**, often splashed white. JUVENILE/1ST-YEAR duller than adult; bill black, soon develops red base.

◉ Great White Pelican (p. 539)

IN FLIGHT, **forewing white, trailing edge and outer half black**, meeting over rump. Soars masterfully: head extended, legs trailed; wings long, broad, **fingered**; held in shallow, taut bow (quite unlike any heron).

ADULT

bill black, becoming red from base with age

JUVENILE
JUL–MAR

ADULT

Rare migrant from S Europe: about 40 per year (<50 records Ireland), all months, most May–Oct; reintroduction project, SE England. Meadows, marshes. Winters in S Europe, Africa.

Black Stork *Ciconia nigra* 545
L 90–105 cm | W 173–205 cm

Huge; **black-and-white**; slim, long-legged, long-necked with long, heavy, dagger-like bill. ADULT **head, neck, breast and upperparts glossy black**, underparts white. Legs and bill red. JUVENILE/1ST-YEAR head and breast brown, upperparts blackish; bill dull, increasingly red from base; legs dusky pink.

ADULT

IN FLIGHT, **black, with white belly and triangle at base of underwing**; soars with head extended, wings long and flat.

bill greenish to brown, becoming dull pink and gaining red from base with age

JUVENILE
JUL–MAR

glossy; bright red bill and legs

ADULT

Very rare migrant from E Europe: <300 records, 5–6 per year (<5 records Ireland), most May–Jun. Scattered. Streams, forest. Winters in Africa.

RARE LARGE WATERSIDE BIRDS

Glossy Ibis *Plegadis falcinellus* 545
L 55–65 cm | W 88–105 cm

Large, dark ibis; resembles a thickset, squat, thick-legged Curlew (p. 218) with a **thick, downcurved bill**, but **very dark** overall.
ADULT BREEDING black, green and copper gloss.
ADULT NON-BREEDING/IMMATURE dark grey-brown with whitish neck streaks and whitish line enclosing eye and base of bill.
VOICE Usually silent.

ADULT

IN FLIGHT, slender, with outstretched head, trailing legs and rounded wings.

glossy dark maroon and green

ADULT MAR–AUG

whitish flecks on head and neck

IMMATURE

Rare migrant/winter visitor from SW Europe: 50–100 per year (<500 records Ireland), sometimes small groups. Mostly in S; increasing. Lakes, marshes, floods, swamps, estuaries.

Purple Heron *Ardea purpurea* 545
L 70–90 cm | W 120–138 cm

Secretive large heron of reedbeds and marshes with long, 'snaky' neck and long, slim bill.
ADULT steely grey with pale-tipped brown plumes on back, **purple-red patch on 'shoulder'** and dark flank. **Neck chestnut with long black and white stripes**. JUVENILE paler, browner with dark streaks. Dark cap, striped face, black-streaked foreneck (pattern like Bittern (p. 261) but much slimmer, longer billed and longer legged).
VOICE Short, harsh croak.

ADULT

IN FLIGHT, **long, bowed wings** with curved trailing edge; wings narrower, **neck 'coil' deeper** and trailing feet longer than Grey Heron (p. 260). (See also p. 256.)

ADULT

tapered neck, head barely wider

rufous neck, black stripes

pale rufous neck

JUVENILE JUN–NOV

Rare migrant from S and W Europe: 25–30 per year (<30 records Ireland), Apr–Aug. Has bred. Marshes. Winters in Africa.

Large waterside birds in flight *p. 256*

IBIS | HERONS

Little Bittern *Ixobrychus minutus* 545

L 33–38 cm | W 49–58 cm

Rare migrant from Europe: >500 records, 3–5 per year (<60 records Ireland), most Apr–May, has bred. Marshes. Winters Africa.

Elusive small bittern (size of Moorhen (*p. 248*)) of dense wetland vegetation. Best seen in flight, although sightings often brief. revealing distinctive **pale wing patch**. May stretch to catch fish, showing elongated neck, otherwise dumpy profile; bill pale. MALE crown/back greenish-black, cheek grey; **neck and underparts bright peach-buff; wing buff**. FEMALE crown/back dark brown, streaked buff; **neck sandy-buff, streaked cream and tawny-buff; wing tawny-buff**. JUVENILE brown, neck broadly streaked brown and white, wing buff with brown streaks.

VOICE Call repeated short croak.

Least Bittern, Squacco Heron (*p. 268*), Green Heron (*p. 270*)

IN FLIGHT, quick action; oval wing patches show in blur; legs trailed (see *p. 256*).

black and buff

brown and buff

streaked pale brown and buff

ADULT ♂

ADULT ♀

JUVENILE JUN–OCT

Night-heron *Nycticorax nycticorax* 545

L 58–65 cm | W 90–100 cm

Rare migrant from Europe: >500 records, 10–20 per year (<100 records Ireland), most spring; some escapes. Marshes, waterside trees. Winters in Africa.

Rather large heron with **short, dagger-like bill**: active at dusk; hidden in foliage by day. ADULT pale grey with black crown/back, white forehead and cheek, and white plumes from nape; **wing plain grey**. JUVENILE dark brown, **spotted buff**; streaked below.

VOICE Call short, croaking "*quark.*"

IN FLIGHT (often at dusk) quicker action than Grey Heron (*p. 260*), regular crow-like wingbeats.

buff spots on grey-brown

JUVENILE JUN–MAR

hint of a dark cap

smooth grey and black

ADULT

spots reduced, darker back, paler wings

yellow legs

1ST-SUMMER MAR–OCT

267

RARE LARGE WATERSIDE BIRDS

Least Bittern ◆
Ixobrychus exilis
L 28–36 cm | W 41–46 cm

Very like Little Bittern (*p. 267*) but more rufous, with **white stripe** each side of back and **rufous/blackish edge** to buff wing.

Vagrant from N America: 1 record (Ireland), Oct (pending). Marshes.

Great Blue Heron
Ardea herodias
L 91–137 cm | W 175–195 cm

Huge heron, like Grey Heron (*p. 260*) but slightly larger with pinkish/brownish-grey neck, and **brownish thigh and 'shoulder'**. ADULT (not recorded) thigh rufous, legs blackish. IMMATURE more pale pinkish-purplish-brown overall than Grey Heron with **brownish 'shoulder' patch**.

Vagrant from N America: <5 records (Britain), Dec, May. Freshwater.

Squacco Heron 545
Ardeola ralloides
L 40–49 cm | W 71–86 cm

Small, **brown-bodied** heron of waterside vegetation, ditches and pools that reveals **white wings** in flight. Inconspicuous and often hard to see. ADULT BREEDING clean **peachy-pink or buff** overall; long, black-edged plumes from nape; bill blue with black tip; legs pinkish. ADULT NON-BREEDING drab sandy-brown, head and neck finely streaked dark grey-brown; bill blackish above, yellowish below. JUVENILE/1ST-WINTER like non-breeding adult but back darker, neck more thickly streaked brown.

VOICE Short, croaking quack.

Vagrant from S Europe: <200 records (<25 Ireland), most Apr–May. Marshes.

⊙ Chinese Pond Heron

HERONS | EGRETS

Chinese Pond Heron
Ardeola bacchus
L 42–52 cm | W 79–90 cm

Small heron with yellow-and-black bill and yellow-green legs; white wings show in flight. ADULT BREEDING (not recorded) head and neck purplish-brown, back blue-grey, wings and underparts white. ADULT NON-BREEDING/IMMATURE very like Squacco Heron but usually has broader dark streaks on duller buff-white neck and breast (narrow streaks on brighter buff on Squacco Heron).

Vagrant from SE Asia: <5 records (Britain), Jan–Mar, Oct–Nov. Marshes/wetlands.

NON-BREEDING

ADULT BREEDING

Snowy Egret
Egretta thula
L 60–65 cm | W 90–105 cm

Like Little Egret (p. 262) but well-defined **bright yellow face patch extending above bill**. ADULT BREEDING (not recorded) bushy head plumes; wispy back plumes. Bright yellow on feet sometimes extends up back of leg. ADULT NON-BREEDING/JUVENILE/1ST-WINTER lack plumes; legs greenish with variable yellow streak up back.

Vagrant from N America: 1 record (Britain), Nov–Sep (long-stayer). Near coast. Marshes/wetland.

wispy plumes

yellow band over bill

bushy head plumes

ADULT BREEDING

NON-BREEDING SEP–APR

back of legs often extensively yellow

double plume

straight plumes

LITTLE EGRET

ADULT BREEDING

legs black

1ST-WINTER

FACE dull yellow/greenish; BILL grey-black

Little Blue Heron ◆
Egretta caerulea
L 60 cm | W 95–105 cm

Small heron. ADULT (not recorded) slaty grey. IMMATURE white, like Little Egret (p. 262) but develops grey patches as it matures; **legs yellow-green**; bill grey with well-defined **black tip**.

Vagrant from N America: 1 record (Ireland), Sep–Dec. Near coast. Marshes/wetland.

1ST-WINTER JUL–MAY

FACE grey; BILL **blue-grey with black tip**

yellow-green

269

RARE LARGE WATERSIDE BIRDS

Green Heron
Butorides virescens
L 45 cm | W 62–70 cm

Very small, dark heron with orange/yellow legs. ADULT dark slaty green above; deep rufous neck with white stripes. JUVENILE/1ST-WINTER brownish-grey with dark cap; broad **rufous and white streaks** on neck/breast; **chestnut cheek**; pale spots on back.

> Vagrant from N America: <15 records (1 Ireland), Sep–Oct. Near coast. Wetlands.

ADULT

1ST-WINTER
AUG–APR

bright pale legs show when flying away

American Bittern
Botaurus lentiginosus
L 59–70 cm | W 95–115 cm

Like Bittern (*p. 261*) but has **browner** crown and neck side, longer black 'moustache' and **bold wide rufous streaks** on breast. IN FLIGHT, plain greyish wingtips without fine bars.

> Vagrant from N America: <75 records (< 25 Ireland), Nov–May, most autumn. Scattered. Marshes.

brown cap

wide streaks

black cap

thinner streaks

BITTERN

Sandhill Crane
Antigone (Grus) canadensis
L 85–95 cm | W 160–180 cm

Large, pale grey crane (often stained ochre-brown) with paler grey flight feathers than Crane (*p. 258*). ADULT **red forehead/cap**, whitish cheek and grey-black bill. 1ST-YEAR grey with rusty crown and feather edges on upperparts.

> Vagrant from N America: <5 records (1 Ireland), Apr, Sep–Oct. Fields.

ADULT

ADULT

'GAMEBIRDS' (partridges, grouse, pheasants and Quail)

GAMEBIRD ID size | tail shape and colour | face pattern | leg colour | voice

A small, diverse group of seed-eating, mostly terrestrial birds (some roost and feed in trees). Essentially chicken-like in basic form and bill shape, generally round-bodied. Fly fast and low if disturbed, with bursts of whirring wingbeats between glides on stiff wings. Young birds may cause confusion since they are able to fly before fully grown.

10 species: 9 resident, 1 summer migrant; 4 introduced, plus 1 reintroduced following extinction.

Partridges (pp. 272–273) include one native species and one long-established introduction, both supplemented by released birds; round head, small bill, round body and short tail.

Grouse (p. 274–279) include four native species, one widespread but declining on heather moors, one restricted to high altitude areas, and two associated with moorland/woodland edge (Capercaillie reintroduced following UK extirpation). They have red eye-wattles and feathered feet, unlike partridges.

Pheasants (p. 278) are all introduced, one released in millions for shooting, some establishing breeding populations; the other two rare and close to extinction. They have rather long, bare legs, short bill and long tail.

Quail (p. 279) unlike the others, is a summer visitor. Most detected are singing males.

Gamebird ageing/sexing

Sexes are dissimilar, in some species markedly. Juveniles look like females and may fly before they are full grown.

PHEASANT

QUAIL

GREY PARTRIDGE

BLACK GROUSE

Escapes and introductions
Several 'gamebird' species may occasionally be seen as escapes and introductions: some have bred (Category E* species, covered on p. 539). Two pheasants were locally established, both now severely declined.

Golden Pheasant *Chrysolophus pictus*
♂ 90–105 cm (incl. tail 60–70 cm) ♀ 60–80 cm (incl. tail 30–35 cm) | W 65–75 cm
MALE largely **red and golden-yellow** with long, 'marbled' tawny tail. FEMALE closely barred black/brown, paler on head and underparts than Lady Amherst's Pheasant.

Lady Amherst's Pheasant *Chrysolophus amherstiae*
♂ 105–120 cm (incl. tail 75–90 cm) ♀ 60–80 cm (incl. tail 25–30 cm) | W 70–85 cm
MALE largely **black-and-white** with **yellow rump** and **long, black-barred silvery tail**. FEMALE closely barred black/buff, darker than Golden Pheasant.

May now be extinct in Britain.

'GAMEBIRDS'

Red-legged Partridge *Alectoris rufa*

L 32–35 cm | W 47–50 cm

Fairly common introduced resident in UK (120,000 breeding pairs, extensively released for shooting); rare in Ireland

Neat, large-bodied partridge with bold colours; introductions persist as wild populations; newly released birds may be approachable. More likely to run than fly if disturbed. Often on downland/heath/sandy fields/dunes, less restricted to grassy meadows than Grey Partridge.

Sexes alike. ADULT pale grey-brown; **plain back**. **White face edged black**, neck closely streaked black and grey. Flank boldly **barred black, white and rufous**. **Bill and legs red**. JUVENILE brown; face buff, soon with whitish stripe over eye and throat; white spots on back, buffish-white bars on brown flank. Bill grey, quickly turning red, legs pinkish.

VOICE Curious, puzzling mix of croaks and rhythmic, grating, mechanical chuffing sounds, often "*chu chu chu chu ka-chekchek ca-chekchek cachekchek…*" sometimes delivered from a high perch.

Farmland, downs, dunes, heaths, sometimes gardens

IN FLIGHT, tail shows dark orange sides against **grey rump**. Glides on **flat wings** (slightly bowed/drooped on Grey Partridge).

ADULT

ADULT

JUVENILE JUN–OCT

ADULT

👁 Chukar Partridge

Chukar Partridge *Alectoris chukar* was also formerly released (now illegal). Similar to, but larger than Red-legged Partridge, plainer on breast without black streaks. These bred and also hybridized with Red-legged Partridge (producing so-called 'ogridges'), some of which may persist.

PARTRIDGES

Grey Partridge *Perdix perdix*

544

L 28–32 cm | W 45–48 cm

Increasingly scarce and local resident in UK (43,000 breeding pairs, declining); rare in Ireland

Arable land, meadows, downs

👁 Pallas's Sandgrouse (p. 284)

Delicate, beautifully marked, native partridge; small, short-legged bantam-like form. Stretches upwards when alarmed (often just shows head above grass), runs, or flies off low and fast.

Sexes look similar although FEMALE duller than MALE. ADULT mid-brown, back and rump finely barred; buff streaks on 'shoulder'. **Large orange face patch**; neck and breast plain blue-grey with dark brown breast patch (largest on MALE); flank barred rust-brown. Bill, legs horn-brown. JUVENILE pale buff-brown, greyer below; face whitish-buff.

VOICE Male calls during slow, springy, upright walk, a creaky, wheezy "*ke-er-it*" or "*cheevit*."

IN FLIGHT, tail spread, **rusty-orange**; barred wings slightly **downcurved** (straighter on Red-legged Partridge). See Red Grouse (p. 274), although grouse are larger, darker, black-tailed and dark-faced; Grey Partridge lacks contrast between back and flight feathers.

ADULT

ADULT ♂

weak head pattern, grey bill

JUVENILE →
1ST-WINTER
JUN–OCT [Sep]

ADULT ♂

dark breast patch biggest on male

ADULT ♀

'GAMEBIRDS'

VU **Red Grouse** *Lagopus lagopus*

L 33–38 cm | W 55–66 cm

Locally common upland resident (150,000 pairs in Britain, declining; 4,200 birds in Ireland)

Dark, shy, crouching, partridge-like grouse with small dark eye and bill, feet feathered white (compare with browner, more barred female Black Grouse (*p. 276*)). Truly wild, native, not reared and released like some other 'gamebirds'.

ADULT MALE rich **dark red-brown** with fine black and buff barring; **red wattle** over eye (rules out Grey Partridge). ADULT FEMALE/JUVENILE paler, more yellowish due to copious broader buff bars.

VOICE Typical moorland sound: loud, abrupt, surprising stutter "*kaa-kaa-kaa – karr-rr-rr-rr-cok cok go-bak go bak bak bak….*"

IN FLIGHT, fast, glides on arched wings, looks very dark except variable **white bars on underwing**. Wings dark; tail black with brown central 'wedge' (tail brown on female Black Grouse; paler with dark orange sides and pale central 'wedge' on partridges).

Extensive heather moorland

British/Irish ssp. *scotica* (Irish birds sometimes treated as ssp. *hibernicus*) of the white-winged European Willow Grouse.

ADULT ♂

ADULT ♂

ADULT ♂

ADULT ♀

can look blackish on moor at long range

GROUSE

Ptarmigan *Lagopus muta* [NT]

ssp. *millaisi* see p.541

L 31–35 cm | W 55–65 cm

Scarce and local resident in the Scottish highlands (10,000 breeding pairs, declining)

Small, delicate grouse of high mountain plateaux in Scotland (sometimes found at lower altitude farther north). Has **white wings** and **black tail** at all times obvious in flight. Only likely to be confused with Red Grouse, which is all-dark and slightly bigger with a larger bill.

Sexes differ and have distinct seasonal colour changes. ADULT MALE SUMMER (May–Oct) peppered pale grey with **white wingtip**, belly and feet; small red eye wattle. ADULT MALE WINTER (Oct–Feb) white except for black tail and patch between eye and bill. In spring and autumn patchy change during moult, often strikingly piebald. ADULT FEMALE changes similarly, but in summer much yellower than male and in winter head **all-white** (no black between eye and bill). JUVENILE grey-black with fine pale fringes above; white with thick, blackish bars below.

VOICE Varied low, belching, croaking notes, typically "*arr-oo-a-karrr.*"

High, stony peaks and plateaux

IN FLIGHT, **white wings** in all plumages.

ADULT ♀ SUMMER [May]

ADULT ♂ SUMMER [Jul]

ADULT ♂ WINTER [Dec]

ADULT ♂ SUMMER [May]

ADULT ♀ WINTER

ADULT ♀ NON-BREEDING → BREEDING [Apr]

ADULT ♂ WINTER

ADULT ♂ NON-BREEDING → BREEDING [Mar]

'GAMEBIRDS'

Black Grouse *Lyrurus (Tetrao) tetrix*

ssp. *britannicus*

L ♂ 49–58 cm | ♀ 40–45 cm | W 65–80 cm

Scarce and local resident, mainly in upland areas (10,000–15,000 (5,000 males)); remnant populations, long-term decline. Absent from Ireland

Big, chicken-like grouse, but 'half size' of Capercaillie and with small, dark bill. May be obvious on grassy meadow in spring, particularly when males displaying, otherwise elusive.

ADULT MALE shiny blue-black with white wingbar and 'shoulder' spot, and **white under tail**. Neck deep blue; large red wattle over eye. In display, long tail raised and fanned, outer feathers **curl outwards**; undertail feathers raised into brilliant white 'cushion'. ADULT FEMALE/JUVENILE brown, finely spotted and barred cream and black; breast pale brown (orange patch on female Capercaillie).

VOICE Calls of male far-carrying: rolling, repeated crooning note and 'sneezing' "*tschuwee*."

IN FLIGHT, large, long and flat-backed. MALE prominent **broad white wingbar**. FEMALE tail fractionally **'notched'** but fanned in flight and same colour as rump (without rufous/grey contrast of Capercaillie and not blackish as on Red Grouse (*p. 274*)). Shows **weak white wingbar**.

Moors, plantations, adjacent hill slopes

ADULT ♂

ADULT ♀

ADULT ♂ DISPLAYING

tail and rump all-brown

MALES display at traditional sites (leks) in spring, with females watching from close by.

MALES may be very obvious on open field, but more often hidden in dense heather/bracken/plantation or foliage.

ADULT ♂

ADULT ♀

Capercaillie *Tetrao urogallus*

GROUSE

● 544

Scarce and local resident in Scotland (1,300 birds, declining); reintroduced. Extinct Ireland

Pine forests and plantations, adjacent heaths

L ♂ 74–90 cm | ♀ 54–63 cm | W 87–125 cm

Huge, turkey-like grouse of pine forests. Reintroduced historically following extinction in UK; elusive and sensitive to disturbance.

ADULT MALE dark grey with white 'shoulder' spot and **curved flank streak**. Bill large, pale greenish. Tail quite long, broad and **rounded**, blackish with scratchy white marks; held closed and low, or **raised in half-circular fan in display**. ADULT FEMALE large, thick-billed; pale brown, heavily **spotted black**, with clear **orange breast patch**. Tail long, broad, rounded; rufous, contrasting with grey rump.

VOICE Various croaking notes; display song unique series of clicks building into 'popped cork' note.

IN FLIGHT, low, bursting from tree or ground, fast and direct, with quick, deep wingbeats; often just a glimpse of large, dark shape disappearing into trees.

ADULT ♂

ADULT ♀

ADULT ♂

ADULT ♂ DISPLAYING

FEMALE has blacker barring and more extensive white than Black Grouse.

MALES display in ones and twos; locally where more common, in small groups, at a lek.

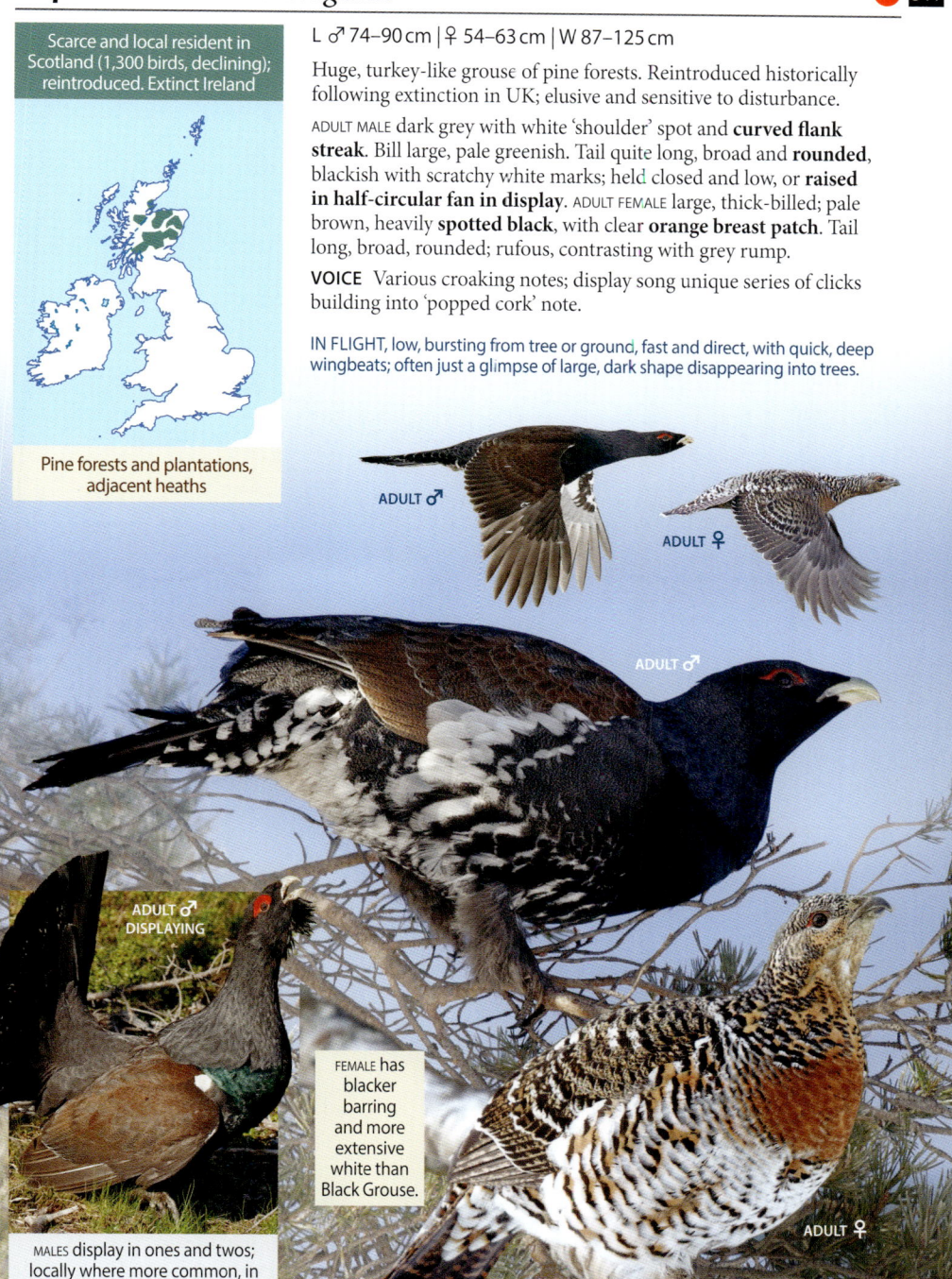

ADULT ♀

'GAMEBIRDS'

Pheasant *Phasianus colchicus*

L ♂ 70–90 cm (incl. tail 35–45 cm) | ♀ 55–70 cm (incl. tail 20–25 cm)
W 70–90 cm

👁 Golden Pheasant, Lady Amherst's Pheasant (*p. 271*)

Large, long-tailed, small-billed 'gamebird'; sexes differ markedly, males individually variable.

ADULT MALE shape and colours unique: big, chicken-like, with **long, tapered tail**. Mostly dark red-brown, often richly golden on flank, purple-red on breast, all spotted inky-black. Rump brown, bronze or pale green. Head green-black with bold **red facial wattle**; often broad white collar. Various subspecies intermixed give great variety within basic colour and pattern. ADULT FEMALE smaller, shorter-tailed; pale brown with cream and black spots and streaks. **Tail long, pointed**, pale brown with dark bars. JUVENILE like short-tailed female.

VOICE Loud "*cor-kok*" followed by a loud flurry of wings; discordant "*ku-cha, kuch-a, kuchok, ok ok.*"

IN FLIGHT, fast and low after initial explosive burst (often almost underfoot); long tail obvious (but beware, half-grown young can fly: more pointed tail than on partridges).

Abundant and widespread introduced resident (>2 million breed in UK (38 million released annually); 300,000 in Ireland)

Mostly lowlands, close to woods, also heaths, reedbeds

ADULT ♀

ADULT ♂

ADULT ♂

ADULT ♀

ADULT ♂ (ring-necked)

Newly released birds often in fields, on roadsides, but established populations more secretive; roosts high in trees.

PHEASANT | QUAIL

Quail *Coturnix coturnix*

L 16–18 cm | W 32–35 cm

Very small 'gamebird' with rounded, partridge-like form on the ground (more upright and elongated when singing or alarmed). Very elusive; heard far more often than seen.

Pale brown with black mottles and **long buff lines** on upperparts; flank striped (long lines rather than vertical bars as on partridges). Dark cap with pale central line and dark eyestripe. Sexes differ slightly: ADULT MALE has **black throat markings**; ADULT FEMALE/JUVENILE a buff/white throat.

VOICE Calls (close range) soft "*miaow*" or "*ma-mah*." Song of male carries far: liquid, rhythmic, low "*quik-wik-ik*" or "*wit-wi-wit*," usually only clue to bird's presence.

IN FLIGHT, quick and direct on long, narrow wings, often puzzling (recalling crake or wader) in brief view or out of context on migration. May take off with sudden burst from underfoot, but usually hard to flush.

ADULT ♂

Generally rare (but erratic) and widespread summer visitor (500 singing males (1,000–2,000 in 'good Quail years'); rare migrant (Apr–Oct); absent in winter

to Africa

Downland, cereal fields; migrants chiefly near coast

ADULT ♂

Occasionally seen at edge of open patch in crop or grass.

ADULT ♂

Singing MALE more upright, still usually hidden from view.

ADULT ♂   ADULT ♀

BUSTARDS

3 species: 1 re-introduction, 2 vagrants.

Bustards are large, stout-legged, short-billed landbirds. All four species found in Europe are declining, and most are now globally threatened. In the UK, the Great Bustard once bred quite widely on open downs, was lost as a breeding species, but is now being reintroduced to Salisbury Plain in Wiltshire; wild birds are now extremely rare vagrants. The most likely bustard to turn up in Britain or Ireland is Little Bustard. Historical records of 'Houbara' Bustard (now known as McQueen's Bustard) highly unlikely to be repeated as the bird is on the brink of extinction in Europe. Since bustards have distinctive white wing patches in flight, other species, especially the odd-looking Egyptian Goose (p. 35), can sometimes cause confusion but in reality, bustards are not much like anything else, and Great Bustard is so big as to be unmistakable.

Macqueen's Bustard
VU | PE
(Asian Houbara)
Chlamydotis macqueenii
L 55–65 cm | W 130–150 cm

Large, long-necked, long-legged bustard; pale sandy-brown above, white below, grey foreneck. ADULT (sexes look alike) thin black cap and black streak down side of neck.

Vagrant from Asia: 1 modern record (Britain), Nov–Dec.

IN FLIGHT, long wings; white 'flash' near wingtip.

ADULT
ADULT

Little Bustard
NT | VU 546
Tetrax tetrax
L 40–45 cm | W 83–91 cm

Small bustard (Pheasant-sized (p. 278), but size remarkably tricky to judge when isolated bird crouches in vegetation) with long legs. ADULT MALE BREEDING **black-and-white neck**. NON-BREEDING MALE/FEMALE like female Pheasant but tail short.

Vagrant from S Europe: <250 records (<10 Ireland), most months. Widespread but declining. Arable fields.

ADULT ♀

IN FLIGHT, unexpectedly fast beats of long, broad, **mostly white wings**.

Crouched bird hidden in tall grass slowly raises round head on slender neck.

ADULT ♂ BREEDING
ADULT ♂ BREEDING
ADULT ♀

BUSTARDS

Great Bustard *Otis tarda*

L ♂ 90–105 cm | W 210–240 cm
♀ 75–85 cm | W 170–190 cm

Long extinct UK breeder, being reintroduced (Wiltshire); very rare wild vagrant (150 records (<5 Ireland): most winter, declining). Grassland, fields.

Huge, heavy bustard, typically on extensive open plains; more-or-less horizontal with erect neck. Elusive: despite size, easily 'lost' in tall crops. Looks dull, greyish at long range; brighter, with richer colours close up. ADULT MALE whiskered grey head with rufous-orange neck and breast; back barred black and **bright ginger-brown**; white below. ADULT FEMALE similar but duller and slimmer; head rounded, greyish, without 'whiskers'. JUVENILE like female but paler and more buffish.

IN FLIGHT, **reveals a lot of white** in wing (beware much smaller Egyptian Goose (*p. 35*)). Flying birds dramatic, with long, straight, fingered wings, crane- or stork-like but body heavy, slender neck outstretched and **tail square with no leg projection**.

ADULT ♀

wingbeats slow, goose-like

tail raised in display: normally held closed and flat

ADULT ♂

cleaner grey on head than any Little Bustard

ADULT ♀

PIGEONS, DOVES and SANDGROUSE

PIGEON and DOVE ID   upperwing pattern | tail pattern above and below | neck pattern

There is no real distinction between a 'pigeon' and a 'dove'. All are short-billed, round-headed, beady-eyed, soft-plumaged birds with broad, tapered wings and a broad, round-tipped tail.
7 pigeons and doves: 4 resident, 1 scarce but has abundant feral derivatives; 1 summer visitor; 2 extremely rare vagrants.
1 sandgrouse: extreme vagrant.

Pigeons (pp. 284–287) are familiar to most people from the ubiquitous street pigeons (Feral Pigeon) that are descendants of domesticated Rock Doves, especially 'racing pigeons' that have 'gone wild' almost everywhere. The truly wild Rock Dove is a handsome bird of northern coasts.

The commonest and, in much of the UK, the commonest large bird, is the Woodpigeon: worth learning well to help identify birds of prey and others at a distance, as high-flying pigeons can be mistaken for several other birds. Stock Dove is smaller, rounder, bluer, with quicker, deeper wingbeats, without the Woodpigeon's white wing marks, and are usually much less numerous – but in most areas regular checking of 'pigeons' will reveal one.

Smaller **doves** (p. 288–290) include one that has been in the UK for millennia, the Turtle Dove, in recent decades declining almost to oblivion in most places, and one that arrived naturally only in the 1950s, the Collared Dove. Turtle Dove is a rural bird, unlikely in most gardens, whereas Collared Dove is a suburban and village bird, favouring dockyards, breweries and distilleries, as well as cereal fields and horse paddocks, wherever there might be seed and grain. All have distinctive flight patterns and also special aerial displays. Only the Collared Dove has a 'flight call' but all coo in one way or another, helping to find and identify them.

Sandgrouse (p. 284) are rounded, short-legged, long-tailed terrestrial birds with a short, curved bill. In flight they have long, narrow wings and fly fast with quick wingbeats. They are social birds of semi-arid regions; the one species recorded has occasional 'eruptions' (from Asia) bringing small numbers ('irruptions') into western Europe, but these have become rare and irregular: recently unknown in Britain.

Pigeon ageing/sexing
Sexes are alike with no seasonal changes; fresh feathers are purer in colour than faded older ones, which tend to become dull and brownish. Juveniles are distinguishable for a few weeks, being duller, without adult head and neck markings; these develop during their first winter.

WOODPIGEON
ADULT
JUVENILE

TURTLE DOVE

PIGEONS and DOVES

Pigeons and doves in flight

Fast-flying pigeons and doves cross open spaces, often allowing good views: check size, tail length and pattern, upperwing. Larger, tighter flocks usually indicate larger pigeons (sometimes mixed) rather than smaller doves.

Some Feral Pigeons look very like Rock Doves, but typically lack a white rump and always have a larger cere

FERAL PIGEON

ROCK DOVE

ROCK DOVE / FERAL PIGEON (p. 284)

FERAL PIGEON

ROCK DOVE

WOODPIGEON (p. 286)

STOCK DOVE (p. 287)

COLLARED DOVE (p. 288)

TURTLE DOVE (p. 289)

ORIENTAL TURTLE DOVE (p. 290)

MOURNING DOVE (p. 290)

283

PIGEONS and DOVES

SANDGROUSE

One species has been recorded, mostly during 'invasions' that now seem to be a thing of the past.

IN FLIGHT, fast; upperwing plain but back/rump strongly barred.

ADULT ♂

EN Pallas's Sandgrouse
Syrrhaptes paradoxus
L 27–32 cm | W 60–71 cm

Pigeon-like, short-legged, terrestrial, shuffling, with **long, pointed tail**. Pale brown-buff with orange head (rather like Grey Partridge (*p. 273*)) and **black belly patch**. ADULT MALE grey neck; plain pink-buff 'shoulder'/lower breast. ADULT FEMALE black spots on neck and 'shoulder'. JUVENILE no tail spike.

ADULT ♀

ADULT ♂

Vagrant from Asia: mostly historical records (<5 records since 1960), May. Open ground.

Rock Dove / Feral Pigeon *Columba livia*

L 30–35 cm | W 62–68 cm

Gone-wild descendants of domesticated Rock Doves are the everyday town or Feral Pigeons, but truly wild Rock Dove is a handsome pigeon of wilder places in the north.

WILD ROCK DOVE pale blue-grey with **white rump** and two black bars across wing. Breast washed purple, neck glossed green. Compared with domestic/town birds, immaculate; **small** white fleshy patch (cere) above **slim bill** (large cere and thick bill on domestic birds). DOMESTIC BIRDS – 'racers' and 'tumblers' – are released in flocks to 'train' above their loft. They will circle in tight flocks, flickering in the sun; racers fly direct in ragged groups, are long-necked and have slimmer, more tapered, swept-back wings than their wild ancestors. Often glide, with wings in a deep 'V', rocking from side to side. JUVENILE dull on neck sides.

Feral Pigeon, common resident in towns (100,000); wild Rock Dove scarce, in north

- Feral Pigeon
- Rock Dove

Feral Pigeon, towns, quarries, cliffs, adjacent fields, waste ground; Rock Dove near coasts

Feral (gone-wild) birds on cliffs are very similar to wild Rock Doves but usually include a proportion of darker individuals, more-or-less dark chequered above, some with patches of white. Town birds, especially, are very variable, with rusty/ginger, blue-grey, blackish and pied types, often with black wingbars, but also white flight feathers or other irregularities. However, even those that are most like Rock Dove always have a larger cere than is found on wild birds.

IN FLIGHT, **white rump/lower back**, dark tail, **white underwing** distinctive on wild birds.

Pigeons and doves in flight *p. 283*

PIGEONS

Feral Pigeon types

Chequered type

Pied type

Blue-grey or black-barred (Rock Dove) type

Rusty/ginger type

'Rock Dove'-like Feral Pigeon – note large cere and lack of white rump

ADULT (Feral Pigeon)

ADULT (Rock Dove)

small cere

two dark bars across wing

large cere

ADULT (Feral Pigeon)

ADULT (Rock Dove)

fleshy white patch on bill (cere) small on wild Rock Doves, larger or bulbous on feral/domestic pigeons

285

PIGEONS and DOVES

Woodpigeon *Columba palumbus*

Widespread, abundant resident (2·7 million pairs, plus 2·6 million birds in Ireland), and migrant

Farmland, woodland, parks

L 38–43 cm | W 68–77 cm

Large, long-winged, long-tailed pigeon; sits upright, motionless, often for hours. Large birds, flying singly or in flocks (sometimes large and high up), over most of Britain and Ireland will often be Woodpigeons. Increasingly bold/tame in towns and gardens.

ADULT grey with **white neck patch** and **white on edge of wing** (often hidden). Greenish gloss on neck, pink breast; red-and-yellow bill; yellow eye; dull pink legs. JUVENILE duller, no white neck patch; dull eye.

VOICE Song loud, rhythmic "*coo, crroo-crroo, cu-coo, cuk crroo-crru, cuk.*" No flight call; various strained cooing, moaning, grunting notes close to nest. Loud wing noise including whistle and clatter in alarm, and sudden 'slap'.

IN FLIGHT, broad **white band** across wing; wide, pale rump; tail has pale central band above, **white band** and black tip below. Long, narrow head; long wings taper to a blunt point; longish, wide-tipped tail, deep chest. Quick, direct; rises with fast, noisy beats; steady beats over longer distances. Often rises to momentary **'stall'**.

ADULT

very young birds still show wispy down; mottled and unkempt-looking

JUVENILE FEB–NOV

ADULT

adult immaculate; often loses small white feathers in noisy, clattering, aggressive encounters

PIGEONS

Stock Dove *Columba oenas*

L 28–32 cm | W 60–66 cm

Common and widespread resident (300,000 pairs, plus 37,000 birds in Ireland)

Small, blue-grey pigeon with rather short wings and tail and soft, rounded outlines. Often over woodland in fast-moving groups, around old parkland trees or on open fields and sandy heaths, but also coastal cliffs and high on hills. Frequently with Woodpigeons, Jackdaws (p. 482) or Rooks (p. 485).

ADULT blue-grey with emerald neck patch, **no striking white**; **two short black bars** on wing (see Rock Dove (p. 284)). Bill red with yellow tip; eye dark; legs bright coral-red. JUVENILE duller.

VOICE Song deep, rolling "*oorr-oo*."

IN FLIGHT dull/matt black around **pale grey midwing**; blue-grey rump, black tail-band. Quick, deep beats of arched wings. Compared with feral/domestic pigeon, rounder-headed and broader-winged with tips curved back, slightly rounded; 'racers' are longer-necked, sharp-faced, sharper-winged and have irregular patterns. Juvenile Woodpigeon has white wing bands and pale tail-band. Display flight has 'stall' and glide like Woodpigeon, but glides/tilts with innerwing raised, outer half flat (straighter wing on Woodpigeon).

Range of habitats from lowlands to upland moors/cliffs/quarries

never has white on wing (unlike juvenile Woodpigeon)

JUVENILE MAY–OCT

ADULT

ADULT

PIGEONS and DOVES

Collared Dove *Streptopelia decaocto*

L 29–33 cm | W 48–53 cm   👁 Mourning Dove *(p. 290)*

Neat, elongated, pale dove, typically on ground, wires, TV aerials, roofs (not so much in leafy trees).

ADULT pale beige/sandy-grey with blue-grey on wing and narrow **black collar**. JUVENILE lacks black collar.

VOICE Diagnostic three-note "*cu-coo-cuk*," middle note strongest; surprisingly varied, with different emphasis, strained or hoarse versions frequent. Flight call nasal, slurred "*kwurrrr*." Wings clatter less than small pigeons but can whistle loudly in short fast flights.

IN FLIGHT almost uniformly pale; diffuse grey on upperwing; uniformly buffish breast and belly. **Underwing soft pale grey**. Underside of tail has small **black base** and **broad white tip**. Upperside has diffuse whitish tip (Turtle Dove has white band contrasted against black base). Strong, fast, direct, flight (less rolling/tilting than Turtle Dove), on bent-back wings; **long tail** catches eye. Display flight steep rise and **long, curving descent**.

Common resident, following rapid spread in second half of 20th century (285,000 pairs, plus 250,000 birds in Ireland)

Suburbs, gardens, farmland

ADULT

ADULT

uppertail with dark base and broad white tip

lacks collar

JUVENILE MAR–OCT

ADULT ♀

black collar

sexes very similar, although FEMALES tend to be buff-grey and MALES pinkish-grey

pale plumage overall, except for darker wingtip

ADULT ♂

DOVES

Turtle Dove *Streptopelia turtur*

L 25–28 cm | W 45–50 cm

Oriental Turtle Dove (p. 290)

Small dove of woodland edge, thickets, old hedgerows on downs, stubble fields; spring–early autumn only.

ADULT upperparts **chequered orange-brown**; neck has small streaked patch, no collar. Breast pale pink, belly white. JUVENILE dull, greyish, with weak dark chequering but broad pale feather edges; no neck patch. **More rufous** than Collared Dove.

VOICE Prolonged, purring, soporific *coo*, "*currr-currurrr-curr.*"

IN FLIGHT, pinkish breast **contrasts** with white belly. Tail grey with blackish band and **bright white tip**; underside has more black than Collared Dove, narrow white tip forms striking rim. Light, agile, **narrow-tipped wings curled back**, often tilting or rolling from side to side. Wings show small, blue-grey cross-band and dark grey underside. Display flight has steep rise and long, gliding descent to tree.

Scarce summer migrant (Apr–Sep) (1,000 pairs Britain; rare migrant Ireland, May, Aug–Sep)

to W Africa

Bushy downland, hedgerows, fields

ADULT

ADULT

slim shape, small head; dull, drab version of adult

uppertail grey with dark band and white tip

often accompanies more distinctive adults

JUVENILE JUN–SEP

streaked neck patch

ADULT

RARE DOVES

Pigeons and doves in flight p.283

Oriental Turtle Dove
Streptopelia orientalis
L 30–35 cm | W 55–60 cm

Like large, heavy Turtle Dove (p. 289). Two subspecies: **ssp. orientalis** dark, heavy, pigeon-like; **ssp. meena** paler, smaller than *orientalis* with broader, paler, rufous fringes to wing coverts. Whitish tips to wing coverts create diffuse wingbars.

Ssp. *orientalis* dark below, undertail greyish. Ssp. *meena* pale belly fades to cream vent/undertail (Turtle Dove has pink breast/flank, distinct white belly/vent/undertail).

Vagrant from Asia: <15 Records (Britain), Nov–Feb. Scattered. Gardens/farmland.

ORIENTAL TURTLE DOVE ssp. *orientalis* — rump grey; tail tip grey-white
ORIENTAL TURTLE DOVE ssp. *meena* — rump grey; tail tip white
TURTLE DOVE — rump brown; tail tip white

ORIENTAL TURTLE DOVE: tail projection beyond wingtip same length as wingtip (**5 tips** show); **TURTLE DOVE**: tail projection shorter than wingtip (**6–7 tips**).

TURTLE DOVE: short tail, 6–7 tips, white under tail
ORIENTAL TURTLE DOVE: long tail, 5 tips, cream under tail

JUVENILE — pinkish-brown; thin ring around eye at most
ADULT — from 1st-winter, **5–6 thin** black bars on grey patch

TURTLE DOVE
JUVENILE — grey; bare 'diamond' around eye
ADULT — **3–4 broad** black bars on white

1ST-WINTER ssp. *meena*
1ST-WINTER ssp. *orientalis*

Mourning Dove
Zenaida macroura
L 28–33 cm | W 37–45 cm

Small, slim dove with long, tapered tail. ADULT/1ST-WINTER pale olive-brown, pinker on head and breast, with a few dark spots on wing coverts. JUVENILE (not recorded) black-centred, pale-fringed wing coverts.

Vagrant from N America: <10 records (<5 Ireland), May, Oct–Jan. Near coasts. Gardens/farmland.

JUVENILE JUN–SEP [Sep]
1ST-WINTER AUG–MAR [Nov]

OWLS and NIGHTJARS

OWL ID size | head shape | eye colour | wing pattern | voice

NIGHTJAR ID wingtip pattern | tail pattern | voice

Broadly nocturnal or active at dawn and dusk, but some owls visible by day.
9 owls: 5 resident, 1 historical introduction, 2 also winter visitors; 4 vagrants, 2 extremely rare.
4 nightjars: 1 breeding visitor; 3 extreme vagrants.

Owls (pp. 292–299) are birds of prey more-or-less specialized to life after dark; they have dense plumage, a large head and a hooked bill largely hidden in deep facial feathers.

Barn and Short-eared (and the exceedingly rare Snowy) Owls hunt by day and Little Owls stand in the open in the daytime, although they feed mostly at dusk. Others, such as the Tawny Owl, are strictly nocturnal and hard to see, unless you find one at roost in a thicket by day. Small birds 'mob' owls and might help lead you to one by their repeated alarm calls.

Short-eared Owls favour marshes, moors and rough pasture and can be searched for in the same way as daytime-hunting harriers. Long-eared Owls hunt in such places but are nocturnal and roost and nest in trees. Tawny Owls prefer woodland or heavily treed parks and gardens: they hoot and call loudly at dusk. Little Owls like old trees in parkland, or tumbledown barns. Barn Owls, farmland or grassland specialists, need several large cavities in trees or buildings for nesting and resting, and hunt small rodents in long grass. On fine afternoons in cold weather, or in the evening in midsummer when nights are short, they hunt over open fields, marshes and grassy verges.

TAWNY OWL

Owl ageing/sexing

Sexes alike (except in Snowy Owl), with no seasonal variation. Juveniles subtly different: some (such as Barn Owl) may be aged over the next 1–3 years by changing patterns during prolonged moult, but doing so is difficult, requiring experience and close examination.

Nightjars (pp. 300–301) are long-winged and long-tailed but very short-legged, and have a tiny bill but very wide gape for catching flying insects.

Nightjar is the only regular species and is active at dusk and dawn, from late spring to late summer, on heaths, in woodland clearings or near plantations, or on higher bracken-covered slopes. It catches moths in flight, with a uniquely acrobatic, buoyant action, sometimes spinning around people and affording close views. The song is the best way to find one: a remarkable 'wooden' churr that can continue for several minutes.

Eagle-owl escapes

The huge (larger than a buzzard) Eurasian Eagle-owl *Bubo bubo* is an escape (about 10 per year) and perhaps an illegal introduction, with a few pairs now breeding (the impact of which is being monitored). It is currently in Category E*, and not on the official British or Irish lists.

NIGHTJAR

OWLS and NIGHTJARS

Owls in flight

With the exception of Short-eared Owl and Barn Owl, views are likely to be brief: concentrate on size, shape (especially length of wing) and the pattern of the hindwing and wingtip.

LONG-EARED OWL (p. 297)

SHORT-EARED OWL (p. 296)

'solid'

barred

TAWNY OWL (p. 294)

SNOWY OWL (p. 298)
ADULT ♂

BARN OWL

LITTLE OWL (p. 295)

Nightjars in flight

NB not to same scale as owls

Nightjars become active (and males begin to sing) soon after sunset, in good but rapidly fading light, so the potential for good views is small. Nighthawks also fly in daylight.

COMMON NIGHTHAWK (p. 301)

NIGHTJAR (p. 300)

RED-NECKED NIGHTJAR (p. 301)

EGYPTIAN NIGHTJAR (p. 301)

OWLS

Barn Owl *Tyto alba*

L 33–39 cm | W 80–95 cm

Medium–large 'white' owl of open countryside, with a narrow body, 'knock-kneed' stance and large, broad head.

Sexes and ages similar. Wide, **heart-shaped face** with black eyes and narrow dark 'V' over bill. Pale sandy or **golden-buff** above with grey 'pepper-and-salt' speckling and dark bars on spread wing (strongest on FEMALE); **white beneath**.

VOICE Shrill, bubbly shriek; various hissing, squealing notes.

Dark-breasted subspecies, rare Britain/Ireland (e.g. **ssp. *guttata*** of N, NE and E Europe), orange-buff with dark flecking including underwing coverts and under tail; greyer above; larger dark patch around eye; many difficult intergrades confuse status.

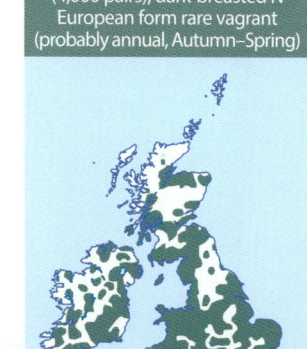

Scarce but widespread resident (4,000 pairs); dark-breasted N European form rare vagrant (probably annual, Autumn–Spring)

Grassland, farmland, marshes

IN FLIGHT, head very large; wings broad-based, tapered to narrow, rounded tip. Wingbeats slightly jerky; **hovers briefly before headlong dive** into vegetation.

ADULT

all-white underwing

colour variable: many darker and greyer than this individual

ADULT

ADULT dark-breasted form

Dark-breasted subspecies are mostly grey above (but some **resident ssp. *alba*** have more grey than normal, so also look for extensive dark areas around the eyes as well as darker underparts).

Tawny Owl *Strix aluco*

L 37–43 cm | W 81–96 cm

The most common large owl in Britain but nocturnal and hard to see; voice and silhouette distinctive. Woodpigeon-sized (p. 286) with big, **round head** and short tail; oval shape when relaxed. Presence can be indicated by small birds noisily mobbing in tree/ivy, or by white droppings under roost (although few disgorged pellets). Appears pale in flight in car headlights (but not as white as Barn Owl (p. 293)).

Sexes/ages similar once fledged. **Rufous-** or **grey-brown**, with row of **white spots diagonally along 'shoulder'**, complex cross-barred streaks beneath. **Rounded facial disk; black eyes**.

VOICE Loud, emphatic "*ke-wick!*" or "*wik-wik-wik*" and variations; pure or breathy, trembling hoot – "*hooo! hu – hu- huwoooo-oo.*" Occasionally sings during day. JUVENILE calls a hissy "*he-wik*" or "*shee-eep*" (see Long-eared Owl (p. 297)).

Fairly common resident (19,000 breeding pairs). Absent from Ireland

Woodland, parks, large gardens

IN FLIGHT, big head, broad wingtips, quick beats; no strong pattern.

ADULT (rufous)

ADULT (grey)

Tawny Owls are mostly rufous in Britain; in the north, and especially farther east in continental Europe, greyer birds are more frequent.

JUVENILE JUN–AUG

Tawny Owls at the nest can be dangerous: adults may attack and are silent, even at very close range.

ADULT (rufous)

Little Owl *Athene noctua*

L 23–27·5 cm | W 50–57 cm

◉ Rare owls (p. 299)

Small, stocky owl, with a large, broad head and low, rounded crown, short legs, short wing and very short tail. Regularly seen perched in the open during the day, standing upright with barrel-shaped body, on branch, stump or rock, but hunts mostly at dusk.

Sexes look similar. ADULT dark brown, **mottled white** above; whitish with dark brown streaks below. **White 'eyebrows'** over **large yellow eyes** set in black rings; facial disk weak. JUVENILE paler brown with buff spots above, lacks white 'eyebrows' and white band beneath cheeks; moults into adult-like plumage soon after fledging.

VOICE Loud, clear, nasal whistles – "*kleee-ow*," "*chi-chi-chi*." Song evenly repeated, rising "*keeeah*."

Scarce resident (5,700 pairs), introduced in 19th century; <5 records Ireland

Old trees, parkland, farmland, quarries, rocky islands

On the ground, stands upright on short, pale legs, sometimes running after prey.

ADULT

IN FLIGHT, quick, **swooping/ bounding**, woodpecker-like action, before **upward sweep to perch**. No strong pattern.

white brows and piercing gaze

ADULT

JUVENILE
JUN–AUG

OWLS and NIGHTJARS Owls in flight p. 292

Short-eared Owl *Asio flammeus*

L 33–40 cm | W 95–105 cm

Large; round-headed owl with sloping stance on ground, more upright on post or rock. Often **flies by day**.

Sexes/ages similar once fledged. Yellowish; some very pale, others darker and more rufous, but belly pale. Facial disk rounded with broad whitish fan around bill; eyes **pale yellow**, set in wide black patch. More marbled than streaked above, with buff blotches (no row of spots on 'shoulder'). Closed wing has pale golden-yellow patch near tip.

VOICE Emphatic, tuneless, wheezy "*eeyah!*," song in flight, deep, booming "*bu-bu-bu-bu*" combined with sharp wing-clap.

Scarce summer (2,300 pairs) and winter visitor (variable numbers, nomadic)

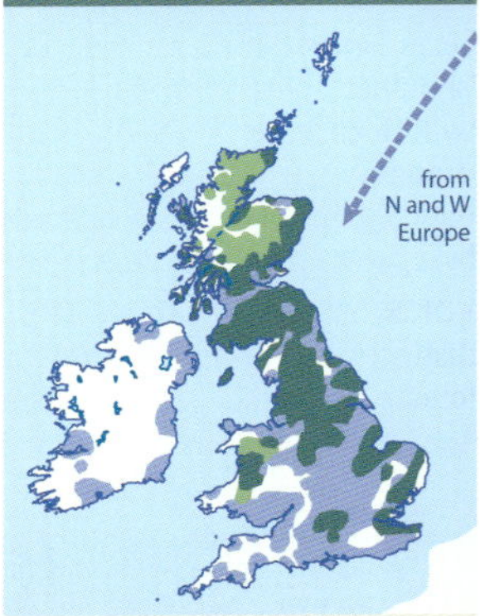

from N and W Europe

Moors, rough meadows, grassland

Asio owls in flight

Both Long-eared and Short-eared Owls have a similar wing pattern: upperwing (see *p. 292*) has **dark 'wrist' and wingtips separated by contrasting golden-buff patch**; underwing is white with a small black mark and dark wing-tips. They can be differentiated, even at distance, as follows:

Short-eared Owl	WINGTIPS: **black, solid** TRAILING EDGE: **white line** TAIL: **broad bars** BELLY: **pale**
Long-eared Owl	WINGTIPS: **barred** TRAILING EDGE: **barred grey** TAIL: **narrow bars** BELLY: **streaked**

IN FLIGHT, **low over open ground**, wavering, harrier-like action with frequent glides.

'solid' black wingtips

pale belly; few streaks

no obvious 'ears'

diffuse feathering around bill

yellow eyes surrounded by black

heavy blotches

ADULT

golden-yellow wing patch

The 'ear' tufts are rarely obvious, usually only seen when a bird is alarmed, and never as long as those of Long-eared Owl.

OWLS

Long-eared Owl *Asio otus*

L 31–37 cm | **W** 86–98 cm

Large, round-headed, upright owl. **Hunts at night**, roosts by day in tree or thicket, marked by droppings and regurgitated grey 'pellets'.

Sexes/ages similar once fledged. Olive or yellowish-brown with pale buff 'shoulder' spots and complex streaks and bars beneath. Wide facial disk with **thick white 'V'**, edged black between eyes, above bill; eyes **deep orange** in narrow, vertical black patch, buff cheek. **'Ear' tufts long**, wide, but often laid flat. Becomes upright when alert, narrowing face. Orange-buff patch towards wingtip.

VOICE Short, moaning, cooing hoot, "*oh*" or "*ooh*." JUVENILE calls distinctive loud, 'squeaky-gate', plaintive "*pee-ee*" or "*pyeee*," louder, sharper, less hissy than juvenile Tawny Owl.

Scarce resident (3,600 pairs) and winter visitor

from Scandinavia

Conifer belts, forests, willow thickets

IN FLIGHT, slow, wavering action similar to Short-eared Owl but wings marginally broader.
Beware – 'ear' tufts usually not apparent in flight.
See table *opposite* for plumage comparison with Short-eared Owl.

barred wingtips

thickly streaked belly

obvious 'ears'

white 'V' between orange eyes

fine freckling

ADULT

orange-buff wing patch

When alert or alarmed, stretches tall, slender and upright, ears raised and face pattern tightened into a narrower shape.

RARE OWLS

Owls in flight *p. 292*

Snowy Owl
Bubo scandiacus
L 53–65 cm | W 125–150 cm

Huge, rounded 'white' owl (but quite unlike Barn Owl (*p. 293*)). Size of Buzzard (*p. 312*), with heavier body and large, round head. **Perches upright on ground**; often hunts by day. Tiny dark bill tip; **yellow eyes** (can look dark from distance). MALE **all-white**, or with a few dark marks on wing and fine flank bars. FEMALE **grey-black bars** on white above, narrower grey bars beneath. IMMATURE like female but white face more contrasted above dense blackish bars below.

Vagrant from N Europe: >500 records (<100 records Ireland), mostly N/W Isles, Cairngorms; has bred.

IN FLIGHT, wingbeats steady, rhythmic with slowish downbeat and quicker upbeat.

IMMATURE ♂

ADULT ♀ similar, but typically has darker nape and more complete tail barring

ADULT ♂

ADULT ♂

1ST-YEAR ♀

298

Rare owls

Only the massive Snowy Owl is at all likely to give good views under normal circumstances: rare smaller owls may be found exhausted or in entirely unsuitable surroundings, such as on remote islands.

Hawk Owl
Surnia ulula   `550`

L 35–43 cm | W 70–80 cm

Smallish, upright, large-headed, **long-tailed**. Diurnal. Dark grey-brown with white mottling; white 'V' above eyes, black 'frame' to white face; **yellow eyes**.

Both **European ssp.** *ulula* and **N American ssp.** *caparoch* (on board ship, Cornwall, Mar 1830) have been recorded.

> Vagrant from N Europe, N America: <5 records (Britain), most historical, Mar, Sep, Nov, Dec. Woodland/heath.

ADULT

IN FLIGHT, wings and tail closely barred, tail longer than Little Owl's (p. 295).

ADULT

Tengmalm's Owl
Aegolius funereus   `550`

L 22–27 cm | W 50–60 cm

Small upright nocturnal forest owl with large, round head and **high-browed**, 'surprised' expression; bright **yellow eyes**; dark-edged pale facial disk (compare face with Little Owl (p. 295)).

> Vagrant from N/E Europe: <50 records (Britain), most old, Jun, Nov–Mar. Scattered. Woodland.

Scops Owl *Otus scops*

L 20 cm | W 47–54 cm

Small, nocturnal, upright, 'eared' owl. Grey-brown or more rufous with row of white spots beside back and bright yellow eyes.

VOICE Call after dusk bright, liquid, ringing "*peoop*" or "*pyup*," repeated every 2–3 seconds.

> Vagrant from S Europe: <100 records (<20 Ireland), most old, summer. Scattered. Woodland/gardens.

'ear' tufts flatten into 'corners' beside crown or raised in points (unlike round-headed Little Owl (p. 295))

ADULT (rufous)

ADULT (grey)

Nightjar *Caprimulgus europaeus*

L 24–28 cm | W 52–59 cm

Rare nightjars

Small (thrush-sized but more slender), **flat-headed**, **long-tailed** nightbird with very short bill and legs. 'Dead-branch' pattern gives marvellous camouflage. Active from dusk to dawn, when usually seen as a silhouette, in flight, or perched on branch or log.

Grey-brown, barred, spotted and marbled with brown and buff; whitish streak beside throat. Band of buff spots along 'shoulder'. Eyes large, black, usually narrow 'slit' by day, round at night.

IN FLIGHT, **long, tapered wings**; **tail long**, narrow or widely spread. Floating swoops, glides and spins. MALE has **white spots on wingtip** and tail corners (eye-catching in twilight) other detail hard to make out. FEMALE/JUVENILE lacks white spots.

VOICE Abrupt, nasal, mechanical "*gooik!*" (beware Tawny Owl (*p. 294*) "*ke-wick*"). Song prolonged vibrating **churr** – 'wooden', hollow, tapping on one note, periodically changing pitch. 'Runs down' before whiplash clap of wings. (Grasshopper Warbler (*p. 428*) has faster, higher, metallic ticking trill.)

Scarce and local summer migrant (4,600 pairs, Apr–Sep)

Open heaths, woodland clearings

ADULT ♂

ADULT ♀

ADULT

Rare nightjars

Good views of nightjars in daylight are unusual: seeing a rare one well will be exceptional. Egyptian Nightjar is distinctive, but a silent Red-necked Nightjar will require good fortune. A Common Nighthawk might be active in daylight.

Common Nighthawk
Chordeiles minor
L 23–25 cm | W 54–60 cm

Like small, dark Nightjar with whitish marbling on wing and streak of white beside throat. IN FLIGHT, (sometimes by day), glides on **wings raised in 'V'**. **Shallow fork** in tail, blackish 'shoulder' and hindwing outline pale panel; white trailing edge and **white bar across blacker outerwing**. MALE white band on tail. FEMALE/JUVENILE tail plain.

Vagrant from N America: <25 records (<5 Ireland), Oct. Scattered. Over open ground/ urban areas.

Red-necked Nightjar
Caprimulgus ruficollis
L 30–34 cm | W 60–65 cm

Dark nightjar with similar shape and actions to Nightjar; but **grey forewing**, **four rows of pale spots** across paler wing coverts (one large row between blacker/browner forewing and plainer hindwing on Nightjar). IN FLIGHT, white wingtip spots and bold white corners to tail.

Vagrant from Iberia: 1 historical record (Britain, 1st-winter, Oct 1856). Open ground.

Egyptian Nightjar
Caprimulgus aegyptius
L 24–27 cm | W 53–58 cm

Pale nightjar with similar shape and actions to Nightjar but **paler, buffier**, with **sandy-buff** spots; underparts finely barred brown on buff. IN FLIGHT, underwing pale with dark tips, white wingtip spots absent or faint.

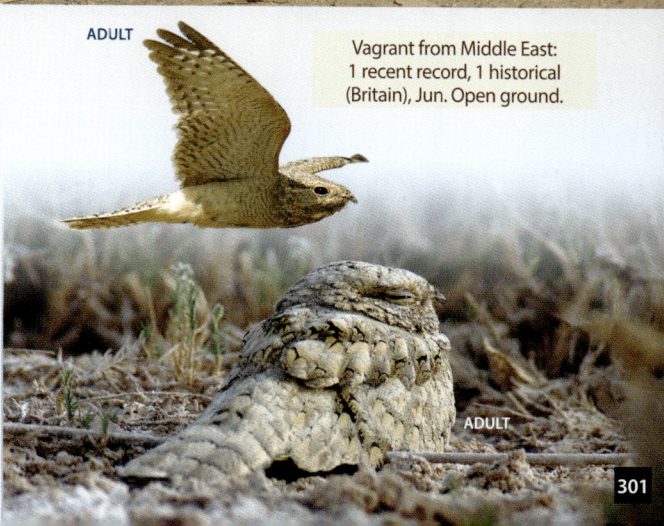

Vagrant from Middle East: 1 recent record, 1 historical (Britain), Jun. Open ground.

BIRDS OF PREY (Raptors)

BIRD OF PREY GROUP ID size | wing shape | tail shape | underwing pattern | flight action/profile

30 species: 15 breed (4 summer visitors, 2 reintroduced as breeders, 1 range expanded by introductions), 2 rare migrants; 13 vagrants (3 historical, incl. 2 vultures); various possible escapes.

A varied group; falcons not closely related to others but included here for ease of comparison. Many spend hours perched but are mostly seen more easily when they fly. Big soaring birds are not all birds of prey – Ravens (p. 486), Rooks (p. 485), Cormorants (p. 80), Grey Herons (p. 260) and gulls (pp. 122–159) are all possible while looking for birds of prey.

Best found by gaining an understanding of behaviour, range and habitats. For some, sit well back from a wood in spring, looking for birds flying up from the trees and carefully assess the likely possibilities.

SPARROWHAWK

Raptor ageing/sexing

In most birds of prey, females are clearly larger than males. Plumages are often similar, but Kestrel, Merlin, hawks and especially harriers show marked sexual differences. Juveniles tend to look more like females but in many species are easily recognized. One-year-old (1st-summer) birds can often be aged, and prolonged moults on larger species (more-or-less continuous in eagles) produce an obvious patchwork of new, dark feathers amongst old, paler ones.

Harris's Hawk *Parabuteo unicinctus* — Escape, has bred

tail tip, undertail, and rump white; thigh and 'shoulder' chestnut-red

Escaped birds of prey

Some hawks and falcons used by falconers or for control of pests may be seen flying free (with straps on the legs) or escape and live wild for a short time. (See pp. 332 and 538 for birds of prey that are classified as escapes or of unknown origin.)

10 falcons plus 2 'escapes' (pp. 326–335): narrow-winged, dark-eyed, most with strong head pattern; fast-flying, in open country, including Kestrel, the bird most likely to be seen hovering as if on a string. Hobby feeds in the air, with tight manoeuvres and changes of pace; Peregrine is increasingly familiar in urban situations (but a bird of prey capturing a dove on the lawn is most likely a Sparrowhawk (with gleaming yellow eye), not a Peregrine).

5 eagles (pp. 304–306, 321–322): very large, dark, with protruding head and broad wings; scan distant ridges and peaks (Golden Eagle) or coastal cliffs (White-tailed Eagle) in Scotland, but do not expect a close view.

Osprey (p. 310) very large, long-winged, short-tailed; usually near water; local breeder, widespread migrant.

5 harriers: (pp. 315–320): large, slim-winged, long-tailed; low-flying, wings in 'V'. Note time of year/location: Hen Harrier on high moors in summer, lowlands in winter; Montagu's Harrier only spring–summer in lowlands; Marsh Harrier most likely over reedbeds, all year in E/S, mostly winter elsewhere.

2 hawks (pp. 323–325): broad-winged, yellow-eyed, secretive/elusive woodland/woodland edge birds that also hunt in open areas (Sparrowhawk visits gardens). Also soar over woods in spring.

2 kites: (pp. 314, 320): large, dark, long-winged, notch-tailed; Red Kite common following reintroductions.

2 buzzards (pp. 308–309, 312–313): large, brownish, broad-winged, round-tailed; one widespread, one rare migrant.

Honey-buzzard (pp. 308, 311): large, with narrow head and long-tail; rare, elusive and only spring–autumn.

INTRODUCTION

Birds of prey groups: flight silhouettes

KITE (p. 314)

EAGLE (pp. 304–306)

OSPREY (p. 300)

RED KITE

WHITE-TAILED EAGLE

OSPREY

HAWK (pp. 323–325)

FALCON (pp. 326–335)

SPARROWHAWK

HOBBY

HARRIER (pp. 315–320)

BUZZARD (pp. 308–309, 312–313)

HONEY-BUZZARD (pp. 308, 311)

MONTAGU'S HARRIER

BUZZARD

HONEY-BUZZARD

CORVIDS (pp. 478–487) (for comparison)

RAVEN

CARRION CROW

303

BIRDS OF PREY

Eagles in flight *p. 306*

White-tailed Eagle *Haliaeetus albicilla*

L 76–92 cm | W 200–244 cm   Bald Eagle (*p. 322*)

Massive, heavy eagle, lacks poise of Golden Eagle but very impressive. Heavily feathered thighs, **bare yellow legs**. ADULT pale brown, whiter on head with huge **yellow bill** and **white tail** (often stained duller). JUVENILE has black teardrop spots above, black lines and 'V's on buff breast; some blacker with rufous tinge. IMMATURE see *below*.

IN FLIGHT, ADULT dark brown, head paler; **tail white**. JUVENILE tail dark, paler streaks revealed if spread. **Long head**, very **short tail**; long, broad wings **flat** in glide (not in 'V') or drooped, with long, flexible 'fingers' upswept. Deep, powerful beats in longer series between glides than Golden Eagle. Can soar to great height.

VOICE Powerful "*kik-rik-rik*" and "*kee-kee-kee*."

Rare resident, reintroduced after extirpation (>100 pairs: NW Scotland, Ireland); rare migrant

Coastal cliffs, islands; big lakes

ADULT

IMMATURE

rich brown, dark eye and bill

dark head, streaked underparts, unlike Golden Eagle

upright stance

JUVENILE/1ST-YEAR

ADULT

IMMATURE (2–4 years old)

neat, dark, new feathers; dull, bleached older ones. Pale eye; bill loses dark tip by 4th-winter

EAGLES

Golden Eagle *Aquila chrysaetos*

L 80–93 cm | W 190–227 cm

Spotted Eagle (*p. 321*)

Rare resident (440 pairs: Scotland; reintroduced Ireland); very rare wanderer N England

Huge eagle, more 'shapely' than square-winged White-tailed Eagle; see Buzzard (*p. 312*). In Scotland, usually a long-range bird of peaks/ old forest (but also adjacent valleys): scan distant skylines! **Crown and nape pale**. Heavily **feathered legs**, yellow feet. Heavy bill **grey** with yellow base. ADULT brown, blotched buff; tail barred dark grey. JUVENILE blacker; tail white with black band.

IN FLIGHT, ADULT dark brown above with **blotchy buff band** across upperwing; tail dark. JUVENILE black-brown, **white midwing band** below, small white patch on upperwing; tail **white with broad black tip**. White reduces with age; IMMATURES retain pale at base of tail. Head, wings and tail relatively longer than Buzzard. Active flight heavy with deep beats, short glides. Long, bulging wings raised in 'V' in glide. Soars to great height. Bounding display, 'teardrop' shape in dives.

VOICE Various short yelps.

wings, tail and head all proportionately longer than Buzzard; trailing edge more bulging

IMMATURE

ADULT

Mountains, moors, forests, coastal cliffs

Precise ageing difficult beyond the broad categories of Juvenile, Immature and Adult

ADULT has several generations of feathers: dark when new, fading paler

ADULT

IMMATURE

BIRDS OF PREY

Eagles in flight

Most eagles are large or very large and broad-winged. In Britain and Ireland, the choice is unlikely to be anything other than between the longer-tailed Golden Eagle, which glides on raised wings, and the shorter-tailed, bulky-headed White-tailed Eagle, which is characteristically flat-winged (like a 'flying door'). Check flight shapes and proportions, underwing and tail patterns.

3–4 year-olds have dark forewing, paler flight feathers below

IMMATURE

IMMATURE

GOLDEN EAGLE (p. 305)

IMMATURE

3–4-YEAR OLD

ADULT

IMMATURE

2-YEAR OLD

ADULT

WHITE-TAILED EAGLE (p. 304)

EAGLES and KITES IN FLIGHT

Kites in flight

Kites need to be separated from buzzards, Honey-buzzard and Harriers and are usually best told by their slow, relaxed beats with angled wings and, viewed from above, a broad, pale diagonal band across the innerwing. Kites' tails are frequently twisted and have sharp corners: when closed they look forked but when spread are more triangular with a straighter rear edge; they never look rounded, as buzzards and Honey-buzzard. Check tail colour and underwing pattern to separate the widespread Red Kite from the rare Black Kite. Harriers are broadly similar but glide on raised wings, have a square/rounded tail and lack large pale patches under the outerwing.

IMMATURE

ADULT

ADULT

RED KITE
(p. 314)

IMMATURE

IMMATURE

BLACK KITE
(p. 320)

ADULT

CARRION CROW

ADULT

IMMATURE

ADULT ♂

BUZZARD
(p. 312)

ADULT ♀/JUVENILE

MARSH HARRIER
(p. 315)

307

BIRDS OF PREY

Buzzards in flight

Buzzards and the unrelated Honey-buzzard can be difficult to tell apart, but are usually easy to tell from the slimmer-winged and longer-tailed harriers, kites and bigger eagles (Buzzards can look remarkably eagle-like at times, but size, habitat and location all help, and the Buzzard's patterned underwing usually leaves no doubt). To separate these large, broad-winged, soaring birds, check shape (including the 'set' of the wings, whether in a 'V', flat or drooped) and flight action, tail pattern and underside coloration.

HEAD/TAIL ON **SOARING** PROFILES

BUZZARDS – WINGS RAISED

HONEY-BUZZARD – WINGS LEVEL

HEAD/TAIL ON **GLIDE** PROFILES

ROUGH-LEGGED BUZZARD – WINGS OFTEN CLEARLY RAISED

BUZZARD – WINGS LEVEL OR SLIGHTLY RAISED

HONEY-BUZZARD – WINGS DOWN

two dark bands at base, dark tip

ADULT ♂

JUVENILE (dark form)

HONEY-BUZZARD (p. 311)

broad dark trailing edge

PALE FORM

two bands at base, dark tip

A variable bird: distinct wing and tail patterns help on typical birds but others look like Buzzard, structure and flight action help more than plumage

ADULT ♂

widely spaced tail-bands

ADULT ♀

dark hindwing

widely spaced tail-bands

JUVENILE

DARK FORM

typical tail

ADULT ♂

heavy barring on forewing

hindwing band diffuse

ADULT ♀

coverts unbarred

hindwing dark

JUVENILE

uniform forewing

few heavy, dark bars across primaries

BUZZARDS IN FLIGHT

BUZZARD (p. 312)

ROUGH-LEGGED BUZZARD (p. 313)

OSPREY (p. 310)

CARRION CROW

- uniform mid-brown above — ADULT
- greyish; white on tail — ADULT ♀
- white on outerwing — JUVENILE
- white tail-band
- ADULT
- black patches on wing and belly — JUVENILE
- TYPICAL TYPE: dark forewing, pale primaries
- fine bars; no tail-band
- ADULT ♀
- very pale
- black wing patches
- JUVENILE
- dark tail-band
- black belly patches
- ADULT ♂
- IMMATURE
- white body
- midwing band
- PALE TYPE: some extremely pale overall — IMMATURE

309

BIRDS OF PREY   Buzzards in flight *p. 308*

Osprey *Pandion haliaetus*

L 52–60 cm | W 150–180 cm   👁 Short-toed Eagle (*p. 321*)

Rare summer visitor (210 pairs: Scotland, locally Wales; introduced C England); rare, widespread migrant (Mar–Oct)

Very large, long-winged bird of prey: between large eagles (*pp. 304–306*) and buzzards (*pp. 308–313*) in size; shape resembles a broad- and blunt-winged 'larger' gull, with wings slightly bowed but wingtips upcurved. Upright, short-tailed on perch.

ADULT dark above, **white below** with dusky breast-band. Head white with **blackish band behind eye**. JUVENILE has bright buff, 'scaly' feather edges all over upperparts.

IN FLIGHT, upperwing dark, short tail broadly barred; **white crown** conspicuous. Underwing white at front with **black 'wrist' patch** and has central dark band. Flight strong, steady, like Great Black-backed Gull (*p. 134*) with relaxed wingbeats and glides on slightly bowed or angled wings. **Hovers** well, body more angled than hovering Buzzard (*p. 312*), wingbeats more forward/back than up/down. **Swoops and dives onto water to catch fish**, resting on surface before flying off.

VOICE High, whistling, "*weilp weilp weilp*" or "*kew kew kew.*"

to W Africa

Lakes, rivers, estuaries, adjacent forested areas

ADULT — tail may look semi-translucent
ADULT
JUVENILE — breast-band less defined in juvenile

JUVENILE JUL–NOV

Juveniles look like adults at a distance: their pale feather edges show in a close view.

uniform brown above
ADULT

pale feather edges on immature birds
pale patch on elbow
JUVENILE

Honey-buzzard *Pernis apivorus*

L 52–59 cm | W 135–150 cm

Large, broad-winged bird of prey: not a buzzard (*pp. 312–313*) but very similar; very variable (see *p. 308*). **Eyes yellow** on adult. ADULT MALE grey head, grey-brown back; some are white below. ADULT FEMALE browner overall. JUVENILE whiter, with dark 'mask'; or more rufous; or black-brown.

IN FLIGHT (ABOVE), ADULT MALE **blackish trailing edge to wing**; tail has **dark tip and two/three bands at base**. ADULT FEMALE pale patch on primaries; tail bands as male or obscure. IN FLIGHT (BENEATH), dark trailing edge, dark bands along hindwing; **tail as above, or single band at base** on MALE. Lacks Buzzard's (*p. 312*) pale breast-band. JUVENILE tail may have more weak bars; darker hindwing, heavier barring across inner primaries than Buzzard; dark eye. Shape like juvenile Buzzard but has **longer, narrower head**; longer tail. Wingtip hooks back, or broadly rounded. Wingbeats **elastic**. Wings smoothly drooped in glide, **flat or slightly raised** when soaring. Display unique: MALE claps wings over back between upward swoops.

VOICE Melodious "*whee-ooo*" or "*whi-whee-oo.*"

Rare summer visitor (40 pairs, May–Oct); scarce autumn migrant (100–400)

to Africa

Extensive forests, wooded farmland, parks; coasts in autumn

SOARING

GLIDING

wings held downwards when seen gliding head on/flying away; flat when soaring

ADULT ♂ — dark bands on wings and tail, weaker on ♀

ADULT ♀ — widely spaced tail-bands on ♀; single band near base on ♂

JUVENILE — compare slim head with chunkier Buzzard; dark hindwing; plain forewing; bars across primaries

ADULT ♂ — yellow eye; most whiter beneath than ♀

ADULT ♀

JUVENILE AUG–OCT

BIRDS OF PREY · Buzzards in flight *p. 308*

Buzzard *Buteo buteo*

L 48–56 cm | W 113–128 cm — Harris's Hawk (*p. 302*)

Large, broad-winged bird of prey; often soars but frequently perches on posts, branches and telegraph poles, and also sits in fields. Creamy-white to very dark, but typically mottled brown. ADULT **pale 'U' below breast**, barred belly. JUVENILE/IMMATURE see annotations *below*.

IN FLIGHT (ABOVE), no strong pattern, most are plain brown, some with paler tail base. IN FLIGHT (BENEATH), **strongly patterned, whitish beyond dark 'wrist'**. ADULT sharply defined dark hindwing band and tail tip. JUVENILE streaked belly, uniformly barred tail, ill-defined hindwing band. Wingbeats quite quick, stiff. Glides with wings hunched in slight kink. Soars with **wings usually in 'V'** (juvenile wings narrower, flatter, more like Honey-buzzard (*p. 311*); soaring Marsh Harrier (*p. 315*) has longer tail, plainer wing). Displays in steep switchbacks, dives.

VOICE Loud, sharp "*pi-yaaa*," explosive close up. Late summer, wails from juveniles (perched or up high).

Common resident in Britain (60,000–70,000 pairs); scarce Ireland (200 pairs)

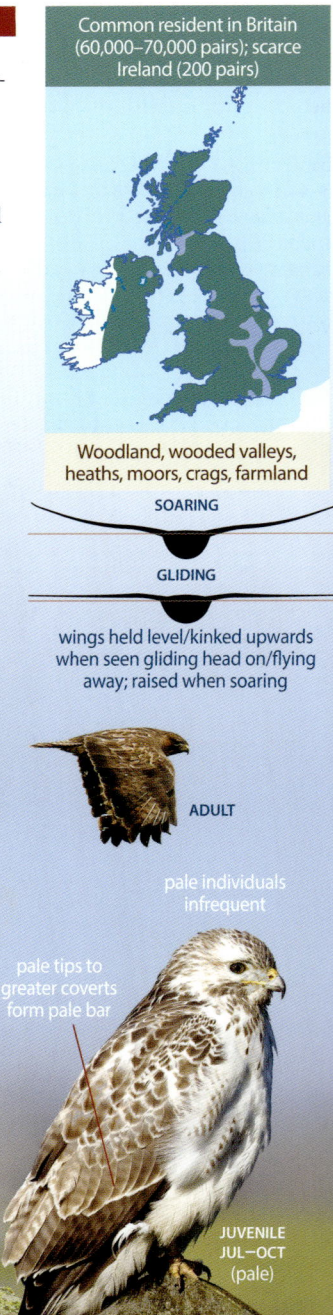

Woodland, wooded valleys, heaths, moors, crags, farmland

SOARING
GLIDING

wings held level/kinked upwards when seen gliding head on/flying away; raised when soaring

IMMATURE (pale) — narrower wings, looks longer-tailed
IMMATURE — diffuse trailing edge and tail-band
JUVENILE (dark) — dark trailing edge and tail-band
hovers well
ADULT

ADULT

ADULT
IMMATURE — 2ND-YEAR has many juvenile feathers, become bleached and faded.
JUVENILE JUL–OCT (pale) — pale individuals infrequent; pale tips to greater coverts form pale bar

Rough-legged Buzzard *Buteo lagopus*

L 49–59 cm | W 120–150 cm

Large, broad-winged bird of prey; often perched on a bare tree or **hovering** over open ground. Typically pale on head and breast; **blackish belly**, pale thighs; feathered lower leg hard to see.
IN FLIGHT (ABOVE), **pale band across primaries** and paler innerwing band (recalling Red Kite (*p. 314*)); **broad white tail base** (ADULT MALE 3–4 bars at tip; ADULT FEMALE narrow, blacker band plus 1–2 fine bars; JUVENILE broad dark band). IN FLIGHT (BENEATH), **black 'wrist' patches**, contrasting with white towards wingtip; black belly; white tail with dark band. Soars like Buzzard with wings raised; glides on more 'bent' wings; active flight more 'elastic'. Hovers more than most Buzzards.

VOICE Silent in winter.

Rare migrant, winter visitor (50 per year, periodically more (up to 185), (<50 records Ireland; Oct–Mar)

from Scandinavia

Regular ssp. is *lagopus*; N American ssp. *sanctijohannis* (one record (Ireland), Oct) others suspected in N and W Britain; identification requires measurements.

wings often clearly raised when seen head on/flying away

Coastal, open areas, moors, farmland

ADULT ♂ — dark tail-band 3–4 bars

ADULT ♀ — dark carpal ('wrist') patches; dark tail-band 1–2 bars

JUVENILE — dark belly

hovers persistently; dark tail-band broad

JUVENILES — pale band across primaries

> Beware Buzzards with a white tail – though in most cases these individuals have more bars on the tail tip and sides.

ADULT ♂

JUVENILE SEP–MAR

BIRDS OF PREY   Kites in flight *p. 307*

NT Red Kite *Milvus milvus*

NT L 61–72 cm | W 175–195 cm   👁 Black Kite (*p. 320*)

A large, fork-tailed bird of prey, with long wings set well forward; more supple action than Buzzard (*p. 312*). Sexes alike. ADULT gingery- or **reddish-brown**, dark streaks; paler feather edgings over wings. Head pale; yellow eye. JUVENILE slightly paler beneath, narrower pale feather edges above.

IN FLIGHT (ABOVE), whitish head may be striking; **diagonal pale band** across innerwing above; tail broad, **forked**, dark-tipped, **rusty-red**.

IN FLIGHT (BENEATH), rufous body and forewing contrast with dark midwing panel and big **white patch before black wingtips**. Tail pale beneath, with dark corners. Flight supremely elegant, with deep, flexible beats; soars on **flat/bowed wings** (not Buzzard's 'V') sometimes to great height. Active flight with wide, curved wings well forward, long, notched/forked tail, twisted sideways.

VOICE Wailing, screaming versions of Buzzard-like notes.

Locally common resident, most reintroduced (1,600 pairs, 20 pairs Ireland); migrant from NW Europe

from S Scandinavia and E Europe

Wooded countryside, villages, forests

ADULTS — long, flat profile, wings pushed forward, recognizable at long range

shallow tail fork

pale colour

JUVENILES — white tips to coverts create white band across midwing

often forages on the ground in open fields

JUVENILE JUL–DEC

ADULT

notice effects of wear and tear on tail

Harriers in flight *p. 316*

KITES | HARRIERS

Marsh Harrier *Circus aeruginosus*

L 43–55 cm | W 120–135 cm

Black Kite (*p. 320*)

546

Buzzard-sized and somewhat buzzard- or kite-like when soaring, but clearly a harrier when gliding low down with wings held in a 'V'. **Tail unbarred**. ADULT MALE brown with pale head, pale **grey wing**, brown back and grey tail. ADULT FEMALE/JUVENILE strikingly dark brown.

IN FLIGHT, ADULT MALE pale **grey midwing**, **black wingtip**; brown back, **pale grey tail**; underside rusty-buff. ADULT FEMALE dark brown with **cream cap and throat**, cream forewing and pale streaks on breast. JUVENILE blackish-brown with pale crown and throat; dark underwing with paler flight feathers. Heavier and broader-winged than other harriers (*pp. 316–320*), but typical **low, direct or wavering** flight, elastic beats between **glides on raised wings**; also soars high up. Striking spring display flight, and typical harrier rolling foot-to-foot 'food pass' between male and female.

VOICE Silent except high chatter over nest in spring.

Rare resident (425 pairs, most E England); scarce migrant, winter visitor

from S Scandinavia and E Europe

Marshes, coastal wetlands

ADULT ♂

typically seen flying low over marsh: supple flaps between glides on raised wings

ADULT ♂

JUVENILE JUL–OCT

♀

MALE **may breed in patchy immature plumage**

♀/juvenile ageing is often impossible on plumage pattern. Compared to older FEMALE, JUVENILE has a darker brown eye (not reddish/yellowish), thicker pale tips to greater coverts, paler tips to upper tail coverts and plainer dark tail (pale spots show on spread tail of ADULT); occasionally all dark.

ADULT ♀

ADULT ♂

BIRDS OF PREY
Harriers in flight

MONTAGU'S HARRIER *(p. 308)*

PALLID HARRIER *(p. 309)*

HEN HARRIER *(p. 307)*

MARSH HARRIER *(p. 305)*

ADULT MALES

ADULT/IMMATURE FEMALES

MONTAGU'S HARRIER

HEN HARRIER

MARSH HARRIER

PALLID HARRIER

3–4 'fingers'

3–4 'fingers'

4–5 'fingers'

JUVENILES WITH WHITE RUMPS

Juveniles are brighter orange-buff below than adult females, upperside feathers edged more rufous.

narrower wings

broad wings

NORTHERN HARRIER *(p. 310)*

plain

dark trailing edge

5 'fingers'

PALLID HARRIER

MONTAGU'S HARRIER

HEN HARRIER

unstreaked

heavily streaked

pale ochre, unstreaked

pale ochre, unstreaked

5 'fingers'

316

Comparison of juvenile harriers *p. 319*

HARRIERS

Hen Harrier *Circus cyaneus*

L 45–55 cm | W 99–121 cm

Northern Harrier (*p. 320*), Pallid Harrier (*p. 319*)

Small-headed bird of prey, smaller than Buzzard (*p. 312*) but long-winged and long-tailed. MALE **grey with black wingtip** and white belly. FEMALE/JUVENILE brown above, buff below with black streaks; dark cheek and white marks around dark eye patch (see *p. 319*).

IN FLIGHT, glides with wings raised between easy, deep wingbeats. Broader wingtip than Montagu's Harrier (*p. 318*), with 4–5 'fingers'. Female heavier, broader-winged than male. MALE **pale grey** with **black wingtips**, white rump and **dark trailing edge to underwing**. IMMATURE MALE has browner back and forewing. FEMALE brown with **white rump**. Pale below with brown streaks. **Tail strongly banded.** JUVENILE similar, streaked black on rusty-buff below.

VOICE Calls on breeding area, chattering "*chet-et-et-et-it-it-et.*"

Rare resident (780 pairs, including 150 in Ireland); scarce but more widespread winter visitor

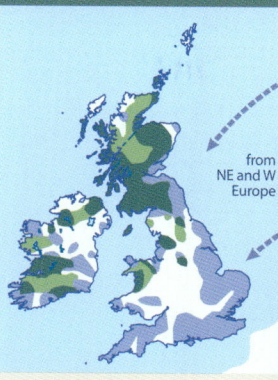

from NE and W Europe

Heather moorland, open grassland, marshes

ADULT ♂

2ND-WINTER ♂

spring display flights include acrobatic tumbling between steep undulations

ADULT ♀

JUVENILE FEMALE
similar but broader-winged

JUVENILE ♂
JUL–OCT

ADULT ♀

IMMATURE MALES
often dull, browner-backed than 'clean and bright' adult

ADULT ♂

BIRDS OF PREY

Harriers in flight *p. 316*

Montagu's Harrier *Circus pygargus*

L 39–50 cm | W 97–115 cm

👁 Pallid Harrier

Rare and very local summer visitor (5–10 pairs, most E England; few migrants, Apr–Sep); <100 records Ireland

Slim, lightweight harrier (like Hen Harrier (*p. 317*) with slender wingtip). MALE grey with **black wingbar and wingtip**. FEMALE brown; underparts buff with black streaks; **dark cheek patch small, isolated** behind white eye-crescents; pale edge to cheek weak or absent. JUVENILE rusty-brown above, plain rufous below, strong head pattern (*opposite*).

IN FLIGHT, tends to glide with tapered wingtips more swept back than Hen Harrier, with particularly light, airy action; elongated, pointed wingtip useful clue (3–4 'fingers'). MALE grey, with **dark forewing/ pale hindwing effect**; extensive black wingtip; **black midwing bar** unique. White rump weak or absent. Underwing has black bar, chestnut blotches on coverts (clean white on Hen Harrier). Outertail lightly barred. FEMALE like Hen Harrier but white rump smaller. JUVENILE **unstreaked buffy-orange below**.

VOICE Calls "*kekekek*" and "*jik-jik-jik*" near nest.

Marshes, rough grassland

JUVENILE JUL–OCT

1ST-SUMMER ♂

intermediate pattern

ADULT ♂

ADULT ♀

ADULT ♂

MALE very lightweight; darker plumage than extremely pale male Hen Harrier

ADULT ♀

NOTE: absent in winter (unlike Hen Harrier).

IMMATURE MALES often dull, browner-backed than 'clean and bright' adult

ADULT ♀

ADULT ♂

HARRIERS

Head patterns of juvenile harriers with white rumps

Juvenile harriers are difficult: structure and plumage must be checked with care and the head pattern is important.

Juvenile harriers have white marks above and below the dark eye and dark cheek crescents.

Hen Harrier has the weakest pattern, small white marks around eye, **streaked neck** beneath narrow pale collar.

Pallid Harrier has a broad, **pale collar contrasting with dark cheek**; unstreaked brown shawl around lower neck.

Montagu's Harrier has white marks above and below dark eye patch, dark cheek, **weak pale collar**; unstreaked throat and breast.

HEN HARRIER

PALLID HARRIERS — strongly marked individual

MONTAGU'S HARRIER

Pallid Harrier
Circus macrourus
546

L 40–50 cm | W 95–120 cm

Slim, lightweight harrier: like a pale Montagu's Harrier but with a shorter, 3–4-'fingered' wingtip.

IN FLIGHT, MALE pale grey with **narrow black 'wedge'** on wingtip. FEMALE like Montagu's Harrier, but plainer above, with barely a hint of a blackish midwing band; darker underwing and hindwing; darker, plainer dark coverts. JUVENILE underside **unmarked orange-buff**; **brown neck patch**; underwing coverts rufous, secondaries grey, broadly barred black.

Vagrant from Asia: <100 records (<10 Ireland), small influxes, Sep–Apr. Scattered. Moors, farmland.

ADULT ♂

ADULT ♀

ADULT ♀

JUVENILE JUL–OCT

ADULT ♀

ADULT ♂

MALE lightweight; pale grey with white underparts

319

RARE BIRDS OF PREY

Rare birds of prey

Black Kite   546
Milvus migrans
L 48–58 cm | W 135–155 cm

Similar to Red Kite (p. 314) but **duller brown**; **tail less forked**, drab brown with short, dark bars; underwing less well marked, **dull primary patch** at best. JUVENILE has paler inner primaries.

IN FLIGHT, less elongated than Red Kite; see Marsh Harrier (p. 315); tail triangular, shallow notch when closed. **Pale band across innerwing** (female Marsh Harrier has pale leading edge; plain, square tail). Active flight with bowed wings, swooping turns, twisting tail, unlike a harrier.

Very rare migrant/vagrant from S Europe: <700 records, 15–25 per year (<25 records Ireland), most Apr–Jun. Winters in Africa.

Kites in flight *p. 307*

JUVENILE
ADULT
ADULT

Eastern ssp. *lineatus* ('Black-eared Kite'), perhaps extreme vagrant to Britain: paler head, dark ear covert patch and slightly paler, barred patch under outerwing than European ssp. *migrans*.

Northern Harrier   546
Circus hudsonius
L 45–55 cm | W 99–121 cm

N American equivalent of Hen Harrier. MALE like Hen Harrier (p. 317) but **browner forewing and back** (SUB-ADULTS mottled brown on grey), **broader dark trailing edge to wing**; hooded appearance; **streaked breast**; fine bars on underwing and tail. FEMALE (not recorded) darker above, **more rufous below** than Hen Harrier. JUVENILE similar to Montagu's Harrier (p. 318) but broad, 5-fingered wingtip like Hen Harrier; usually deeper rufous-buff beneath (closer to Montagu's Harrier), fine streaks restricted to throat. **More (5–6) bars on outer primaries** than Hen Harrier (best seen on photographs); dark brown neck, pale collar; dark hood.

Vagrant from N America: <20 records Britain (<10 Ireland), autumn–winter. Grassland/marshes.

Harriers in flight *p. 316*

ADULT ♂
marked
brown
grey
JUVENILE
HEN HARRIER
2ND-WINTER ♂
little/no marking
JUVENILE JUL–OCT
HEN HARRIER
fine streaks restricted to throat
JUVENILE
streaked

more (5–6) bars on outer primaries than Hen Harrier

NORTHERN HARRIER | HEN HARRIER

KITES | HARRIERS | EAGLES

Short-toed Eagle
Circaetus gallicus
L 62–69 cm | W 170–185 cm

A large eagle, bigger than Osprey (*p. 310*), with a **large, rounded head**, **bright yellow eyes** and short, bare, yellow legs.

IN FLIGHT, long wings, 'bulging' on trailing edge, broadest at 'wrist' and tapered towards tip; rather short tail. Usually looks pale: sandy brown above, **silvery-white below** with variable fine dark bars (some birds have a dark hood). **No dark 'wrist' patch** on underwing. Tail has pale translucent bars. Often hovers with heavy, 'wobbling' action.

Vagrant from S Europe: <10 records (Britain), May–Oct. S England. Heaths, forest.

no dark 'wrist' patch

JUVENILE JUL–OCT

ADULT

ADULT

1ST-SUMMER MAR–SEP

dark 'wrist' patch

BUZZARD IMMATURE (pale)

ADULT

Juvenile pale rufous below – dark hood/ streaked breast after 5–6 years, darkest on females

(Greater) Spotted Eagle
Clanga (Aquila) clanga
L 59–69 cm | W 157–180 cm

Large, dark eagle; like Golden Eagle (*p. 305*) but wide-winged with broad, blunt tips; **short tail**. Pale patch at base of primaries and **small pale rump** above, pale crescent at base of primaries underneath. IMMATURE variable white spotting on wings.

Vagrant from C Europe: 14 records, all pre-1915, Oct–Jan; unlikely now.

JUVENILE

JUVENILE

JUVENILE JUL–DEC

RARE BIRDS OF PREY

Griffon Vulture   546
Gyps fulvus ◆
L 95–105 cm | W 240–280 cm

Enormous, broad-winged, very short-tailed bird of prey. Upperside toffee-brown, flight feathers darker. Brown below with pale lines across wing coverts; flight feathers dark. Soars on raised wings with bulging hindwing and upcurved 'fingers'.

Vagrant from S Europe: 1 historical record (Ireland, 1842).

Egyptian Vulture   546
EN EN
Neophron percnopterus
L 55–65 cm | W 146–175 cm

Very large bird of prey. Fine bill, yellow face, **wedge-tipped tail**; long, rather narrow wings. ADULT **white**, washed yellow/orange; flat wings with **black rear/outerwing** from below. IMMATURE duller, browner.

Vagrant from S Europe: historical records (Britain, last 1868); unlikely now.

Bald Eagle
Haliaeetus leucocephalus ◆
77 cm | W 180–200 cm

Huge, short-tailed eagle; flat-winged like White-tailed Eagle (*p. 304*) but wingtip shows only 6 'fingers' (not 7). ADULT (not recorded) black, with white head and tail. IMMATURE like White-tailed Eagle but body blacker, underwing with whitish bands and tail greyish with blackish tip.

Vagrant from N America: Ireland (<5 records), Jan, Nov.

RARITIES | HAWKS IN FLIGHT

Accipiter hawks in flight

These hawks are relatively broad-winged and long-tailed. **Goshawk** and **Sparrowhawk** can be differentiated by subtleties of shape and size. **Goshawk** can be confused with **Honey-buzzard** (p. 311) and **larger falcons**, particularly a soaring **Peregrine** (p. 329) or **Gyrfalcon** (p. 331) (rare) – check shape and wingset, underwing and head patterns. **Sparrowhawk** can be confused with **Kestrel** (p. 326) and **Merlin** (p. 327), especially if the view is brief. Falcons are relatively longer winged and shorter tailed, with dark eyes.

SPARROWHAWK (p. 324)

ADULT ♂
ADULT ♀
ADULT ♂
ADULT ♀
broad bars
JUVENILE
narrow bars

KESTREL (p. 326)
dark eye

ADULT (scaled as ♂)
broad bars
pale eye
JUVENILE (scaled as ♀)

single tail band
MERLIN (p. 327)
dark eye

GOSHAWK (p. 325)

ADULT ♂
ADULT ♂
ADULT ♀

Goshawk larger, bulkier than Sparrowhawk, hindwing more curved, head longer, tail broader and rounded

JUVENILE ♀

Note Goshawk's variety of profiles: WINGS swept, flexed or straight out; WINGTIPS flat or upswept; TAIL broad, often rounded; HEAD protruding; CHEST deep

JUVENILE
JUVENILE

BIRDS OF PREY   *Accipiter* hawks in flight p.323

Sparrowhawk *Accipiter nisus*

L ♂ 29–34 cm | W 58–65 cm   ♀ 35–41 cm | W 68–77 cm

Small, bird-hunting hawk; elusive but often soars in the open. A frequent brief visitor to gardens. MALE smaller (Collared Dove-sized (p. 288)) and 'snappier' than larger, heavier (Kestrel-sized (p. 326)) FEMALE. **Yellow eye** rules out falcons. MALE bluish-grey; variably pink-orange below. FEMALE grey, fades browner; pale stripe over eye. Underparts **dull white** with grey bars. Legs slim (Goshawk's thick). JUVENILE rusty-brown with paler feather edges, barred rufous below.

IN FLIGHT, **little contrast** above or below except darker tail bands. **Small head**; broad breast; **long, slim tail** (opens in half-fan). Wing broad-based; short outer half spreads to blunt, broad tip, or curves back to short point (compare Kestrel and Merlin (p. 327)). Quick, deep beats between short, flat glides (**flap-flap-glide** unlike Kestrel's erratic action). Hunts in slanting dive, or short, fast chase; sits and waits in thick cover. Does not hover! Evokes frenetic alarm calls from Starlings/ tit flocks. In display, fast, bouncing undulations; patrols with slow, deep beats (suggests Goshawk) before headlong plunge into trees.

VOICE Calls chattering "*kewkewkewkewkew*" around nest.

Fairly common resident (48,000 pairs, including 13,000 in Ireland)

Woodland, extensive forest or scattered trees in farmland, parks; hunts over fields, moors, marshes

JUVENILE (sized as ♀)

ADULT (sized as ♂)

ADULT ♀

JUVENILE

ADULT ♀

The most likely bird of prey to capture a bird in a garden (carries off small prey but may stay to pluck larger birds): takes birds from tits up to Collared Dove size.

ADULT ♂

JUVENILE ♀
JUL–NOV

JUVENILE (scaled as ♂)
JUL–NOV

Goshawk *Accipiter gentilis*

L ♂ 49–56 cm | W 90–105 cm   ♀ 58–64 cm | W 108–127 cm

Large, bird-hunting hawk: see Sparrowhawk, Peregrine (*p. 329*). Female big, long-winged (see Honey-buzzard (*p. 311*)), but 'small Goshawk/large Sparrowhawk' can be problematical. MALE Carrion Crow-sized (*p. 484*); FEMALE near size of Buzzard (*p. 312*).

ADULT greyish above, white below with dark bars; broad white vent; dark face band. JUVENILE brown; **buff** beneath, **streaked black**.

IN FLIGHT, little or **no contrast** above or below except darker tail bands. **Long head**; deep breast/belly; broad rump; **rounded tail**; **bulging innerwing** with **narrow tip**. Taut 'full stretch' in soar (shape like soaring Kestrel (*p. 326*)), flat wings sweep gently upwards. End-on, 'T'-shape, or wings pointed like Peregrine. Displays with deep undulations; slow flight over wood, headlong plunges. Soars, stoops like Peregrine.

VOICE Call near nest recalls Green Woodpecker (*p. 345*), repeated, shouted "*cha-cha-cha-cha-cha*" and high whine.

Rare, local resident (430 pairs); rare migrant; very small numbers but increasing in Ireland

Woodland, adjacent open areas

N American ssp. *atricapillus* [*not illustrated*] (vagrant: <10 records (Ireland), Oct–Feb) likely escape; reduced barring beneath compared with resident ssp. *gentilis*, accurate assessment only likely from photographs.

♂ and ♀ may not be separable without direct size comparison

ADULT ♂

JUVENILE ♂

blue-grey fades browner by late winter

ADULT ♂

NOTE: all birds shown are ssp. *gentilis*.

ADULT ♂

ADULT (scaled as ♀)

JUVENILE

drop-shaped streaks on bright buff

BIRDS OF PREY   Falcons in flight *p. 333*

Kestrel *Falco tinnunculus*

L 31–37 cm | W 65–82 cm

Lesser Kestrel (*p. 334*), Red-footed Falcon (*p. 330*)

Small, long-tailed, upright falcon. MALE head and tail grey; back rufous, spotted black; weak 'moustache'; underparts buff. FEMALE **ginger-brown**, barred above, streaked below. JUVENILE like female; uppertail coverts greyish on male.

IN FLIGHT, **innerwing pale, outerwing dark**. MALE **black band on grey tail**. FEMALE barred rufous; tail/rump often greyer. Wings quite straight, blunt, or angled back to a point. Slender tail opens to full fan. Relaxed or quick beats, with high upstroke, progress erratic, without flap-flap-glide of Sparrowhawk (*p. 324*); slower than Peregrine (*p. 329*) or Merlin, nor so elegant as Hobby (*p. 328*). **Persistent hovering** (sometimes very high, often at dusk): tail spread, wings quivered or flapped. Soars on flat, rather broad wings.

VOICE Sharp, whining "*kee-kee-kee-kee.*"

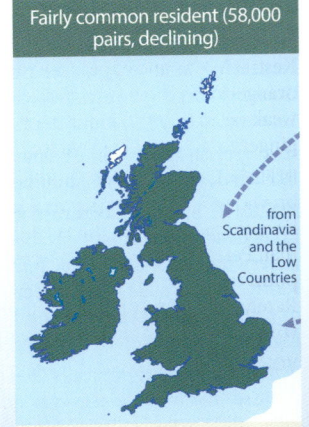

Fairly common resident (58,000 pairs, declining)

from Scandinavia and the Low Countries

Open ground, farmland, heaths, suburban/waste areas

♂

1ST-YEAR ♂

♀

ADULT ♀

JUVENILE ♀

mottled silvery-buff below

striking two-tone effect above

♂

ADULT ♂

A Kestrel watches for prey by hovering, head motionless relative to the ground.

ADULT / JUVENILE ♀

strongly barred

grey head

spotted chestnut back

ADULT ♂

FALCONS

Merlin *Falco columbarius*
ssp. *subaesalon* | 551

L 26–33 cm | W 50–67 cm | American Kestrel (*p. 334*)

Small falcon, male like male Sparrowhawk (*p. 324*), female closer to Kestrel in size and appearance. Chunky, square-headed. MALE blue-grey; orange-buff below with streaks not bars; head pattern/'moustache' weak (as Kestrel). Tail grey with black band. FEMALE/JUVENILE **brown**, less ginger than Kestrel; tail barred cream; dark 'moustache' and rear cheek.

IN FLIGHT, MALE has grey tail with black band. FEMALE/JUVENILE earthy-brown, with **no strong upperwing contrast**; tail barred cream. Fast, low; quick beats, **few glides**; more direct than Kestrel – wings shorter than Peregrine (*p. 329*) and Hobby (*p. 328*), **broad-based but sharper point** than Kestrel's (Sparrowhawk has broader wings with shorter tip). Rarely soars, does not hover. Approaches prey with **flicked, in-out wingtip action** (like Hobby), before **fast, twisting chase**.

VOICE Sharp "*ki-ki-ki-ki;*" "*week-week-week-week-week*."

Ssp. *aesalon* breeds; larger **ssp. *subaesalon*** (breeds Iceland) rare winter migrant; **ssp. *columbarius*** [*not illustrated*] (vagrant from N America: <5 records, Sep, Feb) male has broad black bands on tail.

Rare summer visitor (1,300 pairs, mostly N and W), migrant; widespread, scarce winter visitor

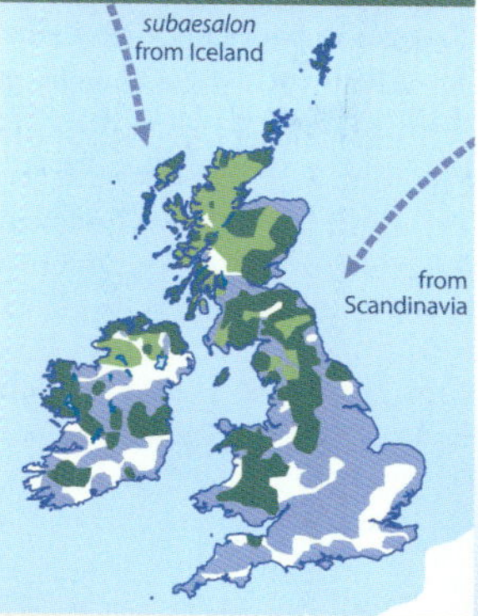

subaesalon from Iceland

from Scandinavia

Moors, open plantations, bushy hillsides; in winter, wetlands, lowland pastures, coasts

compact, sharp-winged, fast and direct

♀ ♂

JUVENILE JUL–NOV

ssp. *subaesalon*

♂ ssp. *subaesalon*

♀

ssp. *aesalon* ADULT ♀

ADULT FEMALES usually brown with narrow buff fringes above (see *below left*), rarely grey like MALE but tail barred; JUVENILE more broadly barred buff on upperparts.

often perches on ground or post

muddier brown than Kestrel; tail barred with cream spots

ADULT ♀

clear blue-grey with fine dark streaks, grey tail with single black band at tip

ADULT ♂ ssp. *aesalon*

Hobby *Falco subbuteo*

L 29–35 cm | W 68–84 cm

Red-footed Falcon (*p. 330*), Eleonora's Falcon (*p. 355*)

Scarce summer migrant, Apr–Oct (1,200–2,800 pairs); <500 records Ireland

Small, aerial falcon (compare with Kestrel (*p. 326*) and especially Peregrine). Elegant in flight: **changes in pace** are evident when hawking insects. Sexes alike; black 'moustache', white cheek. ADULT grey above, tail plain; white below, **thickly streaked** black. Thigh/vent rusty red. JUVENILE browner; buff feather edges above, buff cheek; streaked buff below, no red.

IN FLIGHT, looks **dark**: close view/good light needed to see detail, but **white neck patch** shows well, heavy black streaks below evident at closer range. Patrols on flat/bowed wings, accelerates with **deep, whippy beats** into upward glide/stall, catching insects. Long, slanting, flapping dive into fast, swept-wing stoop when hunting small birds. Long-wings arc to narrow tip, sharper than Kestrel, tail tapered or half-fanned. **Narrower body, especially rump/tail base**, than Peregrine, but can be hard to tell; **head small, squat** into shoulders.

VOICE Rather ringing, bright "*kew-kew-kew-kew*."

to Africa

Open ground, heaths, farmland, moors, around lakes and marshes

narrow tail base is a useful feature
ADULT

barred tail, brown on wings
1ST-SUMMER

dull dark brown above
JUVENILE

JUVENILE AUG–OCT
dark, mottled and streaked below; no rufous

ADULT
streaked below; rufous vent hard to see

white 'hook' on rear cheek
ADULT

Past reliance on heaths/pine copses reduced as Hobbies now occupy farmland and valleys with flooded gravel pits.

FALCONS

Peregrine *Falco peregrinus*

L ♂ 38–45 cm | W 87–100 cm
♀ 46–51 cm | W 104–114 cm

Gyrfalcon (p. 331)

Scarce resident (1,800 pairs, including 300 in Ireland): wanders widely in winter

Large falcon; broad-shouldered, heavily built, FEMALE larger than MALE. **Black beneath eye, white cheek.** MALE blue-grey above, pinkish-white below with black-spotted breast and barred flank. FEMALE duller grey and white. JUVENILE browner; underparts buff, **streaked black**.

IN FLIGHT, rather heavy, broad-bodied; **protruding head with black 'moustache'** and **white neck**; both barred tail and **paler rump** are **broader** than on Hobby. Wings broad, tapered (female's blunt-tipped, male's sharper) or 'anchor' shape; **short, tapered tail**. Flight direct, muscular; **deep, whippy beats**, often with few or no glides. Soars masterfully (wings faintly upswept) to great height. Fast, direct pursuit of prey; swoops from beneath or stoops with closed wings.

VOICE Around nest: loud, coarse "*haar-haair-haair*," chattering "*kek-kek-kek-kek*;" various whining sounds.

from Scandinavia

Cities to wild cliffs, coastal and inland; winter, almost anywhere

broad tail base — ADULT

browner back / pale tail tip — JUVENILE MAY–DEC

JUVENILE — streaked underside

ADULT — barred underside

bright, pale shield-shaped breast above bars and spots

ADULT

ADULT

RARE FALCONS   Falcons in flight *p. 333*

NT **Red-footed Falcon** *Falco vespertinus*   550
NT L 28–34 cm | W 65–76 cm

Very rare migrant from E Europe: <1,000 records, 15–20 per year (<50 records Ireland); Mar–Nov, most May. Open spaces, watersides. Winters in Africa.

Small falcon, between Hobby (*p. 328*) and Kestrel (*p. 326*) in character. Drifts over open space, hovers like Kestrel (migrants rarely do so). Wings shorter than Hobby; red/orange on bill, eyering and legs. ADULT MALE grey with **rufous thigh/belly**. ADULT FEMALE grey back, barred dark; rufous underparts; **buff cap**, **black 'mask'**, white cheek. JUVENILE pale cap, dark 'mask', white cheek; underparts white, streaked black.

◉ Amur Falcon (*p. 335*)

IN FLIGHT, ADULT MALE upperwing grey, with **silvery** tip. IMMATURE MALE (frequent in spring) **rufous on breast**, plainer grey upperwing, **barred/chequered underwing** with old (barred) and new (grey) flight feathers in contrasting patches. ADULT FEMALE grey above, barred darker, with narrowly barred grey tail; rufous cap; underside plain rufous-buff. JUVENILE very like juvenile Hobby but most have **pale collar** and **paler underwing** with dark spots and darker trailing edge and **barred tail**.

flight often slow, dipping

ADULT ♀

ADULT ♂

ADULT ♂

1ST-SUMMER ♂

JUVENILE JUL–OCT

rufous thighs/belly (hard to see in some lights)

ADULT ♀

1ST-SUMMER ♂
MAY–OCT

ADULT ♂

ADULT ♀

grey back with soft dark grey bars

bill base, eyering and legs red

underparts rufous-buff

RARE FALCONS

Gyrfalcon *Falco rusticolus* 550
L 53–63 cm | W 120–134 cm

Very large, heavy falcon: most British/Irish vagrants 'white'. See Peregrine (*p. 329*), Goshawk (*p. 325*). Scandinavian Gyrfalcons dark; Icelandic mid-grey; Greenland 'white'.

IN FLIGHT, big; wingspan equals Buzzard (*p. 312*) or female Goshawk. Slightly rounded wingtips; broad tail; **deep, heavy belly** extending back into deep, **broad undertail area**. Slower, shallower flight action than Peregrine. **Dark coverts/paler flight feathers** below; dark hood but white-face/black 'moustache' weaker than on Peregrine. 'WHITE' ADULT white, with copious dark flecks on some, few on others. JUVENILE grey-brown, underwing very dark, underbody heavily streaked; cheeks dark; legs bluish.

Vagrant from N Europe/Greenland: <500 records (<150 Ireland), Sep–May. Most winter/early spring. Moors/cliffs.

👁 Beware, escaped Saker Falcon (very like juvenile Gyrfalcon), Lanner Falcon, other falcons and hybrids – see *p. 332*.

JUVENILE

JUVENILE

dark cheeks

PEREGRINE
JUVENILE
much smaller; 'moustache' more obvious

IMMATURE 'white form'

ADULT

JUVENILE

IMMATURE (Icelandic)

ADULT (Scandinavian)

ESCAPED FALCONS

Escaped falcons

Falconers, zoos and stately homes often fly birds of prey during displays and some head for freedom: usually identifiable as such by long straps ('jesses') on their legs. Many species are involved, plus a number of irresponsibly bred hybrids, barely identifiable and confusing the issue further. Lanner and Saker Falcons are shown here but other falcons, hawks and eagles are also involved.

EN Lanner Falcon
Falco biarmicus
L 35–50 cm | W 95–105 cm

Long-winged, like huge Kestrel (p.326); rufous cap, rufous/white cheeks. Greyer than Saker Falcon, flanks barred, underwing paler; JUVENILE has densely barred tail.

EN VU Saker Falcon
Falco cherrug
L 45–57 cm | W 95–125 cm

Sandier-brown than Lanner Falcon, buffier on head/breast with dark streaks below and dark thighs. In flight, upperwing has kestrel-like tawny innerwing/dark outerwing.

Falcons in flight ▶

Compared to *Accipiter* hawks (p. 323), falcons are relatively long-winged and short-tailed, and have dark (not yellow) eyes, but a soaring Gyrfalcon or Peregrine can be taken for a Goshawk. Separating commoner falcons is usually straightforward (Peregrine/Hobby less so), but rarer ones may be difficult: patterns and flight shapes important.

GYRFALCON — JUVENILE

LANNER FALCON — dark cheeks — JUVENILE

SAKER FALCON — pale cheeks — JUVENILE

GYRFALCON (p.331) ADULT (SCANDINAVIAN)

LANNER FALCON ADULT

SAKER FALCON 2ND-WINTER ADULT similar but has yellow eyering and cere

PEREGRINE (p.329) ADULT

FALCONS IN FLIGHT

RED-FOOTED FALCON (p. 330)
ADULT ♀
JUVENILE
ADULT ♀
1ST-SUMMER ♂
JUVENILE
ADULT ♂
RED-FOOTED FALCON

HOBBY (p. 328)
ADULT

PEREGRINE (p. 329)
JUVENILE
ADULT
ADULT
ADULT
1ST-SUMMER ♂
HOBBY
JUVENILE

KESTREL (p. 326)
JUVENILE
♂
♂
♀
♀
JUVENILE

MERLIN (p. 327)
♀
♂
JUVENILE

333

RARE FALCONS

Very rare falcons

Lesser Kestrel
Falco naumanni 550
L 27–33 cm | W 58–73 cm

Like slender Kestrel (*p. 326*), with **pale claws**. MALE like Kestrel but bluer head, **unspotted rufous back**, **blue-grey band** across innerwing. Underwing nearly white: small dark tip, fine dark specks. FEMALE/IMMATURE hard to tell from Kestrel but may show a more contrasted paler cheek/darker 'moustache'.

IN FLIGHT, shallow, quick wingbeats, often hovers.

Lesser Kestrel has whitish claws at all ages.

Vagrant from S Europe: <25 records (1 Ireland), Nov–May, most spring. Scattered. Heaths, islands.

1ST-SUMMER ♂ — central tail feathers often protrude
ADULT ♂
♀
1ST-SUMMER ♂
unspotted back
unspotted
ADULT ♀
ADULT ♂
very like Kestrel, more contrast between cheek and 'moustache' ♀
ADULT ♂
black claws — spotted back and wing coverts
KESTREL
ADULT ♀
ADULT ♂

American Kestrel
Falco sparverius
L 23–27 cm | W 51–61 cm

Tiny, dumpy kestrel with fast wingbeats. MALE **multi-coloured head** (white between black 'moustache' and rear cheek; black ear spot); rufous back/tail; **grey upperwing**. FEMALE/IMMATURE like Kestrel (*p. 326*); barred rufous back, wings and tail, but head as male.

IN FLIGHT, rapid, flickery beats of sharp-pointed wings; slightly heavy-bodied/short-winged effect.

Vagrant from N America: <5 records, May–Jun. Scattered. Heaths, islands.

pointed, swept-back wingtips in direct flight
ADULT ♂
ADULT ♀
ADULT ♀
1ST-WINTER SEP–MAR
ADULT ♂

RARE FALCONS

Eleonora's Falcon
Falco eleonorae
L 36–42 cm | W 90–105 cm
550

Large, angular falcon. DARK FORM **brown-black** with bluish bill and legs. PALE FORM sooty brown, **rusty below**, streaked dark; **bold black cap/'moustache', rounded white cheek/throat** (white 'hook' on rear cheek on Hobby (p. 328)).

IN FLIGHT, long, angular wings and narrow tail, but elegant, swooping action when catching insects, fast twists and dives when chasing small birds.

Vagrant from Mediterranean: <10 records (Britain), Jun–Oct. Scattered. Heath/coasts.

In both forms, dark forewing/paler hindwing obvious.

ADULT (pale form) — rounded white cheek

ADULT (dark form)

1ST-SUMMER like adult, with paler spotted underwing

HOBBY — white 'hook' on rear cheek

ADULT (pale form)

Amur Falcon *Falco amurensis*
L 30–36 cm | W 65–75 cm

MALE like Red-footed Falcon (p. 330) with subtly **blacker 'moustache'** and striking **white underwing coverts**, which may show as **white edge** to closed wing. 1ST-YEAR MALE shows variable white marking on underwing coverts. FEMALE white beneath with black streaks; **crown grey** (Red-footed Falcon buff). 1ST-YEAR FEMALE like adult but browner above; underparts greyish-white, streaked grey on breast, barred on flank; **crown grey**.

IN FLIGHT, smooth, relaxed, elegant action.

Vagrant from Asia: <5 records (Britain), Jul, Sep. Open areas.

ADULT ♂

1ST-SUMMER ♂ MAY–OCT

1ST-SUMMER ♂ – barred underwing with tell-tale white adult feathers moulting through

RED-FOOTED FALCON
ADULT ♂
ADULT ♀ — buff, grey

ADULT ♂ NOT RECORDED

1ST-SUMMER ♀

'HIGHER LANDBIRDS' (kingfishers, cuckoos, hoopoes, bee-eaters, rollers and parrots)

This group of birds, often referred to as 'higher landbirds', is placed together partly for convenience, since not all are closely related to the Passerines, as was once thought. The Passerines are perching birds, the 'highest' order in evolutionary terms, and include more than half the world's birds. They all have three toes pointing forwards and one back, helping them to perch. They are also, less accurately, known as 'songbirds'. Most birds that appear earlier in this book – ducks, waders, birds of prey, gulls – are clearly different. In between are the Near-passerines – from pigeons to woodpeckers. All are land birds, mostly associated with trees; they perch, but many may have different arrangements of toes (two forward, two back, or with a more mobile outer toe swinging outwards and backwards). Although many have distinctive voices, they do not 'sing'. This section includes distinctive birds within this intermediate group. Most are related to large numbers of similar species outside Europe.

ID FEATURES all very distinctive species

Kingfishers (pp. 337, 537): 1 widespread resident and 1 vagrant from North America. Birds of watersides, with dagger-like bill, short tail and very short legs. The common Kingfisher is mostly a freshwater bird, but visits saltmarsh creeks or rocky coasts, especially in severe weather. It perches quite low, sometimes hovers, and dives to catch fish.

Cuckoos (pp. 338, 341, 537): 1 widespread species, 1 vagrant from southern Europe and 2 smaller vagrants from North America. Cuckoos have two toes pointing forwards, two back; small, slightly downcurved bill; long wings and tail. The common Cuckoo is a widespread but declining summer visitor from Africa, well known for laying eggs in other species' nests.

Hoopoe (p. 339): 1 species; a rare or scarce migrant, has bred. Large fan-like crest combines with broadly banded black-and-white wings to create a unique appearance, but brief views can suggest a woodpecker or Jay.

Bee-eaters (p. 340): 2 species, one a rare migrant visitor that has bred several times in recent years, one a very rare vagrant. Bee-eaters have a pointed bill, long, pointed wings, long tail (with central 'spike' on adult) and very short legs; they perch prominently and fly with graceful swoops and glides, often calling, on straight, outstretched, pointed wings, catching large insects in flight.

Roller (p. 341): 1 increasingly rare vagrant from Europe (most species of roller are tropical); like a small, pale crow, but showing vivid colours in flight.

Parrots (pp. 342, 539): 1 regular breeding species introduced (or escaped into the wild), thriving in quite restricted parts of southern England; several other species may be seen as 'escapes' and some breed. All have a round head and distinctive short, downcurved bill; short legs and long tail.

Loud, hissing, cheeping calls draw attention to a young Cuckoo demanding food from its smaller foster-parents, such as this Meadow Pipit.

Kingfisher *Alcedo atthis*

L 17–19·5 cm | W 25 cm

ssp. *ispida*

550

👁 Belted Kingfisher (p. 537)

Unmistakable, small, stocky, uniquely coloured waterside bird with dagger-like bill, red legs and very short tail; smaller than Starling (p. 384). Vivid electric blue best in bright light, still wonderfully rich even in deepening evening light, but can be hard to see despite (or because of) bright colours in sun and shade of riverbank. Often heard first: a **sudden 'plop'** of dive, or **sharp whistle** in fly-by.

ADULT **greenish to deep blue** crown, back and wings, and **brilliant blue rump**; white patches behind orange ear coverts; **orange underparts**; orange legs. MALE has black bill; FEMALE two-thirds orange on lower edge. JUVENILE duller, with dark legs.

VOICE High whistle "*chi-k-keee*" or "*ki-kee*," and trilled variants.

IN FLIGHT, blurred wings, **streak of electric blue** immediately obvious (often swings over land to avoid people on bank). Heavy-bellied, but quick flight. Rarely rises to 'tree-top' height, hardly ever above that. Sometimes hovers low over water before diving to catch fish

ADULT ♀

Scarce resident (5,000 breeding pairs UK, plus few 100s in Ireland), winter wanderer; temporary declines after freezing winters

Freshwater margins, also coasts in winter

JUVENILE JUN–DEC

JUVENILE greener, darker on breast sides, crown has buff fringes; legs dull or dark.

all-black

ADULT ♂

some orange

ADULT ♀

'HIGHER LANDBIRDS'

Cuckoo *Cuculus canorus*

L 32–36 cm | W 54–60 cm

American cuckoos (p.537)
Great Spotted Cuckoo (p.341)

Long, slim cuckoo, with typical **small head** and **short, downcurved bill**; when perched can look heavy-bodied with drooped wings and broad, white-spotted tail, which is often swayed sideways or up and down. Tends to perch horizontally on bush, outer branch of tree or on a wire (browner juvenile, begging for food, more upright). Shape and flight action, swooping up to perch, characteristic.

ADULT grey, barred beneath; **white spots** on dark tail. FEMALE most are buffier on neck/underparts but some indistinguishable (rare rufous form – see *inset below*). JUVENILE greyish or rufous-brown, barred dark and scalloped white above; **whitish patch on nape**. See Kestrel (*p. 326*), Sparrowhawk (*p. 324*) (barred but different shape and posture).

VOICE Soft, far-carrying "*cuc-coo*;" FEMALE has loud, bubbling, chuckling trill. MALE also calls low, wheezy, 'laughing' "*gek-eh-eh-eh-eh*."

Scarce summer migrant (Apr–Sep) (14,000 males, plus 12,000 birds in Ireland; declining)

to Africa

Farmland, woodland edge, heaths, in and around reedbeds

wingbeats quick, below body, **slender head raised**

barred underwing has **pale central band**

SPARROWHAWK

no pale band

ADULT

IN FLIGHT, slightly hawk-like; **long wings taper to pointed tip**; tail wider; narrow head **slightly raised; pale central band** along underwing.

ADULT ♀ RUFOUS FORM

Rare rufous FEMALE is red-brown with a black-barred tail.

buffy on neck/breast/ underparts suggests ♀

ADULT

10% of females lack buff on neck, so all-grey birds cannot be sexed.

grey on breast

ADULT

JUVENILE JUN–OCT

JUVENILES may be greyish or more rufous, with pale feather edgings and a pale nape spot.

CUCKOO | HOOPOE

Colourful visitors from Europe

When a high pressure weather system dominates Britain/Ireland and continental Europe (especially in spring) the associated light southerly winds can create conditions in which migratory species normally found in the Mediterranean and southern Europe reach much farther north than usual. These species are known as 'overshoot migrants' and commonly include Hoopoe and Bee-eater (*p. 340*), as well as the less frequent Roller (*p. 341*) and Great Spotted Cuckoo (*p. 341*), amongst others.

Hoopoe *Upupa epops*

L 25–29 cm | W 44–48 cm

Rare migrant from S Europe: 100–160 per year, mostly Mar–Oct; has bred. Woodland edge, open ground. Winters in S Europe, Africa. **550**

Unmistakable mainly ground-feeding bird with **barred black-and-white wings and tail** and **long crest**. **Long, low,** flat-backed shape with short legs; long, **faintly downcurved bill**. Crest usually flattened into **narrow 'wedge'**, briefly raised in broad semicircular **fan of bright orange-buff**. Unobtrusive, blends with shadow and light when on ground; striking pattern suddenly revealed as bird takes flight. Sexes similar. ADULT head and neck more-or-less orange-pink. JUVENILE duller, slightly greyer on nape.

VOICE Simple, far-carrying, soft, quick repetition of quite low, hollow "*poo-poo-poo*."

ADULT

IN FLIGHT, erratic, bounding, settling into a springy, rhythmic bouncy series of in–out flicking beats of broad, rounded wings.

ADULT

ADULT

Fan-like crest raised in display or alarm, more often laid flat in backward-pointing spike.

ADULT

'HIGHER LANDBIRDS'

Bee-eater *Merops apiaster* 550

L 25–29 cm | W 36–40 cm

Long, slim, aerial feeder with long tail, pointed wings and downcurved bill. ADULT bright rusty-brown on back, golden-yellow 'shoulder' and dark rufous head; underparts dull pale blue; **throat yellow**. Pointed central tail spike. JUVENILE duller, square tail without central spike.

VOICE Far-carrying: deep, throaty, soft, rolling whistles, "*prr-up prr-up*."

IN FLIGHT, long, triangular wings (like stretched, elegant Starling (p. 384)), tail with **pointed central spike**. Deep, quick, rowing beats between **flat, straight-winged, circling glides**, with **sudden spurts** to catch flying insects. Underwing has **thick black trailing edge** on inner half, narrower towards tip.

ADULT

1ST-SUMMER MAY–SEP

dull plumage but develops tail-spike

brown

Rare migrant from S Europe: 40–70 per year (<70 records Ireland), most Apr–Jul; very rarely breeds. Dry, sandy, open or bushy spaces. Winters in Africa.

golden back

black 'collar'

ADULT

JUVENILE

feeds in the air but often perches on wire or a bare branch

Blue-cheeked Bee-eater

Merops persicus

L 28–32 cm | W 35–39 cm

Shape and actions like Bee-eater but **greener overall**, and with longer tail spike. Throat has diffuse **red-brown patch** without black border. Green nape. ADULT blue around eye. JUVENILE (not recorded) duller, lacks blue; shorter tail.

VOICE Similar quality to Bee-eater but slightly more 'rolled' "*prrr-rr*" or harsher, more ringing "*prrreep prrreep prrip*;" short, repeated "*chup, chup.*"

Vagrant from Middle East: <15 records (Britain), Jun–Sep. Scattered, near coast.

IN FLIGHT, underwing pale coppery (as Bee-eater) but trailing edge narrow along full length.

ADULT

ADULT

green

green back

no black 'collar'

ADULT

BEE-EATERS | ROLLER | CUCKOOS

Roller
Coracias garrulus
L 29–32 cm | W 35–39 cm

Unmistakable crow-like bird: similar to Jackdaw (*p. 482*) in shape but has **large, broad head**, longer bill, slim tail and very short legs. Can look dull when perched but in flight the vivid colours are obvious: one of Europe's most spectacular birds. ADULT head and body variably dull or brighter green-blue, greener below; **back pale rufous-brown**. JUVENILE/1ST-WINTER duller, with pale sandy back; pale below with subtle streaks; whitish areas around the eye and bill; contrasting dark eyestripe.

VOICE Short, harsh, crow-like, calls.

> Vagrant from S Europe: >300 records (<50 records Ireland) (declining), Apr–Nov, most May–Jun. Farmland/heathland.

dark tips to primary coverts and buff-tinged underside may suggest FEMALE or 1ST-SUMMER

IN FLIGHT, quite long-winged, long-tailed, with square, cross-like form. Upperwing bright turquoise, deep blue and blue-black.

ADULT

ADULT

Great Spotted Cuckoo
Clamator glandarius
L 35–39 cm | W 58–60 cm

Large, slender, strikingly patterned cuckoo with a slight crest; longer wings and tail and relatively longer bill than Cuckoo (*p. 338*). ADULT pale grey cap; **grey above with white spots**, whitish below; long, dark tail. JUVENILE black cap; blackish above, cream below with **rufous outerwing**. 1ST-SUMMER like adult but dark band through eye, beneath grey crown.

VOICE Unlikely from vagrant; loud, rattling chatter "*cher-cher-cher-cher-che-che-che.*"

> Vagrant from S Europe: <75 records (<10 Ireland), Feb–May, Jul–Aug. Most in S; scattered. Bushy open areas.

IN FLIGHT, shape and action like long-winged Magpie (*p. 481*). ADULT has long bands of white spots on slender wings. JUVENILE wings black with white spots and **rufous patch** towards tip. 1ST-SUMMER retains some rufous in wing.

JUVENILE JUL–SEP

1ST-SUMMER

rufous outerwing patches

1ST-SUMMER MAR–SEP

'HIGHER LANDBIRDS'

Ring-necked Parakeet *Psittacula krameri*

L 37–43 cm (incl. tail 18–23 cm)

👁 Alexandrine Parakeet; see also Monk Parakeet (p. 523)

Scarce, locally common introduced resident, Britain (established SE England (8,500 pairs), declining except in London parks); communal roosts winter

Fairly large, slim, long-tailed, round-headed, green parrot. **Pale green** overall, but yellower/paler on belly, bluer on tail, with short, thick, curved **red bill**. MALE black/pink/blue neck ring; black chin. FEMALE/IMMATURE faint neck ring; green chin.

VOICE Loud, frenzied squeals and screeching calls, especially in flight.

IN FLIGHT, fast and direct or twisting; wings quite short but pointed, swept-back; blunt head; long, pointed tail.

ADULT ♀

Parks, gardens, woodland

female has weaker neck ring than male

ADULT ♀

ADULT ♂

IMMATURE ♂

Alexandrine Parakeet *Psittacula eupatria*

Escape, has bred

purplish 'shoulder' patch

ADULT ♂

Easily overlooked as closely resembles Ring-necked Parakeet, but has purplish 'shoulder' patch. MALE has a more prominent neck ring than FEMALE.

WOODPECKERS

WOODPECKER ID size | green/pied/brown colour | head pattern | back pattern | call

6 species: 3 breed (and 1 rare migrant may do so sporadically); 1 extremely rare and 1 possible vagrant from N America.

Woodpeckers (*pp. 345–347, 537, 539*) cling to branches and tree trunks, head-up, tail-down, using their tail as a support. Two are much bigger than a Nuthatch (*p. 474*), less bouncily agile about the trees, but Lesser Spotted Woodpecker is small and more fluttery (it is also now rare).

Green Woodpecker is often seen feeding on the ground or flying up from open grass or heath, taking refuge in nearby trees, but Great Spotted Woodpecker is a bird of trees or at least thick, tall bushes; it is also a common striking black, white and red garden visitor.

The two 'spotted' woodpeckers call often and 'drum' in spring, making a sudden, short, percussion burst against a resonant branch. Green Woodpecker has loud, strident, echoing calls.

The Wryneck (*p. 344*) is a scarce or rare migrant, mostly near the coast. More like a small thrush or large warbler, its square tail is not used much as a prop. It perches quite still for long spells between bouts of feeding on the ground.

Great Spotted Woodpecker is eye-catching and the most striking woodpecker at close range (frequently uses hanging feeders), but it is elusive within woodland, especially in spring/summer foliage. Lesser Spotted Woodpecker is rare on feeders, much smaller, and often extremely elusive. Green Woodpecker is large and easily seen; on a garden lawn, it immediately looks 'different' and unusual, sloping back to rest on the tail and moving with short, leaping hops.

Woodpecker ageing/sexing

Sexes are almost similar except for head patterns (in particular the position and extent of red). JUVENILES duller, more streaked on Green Woodpecker; head pattern different from ADULTS on 'spotted' woodpeckers until autumn moult.

JUVENILE

GREEN WOODPECKER

ADULT ♂

GREAT SPOTTED WOODPECKER

LESSER SPOTTED WOODPECKER

WOODPECKERS

Wryneck *Jynx torquilla*

L 16–18 cm | W 25–27 cm

An unusual and distinctive small, brown woodpecker, which typically sits motionless for long periods in a bush or tree, or hops about on the ground. A forest breeder but migrants usually in low scrub beside open spaces on coast; can sometimes occur in unexpected places such as gardens, searching lawns for ants.

Sexes alike and ADULT, JUVENILE and 1ST-WINTER very similar (see *below*). Cryptic, 'dead wood' pattern; large, pale head with **dark central stripe down nape and upper back**; buff throat with fine dark bars. Broad, **pale grey rump**, and longish, **square, pale grey, finely barred tail** (see Barred Warbler (*p. 453*)). Bill stout, sharp, **quite small**; eye mid-brown, gives staring expression.

VOICE Migrants generally silent; spring song distinctive quick, whining, nasal "*ti-ti-ti-ti-ti-ti*" or "*kyee-kyee-kyee-kyee-kyee*," rather like Kestrel (*p. 326*) or Lesser Spotted Woodpecker (*p. 347*).

Rare migrant, mostly in autumn (300–500 per year); very rare breeder in N (up to 6 males); <400 records Ireland. Woodland, grassland.

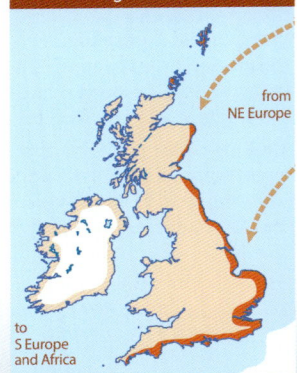

from NE Europe

to S Europe and Africa

Woodlands, heaths, open spaces

ADULT [May] — dark back/nape stripe 'snakes' as bird turns its head

ADULT [Apr]

IN FLIGHT, brown, thrush-like with pale rump and tail, but has marked shallow undulations and long shooting glides on closed wings.

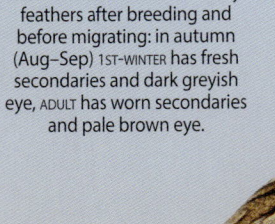

ADULT moults all but secondary feathers after breeding and before migrating: in autumn (Aug–Sep) 1ST-WINTER has fresh secondaries and dark greyish eye, ADULT has worn secondaries and pale brown eye.

Wrynecks look unlike anything else, when perched or foraging on the ground, with a small bill, thin dark eyestripe on the large, round head and dark stripe down the pale grey back.

1ST-WINTER JUL–MAR [Sep]

Green Woodpecker *Picus viridis*

L 30–36 cm | W 45–51 cm

Large woodpecker (size of Jay (*p. 480*)); greenish, with dagger-like bill. On ground, has a peculiar low, short-legged stance, tail down, head up; hops over grass/lawns/anthills, probing with pointed bill and extended tongue. Often clings upright on tree/post, sidling around out of sight.

ADULT **green with glistening red cap, yellow rump**. Dark 'moustache' (black on FEMALE, red-centred on MALE). Pale eye set in black patch gives staring expression. JUVENILE has dark-streaked cheek, dark grey spots on underparts and soft buff-white spots on upperparts.

VOICE   Very distinctive loud, striking, shouted "*kew-kew-kew*" call; song longer, ringing laugh, sudden "*kyu-kyu-kyu!*" or longer "*kyu-yu-yu-yu-yu.*" Soft, 'purring' drum rarely heard. JUVENILE calls short, squeaky "*chiew*," sometimes in chorus from nest hole.

Common resident in Britain (24,000 breeding pairs); <5 records Ireland

IN FLIGHT, **bold yellow rump**; rises with burst of quick beats, then bounds away in long, deep undulations.

Woodlands, heaths, open spaces

ADULT ♂

black

ADULT ♀

red

JUVENILE JUN–OCT

ADULT ♂

JUVENILE (JUN–OCT) greyish, barred and streaked; has a 'primitive', almost snaky look, especially when extending long, slender tongue.

ADULT ♂

Green Woodpeckers feed mostly on ants and their eggs and larvae, taken from burrows by quick pecks and use of the long, sticky tongue.

typically rests on stiff, notched tail

WOODPECKERS

Great Spotted Woodpecker *Dendrocopos major*

ssp. *anglicus* **I**

L 23–26 cm | W 38–44 cm

👁 Yellow-bellied Sapsucker (p.537)

Fairly common resident in Britain (41,000 breeding pairs); rare migrant; very rare in Ireland

Medium-sized woodpecker (size of Blackbird (p.391)), boldly patterned **black, white and red**; easy to identify (but see Lesser Spotted Woodpecker). Bold, jerky movements in trees and on bird feeders; sometimes feeds on fallen branches.

Eye-catching, black-and-white, buff below; unique large **oval white patch** on side of back. **Vivid red under tail** rules out any other bird in Britain. MALE has red patch on nape. FEMALE has all-black nape. JUVENILE has red cap (extends back beyond eye in MALE); weaker red under tail.

VOICE Loud, sharp, abrupt "*tchik*," occasional squeaky rattle of alarm. **Drums often** in spring: loud, hollow-sounding, fast rattle "*brrrrp*" lasting about **half a second**. Young give loud, scratchy, squeaky cacophony from nest hole.

IN FLIGHT, deep, **bounding undulations**. **White oval** on side of back is eye-catching; wings barred black and white.

Woodlands, gardens

ADULT ♂

black

red cap extends beyond eye in ♂

ADULT ♀

red

NOTE: all birds below are **British ssp. *anglicus*.**

JUVENILE ♂ APR–OCT

ADULT ♂

Northern European ssp. *major*
JUVENILE ♂

Northern European ssp. *major*, a scarce migrant, is larger than **British ssp. *anglicus***, with a shorter bill and whiter underparts.

WOODPECKERS

Lesser Spotted Woodpecker *Dryobates minor*

ssp. *comminutus*

L 14–16·5 cm | W 24–29 cm

Small, rather dainty woodpecker (sparrow-sized, but looks bigger due to different shape and broader wings); slightly 'blurred' black-and-white pattern. Unobtrusive, often in tops of trees with dense, thin branches, or in spindly thickets. **Call** helps to locate it.

ADULT black above, **white bars** merge into **whitish patch on back** (no distinct white patch on side of back and **no red under tail** as on Great Spotted Woodpecker). Black patch on white/buff-white cheek. MALE has a red cap and black nape. FEMALE has a buff cap and black nape. JUVENILE like female but MALE has red on rear of crown, FEMALE a few red spots.

VOICE Weak "*tchik*" and **distinctive song**, a nasal "*pee-pee-pee-pee-pee*" (rare Wryneck (*p. 344*) similar but more whining quality). Drum (in spring) a **long** rattling but rather quiet roll (lasting 1·2 to 1·8 seconds), often twice in quick succession (Great Spotted Woodpecker's is louder and more abrupt, but females can give a weaker roll that may sound confusingly similar).

Rare resident (2,000 breeding pairs, declining). Absent from Ireland

Deciduous woodland

red cap

ADULT ♂

ADULT ♂

Flight is fluttery in upper branches (hard to see in full leaf), deeply undulating over longer distance. Relatively large-winged; longer tail than Nuthatch (*p. 474*).

buff cap

ADULT ♀

AERIAL FEEDERS (swifts, swallows and martins)

AERIAL FEEDER ID wing shape | underpart colour | rump colour | throat pattern

8 swifts: 1 regular and breeding, others vagrants, most extremely rare.
8 swallows and martins: 3 breed, 1 rare migrant, 4 very rare.

SWIFTS

Swifts (pp. 349–351) are exclusively aerial. The Swift is a late spring arrival; most are gone by August. A swift's minute legs and forward-pointing toes enable it to hang on to a rough surface but not to grasp a perch; so you will not see a Swift perched on wires or bare twigs – ever. Look for it in the air: stiff bow-and-arrow shapes, with slender tail and long, scythe-like wings. Swift swoops up to nest hole hidden under eaves and in old towers, and dashes around in fast, screeching groups.

Swallows and martins (pp. 352–356), often called 'hirundines', have elegant, swooping, swerving flights and quiet, chirrupy calls. All have tiny legs and bill but broad gape for taking insects in the air. All are long-distance migrants: the Sand Martin is one of the earliest arrivals, in March; the others a few weeks later.

Sand Martin colonies are groups of holes in earth or sand cliffs. House Martins make mud cups tight under eaves and gables on buildings; Swallows use outbuildings, needing a small shelf or beam for their mud-and-straw nests.

Swallows often perch on wires and television aerials; House Martins on wires and rooftops; Sand Martins on bare branches of waterside bushes, and ropes and wires low over water. All three join Swifts over water in cold, wet or windy weather, seeking insects where they can, and Swallows feed in the lee of lines of trees and hedges in difficult conditions. Flocks of Sand Martins, more rarely Swallows, occasionally settle on level areas and even pick insects from open ground, especially in autumn.

Swift ageing/sexing

Sexes of swifts are alike and have no seasonal changes. JUVENILES have white feather edges, obvious when they first fly in late summer. Returning first-summer birds may be identifiable by old, worn flight feathers and pale-edged underwing coverts.

Swallow and martin ageing/sexing

Sexes look alike, but MALE swallows have longer outer tail feathers than FEMALES. JUVENILES are slightly duller and paler; by following spring, returning birds all have fresh plumage and cannot be aged.

Swallows habitually perch on wires, including fences; martins also perch like this but less freely, mostly later in summer/autumn. Swifts cannot perch and are never seen on wires or bare twigs.

SWALLOWS

SWIFTS

Swift *Apus apus*

550

L 17–18.5 cm | W 40–44 cm

Rare swifts (*p. 350–351*)

All-dark aerial feeder, with **stiff**, **scythe-like wings**. The common swift, and an essential comparison for rarer swifts (*pp. 350–351*); also see Swallow (*p. 353*). Entirely aerial, except on hidden nest in a building or cliff (at a few locations); never perches (*e.g.* on a wire, branch or roof).

Sexes alike. ADULT **blackish-brown** except for whitish chin (underwing flashes paler in sun). Fades browner by July (see Pallid Swift (*p. 350*)). JUVENILE white lores and fine whitish feather edgings overall; blacker wings and larger chin patch than adult.

IN FLIGHT, usually high, fast, with deep beats between soaring glides; often slower, erratic, with wings almost beating singly. Beware (infrequent) Swifts with white patches resembling rare species.

VOICE Screeching whistle "*scrrreeee*," FEMALE higher pitched than MALE.

Locally common summer migrant, most Apr–Sep (80,000 pairs in UK, declining)

to Africa

Aerial; breeds in old buildings; feeds over open space, woodland, water.

ADULT — dark

JUVENILE — white, larger chin patch

ADULT — dark lores

ADULT/1ST-SUMMER pale covert fringes and worn, old primaries suggest 1st-summer

JUVENILE JUL–DEC — blacker wings than adult, pale feather edges, white lores, face largely pale

RARE AERIAL FEEDERS

Rare swifts

Pallid Swift
Apus pallidus
L 16–18 cm | W 39–44 cm

Very like Swift (*p. 349*) with same scythe-like wings. ADULT **brown**, with **paler midwing** and **darker 'saddle'** (obscure in poor light) above. From below, paler hindwing, large whitish throat below dark 'mask'. Pale feather edges give **barred/mottled effect** close up in good light. Mottled body vital to exclude pale juvenile Swift. JUVENILE has paler feather edges overall.

IN FLIGHT, silhouette like Swift but slightly blunter wingtips; wider head; broader rear body; tail blunter (outer two pairs of feathers nearly equal, outermost longer on Swift).

NB Brief views/single photographs may mislead, with sunlit/shaded wings looking like different species: prolonged observation from different angles advisable.

Vagrant from S Europe: <100 records (<5 Ireland), Mar–Nov, often much earlier/later than Swift. Scattered.

Alpine Swift
Tachymarptis (Apus) melba
L 20–23 cm | W 57 cm

Shape and flight of Swift (*p. 349*) but **larger**, more powerful, with longer wings and broader body. Dark **brown**, with **dark breast-band** above **white belly** and white chin (harder to see). Blackish under forked tail. Rump/lower back **broader, paler, brighter brown** than Swift. Beware infrequent Swifts with white patches.

VOICE Loud, mechanical, chattering "*chi-it-it-it-it-it,*" unlikely in Britain/Ireland.

Vagrant from S Europe: 10–15 per year (<100 records Ireland), most Mar–Jul. Scattered.

RARE SWIFTS

Pacific Swift *Apus pacificus*
L 17–18 cm | W 40–44 cm

Large swift; long, forked tail held in tight point; **narrow curved white rump**; plain wings; white throat.

Vagrant from Asia: <15 records (Britain), Jun–Oct. Most E coast.

White-rumped Swift
Apus caffer
L 14 cm | W 32–33 cm

Small, slender swift; deeply forked tail; **narrow 'U'-shaped white rump**; narrow, pointed wings straight or swept back; white throat.

Vagrant from SW Europe/NW Africa: 1 record (Britain), Oct.

Little Swift *Apus affinis*
L 12–13.5 cm | W 32–34 cm

Small, stocky swift; all-blackish with square tail; **broad white rump like House Martin** (p.352) (but black beneath); quite broad, scythe-like wings; white throat.

Vagrant from N Africa: <30 records (<5 Ireland), May–Sep. Scattered.

White-throated Needletail
(Needle-tailed Swift)
Hirundapus caudacutus
L 19–21 cm | W 50–54 cm

Large, stocky, sabre-winged swift; dark except for **pale back, white 'U'-shape under tail** and **white throat**.

Vagrant from Asia: <15 records (1 Ireland), May–Jun. Scattered.

Chimney Swift
Chaetura pelagica
L 12–13 cm | W 27–30 cm

Small, chunky swift; dusky grey-brown with slightly paler throat; broad outerwing, narrow at base; short, square-cut tail.

Vagrant from N America: <40 records (<20 Ireland, all in two influxes), Jul–Oct. Scattered, most near coast.

AERIAL FEEDERS

House Martin *Delichon urbicum*

L 13·5–15 cm | W 26–29 cm

👁 Storm Petrel (p. 103), Rare swallows (p. 355–356), Little Swift (p. 351)

Locally common summer migrant, Mar–Oct (379,000 pairs, plus 730,000 birds in Ireland)

Small, stocky, **black-and-white** hirundine. Short, white-feathered legs visible when perched or collecting mud for nest. Sexes alike. ADULT blue-black above with browner wings and broad **white rump**; white below, **from chin to tail**. JUVENILE has duller rump (see Red-rumped Swallow (p. 355)).

IN FLIGHT, **short, forked tail**; **triangular wings**; **white rump**. Blue-black back, browner wings; from below, **white throat, dark underwing**. Stiff action, less fluent than Swallow, **more likely circling above house height** (but the two often mix high up or over water). Wings stiffly outstretched in glide; angled back, fluttered in active flight. Comes to puddles, perches on roofs and wires, but less likely on TV aerials or bare branches than Swallow.

VOICE Short, dry, chattering "*trrrit, trri-it;*" twittering song.

from/to N and W Europe

from/to Africa

to Africa

Suburbs, rural areas, lakes

white rump

ADULT

white throat

JUVENILE JUL–OCT

ADULT

Nest typically under eaves/gable end of building, quarter-sphere with closed top, small entrance.

Small groups gather mud with which they build their nest: a wet patch is therefore essential for successful breeding.

352

SWALLOWS | MARTINS

Swallow *Hirundo rustica*

L 17–21 cm (incl. tail 3·0–6·5 cm);
juv. 14–15 cm | W 29–32 cm

Rare swallows (p. 355–356)

Locally common summer migrant, Mar–Nov (about 1 million pairs in Britain and Ireland); rare in winter

from/to N and W Europe

from/to S Africa

to S Africa

Sleek, slender, fork-tailed hirundine: the familiar swallow, usually seen in flight. ADULT blue-black above; **red forehead and throat, dark breast-band**; cream to pinkish below. MALE has longer tail streamers than FEMALE. JUVENILE rather short-tail, buffish forehead and chin, dull or broken, but still obvious, breast-band.

IN FLIGHT, **deeply forked tail** with row of **white spots**; dark above, pale below with **dark throat**. Often **very low** over fields or water, swerving with wings swept, tail spread; in direct flight, tail less conspicuous. Often rises with momentary pause, or sideways twist. In wind and rain, in lee of hedgerows or trees; on sunny days, chirruping groups at much greater height. Perches on branches, wires, TV aerials.

VOICE Calls sharp "*vit vit*," Goldfinch-like (p. 496) chirrupy "*shrrip*" or "*tritt-it*;" song a rapid musical twitter with quick trill or rattle.

Villages, farmland, freshwater, coasts

deep blue above, often looks black

long, thin tail streamers

ADULT ♂

ADULT ♀

♀ slightly shorter, broader tail streamers

deep peachy-buff to white beneath

short tail streamers

in flight tail often closed into inconspicuous point

JUVENILE

ADULT ♂

Nests in outbuildings, not under open eaves; nest has open top, not side entrance.

JUVENILE MAY–OCT

Swallows have up to three broods per year; juveniles can therefore be seen from late May–Oct.

AERIAL FEEDERS

Sand Martin *Riparia riparia*

L 12–13 cm | W 26–29 cm   ◐ Rare swallows (*p. 355–356*)

Small, slim, **brown-and-white** martin; the smallest breeding hirundine. Sexes alike. ADULT **brown above**, white below with **brown breast-band**. JUVENILE paler with buff feather edges.

IN FLIGHT, wings rather triangular; tail inconspicuous, short, slim, forked. At distance looks dark, with darker breast/underwing, **small white belly**; white lower face (breast-band/white throat harder to see). Quick, flickery, in arrowhead shape, with upward swoops and twists, rise/stall at intervals, little or no gliding. **VOICE** Quick, dry chatter.

Locally common summer migrant, Mar–Oct (164,000 pairs Britain, plus 600,000 birds Ireland)

to Africa

Near/over water, quarries, earth/sand cliffs

In poor weather, in flocks low over water, head into wind. Perches (especially in autumn) along dead branches/wires over water, sometimes swarms on leafy bush or tree.

ADULT

ADULT

breast-band

Often swoops around nest holes in earth/sand cliff, anywhere from soft cliff above beach or large sand quarry to roadside cutting; also makes use of artificial banks with burrows constructed from pipes.

ADULT

JUVENILE JUL–OCT

JUVENILE has sandy-buff feather edging on forehead and throat, and pale fringes on wing coverts.

RARE SWALLOWS and MARTINS

Red-rumped Swallow
Cecropis daurica
L 14–19 cm (incl. tail 3–5 cm)
W 27–32 cm

Obvious swallow with **pale rump**. ADULT **blue cap surrounded by rufous** that extends onto nape; **cheek pale buff**. Blue-glossed upperparts; unstreaked pinkish-buff underparts.

IN FLIGHT **stiffer, less elegant** action than Swallow (p. 353), with straighter wings, steadier glide; thicker tail streamers often in single 'spike'. Tail plain (no white spots). **Rump pale rusty-red** or orange-buff, often whiter towards tail. Underside pale (**no dark throat**). **Black tail coverts** against pale rump and underside give a 'stuck-on-tail' effect. JUVENILE rump dull white, nape pale; black under tail; pale underwings (grey on House Martin (p. 352)).

VOICE Call a useful clue: a short, hard "*djuit*".

Rare migrant from S Europe: >1,000 records, 30–60 per year (<50 records Ireland), most Mar–May, in S England. Winters in Africa.

SWALLOW ADULT — dark rump — red chin and forehead

S European ssp. *rufula* ADULT

ADULT

ADULT — rufous nape with blue centre — uniform rufous rump — streaked below
'Asian Red-rumped Swallow' ssp. *daurica* or *japonica* (vagrant: 1 record (Britain), Jun).

pale rump usually 'two-tone' orange-buff and cream — rufous nape

S European ssp. *rufula* ADULT

Crag Martin
Ptyonoprogne rupestris
L 14–15 cm | W 27–32 cm

Rather like large, robust, grey-brown Sand Martin; underparts drab grey-buff (no breast-band); row of **square white spots** on square tail; contrasting **dark 'wedge'** on underwing coverts. ADULT grey 'bloom' but wears browner by Sep–Oct; throat finely streaked. JUVENILE (Jun–Oct) throat unstreaked, fine pale feather edges above, retained on wing and tail through 1ST-WINTER (Sep–Mar).

Vagrant from S Europe: <15 records (Britain), Apr–Dec. Scattered.

ADULT / 1ST-WINTER [Nov] — contrasting dark underwing coverts — pale throat, no breast-band

ADULT [Apr] — tail spots

ADULT [Apr]

RARE AERIAL FEEDERS

Tree Swallow
Tachycineta bicolor
L 15 cm | W 30–32 cm

ADULT like House Martin (*p. 352*) but **rump dark**; more greenish-blue above. MALE blue-green back. FEMALE duller than male, can be as drab as 1st-winter. JUVENILE/1ST-WINTER (not recorded) like Sand Martin (*p. 354*) but breast-band pale greyish; forehead dark.

Vagrant from N America: <5 records (Britain), May, Jun. Scattered, near coast. Freshwater.

Cliff Swallow
Petrochelidon pyrrhonota
L 13 cm | W 28–30 cm

Small, thickset hirundine; tail shallowly forked, rounded when spread. ADULT (not recorded) upperside dark blue, **rump and collar buff**, forehead white; **throat and cheeks dark rusty-red**. JUVENILE/1ST-WINTER has pale fringes above; dingy dark breast; face variably **whitish with rufous mottles** to **dark rufous**.

Vagrant from N America: <15 records (1 Ireland), Sep–Dec. Scattered, near coast.

Purple Martin *Progne subis*
L 20 cm | W 39–41 cm

A large, heavy hirundine. MALE (not recorded) iridescent dark purple-blue, paler on flight feathers. FEMALE (not recorded) paler beneath. JUVENILE **dark brown** with darker 'mask', some bluish sheen; paler below, whitish on belly. 1ST-WINTER browner, blue on 'shoulders', paler, streaked, below.

Vagrant from N America: 1 record (Britain), Sep. Near coast.

356

LARKS, PIPITS and WAGTAILS

GROUP ID colour/form | tail length | bill size

Largely ground-dwelling birds that walk, do not hop; larks often crouch low to the ground.
10 larks: 2 resident, 1 winter visitor, 1 rare migrant; the rest vagrants.
11 pipits: 3 breed (2 resident (1 with migrant/scarce breeding subspecies)), 1 summer visitor (with migrant subspecies); 1 vagrant.
5 wagtails with several distinct subspecies: 2 resident, 1 summer visitor; 2 vagrants.

STREAKY, BROWN (NB the distinctive Shorelark (p. 359) and MALE Black Lark (p. 363) are exceptions)

Two unrelated groups of 'ground' birds need to be separated. Streaky brown birds on the ground could include finches, buntings, sparrows (pp. 488–523) and the Dunnock (p. 380) but these all **hop**. Larks and pipits **walk**, so anything that hops two-footed can quickly be separated from a lark or pipit.

LARK ID head, tail, wing pattern
PIPIT ID head, back, rump and flank patterns | call

Larks (pp. 358–363) are stockier, bulkier, shorter-tailed than pipits, with a thicker, more triangular bill; many have at least an impression of a crest (flattened or raised as upstanding triangle). Most have a dark tail with a pale centre and white edges. Scapular feathers are more evident than on pipits and are large, pointed and often dark with a drooped, pale upper edge.

Pipits (pp. 364–371) also have a white-sided tail, similar to many buntings. Mostly slighter, longer tailed, thinner-legged and thinner-billed than larks but there are several larger, bulky species. None have even a hint of a crest.

Lark and pipit ageing/sexing

Sexes alike, most with no seasonal change; JUVENILES distinct but 1ST-WINTER after head/body moult practically indistinguishable unless in the hand.

MEADOW PIPIT

SKYLARK

BLACK/WHITE or COLOURFUL

WAGTAIL ID head and other plumage details | call

Wagtails (pp. 372–377) have pipit-like form but are strongly patterned, with a long/very long black tail with broad white sides. Pied and Grey Wagtails are resident, Yellow Wagtail a summer visitor and Citrine and Eastern Yellow Wagtails rare vagrants. White Wagtail, a subspecies of Pied Wagtail, is a migrant. Wagtails prefer open spaces often close to water, or around livestock, and walk on the ground; Pied Wagtail is also an urban bird.

PIED WAGTAIL

Wagtail ageing/sexing

Sexes differ, and seasonal changes marked; JUVENILES distinct; 1ST-WINTER after moult may be identifiable, but plumages complex, variable.

YELLOW WAGTAIL

MALE
FEMALE
JUVENILE

LARKS, PIPITS and WAGTAILS

Larks in flight

Larks fly with bursts of wingbeats – much less undulating than finches; stronger than smaller pipits and buntings. Some have distinctive patterns above or below their broad wings – look especially for presence or absence of a pale trailing edge.; tail pattern less helpful.

Larks in flight – summary of key features

	Underwing	Trailing edge	Tail
Woodlark	whitish; NB UPPERWING black/white patch	plain	short; white 'corners'
Skylark	whitish	whitish (lacking in some worn birds)	long; white edges
Crested	rusty	plain	long; brownish edges
White-winged	black/white	broad, white	long; white edges
Calandra	blackish	broad, white	short; white edges
Bimaculated	grey	plain	short; white tip

NB Both **Black Lark** (MALE) and **Shorelark** are distinctive; the **short-toed larks** both have a plain trailing edge and narrow white sides to the tail.

LARKS

Shorelark *Eremophila alpestris*

L 16–19 cm | W 30–34 cm

Slim, low-slung lark with black cheek and breast-band; creeps/walks/shuffles on flat ground, usually on mud/sand near the coast. Size of Skylark (p. 361). **Black legs** rule out other larks in Britain/Ireland.

ADULT rather plain brown above with **black-and-yellow head**; unstreaked whitish underparts. MALE BREEDING well-defined **black 'mask'**, black cap with distinct 'horns'; **black breast-band**. FEMALE BREEDING black areas more diffuse. ADULT NON-BREEDING/JUVENILE/1ST-WINTER almost alike, duller; breast-band narrow, with browner band beneath, or broader blackish breast patch.

VOICE Short, simple, squeaky "*eeh*," "*tseep*" or "*ee-du*."

Scarce migrant and winter visitor (about 75 per year, 25 in Ireland): Oct–Apr. Has bred once in Scotland

from Scandinavia

♀ [Feb]

ADULT
white underwing

Coastal marshes, tidelines, occasionally ploughed fields

IN FLIGHT, like large pipit or small, slender thrush as much as lark: tapered wings; quick, easy, swerving flight. Fairly uniform except tail: pale centre, black sides, white outer edge.

AMERICAN HORNED LARK (ssp. *alpestris*, *praticola* or *hoyti*) (vagrant: <5 records (Britain), Nov–Apr) similar to **northern European ssp. *flava*** but upperparts streaked darker, stripe over eye whiter, flank darker rufous; sspp. difficult to separate outside normal range.

intensity of yellow and black variable

ADULT ♂ BREEDING

ADULT NON-BREEDING OCT–MAR

359

LARKS, PIPITS and WAGTAILS | Larks in flight p.358

Woodlark *Lullula arborea*

L 13·5–15 cm | W 27–30 cm

◯ Rare larks (pp. 362–363)

Rare resident (3,100 pairs); rare winter visitor or migrant away from breeding range; <20 records Ireland

Small, neat, rounded lark, streaky brown with **black-and-white patch on edge of wing**; **very short tail**; pale legs. Feeds in short heather (looks pale against dark vegetation) or cropped grass/clear-felled areas with bare, sandy patches (where very inconspicuous). Creeps, crouches, leaps up at close range, bounding off before dropping out of sight. Calls draw attention.

ADULT rufous cheek; **white stripes over eyes meet on nape**; black streaks on breast, white underparts; **short, striped crest; black streaks on breast, white underparts**. JUVENILE prominent, rounded, pale buff feather edges on upperparts.

VOICE Quiet, or loud: clear "*t'loo-ee*" (emphasis on second syllable, falling at end). Song melodic, pure series of repeated notes: "*loo-loo-loo, leeu leeu leeu, toodl-oodl-oodl, tlui tlui tlui tlui,*" from perch or very high, circling song flight before steep, silent plunge; often sings at night.

IN FLIGHT, rather rounded wings with **no white trailing edge** but white band below; black/buff patch on leading edge. **Tail very short** with white 'corners'.

Heaths, clear-felled forestry

ADULT

short tail with white 'corners'

wings rounded

ADULT

patch

ADULT

white-black-white patch on edge of wing

short, striped crest

ADULT

'scaly' forehead/crown

striped crown

pale, 'loopy' feather edges

JUVENILE
JUN–OCT

ADULT

Skylark *Alauda arvensis*

L 16–18 cm | W 30–36 cm

ssp. *scotica* | I | 551

Streaky-brown lark, almost size of Starling (p. 384); see Corn Bunting (p. 517). Walks on ground, in open space away from hedge/trees.

ADULT head and upperparts brown, streaked buff; **short, streaked crest**; **brownish breast-band** (paler centre, wears whitish in summer) streaked black; white underparts; longish tail; pale legs. JUVENILE darker, more coarsely marked above than adult.

VOICE Call chirruping "*chrrup*" invariably when flushed, thinner with height/distance; winter flocks give high, thin whistles. Song **unbroken outpouring** of fast trills.

> Rare larks (pp. 362–363), rare 'large' pipits (pp. 370–371)

Locally common resident (1·7 million pairs Britain, plus 365,000 birds in Ireland), winter visitor

from/to N and W Europe

Wide range of habitats with open ground; winter flocks in lowlands

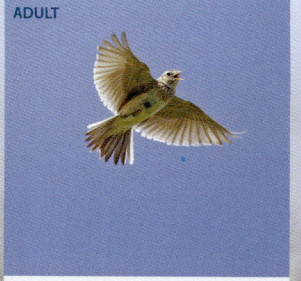

IN FLIGHT, wings broad, angular, with narrow tips; **whitish trailing edge**. Tail quite long, dark either side of pale centre, **broad white sides**.

Winter flocks low over fields; migrants high, in long, straggling lines (autumn or snow-driven in winter), revealed by **frequent calls**.

ADULT

longish tail with white sides

ADULT

wings with narrow tips

raised crest short and blunt

ADULT

Sings in rising hover as if on a string before diving to the ground; deeper notes are lost at distance, leaving a thin, silvery thread of sound.

JUVENILE JUN–OCT

ADULT

Subspecies tentatively recognized, difficult to identify and intergrade: ssp. *arvensis* widespread; supposedly darker/more rufous ssp. *scotica* (Scotland, NW England, Ireland) of uncertain validity; and paler ssp. *intermedia* (historical vagrant from Asia to Ireland). Grey '**Eastern Skylarks**', sspp. *cantarella/intermedia/dulcivox* group suspected but not proven.

RARE LARKS

Short-toed Lark
Calandrella brachydactyla
L 14–16 cm | W 26–31 cm

552

Small, round-headed lark; triangular bill, dark/rufous cap, pale wingbar, **unmarked** white underparts. Yellowish-brown, duller in spring; small **dark/streaky patch at side of breast** (often hidden; faint streaks may join across breast). Row of dark spots on median coverts, long tertials cloak closed wingtip (no obvious primary projection – see *below*) separate from vagrant Lesser Short-toed Lark. ADULT and JUVENILE similar, both have complete moult in summer and are inseparable after Aug.

VOICE Calls dry, chirruping "*drit*" or "*chirrrip*," recalling House Martin (*p. 352*) or snatch of Linnet (*p. 500*), or a hard, sparrowy "*chip chip*."

Migrant 1ST-WINTER and ADULT birds not separable.

Rare migrant from S Europe: 15–25/year (>75 records Ireland), Apr–Oct, rarely overwinters. Mainly in E and S, near coast. Sandy ground, short grass. Winters in Africa.

IN FLIGHT, **no white trailing edge**, unlike Skylark (*p. 361*); tail pale in centre, sides darker, outer edge narrowly white.

SKYLARK — broad white edge, whitish trailing edge

narrow white edge, no white trailing edge

ADULT [Sep]

dark patch at side of breast revealed as head is raised

long tertials cover closed wing

ADULT [Apr]

squats horizontally; pale and nondescript

ADULT [Oct]

Crested Lark *Galerida cristata*
L 17–19 cm | W 29–38 cm

Like bright, pale Skylark (*p. 361*) with short tail and **longer crest** raised in **pointed triangle**.

VOICE Call distinctive, fluty "*ti-torr-tee*" or "*torr-tee*."

Vagrant from S Europe: <30 records (Britain), Apr–Jun, Nov. Most in S. Open ground.

IN FLIGHT, **plain wings** (rusty beneath); **brownish outer tail feathers**.

ADULT

crest never 'pointed'
ADULT
SKYLARK

ADULT

Lesser Short-toed Lark *Alaudala rufescens*
L 14 cm | W 26–31 cm

Like Short-toed Lark but has streaked breast-band and two wingbars; **primaries project well beyond tertials on closed wing**.

VOICE Distinct fast, **buzzing** "*d-r,r,r*" call.

Vagrant from Iberia: 1 record (Britain), May. S coast. Grassland.

PRIMARY PROJECTION
none/minimal — SHORT-TOED LARK
long — LESSER SHORT-TOED LARK

ADULT

Larks in flight *p.358*

RARE LARKS

Calandra Lark *Melanocorypha calandra* 551
L 18–20 cm | W 38–44 cm

Large, thick-billed lark with pale stripe over eye, dark cheek and **blackish neck patch** (compare with much smaller Short-toed Lark); **white sides to tail**.

Vagrant from S Europe: <20 records (Britain), Apr–May. Scattered. Open ground.

IN FLIGHT, **white trailing edge to wing, blackish underwing**

ADULT

lores same tone as crown

ADULT

Bimaculated Lark *Melanocorypha bimaculata*
L 16–18 cm | W 33–36 cm

Like a small Calandra Lark with more contrasting head pattern and more obvious eyestripe; lores darker than crown; **white tip to tail**.

Vagrant from Middle East: <5 records (Britain), May, Jun, Sep. Scattered. Open ground.

IN FLIGHT, **no white trailing edge, greyer underwing**

ADULT

lores darker than crown

ADULT

Black Lark *Melanocorypha yeltoniensis*
L 18–20 cm | W 37 cm

Large, stocky, lark. MALE **blackish**; fresh feathers edged white; heavy, **whitish bill**. FEMALE (not recorded) dull, pale, grey-brown with darker wings; streaked breast; blackish mark on side of neck (as Calandra Lark).

Vagrant from Asia: <5 records (Britain), males, Apr, Jun. Scattered). Coastal heath/grassland.

IN FLIGHT, dark underwing with blackish coverts.

ADULT ♂

ADULT ♂

White-winged Lark *Alauda leucoptera*
L 17–19 cm | W 35 cm

Like rufous Skylark (*p.361*) with **rufous 'shoulder'**, bright **white underparts** and **white collar**. ADULT MALE (not recorded) has rufous forehead. FEMALE/IMMATURE MALE streaked grey-brown on crown, rufous areas duller.

Vagrant from Asia: <5 records (Britain), female and immature male, Oct, Nov. Grassland.

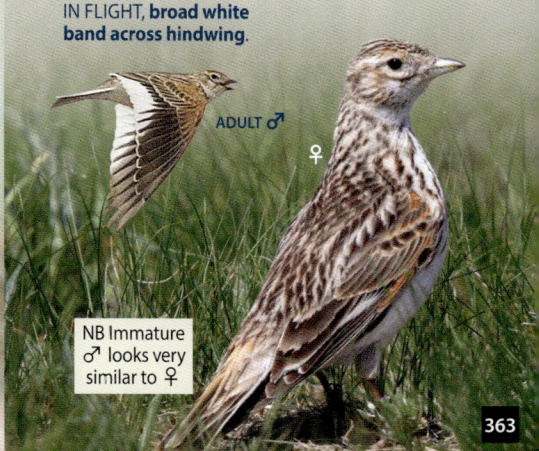

IN FLIGHT, **broad white band across hindwing**.

ADULT ♂

♀

NB Immature ♂ looks very similar to ♀

LARKS, PIPITS and WAGTAILS

Tree Pipit *Anthus trivialis*

L 14–16 cm | W 22–25 cm

Rare pipits (pp. 368–369)

Scarce summer migrant, Apr–Oct (74,000 pairs); absent in winter

Small, slender, streaked, mostly solitary pipit: absent in winter (unlike similar Meadow Pipit). Typical of woodland/heathland edge, clear-fell bordering conifers and adjacent rough grassy areas. Confident walk on branch or ground; dips tail like a wagtail.

ADULT pale olive-brown above, streaked blackish on back; pale yellow-buff below with white belly. Breast streaked black; **sparse thin black streaks on flank**. Long, strong pale stripe above eye, dark line behind eye and faint pale ear-spot; pale eyering broken in front. Bill relatively thick; hind claw short. Legs pink. JUVENILE nearly identical but slightly more buffy, with faint, rounded pale feather edges above.

IN FLIGHT, white sides to tail. If flushed, flight strong; tends to fly far.

VOICE Call buzzy, abrupt, vibrant "*teeess*" or "*speeze*," or "*spiz*." Song **rich, canary-like trills** with **long final notes** "*see-a see-a see-a seee-a*," **from tree** or in song flight.

from/to Scandinavia

from/to Africa

Heaths, plantations, woodland edges

flank streaks noticeably finer than breast streaks

[Jun]

flank streaks usually hard to see

Song flight a steep rise then 'parachuting' descent with tail and wings in 'shuttlecock' shape, usually **starts and finishes on a perch** (sapling or high branch).

hind claw short and curved

Tree Pipit has slightly stronger bill, longer pale stripe over eye, eyering usually broken in front and bolder 'character' than Meadow Pipit.

at all times, difficult to tell age

[Sep]

[Apr]

steady walk; looks large-footed

Pipit flight calls p.352

PIPITS

NT
NT

Meadow Pipit *Anthus pratensis*

L 14–15.5 cm | W 22–25 cm

👁 Rare pipits (*pp. 368–369*)

🟠 🔴 **I**

Small, streaky brown pipit of open spaces and bushy heath: common all year and often forms flocks (similar Tree Pipit is a summer migrant and mostly solitary). Rather nervous, erratic walk/shuffle on ground. Superficially similar to Skylark (*p. 361*) but smaller and with thin bill.

Olive-brown above, streaked blackish on back; buffish below (some more yellow or olive) but fades whiter beneath in summer. Breast buff-white, streaked black; **long, thick black streaks on flank**. Head pattern diffuse, with pale eyering. Bill fine; **hind claw long**. Legs orange-pink. ADULT by Jul–Sep becomes worn, darker above, whiter below. JUVENILE brighter, slightly more boldly streaked, with dark median covert centres more pointed, but by Sep difficult to tell age.

IN FLIGHT, white sides to tail; dark flank streaks usually noticeable. If flushed, rises in **short, springy bounds**; winter flocks circle widely.

VOICE Thin, quick "*seeip-sip-sip*," stronger "*sip sip*." Song simple, **rapidly repeated thin trills**, from ground or in song flight.

Locally common resident (1·9 million pairs, plus 1·7 million birds in Ireland); migrant, winter visitor

from/to Greenland — from/to Iceland — from Scandinavia

Scandinavia / NW Africa

from/to NW Africa

Heaths, bogs, moors; in winter more lowland, fields, marshes *etc.*

flank streaks similar thickness to breast streaks

[Jun]

hind claw long, slightly curved

flank streaks usually noticeable

long hind claw often visible in flight

Song flight a steep rise then 'parachuting' descent with tail and wings in 'shuttlecock' shape, usually **starts and finishes on the ground**.

Meadow Pipit has slimmer bill, shorter pale stripe over eye, complete pale eyering and rather more 'nervous' character than Tree Pipit.

at all times, difficult to tell age

[Oct]

Overall colour varies individually and as feathers become duller and paler with wear.

[Jun]

[Apr]

dips/wags tail; nervy walk, picks side to side from the ground

LARKS, PIPITS and WAGTAILS

Rock Pipit *Anthus petrosus*

L 15·5–17 cm | W 23–28 cm

👁 Buff-bellied Pipit

ssp. *petrosus*

Small, streaky, thickset **dull, dark-legged** pipit with long, **strong bill** and **slurred call**. Walks quickly on the ground. In summer, on **rocks, cliffs, grassy slopes above cliffs**; in winter, often approachable on piers or promenades. Two subspecies, sometimes distinguishable.

BREEDING greyish-brown above, softly streaked darker; dull, yellowish below, with **broad, blurred streaks** (less sharp than Meadow Pipit (*p. 365*)). Head pattern weak, except white eyering. Buff wingbars. Pale grey tail sides. **Legs dark** red-brown or blackish. NON-BREEDING/JUVENILE darker olive-brown above.

VOICE Song, song flight and call resemble Meadow Pipit; call 'thicker', more slurred, "*feest*" or "*sfeep,*" not so often tripled.

Locally common resident (50,000 pairs Britain, Ireland); winter visitor

from Scandinavia

Rocky coasts; scarce migrant inland, frequent winter visitor on coasts beyond breeding range

parachuting display flight

NON-BREEDING
ssp. *petrosus*
JUL–APR

often yellow on bill

[Nov]

BREEDING
APR–JUL
ssp. *petrosus*

pale stripe behind eye short; often weak or mottled

[Jun]

[May]

greyer than in winter; becomes paler with wear

BREEDING
ssp. *petrosus*

BREEDING
ssp. *petrosus*

beware pale individuals!

[Jun]

BREEDING
ssp. *littoralis*

ssp. *littoralis* and ssp. *petrosus* usually inseparable in winter

[Mar]

Scandinavian ssp. *littoralis* on saltmarsh, lakes/reservoirs (vagrant, Ireland) autumn–spring (Oct–Apr). By Mar, pale stripe over eye, greyer nape, but varies individually and with extent of moult. Some are greyer on head and upper back, flushed pink on breast with few streaks: these are unlike **British/Irish ssp.** *petrosus*, but very like Water Pipit.

Water Pipit *Anthus spinoletta*

L 15·5–17 cm | W 23–28 cm

Buff-bellied Pipit

Dark-legged pipit, similar to Rock Pipit but shy, likely to fly far if disturbed (Rock Pipit tends to flit along shore). Alert, wary and upright, full-breasted; dark back, pinkish front, surprisingly like Wheatear (p. 408).

BREEDING head **grey**; **white stripe over eye**; throat and breast **pale pink**. Few flank streaks; back plain brown. NON-BREEDING browner than Rock Pipit and **whiter below** with fewer streaks; **white 'bib'** outlined with grey-brown; **whitish stripe over eye. Dull white wingbars.** White tail sides. Legs dark brown, often paler than Rock Pipit.

VOICE Between Rock Pipit and Meadow Pipit, loud "*tsweeep*" or slightly vibrant "*feest*," fuller, thicker, more slurred than Meadow Pipit (p. 365).

Scarce, very local winter visitor from S/C Europe (190 per year, mostly Sep–Apr; <200 records Ireland).

from Europe

Inland watersides and coastal lagoons or marshes.

ROCK PIPIT
brown head, pale eyering
NON-BREEDING
ssp. *petrosus*
[Nov]

brownish-grey head/nape, pale stripe over eye
BREEDING
ssp. *littoralis*
[Mar]

BREEDING
APR–JUL
[Apr]

NON-BREEDING
JUL–APR
[Oct]

PIPIT FLIGHT CALLS
at a glance

MEADOW PIPIT-LIKE

Meadow Pipit – thin, quick "*seeip-sip-sip*," stronger "*sip sip*." From flocks, short "*pip*" or "*pipit*."

Rock Pipit – as Meadow Pipit but more slurred, "*feest*" or "*sfeep*."

Water Pipit – between Rock and Meadow Pipits: a loud "*tsweeep*" or slightly vibrant "*feest*."

Buff-bellied Pipit – as Meadow Pipit but sharper, "*p-sip*."

TREE-PIPIT-LIKE

Tree Pipit – buzzy, abrupt, vibrant rather than grating, "*teeess*" or "*speeze*," or "*spiz*."

Olive-backed Pipit – "*teess*" or "*tizz*;" similar to Tree Pipit.

DISTINCTIVE

Red-throated Pipit – high, long, thin "*p'seeee!*," with strong start and finely drawn finish, or quiet but explosive "*psee-see-see*."

Pechora Pipit – often silent on migration but occasionally a short, sharp, clicking '*dzep*."

HOUSE SPARROW-LIKE
(large pipits)

Richard's Pipit – throaty "*shrree*;" often softer, flatter or downslurred, "*shrroo*."

Tawny Pipit – harsh, slightly vibrant "*tsreeep*" or "*sfeep*" or shorter "*shilp*," sparrowy "*chwee*" or short "*chup*."

Blyth's Pipit – slightly higher than typical **Richard's Pipit**, less grating or rasping, "*pshiu*" or "*pshee*."

RARE PIPITS

Smaller rare pipits

Four small pipits, resembling Meadow (*p. 365*) and/or Tree Pipits (*p. 364*), are all rare or very rare: **Red-throated Pipit** adult breeding unmistakable, juvenile/1st-winter difficult but has a very distinctive call; **Olive-backed Pipit** has more a distinctive plumage but is easily overlooked; **Pechora Pipit** has a distinctive wing pattern and structure, and also call; **Buff-bellied Pipit** is more like Rock Pipit (*p. 366*) or winter Water Pipit (*p. 367*) and told by pale face and streaked buff underparts.

Small Pipit ID
Combination of structure, plumage and call essential for identification.

TREE   MEADOW   RED-THROATED   PECHORA

Tree Pipit and **Meadow Pipit** have a faintly streaked rump, thin wingbars and short wingtip.

Red-throated Pipit has a **heavily streaked rump**, two pale streaks on the back and short wingtip.

Pechora Pipit has a faintly streaked rump, two broad white wingbars, two pale streaks on the back and **long wingtip extending beyond the tertials**.

Red-throated Pipit
Anthus cervinus

L 14–15 cm | W 25–27 cm

Stocky, relatively short-tailed pipit with **black-and-yellow bill**; bobs tail like wagtail. Breeding adults unmistakable; non-breeding/immature birds very like Meadow Pipit (*p. 365*), except call. ADULT BREEDING **brick-red to pale red-pink face and throat**, weakest on FEMALE. ADULT NON-BREEDING face and throat paler pink or pink-buff, faintly streaked. JUVENILE/1ST-WINTER like greyish Meadow Pipit, with bold black stripes beneath and distinct **pale stripes** on back; **rump heavily streaked** (quite plain on Meadow Pipit).

VOICE Call explosive, high, penetrating "*p'seeee!*"

Very rare migrant from Scandinavia: 8–12 per year, declining (<75 records Ireland), few Apr–May, most Sep–Nov. Mostly coastal. Grassland. Winters in Africa.

Non-breeding adult variably pink-buff or pink on throat but non-breeding female and 1st-winter may be difficult to separate.

ADULT NON-BREEDING / 1ST-WINTER [Nov]

black and cream streaks on back

bold black streaks on flank

BREEDING ♂ [Mar]

Pipit flight calls *p. 367*

SMALLER

Olive-backed Pipit
Anthus hodgsoni

L 14–15·5 cm | W 24–27 cm

Small, elegant, boldly marked pipit; dips tail like wagtail. Feeds in long grass, flying up or into nearby tree/cover if disturbed. Upperparts **greenish-olive with soft, subtle streaks**. Blackish line beside crown; wide, **bright cream stripe over eye**. Black line through eye cuts through drooping end of pale stripe, **creating isolated pale spot at back of cheek**. Breast cream to yellowish with **bold black streaks**. Legs very pale; bill pale at base.

VOICE Call like Tree Pipit's (*p. 364*) hoarse "*teess*" or "*tizz.*"

Vagrant from Asia: <600 records, 20–30 per year (<20 Ireland), most Oct–Nov. Coastal woods, scrub.

Pechora Pipit
Anthus gustavi

L 14–15 cm | W 23–26 cm

Small, boldly streaked pipit; **primaries project beyond tertial tips**. Two **broad whitish stripes on back**, two white wingbars; underparts white, streaked black.

VOICE Call short, clicking "*dzep.*"

Vagrant from Asia: <150 records (<5 Ireland), Sep–Oct. Islands, coasts. Grassland.

Buff-bellied Pipit
Anthus rubescens

L 15–16 cm | W 23–28 cm

Dark-legged pipit, like Water Pipit (*p. 367*) with plain back and **streaked buff** underparts. **Pale between eye and bill** (unlike Water or Rock Pipits (*p. 366*)).

VOICE Similar to Meadow Pipit but sharper, "*p-sip.*"

Vagrant from N America: <100 records (<25 Ireland), most months, most Sep–Apr. Scattered. Waterside/reservoirs.

Tree Pipit (*p. 364*) has a similar, but weakly defined, head pattern; Meadow Pipit (*p. 365*) head pattern weaker still.

TREE PIPIT
ADULT/1ST-WINTER [Oct]
isolated pale ear spot

Pechora Pipits can be very difficult to see well as they often spend a lot of time skulking in thick grass.

ADULT/1ST-WINTER [Oct]

primaries project beyond tertials

ROCK PIPIT [Nov] — dark lores
WATER PIPIT [Oct] — dark lores
less streaking on paler underparts
pale lores
ADULT/1ST-WINTER [Sep]

RARE PIPITS

Larger rare pipits

Three large, wagtail-like pipits, rare or very rare; **Richard's Pipit** in autumn the most likely. All fly up boldly, calling (calls very similar), and drop onto open ground (**Tawny Pipit**) or short grass (**Richard's Pipit** – which may hover briefly first). **Blyth's Pipit** weaker-billed, shorter-legged.

Identification of large pipits – summary of key features	
Richard's Pipit	Big, upright, long-legged; very long hind claw; pale between bill and eye; white belly. 1ST-WINTER has some new adult-type median coverts with **pointed** blackish centre **blurring** into browner fringe. VOICE Loud, cheeping, sparrowy "*speew*."
Tawny Pipit	**Wagtail shape**; wagtail-like bill; **short, arched hind claw; dark from bill to eye.** VOICE Thin, vibrant/rasping "*treeze*" or low "*tsreep*."
Blyth's Pipit	Smaller, slightly shorter tail, weaker bill and legs, and shorter hind claw than Richard's Pipit; buff belly. 1ST-WINTER has some new adult-type median coverts with **blunt** blackish centre and defined whitish fringe. Low, even "*shreeu*," diagnostic "*chup, chup*."

Vagrant from Asia: 100–125 per year (>100 records Ireland), most months, mostly Sep–Nov, occasionally overwinters. Scattered. Grassland.

Richard's Pipit *Anthus richardi*
👁 Blyth's Pipit, Tawny Pipit

L 17–20 cm | W 26–30 cm

Large, round-bodied, upstanding pipit, often very upright, pear-shaped, on long, strong legs. Dull, pale buff-brown or brighter orange-brown. **Mark between eye and bill diffuse, paler** than on Tawny Pipit, but darker than on Blyth's Pipit. Underparts whitish, breast streaks **barely extend onto flank**, unlike smaller Meadow Pipit (p. 365). Dark stripe from bill to blackish neck patch. Bill strong, thrush-like (finer on Tawny Pipit); **hind claw very long**. Walks steadily through long grass; may bob tail, confusingly like Tawny Pipit. ADULT median coverts tipped buff. JUVENILE median coverts tipped white.

VOICE Calls variable: loud, rough or grating, with rolled 'r'; sparrowy "*shrree*" or "*speew*;" softer, flatter or downslurred "*shrroo*." 'Explosive' shouted notes distinctive; quiet notes from undisturbed birds.

IN FLIGHT, strong, bounding, leaping up and away if disturbed; may hover before settling.

'Large' pipit hind claws

RICHARD'S – very long

BLYTH'S – medium–short, fine

TAWNY – medium, arched

Blyth's and Richard's Pipits median and greater coverts

Pattern difficult to assess in the field; median coverts shown here:

JUVENILE — clear-cut, pointed dark centres, buff sides, white tips.

1ST-WINTER NEW

RICHARD'S: pointed blackish centre blends into brown fringe

BLYTH'S: blunter, more distinct centre

ADULT [Mar]

1ST-WINTER AUG–MAR [Oct]

new median covert

paler birds very like Tawny Pipit

diffuse, rather pale lores

Pipit flight calls p.367

LARGER

Blyth's Pipit *Anthus godlewskii*
L 15·5–17 cm | W 23–28 cm

Like small Richard's Pipit but paler between bill and eye, and with shorter, diffuse stripe behind eye; slightly shorter legs, weaker bill, slightly shorter tail, more uniform underparts and whiter wingbar (difficult, but important to assess all these features to confirm identification – see table *opposite*).

VOICE Crucial but hard to judge: slightly higher than Richard's Pipit, longer, less grating "*shreeu*". **Diagnostic "*chup chup.*"**

Vagrant from Asia: <50 records (Britain), Sep–Nov. Most coastal, rare winter inland. Grassland.

NOTE: median coverts all tipped white (still juvenile, none replaced)

1ST-WINTER AUG–MAR [Oct]

very pale lores

Tawny Pipit   554
Anthus campestris
L 15·5–18 cm | W 25–28 cm

Large, full-bodied, **wagtail-like** pipit; often on bare open ground; clearly large (stocky wagtail size) but a little smaller than Richard's Pipit, not often so upright or 'chesty' looking. ADULT BREEDING **pale, plain**: upperparts dull clay-buff, wings darker with buff feather edges and **black spots across 'shoulder'**. **Blackish line from bill through eye** and dark stripe beside throat. JUVENILE streaked, like Richard's Pipit, soon becomes plainer with scattered streaks. Dark **stripe from eye to bill**. Generally colder, greyish-sandy, less rufous than Richard's Pipit. **Shorter, arched hind claw** (see *opposite*), not easy to see in grass!

VOICE Calls harsh, slightly vibrant "*treeze*" or "*tsreep*" or shorter "*shilp*," sparrowy "*chwee*" and short "*chup*" – some confusingly similar to Richard's Pipit.

Vagrant from S Europe: >1,000 records, 7–10 per year, declining (<50 records Ireland), most Apr–May. S coast. Grassland.

BREEDING [Apr]

dark lores

streaked JUVENILE/1ST-WINTER may closely resemble Richard's Pipit

JUVENILE JUN–OCT [Oct]

LARKS, PIPITS and WAGTAILS

Pied/White Wagtail *Motacilla alba*

L 16·5–19 cm | W 28 cm

👁 Imm.: Citrine Wagtail (p. 377), Yellow Wagtail sspp. (p. 375)

🟠 ssp. *yarrellii* 🟠 ssp. *alba*

Common resident (290,000 pairs, plus 500,000 birds in Ireland). White Wagtail frequent migrant, most spring; rare breeder (1–5 pairs, northern isles)

Round-bodied but long-tailed wagtail; walks on the ground, runs and constantly bobs tail. **Black-and-white** tail and **spindly black legs**. Sex, ages and seasonal differences are complex; two regular subspecies occur.

Pied Wagtail (ssp. *yarrellii*): **rump black or dark grey**. MALE BREEDING **black above**; **white face** with extensive **black bib**; underparts white with **sooty-grey** flank. MALE NON-BREEDING back greyer; throat white; black breast-band. FEMALE BREEDING like breeding male but back greyer. FEMALE NON-BREEDING crown grey with blackish sides; throat white. JUVENILE face yellowish; crown dark, edged blacker; side of neck/breast-band black.

White Wagtail (ssp. *alba*): **rump grey**. MALE BREEDING as Pied Wagtail but **pale grey above** and **pale grey** flank. MALE NON-BREEDING throat white, black breast-band. FEMALE BREEDING like breeding male but back drab grey. FEMALE NON-BREEDING crown all-grey; white face, narrow black breast-band. JUVENILE olive-grey above, including crown.

alba from/to Iceland and Greenland

from/to Iberia and N Africa — some *yarrellii* to Iberia

Many habitats, including urban

IN FLIGHT, bounding undulations; long tail with white sides.

- black/dark grey in all plumages — ADULT ♀ [Jan]
- mid- to dark grey
- black
- white/pale yellow
- dark grey
- black, edged white
- JUVENILE JUL–FEB [Jul]

- black — ADULT ♂ BREEDING [May]
- ♀ dark grey / ♂ black
- black
- broad white
- ADULT ♀ NON-BREEDING AUG–FEB [Oct]
- ♂ BREEDING JAN–AUG [Jun]

PIED WAGTAIL ssp. *yarrellii*

- ADULT ♀ BREEDING MAR–AUG [Jul]
- dark grey, often mottled black
- dark grey
- white cheek
- black
- black
- sooty

WAGTAILS

Pied/White Wagtail sspp.

Two regular and two vagrant sspp.: **PIED WAGTAIL** (ssp. *yarrellii*) – resident, Britain/Ireland/near Continent and **WHITE WAGTAIL** (ssp. *alba*) – migrant from continental Europe and Iceland/Greenland. Identification can be problematic in autumn/winter, although easier in spring. **Rump colour** is the most consistent feature, but best identified to subspecies using a suite of characters (see table, descriptions and annotations). Birds of any age can show mixed and/or intermediate features and these individuals are not safely identifiable to subspecies.

Identification of non-breeding Pied/White Wagtails

PIED ssp. *yarrellii*	RUMP ♂ **black**; ♀ **dark grey**; UPPERTAIL COVERTS **black**; FOREHEAD **broad** white; FLANK **dark grey**; BELLY white; often subtle grey spots or streaking; BREAST-BAND **wide**.
WHITE ssp. *alba*	RUMP **grey**; UPPERTAIL COVERTS grey to black; FOREHEAD **narrow** white; FLANK **white to pale grey**; BELLY bright white; rarely any grey markings; BREAST-BAND **narrow**.

1ST-WINTER AUG–MAR [Aug]
- olive-grey (♂ mottled with black)
- olive-grey
- white to yellowish with mottled olive cheek
- dark grey, edged pale grey
- pale grey at darkest
- grey in all plumages — **ADULT ♂** [Nov]

ADULT ♂ BREEDING APR–AUG [Apr] — grey

ADULT ♀ NON-BREEDING AUG–FEB [Aug]
- olive-grey
- olive-grey
- narrow, white

WHITE WAGTAIL ssp. *alba*

ADULT ♂ BREEDING MAR–AUG [May]
- grey
- white/pale grey
- border between black nape and grey back well defined in ♂, diffuse in ♀

ADULT ♂ NON-BREEDING AUG–FEB [Nov]

Isolated black breast patch; extensive white face; large white wing patch with grey feather centres.
ADULT ♂ [Apr]
'Amur Wagtail' ssp. *leucopsis* (from China–Japan) Vagrant: 1 record (Britain), Apr.

Black hood extends onto large black bib; small white 'mask'; grey back; large white wing patch.
ADULT ♂ [May]
'Masked Wagtail' ssp. *personata* (from Central Asia) Vagrant: 1 record (Britain), Nov–Dec.

LARKS, PIPITS and WAGTAILS

Yellow Wagtail *Motacilla flava*

ssp. *flavissima* | ssp. *flava* | ssp. *thunbergi* | **I** | **55**

L 15–16 cm | W 25 cm

👁 Eastern Yellow Wagtail, Citrine Wagtail (p. 377)

Slender 'yellow' wagtail (absent in winter), with spindly **black legs** (legs pale on resident Grey Wagtail (p. 376), which also has yellow below). Subspecies (see *opposite*) show considerable variation, hybridize and intergrade.

ADULT MALE BREEDING green above, **yellow face and underparts** – no other small bird is so **yellow**, unstreaked and habitually **walks** on the ground. FEMALE greyer/browner/more olive than male; pale wingbars; **yellow-buff below**. JUVENILE/1ST-WINTER brownish above, buff below (yellower under tail); dark 'moustache', stripe beside throat and narrow bib (juvenile Pied Wagtail (p. 372) is also yellowish-buff on face with blackish breast-band but is whiter below with grey flank and calls are different). Two whitish wingbars; **long whitish lines** on black wing.

IN FLIGHT, easy, quick; **long, deep undulations. Shorter tail than Pied Wagtail**, but similar **broad white tail sides**.

VOICE Sweet "*tsee*" or "*schlee*," loud "*sfeesp*" or "*sureee*" from perch. Song weak repetition of short, slurred notes.

Scarce and local summer migrant, Apr–Oct (15,000 pairs), scarce migrant Ireland

to W Africa

Wet meadows, cereal fields; migrant elsewhere; absent winter

JUVENILE JUN–OCT

JUVENILES of all subspecies are dull, greyish-brown and yellow-buff: note pale wingbars, long, white-edged black tail and black legs.

British ssp. *flavissima* ADULT ♂ BREEDING

Subspecies are only really distinctive in ADULT MALE plumages.

♀ [May]

British ssp. *flavissima* ♂ BREEDING

NOTE: after Aug, ADULT MALE breast washed brown, belly bright yellow; ADULT FEMALE breast has brown marks, buff-white below. JUVENILE becomes like ADULT FEMALE after Jul–Aug (1st-winter) and most cannot be sexed.

WAGTAIL CALLS AND SONGS at a glance

Pied Wagtail
Cheery, loud, "*tsuwee*," "*churree*" or "*churee-wee*;" also sharper "*tissick*."

White Wagtail
As Pied Wagtail.

Grey Wagtail
Explosive, metallic "*zi-zi*" or "*tsivit!*;" song rapid, sharp "*tiss-iss-iss*" and "*si-si-si*."

Yellow Wagtail
Sweet "*tsee*" or "*schlee*," loud "*sfeesp*" or "*sureee*;" song weak repetition of short, slurred notes.

Citrine Wagtail
Loud, slightly grating "*zrrip*," but 'Black-headed'Yellow Wagtail (ssp. *feldegg*) similar.

Yellow Wagtail subspecies
MALES in spring can usually be identified. FEMALES/JUVENILES may look unlike British birds, but most are probably not identifiable. Hybrids and intergrades create problems.

'BRITISH' ssp. *flavissima*
summer breeder, Apr–Oct. Green head; yellow over eye, yellow throat.

'BLACK-HEADED' ssp. *feldegg*
vagrant, most May; <25 records (1 Ireland). Cap black; chin yellow; back bright green. Call harsh/rasping "*tsee-rr*."

'CHANNEL WAGTAIL'
hybrid *flavissima* × *flava*; rare migrant. Cap and cheek pale blue-grey; white stripe over eye; chin white.

'GREY-HEADED' ssp. *thunbergi*
rare migrant, Apr–Sep (<10 records Ireland). Cap dark grey, nape paler grey, cheek blackish; chin yellow; back grey-green, wings brown.

'IBERIAN' ssp. *iberiae*
vagrant, Apr; <5 records (Britain). Cap grey-blue, cheek darker; thin white line over eye wider behind; chin white. Call like ssp. *flava* or more rasping.

'ASHY-HEADED' ssp. *cinereocapilla*
rare migrant, most Apr–May (has bred) (<15 records Ireland). Cap blue-grey, no white stripe over eye; chin white.

♀ [Jun]

'BLUE-HEADED' ssp. *flava*
rare migrant, Apr–May (has bred) (<100 records Ireland). Cap grey-blue; cheek darker; white over eye; chin yellow. Call "*tswe-ip*."

ADULT ♂ BREEDING

♀ [Jun]

LARKS, PIPITS and WAGTAILS

Grey Wagtail *Motacilla cinerea*

L 17–20 | W 25–27 cm

The wagtail with the **longest tail** and the only one with **yellow that is present in winter** (Yellow Wagtail (p. 374), present Mar–Oct). Legs **short and pale** (longer and black on other wagtails). Lively, active, bobbing and flirting long tail, often on rocks beside fast-flowing river, tree-lined streams with rapids, weirs, *etc*. Easily disturbed – visits to garden ponds often brief, usually first noticed by **distinctive call**.

ADULT slate-grey above; very long, **white-sided tail. Rump yellow-green; yellow under tail.** MALE BREEDING black throat; yellow underparts. MALE NON-BREEDING/FEMALE whiter or mixed black/white throat, paler underparts. JUVENILE/1ST-WINTER pink-buff beneath with whiter flank; **yellow vent**.

VOICE An explosive, metallic "*zi-zi*" or "*tsivit!*;" song rapid, sharp "*tiss-iss-iss*" and "*si-si-si*," penetrating the noise of rushing water.

Locally common resident (50,000 pairs, decline after severe winters), winter visitor

Clean rivers, mill streams; widely scattered outside breeding season, visiting garden ponds, town-centre rooftop puddles

IN FLIGHT, deeply undulating with **long**, slender tail and triangular wings with **white central stripe**.

pale stripe behind eye short; often weak or mottled

ADULT ♂ NON-BREEDING SEP–MAR [Oct]

some females have an unmarked white throat

♂ BREEDING MAR–AUG [Apr]

♀ BREEDING MAR–AUG [Apr]

1ST-WINTER SEP–MAR [Nov]

RARE WAGTAILS

Eastern Yellow Wagtail
Motacilla tschutschensis
L 15–16 cm | W 25 cm

Sleek wagtail; non-breeding birds very like Citrine Wagtail, and very rare (in W Europe) 'grey' female/1st-winter Yellow Wagtail (*p. 374*). Very long hind claw plus late date (Oct–Dec) suggest this species. MALE BREEDING (not recorded) like 'Blue-headed' Yellow Wagtail. MALE NON-BREEDING/FEMALE like dull female Yellow Wagtail, or **grey-and-white** (western sspp. of Yellow Wagtail rarely lack olive/buff, but eastern sspp. do so more frequently). 1ST-WINTER tinged olive/yellow. **Dark cheek joins nape**. Identification usually requires DNA evidence.

VOICE Yellow Wagtail-like "*sfeep*" and rasping "*dzeep*," similar to Citrine Wagtail.

Vagrant from Asia: <10 records (Britain): Oct, Dec. Marshes, coasts.

Citrine Wagtail
Motacilla citreola
L 16 cm | W 25 cm

Slender wagtail; resembles Yellow Wagtail (*p. 374*), Eastern Yellow Wagtail and juvenile Pied/White Wagtails (*p. 372*). MALE BREEDING grey back; yellow head and underparts; **black hindneck**. FEMALE/JUVENILE/1ST-WINTER very like some Yellow Wagtails but **broader white bars** and tertial fringes on blacker wing and pale lores; **pale band** separates dark (or pale-centred) cheek from dark nape; **white** (not yellowish) under tail. (Juvenile Pied/White Wagtails have black breast-band.)

VOICE Grating "*zrrip*" ('Black-headed' Yellow Wagtail (ssp. *feldegg*) similar.

Vagrant from Asia: <350 records, 8–15 per year (<50 Ireland), few spring, most Sep–Oct. Most near coast. Marshy fringes.

ADULT ♂ BREEDING

1ST-WINTER [Oct]

dark cheek joins nape

YELLOW WAGTAIL
shorter hind claw

1ST-WINTER SEP–MAR [Oct]
cheek outlined in white

♀ BREEDING MAR–AUG

ADULT NON-BREEDING [Nov]

♂ BREEDING MAR–AUG

DIPPERS, ACCENTORS, WRENS, ORIOLES, STARLINGS and WAXWINGS

ID each type has a distinct form and plumage features

1 dipper (3 subspecies: 2 resident, 1 a rare winter visitor).
3 accentors: 1 resident (3 subspecies: 2 resident, 1 a regular winter visitor); 2 vagrants.
1 wren (6 subspecies: 5 resident [1 mainland, 4 on islands], 1 a regular winter visitor).
1 Old World oriole: 1 very rare migrant.
2 starlings: 1 resident (2 subspecies); 1 very rare migrant.
2 waxwings: 1 irruptive winter visitor; 1 vagrant.

Ageing/sexing

Dipper, accentors and **Wren** sexes similar; **orioles, starlings** and **waxwings** sexes recognizable.

Accentors, Wren and **Old World oriole** juveniles similar to adults; **Dipper, starlings** and **waxwings** juveniles clearly different from adults.

Dipper (p. 379) is dumpy and short-tailed with a white breast and confined to watersides; has springy up–down action when perched; the only small bird to walk into water, swim and dive.

Wren (pp. 381–382) is tiny, barred brown, with a short tail, tiny wings and loud song; widespread, from low scrub to treetops.

Accentors (pp. 380, 387) are chat-like and thin-billed, hopping/shuffling freely on the ground, rapidly flicking wings and tail. Only one, the widespread Dunnock, is regular in Britain and Ireland.

Golden Oriole (p. 383) is slender and long-bodied but short-legged, with broad tail and long wings; adult male is yellow and black but inconspicuous in dense foliage.

Starlings (pp. 384–385) are small and active, with pointed bill and square-tail; walk and run quickly. In flight, triangular wings and short tail are distinctive: small groups to huge flocks.

Waxwings (pp. 386–387) are crested, heavy-bodied, short-legged and short-billed; sociable berry-eaters in winter, visiting puddles to drink.

DIPPER

WREN

ACCENTOR: DUNNOCK

STARLING

GOLDEN ORIOLE

WAXWINGS

Dipper *Cinclus cinclus*

L 17–20 cm | W 25–30 cm

Unmistakable dumpy, short-tailed, **dark water bird** with **white breast**. **Swims**/drifts buoyantly, **frequently dives** or walks into water. Typically taut **bobbing** action on rock or stony bank by running water. Blinks white membrane across eye. Flies off at least disturbance, or dashes past, following watercourse on jerky, **whirring** wings giving **distinctive call**. Nests under overhang; often flying through spray/waterfalls.

ADULT black-brown with browner head, white breast and **rusty band** under belly (ssp. *gularis*, Britain). JUVENILE dull and mottled, dark feather fringes on breast reduce contrast. 1ST-SUMMER has pale fringes to wing coverts.

VOICE Call (often in flight) hard, thick, oddly rasping "*dzit*" or "*strit*." Song penetrates streamside noise: bright, prolonged, disjointed warble with varied whistles and trills.

Scarce and local resident (13,000 pairs); rare winter visitor from continental Europe

Streams, rivers, rocky lakesides in hilly country. In winter, occasional on lowland rivers, pools, coast

ADULT

IN FLIGHT, low, quick, whirring, slightly jerky: always over water.

ADULT

ssp. *gularis*

ADULT

ADULT

Ssp. *hibernicus* (Ireland, W Scotland): reduced rusty breast-band and blacker back than widespread ssp. *gularis*.

ADULT

JUVENILE JUN–AUG

'BLACK-BELLIED DIPPER' ssp. *cinclus* (rare winter visitor from Europe, Nov–Apr): black belly; darker head than ssp. *gularis*.

DIPPERS, ACCENTORS, WRENS, ORIOLES, STARLINGS and WAXWINGS

Dunnock *Prunella modularis*

except ssp. *modularis* and *hebridium*

L 13–14·5 cm | W 19–21 cm

Alpine Accentor, Siberian Accentor (p. 387)

Small, **dark** accentor; sparrow-like but with **fine bill**. Feeds mainly on the ground, **creeping and shuffling**, with legs flexed, tail flicked (unlike superficially similar pipits, which walk freely). Often in groups of three or four, waving spread wings, sometimes in bush or tree.

Sexes alike. ADULT dark brown, **heavily streaked blackish** above; **grey face and underparts** with dark streaks on browner flank. Thin, orange-brown legs; reddish eye. JUVENILE more streaked beneath, spotted above, like juvenile Robin (p. 400) but darker, more striped, with pale bar across blackish wing. Eye dull.

VOICE Bright, even whistle, "*peeeh*" and thin, vibrant "*si-i-i-i-i-i-i*." Song fast, thin, high, slightly 'flat' warble, even speed and pitch. Shorter, less varied, less rambling than Robin.

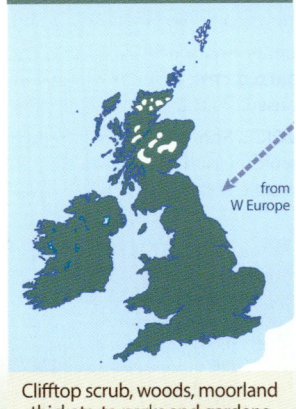

Common and widespread resident (2·1 million pairs, plus 1·7 million birds in Ireland)

from W Europe

Clifftop scrub, woods, moorland thickets, to parks and gardens

ssp. *occidentalis* ADULT

Although mostly inconspicuous and close to the ground, Dunnocks are more obvious when MALES sing from a more-or-less open perch at bush-top (rather than higher tree-top) height.

ssp. *hebridium* ADULT

Ssp. *hebridium* of Ireland and the Hebrides is browner than **British** ssp. *occidentalis* (which is darker than ssp. *modularis*, winter visitor from N/C Europe) [*not illustrated*].

Tiny white tips to coverts (bird *below right*) soon wear off (bird *above left*).

JUVENILE MAY–OCT

ssp. *occidentalis* ADULT

Untidy juvenile soon becomes almost indistinguishable from adult.

Wren *Troglodytes troglodytes*

L 9–10·5 cm | W 13–17 cm

sspp. *fridariensis* and *hirtensis*
sspp. *hebridensis, zetlandicus* and *indigenus*

Tiny, rotund, brown, cock-tailed; the only wren in Britain and Ireland and unmistakable if seen well. Usually in dense cover, where with brief views could be mistaken for Dunnock.

Little variation with age, sex or season. Warm brown, paler below, **barred crosswise**. **Pale stripe over eye**. Tail narrow, often (not always!) raised. Pops up from cover, calls irritably and dives back down again.

VOICE Short "*chek*," longer, rolling/rasping "*cherrrr*" and irregular scolding rattle. Song loud and vibrant, sudden powerful, ringing, rapid warble with low, quick trill at or near the end.

Wren subspecies – see also p. 382 for descriptions
Ssp. *indigenus* is found throughout 'mainland' Britain.
Ssp. *troglodytes* (winter migrant from Europe) is brighter and paler.
Local subspecies on outlying islands: '**SHETLAND**' WREN (ssp. *zetlandicus*), '**FAIR ISLE**' WREN ssp. (*fridariensis*), '**HEBRIDEAN**' WREN (ssp. *hebridensis* – Outer Hebrides) and '**ST KILDA**' WREN (ssp. *hirtensis*) are all more coarsely marked than ssp. *indigenus* found throughout 'mainland' Britain and Ireland; Shetland Wren especially so. St Kilda Wren most distinct, largest, palest and most barred and with a longer bill. Island subspecies told by location.

Widespread and abundant resident (8 million pairs, plus 6 million birds in Ireland)

Anywhere from coastal cliffs to woods, gardens, heaths, moorland thickets; often marshes

Ageing difficult, but in the hand buff bars across secondaries and primaries form long, smooth curves on JUVENILE/1ST-WINTER birds; irregular steps on ADULTS.

A singing Wren is the image of intense effort: tail cocked, its body taut, swaying and vibrating.

DIPPERS, ACCENTORS, WRENS, ORIOLES, STARLINGS and WAXWINGS

The British and Irish subspecies of Wren
6 subspecies of Wren occur: 4 resident (3 on island groups); 1 ('Hebridean') migrates to Ireland; 1 ('European') arrives from continental Europe in winter.

'BRITISH/IRISH WREN' ssp. *indigenus*
Abundant: small, rufous; song loud, disjointed, mechanical; long trill.

'EUROPEAN WREN' ssp. *troglodytes*
Winter migrant from continental Europe: bright, pale, finely barred.

'FAIR ISLE WREN' ssp. *fridariensis*
Restricted to Fair Isle (10–52 pairs; on cliffs): paler than Shetland ssp., darker than mainland birds, neatly barred. Prefers sheltered gullies in coastal cliffs.

'SHETLAND WREN' ssp. *zetlandicus*
Shetland only (common; on cliffs, rocky beaches): rufous, strongly barred, robust; song loud, short.

'ST KILDA WREN' ssp. *hirtensis*
Restricted to St Kilda (200–230 pairs; around cliffs, rocks, ruins): palest, greyest, longest-billed ssp.; song less mechanical, less shrill than ssp. *indigenus*.

'HEBRIDEAN WREN' ssp. *hebridensis*
Outer Hebrides (common; migrates to Ireland): barred, like ssp. *indigenus* but song distinct, fluent, with high, sibilant trills.

Golden Oriole *Oriolus oriolus*

L 19–22 cm | W 44–47 cm

The only Old World oriole recorded in Britain/Ireland and one of Europe's brightest birds; size of Blackbird (p. 391), with elongated, thrush-like form but **longer wings**. Distinctive if seen well, but mostly very secretive and hard to see in leafy canopy.

> Very rare migrant from Europe: 50 per year (<250 records Ireland), most Apr–Jun; past breeder. Mainly near coast. Woodland. Winters in Africa.

ADULT MALE brilliant **yellow and inky black**; black from bill to eye; bill pinkish-red. ADULT FEMALE pale yellow, back greenish, flank faintly streaked grey; grey from bill to eye; greenish-black wing with pale yellow spot near edge; **blackish tail with yellow corners**; green-yellow rump (recalling Green Woodpecker (p. 345)). Dull pink-red bill. JUVENILE greenish, white below with grey streaks, yellow under tail; wing dark with small whitish spot; rump/tail as female. Bill grey. IMMATURE/1ST-YEAR like juvenile but streaking reduced, darker between bill and eye, and bill pink-red.

VOICE Strained, harsh, gaspy "*eee-aahk*." **Song unmistakable** (a bit like a very short snatch of fluty Blackbird): short, rich, fluty, whistling "*ee-dl-oo*," or "*dl'oo*," or "*ee-deeoo-dli-do*" repeated for long periods.

IN FLIGHT, direct, with steady wingbeats (no woodpecker-like undulations).

ADULT ♂

ADULT ♂

ADULT ♀ / 1ST-SUMMER ♂

ADULT ♀ / 1ST-SUMMER ♂

NOTE: **1ST-YEAR** males can resemble females

Starling *Sturnus vulgaris*

L 19–22 cm | W 35–40 cm

Brown-headed Cowbird (p. 536), **Daurian Starling** (p. 539)

Typical starling: fairly small and **short-tailed**, with a longish, pointed bill; usually feeds while **walking or running on the ground**, often in small flocks. Pre-roost gatherings swirl and dive in co-ordinated manoeuvres. Often hawks insects, especially flying ants.

ADULT BREEDING black, with **purple and green gloss**; buff feather edges on wings and around tail. Bill base blue on MALE; pink on FEMALE. ADULT NON-BREEDING **large white spots overall**. Head whitish with **dark eyestripe**. Legs **orange-brown**. JUVENILE brown; **blackish, spiky bill; dark 'wedge'** in front of eye. Develops white spots on black body, as head/neck fade, creating **dark body/pale head**.

VOICE Strident whistles, buzzing "*cheer*." Alarm sharp, clicking "*plik*." Song (puffed-out throat, waving half-open wings) prolonged rattling, whistling, warbling, mimicry; also long, rambling subsong.

Locally common resident (about 2 million pairs Britain and Ireland), temporarily abundant in winter (8·5 million birds, plus 2·7 million in Ireland); much decreased

from W Europe

Farmland, urban and suburban areas; also breeds in woodland

IN FLIGHT, **pointed head, square tail, triangular wings**.

ADULT NON-BREEDING

JUVENILE MOULTING [Aug]

ADULT ♂ BREEDING MAR–AUG — blue

ADULT ♀ BREEDING MAR–AUG — pink

JUVENILE MAY–AUG

Ssp. *zetlandicus* (Shetland) has blacker juvenile plumage than birds in the rest of Britain or Ireland (ssp. *vulgaris*).

ADULT NON-BREEDING JUL–MAR

JUVENILE MOULTING JUL–OCT [Sep]

JUVENILE MAY–AUG — black

Rose-coloured Starling *Pastor roseus*

L 19–22 cm | W 37–42 cm

Similar to Starling in form and behaviour but has a **shorter, blunter bill** and softer, rounder look to the head. ADULT BREEDING unmistakable, **pink-and-black** with **ragged crest**. ADULT NON-BREEDING pink areas washed brown. JUVENILE moults later than Starling so is still unlike adult until late autumn. Pale beige-brown, paler still on rump and underparts, buff fringes to all wing feathers. Note pale rump/dark tail/ dark wing contrast in flight (especially when ruling out not-infrequent sandy-coloured young Starling). Bill distinctively **yellow** with darker tip (blackish on juvenile Starling). Bold dark eye in plain pale face (without juvenile Starling's dark 'wedge'). By late autumn, looks like a dull version of non-breeding adult: grey-brown above, pinkish-buff below.

VOICE Calls like Starling but less harsh.

Very rare migrant from E Europe: 40–50 per year (<150 records Ireland), most May–Nov, occasionally overwinters. Adults often in N/W late summer, juveniles coastal in S in autumn; often with Starlings. Winters in S Asia.

STARLINGS

ADULT
pale belly; short bill

JUVENILE
pale rump, darker wings

ADULT NON-BREEDING SEP–MAR [Sep]
dull bill, pink areas sullied grey

ADULT BREEDING MAR–SEP [May]
spiky crest may be sleeked down

JUVENILE MAY–NOV [Sep]
yellow
pale brown MAY–OCT/NOV (later in autumn than juvenile Starling); most records in Britain/Ireland SEP–OCT

ADULT ♂ BREEDING MAR–SEP [May]
breeding adult brighter, cleaner pink than non-breeding; pinker bill and legs.

DIPPERS, ACCENTORS, WRENS, ORIOLES, STARLINGS and WAXWINGS

Waxwing *Bombycilla garrulus*

L 18–21 cm | W 32–35 cm   👁 Cedar Waxwing

Unmistakable; the only regular waxwing in Europe: stocky, **crested**, **short-billed** and short-legged. Starling-like (*p. 384*) in size and flight profile, but more sedate when perched, often inactive in treetops for lengthy periods, and rarely on the ground unless drinking from a puddle. **Feeds acrobatically** on berries/apples/shoots; occasionally makes flycatching sallies. Greyish-pinkish-brown, paler beneath; foxy-red on face; upstanding **pinkish crest**; **black bib**. **Grey rump** and **rufous under tail**. Black wing marked **white, yellow and red**: extent varies within ages and sexes (see annotations *below*).

VOICE Calls distinctive far-carrying, silvery trill, "*sirrrr.*" Greenfinch (*p. 497*) and Blue Tit (*p. 468*) make remarkably similar sounds in spring.

Scarce, irregular winter visitor, most Nov–Mar; periodic 'invasions' of 100s–1,000s, flocks

from Scandinavia

Ornamental shrubs, berry-bearing trees and bushes

IN FLIGHT, quick, dashing or swooping, with longer body profile/ bigger head than Starling.

1ST-WINTER ♂

ADULT ♀

diffuse edge to chin patch

shorter crest

well-defined edge to chin patch

1ST-WINTER OCT–MAR

ADULT ♂

thin white 'tips' on primaries

no white 'tips' on primaries

thick white 'tips' on primaries

RARE ACCENTORS | WAXWINGS

Alpine Accentor
Prunella collaris
L 16 cm | W 30–32 cm

Large, dark accentor; like large Dunnock (*p. 380*), creeping around in similar fashion. **Two white bars** and **blackish band** across wing; **yellow base** to bill; broad **rufous streaks on flank**.

Vagrant from C Europe: <50 records (Britain), most Mar–May, Nov–Jan. Most coastal. Rocky areas; on ground.

dark band on wing more obvious than rusty flank streaks

pale bill can be eye-catching; pale, spotted throat inconspicuous

ADULT

Siberian Accentor
Prunella montanella
L 13–14 cm | W 19–20 cm

Small, pale accentor; like brightly patterned Dunnock (*p. 380*), feeding on ground in similar way. Dark cap, blackish cheek, **broad orange-buff stripe over eye**; **unmarked orange-buff throat**; rufous streaks on flank.

Vagrant from Asia: <20 records (Britain, all 2016), Oct–Nov. Coasts. Woodland/scrub with open ground/rocky areas.

orange-buff over eye and on throat

greyish flank finely streaked darker

1ST-WINTER (presumed) [Oct]

Cedar Waxwing
Bombycilla cedrorum
L 18 cm | W 22–30 cm

Like Waxwing, with which it may associate. ADULT pale orange-brown, grey rump; tail dark with yellow tip. Grey wing marked with red (no white or yellow); yellow belly and **white under tail**. 1ST-WINTER greyer, with short crest; wing unmarked grey; flank streaked grey, belly yellowish.

Vagrant from N America: <15 records (<5 Ireland), Feb, Jun, Sep–Nov. Scattered. Trees/bushes with berries.

drab wing lacks prominent white flashes

1ST-WINTER OCT–MAR [Nov]

ADULT

yellow beneath (unlike Waxwing)

Easily overlooked amongst Waxwings: pale beneath tail best mark.

387

THRUSHES, CHATS and WHEATEARS

THRUSH ID overall plumage | breast pattern | head pattern | call and song
CHAT ID overall plumage | tail and rump pattern | head patterns | call and song

20 thrushes: 3 common residents, 1 summer visitor, 2 widespread winter visitors that breed occasionally; 14 vagrants, 7 from Asia, 7 from North America.
25 chats and wheatears: 7 breed; 17 rare migrants/vagrants.

Old World thrushes (*pp. 390–397*) are mostly larger, longer-tailed, blunter-billed and rounder-headed than Starling (*p. 384*) and move with a curious mix of walk and hop, or shuffling leaps, not running so freely as Starlings. A typical action is the familiar run–stop–listen–dig for a worm. Flocks are slower, looser, less tightly coordinated than Starling, on the ground and in flight; flying birds have shorter head, rounder wings and longer tail. While some are resident, Ring Ouzel is a summer migrant, Redwing and Fieldfare arrive in autumn and stay until spring, and rarities tend to be autumn birds.

New World thrushes (*pp. 398–399*) include two large, strikingly coloured species and five small, rounded, brownish birds more-or-less spotted on the breast, which are more secretive, and need to be separated from similar Asian chats. All are rare vagrants, occasionally in spring, mostly in autumn.

Chats (*pp. 400–407*) and **Wheatears** (*pp. 408–411*) are like very small, rounded thrushes, with slim bill and rounded head. The Robin is a familiar yardstick: it is adaptable, common and widespread all year in many habitats, whereas the Nightingale is a summer visitor, with a restricted distribution tied to specific habitats. Others are much less skulking birds of heath and moor, preferring more open ground, stones and cliffs, or bushy places. They tend to have strong patterns, at least on breeding males, although females and juveniles may be less easily distinguished. Of these, the wheatears form a distinctive group on account of their form and black-and-white tail/rump patterns.

NIGHTINGALE

WHEATEAR

SONG THRUSH

REDSTART

INTRODUCTION

Thrush and chat ageing/sexing

In 'spotted' thrushes the sexes look alike, in others they differ, as in most small chats/wheatears (but not Robin). Some have seasonal changes, others do not.

Juveniles (*shown here*) are distinct, duller and more spotted than adults. 1st-winter and 1st-summer (one-year-old) birds told from adult by juvenile wing and tail, which become pale and worn.

NIGHTINGALE JUN–AUG

ROBIN MAY–SEP

STONECHAT MAY–AUG
sexes alike in juvenile plumage; differ by 1st-winter after moult

WHEATEAR JUN–JUL

REDSTART JUN–AUG

Post-juvenile moult

JUVENILE → 1ST-WINTER
JUL–SEP: head, body, some wing coverts, from 4–6 weeks, completed at 2–3 months old.

1ST-WINTER ♀ JUL–MAR

1ST-WINTER ♂ JUL–MAR

1st-winter keeps juvenile flight feathers, tail, tertials, many wing coverts, all these browner, more worn than new feathers; difficult to separate from adult by next summer, when heavily worn.

ADULT ♀ SEP–JAN (FRESH) JAN–AUG (WORN)

ADULT ♂ SEP–FEB (FRESH) FEB–AUG (WORN)

Adult moult

ADULT: single complete moult (takes 50 days) JUL/AUG – SEP/OCT; fresh feathers have pale tips, lost by spring.

Rare thrushes, chats and wheatears

Rarities mostly have obvious similarity to common groups, so it is usually easy to tell a 'thrush', a 'wheatear' etc., but separating them, especially in 1st-winter plumage, can be challenging.

GREY-CHEEKED THRUSH

Several similar, small New World thrushes quickly bring to mind 'thrush' (despite their small size and variable spotting on breast); good views and careful observation are needed to tell them apart.

POSSIBLE CONFUSION GROUPS

Dunnock (*p. 380*) fine bill, streaked flank.

Buntings (*pp. 510–523*) thick bill, most have white tail sides, upright on perch or horizontal on ground.

Flycatchers (*pp. 417–421*) upright on very short legs; wide bill.

THRUSHES, CHATS and WHEATEARS

Ring Ouzel *Turdus torquatus*

L 24–27 cm | W 41–45 cm

Black-throated Thrush (*p. 396*), Siberian Thrush (*p. 397*)

Large, dark thrush, resembles Blackbird. Wings and tail long and narrow, flight fast and dashing, disappears over skyline. On ground, looks sleek, flat-backed, with head held up, tail often raised. Favours berried bushes/scattered Rowans on heath/moorland edge in autumn.

MALE BREEDING **black with white breast-band** and pale **silvery-grey panel on wing**. MALE NON-BREEDING pale lacy pattern beneath; white crescent drab. FEMALE duller, dark brownish; **pale feather edges** especially on wings and underparts; dull whitish breast-band. JUVENILE brownish, with extensive pale feather edges and pale wing panel, but obscure breast-band. 1ST-WINTER like adult non-breeding but has juvenile wing and tail feathers.

VOICE Scolding, hard "*tuc tuc tuc*," rolling "*churr*." Song wild, loud, recalls Mistle Thrush (*p. 393*), a few fluty whistles in distinctly separated phrases: "*tuleee tuleee; tiu-lee tiu-lee tiu-lee tiu-lee; schreet schreet*."

Scarce and local summer visitor, Mar–Nov (6,900 pairs, declining); widespread but uncommon on migration spring/autumn

from Scandinavia

to N Africa | to N Africa

Breeds uplands; migrant hills/downs, coastal areas

IN FLIGHT, long wings and tail; upperwing subtly pale, underwing inconspicuous dull whitish.

♂ NON-BREEDING AUG–MAR

NOTE: ADULT and 1ST-SUMMER MALE look similar but the latter has browner wings with thin pale bar on greater coverts.

JUVENILE JUN–SEP

1ST-WINTER ♀ AUG–MAR

JUVENILE lacks a distinct breast-band but has short, whitish bars over dark underparts and short, curved pale streaks above.

1ST-WINTER FEMALE least distinctive; has dull pale wing panel, dull pale 'scaly' feather edges, but only obscure breast-band.

♂ BREEDING MAR–AUG

THRUSHES

Blackbird *Turdus merula*

L 23·5–29 cm | W 40–45 cm

Large, **long-tailed** thrush with run–stop action on ground. **Raises tail** and lowers it slowly as pauses or after a short flight.

👁 Black-throated Thrush (p. 396), Siberian Thrush (p. 397), Red-winged Blackbird (p. 536).

ADULT MALE **black**; **yellow bill** (see Starling (p. 384)) and eyering. 1ST-WINTER MALE bill dark, wings brown. FEMALE **dark brown**, throat often whitish; breast streaked but never has sharp black spots on buff. Bill dark or **yellow with a dark tip**. JUVENILE **rusty-brown**, mottled (tail blacker on MALE); variably spotted below, whitish on throat, but much darker than Song Thrush (p. 392); legs dark.

VOICE Vibrant "*srreee*," soft "*chook*," loud "*chak*" or repeated loud "*pink pwink pwink*" especially at dusk. Mild alarm rhythmic, repeated endlessly; full alarm **clattering, screechy rattle**. Song best at dawn/dusk: varied, musical, throaty and flute-like phrases, which fall into rattles and squeaks, without rigid repetition of Song Thrush.

Very common resident (4-6 million pairs, plus 4·9 million birds in Ireland); migrant, winter visitor

from N and W Europe

Wide range: woods, fields, hedges, parks, gardens, thickets

IN FLIGHT, broad wings, broad tail; MALE shows paler outerwing.

JUVENILE ♂ MAR–SEP

dark bill

1ST-WINTER ♂ AUG–MAR

some juveniles are reddish below; males have a blacker tail than females

NOTE: 1ST-SUMMER MALE is like ADULT but has browner wings.

1ST-WINTER ♀ AUG–MAR

some individuals have a pale breast-band

391

THRUSHES, CHATS and WHEATEARS

Song Thrush *Turdus philomelos*

L 20–22 cm | W 33–36 cm

● except ssp. *philomelos*

👁 Rare American thrushes (*p. 398–399*)

Small, pale, compact thrush (compare with similar Redwing (*p. 395*)). Tends to fly low into a bush if disturbed (unlike larger Mistle Thrush, which flies away over trees).

ADULT **pale, warm brown** above, creamy-buff below with **blackish 'V'-shaped spots**; browner flank, whiter belly (Mistle Thrush is bigger, has pale-edged wing feathers and bolder, rounder spots). Head pattern weaker than Redwing. JUVENILE pale feather edges on upperparts, less regular spots below. 1ST-WINTER as adult but pale wingbar.

VOICE Thin, sharp "*tik*" or "*sip*;" weak, rattling alarm. Song **strident**: rich, fluty whistles, shouted and squeaky notes; **even-paced repetition of short phrases**. Loud 'slap' of snail smashed on stone characteristic.

Locally common resident (1 million pairs, plus 950,000 birds in Ireland); migrant, winter visitor

from N and W Europe

ssp. *hebridensis* 1ST-WINTER

ssp. *philomelos* 1ST-WINTER

Gardens, parks, damp woods, hedgerows

IN FLIGHT, underwing pale orange; tail plain.

Song Thrush subspecies

Three occur in Britain and Ireland but intergrade from south-east to north-west, making it difficult to assign some individuals to subspecies.
Ssp. *philomelos* (passage migrant and winter visitor from Europe) is the palest.
Ssp. *clarkei* (resident in Britain and Ireland) is intermediate in tone and markings.
Ssp. *hebridensis* (resident in the Outer Hebrides and Isle of Skye) is the darkest and also lacks buff on the breast and flank.

dark cap/pale over eye always very subtle, unlike Redwing

pale spots above

JUVENILE APR–SEP

NOTE: ADULT and 1ST-SUMMER very similar but retained juvenile greater covert(s) indicate the latter.

ssp. *clarkei* 1ST-SUMMER

spots 'V'- or fan-shaped, less crosswise than on Mistle Thrush

THRUSHES

Mistle Thrush *Turdus viscivorus*

L 26–29 cm | W 43–45 cm

👁 White's Thrush (p. 396)

Large, pale, long-tailed thrush, often **upright**, hopping with **strong, springy action**. Flies fast, **often high** (goes away high over trees if disturbed): small head, long, squared tail, big wings create distinctive shape, especially as family group or small flock streams by, line astern.

ADULT sandy-grey-brown. **Dark 'shoulder' spots** and **pale feather edges** on wings (Song Thrush more uniform); tail has whitish sides and corners. Underparts uniform yellowish-cream, **round black spots** often merging on sides of breast (creating subtly darker patch at distance). JUVENILE strikingly bright and pale; **dark-edged cream spots above**. 1ST-WINTER as adult but brighter buff below.

VOICE Call dry, rattling "*tchrrr-tchrrr-tchrrr*." Song similar to Blackbird (p. 391) but **less varied**: brief, flowing phrases with far-carrying, wild quality, often from high treetop.

Widespread but thinly spread resident (200,000 pairs, plus 25,000 birds in Ireland)

Gardens, parks, woods, hedgerows, moorland trees with berries, windbreaks, pastures

NOTE: aggressive towards intruders near nest.

IN FLIGHT, **white underwing** (like Fieldfare (p. 394)) flashes prominently.

NOTE: ADULT and 1ST-WINTER similar but 1ST-WINTER brighter buff below.

1ST-WINTER

pale fringes to wing feathers

markedly bigger, but relatively smaller-headed shape, than Song Thrush

JUVENILE APR–AUG

pale spots and dark fringes above

THRUSHES, CHATS and WHEATEARS

Fieldfare *Turdus pilaris*

L 22–27 cm | W 40–42 cm

Large, colourful thrush, often with Redwings in tens/hundreds in winter. Feeds head-to-wind on ground, or on berries; flies into treetops if disturbed. Flocks on ground appear orange-buff head-on; conspicuous grey rumps and black tails from behind.

ADULT grey head, brown back, **grey rump and black tail**. Black around eye and yellow on bill give strong expression. Breast pale to deep **orange**, black streaks and spots (blackish flank in spring). Pale grey rump above broad black tail obvious even on ground. JUVENILE has pale spots on crown, thin buff streaks on back and wing. 1ST-WINTER as adult but some pale-tipped juvenile greater coverts retained.

VOICE Low, throaty, chuckling chatter "*chak-chak-ak*" or "*chuk-uk-uk-uk*," often in chorus from flock; nasal "*swee-eep*" (almost like Lapwing (p. 197)). Occasional low subsong from spring flocks. Song (rare Britain and Ireland) weak, chattering, repetitive sequence.

Common winter visitor, Oct–Apr (680,000); very rare breeder

from NW Europe

from E and C Europe

Woods, hedgerows, orchards, fields, parks

IN FLIGHT, white underwing (Mistle Thrush (p. 393) similar but more elongated, with pale tail).

ADULT

On the ground, the broad, contrastingly pale grey rump is obvious, especially in bright light.

NOTE: ADULT has all greater coverts plain rufous with grey tip; on 1ST-WINTER, inner greater coverts similar but outer ones dull with whitish fringe and tip.

ADULT/ 1ST-WINTER

blacker on flank, brighter orange-buff on breast in spring

white belly/ vent more striking than on other common thrushes

1ST-WINTER

THRUSHES

Redwing *Turdus iliacus*

L 19–23 cm | W 30–34 cm

● except ssp. *coburni*

Rare thrushes (p. 396–397)

Small, dark thrush with **bold head pattern**. Often in flocks with Fieldfares and other thrushes in fields/hedges/orchards. Visits gardens/ornamental shrubberies, especially in severe winters. Flocks usually flighty and wary, slip away through hedge tops. Also feeds deep inside woods and in overgrown ditches.

ADULT dark brown above (darker than Song Thrush (p. 392)). **Cream stripe above eye; dark cheek**, pale 'moustache'. Underparts whitish, with **lines of dark spots**; flank **brick-red**. JUVENILE/1ST-WINTER has pale tips to wing coverts.

VOICE Distinctive high, thin "*seeeeh*" (often heard at night); rattling notes. Song rich, fluty phrase. Rambling 'subsong' chorus from roosting flocks.

Common winter visitor, Sep–Apr (650,000); very rare breeder, Scotland (5–12 pairs)

from Iceland

from N and E Europe

Gardens, parks, fields, woods, orchards, hedgerows

IN FLIGHT, **underwing red**. Small white patch beside dark rump. Smaller than Fieldfare. Flocks overhead (migrants or in hard-weather movements) look like Skylark (p. 361) flocks, but a little more coordinated; individual Redwings sleeker and longer-headed (less 'square') than Skylarks.

ssp. *iliacus*

Icelandic ssp. *coburni* ADULT

strongly striped head always characteristic

N/E European ssp. *iliacus* ADULT

Icelandic ssp. *coburni* (scarce winter migrant, Britain/Ireland) darker than regularly occurring ssp. *iliacus* from N and E Europe: note broad streaks tending to coalesce on browner underparts, darker cheek with thinner pale band beneath, dark streaks on undertail coverts and darker legs.

RARE THRUSHES

Rare Asian thrushes
Vagrant thrushes from the east that tend to arrive in late autumn and sometimes overwinter; they may appear in unlikely places, from sand dunes to gardens.

Black-throated Thrush
Turdus atrogularis
L 23–25·5 cm | W 35–39 cm

Fairly large, greyish thrush with paler underparts; bill **yellow with black tip**. MALE **face/breast black**. FEMALE dull **dark tail** (no rufous); dark mark from eye to bill; **grey mottles on breast** and **pale streaks on flank**. 1ST-WINTER pale wingbar; streaks on throat and flanks coalesce into blacker breast-band on MALE.

Vagrant from Asia: <100 records (Britain), Sep–May. Scattered. Trees/berried bushes, often on ground.

1ST-WINTER ♀ SEP–MAR [Oct]

♂ NON-BREEDING SEP–MAR [Jan]

Red-throated Thrush
Turdus ruficollis
L 23–25·5 cm | W 35–39 cm

Like Black-throated Thrush but **sides of tail rusty/red-brown**. MALE has **brick-red breast and face**, streaked/mottled buff Sep–Mar. FEMALE (not recorded) streaked grey, buff tinge to breast.

Vagrant from Asia: 1 record (Britain), Sep–Oct. On coast. Trees/bushes.

1ST-WINTER ♂ SEP–MAR [Sep]

Siberian Thrush
Geokichla sibirica
L 20–21·5 cm | W 37–42 cm

Small thrush with broad **black and white bands on underwing**, white tips to tail feathers. MALE slate grey with **broad white line over eye**. 1ST-WINTER MALE browner, with buff stripe over eye and throat. FEMALE brown above, **whitish below with dark bars**; pale above and below dark cheek.

Vagrant from Asia: <15 records (<5 Ireland), most Oct–Jan. On coast. Trees/bushes; on ground.

♀

♂

1ST-YEAR ♂

1ST-WINTER ♂ SEP–MAR

[Oct]

paler, browner than adult male

ASIAN

Eyebrowed Thrush
Turdus obscurus
L 20·5–23 cm | W 37–40 cm

Small, pale thrush. ADULT grey head and breast, **white stripes over and below eye**; orange flank. 1ST-WINTER browner, **white over eye**; head grey-brown, dark eyestripe; **pale orange flank**; white belly and vent.

Vagrant from Asia: <25 records (Britain), Apr–Jun, Sep–Dec. Most on coast; often with Redwings (*p. 395*).

1ST-WINTER
OCT–MAR
[Oct]

no spots below

Dusky Thrush
Turdus eunomus
L 21–24 cm | W 34–38 cm

Small, rufous thrush, white below; dark cap; buff-white bands above eye and below dark cheek; blackish spots on breast and 'V'-shapes on flank; rufous wing panel and rump, red underwing. 1ST-WINTER MALE paler edges disrupt duller wing panel. 1ST-WINTER FEMALE duller.

Vagrant from Asia: <15 records (Britain), Sep–Mar, May. Widespread. Trees/bushes.

1ST-WINTER ♂
SEP–MAY
[Feb]

1ST-WINTER ♀
[May]

Dusky and Naumann's Thrush intergrade; it may therefore not be impossible to assign some individuals to either species.

ADULT

Naumann's Thrush
Turdus naumanni
L 21–24 cm | W 35–40 cm

Small, rufous thrush, underparts closely mottled with diamond-shaped **orange-rufous spots**; rusty rump and tail.

Vagrant from Asia: <5 records (Britain), Jan–Mar. Widespread. Trees/bushes.

White's Thrush
Zoothera aurea (dauma)
L 27–31 cm | W 35–40 cm

Large, long, large-billed thrush; pale with **crescentic dark barring** (see juvenile Mistle Thrush (*p. 393*)). Dark bands along upperwing, **black-and-white underwing**; pale tail 'corners'.

Vagrant from Asia: <100 records (<10 Ireland), most Sep–Oct. Most on coast. Trees; feeds on ground.

1ST-WINTER
OCT–MAR
[Oct]

Rare American thrushes

American Robin and Varied Thrush are large thrushes, clearly similar to British/Irish thrushes. But other North American thrushes (*Catharus*) that have been recorded are smaller, more Nightingale-like (p. 401). The most likely species to cross the Atlantic have a large population and wide distribution in eastern North America. Starting their southward autumn migration over the sea they can be caught in strong westerly winds (perhaps resting on an eastbound ship) and make landfall mainly in western Britain, Ireland and the Northern Isles.

American Robin
Turdus migratorius
L 22–25 cm | W 38–40 cm

Fairly large thrush. ADULT slaty-grey above with paler fringes to wing feathers. Blackish hood, with bold **white marks around eye**; throat paler, streaked. Underparts pale **brick-red or orange**, darker on MALE. White with black streaks under tail. Black tail has white 'corners'. IMMATURE paler, with paler edges below.

<50 records (<15 Ireland), May–Jun, most Oct–Apr. Scattered. Trees/bushes; feeds on ground.

mottled paler than adult, white tips to wing coverts

1ST-WINTER ♀ SEP–MAR

Varied Thrush *Ixoreus naevius*
L 24 cm | W 35–40 cm

Grey-and-orange thrush, **orange-buff over eye** and on wingbars; **dark cheek and breast-band**; dark underwing with broad pale band. The bird recorded lacked orange – an extremely rare grey-and-white aberration; any future record likely to be as bird shown here.

1 record (Britain), Nov. On coast. Woodland/scrub.

1ST-WINTER SEP–MAR

NT Wood Thrush
Hylocichla mustelina
L 17–18 cm | W 25–30 cm

Rounded, short-tailed thrush; **uniformly bright brown** above except rustier nape; bold **pale eyering**, dark-flecked cheek. **Large rounded spots** all over pale underparts. Underwing dark with white central band.

1 record (Britain): Oct; on coast. Woodland/scrub.

ADULT/1ST-WINTER

AMERICAN

Swainson's Thrush
Catharus ustulatus
L 16–18 cm | W 22–25 cm

Small, pale thrush, uniformly **sandy-brown above**; wide, bright, **pale eyering**, **pale line** from eye to bill; diffuse dark spots on upper breast, plain grey flank.

<50 records (<10 Ireland), Jun, Sep–Oct. On coast. Woodland/scrub.

- pale eyering
- pale line
- sandy brown
- 1ST-WINTER SEP–MAR

Grey-cheeked Thrush
Catharus minimus
L 15–17 cm | W 25–30 cm

Small thrush, uniformly **dull olive-brown above**; **weak eyering**, **greyish cheek**; diffuse dark spots on buff breast, whiter belly.

<100 records (<10 Ireland), May, Sep–Nov. Most on coast. Woodland/scrub.

SWAINSON'S THRUSH

Catharus thrushes have underwings that are dark with a white central band

- olive brown
- 1ST-WINTER SEP–MAR

Hermit Thrush
Catharus guttatus
L 16–17 cm | W 20–25 cm

Small, dumpy thrush, greyish- or sandy-brown above; **rusty tail** and wing patch (**rufous towards rear**); variable pale eyering; dark spots on throat/breast.

<15 records (<5 Ireland), Apr–Jun, Oct. On coast. Woodland/scrub.

- greyish-brown or sandy-brown
- rufous tail
- ADULT/1ST-WINTER

Hermit Thrush and Veery are similar to Rufous-tailed Robin (*p. 413i*), which has a pale underwing

Veery *Catharus fuscescens*
L 16–18 cm | W 22–27 cm

Small thrush with thick neck and broad tail; **uniformly warm brown** above; bland face, greyish cheek; few diffuse spots on buff throat; pale, unmarked flank.

<15 records (Britain), May, Sep–Nov. On coast. Woodland/scrub.

- warm brown
- few spots
- 1ST-WINTER SEP–MAR
- plain flank

THRUSHES, CHATS and WHEATEARS — Comparison of juvenile chats *p. 389*

Robin *Erithacus rubecula*

L 12·5–14 cm | W 22–25 cm

Bluethroat, Red-flanked Bluetail (*p. 412*)

Familiar garden bird; small chat in mid-level canopy/thickets. Distinctive rounded silhouette (but often looks quite slim if alert or in warmer weather). Curtseys, flicks wings and tail. Hop-and-stop bouncy action, deft flit to ground and up again.

ADULT upperparts mid-brown. **Red-orange face and breast**, flank brownish. Late summer (Jul–Aug) **very faded**; fresh and bright by Aug/Sep, after moult. Red not vivid, but 'glows' in dark recesses.
JUVENILE at first no red: warm brown with pale spots above, buff with dark crescents below, yellowish wingbar, dull tail, pale legs. Quickly develops patchy red on throat/breast during moult. Compare with juvenile Redstart (*p. 402*), Nightingale and Dunnock (*p. 380*).

VOICE Sharp "*tik*;" thin, high "*see*." Song **long**, fluent, melodic, **more-or-less melancholy** (in spring, strong passages like Garden Warbler (*p. 435*)); **frequent changes in speed**; long-drawn notes characteristic. Often **sings at night** near lights.

Very common resident (5·5 million pairs, plus 5·4 million birds in Ireland); common migrant

from N W Europe

Wide range of habitats: forests, gardens, heaths

British/Irish ssp. *melophilus* ADULT

European ssp. *rubecula* ADULT

ssp. *rubecula* (migrant from continental Europe) is paler, more olive and with a bluer neck patch; less approachable than resident **British/Irish ssp. *melophilus*.**

JUVENILE APR–OCT

no red; spotted, but has same character as adult

ROBIN | NIGHTINGALE

Nightingale *Luscinia megarhynchos*

L 15–16·5 cm | W 26–28 cm

👁 Thrush Nightingale (*p. 414*), other rare chats (*pp. 412–415*), Veery (*p. 399*)

Rare, local summer visitor, Apr–Sep (6,700 pairs); rare on migration. Vagrant Ireland (<50 records)

Secretive summer visitor (see Garden Warbler (*p. 435*). Like large Robin without red: tail often raised and conspicuous. Plain pale red-brown head with dark eye and whitish eyering. Easy to hear but hard to see: sings from cover (occasionally exposed perch); typically heard first, then glimpsed on a song post or on the ground under dense thicket with foliage down to ground level.

ADULT rusty-brown, greyer neck, rufous rump and tail (Redstart (*p. 402*) has dark centre). JUVENILE (see *p. 389*) spotted; mottled darker on breast; pale wingbar.

VOICE Low, **grating** "*kerrrr*;" clear, whistled "*wheep*." Song, day or night: **long**, considerable **variation in pace**, pitch and quality; longer pauses than Song Thrush (*p. 392*). Loud, distinctive **deep bubbling**; sudden **change from slow and thin to fast, deep notes** and long **crescendo** "*sseee, ssseee, ssseee seeeee*."

to Africa

Dense thickets, woodland

ADULT

singing bird shows puffy white throat

long tail held down; note long undertail coverts

Eastern ssp. *golzii* (vagrant from Asia: <5 records (Britain), Sep–Oct) greyer than **regularly occurring ssp. *megarhynchos***, with rufous tail, pale line over eye, pale tertial fringes, long tail (see Rufous-tailed Scrub Robin (*p. 414*)).

ADULT

plain and pale, brighter towards tail

THRUSHES, CHATS and WHEATEARS — Comparison of juvenile chats p. 389

Redstart *Phoenicurus phoenicurus*

L 13–14·5 cm | W 25 cm

Rare chats (pp. 412–415), small American thrushes (pp. 398–399)

Locally fairly common summer visitor, Apr–Oct (100,000 pairs, declining); scarce on migration

Slender chat, like a slim Robin (*p. 400*), constantly **quivering orange-red tail**. Elusive in canopy; often around rocks on edge of upland wood, or on heath/woodland edge.

MALE BREEDING distinctively multi-coloured: **white forehead**, **black throat**; **grey back**; rufous breast. Rump and tail sides **rusty-orange**. MALE NON-BREEDING (from Aug) white forehead, black face part-obscured by brown feather fringes; wings dark, often with pale panel; wear during winter/spring produces bright breeding plumage. 1ST-WINTER MALE is browner, and wear produces less bright plumage with browner wings in 1ST-SUMMER. FEMALE orange-buff beneath; plain face, black eye and pale eyering. JUVENILE (see *p. 389*) spotted, **rusty tail** like female. Black legs (unlike Robin and Nightingale (*p. 400*)).

VOICE Sweet, strong "*sweep*" (similar to Chaffinch (*p. 494*) and Chiffchaff (*p. 430*)); often "*wheet-tik tik*" or fast ticking (like Hawfinch (*p. 493*)) in alarm. Song stops short: low, indrawn, vibrant "*srree srree srree*" followed by quick, musical warble.

Breeds old oak woodland, some in stone walls near upland fields; migrants particularly near coasts

1ST-WINTER ♂ AUG–OCT [Oct]

1ST-WINTER ♀ AUG–OCT [Sep]

♂ BREEDING

In 1ST-WINTER plumage, MALE is a browner less bright version of an adult; FEMALE as adult but with pale fringes to the wing feathers.

tail flickered frequently

♀

♂ BREEDING APR–AUG

NOTE: 1ST-SUMMER ♂ has browner wings than ADULT

… REDSTARTS

Black Redstart *Phoenicurus ochruros* 554

L 13–14·5 cm | W 25 cm

Rounded, slim-tailed chat, like Redstart but darker and greyer; terrestrial behaviour more like Wheatear (p. 408); in flight, profile like broad-winged Rock Pipit (p. 366).

ADULT MALE BREEDING **smoky-grey, blacker on face and breast**, white wing panel. Uppertail coverts/sides of tail rusty-orange. ADULT MALE NON-BREEDING (Sep–Mar) black areas duller with greyish feather fringes. 1ST-YEAR MALE (often breeds) greyer, with browner wing. FEMALE/1ST-WINTER **brownish-grey; plain grey head** with pale eyering; wing panel weak. Uppertail coverts and **tail sides rusty-red** (Redstart has more rufous on rump). **Black legs** unlike juvenile Robin (p. 400).

VOICE Sharp "*weet*" or "*weet-t'k t'k*." Song far-carrying but not loud, trill followed by curious dry crackle, musical flourish.

Very rare and local breeder (50 pairs); more widespread but scarce migrant and winter visitor

from Europe

Breeds cities, railway stations, industrial sites; migrant/winter mostly on rocky coasts

'EASTERN BLACK REDSTART'
1ST-WINTER ♂
[Nov]

Black Redstart subspecies

Ssp. *gibraltariensis* is resident and a visitor from Europe.

'EASTERN BLACK REDSTART' – sspp. *phoenicuroides/xerophilus/rufiventris* form a group from Central Asia that winter in NE Africa (vagrant: <10 records (Britain), Nov, all 1st-winter ♂)

1ST-WINTER male 'Eastern' Black Redstart has a grey forehead/back; blackish breast more extensive than male Redstart; reddish below. Females of all subspecies look identical.

Beware hybrids and S European 'red-bellied' Black Redstarts.

ADULT ♂ NON-BREEDING SEP–MAR [Feb]

NOTE: grey feather fringes wear off by Mar to reveal black beneath.

ADULT ♂ BREEDING MAR–AUG [Apr]

♀ [Dec]

NOTE: both sexes in 1ST-WINTER mostly look like ♀, but some ♂♂ more like ADULT.

♀/1ST-WINTER AUG–MAR [Nov]

wing panel variable

mid-grey overall

403

THRUSHES, CHATS and WHEATEARS　　　　　　　　　Comparison of juvenile chats p. 389

Whinchat *Saxicola rubetra*

L 12–14 cm | W 22–24 cm

> Siberian and Stejneger's Stonechats (pp. 406–407)

Small chat; upright, on bush-top or isolated tall stem; less squat/pot-bellied than Stonechat. May perch high on tree but usually low down. **Pale stripe over eye**, **white at sides of tail** useful features.

ADULT MALE BREEDING **streaked brown and cream above, pale below**. **Long white stripes** above and below **black cheek**; apricot throat and breast. White patch on edge of wing. Looks more black-and-white by Jul–Aug. FEMALE BREEDING long dark brown streaks and creamy feather edges on **buffy-brown** upperparts; long **buff line over eye**. ADULTS NON-BREEDING like female breeding, male with more white on primary coverts. JUVENILE/1ST-WINTER more buff, with pale feather edges creating scalloped effect above; stripe over eye less striking; throat/cheek contrast reduced, approaching some Stonechats.

VOICE Sweet "*siu*" and "*siu-tek tek*." Song variable, sometimes like Robin (*p. 400*) with added rattles and clicks, often dry, ticking sequence before more musical, fast flourish.

Scarce summer visitor, Apr–Oct (47,000 pairs Britain, mainly in N and W, declining, rare breeder Ireland)

from/to Scandinavia

to Africa

Grassy heaths, bracken stands, young plantations

white wing patch broad on ADULT ♂, narrow on ADULT ♀, lacking on JUVENILE/1ST-WINTER

black cheek bordered by white

1ST-SUMMER ♂ APR–AUG

browner cheek than adult male

Whinchat in all plumages shows white panel each side of base of tail, unlike all stonechats.

ADULT ♂ BREEDING APR–AUG

head pattern relatively weak but still distinctive

1ST-WINTER AUG–MAR

pale stripe over dark cheek

♀ BREEDING APR–AUG

migrants Aug–Oct bright, buffish; age and sex quite difficult to determine

Stonechat *Saxicola rubicola (torquatus)*

L 11·5–13 cm | W 21–23 cm

Siberian and Stejneger's Stonechats (pp. 406–407)

Locally fairly common resident (56,000 pairs, plus 120,000 birds in Ireland); scarce migrant/winter visitor outside breeding range

Small, dark, upright, dumpy and pot-bellied chat with **all-dark tail**. Usually on top of Gorse/Heather, sometimes on wire, occasionally in a tree; can skulk low down.

MALE BREEDING dark black-brown above, rufous and white below; **black hood, white neck patch**; rufous breast, white belly; **rump mixed white and brownish, streaked black**; uppertail coverts spotted. White wing patches spread in display; underwing coverts and axillaries whitish.
MALE NON-BREEDING dark areas suffused brown. FEMALE/1ST-WINTER browner; **dark hood**; weak neck patch; pale crescent under throat; rump brown, thickly streaked black. JUVENILE has pale stripe over eye (shorter/thinner than Whinchat), whitish crescent below streaked throat and **dark tail**.

VOICE Sharp whistle with or without hard "*tak*" notes: "*whee-tak*." Song fast, chattering, squeaky warble.

Heaths, scrubby areas

ssp. *rubicola*
♂ BREEDING

♂ NON-BREEDING

underwing coverts and axillaries whitish with variable blackish marks (all plumages)

♀ [Jan]

weak pale line over eye and under throat

Continental ssp. *rubicola* is presumed migrant: MALE shows less rufous on breast, bigger white neck and wing patches, more white on rump than **British/Irish ssp. *hibernans*** but overlap makes identification uncertain.

NOTE: BREEDING ♂ may have small white rump, but spotted uppertail coverts

dark flank against white vent

big white neck patch

British/Irish ssp. *hibernans*
♂ BREEDING
MAR–SEP

small neck patch

ADULT ♀

♂ NON-BREEDING
SEP–MAR

NOTE: 1ST-SUMMER ♂ has browner wings than ADULT

THRUSHES, CHATS and WHEATEARS

'Siberian' stonechats

'Siberian' stonechats have long been known as autumn/winter vagrants, but a recent 'split' into two species – Siberian Stonechat (with two subspecies) and Stejneger's Stonechat – has complicated matters. Separation of the two species is often impossible without DNA analysis, although Stejneger's Stonechat can have a distinctively wider bill (4·7–5·7 mm; Siberian Stonechat 4·2–4·9 mm). Autumn individuals, with buff over the eye and a pale throat, may suggest Whinchat (p. 404) as much as Stonechat (p. 405), but have a pale rump and all-dark tail. Adult males have black underwing coverts and silvery flight feathers (on Stonechat, whitish underwing coverts are variably marked black especially on primary coverts, and flight feathers are brownish).

brownish — ♂ NON-BREEDING ssp. *rubicola*

whitish, primary coverts marked black

dark markings on rump

extensive rufous

flank sullied grey with very thin dark streaks

STONECHAT British/Irish ssp. *hibernans* ♂ BREEDING

Siberian Stonechat
Saxicola maurus
L 12–13 cm | W 22–23 cm

MALE BREEDING (very rare) like male Stonechat (p. 405) but small rufous breast patch; **whiter underparts unstreaked; broad, unstreaked white rump. Black underwing coverts and axillaries.** FEMALE/1ST-WINTER **pale grey-buff** with blacker wings; buffish line over eye, buff throat. **Rump plain pale orange, fades to white** (1st-winter (Sep–Mar)); underwing coverts **black** on MALE, grey on FEMALE.

Vagrant from Asia: <400 records (<10 Ireland), Sep–May, most Oct (majority ssp. *maurus*; <5 records of ssp. *hemprichii*). Mainly on coast. Scrubby areas.

ssp. *maurus* ♂ BREEDING

silvery — black — unmarked rump

'CASPIAN' ssp. *hemprichii* ♂ BREEDING

ssp. *maurus* ♂ BREEDING

white sides to base of tail — dark

'CASPIAN STONECHAT' ssp. *hemprichii* has more white in base of tail than more frequent W Siberian ssp. *maurus*.

On both species, adult male has smaller rufous breast patch, whiter flank and whiter rump than Stonechat.

Stejneger's Stonechat
Saxicola stejnegeri
L 12–13 cm | W 22–23 cm

Very similar to Siberian Stonechat, separation from which is often not possible without DNA analysis; in the hand, bill may be distinctively wider. MALE BREEDING (not recorded) as Siberian Stonechat ssp. *maurus* but tends to have a slightly smaller white neck patch and narrower white rump. FEMALE/1ST-WINTER tends to be darker, warmer rufous-brown than Siberian Stonechat.

Vagrant from Asia: <5 records (Britain), Oct, Nov. Coastal bushes.

NOTE: 1ST-SUMMER MALES have browner wings than ADULTS

♂ BREEDING [not recorded]

dark tail

CHATS

Identification of female/1st-winter stonechats

Female and first-winter Siberian and Stejneger's Stonechats may be near-impossible to separate and may be difficult to tell from Stonechat. Very pale individuals in Britain or Ireland in Sep–Oct are most likely Siberian Stonechat ssp. *maurus*; darker late Oct/Nov arrivals may be Stejneger's Stonechat. On both, underwing coverts are black with paler fringes on 1st-winter male, blackish-grey with paler fringes on female (on Stonechat, underwing coverts greyer/buffier with blackish mark near bend of wing). Measurements in the hand are of no value, although the larger bill-width of Stejneger's may be distinctive (see introduction *opposite*). DNA (*e.g. from lost feathers*) is essential.

STONECHAT ssp. *hibernans* 1ST-WINTER

underwing coverts/axillaries never solidly black as on 'siberian' stonechats

warm brown overall

rump orange, **streaked**; uppertail coverts **spotted** dark

ssp. *maurus* 1ST-WINTER ♂

'CASPIAN' ssp. *hemprichii* 1ST-WINTER ♂

ssp. *maurus* (presumed but could possibly be Stejneger's Stonechat) 1ST-WINTER ♂

underwing coverts and axillaries black

ssp. *maurus* (presumed but could well be Stejneger's Stonechat) 1ST-WINTER ♂

white sides

dark

dark

On both species, **rump and uppertail coverts unspotted** pale orange (wear to white by Mar/Apr).

♂ NON-BREEDING [not recorded]

STEJNEGER'S STONECHAT

1ST-WINTER

underwing coverts and axillaries black, as Siberian Stonechat

tends to be darker and warmer in hue than Siberian Stonechat

dark

407

THRUSHES, CHATS and WHEATEARS　　　　　　　　Comparison of juvenile chats p. 389

Wheatear *Oenanthe oenanthe*

L 14–16·5 cm | W 27–28 cm

👁 Rare wheatears (p. 410–411)

Small, angled, strong-legged, short-tailed: the only common wheatear, typically on the ground, repeatedly flying ahead if disturbed, revealing **broad white patch above black 'T' on tail**. All plumages have white rump/black tail pattern – in flight, white makes a big, eye-catching patch unlike anything except other, very rare, wheatears.

MALE BREEDING pale blue-grey above, variably pink/yellow-buff below, fading whiter by Jul; **black 'mask'**, blackish wings. Large 'Greenland' ssp. *leucorhoa* (mostly May): browner back, stronger orange-buff underparts than British/Irish breeders (ssp. *oenanthe*). FEMALE grey-brown above, buff below; paler stripe over eye, only slightly **darker ear coverts** and **plain dark brown wings**. Greyish bloom wears off back, fades to brown and white by Jul; by Sep strikingly different, with broad, **bright buff edges to wing feathers**. JUVENILE/1ST-WINTER/NON-BREEDING ADULTS wider pale tips to primaries (for juvenile, see p. 389).

VOICE Whistled "*wheet*" and hard "*chak*." Song often given in short **fluttery song flight**, or from low perch, quick-fire phrase of chattering and ticking notes with musical chirps.

Locally common summer visitor, Mar–Oct (230,000 pairs, plus 48,000 birds in Ireland); widespread on migration

from/to Iceland
from/to N and W Europe
to Africa

Breeds mainly uplands, few on sandy heaths and downs; migrant particularly on coast

♂ (DISPLAY FLIGHT)

NOTE: all birds below are widespread ssp. *oenanthe*.

1ST-SUMMER ♂ [Apr]

'mask' and wings brownish

ADULT ♀ [May]

ADULT ♂ BREEDING MAR–AUG [Apr]

Pale above and below with broad black band from 'shoulder' to tail.

WHEATEAR

Wheatear tail patterns
Typical tail patterns shown: there is some variation, and detail can be hard to observe as pattern hidden when tail is tightly closed when perched.

PIED WHEATEAR: black forms narrow, broken tip and extends onto corners

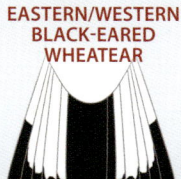

EASTERN/WESTERN BLACK-EARED WHEATEAR: black forms narrow tip and 'curls' up sides

WHEATEAR: black forms basic 'T'-shape; tip of even width

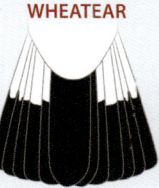

ISABELLINE WHEATEAR: black forms broad tip; small white basal panels

DESERT WHEATEAR: almost entirely black

NOTE: ADULT ♀, 1ST-WINTER ♂ and 1ST-WINTER ♀ may be impossible to separate in autumn.

autumn males show black 'mask', subdued by buff feather edges

ssp. *oenanthe*
ADULT ♂ NON-BREEDING
AUG–FEB [Sep]

ssp. *oenanthe*
1ST-WINTER ♀
JUL–MAR [Sep]

'GREENLAND WHEATEAR'
ssp. *leucorhoa*

brownish ear coverts

back tinged brown

ssp. *oenanthe*

≤7 tips

long wings; shows 7–8 primary tips

buffy underparts

ssp. *leucorhoa*
ADULT ♂ BREEDING
MAR–AUG [Apr]

ssp. *leucorhoa*
1ST-WINTER ♀
[Oct]

longer legs

409

RARE CHATS and WHEATEARS

Wheatear tail patterns *p. 409*

Black-eared wheatears

Western Black-eared Wheatear [WBEW] |
Eastern Black-eared Wheatear [EBEW]

L 13·5–15·5 cm | W 25–26 cm

Two closely related species; small and slender; often perch on bushes. Breeding males are usually identifiable; other plumages difficult to separate; vagrants may be best left unidentified. In all plumages both have a white rump and white tail with a **narrow black terminal band that curls up onto the sides** (anchor-shaped), and **blackish underwing coverts** (greyer on female). Both species have dark-throated and pale-throated forms. MALE BREEDING **blackish wing** extends onto scapulars ('shoulder'), creating a **broader band** than on Wheatear (*p. 408*) with less extensive pale back (especially EBEW); underparts pale buff. MALE NON-BREEDING buff/white fringes on black 'mask' and wing. FEMALE BREEDING upperparts brown, wing and scapulars darker; breast buff, underparts buff-white or pale orange; throat whitish or dark brown. 1ST-WINTER MALE like non-breeding male, with buff scapulars and broader buff fringes concealing most of the black on head and wing. NON-BREEDING/1ST-WINTER FEMALE have buff fringes. Key differences between the two species are highlighted below.

Western Black-eared Wheatear
Oenanthe hispanica

Vagrant from SW Europe: <100 records (<10 Ireland), Apr–Oct. Open ground.

MALE BREEDING **crown, nape and back brownish-buff, brighter ochre** Apr/May, whiter by Jun/Jul. Black 'shoulder'/wing (with thin buff fringes when fresh) isolated from blackish cheek/throat. **Black 'mask'**, or **black face and bib** not extending below angle of throat. **Little or no black above bill.** MALE NON-BREEDING like breeding male with **bright buff** upperparts, most black feathers tipped pale buff. FEMALE BREEDING/NON-BREEDING/1ST-WINTER brown upperparts (some more rusty), wing darker; dark brown/blackish through eye; most pale below from chin to tail (some have pale chin/dark throat), with **little contrast**.

Eastern Black-eared Wheatear
Oenanthe melanoleuca

Vagrant from SE Europe: <20 records (Britain), Apr–Oct. Open ground.

MALE BREEDING **dull** white/pale grey above, white by Mar/Apr but often **grey crown**/pale ochre back. 'Shoulder'/wing like WBEW but broader pale fringes when fresh. **Broader black 'mask'** or extensive black bib just extending onto upper breast. **Thin black band above bill.** MALE NON-BREEDING duller, **greyer** and darker than breeding male; fewer pale fringes on head and wing coverts than WBEW; some have darker/greyer crown, paler/browner back. FEMALE BREEDING/NON-BREEDING/1ST-WINTER like WBEW but back often **less rusty**, more contrast between orange breast and paler belly. Some have faint pale fringes on back (like Pied Wheatear, from which may be inseparable).

underwing coverts dark

1ST-WINTER ♀
AUG–MAR
[Oct]

1ST-WINTER ♂
AUG–MAR
[Oct]

[May]

1ST-WINTER ♂
AUG–MAR
[Oct]

EBEW generally less 'rusty' on back than WBEW, but subjective and changes with light conditions

♀ [Mar]

orange-buff back

narrow black 'mask' or black face/bib

♂ BREEDING

whiter above

black 'mask'/throat more extensive; **black above bill**

♂ BREEDING

Isabelline Wheatear
Oenanthe isabellina
L 15–16·5 cm | W 26–28 cm

Large, upright wheatear; pale sandy brown; relatively thick-billed. Broad black tail-band but short 'T'-stem; wings plain, except **blackish alula**. White stripe over eye short and thin behind eye; dark line from bill to eye (both extend behind eye on Wheatear (*p. 408*)).

Vagrant from E Europe: <50 records (1 Ireland), May, Sep–Nov. Most on coast. Open ground.

NT

Desert Wheatear
Oenanthe deserti
L 14·5–15·5 cm | W 25–26 cm

Small, pale wheatear with **all-black tail** and white rump. MALE **black face/throat joins black wing**. FEMALE/1ST-WINTER sandy above, whiter below; pale 'shoulder', darker midwing, black wingtip. Underwing coverts dark.

Three subspecies recorded: *deserti* (Middle East) described above; *homochroa* (N Africa) smaller, paler, pinkish; *atrogularis* (Asia) larger, browner. Most records in Britain/Ireland impossible to assign to ssp.

Vagrant from E Europe: <150 records (<10 Ireland), autumn–spring, most Nov–Dec. Most on coast. Open ground.

Pied Wheatear
Oenanthe pleschanka
L 14–16·5 cm | W 25–26 cm

Small wheatear. White rump and tail sides; **narrow tail-band extends around corners**. MALE BREEDING (see *inset*). FEMALE/1ST-WINTER cold grey-brown; **pale fringes** on back unlike Western Black-eared Wheatear (some Eastern Black-eared Wheatears very similar). Face, throat and breast dusky grey-brown.

Vagrant from E Europe: <100 records (<10 Ireland), May–Jul, most Sep–Dec. Open ground.

WHEATEARS

underwing silvery-grey/whitish – hard to see

underwing coverts white, dark centres (fresh), darker overall when worn

ADULT / 1ST-WINTER [Oct]

WHEATEAR ♀ / 1ST-WINTER AUG–MAR

black alula

1st-winter like adult with pale fringes on wings; male has blackish face obscured by pale tips, wearing off by spring

1ST-WINTER ♂ AUG–MAR [Oct]

1ST-WINTER ♂ [Dec]

1ST-WINTER ♀ AUG–MAR [Nov]

pale wheatear with small white rump and black tail

1ST-WINTER ♂ AUG–MAR [Nov]

♀ / 1ST-WINTER AUG–MAR [Oct]

blackish; whitish cap; white below, buff on breast

'scaly' on back

♂ BREEDING

RARE CHATS and WHEATEARS

Rare chats

Warm winds from the south in spring might bring exciting birds to Britain and Ireland: along with rare herons, Hoopoes, Bee-eaters and Red-rumped Swallows, there may perhaps be a rare chat or wheatear (see pp. 410–411). These can be more difficult to identify in autumn, when other very rare, more-or-less Robin-like chats may arrive from the far north or east.

Bluethroat *Luscinia svecica* 554
L 13–14 cm | W 23–25 cm

Small chat; shape and actions resemble Robin (*p. 400*) but also runs/hops, raises and dips **slender tail** with exaggerated action. MALE BREEDING **white stripe over eye**, **electric-blue throat/upper breast** above black, white and rufous bands. Red spot on ssp. *svecica* (N Europe), white on ssp. *cyanecula* (C and S Europe), rarely all-blue. FEMALE/1ST-WINTER **white stripe** over eye, black-and-white throat, **rusty across breast**; most FEMALES lack blue but variable on young MALE.

VOICE Loud "*shlak*." Song strong, clear whistle with fast, variable flourish, including mimicry.

IN FLIGHT, **rusty-red sides to base of tail**.

Rare migrant from Europe: 40–60 per year (<50 records Ireland), Mar–May, Aug–Oct. Mainly on coast; declining; has bred. Often in reedbeds, willows; on muddy paths. Winters in Africa.

White-spotted ssp. *cyanecula* ♂ BREEDING

Red-spotted ssp. *svecica* ♂ BREEDING

blue on throat/breast

white stripe over eye

1ST-WINTER ♂ AUG–NOV

♀

Red-flanked Bluetail
Tarsiger cyanurus
L 14 cm | W 25–26 cm

Small, unobtrusive chat in trees/bushes, **bluish rump and tail**. MALE blue above, white below, orange flank. FEMALE/1ST-WINTER olive-brown; greyish-buff below, paler throat, **pale orange flank**; white eyering. Female White-throated Robin (*p. 415*) greyer; blackish tail, darker grey breast-band.

Vagrant from NE Europe: <150 records (<10 Ireland), most Sep–Nov, extremely rare Dec–May; increasing. Most on coast. Trees.

ADULT ♂ BREEDING

Shape and actions like slim Robin (*p. 400*) or Redstart (*p. 402*).

1ST-WINTER AUG–MAR

pale eyering, plain head

orange flank

slaty-blue tail

CHATS

Siberian Rubythroat
Calliope calliope
L 15 cm | W 26–27 cm

Robust, long-legged, upright chat; hops on the ground. ADULT MALE pale brown above, grey on breast; white stripe over eye, black between eye and bill, short white 'moustache', edged black; **vivid red throat** with variable black border. FEMALE similar head pattern in brown, whitish and grey. 1ST-WINTER as female with pale spots on wing; MALE develops red throat.

Vagrant from Asia: <15 records (Britain), Oct–Nov. On coast. Scrubby areas.

white stripe over eye

1ST-WINTER ♀
AUG–MAR

1ST-WINTER ♂
AUG–MAR

long legs pale pink to dark brown

Tail plain (female/1st-winter Bluethroats that lack blue have rufous tail sides).

Rufous-tailed Robin
Larvivora sibilans
L 14 cm | W 21–22 cm

Small, rounded chat with long, pale pink legs; hops on the ground. Grey-brown with **broad buff eyering**; breast pale, **scaled olive-brown**, flank brown; rump and short tail **rufous-brown**. Underwing plain (dark with pale band on similar Veery and Hermit Thrush (*p. 399*)).

Vagrant from Asia: <5 records (Britain), Sep–Oct. On coast. Scrubby areas.

👁 Veery, Hermit Thrush (*p. 399*)

tail brighter rufous-brown than back

broad buff eyering

long, pale legs

'scaly' brown marks on breast

1ST-WINTER
AUG–MAR

Siberian Blue Robin
Larvivora cyane
L 12 cm | W 20–22 cm

Small, short-tailed chat with long, pale pinkish legs; hops on the ground. MALE unmistakable; **dark blue above, white below**. FEMALE/1ST-WINTER brown above; dark mottling on buff breast, white belly; bluish tail.

Vagrant from Asia: <5 records (Britain), Sep–Oct. On coast. Scrubby areas.

ADULT ♂ BREEDING

bluish tail

mottled breast

long, pale legs

1ST-WINTER ♀
AUG–MAR

RARE CHATS and WHEATEARS

Thrush Nightingale
Luscinia luscinia
L 16 cm | W 27–28 cm

Very like Nightingale (p. 401) and just as elusive in dense thickets. Dull grey-brown above, with contrasted brighter rufous tail (Nightingale more rufous overall). Close views/photographs may confirm longer yellow gape and **minute first (outermost) primary**, usually hidden beneath primary coverts (on Nightingale, short but visible just beyond primary coverts). Alula may show pale outer/dark inner half (uniform on Nightingale). Closed wingtip shows **eight primary tips** (seven on Nightingale). ADULT hint of dark smudge beside throat; slight **soft, olive-grey mottled breast-band**; vague dusky bars under tail. JUVENILE pale spots above, mottled darker on breast.

> Very rare migrant from N Europe: <250 records (<5 Ireland), most Apr–May, Sep. Mainly on coast. Scrubby areas.

NIGHTINGALE — 7 primary tips show — plain — plain

THRUSH NIGHTINGALE — 8 primary tips show — may be two-tone — faint stripe — mottled

dull rufous tail — plain head — mottled breast

Rufous-tailed Scrub Robin
(Rufous Bush Chat)
Cercotrichas galactotes
L 16 cm | W 26–28 cm

Slim, long-tailed chat, upright on long, pink legs. Pale line over eye, dark eyestripe; **rufous rump and tail with black-and-white tip; tail often raised**. Underparts buff-white. Two 'forms' recorded: ssp. *galactotes* (from SW Europe) orange-brown above; and either ssp. *familiaris* or *syriaca* (from SE Europe/Asia) grey-brown above.

> Vagrant from S Europe/Asia: **ssp. *galactotes*** <15 records (<5 Ireland); **ssp. *familiaris*** or **syriacus** 1 record (Ireland), Apr–Oct. On coast. Open scrub, feeds on ground.

rufous tail tipped black and white — strong head pattern

CHATS | WHEATEAR

White-throated Robin
Irania gutturalis
L 14 cm | W 25–27 cm

Structure and form rather like Redstart (*p. 402*). MALE blue-grey above, pale rusty-orange below; white stripe over eye; **black lower face, narrow white throat**. FEMALE/1ST-WINTER pale; face grey; whitish throat; **orange flank; blackish tail**; black legs.

Vagrant from S Europe: <5 records (Britain), May–Jun. On coast. Open scrub, feeds on ground.

ADULT ♂

Longer-tailed, more thrush-like stance than Red-flanked Bluetail (*p. 412*).

♀

Moussier's Redstart
Phoenicurus moussieri
L 12 cm | W 20–22 cm

Small, short-tailed chat. MALE black above with **long white stripe over eye** and **white wing panel**; orange beneath. FEMALE/1ST-WINTER (not recorded) grey-brown above, **pale rufous on belly, rump and sides of tail**; whitish eyering.

Vagrant from N Africa: 1 record (male) (Britain), April. On coast. Open ground.

ADULT ♂

ADULT ♀
(not recorded)

White-crowned Black Wheatear
Oenanthe leucopyga
L 18 cm | W 26–29 cm

Large **black** wheatear with white rump; white tail with short black centre, **dark spots across tip** (not complete band). Large white vent. ADULT glossy, usually (not always) with obvious **white crown**; JUVENILE/1ST-YEAR dull with black crown. **Tail pattern critical**.

Vagrant from N Africa (1 record: Jun; on coast). Open ground. Also a Jun record from Ireland, which was either this species or Black Wheatear *O. leucura*.

1ST-WINTER
(black-crowned form)

NOTE: beware black-crowned individuals (recorded) must be separated from Black Wheatear (not certainly recorded), which has broad black tip to tail.

415

RARE CHATS and WHEATEARS

Rock Thrush
Monticola saxatilis
L 18 cm | W 32–35 cm

Small, short-tailed, spike-billed, thrush-like chat. MALE BREEDING grey hood, **white patch on back**, rufous underparts. ADULT MALE NON-BREEDING upperparts brown with extensive buff fringes; underparts buff with brown bars and orange mottling. FEMALE/1ST-WINTER brown, with close pale bars above and **dark bars on rusty-buff** below. **Tail rufous**.

♂ BREEDING

ADULT ♀

Vagrant from S Europe: <50 records (<5 Ireland), Feb–Nov, most Apr–Jun. On coast. Rocky areas/cliffs.

Blue Rock Thrush
Monticola solitarius
L 21–23 cm | W 37–40 cm

Long-bodied, tapered, thrush-like chat with a markedly **long bill**. ADULT MALE **slaty blue**, wings blackish-brown. FEMALE/1ST-WINTER **dark brown** above, dusky **buff below with close dark bars**. **Tail dark** (not rufous as Rock Thrush).

ADULT ♂

ADULT ♀

Vagrant from S Europe: <10 records (Britain), Apr, Jun, Oct–Dec. On coast. Rocky areas/cliffs.

FLYCATCHERS

FLYCATCHER ID overall colour | wing pattern | tail pattern

Flycatchers are small, slender or rounded, with long wings, slim tail and short legs; they perch upright and are much less mobile in foliage than warblers. Catch insects in wide-based bill that looks slightly thicker than on many warblers.
6 species: 2 breeding summer visitors; others rare migrants/vagrants.

Flycatchers (pp. 418–421) are small woodland, park or garden birds that sit still on perches for long spells and fly out to catch insects in the air, or drop to the ground to find food. They are less likely to glean food from foliage, as do warblers, Robins and small chats. The small bill is slender when seen from the side, but quite broad-based, with a wide gape. Wings are long, held alongside the slim tail, sometimes drooped rather low. All are migrants and may be seen outside their normal breeding ranges in spring and autumn.

Flycatcher ageing/sexing
Male and female differ, except in Spotted Flycatcher; juveniles, 1st-winters and 1st-summer males recognizable.

POSSIBLE CONFUSION GROUPS
Warblers (pp. 422–457) have a similar slender bill, some (e.g. *Hippolais*, *Iduna*) also similarly wide-based, but short-legged, upright stance is characteristic of flycatchers; bold patterns of 'pied' group unlike any warbler. Small chats (pp. 400–415) are also upright, but shorter-tailed, rounder-bodied.

American 'flycatchers'
Four species of American flycatcher (p. 530) have been recorded; although they have a basic similarity of shape, structure and behaviour to Old World Flycatchers they are not closely related. Their large head and more-or-less crested appearance separate them. All are exceptionally rare vagrants.

PIED FLYCATCHER

ALDER FLYCATCHER

FLYCATCHERS

Spotted Flycatcher *Muscicapa striata*

L 13·5–15 cm | W 23–25·5 cm

Red-breasted/Taiga (*p. 420*), Asian Brown (*p. 421*) Flycatchers

Small, pale brown, upright flycatcher with a thickish bill, neither quite like a warbler nor a chat. Quietly alert, mostly inactive. Large head (flattened forehead/rounded nape), large dark eye; **long wingtip** and tail; short, dark legs. Quick, jerky wing-flick and/or tail dip. Perches in open on post, fence, branch or wire, **flies out to snatch flying insect** with obvious 'snap', **returning to same perch** or one close by.

ADULT dull grey-brown (not so plain as Garden Warbler (*p. 435*)) with **streaked crown**. Wings have silvery-buff feather edges (white on Pied Flycatcher). Underparts grey-buff or whitish with **grey-brown streaks** on breast; white under tail. **Short black legs**. JUVENILE buff spots over back; yellow-buff wingbar.

VOICE Calls, from perch or in flight, thin, scratchy or slightly vibrant "*sirrr*" or "*tseeet*." Song variable, weak repetition of calls, or longer, more musical, thin, squeaky phrases.

Scarce summer visitor, most May–Sep (30,000 pairs, plus 40,000 birds in Ireland, declining)

from/to Scandinavia

to Africa

from/to Africa

Woods, parks, gardens; elsewhere on migration (spring, autumn)

small pale bird; flies out to catch insect and returns to perch

ADULT [Jun]

ADULT / 1ST-WINTER [Sep]

Upright; pale with spotted breast

1ST-WINTER AUG–MAR [Sep]

only a trace of a wingbar compared with Pied Flycatcher

JUVENILE JUL–SEP [Aug]

JUVENILE has spotting above and buff wingbar (which is never so white as on Pied Flycatcher).

FLYCATCHERS

Pied Flycatcher *Ficedula hypoleuca*

L 12–13·5 cm | W 21·5–24 cm

👁 **Collared Flycatcher** (p. 421)

554

Small, round-headed, short-tailed flycatcher with **extensive white** in long wing (compare with Spotted Flycatcher and see Chaffinch (p. 494)). **Wingtips** often drooped. **Short, dark legs.** Frequently inconspicuous in foliage, **drops to ground to feed**, returns to new perch.

BREEDING MALE **black above**, **white below**: one or two white forehead spots, **white panel on wing**. 1ST-SUMMER MALE (breeds) duller, wings browner. FEMALE **brown above**, **buff-white below**, blacker on wings; wing panel small. Brownish beside throat, more-or-less joined across breast. NON-BREEDING MALE (Jul–Oct) like female, except blacker tail. JUVENILE drabber, throat marks darker, less white on wing.

VOICE Sharp "*pwit*," sweet "*huit*" or often "*huit-tik*." Song staccato, whistled phrase (less free-flowing than similar-sounding Redstart (p. 402) in same habitat), some mimicry; several variants in irregular sequence.

> **Siberian ssp.** *sibirica* (vagrant, 1 record (Britain): Sep; on E coast) can only be told from regularly occurring breeding ssp. *hypoleuca* when examined in the hand (fractionally larger and less intensely black, but subspecies intergrade).

Scarce to locally common summer visitor, Apr–Aug (19,000 pairs); scarce Ireland

from/to Scandinavia

to Africa — from/to Africa

Breeds mainly in oak woods; mostly near coasts on migration (spring and especially autumn)

no other small bird is so plain black above and clean white below

♂ NON-BREEDING AUG–MAR [Sep]

narrow patch at base of primaries falls well short of wing edge

variable dark patch beside throat

ADULT ♂ BREEDING MAR–AUG [Apr]

NOTE: ADULT ♂ BREEDING can show brown on black upperparts

ADULT ♀ [May]

very short dark legs

ADULT ♂ BREEDING / 1ST-SUMMER ♂ MAR–AUG [Apr]

RARE FLYCATCHERS

Red-breasted Flycatcher *Ficedula parva*   554
L 11–12 cm | W 18·5–21 cm

Tiny flycatcher with bold dark eye and **distinctive tail pattern**. Perches quietly low down on edge of clearing, or moves about restlessly higher in trees. Often droops wingtips and raises tail; legs very short. Grey-brown above, buffish-white below. Dark rump, black tail with **rectangular white panel each side** (white often inconspicuous on perched bird, eye-catching flash in flight). ADULT MALE greyish head; **orange-red chin and throat**. FEMALE pale olive-brown; **prominent white eyering**; pale throat. 1ST-WINTER like female but peachy-buff on throat and breast, white beneath; dull, thin, rusty-buff wingbar and tertial fringes; paler uppertail coverts than Taiga Flycatcher.

VOICE Soft "*tuc*" or "*tic;*" short, hard "*t't;*" or longer, dry, "*t-trrt.*"

Rare migrant from E Europe: 30–100 per year (<300 records Ireland), most Sep–Oct. Mostly on coast. Woods. Winters in Africa.

White sides to base of tail is a key identification feature of Red-breasted and Taiga Flycatchers.

1ST WINTER AUG–MAR [Sep]

ADULT ♂ [Oct]

Identification of 1st-winter 'red-breasted' flycatchers	RED-BREASTED	TAIGA
Rump	pale	pale
Uppertail coverts	pale	black
Tail	black	black

Taiga Flycatcher
Ficedula albicilla
L 11–12·5 cm | W 18·5–21 cm

Extremely similar to Red-breasted Flycatcher. ADULT MALE has small orange throat patch surrounded by **grey cheek and breast-band**. 1ST-WINTER has white wingbar and tertial fringes; **blacker uppertail coverts** and greyer breast than Red-breasted Flycatcher.

VOICE Fast rattling chatter like dry, buzzy Red-breasted Flycatcher.

Vagrant from Asia: <5 records (Britain), Apr, Oct–Nov. On coast. Woods.

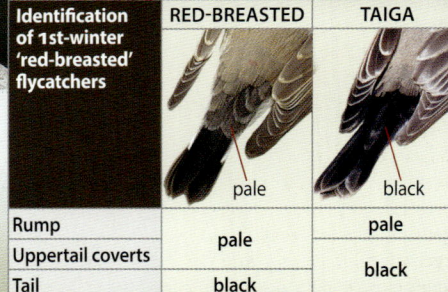

1ST WINTER AUG–MAR [Sep]

ADULT ♂ [Feb]

RARE FLYCATCHERS

Asian Brown Flycatcher
Muscicapa dauurica
L 12–13 cm | W 19·5–21·5 cm

Like small, greyish, plain Spotted Flycatcher (*p. 418*). Head and breast **unstreaked**; **large eye** and **white eyering**; clearly **broad-based bill** with **extensive** pale pink at base.

Vagrant from Asia: <5 records (Britain), Sep–Oct. On coast. Woods.

white eyering

broad-based bill with extensive pale base

buff eyering

SPOTTED FLYCATCHER

relatively narrow bill with restricted pale base

ADULT / 1ST-WINTER [Feb]

Collared Flycatcher   554
Ficedula albicollis
L 12–13·5 cm | W 22·5–24·5 cm

Similar to Pied Flycatcher (*p. 419*) in all plumages, although shorter tail may be evident. MALE BREEDING compared to Pied Flycatcher, **broad white collar**, bigger white forehead patch, broader white wing panel, wider white band across primaries and **white rump**. 1ST-SUMMER MALE has a collar but forehead and wing very like Pied Flycatcher. MALE NON-BREEDING/ FEMALE/1ST-WINTER wider, longer extension of pale throat onto neck; **larger white patch on primaries** widens close to edge of wing (some have subtly whiter rump).

Vagrant from E Europe: <50 records (1 Ireland), most Apr–Jun, few Sep. Mostly on coast. Usually woods.

PIED FLYCATCHER ♀
narrow patch at base of primaries falls well short of wing edge

primary patch widens close to wing edge

1ST-SUMMER ♂
APR–AUG
[May]

First-summer (one year-old) males retain brown wings and have reduced white wing and forehead patches.

ADULT ♂
NON-BREEDING
AUG–MAR
[Sep]

hint of pale rump

white rump

ADULT ♂
BREEDING
APR–AUG
[May]

(OLD WORLD) WARBLERS, CISTICOLAS and CRESTS

GROUP ID general structure and coloration | tail shape | behaviour

Warblers are complex and their taxonomic relationships are still being investigated. All have relatively thin 'insect-eater' bills. They tend to be slender-legged and tapered, unlike the more chunky tits (p. 465–473). Some are dull, some bright, some uniform, others patterned;

52 old world warblers: 13 breed (2 erratically, 2 resident, 2 others regular in winter); 39 scarce migrants/vagrants.
1 cisticola: vagrant.
3 crests: 2 resident; 1 (kinglet) vagrant from America.

Warbler ageing/sexing
Sexes alike in most species, differ in others (especially *Sylvia* species). Juveniles differ slightly from adults (*e.g.* pale fringes to feathers or richer colours); plumage is quickly replaced (giving 1st-winter). Spring migrants less than a year old (1st-summer) are like adult but have old juvenile wing feathers.

Regulus (crests) – 2 species (*pp. 424–425*) plus 1 vagrant (*p. 525*): favour trees and bushes. CALLS: high, thin, sharp notes. SONGS: simple, rhythmic phrase or trill. STRUCTURE: tiny, with slim, sharp bill; square/notched tail; short wings. PLUMAGE: sexes almost alike; greenish; head patterns diagnostic – **crown with yellow/orange/red centre**; pale below, unstreaked; wings barred blackish/cream.

ID head pattern

Regulus | FIRECREST

Phylloscopus: – 17 species (*pp. 430–433, 448–452*): favour treetop foliage, where they are very active, gleaning insects from the leaves (some hover), not seen much on the ground; in scrub/bushes on migration. CALLS: variations on sweet, more-or-less two-syllable notes. SONGS: musical cadence, or repeated, staccato notes, or metallic trill; no harsh notes. STRUCTURE: slim, sharp bill; **thin legs**; **tail square/notched, undertail coverts (UTCs) short**. PLUMAGE: sexes alike; greenish/yellow or brownish; head patterns important: most have stripes over and through eye, some rarer species have wingbars.

ID leg colour | wingbars | head pattern | call and song

Phylloscopus | CHIFFCHAFF
thin bill
square tail
UTCs short
thin legs

Sylvia – 15 species (*pp. 434–438, 453–457*): favour thick scrub/hedges/low vegetation. CALLS: short, hard notes. SONGS: fast, irregular, harsh or very musical. STRUCTURE: strong; **heavy bill**; **thick legs**; **tail square, some long and slim**. PLUMAGE: sexes differ in most species, especially in head pattern; brown/grey above; buff/pale beneath, unstreaked.

ID head pattern | back colour | call and song

Sylvia | WHITETHROAT
heavy bill
square tail
thick legs

WARBLERS, CISTCOLAS and CRESTS

Acrocephalus | SEDGE WARBLER

- slightly rounded tail
- UTCs long

Acrocephalus – 7 species (pp. 426–427, 440–443): favour waterside vegetation, often clinging to vertical stems, but in bushes/scrub on migration. CALLS: short, hard notes and churrs. SONGS: fast, repetitive, rhythmic phrasing, include musical and harsh notes, mimicry. STRUCTURE: low, sloping forehead, sharp bill, strong legs; **tail slightly rounded, undertail coverts (UTCs) medium-long**. PLUMAGE: sexes alike; plain or streaked brown above, unstreaked buff below.

ID wing detail | subtle structure and plumage differences, especially head patterns and rump colour

Locustella | GRASSHOPPER WARBLER

- rounded tail
- curved edge to wing
- UTCs long

Locustella and **Helopsaltes** – 5 species (pp. 428–429, 444): favour dense, low vegetation/scrub, creeping, elusive, low down; in bushes/grass on migration. SONGS: remarkable prolonged, trilling or reeling, insect-like song, often at dusk or at night. STRUCTURE: sharp bill, flat head; wings short, **curved outer edge**; tail long and rounded, **undertail coverts (UTCs) long**. PLUMAGE: sexes alike; brown, plain or streaked.

ID subtle plumage differences, especially underpart and tail patterns

Hippolais | MELODIOUS WARBLER

- strong, broad bill
- square tail
- strong legs
- UTCs short

Hippolais, **Iduna** and **Arundinax** – 7 species (pp. 443, 445–447): all rare migrants/vagrants, favour bushes and trees. CALLS: short, hard notes. STRUCTURE: between *Acrocephalus* and *Phylloscopus*: strong, wide bill; **strong legs**; wings long- or short-tipped; **tail square, undertail coverts (UTCs) short**. PLUMAGE: sexes alike; greenish/yellow or brown/buff, unstreaked; most pale between eye and bill (lores).

ID wing detail | subtle plumage and behavioural differences

Cettia – 1 species (p. 429): in thick waterside vegetation: dark red-brown above, paler below with rounded wings and a **broad, square-ended tail (often raised)**; outburst of abrupt song diagnostic.

- broad tail

Cettia | CETTI'S WARBLER

Cisticola – 1 species, rare vagrant (p. 443): found in scrub/bushes, with a preference for wetlands. SONG: repeated sharp, high note. STRUCTURE: round wings; **short, round tail**. PLUMAGE: sexes alike; pale buff-brown, streaked; **spots under tip of tail**.

- short, rounded tail

Cisticola | FAN-TAILED WARBLER

American Warblers and Vireos (pp. 525–529)

Vagrants from North America that bear a structural resemblance to Old World Warblers. They occur mainly in autumn in first-winter plumages that come in a variety of often quite striking patterns that are generally noticeably very different from the region's regular species.

Setophaga | MYRTLE WARBLER

WARBLERS, CISTICOLAS and CRESTS

Goldcrest *Regulus regulus*

L 8·5–9·5 cm | W 14–15 cm

▶ Ruby-crowned Kinglet (p. 525)

Minute; typical 'crest', like tiny, dumpy, olive-green warbler with well-marked wings and a 'plain' face. (Firecrest similar but more richly coloured and with a boldly patterned head). Distinctive song is always a good indication of presence. Can skulk but often feeds high in trees.

ADULT olive-green, whiter beneath, **black/white wing bands**. Face pale, weak **dark 'moustache'** from base of bill. Crown has **streak of yellow narrowly edged black**. MALE crown brighter than FEMALE, with orange, which is particularly evident when crown is spread in display in similar manner to Firecrest (see *opposite*). JUVENILE lacks crown stripe.

VOICE Song rhythmic, very high-pitched, with 'di-diddle' element and **slight terminal flourish** (usually lacking in Firecrest): "*si-sissi si-sissi si-sissi sissi-si-siswee-it*" (resembles Treecreeper (p. 475)). Call slightly less shrill, slightly more emphatic, slower than Long-tailed Tit (p. 467): "*ssee-ssee-ssee*" or "*zree-zree-zree*" (3–4 notes, sometimes single, stronger call). Feeding flocks make tiny sharp "*sit*" notes.

Very common resident (770,000 pairs, plus 720,000 birds in Ireland), migrant, winter visitor

from N and W Europe

Woodlands, thickets, hedgerows; migrants often in coastal bushes

yellow

ADULT ♀

Goldcrests and Firecrests both hover to feed, often just outside the foliage of trees and thickets.

JUVENILE JUN–AUG

ADULT ♂

more orange

See also warbler introduction *pp. 422–423*

CRESTS

Firecrest *Regulus ignicapilla*

L 9–10 cm | W 14–15 cm

Pallas's Warbler (*p. 452*)

Rare and local breeder (at least 1,500 pairs); scarce migrant/winter visitor (few 100s per year)

Minute; typical 'crest', richly coloured; **white beneath**; **distinctive head pattern** (Goldcrest similar but more olive, less white beneath, with much plainer face). Song always a good indication of presence. Breeding birds best located by song, often high in Ivy, Holly or conifers; at other times, also low down in bushes.

ADULT bright green above, sides of breast/'shoulder' gleams bronzy yellow in good light. Bold **white, wedge-shaped stripe over eye**; narrow white crescent beneath; **black eyestripe**, dark 'moustache'. Crown has **broad black sides**, central streak orange in MALE (widens into broad fan in display), yellow with orange centre in FEMALE. JUVENILE lacks crown stripe.

VOICE Song varies, but typical form fast, accelerating, slightly rising, simple trill (without rhythmic 'te-diddle' form or terminal flourish of Goldcrest): "*zi-zi-zi-zizizizizizi*." Call like Goldcrest, sometimes single, often 2–3 notes, first longer, "*zee-zi-zi*," but calls often indistinguishable.

from Europe

Woods, thickets, dense evergreens (favours Holly/Ivy/Yew stands)

crown spread into orange-red fan in display

more contrasted green above/white below than Goldcrest

black and white stripes on head, unlike Goldcrest's bland face

ADULT

ADULT ♂

ADULT ♂

JUVENILE JUN–AUG

WARBLERS, CISTICOLAS and CRESTS

Sedge Warbler *Acrocephalus schoenobaenus*

L 11·5–13 cm | W 18–20 cm

👁 Aquatic Warbler (p. 442), Fan-tailed Warbler (p. 443)

Small, subtly streaked brownish warbler with white stripe over eye; often flies low between bushes in rough wetland/riverside vegetation.

ADULT dark cap and eyestripe; **broad white stripe over eye**. Back olive-brown with **soft streaks**; wings dark with pale fringes (Reed Warbler much plainer); plain, **pale sandy rump**. By Jul–Aug, becomes duller, darker, more uniform. **Silky white throat**; bright buff rear flank.

JUVENILE/1ST-WINTER slightly yellower or pale gingery; paler central crown stripe; small, faint, dark streaks on breast.

VOICE Hard "*tuk*" and short, flat "*trrrr*." Song energetic, varied, scratchy and irritable, or more musical. Less repetitive and rhythmic than Reed Warbler. Often short whirry **song flight** (not seen in Reed Warbler). Typically begins with **sweet, musical notes** often like Yellow Wagtail (p. 374) call.

Locally fairly common summer visitor, Apr–Oct (260,000 pairs, plus 130,000 birds in Ireland)

from/to Scandinavia

to Africa

from/to Africa

Waterside reed/nettle beds, bramble thickets; damp rushy moors; scrub on migration

frequently sings in rising, wing-whirring song flight (unlike Reed Warbler)

ADULT

Sings upright on exposed perch or hidden in bushy tangle: bright pale throat often catches the eye.

ADULT [Apr]

plain rump and uppertail coverts

pale feather fringes; pale centre to crown

JUVENILE JUL–SEP [Sep]

ACROCEPHALUS WARBLERS

Reed Warbler *Acrocephalus scirpaceus*

L 12·5–14 cm | W 18–20 cm

Small, slim, **plain** brown warbler; the 'baseline' against which to compare Marsh Warbler and other rare unstreaked *Acrocephalus* warblers (*pp. 440–443*); Garden Warbler (*p. 435*) easily separated by **song**. Sidles up reed, dashes across open space; forages in trees.

Rare *Acrocephalus* warblers (*pp. 440–443*), Eastern Olivaceous Warbler (*p. 446*), Savi's Warbler (*p. 429*)

Unstreaked; **weak** pale stripe over eye and pale eyering (Sedge Warbler is often in same habitat but is streaked and has broad white stripe over eye). Slender, spike-like bill (Garden Warbler has thicker bill, rounder head). Legs grey-brown to blue-grey. ADULT mid-brown with **pale rusty rump and tail**; pale tertial fringes diffuse; pale buff below with **white throat**, puffed out when singing, in larger white bib than Whitethroat (*p. 436*). Eye red-brown. JUVENILE more uniformly rufous above; flank orange-buff. 1ST-WINTER like adult but wing feathers unworn, eye dark grey.

VOICE Low, slurred "*tcharr*," softer "*kresh*" and grating "*krrrr*." Song invaluable clue: **rhythmic, repetitive**, each phrase repeated 2–4 times, lower, more even than Sedge Warbler without high trills: "*chara-chara-krrik-krrik-krrik charee charee charee*," etc.

Locally very common summer visitor, Apr–Oct (130,000 pairs, uncommon in Ireland)

from/to NW Europe

to Africa

from/to Africa

Reedbeds, swamps, adjacent trees; scrub on migration

Variation in **Asian ssp.** *fuscus* greater than difference from **British/Irish ssp.** *scirpaceus*, and usually indistinguishable; majority paler above, nape often greyer; brighter only on rump and uppertail coverts. Two records (Britain), confirmed by DNA analysis, Nov, Dec.

1ST-WINTER JUL–MAR [Sep]

Reed Warblers are adapted to sidling up vertical perches, but migrants may turn up almost anywhere, looking oddly out of context and 'uncomfortable'.

sings from upright stem; often a chorus before dawn

ADULT [May]

often well hidden in reeds, but rustle of stems may give it away before short, low flight across open space

1ST-WINTER JUL–MAR [Oct]

WARBLERS, CISTICOLAS and CRESTS

Grasshopper Warbler *Locustella naevia*

L 12·5–13·5 cm | W 16–18 cm

◉ River, Lanceolated, Pallas's Grasshopper Warblers (p. 444)

Secretive, rather elongated warbler best located by **distinctive song**. Creeps mouse-like, skulking in low, dense vegetation. May flush at close range, flits ahead and dives back down; looks **pale, yellowish, round-tailed**.

ADULT olive- to yellowish-brown, subtly marked with **soft streaks** on crown and back; some have diffuse flank streaks. **Dark streaks under tail** may be conspicuous as bird tilts and drops out of sight. **Undertail coverts long**, extending well down tail. JUVENILE/1ST-WINTER often more yellow; some have slight fine streaking on throat or breast. (Sedge Warbler (p. 426) has stronger back/rump contrast and bolder pale stripe over eye.)

VOICE Sharp "*tik*" or "*psit*." **Song remarkable**, at dusk or in warm, sultry weather: **prolonged reeling trill**, often for minutes on end; **mechanical**, more like old-fashioned freewheeling bicycle than insect; at distance, thinner, whirring trill on one note (volume changes occasionally). Savi's Warbler similar; also see Nightjar (p. 300) (although quality very different).

Rare and local summer visitor, Apr–Oct (11,000 pairs, plus 24,000 birds in Ireland); scarce on migration, mostly coastal

to Africa

Tall grass, often growing through scrub/brambles; reedbeds

'Eastern Grasshopper Warbler' ssp. *straminea* (vagrant: 1 record (Britain), Sep; N Isles) typically small, greyish, heavily streaked, pale lores, but similar birds in western European ssp. *naevia*, makes identification near-impossible without DNA analysis.

ADULT [Jun]

Song helps locate a singing bird in thicket or on low, exposed perch.

Some juvenile and 1st-winter birds are quite yellowish overall; ageing difficult as post-juvenile moult is late, from Oct–Feb.

long, streaked undertail coverts

tapered both ends; long, low crown profile

JUVENILE/ 1ST-WINTER (both) AUG–MAR [Oct]

See also warbler introduction pp. 422–423

LOCUSTELLA | CETTI'S WARBLERS

Cetti's Warbler *Cettia cetti*

552

L 13–14 cm | W 18–20 cm

Small, dark, dumpy warbler; **easy to hear**, hard to see. Skulks in dense vegetation: perches briefly in open, sings, disappears, sings again somewhere else! (Wren (*p. 381*) is often in same watery habitat and flies across open spaces in a similar way.)

Dark rufous-brown (Reed Warbler (*p. 427*) is paler). Whitish throat, **grey cheek and breast**; **pale stripe over eye**; dull underparts, otherwise plain. **Tail long, square, dark rufous**; often held up revealing dark undertail coverts with pale tips. IN FLIGHT, low, quick; rounded wings.

VOICE Short, hard, sharp "*quilp!*" or "*plit*" from dense waterside vegetation (especially in winter) but can be a quiet note. Song **loud outburst** of short notes, momentary pause, then **fast** "*chwee; chwee: chuwee-wee-wee-wee-wee chwit-it!*" unlike any similar birds nearby.

Scarce and local resident (1,900 singing males, mostly S England). Vagrant Ireland (<5 records)

Sometimes appears on edge of thicket, perched with tail raised; may hop across gaps in reeds, over leaf-litter.

Dense waterside vegetation: overgrown ditches, reedbeds, scrubby tangles

dark undertail coverts

ADULT [Jun]

ADULT [Apr]

Sings from hidden perch with great gusto, often moving to another spot nearby before delivering the next phrase.

Savi's Warbler *Locustella luscinioides* 🔴 552

River Warbler (*p. 444*)

L 13·5–15 cm | W 16–18 cm

Brownish warbler, **located by song, from dense reeds**. Sandy-brown above, paler buffish below with **very long brown undertail coverts** and **broad tail**. Obvious curve to edge of closed wing. Most like Reed Warbler (*p. 427*), which has shorter, slimmer, whiter undertail coverts. Plumage more **uniform** than Grasshopper and Sedge (*p. 426*) Warblers.

VOICE Sharp, metallic "*pvit*." Song like Grasshopper Warbler, often at night, but **lower and faster**, more purring or buzzing than ticking/reeling.

'thick' rear-end, broad tail

ADULT [Apr]

underparts browner towards tail

Very rare summer visitor, Apr–Aug (up to 5 pairs). Very rare, mostly coastal on migration (<10 per year; <15 records Ireland). Mainly large reedbeds near coast. Winters in Africa.

WARBLERS, CISTICOLAS and CRESTS

Chiffchaff *Phylloscopus collybita*

L 10–12 cm | W 15–21 cm

👁 Iberian Chiffchaff (p.449), other rare *Phylloscopus* warblers (pp.448–451)

Very common summer visitor, most Mar–Oct (1·1 million pairs, plus 300,000 birds in Ireland) and migrant; rare winter (few 100s)

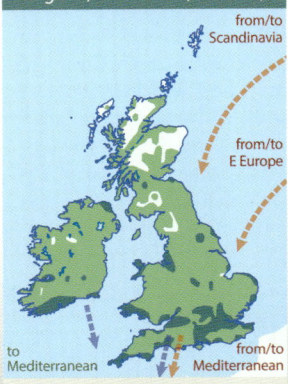

Very small, active, 'tail-dipping' woodland warbler. Fine bill, round head; short primary projection; dark legs (very similar Willow Warbler (p.432) has a slightly thicker bill, paler legs, longer primary projection and genrally a slightly flatter head). Frequent **downward tail 'dips'** more obvious than Willow Warbler's tail flourish.

ADULT ssp. *collybita* (majority of British/Irish birds) green or dull, **dusky olive** with pale edges to dark wing and tail. Pale stripe over eye; dark eyestripe; **white crescent under eye**. Underparts dull, yellowish, whiter under tail. Legs **thin, dark** brown–black. (Willow Warbler's legs typically pale, sometimes dark with paler feet, not so spindly.) Fresh autumn plumage, brighter, yellower, more buff beneath. JUVENILE/1ST-WINTER greener, yellower below; pale orange bill base.

VOICE Simple "*hweet*," less disyllabic than Willow Warbler, less forceful than similar note of Chaffinch (p.494). In Jul–Sep, slurred "*shrilip*" or "*shlip*." Short "*hoot*" in Sep–Oct. Song obvious: well-defined, even-paced notes in random sequence, "*chip-chap-chiff-chap-chap-chiff-chee*." Interspersed with low "*grrt-grrt*." Song frequent in autumn.

Woodland; willows close to water; well-wooded gardens, parks

An odd-sounding 'chiffchaff' in spring may simply be a Chiffchaff with an aberrant song, but the closely similar **Iberian Chiffchaff** (p.449) can usually be identified by consistent differences in the song's structure.
NOTE: Individuals with confusing call/plumage features may remain unidentifiable and can only be confirmed by DNA analysis.

ssp. *collybita* ADULT [Apr]

ssp. *collybita* ADULT / 1ST-WINTER [Jan]

Chiffchaffs regularly overwinter, in woodland, low scrub and gardens, but favour willows close to water, with abundant insects. (Willow Warbler very rarely winters.) ADULT in midwinter has dark wing feathers, edged green; 1ST-WINTER's edged yellowish. After moult Dec–Feb, may be impossible to age.

ssp. *collybita* ADULT / 1ST-WINTER [Oct]

See also warbler introduction *pp. 422–423*

PHYLLOSCOPUS WARBLERS

Chiffchaff and Willow Warbler compared

Chiffchaff and **Willow Warbler** are a difficult pair: look for leg colour (bearing in mind that there is variation), head shape, primary projection, tail movement and Chiffchaff's more olive/yellow, less grey-green/cream, appearance.

round head — **WILLOW WARBLER** — flattish head
short primary projection — [Apr] — long primary projection — [May]
CHIFFCHAFF ssp. *collybita* — dark legs — pale legs

Chiffchaff subspecies
– 'eastern' Chiffchaffs intergrade across their range and not all are assignable to a subspecies; call is important in identification. All have a similar structure, pale crescent under eye and frequent tail dip.

Ssp. *collybita* is the common Chiffchaff in Britain and Ireland: rather olive-green, pale yellowish below. Wing and tail edged dull green. Thin yellowish stripe over eye. Bill pinkish at base; legs dark brown; often paler under toes. Call a bright, rising, practically monosyllabic *"hweet."*

'SIBERIAN CHIFFCHAFF' ssp. *tristis* is rare (100–145 per year, most Sep–Oct, few Nov–Mar). Best identified by voice and/or DNA sample. Certain ssp. *tristis* are **pale greyish khaki-brown** with no green on head or back, but wing, sides of rump and tail feathers edged green. Whitish below with buff flank, **no yellow** (but yellow underwing may show). 'Cold grey' effect becomes more buff-brown in bright light. Broad warm **buff stripe over eye**, dark eyestripe; **buff-brown patch on cheek**, rusty in good light. Bill **mostly black** with paler base; legs black. Call Dunnock-like flat or falling, monosyllabic, 'off-key' or 'sad' *"eep"* or *"speep."* Spring song unlike ssp. *collybita*: *"chivvi-tee, chooee, chivvi-tee, chooee-tee, chivvy."* Pre-breeding moult still evident Mar–Apr, when complete in other subspecies. Green fringes on wing of ssp. *tristis* in Sep/Oct may bring to mind Western and Eastern Bonelli's Warblers (*p. 448*), but worn off by Mar, when reminiscent of Booted Warbler (*p. 447*). Variation/hybrids/intergrades make boundary of ssp. *tristis* hard to define: debatable individuals are more greyish-olive (sometimes termed '*fulvescens*'), or greyer with white underparts.

N/E European ssp. *abietinus* (rare, status uncertain but fewer than ssp. *tristis*; some Sep–Mar birds proven as this subspecies). **Identifiable only by DNA analysis**. Greyish and brownish forms: wing and tail edged brownish; dull grey-buff underparts; yellowish/white stripe over eye; bill and legs blackish. Call similar to ssp. *collybita*.

ssp. *tristis* or ssp. *abietinus*
ADULT / **1ST-WINTER**
[Oct]

ssp. *collybita*
ADULT / **1ST-WINTER**
[Dec]

ssp. *tristis*
ADULT / **1ST-WINTER**
[Nov]

WARBLERS, CISTICOLAS and CRESTS

Comparison with Chiffchaff *p. 431*

Willow Warbler *Phylloscopus trochilus*

L 11–12·5 cm | W 15–21 cm

except ssp. *acredula*

Iberian Chiffchaff (*p. 449*), other rare *Phylloscopus* warblers (*pp. 448–451*)

Small, slim, pale warbler of trees and bushy heaths, difficult to separate from Chiffchaff (*p. 430*) unless by **song**, but has a long primary projection and typically pale legs, and generally a flattish head. Wings and tail flicked/twitched, but tail is not 'dipped' like Chiffchaff.

ADULT brighter, cleaner than average Chiffchaff (often subtle). Greenish above; pale yellow-cream breast, whiter belly. Quite **strong yellowish line over eye**; weaker eyering above paler cheek than Chiffchaff. Bill more extensively pale. **Legs pale orange-brown**, sometimes darker with pale feet. Wings quite plain, lack bright yellow edges of Wood Warbler. JUVENILE greenish above, **yellow** below; prominent yellow stripe over eye. 1ST-WINTER underparts bright yellow, from chin to tail.

VOICE Call more firmly two syllables than Chiffchaff: "*hoo-eet*," like Redstart (*p. 402*). Song immediately distinctive: short, sweet, lilting, whistling descending cadence.

Locally very common summer visitor, Apr–Oct (2 million pairs, plus 1·6 million birds in Ireland), passage migrant

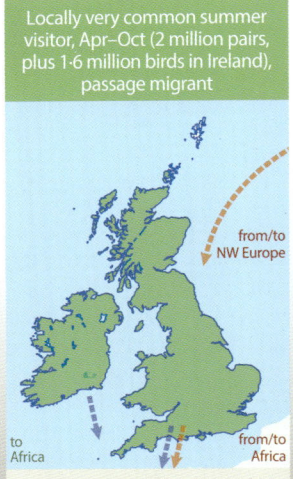

from/to NW Europe

to Africa

from/to Africa

Woods, scattered birches/oaks/willows on heaths, moors

ADULT [Apr]

Frequently sings from top or side of bush on exposed perch; allows close views with careful approach.

ssp. *trochilus* ADULT [May]

legs nearly always paler, browner than Chiffchaff's

'clean' and pale compared with Chiffchaff

strong yellow stripe over eye; pale bill

ssp. *trochilus* ADULT/1ST-WINTER [Aug]

ssp. *acredula* ADULT/1ST-WINTER [Sep]

Scandinavian ssp. *acredula* (scarce migrant) is greyer above, whiter below than British/Irish breeders (widespread European ssp. *trochilus*).

See also warbler introduction pp. 422–423

PHYLLOSCOPUS WARBLERS

Wood Warbler *Phylloscopus sibilatrix*

L 11–12·5 cm | W 16–22 cm

👁 Bonelli's warblers (p. 448)

A bright 'green' warbler of dense woodland canopy above open ground/leaf-litter, most easily **located by song**.

Stocky, long, wide-bellied; long wings often drooped beside **short, broad tail**. ADULT bright, clear green above, white below; **long yellow stripe over eye** and broad, dark eyestripe. Lower face and upper breast pale lemon-yellow, against white underparts. Brighter, more contrasted than Willow Warbler, but many are pale yellow only on throat. Wings **contrasted** with black-brown feathers edged yellow-green (Willow Warbler and Chiffchaff (p. 430) plainer). JUVENILE/ 1ST-WINTER has **white** tertial fringes, minute white primary tips.

VOICE Call high, sweet, sad "*siuuh*." Song a rhythmic repetition of call note (resembling Willow Tit (p. 473)), between more frequent trills: metallic ticking firming up into **short, fast trill** (see also Western and Eastern Bonelli's warblers (p. 448)).

Scarce and local summer visitor, Apr–Sep (6,500 pairs; very rare Ireland); rare migrant outside breeding areas

to Africa

Oak, Beech, Larch woods

ADULT [May]

Wood Warbler in early summer is best found by following up the silvery trilled song in broadleaved woodland without an understorey.

strength of yellow throat variable; some very pale

ADULT [May]

ADULT [May]

1ST-WINTER JUN–MAR [Sep]

long wingtip often drooped beside tail

'clean' white underparts; no hint of buff or yellow

WARBLERS, CISTICOLAS and CRESTS

Blackcap *Sylvia atricapilla*

L 13·5–15 cm | W 20–23 cm

Orphean warblers (p. 456)

Common summer visitor (1·1 million pairs, plus 260,000 birds in Ireland) and passage migrant; small numbers winter

Small, stocky, slightly sluggish woodland warbler with heavy movements. Marsh Tit (*p. 472*) superficially similar (but has black bib). Wintering birds visit bird tables. Jerks/flicks square tail upwards.

MALE plain grey-brown, paler below, with **round black cap** (falls short of gape). Pale grey collar when seen from rear. FEMALE pale grey-brown, brighter buffish below with pale under tail that may show as a streak; **bright rusty cap**; eye red-brown. JUVENILE has dull brown cap; eye grey-brown. 1ST-WINTER has inner greater coverts fringed greenish-grey, outer ones browner (adult's all-brown); MALE cap black with brown tips.

VOICE Hard, unmusical "*tek*" or "*tak*;" quick, anxious series if alarmed. Compare song with Garden Warbler, which it may mimic – a rich, throaty, fast, **fluty warble, vigorous and musical**, typically low start increases in speed and volume, more strident, more forceful than Garden Warbler. Faster, less varied, shorter than Nightingale (*p. 401*). May mimic a wide range of other species.

from NW Europe

from C Europe

to Mediterranean

Woodland, thickets, parkland

JUVENILE JUN–SEP [Jun]

cap brighter rufous than juvenile's

♀ [May]

cap mixed black and rufous

1ST-WINTER ♂ AUG–MAR [Aug]

MALES sing from bush-top to tall tree-top height; sometimes two or three together in brief skirmish, with prolonged songs.

♂ [May]

MARSH TIT (*p. 472*) – possible confusion species – note black nape; more extensive black cap; black in front of eye, black bib

SYLVIA WARBLERS

Garden Warbler *Sylvia borin*

L 13–14·5 cm | W 20–22 cm

Small, **plain, pale brownish** woodland warbler (no green or yellow and no contrasted cap – see Blackcap, more upright Spotted Flycatcher (p. 418) and slimmer-billed Reed Warbler (p. 427)). Quite skulking, slow and sedate; sits still for lengthy spells, but flies rapidly between songposts. Has wing-flick and tail-dip like Chiffchaff (p. 430) but clearly bigger and more sluggish.

Sexes look alike. ADULT upperparts sandy-grey-brown; less rusty than Reed Warbler (which has longer head/bill profile). **Bland head pattern** with thin whitish eyering and usually a faint pale stripe over eye; diffuse greyish neck. Large, dark eye prominent. Bill dark blue-grey, slightly **thick and stubby** for a warbler; legs dark grey. JUVENILE/1ST-WINTER like adult but well-defined very narrow pale feather edges on wing and tail.

VOICE Call "*chek*" or "*tsak*," a little softer, more wooden than Blackcap; alarm call more 'chuffing' "*chuff-chuff-chuff*" or "*cha cha cha*." Song may be like Blackcap but phrases generally longer, simpler with more even delivery: **fast, flowing/bubbling tempo** (less acceleration in middle, less forceful finish).

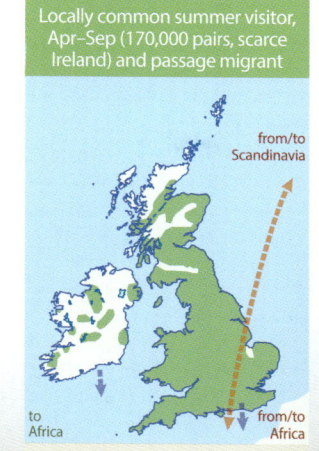

Locally common summer visitor, Apr–Sep (170,000 pairs, scarce Ireland) and passage migrant

from/to Scandinavia

to Africa

from/to Africa

Woodland, thickets, scrub

plumage resembles Spotted Flycatcher, but has a more horizontal stance and skulking behaviour

ADULT
[Apr]

MALES sing from low bramble to tall tree height; inconspicuous but may fly a long distance to a new song perch.

fresh autumn feathers have immaculate pale fringes

1ST-WINTER
AUG–MAR
[Sep]

WARBLERS, CISTICOLAS and CRESTS

Whitethroat *Sylvia communis*

L 13–15 cm | W 18–22 cm

Rare *Sylvia* warblers (p. 453–457)

Bright, pale warbler with **rufous wings** and **white throat**. Alert, perky; raises and swings tail before diving into cover. Sings from wire or twig, or from cover, or in **bouncy song flight**.

Upperparts pale olive-brown; brighter **rufous wing patch**; tertials with broad, rounded dark centre and rufous-buff fringe. Underparts pinkish. ADULT eye pale brown; legs pale yellow-orange. MALE head grey with broken white eyering; white throat. FEMALE browner; head greyish-brown, although some nearly as grey as male. JUVENILE bright; head buff-brown; dark wing coverts with diffuse sandy fringes; eye dark. 1ST-WINTER some coverts contrasted adult-type.

VOICE Varied; including nasal, slightly buzzy, breathy "*aid-aid-aid*", longer, buzzy "*churrr*" and rhythmic "*wichety-wichety*." Song (perched or in wing-waving song flight) fast, **churring, scratchy warble** with fast rise-fall rhythm.

Locally common summer visitor, Apr–Oct (930,000 pairs, plus 95,000 birds in Ireland), migrant

from/to NW Europe

to Africa — from/to Africa

Hedgerows, scrub, thickets, dense bramble patches, nettle beds

IN FLIGHT, slender brown tail with narrow white sides.

♂ song flight

MALES sing from wires or tall perches, or well hidden in dense hedgerow, bramble patch or nettle bed, but periodically rise into fluttery song flight (*right*).

grey head

ADULT ♂ [Apr]

head usually greyish-brown with gingery cheeks

1ST-WINTER JUL–MAR [Sep]

ADULT ♀ [May]

436

See also warbler introduction *pp. 422–423*

SYLVIA WARBLERS

Lesser Whitethroat *Sylvia curruca*

L 11·5–13·5 cm | W 17–22 cm

Small, sleek warbler lacking bright colours. Skulking, often disappears out of back of bush.

Rare *Sylvia* warblers (*p. 453–457*)

Sexes look alike. ADULT head grey; **darker cheek contrasts with white throat**. Upperparts dull grey-brown, **no rufous on wing**; underparts whitish, pinkish-buff on flank. **Legs blue-grey**; eyes dark. JUVENILE like adult but 'clean', bright impression; white eyering (sometimes broken); dark mark from eye to bill; pale fringes to flight feathers; greater coverts edged brownish. 1ST-WINTER has some adult-type greater coverts, edged greyish. IN FLIGHT, dark tail with narrow white sides.

VOICE Clicking, hard "*tet*" or "*tuk*," sharper than Blackcap (*p. 434*); high "*see*." Song low warble before loud, wooden rattle "*tuk-atuk-atuk-atuk-atuk-atuk-atuk*."

Scarce summer visitor, Apr–Oct (64,000 pairs), passage migrant; has bred in Ireland

to E Africa

Tall, dense hedgerows, thickets

some individuals have a broken white eyering and a pale stripe over the eye

ssp. *curruca* ADULT [Mar]

ssp. *curruca* 1ST-WINTER AUG–NOV [Aug]

ssp. *blythi* [Jan]

ssp. *halimodendri* [Nov]

ssp. *halimodendri* (probably) [Oct]

Eastern subspecies sometimes suspected but rarely confirmed, as identification not straightforward; sometimes impossible without DNA analysis. '**SIBERIAN LESSER WHITETHROAT**' ssp. *blythi* (vagrant; <100 records, Oct–Feb) paler head, whiter line over eye compared to breeding birds (**European** ssp. *curruca*).
'**CENTRAL ASIAN LESSER WHITETHROAT**' ssp. *halimodendri* (vagrant; <5 records, Oct–Nov) brown nape, buff flank, pale lores, short wing/long tail, much white in outer tail; tit-like call.

WARBLERS, CISTICOLAS and CRESTS

NT Dartford Warbler *Sylvia undata*

NT L 13–14 cm | W 16–18 cm 👁 Marmora's Warbler (*p. 453*)

Rare and very local resident (3,000 pairs, declines in severe winters); very rare migrant. Vagrant Ireland (<15 records)

Small, long-tailed warbler, elusive and secretive in heather/gorse. Tail exaggerates size, often but not always raised. Best located by call or song but often hard to see well. Flies **low and fast over heather**, tail dipping, swooping into gorse, small pine, or deep heather.

Greyish head and upperparts; reddish underparts. Long-tailed, short-winged, pot-bellied (but can look slim). Dark, with long, thin tail (Whitethroat (*p. 436*) paler, and short-tailed); **red eyering**. MALE dark blue-grey head; throat and **breast brownish-red**. FEMALE paler, duller, brownish-grey; throat pale. JUVENILE/1ST-WINTER like female but paler, greyer-brown, buff (less orange) below.

VOICE Call distinctive (but Whitethroat comes close) **buzzing churr**: low, soft, simple, nasal "*chairrrr*." Song brighter, fast sequence, whistles and buzzy notes in jumbled warble, usually from half- or fully hidden perch in gorse.

Heather/gorse heath (mostly S England, coastal East Anglia; rare S Wales, Midlands)

1ST-WINTER AUG–MAR

Dispersing 1st-winter birds appear in coastal brambles, scrub and gorse bushes, but long tail, dark head and back, and rusty flank should dispel thoughts of rarer species.

classic gorse-top pose, but more often hidden deep inside bush or heather

ADULT ♂

tail often slightly raised, sometimes flat or held very high

♀

See also warbler introduction *pp. 422–423*

Rare warblers

Rare warblers have a special appeal to many people: the glimpse of a wingbar in a coastal copse, a strange call from a willow thicket, the sight of a 'tail end' diving out of sight into a bramble patch on some far-flung island in autumn all start the adrenalin flowing. The same feeling may be replicated by a scarce migrant on a local 'patch'.

Some 41 species of warbler are scarce migrants or vagrants to Britain and/or Ireland (excluding New World warblers, covered separately on *pp. 526–529*). Most are spring or autumn migrants (a very few also breed in tiny numbers). They include species from all of the main groups introduced on *pp. 422–423*, but vagrants often appear in unlikely places (*e.g.* coastal headlands or barren islands). Concentrating on structure and calls, to help narrow the options to the correct genus, is important in such cases where normal habitat choices and behaviour are less relevant. As with any rarity, careful, objective observation and detailed records of calls, plumage features and structural characters (*e.g.* bill shape and primary projection) remain vitally important.

Rare *Phylloscopus* warblers from Asia

from Siberia

Migrant **Lanceolated Warblers** are usually very skulking, and brief views of small parts at a time are most likely!

A male '**subalpine**' warbler is distinctive, but raises difficult identification issues due to recent taxonomic changes (see *p. 454*).

Icterine Warbler is a striking representative of a difficult group, now split into *Hippolais* and *Iduna* warblers.

Marsh Warbler still breeds but is now mostly a rare coastal migrant that is hard to identify, and can turn up in strange places!

Until recently, **Yellow-browed Warbler** was a rare 'Siberian' vagrant, but numbers have steadily increased and now several hundred might be expected in an autumn. Some penetrate far inland and a few remain to winter, but the vast majority are late September–October birds of coasts, headlands and islands. Usually later than the main influx of Yellow-browed Warblers a few **Pallas's Warblers** can be expected; **Hume's Warblers** remain very rare and are often later arrivals. **Dusky** and **Radde's Warblers** used to be a 'pair', difficult to separate and with almost equal numbers of records in Britain in late autumn: more recently, numbers of Dusky Warblers have increased markedly. With increased awareness of possibilities, plus undoubted changes affecting bird's movements, several other 'extreme' vagrants have been identified, such as **Eastern Crowned** and **Pale-legged Leaf Warblers**.

Yellow-browed Warbler is the classic 'Sibe' that has increased from a few tens to several hundreds per year in recent decades. Although Yellow-browed Warblers hover at times (but less so than Firecrests (*p. 425*); **Pallas's Warblers** do so frequently, when they may reveal a diagnostic pale yellow rump (*right*).

PALLAS'S WARBLER

RARE WARBLERS

Warblers | *Acrocephalus*

While some are straightforward, several species are difficult, even when photographed: details of wing may be vital, but require careful interpretation (*e.g.* raised tertials may reveal an extra primary tip).

REED WARBLER

weakly contrasted pale tertial fringes

primary tips only slightly paler

darkish legs

1ST-WINTER
JUL—MAR
[Sep]

Reed Warbler is the usual plain *Acrocephalus* warbler in reedbeds all summer: however, migrants might include a rarity, typically near the coast in autumn. Note down (or record) calls carefully; look at the wingtip for length, number of visible primary tips, contrasting paler feather fringes, *etc.*

Plain brown *Acrocephalus* warblers – key features

	General appearance	Head pattern	Tertials	Wingtip	
Marsh Warbler	Olive; barely brighter rump	Weak stripe over eye; bolder eyering	Strongly contrasted pale fringes; just longer than secondaries	Primary projection long; 8 visible pale tips (wear off in summer)	sharp contrast
Reed Warbler (p. 427)	Warm brown; rustier rump/tail	Weak stripe over eye; white throat	Weakly contrasted paler fringes; same length as secondaries	Primary projection long; 7 visible dull pale tips	diffuse contrast
Blyth's Reed Warbler	Olive; very uniform	Stripe over eye bulbous in front	Very plain	Primary projection short; 6 visible pale tips. 1ST-WINTER has bronzy panel on secondaries	plain
Paddyfield Warbler (p. 443)	Bright; sandy/rusty. Long tail	Stripe over eye edged dark above and below	Obvious paler fringes	Primary projection short; 5–7 visible pale tips	pale fringes

ACROCEPHALUS WARBLERS

See also warbler introduction pp. 422–423

Marsh Warbler *Acrocephalus palustris* 🔴   552
L 13–15 cm | W 18–20 cm

Small, unstreaked brownish warbler. Separation from Reed Warbler (p. 427) difficult without **song** but Marsh Warbler duller, **less rufous**, with more **clearly defined pale tertial fringes**, shorter bill and rounder head. Legs pale straw to greyish. ADULT sandy-olive; rump yellow-brown; lemon-buff below. Whitish eyering. JUVENILE/1ST-WINTER pale olive-brown, rump warm brown; primaries tipped whitish (dull on autumn adult).

VOICE Dry, rattling "*terrrr*" and soft "*chek*." Song lively, flowing, including **great variety of accurate mimicry** and distinctive nasal "*tzay-beeee*," but also many grating notes.

Very rare, erratic summer visitor, May–Sep (<10 pairs). Very rare, mostly coastal on migration (30–50 per year; <10 records Ireland). Marsh vegetation; scrub. Winters in SE Africa.

ADULT [Jun]

strongly contrasted pale tertial fringes

pale-tipped primaries

ADULT [Jul]

strong pale legs and claws

Late spring arrivals (late May–Jun) may sing: best at dawn and dusk, often hesitant, quieter during day.

👁 Paddyfield Warbler (p. 443)
Iduna Warblers (pp. 446–447)

Blyth's Reed Warbler
Acrocephalus dumetorum
L 12·5–14 cm | W 16–18 cm

Very like Reed (p. 427) and Marsh Warblers; may perch with head and tail raised ('banana' shape). Broad **pale stripe from eye to bill** ('blob'), short/absent behind eye; **long, pale bill darkens towards tip**. Dull greyish-olive-brown above; **wings very plain** but slight bronzy lengthwise panel on 1ST-WINTER. Legs greyish or brown (Marsh Warbler pinker).

VOICE Call short, hard "*tchlit*."

Vagrant from E Europe: <200 records (<15 Ireland), most months, mainly Oct. Most on coast. Reedbeds, scrub.

1ST-WINTER AUG–MAR [Nov]

1ST-WINTER birds often show paler bronzy panel on secondaries

RARE WARBLERS

See also warbler introduction *pp. 422–423*

VU Aquatic Warbler 🔴 552
VU *Acrocephalus paludicola*
L 11·5–13 cm | W 16–18 cm

Small, streaked wetland warbler; more secretive than very similar Sedge Warbler (*p. 426*): requires close observation to see key features. **Unmarked buff central crown stripe**, broad buff stripe over eye; **cream stripes on blackish back**; **streaks on rump** and pointed uppertail coverts. **Pale-faced**: dark eyestripe **short of bill**. legs pale pink. ADULT **fine streaks on breast and flank.** JUVENILE underparts unmarked; buff marks on blackish crown sides.

VOICE Ticking "*chak*" or "*chek*," or deep "*tuk*."

> Very rare migrant from E Europe: 7–10 per year (<20 records Ireland), Aug–Sep; most records juveniles. Mostly coastal S, SW England (declining). Reedbeds, tall marshy vegetation. Winters in Africa.

dark streaks in pale
JUVENILE
SEDGE WARBLER

unmarked buff
ADULT [Apr]

JUVENILE JUL–DEC [Aug]

streaked rump and uppertail coverts

Great Reed Warbler
Acrocephalus arundinaceus
L 16–20 cm | W 25–30 cm

Large brown warbler, much larger than Reed Warbler (*p. 427*); **crashes** through reeds. Short flights over reeds: long wings; long, broad, slightly raised tail. Plain brown above, buff below; bold **pale stripe over eye**, fading out quickly behind; **broad dark eyestripe. Strong, two-toned bill.**

VOICE Call hard "*crek*." Song **loud, coarse, repetitive**, with **deeper** notes than Reed Warbler but also high squeaky ones; sometimes hesitant, but unique in full flow: "*krr-krr kreek kreek kreek krrr krr grik grik chweee chweee chweee kerra kerra kerra….*"

> Very rare migrant/vagrant from Europe: <300 records (<10 Ireland), most May–Jun. Sometimes sings for a few days. Reedbeds, scrub. Winters in Africa.

bold head pattern
thick bill
ADULT [Jun]

ACROCEPHALUS | CISTICOLA | ARUNDINAX

Paddyfield Warbler
Acrocephalus agricola
L 12–13·5 cm | W 15–17 cm

Like small, pale, tawny Reed Warbler (p. 427), with **short bill and long tail**. **Bold pale stripe over eye**, fading to rear (recalls Sedge Warbler (p. 426)); slightly **darker sides** to plain brown crown; dark eyestripe. Bill dark with **yellowish base/sharp black tip**. Wings brown with distinct **darker feather centres** on tertials (plainer on Blyth's Reed Warbler (p. 441)). Primary projection short. Rump/uppertail often bright sandy/rusty.

Vagrant from E Europe: <150 records (<10 Ireland), most Aug–Oct. Reeds, scrub. Mostly on coast.

bold pale stripe over eye, below dark sides to crown

yellowish base to short, dark bill

pale edges to dark tertials

much 'plainer' face

1ST-WINTER
REED WARBLER

ADULT [Jun]

Marsh & Blyth's Reed Warblers (p. 441)
Iduna Warblers (pp. 446–447)

Fan-tailed Warbler
(Zitting Cisticola)
Cisticola juncidis
L 10–11 cm | W 12–15 cm

Tiny, pale brownish warbler, finely streaked on crown; bolder black and buff streaks on back. Short, round tail has **black spots and white feather tips**. Bright, sandy-buff Oct–Nov; darker, more uniform appearance by Apr–May.

VOICE Song in high, bounding flight, repeated "*dzeep… dzeep….*"

Vagrant from S Europe: <15 records (<5 Ireland), Mar–Dec. Most S, SE England. Coastal grass/wetlands.

JUVENILE → 1ST-WINTER
JUN–MAR
[Sep]

streaked above

tail feathers with black spots and white tips

very short wing

ADULT [Feb]

Thick-billed Warbler
Arundinax (Iduna) aedon
L 16–17 cm | W 24–28 cm

Like a pale Great Reed Warbler with a **stout, slightly arched, pale-based bill** and thick gape. Slightly **darker cap**. **Pale** between eye and bill; white throat above rusty-buff breast. **Short wings and primary projection; long, rounded, bright rufous-brown tail**.

Vagrant from Asia: <10 records (Britain), May, Sep–Oct. N Isles. Scrub, dense vegetation.

big, long-tailed, short-winged, plain warbler; bland head, beady eye, deep bill

ADULT [May]

RARE WARBLERS

River Warbler
Locustella fluviatilis
L 14·5–16 cm | W 16–18 cm

Resembles Savi's Warbler (*p. 429*), but long undertail coverts **darker** with prominent **pale crescentic tips**; **throat and breast subtly streaked**.

VOICE Song sharp, metallic, shaking trill, fast, rhythmic or mechanical "*schili-schili-schili-schili-schili-schili….*" Call "*zic zic.*"

> Very rare migrant/vagrant from N Europe: <50 records (Britain), May–Oct. Widespread. Damp bushy places.

broad, plain wing; long, curved outer edge often noticeably pale

ADULT [May]

long, sharp bill

streaked throat and breast

undertail coverts dark with pale tips

Lanceolated Warbler
Locustella lanceolata
L 12 cm | W 16–18 cm

Like small, extremely skulking, short-tailed Grasshopper Warbler (*p. 428*) but more distinctly streaked; **tertials have sharper, narrow pale fringes**; **diffuse streaking beneath** on autumn immatures more extensive than on young Grasshopper Warbler.

VOICE Call quick, soft, "*tssk tssk tssk.*"

> Vagrant from NE Europe and Asia: <200 records, about 4 per year (Britain), Sep–Oct. Mostly N Isles. Dense vegetation.

GRASSHOPPER WARBLER

broad pale fringes

JUVENILE AUG–OCT [Oct]

wide plumage variation

striking black tertials with narrow pale fringes

JUVENILE AUG–OCT [Oct]

Pallas's Grasshopper Warbler
Helopsaltes (Locustella) certhiola
L 13–14 cm | W 18–20 cm

Like Grasshopper Warbler (*p. 428*) and similarly skulking, difficult to observe in low vegetation. Dark cap, pale stripe over eye; more sharply defined white edges/tips on blackish tertials; **white tips beyond blackish band on tail feathers**.

VOICE Call sharp, thin "*tsik tsik.*"

> Vagrant from Asia: <75 records (<5 Ireland), Sep–Oct. Mostly N Isles. Dense vegetation.

bright, yellow-buff-olive underparts, warm chestnut/rufous rump, contrasting with long, very dark tail

JUVENILE JUL–OCT [Sep]

white tips to dark tail

'LOCUSTELLA' AND ALLIES | HIPPOLAIS

Icterine Warbler
Hippolais icterina
L 12–13·5 cm | W 22 cm

Rare migrant from Europe: 50–80 per year (<250 records Ireland), mostly Aug–Oct on coast in E/SE England. Trees, scrub. Winters in Africa.

Olive-and-yellow warbler, larger, bulkier than Willow Warbler (*p. 432*), more lively and active than Melodious Warbler. Strong, broad bill and thick legs; angular nape. **Pale between eye and bill** (as Melodious Warbler; Willow Warbler has darker stripe). **Long wingtip; pale wing panel** (occasionally worn off on adults, weaker on juveniles). ADULT grey-green above, pale yellow below (brightest in spring). JUVENILE pale brownish-green above; pale yellow throat and breast, underparts white.

VOICE Infrequent hard "*tek*" (Reed Warbler (*p. 427*) calls more often).

Melodious Warbler
Hippolais polyglotta
L 12–13 cm | W 20–21 cm

Very rare migrant from SW Europe: 20–30 per year, declining (<250 records Ireland), mostly Aug–Oct on coast in S/SW England. Trees, scrub. Winters in Africa.

Olive-and-yellow warbler, like Icterine Warbler (but also see Willow Warbler (*p. 432*) and Reed Warbler (*p. 427*)). Skulking (Icterine Warbler less subdued), body rounded/pear-shaped (Icterine Warbler more angular). Typically rounded head. **Short wingtip**, wings almost plain. ADULT green above, uniformly yellowish below, even in autumn. JUVENILE paler fringes on wing, but striking pale panel not usual.

VOICE Call subdued sparrow-like chattering, and short "*tchret-tret.*"

Note the varying head-shapes on Icterine and Melodious Warblers: 'typical' shapes may change briefly.

MELODIOUS — short
Primary projection half length of longest tertial (**short wing**); usually no pale wing panel.

ICTERINE — long
Primary projection equals longest tertial (**long-winged** effect); usually prominent pale wing panel.

broad pale edges to feathers merge to form lengthwise pale panel on wing

ADULT [May]

pale bill

bill pink-orange; large, pointed, wide-based

JUVENILE JUL–DEC [Sep]

legs bluish-grey

NB Willow Warbler has orange-brown legs

crown feathers may be raised when singing/alarmed

ADULT [May]

pale bill

plain wing

Compared to Icterine Warbler, the bill of Melodious Warbler is slightly smaller and the legs are browner.

JUVENILE JUL–OCT [Aug]

RARE WARBLERS

Olive-tree Warbler 552
Hippolais olivetorum
L 16–18 cm | W 26–28 cm

Large, pale, grey warbler, size much as Barred Warbler (*p. 453*) but less heavy-bodied; larger and greyer than Eastern Olivaceous Warbler. **Long wings**, **long primary projection** (8 primary tips show); **long tail**. Weak dark mark between eye and bill, short pale stripe above; long, deep bill, **orange-yellow** at base; greyish upperparts, darker wings with strong **pale panel**; whitish tail sides.

VOICE Call deep "*tuc.*"

Vagrant: 1 record (Britain), Aug. N Isles. Trees, scrub.

👁 Eastern Olivaceous Warbler

1ST-WINTER JUL–MAR [Aug]

Pale, grey and heavy up-front; bigger, greyer than Eastern Olivaceous Warbler.

long, deep bill orange-yellow at base

ADULT [May]

long tail (may be dipped like Eastern Olivaceous Warbler)

Iduna warblers Three species that are similar to one another, with overlapping, subtle and variable features.

Booted and **Sykes's Warblers** are extremely similar; **Sykes's** and **Eastern Olivaceous Warblers** can be very difficult to tell apart. Furthermore, these two can also look very similar to *Acrocephalus* warblers, although *Iduna* warblers have shorter undertail coverts. Differences between the species are summarized below.

👁 Marsh & Blyth's Reed Warblers (*p. 441*)
Paddyfield Warbler (*p. 443*)

Comparison of *Iduna* warblers

	Booted Warbler	Sykes's Warbler	Eastern Olivaceous Warbler
Jizz	*Phylloscopus* warbler-like	longer body shape than Booted Warbler; *Acrocephalus* warbler-like	long body shape; *Acrocephalus* warbler-like
Behaviour	twitch wings and tail nervously but lack repetitive tail-dip		tail-dips repeatedly
	forages low (like an *Acrocephalus* warbler)	forages higher (like a *Phylloscopus* warbler); 'nervous', quick actions	forages at all levels; relaxed, less 'nervous' actions
Call	sharp, clicking "*chek*"		Call short, low "*tch't.*"
Head	PALE STRIPE OVER EYE **distinct** (whitish to rusty-buff), **extends behind eye**; CROWN **dark on side**; LORES **slight dark spot**; EYE large.	PALE STRIPE OVER EYE **diffuse** (variable but never rusty-buff), **very short behind eye**; CROWN **scarcely darker** on side; LORES **pale**.	thick-necked, large-headed effect PALE STRIPE OVER EYE weak, short (buff); LORES **slight dark line** from bill to eye.
Bill	typically **shortish** to medium-long, lower mandible with diffuse darker tip (may be faint or absent)	**long, thin**, straight; pale tip (may be faint dark smudge)	long, broad-based, orange-yellow; slight downcurve, curved cutting edge
Upperparts	**pale tawny-** to **sandy-brown**	plain greyish-brown	pale brownish-grey
Underparts	whitish below, **flank brighter buff/ochre**	whitish below without brighter flank	bright, pale and 'clean'
Legs	pinkish-brown	pale greyish-pink	greyish
Wing	TERTIALS (+ GREATER COVERTS) dark with **contrasting paler edges**; TERTIAL TIPS **evenly** spaced	TERTIALS **plain**; TERTIAL TIPS **unevenly** spaced	TERTIALS plain; may show **slight pale panel** on secondaries TERTIAL TIPS **evenly** spaced
Wingtip	WINGTIP short; tips < half tertial length		longer; tips ± half tertial length
Tail	moderate length, diffuse/very little white on outer two pairs, does not extend onto inner web	clearly long, diffuse white on tip of outer two pairs may extend onto inner web	long; **whitish edges and tips** to outer feathers

HIPPOLAIS | IDUNA

Booted Warbler
Iduna caligata
L 11–12·5 cm | W 18–21 cm

Small pale warbler; size and shape like a *Phylloscopus* warbler; shorter bodied than Sykes's Warbler. (**See table opposite for details.**)

Vagrant from Asia: <200 records (<10 Ireland), most Aug–Oct. On coast. Scrub, tall vegetation.

Sykes's Warbler *Iduna rama*
L 11·5–13 cm | W 18–21 cm

Small pale warbler; subtle, variable features affected by angle of view and light but size and shape like an *Acrocephalus* warbler; longer bodied than Booted Warbler; undertail coverts shorter than Paddyfield (p. 443) and Blyth's Reed Warblers (p. 441). (**See table opposite for details.**)

Vagrant from Asia: <25 records (<5 Ireland), Aug–Oct. On coast. Scrub, tall vegetation.

1ST-WINTER AUG–OCT [Aug]

TERTIALS dark/pale contrast; tips evenly spaced

more distinct pale stripe longer behind eye

at least a hint of buff/ochre on flank

neither species repeatedly dips tail

1ST-WINTER AUG–OCT [Sep]

weakly defined pale stripe short behind eye

TERTIALS plainer; tips unevenly spaced

flank and underparts whitish

Iduna wings and bills compared

wingtip < half tertial length

BOOTED

BOTH HAVE PINKISH BASE

wingtip ± half tertial length

EASTERN OLIVACEOUS

orange-yellow base

BOOTED/SYKES'S

SYKES'S

dark smudge (may be absent)

pale (may show faint dark smudge)

Eastern Olivaceous Warbler
Iduna pallida
L 12–13·5 cm | W 18–21 cm

Small, slim, square-tailed, plain brownish-grey warbler. Strongly resembles Reed Warbler (p. 427), especially paler individuals of ssp. *fuscus* and Marsh Warbler (p. 441) but is greyer and has a broader bill and shorter undertail coverts. (**See table opposite for details.**)

VOICE Call short, low "*tch't.*"

Vagrant from SE Europe: <25 records (<5 Ireland), May–Nov, most Sep–Oct. On coast. Trees, scrub.

1ST-WINTER AUG–OCT [Sep]

Frequently dips tail downwards (like Chiffchaff (p. 430)).

long bill broad at base, shows much pale orange-yellow.

ADULT [May]

particularly bright, pale and clean below

plain pale brown; faint or no pale wing panel

447

RARE WARBLERS

Beware 'grey' Chiffchaff of sspp. *tristis* or *abietinus* (*p. 430*) with green fringes on wing.

Western Bonelli's Warbler
Phylloscopus bonelli
L 10·5–11·5 cm | W 18–20 cm

Slender, pale warbler, Chiffchaff (*p. 430*) size. ADULT (SPRING) grey-green; rump **brighter yellowish-green**; **silky white below. Head rather plain**; weak line behind eye; short pale stripe over eye. Wing and tail feathers edged pale green. Bill sturdy, pale base, dark tip; legs mid- or dark brown. JUVENILE/1ST-WINTER greyish on back and 'shoulder'.

VOICE Call long "*tu-eee.*" Song fast, soft, **bubbling trill**, even speed and pitch, "*prr-r-r-r-r-r-r-r-r-r*" (resembles Wood Warbler (*p. 433*); song of Cirl Bunting (*p. 515*) also similar but more metallic).

Vagrant from SW Europe: <200 records (< 25 Ireland), few May, most Aug–Oct. Mostly on coast. Trees/bushes.

1ST-WINTER AUG–MAR [Oct]

ADULT [Apr]

Bonelli's warbler calls	
WESTERN	"*tu-eee*"
EASTERN	short "*chip*"

Eastern Bonelli's Warbler
Phylloscopus orientalis
L 11–12 cm | W 18–20 cm

Small, pale warbler almost identical to Western Bonelli's Warbler; **call vital**. ADULT (SPRING) greyish above, brighter, greener wings and rump; white underparts. JUVENILE/1ST-WINTER pale brownish-grey on back and 'shoulder'.

VOICE Call **distinctive short** "*chip.*

Vagrant from SE Europe: <10 records (Britain), Apr, May, Aug–Oct. On coast. Trees/bushes.

1ST-WINTER AUG–MAR [Oct]

ADULT [Apr]

Iberian Chiffchaff
Phylloscopus ibericus
L 11–12 cm | W 15–21 cm

Very like Chiffchaff (*p. 430*) but slightly greener; buffish-yellow breast contrasts with whiter belly, pale fringes to wing feathers brighter yellow and primary projection usually slightly longer. Yellow line over eye/dark eyestripe like Willow Warbler (*p. 432*).

VOICE Call **downslurred** "*wee-oo.*" **Song distinctive**, typically in three parts: "*djup djup djup wheep wheep chittichittichittichitta.*"

Vagrant from Iberia: <75 records (1 Ireland), Mar–Jul. Woodland.

Colours and longish primary projection close to Willow Warbler; hard to tell from Chiffchaff without voice.

ADULT [Apr]

yellow stripe over eye · weak eyering · yellowish base to bill · yellow throat · white belly · yellow vent

NOTE: southern Iberian populations have shorter primary projection, like Chiffchaff.

Dusky Warbler
Phylloscopus fuscatus
L 10·5–12 cm | W 16–19 cm

Like a **brown Chiffchaff** (*p. 430*) with 'hard' call; very like Radde's Warbler. Grey-brown above, buffy below, brighter under tail. **Bold stripe over eye,** white in front, buff behind. **Bill fine**; legs brown.

VOICE Hard "*tek*" or fast clicking notes (beware Wren (*p. 381*)!), or softer, sucked, "*ch'k*" or "*tsuc.*"

Vagrant from Asia: <600 records (<15 Ireland), most Sep–Nov. Coastal scrub, woods.

ADULT/ 1ST-WINTER [Nov]

buff behind eye only · grey-brown · buff

Dusky Warbler tends to have a low forehead, noticeable 'chin' and fine bill; **Radde's Warbler** has a rounded forehead, receding 'chin' and relatively thick bill.

DUSKY — fine · **RADDE'S** — thick

Radde's Warbler
Phylloscopus schwarzi
L 11·5–12·5 cm | W 17–19 cm

Stocky, thick-legged; skulking. Very like Dusky Warbler, even in the hand. Olive-brown above, yellowish/buff below, flank brighter, **apricot-buff** under tail. **Long buff stripe over eye**; broad dark eyestripe; mottled cheek. **Bill quite thick**, legs orange-yellow.

VOICE Soft "*chuc,*" often repeated; "*chrep*" or "*chett.*"

Vagrant from Asia: <500 records (<25 Ireland), most Sep–Oct. Coastal scrub, woods.

buff in front of eye · olive-brown · apricot-buff

1ST-WINTER SEP–MAR [Oct]

RARE WARBLERS

Greenish Warbler
Phylloscopus trochiloides
L 9·5–10·5 cm | W 16–18 cm

Small, delicate warbler; **thin pale wingbar**. Very like Arctic Warbler but dark eyestripe **does not quite reach bill**; cream stripe over eye thin in front, **stripes meet over bill**. Whitish below. Bill small, lower half **all-pale**.

VOICE Bright "*tsi-li*" or "*chilip*." Rare spring/summer migrant may sing: slightly jerky, piercing notes, break in middle and trill at end.

> Very rare migrant from NE Europe: <1,000 records, 15–40 per year (<50 records Ireland), May–Oct, most Aug–Sep. Mostly coastal. Woods, scrubby thickets. Winters in S Asia.

ADULT [May]

Most Greenish Warblers are seen in Aug–Sep, but a few arrive in late May or Jun and are heard singing.

pale stripe over eyes meet over bill; dark eyestripe does not reach bill (but detail may be indistinct)

in autumn the wingbar is broader on fresher-plumaged immature birds than on adults with worn plumage

1ST-WINTER AUG–MAR [Aug]

Two-barred Greenish Warbler
Phylloscopus plumbeitarsus
L 10–11 cm | W 15–17 cm

Small warbler, like Yellow-browed Warbler (*p. 452*) but wings paler, tertials plain. Dull green; pale stripe over eye falling short of bill and mottled cheek (like Arctic Warbler). Dark wing has well-defined **long, broad, even-width** lower wingbar; usually also short upper wingbar. Lower mandible all yellow-pink. Legs reddish-brown.

VOICE Two-syllable "*chew-wee*" and monosyllabic notes.

> Vagrant from Asia: <10 records (Britain), May, Sep–Oct. Woods, scrub.

Eyestripe and mottled cheek more like Arctic than Greenish Warbler.

tertials plain

lower wingbar long, broad, even width

1ST-WINTER AUG–MAR [Aug]

Green Warbler
Phylloscopus nitidus
L 10–11 cm | W 15–17 cm

Small, yellow-and-green warbler, brighter above, **yellower below** than Greenish Warbler and Yellow-browed Warbler (*p. 452*), with **two thin, pale yellow wingbars**; long pale yellow stripe over eye; yellowish throat and cheek.

VOICE Bright, slurred "*tslu-ree*."

> Vagrant from Asia: <5 records (Britain), May–Jul, Sep–Oct. Woods.

Brighter above and yellower below than Greenish Warbler

ADULT [May]

two thin, pale yellow wingbars

Arctic Warbler
Phylloscopus borealis
L 11·5–13 cm | W 17–19 cm

Stocky warbler; green above; greyish breast, paler belly faintly streaked. **Pale midwing bar**; often shorter upper bar (worn adults may not show any wingbar). Long, **broad, dark eyestripe reaches bill**; mottled cheek. Long **yellow-cream stripe** over eye to nape **falls short of bill**. Bill strong; **dark tip to lower mandible**.

VOICE Hard "*dzit.*"

> Very rare migrant from N Europe: <400 records, 8–10 per year (<15 records Ireland). Most Aug–Oct. Mostly on coast. Woods, scrubby thickets.

ADULT (worn plumage) [Sep]

In autumn, adults are duller and have a less distinct wingbar than fresh-plumaged immature birds.

pale stripes meet over bill

dark eyestripe short of bill

GREENISH WARBLER

pale stripe over eye falls short of bill; dark eyestripe reaches bill

1ST-WINTER AUG–MAR [Sep]

Eastern Crowned Warbler
Phylloscopus plumbeitarsus
L 12 cm | W 16–18 cm

Resembles Arctic Warbler with strong bill, two weak whitish wingbars, long stripe over eye; but **dark cap has pale central stripe**.

VOICE Loud, downslurred "*schleuw.*"

> Vagrant from Asia: <5 records (Britain), Oct–Nov. Woods, scrubby thickets.

Like Arctic Warbler with a darker cap and pale central crown stripe.

1ST-WINTER AUG–MAR [Oct]

Pale-legged Leaf Warbler
Phylloscopus nitidus
L 0–11 cm | W 18–20 cm

Small, brownish-green warbler, with **dark grey-olive crown and eyestripe**; **long**, cream stripe over eye falls short of forehead; creamy-white beneath eye above dark 'moustache' and mottled cheek; two **pale wingbars** (upper obscure); **white underparts**; **pale pink legs**.

VOICE High thin, short "*tseep.*"

> Vagrant from Asia: 1 record (Britain) (plus 1 record of either Pale-legged Leaf Warbler or Sakhalin Leaf Warbler), Oct. On coast. Woods.

ADULT

SAKHALIN LEAF WARBLER

The two species shown here are extremely similar; confirming identification may require examination in the hand or DNA analysis.

ADULT/ 1ST-WINTER [Sep]

RARE WARBLERS

Pallas's Warbler
Phylloscopus proregulus
L 9–9.5 cm | W 14–16 cm

Tiny, bright warbler (see Firecrest (*p. 425*)). Greenish above, whitish below; short upper wingbar, **broad yellowish midwing bar**. **Long yellow stripe over eye**, black eyestripe, **pale central stripe** on dark crown. **Pale yellow rump**.

VOICE Calls infrequently, soft, rising "*chuee*."

> Vagrant from Asia: 50–100 per year (<50 records Ireland), Oct–Nov, occasionally winters. Mostly on coast. Woods, thickets.

Yellow-browed Warbler
Phylloscopus inornatus
L 9–10.5 cm | W 15–16 cm

Small; active but inconspicuous, calls often and constantly twitches wing/tail. Greenish above, whitish below, faintly streaked greyish; short upper wingbar, broad **creamy-yellow midwing bar**; tertials tipped white. **Long cream/yellow stripe over eye**, dark eyestripe, plain dark crown. Bill pink at base; legs dark, feet yellow.

VOICE Sharp, high, loud, rising "*tchu-wee!*," "*tssooee*" or "*tsweest*;" weaker, whispy, at distance.

> Vagrant from Asia: 1,000 (recently 2,000) per year, Sep–Oct, a few winter. Widespread, mostly on coast. Woods, thickets.

Hume's Warbler
Phylloscopus humei
L 9–10.5 cm | W 15–16 cm

Like **greyish/brownish** Yellow-browed Warbler. Stripe over eye and wingbars tinged buff; tertial tips **dull**; bill blacker, legs and feet darker. **Call** essential.

VOICE Call dull, flat "*dsweet*" or longish, slightly falling "*dsee-o*."

> Vagrant from Asia: <150 records (<5 Ireland), Oct–May, most Oct–Nov. Mostly on coast. Woods, thickets.

---

bold, striking head pattern with central crown stripe

brighter than most Yellow-browed Warblers

yellow rump

ADULT/1ST-WINTER [Oct]

many individuals have a hint of a crown stripe

bright greenish to grey-green; wingbar often the feature initially most obvious

tertial tips white

ADULT/1ST-WINTER [Oct]

'Double' wing-barred warbler calls

PALLAS'S WARBLER Infrequent soft, rising "*chuee*"

YELLOW-BROWED WARBLER Sharp, rising "*tchu-wee!*" or "*tsweest*"

HUME'S WARBLER Dull, flat "*dsweet*" or longish, descending "*dsee-o*"

if present, faint crown stripe greyish-green

duller than most Yellow-browed Warblers: call is a vital clue

tertial tips dull

ADULT/1ST-WINTER [Nov]

PHYLLOSCOPUS | SYLVIA

See also warbler introduction *pp. 422–423*

Barred Warbler 552
Sylvia nisoria
L 15·5–17 cm | W 22–25 cm

Heavy, square-tailed warbler; moves slowly in thick scrub (stays still for long spells). MALE steely-grey with **two white wingbars** and **white tertial tips**; grey bars below. Yellow eye in dark face. FEMALE incomplete bars; duller eye. JUVENILE (most frequent in autumn) **grey-buff**, paler below. Pale eyering; short pale line over **dark eye**; thrush-like bill. **Thin wingbars**; pale tertial tips. Pale bars on rump; tail long and dark with white sides. Underparts pale; faint 'scaly' bars on rear flank, **stronger under tail**.
VOICE Call long, loud, fading rattle "*trr-rr-rr-t-t-t*."

Rare migrant from E Europe: 150–350 per year (<250 records Ireland), most Aug–Oct. Mostly on coast. Dense scrub. Winters in E Africa.

BREEDING MALE distinctly barred; pale wingbar; has rising, fluttering song flight.

big, pale, long-tailed, heavy warbler with bold dark eye

JUVENILE JUL–NOV [Sep]

Marmora's Warbler 553
Sylvia sarda
L 13–14 cm | W 16–18 cm

Resembles Dartford Warbler (*p. 438*) but **pale grey**. JUVENILE difficult, but whiter throat and belly and greyer flank.
VOICE Call short, dry "*chr't*." Song like short, fast, churring phrase of Robin (*p. 400*).

Vagrant from Mediterranean: <10 records (Britain), May–Jul. Upland/coastal heath.

♂ [Jun]

shape and actions like Dartford Warbler, but all-grey

Asian Desert Warbler
Sylvia nana
L 11·5–12·5 cm | W 18–20 cm

Small, pale warbler, like browner Whitethroat (*p. 436*) with pale, bland face. Pale grey-brown above, **rump and tail rufous** with dark feather centres and white sides; bill and legs yellowish; **eye yellow**.
VOICE Call fast, nasal "*tr-r-r-chair-chair*." Song a rich, fluty warble.

Vagrant from Asia: <15 records (Britain), May, Oct–Jan. On coast. Scrub.

like washed-out Whitethroat with rusty rump and tail

ADULT [Apr]

RARE WARBLERS

Subalpine warblers
The subalpine warbler complex from S Europe comprises two very similar species. Moltoni's Subalpine Warbler (monotypic) and **Subalpine Warbler** (four subspecies – three recorded in Britain: '**Western**' (ssp. *iberiae*) and '**Eastern**' (sspp. *cantillans* and *albistriata*)). **Identification is not straightforward.**
MALES: apart from tail pattern and call, differences are subtle and colours can look different, depending on light conditions; see table for descriptions. **FEMALES/IMMATURES:** all very similar; tail pattern essential for ID (see table).

Identification of subalpine warblers – summary of key features				
	ID Criteria	Call	Tail pattern	Male
'Eastern' SUBALPINE ssp. *albistriata*	FROM 'WESTERN' SUBALPINE and MOLTONI'S SUBALPINE: tail pattern	**Dry, hard click, "*tet*"** or rolling "*trret*"	White on 2nd outermost feather (T5) extends **up shaft** on inner web forming large white 'wedge'; **much white** on 3rd outermost feather (T4)	UPPERPARTS: pale grey; UNDERPARTS: pale brownish or buffish pink extending to belly; WHITE 'MOUSTACHE': broader
'Eastern' SUBALPINE ssp. *cantillans*	DNA often required to confirm subspecies	similar to 'Western' Subalpine		
'Western' SUBALPINE ssp. *iberiae*	FROM 'EASTERN' SUBALPINE: tail pattern FROM MOLTONI'S SUBALPINE: call	Soft "*chuk*" and harder "*tek*" or "*tek-tek-tek*"	Small white tip on 2nd outermost feather (T5) curves **up inner edge, not up shaft**; little white on 3rd outermost feather (T4)	UPPERPARTS: blue-grey, dusky or purplish; wings browner grey; UNDERPARTS: brick-red to deep pink breast and flank; paler belly; WHITE 'MOUSTACHE': thinner
MOLTONI'S SUBALPINE WARBLER	FROM 'EASTERN' SUBALPINE: tail pattern FROM 'WESTERN' SUBALPINE: call	**Rolling, dry "*ttrrrrr*,"** like Wren (p. 381), fading at end		UPPERPARTS: pale grey; UNDERPARTS: pale brownish or buffish pink extending to belly; WHITE 'MOUSTACHE': intermediate

Subalpine Warbler *Sylvia cantillans*
L 12–13 cm | W 17–21 cm

MALE greyish above, with **white 'moustache'**; pinkish below. FEMALE/1ST-WINTER paler, browner than male; slight white 'moustache'. Red around eye inside whitish eyering; legs pale yellowish. *See table for summary of key features*.

Very rare migrant/vagrant: ssp. *iberiae* (from Iberia, S France and Italy) and ssp. *cantillans* (from Italy) presumed to form the majority of occurrences (past records mostly unassignable to ssp.), >500 records (>50 Ireland), 25–35 per year, mostly in S in spring; ssp. *albistriata* from SE Europe <50 records, Apr–Oct. Most on coast. Scrub.

'Eastern' SUBALPINE ssp. *albistriata*

'Western' SUBALPINE ssp. *iberiae*

'Western' SUBALPINE ssp. *iberiae*

Moltoni's Subalpine Warbler
Sylvia subalpina
L 11·5–13 cm | W 18–21 cm

Very like Subalpine Warbler. *See table for differences.*

Vagrant (breeds Mallorca, Corsica, Sardinia, N Italy): <10 records (Britain), May–Jun. On coast. Scrub.

'Western' Subalpine Warbler and Moltoni's Subalpine Warbler only separable in the field by call.

See also warbler introduction *pp. 422–423*

SYLVIA

Spectacled Warbler
Sylvia conspicillata
L 12–13 cm | W 18–20 cm

Like small, dark Whitethroat (*p. 436*) with similar or more contrasted white eyering. MALE **black between eye and bill**, blue-grey hood, white throat, dusky pink underparts, unstreaked rufous wing patch. FEMALE/1ST-WINTER like Whitethroat and subalpine warblers but **more extensive rufous** on wing, tertials with **pointed dark centres**; little or no dark on centres of coverts (unlike Whitethroat); shorter primary projection; yellower legs, dark tail with broad white sides. VOICE Call "*tchhh tchhh.*" Song short, fast, even warble.

Vagrant from S Europe: <10 records (Britain), Apr–Jun, Oct. On coast, inland. Low scrub.

WHITETHROAT
tertials edged **rufous** with more rounded dark centres
grey
dark centres
long
♂

tertials edged **rufous** with **pointed** dark centres
black
♀
♂
short
little or no dark on centres of coverts
legs yellowish

'Rufous' *Sylvia* immatures

Juvenile/1st-winter **Subalpine, Moltoni's** and **Spectacled Warblers** all look broadly similar to the common **Whitethroat** (*p. 436*) and care needs to be taken to distinguish between them. The pattern of the tertials is one reliable feature that can be used.

WHITETHROAT
dark tertials edged **rufous**; centres **rounded**
primary projection **long**
dark centres to rufous coverts
1ST-WINTER
JUL–MAR
[Sep]

MOLTONI'S SUBALPINE WARBLER
dark tertials edged **tawny-brown**
no rufous patch
JUVENILE → 1ST-WINTER
JUN–APR [Sep]

SPECTACLED WARBLER
dark tertials edged **rufous**; centres **pointed**
primary projection **short**
JUVENILE
JUN–SEP [Jun]
little or no dark on centres of coverts

RARE WARBLERS

Orphean warblers

The two orphean warblers from Iberia/S Europe have both occurred in Britain. They are very similar and best told by details of the tail pattern and undertail coverts. MALE like large, grey, stout-legged Blackcap (p. 434) but dark cap extends below eye onto cheek; **whitish eye**; white throat, pinkish-white underparts. 1ST-YEAR and 2ND-YEAR MALES have paler ear coverts (like a large Lesser Whitethroat (p. 437) with a stouter, pale-based bill and a longer, wider tail); eyes grey-brown to dirty whitish. FEMALE crown grey, ear coverts blackish-grey (paler than on male); upperparts grey-brown (less pure grey than male). JUVENILE crown and cheek all greyish, upperparts grey-brown; eye dark brown. 1ST-WINTER like juvenile but has some greyer adult-type wing coverts.

EASTERN ORPHEAN WARBLER
1ST-WINTER [Jul]

in both species all plumages have a diffuse dark hood rather than a sharp cap

showing the diagnostic undertail markings and tail pattern of that species

♂ **WESTERN ORPHEAN WARBLER**

plumages for both species similar at all comparable ages/sexes

JUVENILE JUN–AUG [Jul]

Western Orphean Warbler
Sylvia hortensis
L 15 cm | W 25 cm

See above for general plumage descriptions. Very similar to Eastern Orphean Warbler at all ages but **undertail coverts pale and unmarked** and outermost tail feather has long, **thin white streak**.

VOICE Dry, churred "*trr-trr-t*" and "*tak.*"

Vagrant from S Europe: <5 records (Britain), May, Sep–Dec. On coast. Trees, bushes.

1ST-WINTER AUG–OCT [Nov]

plain under tail

WESTERN OUTERMOST TAIL FEATHER (T6) **long white streak** T6

EASTERN OUTERMOST TAIL FEATHER (T6) **broad white patch** T6

Eastern Orphean Warbler
Sylvia crassirostris
L 15 cm | W 25 cm

See above for general plumage descriptions. Very similar to Western Orphean Warbler at all ages but **undertail coverts marked with grey chevrons** and outermost tail feather has **short, broad white patch** and next three feathers have small white tips.

VOICE Hard "*tak.*"

Vagrant from SE Europe: 1 record (Britain), Oct. On coast. Trees, bushes.

grey chevrons under tail

1ST-WINTER AUG–MAR [Jul]

See also warbler introduction pp. 422–423

SYLVIA

Sardinian Warbler
Sylvia melanocephala
L 13–14 cm | W 18–22 cm

Small, long-tailed warbler that tends to keep low; male easily identified, female and immatures confusing. Compare subalpine warblers (*p. 454*) and Whitethroat (*p. 436*). Tail long, slender, **blackish with white sides** (white 'corners' or spotted rim in low, fast flight to next bush). MALE grey, with **blackish hood** extending over cheek, white throat and **red eyering**. FEMALE drab, browner: **hood grey**, red eyering paler, throat greyish. 1ST-WINTER even browner; white throat against dark underparts (see Rüppell's Warbler).

VOICE Loud, hard "*tsek*" and distinctive longer, grating rattle, varying in pitch and pace, "*tuet-et-et-et-et-et-et-et*."

Vagrant from S Europe: <100 records (<5 Ireland), most months, mainly Apr–Jun. Mostly on coast. Low scrub, thickets.

All plumages have striking white throat and a red eyering

ADULT / 1ST-WINTER ♀ [Dec]

head dull brownish (darker and greyer on 1ST-WINTER MALE)

1ST-WINTER ♀ AUG–MAR [Nov]

ADULT ♂ [Dec]

Rüppell's Warbler
Sylvia ruppeli   553
L 14 cm | W 23–25 cm

Small **grey** warbler with slightly downcurved bill. MALE **black cap/lores and throat, white 'moustache'**; red eye. FEMALE/1ST-WINTER pale throat but whiter 'moustache' stands out; pale blue-grey bill; dark tail with white sides; **well-defined pale edges to wing coverts** and tertials. See subalpine (*p. 454*) and Sardinian Warblers.

VOICE Call a dry, fast chatter. Song slower, deeper rattle than Sardinian Warbler.

Vagrant from SE Europe: <10 records (Britain), Jun, Aug–Oct. On coast. Dense scrub.

plain grey head, white 'moustache', whitish throat

♀

grey underparts

♂

1ST-SUMMER MALE has dull eye/eyering

457

SHRIKES

SHRIKE ID | head pattern | crown/back/rump colour | wing details | upper/undertail colour

Shrikes are roughly the same size or smaller than common thrushes (pp. 390–395), much smaller than any bird of prey (pp. 302–335). They perch quite upright and have a round head, short wings and long tail; their bill is thick and very slightly hooked. In flight, they look round-winged and long-tailed; may hover momentarily (Great Grey Shrike sometimes for 30–40 seconds or more).

9 species: 1 regular migrant (and rare breeder); 1 regular migrant/winter visitor; 7 rare or very rare vagrants.

Shrikes are charismatic yet perch quietly doing nothing for long spells and can be very elusive. When they do feed, they behave like birds of prey, dropping to the ground for an insect, reptile or vole, or chasing small birds. They impale prey on thorns, both as a 'larder' and to help dismember larger items.

Red-backed Shrike used to breed but is now a scarce migrant: spring males are striking and obvious but females and immature birds are rufous-brown and must be told both from small thrushes and other, rarer shrikes.

Great Grey Shrike is an autumn migrant and winter visitor on heaths and open land with bushes or tall trees. A distant 'whitish spot' on a bush top is worth checking: nothing else shares the pale grey, black and soft greyish-white pattern, including a typical shrike 'mask', except for the exceedingly rare Lesser Grey Shrike, a vagrant in summer. Woodchat Shrike is the most frequent of the rare shrikes: usually spring adults, black-and-white with a distinctive rufous cap; like all shrikes they tend to perch upright on bush tops or wires, keeping still, often elusive but very obvious once found.

GREAT GREY SHRIKE

Shrike ageing/sexing

Some species of shrike have markedly different male and female plumages, others not; juveniles become difficult to distinguish from adult females.

Red-backed Shrike
JUVENILE — JUVENILE [Aug]
Redder than adult female, with dark crescentic marks on crown and upperpart feathers, extensive barring beneath. Feathers almost new, fresh and neat. Will moult body feathers, variable number of coverts Aug–Sep, and complete moult from Nov/Jan–Mar/Apr.

ADULT FEMALE BREEDING — ADULT ♀ [Jul]
Unmarked back but streaky marks on forehead and crown, hint of dark 'mask'; fine crescentic bars on breast and flank. All plumage shows signs of wear, with loose, wispy or coarse, abraded tips to feathers several months old. Will moult body and some covert feathers, and variable number of tail, secondary and primary feathers, Jul–Sep, then complete moult from Nov/Jan–Mar/Apr.

ADULT MALE BREEDING — ADULT ♂ [May]
Clear blue-grey head, black 'mask', rufous back, black-and-white tail. Plumage quite fresh, signs of wear on fringes of some wing feathers.

Great Grey Shrike
Ageing is less straightforward. **ADULT** has complete moult Jul–Nov and some body feathers also replaced Mar–May. **JUVENILE** moults body and some covert feathers, and variable number of tail and wing feathers, Jul–Nov, and some body and tail feathers through to May before complete moult Jul–Nov. **1ST-WINTER** therefore has some outer greater coverts (diffusely tipped buff) and primary coverts dull brownish, but fresh black median and inner greater coverts; **ADULT** has these coverts all fresh, strong black, some greater coverts with clear white fringe.

SHRIKES

Great Grey Shrike *Lanius excubitor*

L 21–26 cm | W 30–34 cm

Lesser Grey Shrike (p. 464)

Large (about Blackbird-sized (*p. 391*)) shrike; **pale grey, white and black**. Often perched in open on bush-top, tree or overhead wire – a 'white blob' at long range (see *opposite*), but can be very unobtrusive. Long, slim tail (spread, tilted or twisted for balance), rather large head, very short primary projection and stout, slightly hooked bill.

ADULT **very pale grey**; black 'mask' (with thin white line above); **black-and-white wings and tail**. Whitish patch above closed wing obvious or part-hidden. FEMALE slightly duller than MALE: greyer below, very faint bars. JUVENILE has pale grey crown and back; whitish underparts with faint bars; bill dark grey, pinkish at base.

VOICE Short harsh calls; sometimes low, rambling subsong.

IN FLIGHT, striking, **long white band** across outerwing, sometimes extending inwards, white sides to tail. Bounding flight, **sweeping up to perch**; if repeatedly disturbed will move far away in long, high, swooping flight.

Scarce autumn migrant, winter visitor (150–300 per year). Vagrant Ireland (<50 records)

from Scandinavia

from Europe

Heaths, forest edge, bushy areas

ssp. *excubitor*

crown plain

1ST-WINTER
ssp. *excubitor*
SEP–NOV
[Nov]

sits on open perches: at a distance an obvious pale 'blob' with black band across middle

1ST-WINTER
SEP–NOV
[Nov]

underparts faintly barred

ADULT
ssp. *excubitor*

'STEPPE GREY SHRIKE'
ssp. *pallidirostris* (vagrant from Asia: <25 records (Britain), Apr, Jun, Sep–Dec) – sometimes treated as a separate species – is very pale, and has **paler bill, weaker 'mask', more extensive white primary patch** and **longer wingtip** than regular ssp. *excubitor*.

SHRIKES 'Brown' shrikes compared p.462

Red-backed Shrike *Lanius collurio*

L 16–18 cm | W 24–27 cm

👁 Rare shrikes (pp. 461–464)

Small, delicate shrike: male unmistakable, other plumages may lead to confusion with rarer shrikes. Has typical shrike's broad, rounded head and thick, hook-tipped bill; strong feet; upright stance. Long, slim tail often spread, sometimes flaunted with a sideways twist. Perches on exposed twigs but can be inconspicuous on side of bush/hedge, where easily overlooked.

MALE **blue-grey head** with prominent black 'mask'; reddish back; white throat, pale pink breast. **White sides to base of black tail**; grey rump. FEMALE upperpart/underpart contrast strong: rufous back, dark cheek; grey crown, nape and rump; whitish underparts with dark 'scaly' bars. JUVENILE/1ST-WINTER (see *pp. 462–463*) reddish with dark barring above; greyer crown and nape; plain greyish rump. Pale between bill and large, dark eye; **dark cheek** contrasts with pale throat. Tail dull to rufous-brown, grey beneath. Underparts cold whitish with dark flank bars.

VOICE Short, harsh notes.

Scarce migrant from Europe, Apr–Oct; very rare summer visitor (irregular breeder, <5 pairs); <200 records Ireland. Winters in Africa.

from Scandinavia and Europe

to E and S Africa

Bushy heaths, scrubby areas

IN FLIGHT, thrush-like, but long, straight wings; pale grey rump; dark tail. MALE has black tail with white side panels at base.

greyish crown
dark cheek
barred back
ADULT ♂
barred flank
grey crown
dark cheek
ADULT ♀
1ST-WINTER SEP–MAR [Sep]
NOTE: rarely, ADULT ♀ shows a small white primary patch.
rufous back
ADULT ♀
upright, large-headed, slim-tailed
black 'mask'
pink breast
ADULT ♂

RARE SHRIKES

Woodchat Shrike *Lanius senator*
L 17–19 cm | W 25–27 cm

👁 Masked Shrike (p. 464)

Smallish, **black-and-white** shrike with **rufous cap**. Stocky and relatively short-tailed; often perches on wire or bush top. Most records are of C/S European ssp. *senator*.

MALE black 'mask'; rufous cap and nape; black back. FEMALE similar to male but black 'mask' interrupted by whitish marks; paler cap. Both sexes have **white oval each side of back** and broad white patch at base of primaries (absent on vagrant W Mediterranean island ssp. *badius*). JUVENILE/1ST-WINTER 'cold' greyish above with **barred, whitish rump** (plain grey-brown on Red-backed Shrike); line of **whitish feathers**, each with black crescent, along 'shoulder' (rufous with darker centres on Red-backed Shrike).

Rare migrant from Europe: >1,000 records, 20–35 per year (<120 records Ireland), mostly Apr–Jun. Open bushy areas. Winters in Africa.

IN FLIGHT, white in wings and on rump **striking pied effect**.

1ST-SUMMER ssp. *senator*

ADULT ♀ ssp. *senator* — 'scruffy' black 'mask'; greyer back than male

1ST-SUMMER ♂ [Sep] ssp. *senator* — blacker back than female

1ST-SUMMER ♀ [Apr] ssp. *senator*

ADULT ♂ ssp. *senator* — 'clean' black 'mask'; black back

brownish back

JUVENILE JUN–AUG [Jul] ssp. *senator* — 'cold', greyish, 'scaly'; white along 'shoulder'

ADULT ♂ — W Mediterranean island ssp. *badius* (spring vagrant, <20 records (<5 Ireland), Apr–Jul) lacks white patch on primaries.

461

RARE SHRIKES

'Brown' shrikes

One species, Red-backed Shrike (p. 460), is scarce but regular; three are very rare, two of which, Daurian and Turkestan Shrikes, are extremely similar (formerly treated as the same species): start by ruling out female/immature Red-backed Shrike, then check subtle structural and plumage features.

Adult 'brown' shrikes – summary of key features	
Red-backed Shrike (p. 460)	MALE: unmistakable. FEMALE: rufous, darker 'mask', grey head and rump; no white primary patch. VISIBLE PRIMARY TIPS: 7–8
Daurian Shrike	Greyish-sandy, little contrast; weak buff stripe over eye; rufous tail; white primary patch small/absent. VIS. PR. TIPS: 6–7
Turkestan Shrike	Sandy-brown, paler below; white stripe over eye; rufous tail; prominent white primary patch. VISIBLE PRIMARY TIPS: 6–7
Brown Shrike	Brown and buff; greyish stripe over eye; rusty rump, darker tail; no white primary patch. VISIBLE PRIMARY TIPS: 5–6

Daurian (Isabelline) Shrike
Lanius isabellinus
L 16·5–18 cm | W 26–28 cm

Very similar to Turkestan Shrike but more uniformly pale; **tail rufous above and below**. MALE greyish above, buff below; buff stripe over black 'mask'; small white primary patch. FEMALE sandy-grey; weak buffish stripe over eye; rump rusty. Small white primary patch (sometimes absent). JUVENILE/1ST-WINTER **sandy-buff above and below**; crown faintly scaled; **no strong 'mask'**; rump rusty; wing feathers edged buff. Underparts buff-white with ginger scaling.

Vagrant form Asia: <100 records (<10 Ireland), Mar–Nov, most Aug–Oct. Mostly coastal. Scrubby areas.

buffish stripe above eye obscure over bill

ADULT (presumed ♂) [Oct]

ADULT ♀

ADULT ♀

Turkestan (Red-tailed) Shrike
Lanius phoenicuroides
L 16·5–18 cm | W 26–28 cm

Very similar to Daurian Shrike, with same **rusty rump and tail**; **darker upperparts** contrast more with **whiter underparts**. more **rufous crown**, nape and rump. ADULT clear **white stripe** over black 'mask' (duller on FEMALE). White primary patch. JUVENILE/1ST-WINTER brown above, **whiter below**; **crown more rufous than back**, **blackish 'mask'**; rump rusty; wing feathers edged white; underparts buff-white with brown scaling.

Vagrant from Asia: <10 records (Britain) May, Aug–Oct. Mostly coastal. Scrubby areas.

ADULT ♀

clear white stripe above eye continues over bill

ADULT ♂

'BROWN' SHRIKES

Juvenile / 1st-winter 'brown' shrikes

Autumn migrant shrikes can be very difficult and require careful study: focus on the overall structure (see *opposite*), and colours and patterning (see *below*).

Juvenile / 1st-winter 'brown' shrikes – summary of plumage features	
Red-backed Shrike (p. 460)	Most likely. HEAD: barred; greyish; dark 'mask'. TAIL: brown/rufous above, greyish beneath. UPPERPARTS: rusty, barred; greyish nape and rump. UNDERPARTS: whitish; crescentic bars.
Daurian Shrike	HEAD: buffish over eye; no strong 'mask'. TAIL: rufous above and below. UPPERPARTS: pale as underparts; nape as back, rump rusty. UNDERPARTS: buff, pale ginger scaling.
Turkestan Shrike	HEAD: whitish over eye; dark 'mask'. TAIL: rufous above and below. UPPERPARTS: darker than underparts; nape/rump rufous. UNDERPARTS: buff-white with brown scaling.
Brown Shrike	HEAD: brown crown; strong 'mask'. TAIL: long, dark rufous-brown. UPPERPARTS: darker warm brown than underparts. UNDERPARTS: buff, finely barred brown.

RED-BACKED SHRIKE 1ST-WINTER
7–8 primary tips show
7 tips showing on this bird

DAURIAN SHRIKE 1ST-WINTER SEP–MAR [Oct]

TURKESTAN SHRIKE 1ST-WINTER SEP–MAR [Oct]

BROWN SHRIKE 1ST-WINTER SEP–MAR [Dec]

Brown Shrike *Lanius cristatus*
L 18–20 cm | W 25–28 cm

Resembles female Red-backed (p. 460), Daurian and Turkestan Shrikes but has larger head, **thicker bill**, **shorter primary projection** (see *inset*) and **longer, graduated tail**. MALE rich brown above, buff below, throat whiter; black 'mask'. FEMALE / 1ST-WINTER uniformly **warm brown from crown to rump**; **strong grey/black 'mask'**; wing feathers edged dull brown. Underparts buff, barred brown.

short wings: only 5–6 primary tips show (6–8 on other 'brown' shrikes)

ADULT ♂

Vagrant from Asia: <30 records (1 Ireland), May, Sep–Jan. Mostly on coast. Scrubby areas, heaths.

RARE SHRIKES

Lesser Grey Shrike   551
Lanius minor
L 19–21 cm | W 28–30 cm

Medium-sized 'grey, black and white' shrike. Compared with Great Grey Shrike (*p. 459*): slightly stockier, more bull-necked and thicker-billed; wing long, more pointed with **longer primary projection**; often sits bolt-upright. MALE grey above, white flushed pink below, white throat. Black 'mask' extends as **broad band across forehead**. FEMALE 'mask' brownish-black, underparts dull whitish. JUVENILE has pale edges to blackish wing feathers. Crown and back pale grey with faint barring; underparts plain; no forehead band; weak blackish 'mask'; bill paler than Great Grey Shrike.

> Vagrant from SE Europe: <200 records (<10 Ireland), Jun–Oct. Mostly on coast. Open scrubby areas.

IN FLIGHT, broad white wing patch and tail sides.
forehead grey
crown and back faintly barred
JUVENILE JUN–AUG [Jul]
ADULT
black 'blob' on face at distance
ADULT ♂

Long-tailed Shrike
Lanius schach
L 22–27 cm | W 25–26 cm

Large shrike with strikingly **long tail**. Grey crown/back, **brown rump**, black 'mask', white throat and **deep buff underparts**.

> Vagrant from Asia: 1 record (Britain), Nov. On coast. Scrub.

1ST-WINTER AUG–MAR [Jan]

Masked Shrike
Lanius nubicus
L 17–18 cm | W 18–20 cm

Slender shrike with long, narrow tail. ADULT (not recorded) black-and-white with orange-buff flank. JUVENILE like juvenile Woodchat Shrike (*p. 461*) but darker, with blacker 'mask', **whiter 'shoulder' patch** and **slimmer, blacker tail with white edges**.

> Vagrant from SE Europe: <5 records (Britain), Sep–Nov. On coast. Scrub.

♀

JUVENILE JUN–NOV [Nov]

TITS, NUTHATCHES and 'CREEPERS'

TIT ID   overall plumage | head pattern | call and song

Tits are small, rather bulky-bodied and short-winged with a rounded head and small, slightly bulbous, bluntly triangular bill (sharper on Bearded and Penduline Tits). They are sociable, often in loose, mixed flocks when not breeding.

6 tits: all resident, 3 common, 2 declining, 1 Scotland only
Long-tailed Tit, Bearded Tit (both resident) and **Penduline Tit** (vagrant) are similar in form but unrelated to the tit family, each belonging to their own individual family.

Tits (pp. 468–473) are either green, blue-and-yellow, or drab brownish with black on the head. They have a bolder, more stop-start or leaping progress through trees or across spaces than most warblers, pausing to explore, often hanging from slender twigs. Calls are strident, whistling, or buzzing, with many high, thin, contact notes. Marsh and Willow Tits are a very difficult pair to identify: calls and songs are invaluable. Both seem destined to disappear from most of Britain quite soon. Crested Tit is restricted to pine woods in northern Scotland: best discovered by purring calls.
Long-tailed Tit (p. 467) is not closely related, but has a basic tit-like form, with a very long, slim tail; social, vocal and easy to see.
Bearded Tit (or Bearded Reedling) (p. 466) is also an unrelated bird of reedbeds and fen vegetation, discovered by its calls and usually seen flitting over the reed tops.
Penduline Tit (p. 477) favours poplars and willows in summer, reedbeds and areas of reedmace in winter.

Tit ageing/sexing
Sexes differ slightly (males brighter) or look identical; juveniles are duller and in some species can be separated through their first winter.

JUVENILE
BLUE TIT
LONG-TAILED TIT
BEARDED TIT
PENDULINE TIT

NUTHATCH and 'CREEPER' ID   overall plumage | wing pattern | call and song

Much smaller than woodpeckers and unlikely to be confused although they spend their lives creeping about on tree branches and climbing tree trunks (Wallcreeper on rock faces).
2 nuthatches: 1 resident; 1 vagrant
3 'creepers': **2 treecreepers**: 1 resident; 1 vagrant, and the unrelated **Wallcreeper** (vagrant – p. 477)

The **Nuthatch** (p. 474) is distinctive in the UK: small, stout, short-tailed, spike-billed and strongly patterned. It climbs up and down with equal ease, without using its tail, relying on the strength of its feet and claws. It is noisy, especially in spring.
Treecreepers (pp. 475–476) include two nearly identical species, only one at all likely to be seen: Treecreeper is common and widespread; Short-toed Treecreeper very rare. They use the tail for support as they creep upwards or spiral around branches (rarely rocks or walls): they can hang beneath, but rarely descend head first as do nuthatches. They come to the ground much less often, and cannot properly walk or hop.

NUTHATCH
TREECREEPER

TITS, NUTHATCHES and TREECREEPERS

Bearded Tit (Bearded Reedling) *Panurus biarmicus*

L 14–15·5 cm | W 16–18 cm   Penduline Tit (*p. 477*)

Scarce, local resident (550–600 pairs) and winter dispersal; <200 records Ireland

Small, elongated, **long-tailed** 'tit', generally found in **reeds** and reedmace (not closely related to other tits). Often a succession of calls and rustling, but hard to see. Acrobatic among stems; feeds on ground beneath, with double-footed shuffle.

Bright tawny with **black and cream wing streaks** and short, triangular, bright golden-orange bill. MALE striking, with narrow-crowned **blue-grey head** and long, pointed, **black 'moustache'**. Black patch under tail. FEMALE has plain head, pale undertail; **long brown tail has narrow white sides**. JUVENILE blackish on back, black streaks on outertail; MALE has a yellow bill and black stripe to pale eye, FEMALE has a dark bill and faint eye patch.

VOICE Calls are very distinctive, quite loud, metallic, pinging "*ching*" or "*p-chink*."

May fly short distance low over reeds, whirring flight before diving out of sight.

Reedbeds; more widespread in some winters, in varied wetlands

dark bill; faint eye patch

yellow bill; dark eye patch

JUVENILE ♀
MAY–AUG

JUVENILE ♂
MAY–AUG

ADULT ♂

ADULT ♀

Long-tailed Tit *Aegithalos caudatus*

ssp. *rosaceus*

L 13–15 cm | W 16–19 cm

Unmistakable: tiny, acrobatic 'tit' with a **long, slim tail** (despite its name, not closely related to other tits). Often flies single-file across spaces on round, audibly whirring wings, revealing flocks of 10–20 or so. Often in mixed flocks with tits, Goldcrests (*p. 424*) and other birds.

ADULT black and dull pinkish-white. **Black stripes** beside crown blend into dark back; **pink 'shoulder'**; pinkish underparts; white-sided black tail. JUVENILE duller, lacking pink and with brown face.

VOICE High, thin, unemphatic "*see-see-see*" or "*si-si-si*" (quicker, less 'body' than Goldcrest); distinctive short, abrupt "*brr-p*" mixed with dry, trilled "*ts-rreet*" and metallic "*pit*."

Fairly common resident (330,000 pairs, plus 115,000 birds in Ireland)

Woodland, hedgerows, thickets, large gardens

In recent years, Long-tailed Tits have become more frequent at feeders and seed put out for garden birds.

once the first autumn moult is completed, young birds are indistinguishable from adults

JUVENILE MAY–AUG

Northern ssp. *caudatus*

ADULT

Northern ssp. *caudatus* (rare migrant/vagrant from N Europe, Oct–Mar) has pure white head; strikingly different from resident **British/Irish ssp. *rosaceus***, but status confused by intermediate birds.

British/Irish ssp. *rosaceus*

ADULT

No other small bird in a tree has such a long tail, but beware winter roosts of Pied Wagtails (*p. 372*) in urban treetops.

TITS, NUTHATCHES and TREECREEPERS

Blue Tit *Cyanistes (Parus) caeruleus*

ssp. *obscurus*

Common, widespread resident (3·3 million pairs, plus 2·2 million birds in Ireland)

L 10·5–12 cm | W 17–18 cm

Tiny, chunky tit; an acrobatic feeder in high canopy and often on feeders. Leaps through foliage and hangs down from its perch more than warblers, its strong grip allowing it to rest at any angle; frequent jerky wing flicks. Flight fast, direct, 'stops dead' on perch. Often in mixed flocks. Barrel-bodied, pale; 'green' or 'yellow' with white face, depending on view.

ADULT pale blue wings and tail; often dull but more vivid in spring MALE; some FEMALES faintly greener. MALE **blue cap inside white band**, white face, black chin obvious marks. Smaller, paler than Great Tit and underparts with slight streak down centre (not bold black band); **tail blue** without white sides. JUVENILE greener, with greenish cap; yellow cheek and throat. 1ST-WINTER like adult after Sep, but retains some duller juvenile wing coverts.

VOICE High, sharp "*si-si-si*," frequent rhythmic "*sisi-du*" or "*tzisi-di-di-di*." Song slurred, trilled "*see-see-si-surrrrr*."

Woodland, gardens, scrub, hedgerows, reedbeds

Continental ssp. *caeruleus* (winter visitor [*not illustrated*]) differs so slightly (*e.g.* 10% shorter wing length) that it cannot be reliably distinguished in the field from the sedentary **British/Irish ssp. *obscurus*.**

NOTE: all birds shown are **British/Irish ssp. *obscurus*.**

pale above eye

ADULT

JUVENILE
MAY–JUL

weak dark line on breast

blue cap

white forehead

blue tail

dark eyestripe

ADULT

468

Great Tit *Parus major*

ssp. *newtoni*

L 13·5–15 cm | W 18–20 cm

Common, widespread resident (2 million pairs plus 1·3 million birds in Ireland); winter visitor

Bulky tit, larger, longer-looking, more boldly patterned than Blue or Coal Tit (p. 471). Acrobatic feeder, but also moves through low vegetation, probes under bark, and feeds on the ground.

Black head with oval **white cheek** distinctive (but see Coal Tit). ADULT pale yellow or buffish-yellow beneath. Green above with bluer wings and white wingbar. **Black stripe down centre of belly** (tapers on FEMALE, widens between legs on MALE). **White sides to tail** (unlike Blue Tit). JUVENILE pale, dull; cap greenish-black, cheek greenish-yellow. 1ST-WINTER like adult after Sep, but retains some duller juvenile wing coverts.

VOICE Very varied, many strident, off-key notes: "*pink*" or "*chink*" (like Chaffinch (p. 494)), "*pink-a-tchee tchee*;" "*tsweet*" or "*tsi-uti-uti*." Song loud, see-sawing two- or three-note, whistle, "*tsee-tsoo tsee-tsoo tsee-tsoo*" or "*tchee-tchu*" or "*tchi-too-tcha*." Taps bill loudly.

Woodland, gardens

Partially melanistic birds with black cheek are occasionally seen, particularly in the home counties.

Continental ssp. *major*

Continental ssp. *major* tends to have a smaller bill, yellower back and duller underparts than resident **British/Irish ssp. *newtoni***, but features variable and most individuals cannot be assigned to ssp.

ADULT ♀

NOTE: all birds below are British/Irish ssp. *newtoni*.

FEMALE: black narrows towards legs

green-black cap, yellow cheek

ADULT ♂

black forehead

white cheek

white sides to tail

MALE: black widens between legs

JUVENILE MAY–JUL

TITS, NUTHATCHES and TREECREEPERS

Crested Tit *Lophophanes (Parus) cristatus*

ssp. *scoticus*

L 10·5–12 cm | W 17–20 cm

Tiny, buff-brown tit; has no bright colours but a **striking head shape**. Listen/look in Scottish pine forests/plantations – found nowhere else.

Superficially similar to Marsh Tit (*p. 472*), but has sharp-**pointed crest** (barred black and white), black eyestripe extending around cheek and black throat continuing as collar. ADULT MALE has slightly longer crest and broader head stripes than ADULT FEMALE. JUVENILE slightly browner on head, crest blunt.

VOICE Useful clue to presence: a thin, trilling, rolling or purring note with a distinct rhythm: "*p'trrr-up*" or "*burrur-ur-eet.*" Also high, thin "*seeet*" call notes.

Scarce and local resident, N Scotland (1,500 pairs)

Pine forests

Northern European ssp. *cristatus*

Central European ssp. *mitratus*

Central European **ssp.** *mitratus* (similar to **ssp.** *scoticus*), and **northern European ssp.** *cristatus* (paler, more 'grey-and-white') both recorded in 19th century, very rarely since (<10 records), but frequent intergrades make identification in isolation unsafe.

British ssp. *scoticus*

In Britain, restricted to native Scots Pine and plantations in Scotland.

cheek pattern and collar as distinctive as upstanding crest

British ssp. *scoticus*

Coal Tit *Periparus (Parus) ater*

L 10–11·5 cm | W 17–21 cm

ssp. *britannicus*

Tiny tit, close to Goldcrest (*p. 424*) in size. **No bright yellow, blue or green**, but adults fade to drab greenish after breeding and juvenile yellowish below and on cheek. Favours conifers but also feeds on the ground. Acrobatic, often in mixed flocks. Visits feeders but takes food away to eat nearby or hide in cache.

ADULT large black head with prominent **white cheek**; unique **clear-cut white patch on back of head**; extensive black chin; **buff underparts** without central streak. Back olive-grey; **two white bars** across wing; plain tail. JUVENILE has smaller bib and dull crown, and is dull greenish-yellow on nape, cheek and underparts. 1ST-WINTER has mixed old brownish juvenile and new bluish-grey adult-type greater coverts.

VOICE Sharp "*tsooo*" or "*tsee*" and melancholy variations; short, sharp, hard 'spitting' note. Song resembles Great Tit (*p. 469*) in emphatic two-note rhythm, but simpler, sharper, less strident "*see-too see-too.*"

Common, widespread resident (600,000 pairs, plus 925,000 birds in Ireland); migrant, winter visitor

Woodland with some pine/spruce/Larch, scrub, thickets

yellowish tinge to cheek

Irish ssp. *hibernicus*

Irish ssp. *hibernicus* (vagrant in Britain) slightly browner; yellower on cheeks and underparts than British ssp. *britannicus*.

White nape may be hidden in side view, but will quickly be seen as bird is constantly on the move.

bluish-grey above

ssp. *ater*

Continental ssp. *ater*

tiny crest

Continental ssp. *ater* (regular migrant from continental Europe) – tiny crest on nape; bluish-grey on back and wings; uniformly pale underparts.

olive above, flank darker than belly

British ssp. *britannicus*

NOTE: 1ST-WINTER IS like ADULT but retains some duller JUVENILE wing coverts

TITS, NUTHATCHES and TREECREEPERS

Marsh Tit *Poecile (Parus) palustris*

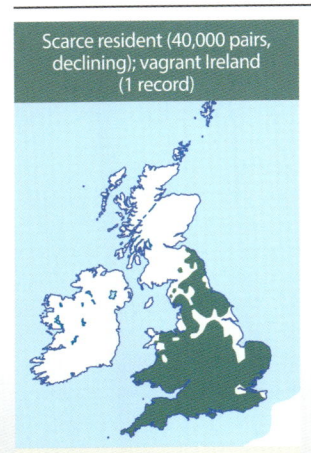

Scarce resident (40,000 pairs, declining); vagrant Ireland (1 record)

Mature woodland and associated secondary growth, hedgerows, old gardens; comes to feeders

L 11·5–13 cm | W 18–19·5 cm

Small, brown, **black-capped** tit; no green, blue or yellow. Very like Willow Tit; identification requires care but **call** invaluable. (See also Blackcap (*p. 434*), which lacks a black bib.)

Slightly colder and duller overall than Willow Tit. ADULT compared with Willow Tit has smaller, more clearly defined white cheek against grey-brown neck; often (not always) a glossier black cap and smaller, squarer black bib. Underparts often plainer without strong buff flank (but much overlap); usually **plainer wing** with weak lengthwise panel (but some individuals are well marked). Bill usually has **pale patch at base of upper mandible** (usually absent on Willow Tit). JUVENILE has duller, greyer cap. A combination of features plus call is ideally needed to confirm identification.

VOICE Bright, cheery, whistled "*pit-chew!*" is the best instant clue and rules out Willow Tit. Various thin "*si-si*" notes, quick, easy, lightweight "*tsi-tsi-dee-dee-dee*" (clearly related but lacking harsh nasal quality of Willow Tit). Song simple, flat, even rattle, "*chi-ip-ip-ip-ip*" or more ringing "*witawitawitawitawita*".

Marsh/Willow Tit calls compared
MARSH TIT – Whistled "***pit-chew***;" light "***tsi-tsi dee dee dee***"
WILLOW TIT – Deep, buzzy "***tsi-tsi chair chair chair***"

BLACKCAP ♂ (*p. 434*) – possible confusion species – note grey cheek and nape, smaller black cap, pale in front of eye and no bib

Willow Tit *Poecile (Parus) montana*

Rare resident (3,500 pairs, rapid decline); absent from Ireland

L 12–13 cm | W 17–20·5 cm

Small, grey-brown and buff tit with **black cap** and **distinctive calls**. See Marsh Tit: requires careful study to confirm identification as most features overlap. Increasingly scarce and hard to find.

ADULT dull brown, buffish below. Compared with Marsh Tit, more often has a dull black cap; often wider inverted-'V'-shaped black chin (but much overlap); thick-necked. Invariably has buff flank, but some birds are **rusty-buff** (unlike Marsh Tit). Whitish cheek blends to buff before greyish 'shoulder'. Wing more often has distinct **pale panel** lengthwise along middle. Bill all-dark. JUVENILE has paler, greyer cap

VOICE Deep, buzzy "*tsi-tsi chair chair chair*;" basic "*tchairr*" note more buzzing, nasal than lighter notes of Marsh Tit and **never** gives bright, clear "*pit-chew*" call of Marsh Tit. Short, sharp "*tsi tsi*." Song "*tsew-tsew-tsew*" (like call of Wood Warbler (*p. 433*)) or rare brief, melodic, rich warble.

Woodlands, willow/Alder scrub, old hedgerows, woodland edges; comes to feeders

MARSH TIT
- Less 'bull-necked'
- cap often glossy
- most have pale patch at base of bill
- black bib often 'neater'

Northern European ssp. *borealis*

Northern European ssp. *borealis* (rare vagrant from N Europe, Oct–Mar) is relatively distinctive: whiter than resident **British ssp.** *kleinschmidti*.

- bill all-dark on most
- **British ssp.** *kleinschmidti*
- some individuals have rusty-buff flank

TITS, NUTHATCHES and TREECREEPERS

Nuthatch *Sitta europaea*

L 12–14·5 cm | W 22·5–27 cm

👁 Red-breasted Nuthatch (p.477)

Fairly common resident (220,000 pairs). Absent from Ireland.

Distinctive small, short-tailed bird associated with trees. Alert, bouncy, agile, climbing up and down trunks, often hanging upside down; sometimes explores stone walls, roofs and gutters, and occasionally feeds on the ground.

Unique pale **blue-grey** above, buff below with **bold black eyestripe** and rusty flank. Wedge-shaped head and bill. **Tail short and square**, with black-and-white 'corners'. MALE chestnut flank and undertail. FEMALE buff flank and undertail. JUVENILE duller, less blue than adult, bill shorter at first. IN FLIGHT, usually over clearings, flitting and flying straight with no agility and showing a markedly spike-billed/heavy bodied/short tailed profile.

VOICE Distinctive (from treetop to ground level): loud, clear, ringing or shouted whistles, often in fast series – "*ch'wit;*" "*hwit hwit hwit*" or tit-like "*sit.*" Song clear "*wheee wheee wheee.*"

Woodland/parkland; comes to feeders

distinctive flat, wedge-shaped profile with short, square tail

♂

chestnut flank and undertail

♀

buff flank and undertail

NUTHATCH | TREECREEPER

Treecreeper *Certhia familiaris*

L 12·5–14 cm | W 17·5–21 cm

◉ Short-toed Treecreeper (p. 476)

Common resident (200,000 pairs); N European ssp. rare vagrant (most N Isles, NE coasts; autumn)

Small, brown-backed 'creeper' with white underparts; **pressed to bark** or hanging from below branch. Occasionally forages on walls; rarely, briefly, on the ground (cannot properly walk). **Climbs (often spirals) upwards, using tail as support** even under branch.

Sexes and ages alike. Dark brown, **mottled buff** above with **whitish stripe over eye**; **spiky brown tail**; narrow **buff bar with blackish borders** across wing; small white tips to primaries. **White underparts**. IN FLIGHT, weak, undulating, hesitant; shows obvious broad **pale band along length of wing** both above and below.

VOICE Thin, long, faintly vibrant "*srreeee*." Song thin, high, quiet but far-carrying: a sweet free-flowing phrase with a flourish at the end (less rhythmic than Goldcrest (p. 424) and quieter, less rattling than Chaffinch (p. 494)).

Woodland

creeps jerkily up trunks and branches, but equally often clings underneath

British/Irish ssp. *britannica*

Northern European ssp. *familiaris*

Northern European ssp. *familiaris* (vagrant (but status confused by intergrades): N Isles, E coast, Oct–Mar), bright white beneath, copious white spots above, paler claws compared to resident **British/Irish ssp.** *britannica*.

RARE TITS, NUTHATCHES and 'CREEPERS'

Vagrant from Europe: <30 records (Britain), Sep–Apr. On coast. Woodland.

Short-toed Treecreeper 553
Certhia brachydactyla
L 13 cm | W 17·5–21 cm

Very hard to separate from Treecreeper (*p. 475*) without **calls or song**. Drabber, with whiter throat above dull, **off-white or buff underparts**.

VOICE Call strong, penetrating "*tsoot*;" song has **distinct pattern of individual notes**, staccato, without terminal flourish: "*tseet tseet, tseet-it-eeroit-it*" (some mimic Treecreeper too!).

Focus on the shape of the broad buff bar across the primaries, and Short-toed Treecreeper's larger pale primary tips (best determined from photographs).

Identification of treecreepers – summary of key features		
	Short-toed Treecreeper	Treecreeper (*p. 475*)
Stripe over eye	Dull, indistinct in front; **does not reach** forehead	Long, broad, whitish/white; **reaches** forehead
Forehead	Plain brown	Streaked white
Throat	White; contrasts with underparts	White; no contrast with underparts
Underparts	Grey/buff; FLANK more rufous	Silky-white; FLANK grey/buff
Primaries: rear edge of buff bar	**sharp points or 'sawtooth' against black-brown**	**evenly stepped against black-brown**
Primary tips	White; large (see inset *below left*)	White; small (see inset *below right*)
Call	Strong, penetrating "**tsoot**"	Thin, long, faintly vibrant "**srreeee**"
Song	Distinct separate notes, without terminal flourish – "*tseet tseet, tseet-it eeroit-it*" (some mimic Treecreeper!)	Thin, high, quiet but far-carrying, sweet, free-flowing phrase with a flourish at the end

hind claw shorter on Short-toed Treecreeper (*left*)

TREECREEPER

RARE TITS and 'CREEPERS'

Red-breasted Nuthatch
Sitta canadensis
L 11 cm | W 19–21 cm

Shape and actions as Nuthatch (*p. 452*) but smaller. Grey above, bright buff below with **dark cap** and eyestripe and **bold white stripe over eye**.

> Vagrant from N America: 1 record (Britain), Oct–May. On coast. Pine woodland.

ADULT

Wallcreeper
Tichodroma muraria
L 16 cm | W 27–32 cm

Unique and unmistakable 'creeper', fluttering/climbing around cliffs and rocks; springy, bouncy action, flicks wings. Pale grey; **crimson on wings**; very short, square tail; thin bill. MALE extensive black throat in summer (narrow black line on FEMALE); throat white in winter.

IN FLIGHT, bounding, fluttering; very **broad, rounded wings**: **crimson on upperwing**; outerwing black with row of **round white spots**.

> Vagrant from C/S Europe: <15 records (Britain), May–Jun, Sep–Apr. Cliffs/quarries.

ADULT NON-BREEDING

Perches with wings tightly closed, but searches for food with frequent rhythmic in–out flicks of outerwing.

Penduline Tit
Remiz pendulinus
L 10–11.5 cm | W 16–17.5 cm

Small, acrobatic 'tit', with finely pointed bill and black legs (despite name, in different family to other tits). ADULT striking pattern: rusty-brown above, buff below, **pale grey head**, **broad black 'mask'**. Rusty band across wing usually distinct. JUVENILE buffier, with paler back, plain buff head; black eye in plain face; **rusty wing band**.

VOICE Call distinctive (beware thin, high Reed Bunting (*p. 516*) notes): long, downward "*tseeeee*."

> Vagrant from Europe: >300 records (Britain), most months, some overwinter. Most on coast. Reedbeds, reedmace.

A reedbed bird in winter, but found high in riverside willows/poplars in summer. The nest is a hanging pouch of willow/poplar down and cobwebs with a side-entrance 'porch'; has not bred in Britain but in 1990 a lone male built a nest.

ADULT ♀

ADULT ♂
resembles a tiny male Red-backed Shrike (*p. 460*)

JUVENILE MAY–NOV

CORVIDS (crows, Jay, Magpie and Nutcracker)

CORVID ID overall colour | wing and tail shape | size | calls

Large, strongly built, with short, arched bill, and feet that are strong but suited to perching rather than grasping prey.
9 species: 6 common residents, 2 less common; 1 rare/sporadic vagrant.

Crows (pp. 482–487) are 'black', with a colourful sheen in the right conditions. The largest is the Raven, nesting on cliff ledges or in trees, and which uniquely rolls over momentarily in flight. Size may not be obvious, so shape and calls help separate it, especially from the Rook, which is a consistently social bird, breeding in treetop colonies up to hundreds strong. Rook and Jackdaw feed, fly and roost together, sometimes in big, noisy flocks. Jackdaw is bold, noisy, inquisitive and an excellent flier. Carrion Crow is frequently more solitary, but scores gather on beaches and in fields. In the north, in Ireland and on the Isle of Man the Carrion Crow is replaced by the Hooded Crow, once a winter visitor in England but now rare. The Chough is 'finger-winged', square-tailed and glossy with a red bill and legs: a cliff bird of coasts and quarries or mineshafts, rare outside its breeding range. Choughs are wonderfully adept fliers, but Jackdaws and Rooks fly over coastal clifftops and may briefly cause confusion.

Corvid ageing/sexing
Sexes alike, no seasonal changes; juveniles generally duller but difficult to distinguish beyond first moult.

Jay (p. 480) is a boldly patterned but secretive woodland bird that draws attention by its calls and frequently flies overhead in autumn, often carrying acorns.
Magpie (p. 481) is black-and-white, glossy and long-tailed, not confusable with any other bird.
Nutcracker (p. 487) is a distinctive but rare vagrant, uniquely patterned with white streaks and drop-shaped spots.

JACKDAWS

ROOKS

Some corvid nests are easily visible – indeed the grouped nests of a rookery, the solitary nests of Carrion and Hooded Crows and a Magpie's domed treetop nest are part of the landscape.

Corvids in flight

Concentrate on size, tail shape, wingbeats and plumage contrasts.

RAVEN (p. 486)

CARRION CROW (p. 484)

HOODED CROW (p. 483)

JUVENILE

ROOK (p. 485)

CHOUGH (p. 487)

JACKDAW (p. 482)

NUTCRACKER (p. 487)

JAY (p. 480)

MAGPIE (p. 481)

CORVIDS

479

CORVIDS — Corvids in flight p.479

Jay *Garrulus glandarius*

sspp. *hibernicus* and *rufitergum*

L 32–35 cm | W 50 cm   ⓘ Hoopoe (p. 339)

Fairly common resident (160,000 pairs); irregular migrant

Medium-sized, wide-winged, strongly contrasted corvid of woodland and gardens. Obvious **large white rump** as it flies across road or clearing, often followed by another.

Pinkish, with greyer back, **black-and-white wings**, **white rump** and black tail. Streaked crown, **black 'moustache'**. Patch of **electric blue** on wing with dark bars. ADULT dark bars on blue wing patch evenly spaced. JUVENILE dark bars on blue wing patch spaced unevenly.

VOICE Subdued or loud 'mewing'; more frequent harsh screech of alarm or irritation, hoarse, tearing "*shraairk!*"

IN FLIGHT, quick, elusive in dense trees. Flies higher, with springy, elastic beats, between feeding woods and during regular autumn movements.

European ssp. *glandarius* ADULT
white rump
black tail
black-and-white wings

Woodland, parks

Irish ssp. *hibernicus* ADULT

Irish ssp. *hibernicus* (above) darker, more rufous back and cheek than **resident ssp. *rufitergum***.

Northern/central European ssp. *glandarius* (bird in flight *above*) is greyer; reaches Britain/Ireland in some years.

Scottish ssp. *caledonicus* also greyish: gradation between forms prevents firm identification.

black 'moustache'
grey-pink body
British ssp. *rufitergum* ADULT

Magpie *Pica pica*

L 40–51 cm (incl. tail 20–30 cm) | W 56–61 cm

Unmistakable, **long-tailed**, pied corvid: often in small groups, but also singly or in pairs; sometimes larger treetop gatherings.

ADULT head and breast dull black; wings glossed blue; **long tail** glossed green, blue and intense purple. **Large white 'shoulder' patch**, **white belly** and wingtip. JUVENILE has shorter tail but still cannot be mistaken for any other bird.

VOICE Loud, chattering, staccato "*cha-cha-cha*" and variations.

IN FLIGHT, can be overlooked when seen head-on and tail not obvious, but steady, quick beats and frequent steep, closed-winged dives to ground or perch characteristic.

spread wings reveal streaky white outer half

ADULT

Common resident (590,000 pairs, plus 750,000 birds in Ireland)

Widespread, woods, farmland, bushy areas, suburbs, parks

Frequent spring gatherings in bare treetops.

unique black and white pattern

long tail

ADULT

Jackdaw *Coloeus (Corvus) monedula*

L 30–34 cm | W 70–75 cm   ◯ Chough (*p. 487*)

Small, grey-black crow; somewhat resembles a pigeon but stouter, stronger, longer-legged and more upright. **Bill short and stout**, head rounded but broad.

ADULT grey-black with slight gloss; **inky black face and cap** against **pale grey shawl**. **Whitish eye** obvious close up. JUVENILE dull greyish; eye bluish, bill pale. 1ST-YEAR duller than adult with less well-defined cap. IN FLIGHT, quick, with **flickery beats**; frequently soars, often in large groups, swirling out from trees or cliff, swinging around with noisy outburst and returning. Often mixes with bigger Rooks (*p. 485*). Wings and tail more rounded than slightly larger Chough (*p. 487*).

VOICE Metallic "*jak*," "*chak*" or "*kya*," but very varied: a single bird can create a prolonged, rapid, bouncy cacophony, with short, sharp, barked, shouted or squeaky notes. Noisy, quick-fire, staccato chorus from flocks going to roost.

Common resident (1·3 million pairs, plus 2·8 million birds in Ireland); ssp. *monedula* scarce visitor from N Europe, Oct–Mar

Town centres to cliffs, farmland, parks, old woodland

Wings slightly rounded, often slightly curled back; smoother, rounder, gentler shapes than Rook (*p. 485*) or Chough (*p. 487*).

Ssp. *monedula* (often referred to as 'Nordic' Jackdaw), rare/scarce visitor from N Europe (Oct–Mar), greyer than resident **British/Irish** ssp. *spermologus*, with **paler band on side of neck**. Some birds darker above with pale neck band, perhaps from farther east.

white eye
dark cap and chin
grey neck

British/Irish ssp. *spermologus* ADULT

immature duller than adult

CROWS

Hooded Crow *Corvus cornix*

L 44–51 cm | W 85–95 cm

👁 *Sometimes treated as a subspecies of Carrion Crow (p. 484).*

Striking **two-tone, grey-and-black crow** (grey faintly washed fawn/pinkish-buff in some lights). Social where common but often isolated pairs on moors. IN FLIGHT, action and shapes like Carrion Crow, without quicker, more determined impression of Jackdaw, or rounder tail of Rook (*p. 486*), or 'presence' of larger Raven (*p. 484*).

Narrow zone of Hooded × Carrion Crow hybridization crosses N Scotland. Hybrids have 'shadow' of Hooded Crow pattern, but grey areas darker, or streaked black. Occasional hybrid pairs elsewhere, and hybrid patterns may persist for generations.

VOICE Repeated "*kraa kraa kraa*" on even pitch.

Common resident (160,000 pairs, plus 540,000 birds in Ireland); scarce (declined) winter visitor outside breeding range

from Scandinavia

Low-lying coasts, beaches, moors, fields, mountains, woodland edge

Square-winged, square-tailed shape combined with pale body easily recognized.

ADULT

Hybrid Hooded × Carrion Crows are usually obviously intermediate, but subsequent generations may be more-or-less like one of the parents.

grey with black head and breast

NOTE: JUVENILE has browner plumage and eye paler at first than ADULT.

black wings and tail

ADULT

Carrion Crow *Corvus corone*

L 44–51 cm | W 85–90 cm

Raven (p. 486), Hooded Crow (p. 483)

Common resident (1 million pairs). Generally rare Ireland but locally common in NE

Large, black, short-billed and short-legged crow; long wingtip/tail gives sleek shape (compare with Rook and Raven). Small numbers mix with Rook flocks (although not at nesting colony), but found in flocks of scores to 100s where food plentiful (*e.g.* rubbish tips, fields spread with manure, beaches).

Neat, smooth plumage. Broad, low crown; **short, arched, black bill** (excited bird raises forehead/crown in steep, smooth dome, less peaked than Rook); **black face**. Hard to tell from juvenile Rook but body plumage tighter; bill less pointed, blacker; basal bristles smoother (less obvious 'bump'); and thicker neck and shoulders. IN FLIGHT, soars less than Rook: fairly sedate, straight (unless chasing bird of prey).

VOICE Hard, rough, "*kraang-kraang-kraang*" or "*kraaa*," or soft "*krr-krr-krr*." Other calls varied, not so 'musical' as Rook.

ADULT

On/near open ground anywhere: woodland edge, fields, beaches

Rook (juvenile): thin, pointed bill; basal bristles prominent; neck relatively slender

Carrion Crow: heavy bill, basal bristle profile smooth; neck thick

Raven: very heavy bill, basal bristles prominent; neck very thick

Short head/neck/bill; short, **square tail**; wings oblong, broad at tip, held rather straight.

NOTE: some birds have whitish bands across wings (due to deficient diet), obvious in flight.

NOTE: JUVENILE has browner plumage and eye paler at first than ADULT.

ADULT

smoother curve to belly profile, less angular than Rook

CROWS

Rook *Corvus frugilegus*

L 41–49 cm | W 80–90 cm

Raven (p. 486), Chough (p. 487)

Very common resident (990,000 pairs Britain, common in Ireland)

Common large crow; see Carrion Crow, Raven (*p. 486*). **Always social**, often with Jackdaws (*p. 482*); nests in **treetop colonies** (Jackdaws mix at colony, but not Carrion Crows).

'Loose' body plumage, **wide, shaggy flank**; steep forehead, **peaked crown**; tapered, very wide-based bill. ADULT black, purple gloss, except **bare grey-buff face**; grey bill. JUVENILE black face, best told from Carrion Crow by shape and structure (see *annotations below*).

IN FLIGHT, capable of acrobatics in wind and much **more likely to soar** to great height, than Carrion Crow. Flocks swirl over colony at any time of year. May glide with wings raised in 'V' or stiffly downtilted, giving greater range of profiles than Carrion Crow. Wings and tail more rounded than smaller Chough (*p. 487*).

VOICE Varied: around colony, deep, 'comfortable' caws and croaks; typical "*craa-craa-craa*." Frequent loud, far-carrying, high "*crroo-crroo-crroo*," choked trumpeting notes, musical squeaks and squeals; deep, mechanical, wooden rattle in flight.

Farmland, woodland edge, copses, clifftops, urban areas

ADULT

Juvenile has black face and is very like Carrion Crow: differences as shown here:

basal bristles form more prominent 'bump'

neck and shoulders not as thickset

long, more pointed bill

JUVENILE JUN–JAN

Long head and bill; **long, round or wedge-shaped tail** (closer to Raven); tapered wingtips often curve back.

from the side, broad head/bill looks long and tapered

ADULT

CORVIDS Corvids in flight *p. 479*

Raven *Corvus corax*

L 54–67 cm | W 125–135 cm

Huge crow (size often obvious but can be hard to judge); see Carrion Crow and particularly Rook. May form flocks (scores) where common.

👁 Carrion Crow (*p. 484*), Rook (*p. 485*)

Scarce resident, locally common (7,400 pairs, plus 70,000 birds in Ireland)

All black. Very large; crown round, peaked or flattened, smooth profile. Throat raised in 'beard', uniquely bulbous in flight. **Bill long, deeply arched**. IN FLIGHT, size approaches Buzzard (*p. 312*); soars masterfully, with diagnostic **momentary roll onto back** with angled wings. May twist primaries to create loud, rasping thrum. Most soaring birds are not as black (but beware high-flying Cormorant (*p. 78*)); Buzzard broader-winged. ADULT in moult has gaps in trailing edge, with swept-back 'fingers'; JUVENILES have shorter, neater wings and a less bulging trailing edge.

VOICE Carries far: loud, echoing, abrupt, hollow quality "*prruk-prruk-prruk*;" higher, more ringing "*tonk!*" Loud "*quak quak*;" subdued notes, rattles and clicks at close range.

Upland areas, chalk downs, forest, coastal cliffs

Long wings with long, narrow tips, slightly bulging trailing edge; straight or angled leading edge. **Tail long, broad; rounded or wedge-shaped**: at times, distinctive 'diamond' (more like Rook's when closed).

ADULT

pair often fly close together, fast, shoulder-to-shoulder

1ST-WINTER

heavy, arched bill

close up, paler feather edges give 'scaly' effect

NOTE: 1ST-YEAR birds have mixed glossy black and dull brown (juvenile) wing coverts and tertials.

CROWS | NUTCRACKER

Chough *Pyrrhocorax pyrrhocorax*

ssp. *pyrrhocorax* see p.541

551

L 37–41 cm | W 75–90 cm

Small, glossy black crow of cliffs and quarries. Long, slim, curved bill; long, broad, square wings and tail. Extravagant, acrobatic flight around cliffs, often in flocks. On ground, bouncy hops and walk; **long wingtips** flicked, head bowed.

ADULT black with steely-blue sheen; **bill and legs red**. JUVENILE bill shorter, orange; narrower wings and slightly notched tail. IN FLIGHT, square shape (Jackdaw (*p.482*) and Rook (*p.485*) both have more rounded wings and tail, but also soar and dive around coastal cliffs). Often dives with half-closed wings, frequently swooping back up in steep, bounding climb.

VOICE Jackdaw-like but longer, more **ringing, piercing**, shouted "*chee-aah*," "*chaaa*" or "*chrri*."

◉ Jackdaw (*p.482*), Rook (*p.485*)

Rare and very local resident (300 pairs, plus 2,400 birds in Ireland); very rare outside breeding range

Mostly coastal cliffs, islands, rare inland; feeds on nearby pastures, piles of seaweed on beaches

NOTE: **1ST-WINTER** birds have browner wings than ADULTS

1ST-WINTER

slim, curved, red bill

inky black, variably glossy body

'triangular' shape

red legs

Broad, **square-tipped** deeply fingered wings (two-tone beneath with **blacker coverts**); head quite long, narrow; tail short, square.

ADULT

Nutcracker *Nucifraga caryocatactes*
L 32–38 cm | W 49–53 cm

Unlike any other corvid: dark brown with lines of copious **white spots**; **white vent and tail tip**; white bars under wing.

Two subspecies recorded: '**thin-billed**' ssp. *macrorhynchos* (most frequent) and '**thick-billed**' ssp. *caryocatactes* (two records); told by bill size, but overlap.

Vagrant from C Europe: <500 records (Britain), Aug–Mar. Widespread; infrequent invasions. Pines; often on ground.

ADULT 'thick-billed' ssp. *caryocatactes*

ADULT 'thin-billed' ssp. *macrorhynchos*

SPARROWS and FINCHES

SPARROW ID head pattern | tail pattern
FINCH ID bill shape/colour | wing and tail pattern | streaking | rump colour | calls and song

4 sparrows: 2 resident; 2 vagrants.
21 finches: 12 resident (2 Scotland only, 1 very rare); 2 winter visitors; 2 migrants; 5 vagrants (plus vagrant sparrows and finches from America).

Finch, Sparrow or Bunting?

Finches, **sparrows** and **buntings** (see *p. 510*) can be told from other perching birds by their triangular bill and short legs.

Sparrows (*pp. 490–491, 509*) all have plain, unstreaked underparts, ruling out most finches and buntings, except Chaffinch, which is easily told by the extensive white in its wings and tail.

Finches (*pp. 492–509*) are distinguished from the similar buntings with more difficulty: many buntings have a blackish tail with white outer feathers, while finches have thin, pale feather edges or patches of colour on the tail. There are more detailed differences, such as the shape of the bill (on buntings, the upper mandible often makes a smaller 'lid' on the big, broad lower one) and the pattern of the dark centres on the tertials (a marked 'stepped' shape on buntings). Some finches have fine songs; a few, unlike any bunting, display by using song flights. Many finches are also more acrobatic feeders, on tall stems and in trees, than the buntings. Finches as a group have a remarkable variety of bill shapes, adapted primarily for shelling seeds; from the beech-mast-crunching Hawfinch to the pine-seed-extracting crossbills.

upper mandible generally smaller than lower; backward point at gape

REED BUNTING

BRAMBLING (FINCH)

backward point at base

square at base

HOUSE SPARROW

Sparrow ageing/sexing
House Sparrows have marked sexual differences but male and female Tree Sparrows look the same, both with a black bib. Juveniles can be separated but look like adults by their first summer.

Finch ageing/sexing Some have marked differences between male and female, and also between breeding and non-breeding plumages. Breeding colours are often obscured by dull feather tips in winter, revealed as these fall away in spring. Juveniles and first-winter birds are mostly identifiable.

Adults and juveniles have a single moult each year.

Post-juvenile moult
JUL–SEP: flight feathers and some coverts retained for a full year, becoming very abraded.

Adult moult
JUL–SEP (body moult may rarely continue into spring): complete moult after breeding; breeding plumage assumed by abrasion/disintegration of dull feather tips.

SISKIN

JUVENILE APR–SEP

♀

♂ ADULT SEP–JAN (fresh) JAN–AUG (worn)

INTRODUCTION

The types of finches

Finches fall into several groups and can be told apart by their frequent flight calls, with experience, or by their songs.

Greenfinch, **Linnet** and **Twite** all have pale (yellow or white) streaks on the outer edges of their wing and tail feathers. **Greenfinch** is uniquely largely plain, unstreaked green in most plumages. **Siskin** (*opposite*) is green but strongly streaked, with boldly barred wings.

Goldfinch and **Siskin**, and the streaky brown **redpolls**, cling to tall stems and seedheads to feed, while **Linnet** and **Twite** stand on the ground and reach up to seedheads with their bill, or pull them down under one foot. **Siskin**, **redpolls** and **Goldfinch** also feed in treetops. Some species visit bird tables and the ground beneath, while others specialize in artificial feeders, especially **Siskin**, **Goldfinch**, **redpolls** and **Greenfinch**.

Crossbills are treetop feeders, prising open scales of cones with crossed bill tips. When they fly off, they can be extremely vocal.

Hawfinch is large-billed, capable of dealing with cherry stones and other tough foods, but also feeds a good deal on beech mast under trees. **Bullfinch** is a quieter, more secretive feeder on soft buds, shoots and berries.

Chaffinch and **Brambling** are remarkably similar in shape, structure and pattern but differ in colour details: **Chaffinch** is widespread all year, **Brambling** is a winter visitor. They tend to feed on the ground, or take caterpillars from foliage in summer.

American Sparrows

Vagrants from North America (see *pp. 532–533*), mainly in spring and probably mostly crossing the Atlantic at least partly on board ships, include sparrows (such as White-throated Sparrow) and finches (such as Evening Grosbeak, Dark-eyed Junco and Eastern Towhee), as well as 'sparrows' that are more closely related to Old World buntings, such as Savannah Sparrow.

SPARROWS and FINCHES

House Sparrow *Passer domesticus*

L 14–16 cm | W 18–25 cm

👁 Spanish Sparrow, Rock Sparrow (p. 509)

Common resident (5 million pairs, plus 2·4 million birds in Ireland); much decreased, now rare/absent in some areas

The familiar sparrow: small, finch-like, with **thick bill** and **short, pale legs**; **unstreaked underparts**. Very social, family groups to hundreds where abundant keep loosely together; noisy, squabbling groups in hedgerows and thickets. Flies from field to hedge in **tight whirring groups**, rather tail-down.

MALE BREEDING **grey band on crown**, red-brown hindneck; pale grey cheek, **black throat and bib**. Underparts **unmarked** pale grey. Broad white wingbar. Bill thick, triangular, black. MALE NON-BREEDING has **small black chin** (bib lost) and crown pattern obscured by buff tips; **whitish ring around sides of neck** and yellowish bill. FEMALE less conspicuous, **pale brown** with **broad buff stripe** from eye over cheek. **Unstreaked** pale grey-buff underparts. Two pale buff streaks on back. Bill pale buffish. JUVENILE like pale, rather 'fluffy' female.

VOICE Loud chirrups and cheeps: "*cheep*," "*chwilp*" or "*shreep*;" song includes calls in prolonged, rich, loud, emphatic but unmusical performance.

IN FLIGHT, chunky, square-tailed, broad-winged; whirring bursts of wingbeats but little undulation; often low down.

Suburban areas, gardens, parks, farmland, coastal grassland/scrub

♂ BREEDING

greyish-brown cap over broad pale stripe

ADULT ♀

ADULT ♂ NON-BREEDING JUL–MAR

hint of pale collar

yellowish on bill

grey feather edges obscure head pattern and bib in winter

grey feather edges wear away to reveal colour beneath in spring

grey crown

unstreaked underparts

white cheeks; large black bib

ADULT ♂ BREEDING FEB–AUG

SPARROWS

Tree Sparrow *Passer montanus* 554

L 12–14 cm | W 20–22 cm

Spanish Sparrow (p.509)

Small sparrow: thick-billed and streaky brown; resembles male House Sparrow. Mixes with finches, House Sparrow and buntings, often feeding on waterside 'tideline'. Hops with tail cocked; crown feathers often raised, giving rounder-headed, small-billed appearance. Fast, whirring, agile flight.

Sexes alike. ADULT **all-brown cap**; white cheek with **black spot**. Black bib always small and neat (not so extensive or streaked as breeding male House Sparrow). Almost complete white collar. Bill black in summer, buffish/grey in winter. JUVENILE duller, with centre of crown diffusely paler/greyer.

VOICE Distinctive hard "*tek*" or "*tet-et-et*" in flight, and cheerful "*tsuwit*". Song higher, more chattering, less dynamic than House Sparrow.

Scarce, local resident (180,000 pairs Britain, scarce Ireland)

Woods, farmland, waterside thickets

IN FLIGHT, short-tailed, broad-winged; direct, often rather high, with bursts of wingbeats.

dull cap, small cheek spot

JUVENILE JUN–AUG

yellowish on bill

ADULT NON-BREEDING JUL–MAR

Readily comes to feeders.

brown crown

pale collar; black cheek spot

black bill

small black bib

ADULT BREEDING FEB–AUG

unstreaked underparts

SPARROWS and FINCHES

Bullfinch *Pyrrhula pyrrhula*

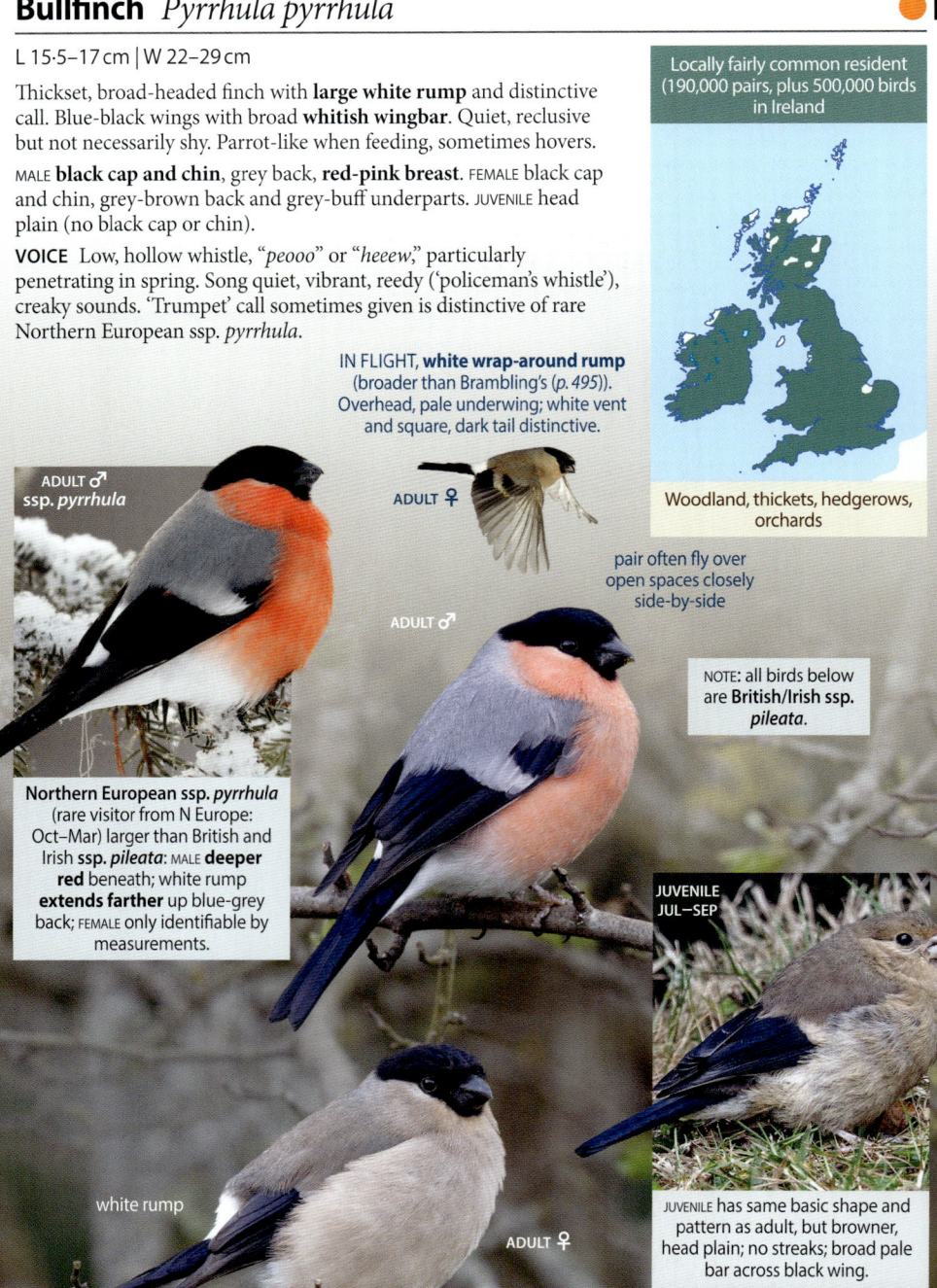

L 15·5–17 cm | W 22–29 cm

Thickset, broad-headed finch with **large white rump** and distinctive call. Blue-black wings with broad **whitish wingbar**. Quiet, reclusive but not necessarily shy. Parrot-like when feeding, sometimes hovers.

MALE **black cap and chin**, grey back, **red-pink breast**. FEMALE black cap and chin, grey-brown back and grey-buff underparts. JUVENILE head plain (no black cap or chin).

VOICE Low, hollow whistle, "*peooo*" or "*heeew*," particularly penetrating in spring. Song quiet, vibrant, reedy ('policeman's whistle'), creaky sounds. 'Trumpet' call sometimes given is distinctive of rare Northern European ssp. *pyrrhula*.

Locally fairly common resident (190,000 pairs, plus 500,000 birds in Ireland)

IN FLIGHT, **white wrap-around rump** (broader than Brambling's (*p. 495*)). Overhead, pale underwing; white vent and square, dark tail distinctive.

ADULT ♂ ssp. *pyrrhula*

ADULT ♀

Woodland, thickets, hedgerows, orchards

ADULT ♂

pair often fly over open spaces closely side-by-side

NOTE: all birds below are **British/Irish ssp. *pileata*.**

Northern European ssp. *pyrrhula* (rare visitor from N Europe: Oct–Mar) larger than British and Irish ssp. *pileata*: MALE **deeper red** beneath; white rump **extends farther** up blue-grey back; FEMALE only identifiable by measurements.

JUVENILE JUL–SEP

white rump

ADULT ♀

JUVENILE has same basic shape and pattern as adult, but browner, head plain; no streaks; broad pale bar across black wing.

FINCHES

Hawfinch *Coccothraustes coccothraustes*

L 16·5–18 cm | W 29–33 cm   👁 Evening Grosbeak (*p. 534*)

Large, striking finch, but shy and hard to find; faithful to a few traditional sites. May sit upright on treetop (like Crossbill (*p. 506*)); feeds on the ground.

Bright crown, pale cheek, black chin; **pale wing band**. Bill large (although not grotesquely so), blue-grey or pinkish with dark tip (yellowish in winter). MALE bright forehead and cheek, darker cap, grey hindneck; rump pale tawny. Wings steely-blue. FEMALE duller, less pinkish below, browner between eye and bill. JUVENILE may be perplexing: pale throat, blackish barring below, but broad white wing panel and **white tail tip**.

VOICE Call hard, dry, clicking or ticking "*tik!*" (often louder than Robin (*p. 400*) but very like Redstart (*p. 402*)), or "*tik-ik-ik*." Quiet, variable song.

Rare and local resident (800 pairs, declining); <300 records Ireland

Old woodland, parks with lines of tall trees, especially Beech, Hornbeam, cherries

JUVENILE JUL–SEP

♂ BREEDING

IN FLIGHT, **white tail tip** eye-catching especially in shade under trees; overhead, fast, **long-winged/short-tailed**, with angular white patch across wing.

head and bill duller in winter

NON-BREEDING SEP–FEB [Oct]

JUVENILE has same basic pattern as adult but dull, pale, marked by mottles and bars beneath.

ADULT ♀ [Jan]

bright cap and cheek

pale band on wing

ADULT ♂ [Feb]

SPARROWS and FINCHES

Chaffinch *Fringilla coelebs*

L 14–16 cm | W 24–28 cm

ssp. *gengleri*

Sparrow-sized, long-bodied finch with **white on wing and tail** (white 'shoulder' often hidden but white midwing bar prominent), underparts unstreaked. Tame around car parks, picnic sites, gardens.

MALE BREEDING orange-pink cheek and breast, bluish cap; greenish rump; bill blue-grey. MALE NON-BREEDING colours obscured by buff feather edges from Sep, which wear away by Mar; bill yellowish. FEMALE/JUVENILE dull, olive-grey above, unstreaked olive-buff below. Dark sides to crown.

VOICE High, ringing "*pink*;" in flight, "*chup*" characteristic. In Apr–Jun, monotonous "*huit*" for long periods, slightly like Chiffchaff (p. 430). Song bright, rattling "*chip-chip-chip cherry-erry-erry*," accelerating into final flourish.

Very common resident (5·6 million pairs, plus 4·2 million birds in Ireland), winter visitor

from N and W Europe

Woodland, farmland, gardens

IN FLIGHT, striking white on wings and tail; greenish rump; flocks loose, uncoordinated.

European ssp. *coelebs*

♀

♂ BREEDING

♂ NON-BREEDING

NOTE: all birds below are British/Irish ssp. *gengleri*.

ADULT ♂ NON-BREEDING

European ssp. *coelebs* (winter visitor) slightly paler and 'cleaner' than resident **British and Irish ssp. gengleri**. The difference is subtle and best noted when a mixed flock allows direct comparison.

ADULT ♂ NON-BREEDING AUG–MAR [Mar]

bill never yellow

ADULT ♂ BREEDING MAR–AUG [May]

ADULT ♀

white bar across middle of wing

white 'shoulder' (can be hidden)

plain flank

FINCHES

Brambling *Fringilla montifringilla*

L 14–16 cm | W 25–26 cm

Colourful finch; size and structure as Chaffinch but has an **orange 'shoulder'** and **white rump**. Often with Chaffinches; feeds under trees, in fields; beneath bird tables on spilled seed.

MALE BREEDING black hood, orange 'shoulder' and breast, black/white/buff wings, white belly. MALE NON-BREEDING dark cap with dark bands beside grey nape; bright yellow bill. Rusty-brown on back, fading whiter; hoary look to head (pale fringes to feathers wear away by Apr, revealing black). Pale **orange breast against white belly**; **flank spotted**. FEMALE subdued but similar pattern: **dark band beside pale nape**; pale grey collar; dull orange breast against **white belly**, dark **flank spots**; buff 'shoulder' and wingbar.

VOICE Twangy, 'vulgar', coarse "*tswairk*" or "*tsweep*" and harder "*chup*" than Chaffinch. Song (rare) includes deep buzzing note.

Scarce winter visitor (erratic, locally common in some years)

from N and W Europe

Woodland, farmland

IN FLIGHT, narrow **white rump** distinctive.

Flight like Chaffinch: slightly jerky/hesitant; flocks quite loose.

1ST-WINTER ♂
AUG–FEB [Dec]

bright colours obscured by whitish fringes from Aug; by Apr (*below*) abrasion of pale tips almost complete

1ST-WINTER ♀
SEP–MAR [Nov]

orange-buff 'shoulder'

yellow on bill

♂ BREEDING
MAR–SEP [Jul]

black head, back, obscured by whitish fringes

grey band on neck

1ST-WINTER ♂
FEB–APR [Apr]

orange 'shoulder'

♀ [Oct]

white belly

white belly, dark flank spots

495

SPARROWS and FINCHES

Goldfinch *Carduelis carduelis*

L 12–13·5 cm | W 20–25 cm

ssp. *britannica*

Unmistakable small, dainty, distinctive finch with a **broad yellow band on the wing**. Sociable; slim; tail deeply notched. Feeds on seedheads, thistles and also in trees (Alder, birches) sometimes with Siskins (*p. 498*) or redpolls (*p. 502*). Perches high, often inconspicuously, inside leafy canopy; frequent on garden feeders. Often groups of 5–10; sometimes many more in good feeding areas.

Dull pale brown above, buff-white below with dark brownish breast patches. Black wing with broad **yellow band**. Rump white; tail black with white spots at tip. ADULT has **red, white and black face**. JUVENILE plain greyish head and buff feather tips on dull black wing and tail.

VOICE Call a slurred, sweet, musical "*swilp*," "*swilip*," or "*sililip*," quite like Swallow (*p. 353*); also harsh, churring rasp. Song fast, tinkling trills, chattery notes from tree.

Common resident (1·2 million pairs, plus 915,000 birds in Ireland) and winter visitor

from W Europe

to Low Countries

Farmland, open spaces, heaths, scrub, areas with seeding thistles

IN FLIGHT, light, airy, sometimes erratic as if bounced by gust of wind. Broad pale band across black wing; obvious pale body/dark hindwing from below.

ADULT

Separating MALE and FEMALE difficult/impossible; compared to MALE, FEMALE may have less red on face (not extending behind eye) and greyer patch between eye and bill, such as on the left hand adult shown here – but there is considerable overlap.

ADULT ♀

unique black/white/red head

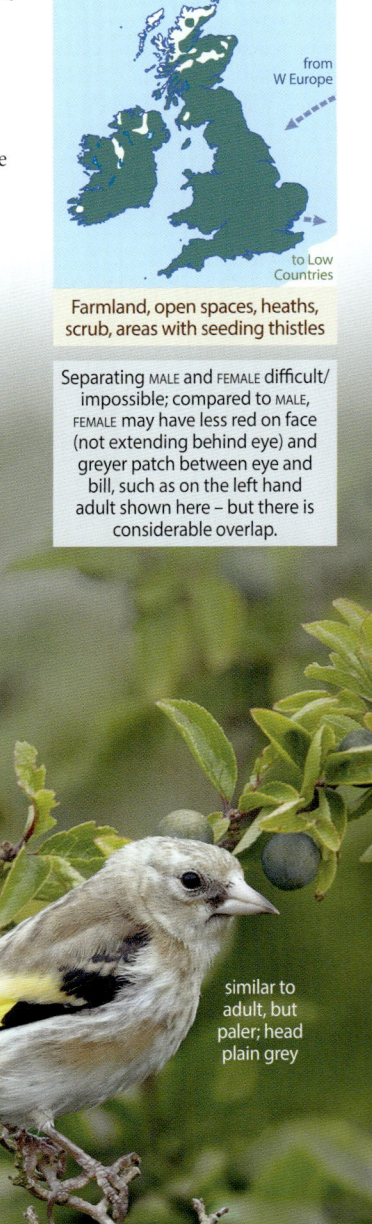

ADULT

dark breast patch

yellow band on wing

no yellow on tail

similar to adult, but paler; head plain grey

JUVENILE JUL–OCT

FINCHES

Greenfinch *Chloris (Carduelis) chloris*

L 14–16 cm | W 24–27 cm   ◉ Citril Finch (p. 499)

● ssp. *harrisoni*   I

Large, **thick-billed**, upright finch with a **yellow streak along edge of wing**. Feeds in fields, on feeders, under trees; flocks in flight bunch more tightly than Chaffinch (p. 494).

MALE **apple green**; grey on wing. **Pale bill**, dark 'frown'; **broad yellow streak** along wing and side of tail. In winter (Sep–Mar) dull feather fringes. FEMALE brownish-green, softly streaked above; narrow yellow streak along wing. JUVENILE like female but paler and streaked below; thin yellow streak along wing still characteristic.

VOICE Call short "*jup*;" erratic trill "*jup-jup-up-up*," heavier, louder than Linnet (p. 500), less metallic than redpolls (p. 502). Juvenile loud "*chup*," like Crossbill (p. 506). Song, perched or in **stretched-winged rolling, bat-like song flight**, includes loud, nasal "*dweeez*;" **ringing, musical trills**, varying speed, rhythm.

Common resident (1·7 million pairs, plus 830,000 birds in Ireland) and winter visitor

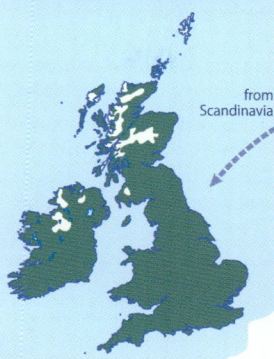

from Scandinavia

Parks, woods, farmland, open spaces, heathland scrub; winter flocks, even on tidelines

Ssp. *harrisoni* (Britain and Ireland) uniform green below; **ssp. *chloris*.** (N Scotland and winter migrants) green with yellower chin and belly.

IN FLIGHT, yellow streaks on wing, but **yellow beside base of tail** more striking in rear view. Wingbeats more emphatic than Chaffinch: long undulations.

1ST-WINTER ♂
AUG–MAR
[Dec]

♂

FEMALE and NON-BREEDING MALE can look dark green-grey in dull light

JUVENILE
JUN–SEP

faint streaks on breast

Judging age/sex can be difficult: 1ST-WINTER has narrower yellow streak on wing than ADULT; MALE'S broader than FEMALE'S of same age.

ADULT ♂

thick pale bill

♀

yellow on side of tail

497

SPARROWS and FINCHES

Siskin *Spinus (Carduelis) spinus*

L 11–12·5 cm | W 18–22 cm

👁 Citril Finch, Atlantic Canary (*p. 539*)

Tiny, slender, streaky, greenish finch with a notched tail, fine, pointed bill and **black and yellow** wingbars. Acrobatic feeder in twigs, often with other finches and tit flocks. Often inconspicuous in treetops, giving chorus of soft calls. Disturbed flocks twist and turn tightly together.

Broad **black and yellow bands** across wing, yellow side to tail. MALE **black cap and chin**, yellow over eye, yellow breast, white belly with few streaks; rump yellow. FEMALE paler, with duller head, greyer back, whiter below with more dark streaks. JUVENILE duller, streaky, narrower yellow wingbars, but same character.

VOICE Call distinctive, ringing, squeaky "*tluee*," "*tilu*" or "*tzsy-ee*." Also hard, harsh rattle or churr; fast medley from treetop flocks. Song fast, twittery, squeaky with trills and light, buzzy, wheezy notes.

Locally fairly common resident (410,000 pairs, Britain; 60,000 pairs, Ireland) and winter visitor

from N and W Europe

Localized breeder; more widely in winter in conifers, Alder, birches; comes to feeders

IN FLIGHT, long yellow stripe along blackish wing.

♂

black cap, yellow behind eye

yellow-green bar across blackish wing

black chin

ADULT ♂

♂

In late winter/spring, MALES frequently break from feeding to sing.

♀ lacks cap

pale bar on blackish wing

JUVENILE JUN–SEP

whitish beneath, streaked black; looks a grey bird on feeders (redpolls (*p. 502*) look brown)

JUVENILE is much duller than ADULT, slightly browner above and with a plainer head.

FINCHES

Serin *Serinus serinus*
L 11–12 cm | W 18–22 cm

Tiny, round-headed, greenish/yellowish, streaky finch; calls draw attention. **Tiny bill**, **yellow rump**. Pale crescent under eye; pale lower cheek; dark 'moustache'. See Siskin, beware escaped Atlantic Canary (*p. 539*). Sits upright, hard to see in treetops; crouches/hops on ground. MALE **yellow forehead**, over eye and on throat; **white belly**, flank streaked black. FEMALE greyer, less yellow. JUVENILE buff-brown, streaked; head grey-brown with pale crescents above and below eye, pale throat, pale cheek spot. Curved, **buff wingbar**; pale buffish rump (see Linnet (*p. 500*)). IN FLIGHT, light, fast, buoyant, bouncy.

VOICE Call jingling trill; upswept "*tu-wee*." Song fast, 'splintering glass' jingle, often in song flight.

> **Atlantic Canary (*p. 539*)**
> Very rare migrant from Europe: 30–40 per year (<15 records Ireland), most Apr–May; very rare breeder. Mostly woods and villages near S coast.

ADULT ♂

Males are easy to see in spring when singing from a high perch.

1ST-WINTER ♀
AUG–MAR [Dec]

densely streaked; weak wingbars

♀

♂
yellow rump

head more like Linnet than Siskin

two pale bars on dark wing

JUVENILE
JUN–SEP

Citril Finch *Carduelis citrinella*
L 11·5–13 cm | W 20–22 cm

Most resembles Siskin in size/structure, but adults **not streaked**; **two broad greenish-yellow bars** on blackish wing. MALE yellowish face, **grey nape**; yellow-green underparts. FEMALE (not recorded) greyer. JUVENILE (not recorded) browner, wingbars narrower, underparts narrowly streaked.

Vagrant from S Europe: <5 records (Britain) (males), May, Jun. On coast. Woods.

May feed on the ground like Linnet (*p. 500*).

ADULT ♂

SPARROWS and FINCHES

Linnet *Linaria (Carduelis) cannabina*

ssp. *autochthona* 555

L 12·5–14 cm | W 20–24 cm

Serin (p. 499), Common Rosefinch (p. 505)

Small, short-billed finch with **white streaks** on wing and tail. Distinct face patterns with whitish crescent above and below eye and spot on cheek; grey bill. Flocks fly high, bounding, co-ordinated, drop into low vegetation; stand up to feed, not clinging onto stems like other finches.

MALE **grey head**, red forehead; **plain red-brown back**; **white streaks along wing and tail** sides. Underparts plain buff, breast red (extensive, bright Mar–May). FEMALE no red; greyish head, lightly streaked back; fine streaks on breast, belly white. In dull light, looks dark, greyish with **whitish crescents** above and below eye and **pale cheek spot**.

VOICE Twittering, dry "*chet-et-et*;" twangy "*tsooee*," less forceful than Greenfinch (p. 497), less hard than redpolls (p. 502). Song musical sweet warbling.

IN FLIGHT, bounding, lightweight; white edges to primaries, broad white triangle each side of tail (see Twite).

Scottish ssp. *autochthona* [not illustrated] darker, more slender bill, but grades into ssp. *cannabina* farther south.

Locally common resident (410,000 pairs, plus 550,000 birds in Ireland), migrant and winter visitor

from Scandinavia

to Low Countries

Heaths, rough grassland and 'waste' ground; farmland stubbles

JUVENILE JUN–OCT

whitish throat

grey bill (all plumages)

ADULT ♂ AUG–MAY [May]

colours obscured by pale feather edges, sometimes until May

ADULT ♀

♂ BREEDING MAR–JUL

unstreaked back

red forehead and breast

pale crescents above and below eye; pale cheek spot in all plumages

broad white side to tail

FINCHES

Twite *Linaria (Carduelis) flavirostris* 🔴 Ⓘ 555

L 12·5–14 cm | W 22–24 cm

Small, short-billed finch; white streaks on wing like Linnet, but **buff wingbar** like redpolls (*pp. 502–504*); **tawny-buff throat**. Flocks feed low down in herbs; often circle saltmarsh before dropping down. MALE BREEDING boldly streaked; large tawny-buff throat patch; **deep pink rump**. Bill greyish. FEMALE lacks pink. NON-BREEDING (both sexes) **buff throat patch**, **yellow bill** (grey on Linnet), buff wingbar; long white streak along closed wing and side of tail (more conspicuous than on Linnet). Brighter beneath but spread wing and tail similar to Linnet.

VOICE Distinctive: harder flight note than Linnet, closer to redpolls: **twangy, nasal, buzzing** "*twaa-it.*" Song fast, twittering, mixing twangy call and rattling trills.

Scarce resident and summer visitor (7,800 pairs, plus 50 pairs Ireland); rare and declining winter migrant in S

Breeds uplands/coastal areas; winters on low-lying coasts

'HEBRIDEAN' TWITE [ssp.] '*bensonorum*'

ssp. *pipilans* of N Britain, Ireland, slightly darker than ssp. *flavirostris* (winter migrant from Scandinavia); birds from the Outer Hebrides ([ssp.] '*bensonorum*') dark and heavily streaked, but differences are slight and not easy to assign individuals to ssp. unless comparison is possible.

IN FLIGHT, bouncy, with whirring wingbeats; white edges to primaries, narrow white streak on side of tail (see Linnet).

1ST-WINTER/ NON-BREEDING [Oct]

in winter both sexes have a yellow bill, male has pink on rump

yellow bill

stubby bill

dull, softly streaked

buff wingbar

glimpse of pink rump indicates ♂

no pink on rump indicates ♀

pale greyish bill

pale tawny-buff throat

♀ BREEDING MAR–OCT [Oct]

♂ BREEDING MAR–OCT [Apr]

thin white side to tail

501

SPARROWS and FINCHES

Redpolls

Redpolls split opinion amongst taxonomic authorities; some regard the complex as comprising several species; some just one or two. Although often difficult to tell apart, the differences between the various forms are appreciable. Here, redpolls are treated as three species.

Redpolls are small, slim, streaky finches with broad **buff or white wingbar**, **red cap** and **black chin**. Distinguished from other finches by dark wing with pale wingbar (not a streak along the wing as Linnet and Twite (pp. 500–501)), tiny yellow bill, **short dark legs**. Active, acrobatic; often with Siskins (p. 498), but less addicted to feeders, often feeding on the ground.

From late winter or spring male redpolls become extensively pink or red: some very red on the breast, pink on underparts and rump, almost like Common Rosefinch (p. 505). Winter plumages are generally duller – see p. 504.

1ST-WINTER/ADULT ♀ [Apr]

LESSER REDPOLL

legs may be pink

LESSER REDPOLL

small black chin

LESSER REDPOLL

red cap

curved pale bar across wing

1ST-WINTER SEP–JUN [Feb]

ADULT ♂ BREEDING JAN–JUL [Apr]

neat, rounded tail feathers in winter indicate adult; worn, pointed tips indicate 1st-winter

late winter/spring male can be extensively red-pink from Jan onwards

COMMON (MEALY) REDPOLL

ssp. *flammea* ♂ BREEDING FEB–JUL [Jun]

ns in winter *p.490*

FINCHES

Lesser Redpoll *Acanthis (Carduelis) cabaret*

L 11–14 cm | W 16–20 cm

👁 Common Rosefinch (*p.505*)

Small, brown, very short-billed finch, and the smallest, darkest redpoll; broad **buff wingbar** (fades whiter by Feb), shiny **red cap** and **black chin**. MALE BREEDING (from Jan–Jul) **pink-red all over breast**, pink on rump. MALE NON-BREEDING pink on face and breast obscured by buff fringes. FEMALE small red cap, black around bill, streak through eye; long **streaks on buff flank** beside white belly. JUVENILE lacks red cap, sometimes through winter.

VOICE Hard, fast metallic "*chuch-uch-uch-uch-uch;*" twangy "*tsooeee*." Song (often long, bouncy song flight) mixes calls with jingly trill "*trrrreeee.*"

Scarce and local resident (190,000 pairs Britain), winter visitor (numbers vary year to year)

Redpolls – summary of key identification features	
Lesser Redpoll	Smallest, darkest; darkest buff wingbar (fades); rump brown/pink; buff edges on wing feathers; streaks under tail.
Common (Mealy) Redpoll	Large, pale; white wingbar; rump grey-white/dark streaks; white edges on blacker wing feathers; streaks under tail.
Arctic Redpoll	Large, pale; large head/neck, tiny bill; white rump or white upper band; white under tail with one streak at most.

Woodland, scrub, heaths, moors; favours birches; widely in winter

Common (Mealy) Redpoll
Acanthis (Carduelis) flammea

L 11.5–14 cm | W 18–20 cm

ssp. *flammea*

Scarce/rare winter visitor from N Europe; mostly N & E Britain. Woodland

Slightly larger than Lesser Redpoll; **paler**, less buff, especially on head; whiter lines on back; **whiter wingbar**. **Rump white/greyish** with short, dark streaks (streaked brown/buff on Lesser Redpoll); blacker wings have whitish fringes (buff on Lesser Redpoll); flank whiter. Much variation (and note that buff on Lesser Redpoll fades whiter by late winter). Ssp. *rostrata* (rare migrant, has bred) is larger and browner, with blacker streaks and broader flank steaks (more like Twite (*p.501*).

VOICE Much like Lesser Redpoll but variable deeper notes.

Two **subspecies**: *flammea* (N Europe to Alaska); *rostrata* (Greenland/Iceland).

streaks on whitish rump

ssp. *flammea* NON-BREEDING

Arctic Redpoll *Acanthis (Carduelis) hornemanni*

L 12–14 cm | W 20–26 cm

Very rare migrant/vagrant from N Europe, Greenland: 5–35 per year (<10 records Ireland), Oct–Apr. Mostly N & E Britain. Trees.

Large head, thick neck; **very short bill**. **Narrow grey streak or all-white under tail** (dark streaks on Lesser and Common Redpolls). Some have **bright buff head** and upper back, whiter body. Male ssp. *exilipes* can be obvious 'snowball'; other plumages less distinct. ADULT broad white wingbar, **large white rump**. MALE breast pale pink; rump pink Feb–Jun. JUVENILE **unmarked white band on rump**, streaked upper edge, or fine streaks overall, more like Common Redpoll. Some ssp. *hornemanni* in Greenland have broad dark flank streaks, lightly streaked rump, 1–3 streaks under tail, so identification problematical.

VOICE Like other redpolls.

Two **subspecies**: *hornemanni* (NE Canada, Greenland) and *exilipes* (N Eurasia).

large white rump

ssp. *hornemanni* NON-BREEDING

SPARROWS and FINCHES

Redpolls in winter

Redpolls feed in high tops of birches, Alder and other trees, or on fallen seed beneath, sometimes joining finch flocks in fields: they can be hard to see well. Fortunately, they also come to feeders where they can be examined closely.

Plumages vary with age, sex and season and differences between subspecies sometimes overlap, so many will be hard to identify with precision beyond 'redpoll'.

Check size, bulk; bill size. Look carefully at head and wingbars; pale buff areas tend to fade whiter towards spring. Examine the rump and undertail coverts if you suspect a scarce or rare redpoll. Compare with other redpolls nearby if possible.

IN FLIGHT, stubby, short-headed, slim-tailed; quick, bouncy undulations.

1ST-WINTER
SEP–JUN [Feb]

LESSER REDPOLL

ARCTIC REDPOLL
faint or no streaks

COMMON (MEALY) REDPOLL
dark streaks

ssp. *flammea*
ADULT NON-BREEDING
SEP–MAR [Nov]

winter adult typically more 'frosty' than 1st-winter Lesser Redpoll

COMMON (MEALY) REDPOLL

ssp. *rostrata*
ADULT / 1ST-WINTER
SEP–MAR [Sep]

ARCTIC REDPOLL

Arctic Redpolls have a large, round head and tiny bill seemingly 'pushed in' to the face. Adult males may be obvious, females and juveniles much less so.

ssp. *hornemanni*
ADULT NON-BREEDING
SEP–MAR [Oct]

ssp. *exilipes*
ADULT / 1ST-WINTER
SEP–MAR [Nov]

Common Rosefinch
Carpodacus erythrinus (Erythrina erythrina)
L 13·5–15 cm | W 24–25 cm

555

Round-headed, long-tailed, sparrow-like finch with large, slightly bulbous bill; **bold dark eye in plain face** rules out female House Sparrow (*p. 490*) and redpolls. Pale tertial edges but all-dark tail rules out most buntings, but see Corn Bunting (*p. 517*).

MALE **bright deep red on head, breast and rump**, otherwise mid-brown with whiter belly and tertial tips. Raises crown feathers in distinct peak. FEMALE olive-brown, subtly streaked; **two thin, pale wingbars**. JUVENILE like female but brighter, buffier on flank; slightly sandier above, more sharply defined streaks beneath; **two broader, pale buff, parallel wingbars**; whitish eyering.

VOICE Call soft, upswept "*tiu-eek.*" Rhythmic, whistling song with simple phrases: "*weedy-weedy-weedy-wu.*"

Indigo Bunting (p. 534)

Rare/scarce migrant from NE Europe: 100–250 per year (<250 records Ireland), most Apr–May, Sep–Oct; has bred. Woodland edge, scrub. Winters in S Asia.

IN FLIGHT, like House Sparrow but less energetic with short, regular undulations; often flies high (above tree-tops).

ADULT ♂ — stout, bulbous bill

ADULT ♀ — dark eye in plain, pale face; two thin pale wingbars

JUVENILE JUN–OCT — pale wingbars and tertial edges; faint, soft streaks

SPARROWS and FINCHES

Crossbill *Loxia curvirostra*

L 15–17 cm | W 27–30 cm   ◉ Two-barred Crossbill (p. 508)

Large, round-headed finch; **arched** bill with **crossed tips**. Often upright on treetop (see Hawfinch (p. 493)); groups fly high above trees. Feeds quietly with parrot-like agility; bursts of calls draw attention. Frequently drinks from puddles. 'Irruptions' irregular. Some long-bodied (so look longer-tailed); others short-bodied, tail looks shorter.

MALE **dull red** with **brighter rump**. IMMATURE MALE greenish, variably streaked, and patched orange-red. FEMALE greenish, **rump yellower**; plain wing (unlike Greenfinch (p. 497)). JUVENILE dull, streaked; may have white wingbars, thin tertial fringes (see p. 508).

VOICE Calls deep purring notes from perch, building to ringing "*jip-jip-jip*" as flies off; forceful "*djeep-djeep-djeep*" generally higher pitched than Parrot Crossbill. Often excited chorus, typical of all crossbills. Song buzzing, trilling, whistled sounds.

Scarce and local resident (11,000 pairs); widespread irregular migrant/immigrant elsewhere, occasionally breeding

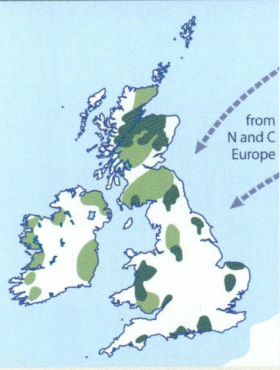

from N and C Europe

Coniferous woods, windbreaks; favours spruce

IN FLIGHT, dynamic, bounding flight over treetops, often over long distances.

JUVENILE JAN–OCT

IMMATURE ♂

JUVENILES are dull grey-brown with plain wing and finely streaked elsewhere; IMMATURE MALES combine juvenile streaks with adult colour, especially on the rump. The amount of adult colour increases with age.

basically green and grey ♀

variably orange-red and brown ♂

Crossbill identification

Common, Scottish and Parrot Crossbills share similar plumages and general character and are not easily identifiable: concentrate on head, bill and calls. Even Parrot and Common Crossbills can be very difficult, while Scottish Crossbills are intermediate, often impossible without analysis of sound recordings. Look for them in conifers and listen for falling cones; they feed very quietly but may suddenly create an outburst of loud calls, often before flying away.

- Scottish Crossbill 
- both species
- Parrot Crossbill

CROSSBILL — smallest; tip often long, curved

SCOTTISH CROSSBILL — bill deep; cheek 'bulging'

PARROT CROSSBILL — bill deepest, roundest; tips barely cross

FINCHES

Scottish Crossbill *Loxia scotica* 555

L 16–18 cm | W 27–30 cm

Size and structure more-or-less intermediate between Crossbill and Parrot Crossbill. Found in same forests, including coniferous plantations. Plumages as Crossbill but underwing typically paler. **Bill deep**, heavy; head may appear rather 'fat-cheeked'.

VOICE Between Crossbill and Parrot Crossbill: often impossible to separate from these species without analysis of voice.

fat, 'bulging' cheek

♂ ♀

Rare and local resident (<5,000 pairs) restricted to Scottish Highlands; movements obscure. Pine forest, particularly Scots pine

Parrot Crossbill *Loxia pytyopsittacus* 555

L 17–18 cm | W 30–33 cm

Biggest crossbill, feeds on seeds from large pine cones. FEMALE smaller bill than MALE, but on average Parrot Crossbill has **bigger, deeper, blunter bill**, wider head (thicker neck, often shows 'ruff' when hunched) and smaller eye than Crossbill. Bill deep, **bulging** (like ball pressed into face), slightly 'hanging'.

VOICE Like Crossbill, but typically deeper, harder quality, "*tup*" (rather than "*klip*" or "*jip*") – "*tup-tup-tup-tup….*"

'flat' cheek

♀ ♂

Very rare breeder N Scotland; vagrant from N Europe (<10 per year). Pines.

507

RARE SPARROWS and FINCHES

Two-barred Crossbill   555
Loxia leucoptera
L 14–16 cm | W 25–29 cm

Small crossbill with slender bill, white wingbars and broad white tips to tertials. See Crossbill (*p. 506*). MALE **raspberry-red; blackish wings, two broad white wingbars**. Tertials **boldly tipped white**. FEMALE pale grey-green, smaller tertial tips. JUVENILE olive-grey, dull wing, fine white wingbars.

VOICE High, sharp "*chip-chip-chip.*" Vibrant, piping "*feet*" distinctive.

> Very rare, irregular migrant from N Europe: usually 8–10 per year (<5 records Ireland), most Sep–Mar. Widespread. Coniferous woodland, particularly Larch.

1ST-WINTER ♂
dark tips

CROSSBILL – a few individuals have very thin pale wingbars on fresh feathers, but never a broad double bar and obvious white tertial tips.

ADULT ♂

♂ broad white wingbars and large white tertial spots

ADULT ♀

♀ double white wingbar; tertial spots

JUVENILE FEB–JUL

JUVENILE thin wingbars; white on tertials

Pine Grosbeak
Pinicola enucleator
L 18–20 cm | W 30–35 cm

Very large, bulky (in cold weather) or rather slender, slim-tailed finch with **bulbous bill** and **white wingbars**. MALE pale red and grey with blacker wings. FEMALE bronzy-yellow and grey. JUVENILE like female but male gradually develops orange-red, recalling immature male Crossbill (*p. 506*).

> Vagrant from N Europe: <15 records (Britain), Oct–May. Widespread. Woods, gardens.

ADULT ♂

Shape round (cold, inactive) or slim (active); bulbous bill.

ADULT ♀

RARE SPARROWS and FINCHES

Spanish Sparrow
Passer hispaniolensis
L 14–16 cm | W 22–24 cm

MALE like dark male House Sparrow (p. 490), but **cap all red-brown**, strikingly **white cheek**, broad black streaks on back and black bib that breaks into broad **black streaks over whole of underparts**. FEMALE often indistinguishable from House Sparrow; some show faint streaks below and may have weaker hint of male's pale cheek and dark bib.

Vagrant from SE Europe: <15 records (Britain), most months. Widespread. Usually with House Sparrows.

ADULT ♀

♀ very like House Sparrow; faint streaks (on some) below point to Spanish Sparrow

brown cap, white cheek

♂ BREEDING grey cap

♂ BREEDING FEB–AUG

unstreaked

HOUSE SPARROW

♂ NON-BREEDING AUG–FEB

bold black streaks above and below

NON-BREEDING: pattern obscured by pale fringes but crown still brown; heavily streaked below.

Trumpeter Finch   555
Bucanetes githagineus
L 11·5–13 cm | W 22–26 cm

Small, pale, round-headed finch; like unstreaked Linnet (p. 500) with **bulbous bill**. MALE orange-red bill; pink on wings and rump. FEMALE/JUVENILE paler, no pink; bill pale pink.

VOICE Call nasal, grating "*tchep, tchairp*;" song short, vibrant buzz "*airr.*"

Vagrant from N Africa: <20 records (Britain), May–Jun, Aug–Sep. Widespread. Bare ground; rocks.

pale and plain except for dark brown on wings and tail

♂

Rock Sparrow
Petronia petronia
L 14–16 cm | W 28–32 cm

Like female House Sparrow (p. 490) but bolder **dark band each side of crown** and broad pale stripe over eye; long **brown streaks on whitish underparts**; white spots on tail tip.

VOICE Nasal/twangy "*pee*," harder "*pi-eet*," fast twitter.

Vagrant from S Europe: 1 record (Britain), Jun. On coast. Open, rocky/stony areas.

pale but broadly streaked, with obvious head pattern

ADULT

509

BUNTINGS

BUNTING ID head, wing, rump and tail patterns | streaking | leg colour | calls and song

19 species: 5 resident –1 local SW England, 1 rare breeder Scotland (also a winter visitor); 1 scarce migrant, 13 rare migrants/ vagrants.
NB the vagrant American sparrows are most closely related to buntings – see *pp. 489, 532–535*

Buntings (*pp. 511–523*) look much like finches (see *p. 488* for more information) but have a slightly longer, slimmer tail and different detailed bill shapes, with a narrow upper mandible fitting like a lid on a broader, deeper lower one, adapted for feeding on seeds, particularly grasses.

The shape and pattern of the tertials also differs from finches, often with a distinctly 'stepped' black central patch. Many have bold white tail sides, not unlike some larks and pipits (see *p. 357*). However, buntings hop and shuffle; larks and pipits walk. The most lark-like in other ways, the Corn Bunting, is easily told from them by its plain tail. Some are farmland birds, Reed Bunting is a marsh or wetland bird, while the two non-*Emberiza* species (Snow and Lapland Buntings) are found mainly around the coast in winter. Unlike some finches, buntings have simple songs, with monotonous, rather unmusical phrases given from a low perch.

An impressive list of buntings, including many rare species from Europe and Asia, has been recorded in Britain and Ireland – they can, however, be difficult to identify. Throughout this book, simple, everyday language has been used wherever possible to describe the parts of a bird, but with buntings learning a few technical terms helps to improve precision when looking for the key, often subtle, identification features of some species. This Little Bunting, with its component parts pointed out, aims to clarify the meaning of these terms.

Bunting ageing/sexing In most species, males and females differ and have distinct breeding and non-breeding plumages. Juveniles are often identifiable through their first winter. **Adults and juveniles have a single moult each year.**

Post-juvenile moult
JUL–SEP: usually retaining most secondaries, primaries and tail feathers and some coverts. Unmoulted juvenile primary coverts dark brown, edged rufous, worn and frayed. Iris dark grey-brown, slowly becoming chestnut.

1ST-WINTER SEP–MAR

ADULT (FRESH) SEP–MAR

Adult moult
JUL–SEP: complete moult after breeding. Fresh primary coverts have firm grey tips. Iris dark chestnut. Fresh plumage has pale feather tips obscuring pattern beneath. Tips break away or wear off in spring to give bolder breeding season patterns.

ADULT (WORN) APR–AUG

REED BUNTING

LITTLE BUNTING

Labels: stripe over eye, eyestripe, crown, side of crown, eyering, nape (hindneck), pale cheek spot, cheek, back, throat, dark line by throat, 'moustache', lesser coverts ('shoulder'), median coverts (upper wingbar), greater coverts (lower wingbar), breast, tertials, rump [obscured], wingtip, vent, flank, outer tail feather

BUNTINGS

Lapland Bunting *Calcarius lapponicus* 555

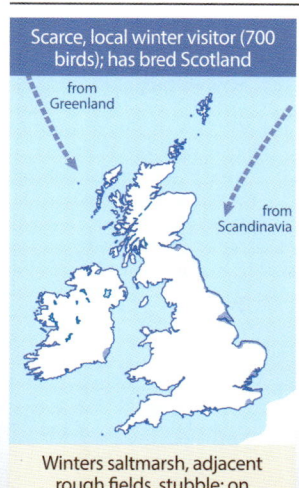

Scarce, local winter visitor (700 birds); has bred Scotland

from Greenland

from Scandinavia

Winters saltmarsh, adjacent rough fields, stubble; on migration, also rocky coastal grasslands; breeds moorland

L 15–16 cm | W 24–27 cm

Low-slung, black-legged bunting, always perches on the ground: see Snow Bunting (*p. 512*) and Reed Bunting (*p. 516*). Autumn/winter birds (most likely) dull, obscure; breeding male (rare) striking.

Rustic Bunting (*p. 519*), N American sparrows (*p. 532–533*)

MALE BREEDING black cap, face and bib; white line on neck. MALE NON-BREEDING broad pale stripe over eye curving under cheek; **black line around cheek**, rusty-red hindneck; **mottled blackish bib** and breast-sides; **striped flank**. FEMALE/1ST-WINTER subdued (more closely resemble Reed Bunting): **pale central crown** with darker sides. Reddish-buff face, triangular **blackish 'corners' to cheek**; nape dull or dusky rufous. Back has long blackish streaks and long creamy stripes; two thin **white wingbars outline reddish panel**.

VOICE Dry, hard, low rattling trill "*trrr-r-r-r-t* or *trr-r-r-t'k*" (lighter "*ticky-ticky-tik*" at distance); soft, or longer, loud "*teu*."

IN FLIGHT, long-winged (more like Snow Bunting than Reed Bunting); best told by call.

♂ NON-BREEDING JUL–MAR [Sep]

crown with pale centre and dark sides

ADULT / 1ST-WINTER ♀ [Oct]

streaks on side of breast extend onto flank

whitish upper and lower wingbars enclose bright chestnut greater coverts

dusky rufous nape

♀ BREEDING MAR–JUL [Jul]

white crescent between black face and chestnut hindneck

ADULT ♂ BREEDING MAR–JUL [Jun]

BUNTINGS

Snow Bunting *Plectrophenax nivalis*

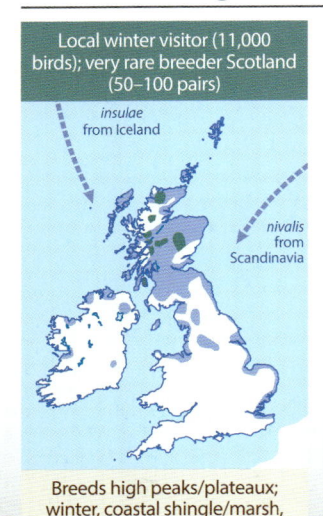

555

Local winter visitor (11,000 birds); very rare breeder Scotland (50–100 pairs)

insulae from Iceland

nivalis from Scandinavia

Breeds high peaks/plateaux; winter, coastal shingle/marsh, also peaks/moors inland

L 15·5–18 cm | W 32–38 cm

Short-legged bunting, always perches on ground (or low roofs around ski lifts, *etc.*). **Unstreaked below, white on wings in flight**. Often tame, inconspicuous.

MALE BREEDING **black-and-white**. FEMALE back buff streaked black. NON-BREEDING (both sexes) **tawny-brown** on crown, cheek and breast; **yellow bill; black legs**. Tawny feather fringes wear off by spring. 1ST-WINTER paler buff tertial tips than adult, more pointed tail feathers.

VOICE Characteristic rippling, rhythmic "*til-lil-il-it!*;" bright, whistled "*peu*," often combined.

Two subspecies breed and winter: **ssp.** *nivalis* (Scandinavia eastwards to Greenland) and **ssp.** *insulae* (Iceland; usually commoner in Britain). NON-BREEDING ssp. *nivalis* back frosty greyish in centre with browner sides and pale rump; ssp. *insulae* back uniformly darker and browner, darker rump and breast-band. BREEDING MALE ssp. *nivalis* has white rump; ssp. *insulae* shows dark feather tips on rump.

ssp. *nivalis* ♀ BREEDING MAR–AUG [Jul]

ssp. *insulae* ♀ BREEDING MAR–AUG [Jun]

ssp. *nivalis* ♂ BREEDING MAR–AUG [May]

unmarked white rump

ssp. *insulae* ♂ BREEDING MAR–AUG [Jun]

dark marks on rump

BUNTINGS

IN FLIGHT, MALE has **white wings**, black tips; FEMALE shorter white band on wing; 1ST-WINTER less white in wing than adults.

[Mar]
ssp. *nivalis*

Determining the age and sex of winter birds can be difficult due to subtle differences between subspecies. White in outer primaries indicates male, but extent depends on age and subspecies. Blunt dark centres to scapulars = male; pointed centres = female. On females, >60% white on base of the second innermost primary indicates **ssp. *nivalis***; <40% white is diagnostic for **ssp. *insulae***.

ssp. *insulae*
NON-BREEDING /
1ST-WINTER ♀
AUG–MAR [Nov]

ssp. *nivalis* (probably)
NON-BREEDING /
1ST-WINTER ♂
AUG–MAR [Oct]

ssp. *nivalis* (probably)
NON-BREEDING /
1ST-WINTER ♂
AUG–MAR [Jan]

ssp. *nivalis*
1ST-WINTER ♀
SEP–MAR [Nov]

ssp. *nivalis*
NON-BREEDING /
1ST-WINTER ♂
FEB–MAR [Mar]

BUNTINGS

Yellowhammer *Emberiza citrinella*

Locally common resident (790,000 pairs, plus 230,000 birds in Ireland; declining)

to/from Scandinavia

Heaths, downs, farmland, moorland edge; more widely in winter

L 16–17 cm | W 23–29 cm

Long, slim, sharp-billed 'yellow' bunting. Feeds on the ground, perches freely, often very upright.

Cirl Bunting, Pine Bunting (p.523) and other rare buntings (pp. 518–523)

Rufous-orange rump, blackish tail with white sides. MALE BREEDING **yellow head** and breast; blackish lines on head; orange-brown on breast and flank. MALE NON-BREEDING head more prominently striped. FEMALE streaked black; thin pale wingbars. Pale **yellowish** below, with dark flank streaks. **Yellowish crown with dark sides**, dark cheek with pale spot. Yellow tinge overall, **rusty rump** and **black-and-white tail**. JUVENILE like female but paler on head and whiter underparts. 1ST-WINTER yellower below but age/sex difficult to tell.

VOICE Call clicking "*tswik*," "*tik*" or rasping "*tzu*." Song high, metallic notes, one or two high/low at end: "*sip-ip-ip-ip-ip-ip-seee-u*" or ending "*-seeee*." Also faster, trilling version.

NOTE: all birds below are ssp. *citrinella*.

1ST-WINTER ♂
SEP–MAR [Oct]

♂ NON-BREEDING
SEP–MAR [Feb]

♂ BREEDING
MAR–SEP [May]

Ssp. *caliginosa* in N/W darker, more greenish on head, rufous on breast/flank than ssp. *citrinella* of S/E, but subspecies intergrade.

♀ BREEDING
MAR–SEP [May]

NON-BREEDING /
1ST-WINTER ♂
SEP–MAR [Oct]

ginger/
chestnut
rump

1ST-WINTER ♀
SEP–MAR [Oct]

BUNTINGS

Cirl Bunting *Emberiza cirlus*

L 16–16·5 cm | W 22–25 cm

Pine Bunting (*p. 523*), other rare buntings (*pp. 518–523*)

Slim, sharp-billed, reddish/yellowish bunting; resembles Yellowhammer and also feeds on the ground (sometimes together), frequently perching in bushes.

Dull olive rump, blackish tail with white sides. MALE BREEDING **black-and-yellow face**, black throat; greenish breast-band. MALE NON-BREEDING black throat obscured by grey feather fringes. FEMALE/JUVENILE/1ST-WINTER like female Yellowhammer, but **rump dull olive-grey**; chestnut more confined to 'shoulder'; underparts have finer streaks, densest around upper breast; plainer dark crown; dark line behind eye and dark edge to cheek with prominent whitish spot; pale eyering.

VOICE Call distinct but elusive: high, thin, quiet "*si*" or "*zit*." Song locates male (but see Yellowhammer and Lesser Whitethroat (*p. 437*)) – a short trill on one note; fast, thin and metallic "*ts-r-r-r-r-r-r-r-r*" or slightly slower, more distinct "*tsi-tsi-tsi-tsi-tsi-tsi-tsi-tsi*," without Yellowhammer's usual flourish. Less wooden, hollow or rattling than Lesser Whitethroat.

Rare and local resident (1,100 pairs); rare migrant/vagrant elsewhere. Vagrant Ireland (1 record).

Farmland, old meadows, tall hedgerows

♂ BREEDING MAR–SEP [May]

♂ NON-BREEDING SEP–MAR [Dec]

NON-BREEDING / 1ST-WINTER ♀ SEP–MAR [Nov]

whitish cheek-spot usually more prominent than on Yellowhammer

olive-grey rump

♀ BREEDING MAR–SEP [Apr]

BUNTINGS

Reed Bunting *Emberiza schoeniclus*

L 14–16 cm | W 21–28 cm

Lapland Bunting (p. 511), rare buntings (pp. 518–523), N American sparrows (pp. 532–533)

Locally common resident (230,000 pairs, plus 220,000 birds Ireland) migrant; winter visitor

Slim, streaky, bunting with **long blackish tail with broad white sides**, revealed in out–in flicks.

MALE BREEDING **black head, white neck and 'moustache'**; upperparts black. MALE NON-BREEDING buff/brown fringes to feathers obscure pattern but wear away by spring to reveal black (variable intermediate stages). FEMALE like non-breeding male; back often has two cream stripes; rump browner. Crown all-dark; **pale stripe over eye**; cheek dark with **blacker surround** ('masked' effect); **broad black stripe** from bill beside white throat. JUVENILE/1ST-WINTER drab; buff stripe over eye, paler cheek; long dark stripes on face reach bill; grey-brown rump; dark legs. White in tail rules out Corn Bunting, sparrows and most finches.

VOICE Call simple "*tseup*" or high, thin "*tseee*." Song, monotonously repeated from low perch, disjointed, short, simple, slow phrase "*sup-jip-chilee-up*."

from Scandinavia
from N Europe

Watersides, wet heaths, moors; gardens in winter

♀ BREEDING
FEB–AUG [Mar]

ADULT ♂
FEB–JUL [Jun]

1ST-WINTER ♀
AUG–MAR [Dec]

changes from winter to summer through wear of dull feather fringes; summer plumages wear gradually darker

rump dull olive in autumn; by Feb–Mar worn to greyish, streaked brown, but ADULT MALE's unstreaked pale grey

♀ rump is generally browner than than that of the male at all ages.

NON-BREEDING/
1ST-WINTER ♂
AUG–FEB [Nov]

NON-BREEDING/
1ST-WINTER ♀
AUG–MAR [Dec]

1ST-WINTER ♂
AUG–MAR [Jan]

BUNTINGS

Corn Bunting *Emberiza calandra*

L 16–19 cm | W 26–32 cm

Large, brown, streaked, **plain-tailed** bunting; no bold colours. Keeps low, **hops** (unlike larks); often on fence or mound of earth in open field, or isolated bush on grassy downland, or sings from overhead wire (tail tilted down, head often tipped back).

Pale buff-brown, streaked dark; streaks merge into central patch on whitish breast. **Large pinkish-buff bill, plain brown tail** and **plain wings** (rules out Skylark (p. 361)). No seasonal differences. ADULT greyish-brown, some with darker sides to crown; breast streaks short. (Breeding adults in W Scotland more heavily streaked and darker above, yellower below than elsewhere.) JUVENILE yellower, sides of crown dark; breast streaks long. IN FLIGHT, groups fly up to perch (Skylarks fly off higher); may briefly dangle legs when taking flight.

VOICE Call loud, full "*quik*" or "*plip*." Song highly characteristic: short, monotonous, crunching glass/shaking keys quality – **short** notes followed by rising, straining trill "*tuc-tuc-tuc-tss-rr-rreeeee*," given in upright, open-billed pose.

Scarce and local resident (10,000 pairs, declining). Now only vagrant in Ireland

Farmland, grassy downs

ADULT ♂

Singing MALE distinctive even at long range: head back, bill open; on exposed perch in open landscape.

ADULT
streaks on breast often merge to form dark patch

forehead slopes to thick, pale bill

no bright colours or strong pattern

closely streaked all over

ADULT
plain tail

ADULT

517

RARE BUNTINGS

Little Bunting
Emberiza pusilla
L 12–13·5 cm | W 18–20 cm

👁 N American sparrows (pp. 532–533)

Small, neat bunting, subtle but distinctive (but see Rustic Bunting). Resembles female Reed Bunting (*p. 516*) except: small, sharp, **straight-edged bill**; distinct **white eyering** in plain face; **rusty cheek** with whitish spot at rear; **pale/rufous between eye and bill**; dark eyestripe, blackish edge of cheek **does not reach bill**; dull grey-brown lesser coverts; two thin, whitish wingbars and pale **pink legs**. MALE rufous central stripe on black crown; rufous face. FEMALE duller, face less red. 1ST-WINTER may have rufous nape, usually rufous cheek, central crown and nape between darker sides – bill shape, eyering and plain face all useful features.

VOICE Call important: sharp, clicking "*zik*" or "*tik*".

Rare autumn migrant/vagrant from NE Europe: <2,000 records, 30–50 per year (<100 records Ireland). Most Sep–Mar. Coastal grassland, bushes. Most winter in SE Asia.

REED BUNTING – common species most likely to cause confusion in the autumn plumages shown here. Note bill shape and long dark streaks on cheek and throat reaching bill.

♂ NON-BREEDING like Rustic Bunting

1ST-WINTER ♂ like Black-faced Bunting

JUVENILE / ♀ like Little, Pallas's Reed and Black-faced Buntings

pale eyering
NON-BREEDING / 1ST-WINTER SEP–MAR [Oct]

sharp, straight-edged bill
NON-BREEDING / 1ST-WINTER SEP–MAR [Sep]

dark surround on rear edge of cheek

Chestnut-eared Bunting
Emberiza fucata
L 15–16 cm | W 20–22 cm

Much like Little Bunting, but larger: similar chestnut cheek with **pale buff spot** and **bright, pale eyering** – but **lacks dark eyestripe and dark edge to cheek**. Yellowish breast; dark streaking on breast, hint of chestnut band below; chestnut lower back and rump (dull on Little Bunting); longer tail.

VOICE Call explosive "*tzic*" similar to Rustic Bunting.

Vagrant from Asia: <5 records (Britain), Oct. On coast. Scrub.

👁 N American sparrows (pp. 532–533)

1ST-WINTER SEP–MAR [Oct]

Size of Reed Bunting, but pattern like Little Bunting with a weaker pale stripe over eye, stronger eyering and less black on cheek edge.

RARE BUNTINGS

Rustic Bunting
Emberiza rustica
L 13–14·5 cm | W 20–24 cm

N American sparrows (pp. 532–533)

Very rare migrant/vagrant from NE Europe: <600 records, 6–8 per year, declining (<25 records Ireland). May–Jun, most Sep–Oct. Marshy scrub, thickets, woods. Winters in SE Asia.

Neat, peak-crowned bunting. Migrants inconspicuous. See Little Bunting. Bold face pattern; streaked rufous breast band and **rufous flank stripes**. Unstreaked **red-brown rump** (redder than Yellowhammer (*p. 514*), brighter than Reed Bunting (*p. 516*)). Thin white wingbars. Bill pink with dark tip (grey on Reed Bunting). MALE BREEDING **black head, white stripe over eye**, white nape, cheek spot and throat. MALE NON-BREEDING/FEMALE head pattern similar to breeding male but slightly obscured; streaked red-brown below. 1ST-WINTER **pale crown with blacker streaks on sides**; long, **broad, buff stripe behind eye**; black eyestripe and edge of cheek; white cheek spot. Rufous streaks across breast; broader **red-brown streaks** on flank.

VOICE Call sharp "*zit*."

♀ BREEDING MAR–SEP [May]

1ST-WINTER SEP–MAR [Sep]

pale stripes above and below dark cheek

♂ BREEDING MAR–SEP [May]

brick-red rump

white underparts

Pallas's Reed Bunting
Emberiza pallasi
L 13–13·5 cm | W 20–25 cm

1ST-WINTER ♂ SEP–MAR [Sep]

Vagrant from Asia: <10 records (Britain), Sep–Oct, Jun. Widespread. Scrub.

Only likely in autumn at migration watchpoint: look for 'small dull Reed Bunting' with pale rump.

Like **small** Reed Bunting (*p. 516*); straight-edged bill, long tail. Black streaks on grey-buff upperparts, paler rump, dull **grey patch on lesser coverts**. Weak head pattern: pale brown cap without dark sides or dark eyestripe; **pale cheek above black spot**. 1ST-WINTER almost **unmarked** below but some migrate in JUVENILE plumage, streaked blackish on breast, browner lesser coverts and rump, **two whitish wingbars**; pink-based bill.

VOICE Call sparrow-like "*chee-ulp*."

1ST-WINTER ♂ SEP–MAR [Sep]

pale rump

grey

REED BUNTING ♀

bright rufous lesser coverts

brown rump

streaked

RARE BUNTINGS

Black-headed Bunting *Emberiza melanocephala*
L 14–15·5 cm | W 20–23 cm

Slim, rather long-billed bunting. MALE BREEDING red-brown above, **yellow below**; **black hood**. FEMALE dull; hood greyish, throat and underparts pale yellow; **rump rusty** (greenish/yellowish on Red-headed Bunting (*p. 538*)). 1ST-WINTER duller; greyish-buff below, **yellow under tail**; brown tail lacks white. May be impossible to separate from escaped/possible vagrant Red-headed Bunting unless rusty rump and finely streaked crown of Black-headed Bunting can be seen.

VOICE Call fine high "*psip*."

👁 Red-headed Bunting (*p. 538*)

Vagrant from Asia: <250 records (<15 records Ireland), spring/summer, most May–Jun. Scattered. Grassland, bushes.

♂ BREEDING FEB–AUG [May]

♀ BREEDING FEB–AUG [May]

finely streaked crown

rusty coloured rump

1ST-WINTER SEP–MAR [Oct]

Yellow-breasted Bunting *Emberiza aureola*
EN CR
L 15 cm | W 20–22 cm

Slim, rather long-billed bunting. MALE BREEDING (very rare) chestnut above, yellow below; broad white 'shoulder' patch (often hidden); black face. JUVENILE/1ST-WINTER **yellowish**, closely streaked blackish; two pale bands down back; **pale central stripe on dark crown**; yellowish cheek spot, yellow-buff band beneath black-edged greyish cheek; **two white wingbars**. Rump grey-brown, streaked; white side to tail.

VOICE Call high, sharp, metallic "*tsip*."

Very rare migrant from NE Europe: <250 records (<10 Ireland), fast declining, most Sep–Oct. On coast, most N Isles. Scrub, stubbles.

♂ BREEDING FEB–AUG [May]

JUVENILE JUL–SEP [Sep]

pale crown stripe

RARE BUNTINGS

Yellow-browed Bunting
Emberiza chrysophrys
L 13–14 cm | W 20–25 cm

Small bunting with striped head pattern. ADULT/1ST-WINTER black crown, **white stripe on nape**; broad pale stripe over eye, **yellow, fading out to white** behind; chestnut cheek with whitish spot at rear. Narrow black streaks on pale underparts.

VOICE Call thin, high "*sip*."

Vagrant from Asia: <10 records (Britain), May, Sep–Oct. On coast. Scrub.

N American sparrows (pp. 532–533)

ADULT / 1ST-WINTER
SEP–MAR [Sep]

Black-faced Bunting
Emberiza spodocephala
L 14–15·5 cm | W 20–23 cm

Slim, 'dull' bunting with white tail sides. MALE grey on head (black on face from Dec); resembles Dunnock (p. 380). ADULT/1ST-WINTER FEMALE like dull olive-grey Reed Bunting (p. 516) with greyer neck and greyish rump; dark stripe beside throat beneath pale 'moustache'; dull greyish or yellowish underparts.

VOICE Call thin, metallic "*tip*."

Vagrant from Asia: <10 records (Britain), Mar–Apr, Oct. On coast. Scrub.

♂ black on face

ADULT / 1ST-WINTER ♀

[Dec]

♂ [Apr]

Chestnut Bunting
Emberiza rutila
L 14–15 cm | W 20–21 cm

Small bunting with rather domed head and small bill. **Rump chestnut; tail lacks prominent white sides.** 1ST-WINTER streaked black and grey-buff; wings **rusty** with two buff wingbars. Crown and rear cheek rusty, cheek grey-centred. Underparts yellowish with blackish streaks on breast and flank.

VOICE Call a sharp "*zik*."

Vagrant from Asia: 1 record (Britain), Oct. On coast. Status confused by occasional escapes. Scrub.

1ST-WINTER ♂
SEP–MAR [Oct]

RARE BUNTINGS

Ortolan Bunting *Emberiza hortulana*
L 15–16·5 cm | W 21–27 cm

Slender, delicate, pale bunting with soft, pastel shades and distinctive expression; black-and-white tail. Yellowhammer (*p. 514*) shape, with slim bill and notched tail. White or **yellowish eyering in plain face**; yellow chin and throat; rather sharp, pointed **pinkish bill** and pink legs. Feeds on the ground. MALE **pale green head; yellow throat and line under cheek**; pale orange underparts, browner upperparts (no great contrast); wears darker overall by May. FEMALE similar but duller, finely streaked on crown and breast. 1ST-WINTER like female, with **yellowish eyering**, more streaks below, hint of grey-green on head and pale orange beneath.

VOICE Metallic "*chip*" or "*sli*" alternating with fuller "*plit*."

Cretzschmar's Bunting 555
Very rare migrant from Europe: <3,000 records, 35–75 per year, declining (<150 records Ireland), most Apr–Oct. On coast. Grassland, bushes. Winters in Africa.

♀ [May]

1ST-WINTER SEP–MAR [Sep]

bright pale eyering; bill pink and chin yellow by April on ♂

1ST-SUMMER [May]

♂ [May]

'cold' brown rump

unique green/yellow/orange combination; look for eyering, pink bill

Cretzschmar's Bunting 555
Emberiza caesia
L 14–15·5 cm | W 23–26 cm

Like Ortolan Bunting; eyering white, bill pink. MALE head and breast **blue-grey**; throat **rusty**. (obscured by greenish-buff fringes Aug–Apr). FEMALE (not recorded) head and breast paler, less blue, finely streaked black; throat orange-buff; 'warm' brown rump. 1ST-WINTER as non-breeding adult.

VOICE Metallic "*tchip*" or "*schip*."

Vagrant from SE Europe: <10 records (Britain), Apr–Jun, Sep. On coast. Grassland, rocky areas.

'warm' brown rump

♀ [Mar]

blue-grey head and rusty throat

♂ [Jun]

RARE BUNTINGS

Pine Bunting *Emberiza leucephalos* [VU]
L 16–17·5 cm | W 25–30 cm

Long, slim bunting; size and shape of Yellowhammer (*p. 514*). MALE **white crown, cheek** and **breast-band**; broad chestnut stripe over eye, edged black, and chestnut throat; **rufous streaks beneath**. Colours partly obscured by buff-white fringes Sep–Mar. FEMALE/1ST-WINTER like pale Yellowhammer but **lacking yellow**; **primaries edged white**. Beware infrequent pale Yellowhammer and hybrids/ intergrades, which have pale yellow feather edges on wings.

VOICE Sharp "*tswik*" notes, like Yellowhammer.

pale Yellowhammers have some yellow, most reliably on edge of primaries

YELLOWHAMMER ♀ [Jan]

PINE BUNTING

white (no yellow)

NON-BREEDING / 1ST-WINTER ♂ SEP–MAR [Nov]

1ST-WINTER ♂ SEP–MAR [Nov]

1ST-WINTER ♀ SEP–MAR [Dec]

Vagrant from NE Europe/Asia: <75 records (<5 Ireland), most months, most Oct. Widespread. Farmland, scrub.

Compared with Yellowhammer, whiter beneath with rufous streaks and pale orange flank; wing feathers narrowly edged white, never yellow.

Rock Bunting *Emberiza cia*
L 16 cm | W 20–27 cm

Slim, terrestrial bunting; rusty-brown with black streaks above, **plain orange-brown below**. ADULT head/breast grey; **black bands** beside crown, through eye and under cheek; MALE brighter than FEMALE (not recorded). JUVENILE/ 1ST-WINTER (not recorded) drabber still, crown streaked brown, head stripes less distinct.

VOICE Call thin, high, short "*si*."

Vagrant from S Europe: <10 records (Britain), Feb–Jun, Oct. Widespread. Grassland, rocky areas.

ADULT ♂

523

VAGRANT LANDBIRDS FROM NORTH AMERICA

Rare birds from North America are exciting to see in Britain and Ireland. Some species are regular visitors from the Canadian Arctic, but from Canada and the USA a remarkable total of 135 North American (Nearctic) species (excluding pelagic seabirds) have occurred as vagrants in Britain and/or Ireland.

More than 80% of all individual American landbirds have been recorded in autumn, centred on mid-October. In south-west England, 95% are in autumn; in the Northern Isles autumn arrivals still predominate, but more than 35% have been in spring. In autumn, eastbound transatlantic weather systems bring small birds across quickly: in spring, when seed-eaters are more frequent, such conditions are rare. Consequently, birds that arrive in the autumn (including the insectivorous warblers, vireos, thrushes, cuckoos and flycatchers) are very likely to have made the Atlantic crossing without stopping, although spring arrivals, particularly the granivorous American sparrows (especially those records close to British and Irish ports), may have made all or part of the crossing on board vessels. Birds that are thought to have arrived in this way are often termed 'ship-assisted' vagrants.

In the past, south-west England – including renowned areas such as the Isles of Scilly – was favoured by American landbirds, although they have been widely spread across islands and headlands from south-west Ireland and Dyfed to North Wales. More recently, the Western Isles, Orkney and Shetland have earned a special place for such birds. In the north, autumn arrivals tend to be earlier than in the south, and there is a greater proportion of seed-eating birds – finches, buntings, sparrows – in the overall mix. Yet American landbirds turn up at widely scattered sites across Britain and Ireland, even on bird feeders in gardens.

The following table summarizes the Nearctic bird species that have been recorded (the figures do not include European species with Nearctic subspecies that have been recorded (e.g. Brent Goose (Black Brant), Bewick's Swan (Tundra Swan) and Iceland Gull ('Thayer's Gull')). Green shading indicates those 52 species covered in the following section; buff shading indicates species covered elsewhere in the book, all cross-referenced to the relevant page(s).

'Type' of bird	Species	Pages
Wildfowl	14	64–75
Divers	1	91
Grebes	1	91
Cormorants	1	92
Auks	3	113
Frigatebirds	1	115
Gulls	6	152–154, 156, 158
Terns	4	161, 169–171, 173
Waders	23*	226, 228, 230–245
Rails	3	253–254
Herons and egrets	6	268–270
Cranes	1	270
Doves	1	290
Nightjars	1	301
Large birds of prey	2	320, 322
Falcons	1	334
Swifts	1	351
Swallows and martins	3	356
Pipits	1	369
Waxwings	1	387
Thrushes	7	398–399
Nuthatches	1	477
Vireos	3	525
Crests (kinglets)	1	525
N American warblers	20	526–529
Tyrant flycatchers	4	530
Mimids (mockingbird, thrasher, catbird)	3	531
American sparrows (incl. Eastern Towhee, Dark-eyed Junco)	8	532–533, 535
Grosbeaks and buntings	2	534
Finches (Evening Grosbeak)	1	534
Tanagers	2	535
Icterids (American orioles and blackbirds, Bobolink, Brown-headed Cowbird)	4	536
Kingfishers	1	537
Woodpeckers	1	537
Cuckoos	2	537

* including Eskimo Curlew (now probably extinct)

VIREOS | CRESTS

Vireos

Like sluggish, heavy-moving warblers; round head and thick, wide bill; stout legs. They inhabit forest and undergrowth in North America. Look for precise head patterns, overall colour and presence or absence of wingbars. They have occurred widely in Britain and Ireland, mostly near coasts.

Red-eyed Vireo *Vireo olivaceus*

L 13–14 cm | W 22–24 cm

ADULT (Sep–Mar) red eye; worn primaries. 1ST-WINTER dark brown eye until late winter; unworn primary tips.

- grey cap with blackish sides
- bold white stripe over eye
- plain wing
- 1ST-WINTER

Most regular North American landbird (3–4 per year). <200 records (>50 Ireland), Sep–Nov. Scattered (most on coast).

Yellow-throated Vireo
Vireo flavifrons
L 14 cm | W 20–24 cm

1 record (Britain), Sep. On coast.

- 1ST-WINTER
- pale yellow 'spectacles'
- two white wingbars
- yellow throat
- white underparts

Philadelphia Vireo
Vireo philadelphicus
L 13 cm | W 20–23 cm

<5 records (1 Britain), Oct. On coast.

- 1ST-WINTER
- plain grey crown; diffuse pale stripe over eye
- dark from bill through eye
- yellow underparts

Crests (kinglets)

Like tiny warblers; kinglets are the North American equivalent of the regular 'crests' (see p. 422): one species has occurred, but only once, so not frequently enough to establish any pattern; future occurrences are most likely in late autumn.

Ruby-crowned Kinglet *Regulus calendula* ◆

L 9–11 cm | W 16–18 cm

Tiny, like grey-green Goldcrest (p. 424) without crown stripes. MALE (not recorded) small red nape, usually hidden. FEMALE lacks red; 1ST-WINTER a little greyer overall.

1 record (Ireland), Oct. On coast.

- white eyering
- black-and-white wingbars
- dull greyish face, no 'moustache' or eyestripe

RARE NORTH AMERICAN LANDBIRDS

North American Warblers

Not related to Old World warblers, but similar-looking small, slender, slim-billed birds that favour trees and dense foliage. They arrive, particularly after strong winds from the west, most often on western headlands and islands. Summer adults (very rare) are brightly coloured but autumn juveniles/first-winter birds are much duller and more difficult to identify.

LOOK FOR head patterns | wing and tail markings | upperpart/underpart streaking

♂ BREEDING

Blackpoll Warbler
Setophaga striata
L 13–15 cm | W 20–25 cm

Bay-breasted Warbler
<60 records (<15 Ireland), Jun, Sep–Dec (most Oct). On coast.

1ST-WINTER

olive head; faint dark streaks on olive back

white edge to outer tail feathers; white under tail

breast yellowest at front

faint streaks

Full black cap, white cheek; wingbars

two long, curved white wingbars

long wings

orange legs

♂ BREEDING

Myrtle Warbler
(Yellow-rumped Warbler)
Setophaga coronata
L 12–15 cm | W 19–24 cm

<50 records (<20 Ireland), Jan–Feb, May–Jun, Sep–Nov. Mostly on coast.

1ST-WINTER

two long, white wingbars

pale yellow rump

white crescents above and below eye

yellow rump, breast sides and crown; eye crescents, wingbars

dark streaks on flank

black legs

Cape May Warbler
Setophaga tigrina
L 12–14 cm | W 19–22 cm

<5 records (Britain), Jun, Oct–Nov. Scattered.

plain greyish head/back

1ST-WINTER ♀

greenish wings, diffuse pale wingbars

white crescents above and below eye

♂ BREEDING

yellow collar, chestnut cheeks, black cap, wingbar

olive rump

underparts white, flank streaked grey

darkish legs, yellow soles to feet

WARBLERS

Nearctic warblers – preferred habitats

Trees	Blackpoll, Myrtle, Cape May, Bay-breasted, Blackburnian, Magnolia, Canada, Tennessee and Golden-winged Black-and-white Warblers, American Redstart, Northern Parula	Bushes	Wilson's Warbler, Blue-winged Warbler, Yellow Warbler, Myrtle Warbler
		Wet vegetation	Hooded Warbler, Common Yellowthroat
		Ground	Northern Waterthrush, Ovenbird

Bay-breasted Warbler
Setophaga castanea
L 13–15 cm | W 20–23 cm

1 record (Britain), Oct. On coast.

1ST-WINTER

- faint dark streaks on back
- strong bill
- buff under tail
- two long, curved white wingbars
- unstreaked

Blackburnian Warbler
Setophaga fusca
L 11–13 cm | W 20–22 cm

<5 records (Britain), Sep, Oct. On coast.

1ST-WINTER

- **broad pale yellow** stripe over eye
- dark, triangular cheek patch
- two wide, white wingbars
- orange-yellow throat
- long dark streaks on flank

Chestnut-sided Warbler
Setophaga pensylvanica
L 10–14 cm | W 16–21 cm

<5 records (Britain), Sep, Oct. On coast.

1ST-WINTER / ADULT ♀

- lime-green crown/back
- grey cheek
- 'pot-bellied'
- unstreaked grey-white underparts; hint of **chestnut on flank** suggests ♂

Magnolia Warbler
Setophaga magnolia
L 11–13 cm | W 16–20 cm

<5 records (Britain), Sep. On coast.

Clear view of the tail most important.

- white eyering
- scarcely streaked back
- two narrow white wingbars
- white band across tail
- yellow underparts; few soft streaks

1ST-WINTER

American Redstart
Setophaga ruticilla
L 13 cm | W 16–23 cm

<10 records (<5 Ireland), Sep–Dec. Scattered.

- yellow sides to tail
- pale yellow band on wing (may be absent)
- flank yellow (♀) or orange (♂)

1ST-WINTER ♀

Northern Parula
Setophaga americana
L 11–12 cm | W 16–18 cm

- green-yellow patch on back

1ST-WINTER ♂ — brighter than ♀

- white crescents above/below eye
- pale yellow throat/breast

1ST-WINTER ♀

- blue-grey wings; two wingbars

<20 records (<5 Ireland), Sep–Nov. On coast.

RARE NORTH AMERICAN LANDBIRDS

Preferred habitats *p. 513*

Hooded Warbler
Setophaga citrina
L 13 cm | W 18–20 cm

<5 records (Britain), Sep. On coast.

long white spots under tail visible from below or when tail fanned

broad yellow patch above large dark eye

very pale legs/feet

Wilson's Warbler
Cardellina pusilla
L 10–12 cm | W 16–20 cm

<5 records (1 Ireland), Sep, Oct. On coast.

dark cap; black eye in yellow face

relatively long tail; no white markings

pale legs/feet, yellow soles

1ST-WINTER ♂

Yellow Warbler
Setophaga aestiva (petechia)
L 12–13 cm | W 16–20 cm

<10 records (<5 Ireland), Aug–Nov. On coast.

plain face

pale-fringed tertials

yellow edges to tail; no white markings

yellow underparts – may have **chestnut** streaks

1ST-WINTER ♂

Common Yellowthroat
Geothlypis trichas
L 14 cm | W 20–22 cm

<15 records (1 Ireland), Feb–Jun, Oct–Nov. On coast.

black cheek yellow throat

1ST-WINTER ♂

1ST-WINTER ♀ [probably]

pale yellow throat

pale brownish underparts

Black-and-white Warbler *Mniotilta varia*
L 11–13 cm | W 20–22 cm

<20 records (<5 Ireland), Mar, Sep–Dec. Scattered.

Unmistakable tiny, black-and-white-striped warbler; behaves like Nuthatch/Treecreeper (*pp. 474–475*). Pale crown stripe rules out adult male Blackpoll Warbler (*p. 526*). FEMALE/1ST-WINTER have paler ear coverts than MALE. Looks blue-grey in flight or quick glimpse.

1ST-WINTER ♀

buffy cheek/flank and more diffuse stripes suggest ♀

black and white stripes all over

black crown with white central stripe

1ST-WINTER ♂

WARBLERS

Canada Warbler *Cardellina canadensis* ◆
13 cm | WS 19–21 cm

1ST-WINTER ♀
- white eyering
- long, plain grey tail
- plain grey wings
- pale legs
- variable breast-band

1 record (Ireland), Oct. On coast.

Tennessee Warbler
Leiothlypis (Oreothlypis) peregrina
L 11·5 cm | W 18–20 cm

Small, greenish warbler, somewhat like Arctic Warbler (p. 451) but **yellower**.
- faint wingbar
- weak stripe over eye
- white undertail
- fine, grey-based bill

<5 records (Britain), Sep. On coast.

1ST-WINTER

NT Golden-winged Warbler
Vermivora chrysoptera
L 11·5 cm | W 18–20 cm

1 record (Britain), Jan. Inland.

- broad black 'mask' and throat
- yellow on wing

♂

Blue-winged Warbler ◆
Vermivora cyanoptera
L 11·5 cm | W 18–20 cm

1 record (Ireland), Oct. On coast.

- bluish-grey wings, two pale wingbars
- dark stripe from bill to eye

1ST-WINTER ♂

Northern Waterthrush
Parkesia noveboracensis
L 12–15 cm | W 21–24 cm

Small, pipit-like; **walks on the ground**, **bobbing tail** like wagtail. **VOICE** loud, sharp "*chink*."

<10 records (<5 Ireland), Aug–Oct. On coast.

- very long pale stripe over eye tapers to nape
- dark streaks on buff/white underparts

1ST-WINTER

Ovenbird
Seiurus aurocapilla
L 11–14 cm | W 19–26 cm

Small, rounded warbler, **walks on the ground** with deliberate steps; bobs tail; tosses leaves aside.

<10 records (<5 Ireland), Sep, Oct, Dec–Feb. Most on coast.

- rusty crown stripe, edged black
- white eyering
- long black stripes on white breast

1ST-WINTER

529

RARE NORTH AMERICAN LANDBIRDS

Tyrant Flycatchers

Despite the name, this group has no close equivalent in Britain and Ireland; it includes various upright, large-headed, large-billed flycatching birds of woods and bushes. In autumn the smaller species can pose almost insuperable identification problems, as they are extremely similar and best separated by their songs and calls.

Eastern Kingbird *Tyrannus tyrannus*
L 19–23 cm | W 33–38 cm

Rather upright, slender, big-headed, long-tailed flycatcher; blackish head and upperparts, white underparts; **white tip** to tail, striking in flight.
1ST-WINTER dull smoky-grey above, wing feathers edged white.
VOICE Harsh "*kit*" or "*kitter.*"

<5 records (2 Ireland), Sep–Oct. On coast. Bushes, trees.

strong, wide bill
dark 'hood'
greyish upperparts
1ST-WINTER [Aug]
long, black tail with white tip
white underparts

Eastern Phoebe *Sayornis phoebe*
L 14–17 cm | W 26–28 cm

Upright, **large-headed**, long-tailed flycatcher; blackish head, grey-brown upperparts, white throat, buffish underparts.
VOICE Sharp "*chip.*"

1 record (Britain), Apr. On coast. Exposed perches.

dark 'hood'; no eyering
all-dark bill
grey-brown upperparts; two indistinct buff wingbars
white throat; grey breast
1ST-WINTER [Nov]
buffish underparts
pumps tail up and down

Alder Flycatcher *Empidonax alnorum*
L 13–14 cm | W 18–22 cm

Small, olive-and-yellowish flycatcher; two white wingbars, **short primary projection**.
(NOTE: Alder and Willow Flycatchers *E. traillii* (not recorded) very difficult, even when trapped and measured.)
VOICE Call "*pip*" (Willow Flycatcher "*whit*").

<5 records (Britain), Sep, Oct. On coast. Bushes.

1ST-WINTER [Sep]
round, dusky head
bill grey
greyish back and wings
whitish throat and underparts
pale tertial fringes
two white wingbars
short primary projection

Acadian Flycatcher *Empidonax virescens*
L 12–13 cm | W 17–20 cm

Large-headed, stout-billed flycatcher; two white wingbars, **long primary projection**.
VOICE Call explosive "*peet-sah.*"

1 record (Britain), Sep. On coast. Bushes.

thin eyering
bill long, pink at base
olive-green head and back, greyer wings
yellowish throat and underparts
pale tertial fringes
two white wingbars
ADULT / 1ST-WINTER [Sep]
long primary projection

TYRANT FLYCATCHERS | MIMIDS

Mockingbirds and Thrashers (mimids)

A very varied group of long-tailed, thrush-like birds: those that have occurred being relatively distinctive (although there are other species in North America that are closely similar).

1ST-WINTER

Brown Thrasher
Toxostoma rufum
L 23–30 cm | W 29–33 cm

Large (Blackbird-sized (*p. 391*)), thrush-like; skulks on ground/under thickets. **Long tail**; slightly downcurved bill; yellow eye; strong, pale legs. **Bright rufous** above, with **two black-and-white wingbars**; buffy-white below with rows of short **blackish streaks**.
VOICE Loud, 'smacking' "*tsak*."

1 record (Britain), Nov. Coastal thicket.

Northern Mockingbird
Mimus polyglottos
L 21–28 cm | W 31–38 cm

Slender (Blackbird-sized (*p. 391*)), thrush-like; perches boldly in open. Long tail, curved bill, dark legs, pale eye. Pale grey above, whitish below with two white wingbars and white patch on spread wing; white-sided tail. (Great Grey Shrike (*p. 459*) also pale grey-and-white, but has black 'mask' and blacker wings and tail).
VOICE Harsh, grating "*schew*" or "*scair*."

<5 records (Britain), May, Aug. Coasts.

ADULT

Grey Catbird
Dumetella carolinensis
L 20–24 cm | W 22–30 cm

Slender, dark, small-headed, elusive bird of dense thickets. Smoky-grey with **black cap**; **long, broad, slightly rounded tail, often raised**, when shows **dark rufous undertail coverts**.

<5 records (1 Ireland), Oct, Nov. Coastal thicket.

1ST-WINTER

531

RARE NORTH AMERICAN LANDBIRDS

American Sparrows

A varied group, some strikingly patterned, others presenting real identification problems as there are several similar species and subspecies in North America. They are small terrestrial birds, likely to be found in varied open habitats: some records are close to dockyards, indicating likely 'ship-assisted' transatlantic passage.

Summary of favoured habitats and key features of American sparrows					
Lark Sparrow	Savannah Sparrow	Red Fox Sparrow	Song Sparrow	White-throated Sparrow	White-crowned Sparrow
Grassland			Scrub		
Slim, long-tailed; dull buff-brown; unstreaked below; unique striped head pattern	Dumpy, short-tailed, 'neckless'; pale brown, thickly streaked; pale stripe over eye (yellowish in front)	Thickset; rufous, white below with rusty streaks; broad grey stripe over eye, grey collar	Long-tailed; greyish to rufous, white below streaked rufous/black; broad grey stripe over eye, grey cheek	Stocky; brown above, grey below; broad yellow-and-white stripe over eye; white throat	Stocky; brown above, grey below; black-and-white-striped crown, grey throat

White-crowned Sparrow
Zonotrichia leucophrys
L 18 cm | W 24–25 cm

Stocky brown-and-grey sparrow. ADULT head **striped black-and-white** with narrow white central crown stripe; cheek and throat grey. Streaked brown, buff, black above; two white wingbars; underparts uniform grey. JUVENILE/1ST-WINTER head stripes **red-brown** and pale grey.

<10 records (1 Ireland), Jan–Mar, Apr, May, Oct. On coast.

1ST-WINTER
crown stripes grey and rufous

ADULT
Western ssp.
gambelli

ADULT
Eastern ssp.
leucophrys

Western birds lack black between eye and bill

White-throated Sparrow
Zonotrichia albicollis
L 18 cm | W 24–25 cm

Stocky brown-and-grey sparrow. ADULT **cap black** with **thin** white central stripe; **broad white stripe** over eye, **bright yellow** at front; **white throat** (edged black); dark rufous 'shoulder'; two white wingbars; underparts unstreaked grey, flank softly streaked brown. JUVENILE/1ST-WINTER drab and browner, head stripes **black and buff** with **yellow spot** near bill; grey cheek; underparts streaked grey.

<60 records (<5 Ireland), most months, mainly May–Jun. Scattered, mostly near coast.

minority 'tan-striped' form is black-brown and buff on head

ADULT/
1ST-SUMMER

ADULT/
1ST-SUMMER

AMERICAN SPARROWS

Red Fox Sparrow ◆
Passerella iliaca
L 15–19 cm | W 26–28 cm

Thickset, **rusty-and-white** sparrow with broad **grey stripe over eye** and grey collar. Rufous cheek; **bright rufous rump and tail**. Underparts white, with heavy arrow-shaped streaks of rusty-brown and blackish.

1 record (Ireland), Jun. On coast.

ADULT

Song Sparrow
Melospiza melodia
L 11–18 cm | W 18–25 cm

Long-tailed, bright, **rusty, grey and buff** sparrow. Pale buff and rufous streaks above; buff below with long streaks of dark rufous, extensive **white belly. Cap rufous** with thin, **grey-buff central stripe**. Broad grey stripe over eye; grey cheek edged dark rufous. Long, rounded tail.

<10 records (Britain), Apr–Jun (most), Oct. On coast.

ADULT

Savannah Sparrow
Passerculus sandwichensis
L 11–17 cm | W 18–25 cm

Small, dumpy, rather 'neckless', short-tailed, streaky sparrow. Streaked brown and black above; white below, streaked blackish. **Crown dark with whitish central stripe**; pale stripe over eye may be **yellow** at front; yellow-white eyering. Brown cheek edged black above and below, and black 'moustache', in bunting-like pattern. Slender tail edged buffish.

<5 records (Britain), Apr, Sep, Oct. On coast.

Two subspecies recorded: ssp. *labradorius* and ssp. *princeps*, which is larger, paler and has narrower, browner streaks.

1ST-WINTER

Lark Sparrow
Chondestes grammacus
L 15–17 cm | W 28 cm

Long-tailed, elongated sparrow. Pointed grey bill; strong pink legs. Buff-brown, streaked black above. **Head boldly striped rufous, black and buff with black, white and chestnut cheek stripes**. Grey-buff below with black breast spot.

<5 records (Britain), May, Jun–Jul. On coast.

ADULT

RARE NORTH AMERICAN LANDBIRDS

'Finches', Buntings, Tanagers & 'New World Blackbirds' (icterids)

A mixed group, some species resembling Old World finches and buntings. **Tanagers** are slender, finch-like, thick-billed, fruit-eating species of forest canopy; **'New World Blackbirds'** (icterids) include sharp-billed American orioles and blackbirds, cowbirds and Bobolink. They find what cover they can where they arrive on coasts and islands, most favouring trees and bushes.

Rose-breasted Grosbeak
Pheucticus ludovicianus
L 18–22 cm | W 29–33 cm

Large, heavy, thick-billed, finch-like. ADULT MALE **black-and-white** with black hood, **red breast patch**, whitish bill. FEMALE/1ST-WINTER warm brown streaked black above; two wingbars of white spots; brown crown with paler central stripe, **broad white stripe over eye**, brown cheek; underparts yellow-buff, streaked dark brown. 1ST-WINTER MALE has blacker crown and cheek, some pale red on breast.

<40 records (<10 Ireland), Apr–May, Sep–Jan (most Oct). On coast. Trees/bushes.

ADULT ♂

Unique; striking black-and-white plumage

1ST-WINTER ♀

Evening Grosbeak
Hesperiphona vespertina
L 20 cm | W 30–33 cm

Large, heavy finch with massive **pale, conical bill**. MALE yellowish with **dark grey head**, broad **yellow stripe over forehead and eye**; yellow 'shoulder' and underparts, large **white patch** above **black wing**; black tail. FEMALE/1ST-WINTER paler, greyer, with plain grey head.

<5 records (Britain), Mar. Most on coast. Trees.

1ST-WINTER ♂

Indigo Bunting
Passerina cyanea
L 11–15 cm | W 18–23 cm

Small, round-headed, finch-like with small, pointed bill and **blackish legs**. MALE BREEDING vivid blue. MALE NON-BREEDING blue, suffused with brown. FEMALE pale brown above, buff below with soft brown streaks; black eye in plain head; tan wingbars; steely-blue sheen on tail. 1ST-WINTER as female, males increasingly with and scattered **blue mottling**.

<5 records (1 Ireland), May, Oct. On coast. Trees.

1ST-SUMMER ♂

1ST-YEAR ♂

1ST-WINTER

Vivid blue plumage of breeding male is unmistakable.

FINCHES | BUNTINGS | TANAGERS

Dark-eyed Junco
Junco hyemalis
L 13–17 cm | W 18–25 cm

Small, neat, sparrow-like with simple contrasted pattern: **dark** with rounded **white belly**, white sides to tail and **whitish bill**. ADULT MALE **slate-grey**; darker face. FEMALE/1ST-WINTER slightly browner.

<60 records (<5 Ireland), all months, most May. Scattered. Trees; feeds on ground.

1ST-SUMMER ♂

Eastern Towhee
Pipilo erythrophthalmus
L 17–23 cm | W 20–28 cm

Rounded, large-headed, long-tailed, finch-like; dark with **deep orange flank** and **bright white belly**. ADULT MALE (not recorded) blue-black, orange and white. FEMALE/1ST-WINTER dark brown, rufous and white.

1 record (Britain), Jun. On coast. Scrub/woodland; feeds on ground.

ADULT ♀

Summer Tanager
Piranga rubra
L 17 cm | W 25–27 cm

Elongated, finch-like with pale conical bill; plain plumage. ADULT MALE (not recorded) rose-red. FEMALE/1ST-WINTER brownish or orange-brown above, wings **plain olive** with dark brown wingtip; **dull orange-yellow below**. **Underwing yellow.**

1 record (Britain), Sep. On coast. Trees.

1ST-WINTER

Scarlet Tanager
Piranga olivacea
L 16–19 cm | W 25–30 cm

Elongated, finch-like with dark conical bill; plain plumage. ADULT MALE (not recorded) scarlet with black wings and tail. FEMALE/1ST-WINTER yellow-green above, wings greyish **darker than back**; pale yellow below, deepest on throat and under tail. **Underwing white.**

<15 records (<5 Ireland), Sep–Oct. On coast. Trees.

1ST-WINTER ♂   1ST-WINTER ♀

RARE NORTH AMERICAN LANDBIRDS

Baltimore Oriole
Icterus galbula
L 17–22 cm | W 23–30 cm

Small, sharp-billed icterid, shape and size like Starling (p. 384). ADULT MALE (not recorded) black with orange underparts and white wingbars. FEMALE/1ST-WINTER browner above, **two pale bars** on brown wing, **orange rump**; throat bright orange, blends into **yellow underparts**; yellow-sided tail.

<30 records (<5 Ireland), May, Sep–Jan. Scattered. Trees, gardens.

Bobolink
Dolichonyx oryzivorus
L 16–18 cm | W 19–26 cm

Small, bunting-like icterid with short, sharp bill and spiky tail. 1ST-WINTER bright yellow-buff, streaked black on back and wings with **two cream stripes on back**; brown crown with **bright buff central stripe**, yellow-buff stripe above dark eyestripe. Underparts yellowish with fine black streaks.

<40 records (<5 Ireland), Sep–Nov. On coast. Grassland, bushes.

Brown-headed Cowbird
Molothrus ater
L 16–22 cm | W 34–36 cm

Small, dark, stocky icterid; recalls Blackbird (p. 391) but smaller and with shorter, slimmer tail (often raised), sturdy legs and **triangular bill**. MALE black, glossed blue-green, **head and neck dull brown**. FEMALE/1ST-WINTER (not recorded) brown overall, bold dark eye in **paler plain head**; like juvenile Starling (p. 384) with a thick black bill.

<10 records (Britain), Apr, May, Jul. On coast. Grassland, bushes.

Red-winged Blackbird
Agelaius phoeniceus
L 17–23 cm | W 31–40 cm

Stocky icterid with sharp, conical bill and square tail. MALE (not recorded) black; red 'shoulder' patch edged yellow. FEMALE dark brown, white below, densely streaked rufous and black; head brown with whitish stripe behind eye, orange-buff around bill.

Vagrant from N America: 1 record (Britain), Apr–May. Bushy areas.

ICTERIDS | WOODPECKERS | KINGFISHERS | CUCKOOS

North American cuckoos, kingfishers and woodpeckers

Yellow-bellied Sapsucker
Sphyrapicus varius
L 18–21 cm | W 35–40 cm

Small woodpecker; black-and-white with long white band on wing. ADULT red forehead and black-and-white-striped head and red (MALE) or white (FEMALE) throat; black breast; back black mottled with white. JUVENILE as adult but drabber, lacks obvious red on crown and black on breast; contrast reduced by pale feather edges; MALE with reddish tinge to throat.

1 record Britain, 1 Ireland, Sep–Oct. On coast. Woodland.

Belted Kingfisher
Megaceryle alcyon
L 31–34 cm | W 48–58 cm

Large, crested, grey-and-white kingfisher with dark breast-bands. **VOICE** Piercing, squeaky, chattering rattle.

<15 records (<5 Ireland), Oct–Jun. Scattered. Rivers.

Black-billed Cuckoo
Coccyzus erythrophthalmus
L 28–31 cm | W 40–44 cm

Grey-brown and white cuckoo with a little **dull** rufous on wing. Long grey-brown tail with small white tips on outer feathers, creating **no strong pattern** from below. White breast, but throat and undertail buff. **Bill grey**.

<20 records (1 Ireland), May, Aug–Nov. Scattered, coastal.

Yellow-billed Cuckoo
Coccyzus americanus
L 29–32 cm | W 38–43 cm

Grey-brown and white cuckoo with much **rufous on wing**; long tail with brown centre, **large white tips** to blackish outer feathers, which make **bold black-and-white pattern** from below; white edge to outermost tail feather from above. White from throat to tail. **Bill yellow-and-black**.

<80 records (<15 Ireland), Sep–Oct. Scattered, mostly coastal.

IN FLIGHT bold tail pattern and rufous wing flash are striking.

CATEGORIES D and E

Birds of uncertain origin and escapes/introductions

The official British and Irish Lists (see *p. 540*) are subdivided into Categories A, B and C. Not forming part of the Lists are Categories D (birds of uncertain origin) and E (those known to have escaped from captivity). Category D is a 'holding' category for species that have been reliably identified, but for which a truly wild origin is questionable. Category D species may be upgraded to A if further evidence comes to light or new records are acceptably of wild birds, or demoted to Category E if there is no likelihood that the birds recorded were wild. Indeed, most Category D species are also on Category E, as known escapes have occurred.

At the end of October 2019, 13 species were placed solely in Category D in Britain, one of which (Bald Eagle) is in Category A in Ireland. There are 11 species in Category D in Ireland, of which four (Falcated Duck, Red-legged Partridge, Bridled Tern and Purple Martin) are on the British list. Overall, 20 species are in Category D in either Britain or Ireland. Following is an annotated list of all the birds currently in Category D in Britain (■) and/or Ireland (■) (where Category D is subdivided – see *p. 540*). The ten species included elsewhere in the book, either because they are also on the official British List or Irish List, or in order to highlight potential identification pitfalls as they occur frequently, are listed; the remaining ten species are illustrated here.

Category D

Ross's Goose *Anser rossii* (*p. 62*) **D**
<50 records (Britain). Usually recorded with Pink-footed Geese (*p. 31*) autumn–spring (status unclear due to escapes from captivity, which have bred).

Falcated Duck *Mareca falcata* (*p. 65*) **D1**
1 record (Ireland). (Vagrant Britain: 1 record (Cat A).)

Marbled Duck *Marmaronetta angustirostris* (*p. 62*) **D**
<50 records (Britain).

Wood Duck *Aix sponsa* (*p. 61*) **D** **D1**
British birds considered escapes from captivity; has bred. <50 records (Ireland), including 1 possible vagrant.

White-headed Duck *Oxyura leucocephala* (*p. 60*) **D**
<10 records (Britain).

Red-legged Partridge *Alectoris rufa* (*p. 272*) **D4**
Unsuccessful introductions in Ireland where small population not self-sustaining. (Established introduction Britain (Cat C1).)

Bald Eagle *Hieraaetus pennatus* (*p. 322*) **D**
<5 records (Britain). (Vagrant Ireland: <5 records (Cat A).)

Bridled Tern *Onychoprion anaethetus* (*p. 172*) **D3**
1 record (Ireland). (Vagrant Britain: <25 records (Cat A).)

Saker Falcon *Falco cherrug* (*p. 332*) **D**
Occasional records (Britain); confusion due to escapes/hybrids.

Purple Martin *Progne subis* (*p. 356*) **D1**
1 old record (Ireland), 1840. (Vagrant Britain: 1 record (Cat A).)

Booted Eagle *Hieraaetus pennatus* 546
L 45–55 cm | W 110–130 cm **D** **D1**
size of Buzzard (*p. 312*), dark brown or whitish below, white rump, pale band on upperwing

ADULT pale form
white spot beside neck
JUVENILE pale form
JUVENILE pale form

1 (Ireland and Britain), Mar: considered to be an escape.

Red-headed Bunting *Emberiza bruniceps* **D** **D1**
L 16 cm
Infrequent: status confused by likely escaped cagebirds.

FEMALE **unmarked pale yellow** below. 1ST-WINTER duller greyish-buff below, **yellow under tail**; brown tail lacks white; may be inseparable from Black-headed Bunting (*p. 520*).

1ST-WINTER
MALE **yellow below, red-brown hood**.

CATEGORIES D and E

Great White Pelican
Pelecanus onocrotalus
L 140–180 cm

D

Occasional (Britain): most known escapes, none certainly of wild origin.

Greater Flamingo
Phoenicopterus ruber
L 120–145 cm

D D1
545

pink legs

NB Most flamingos in Britain/Ireland escaped Chilean Flamingo *Phoenicopterus chilensis*: like Greater Flamingo but **legs grey, pink joint**.

Infrequent: no proof of wild origin.

Northern Flicker
Colaptes auratus
L 30–35 cm

D2

♂

1 record (Ireland), Oct: arrived on board ship.

546

peaked forehead
pale neck

House Crow
Corvus splendens
L 41–43 cm

D2

long bill

black cap, face and throat

<5 records (Ireland): likely ship-assisted.

Daurian Starling
Agropsar sturninus
L 17 cm

D

1ST-WINTER ♂

<5 records (Britain): May, Oct: possible vagrant – status confused by escapes.

Mugimaki Flycatcher
Ficedula mugimaki
L 13 cm

D

♂ NON-BREEDING

1 record (Britain), Nov: potentially escaped bird.

American Goldfinch
Spinus (Carduelis) tristis
L 11–13 cm

D1

Resembles female Chaffinch (p. 494) but yellow on face.

♀ / NON-BREEDING

1 old record (Ireland), Sep 1894.

Yellow-headed Blackbird
Xanthocephalus xanthocephalus
L 22–26 cm

D

♂

<10 records (Britain) when commonly sold as cagebird: unlikely vagrant.

Category E*

These species have been recorded 'flying free' and have bred, but are mostly obvious escapes from captivity. They are of importance, as they may become established and self-sustaining over time. They could potentially compete with native species or be damaging to commercial crops, and records of these species are therefore maintained more carefully. Introductions of non-native species are always unwise, and unlicensed releases are illegal. Species can be categorized as E* as well as other categories (*e.g.* Quail – see table pp. 543–556), but there are 27 solely in Category E*. Those that are similar to wild species or are regularly encountered are illustrated.

Helmeted Guineafowl *Numida meleagris*
Chukar Partridge *Alectoris chukar* (p. 272)
Silver Pheasant *Lophura nycthemera*
Reeves's Pheasant *Syrmaticus reevesii*
Wild Turkey *Meleagris gallopavo*
Indian Peafowl *Pavo cristatus*
Black Swan *Cygnus atratus* (p. 62)
Trumpeter Swan *Cygnus buccinator* (p. 62)
Swan Goose *Anser cygnoides*
Bar-headed Goose *Anser indicus* (p. 62)
Emperor Goose *Anser (Chen) canagica* (p. 62)
Upland Goose *Chloephaga picta*
South African Shelduck *Tadorna cana*
Muscovy Duck *Cairina moschata* (p. 62)
Wood Duck *Aix sponsa* (p. 61)
Cinnamon Teal *Spatula cyanoptera* (p. 62)
Yellow-billed Teal *Anas flavirostris*
Harris's Hawk *Parabuteo unicinctus* (p. 302)
Budgerigar *Melopsittacus undulatus*
Rosy-faced Lovebird *Agapornis roseicollis*
Alexandrine Parakeet *Psittacula eupatria* (p. 342)
Blue-crowned Parakeet *Thectocercus acuticaudatus*
Monk Parakeet *Myiopsitta monachus*
Eurasian Eagle-Owl *Bubo bubo* (p. 291)
Red-winged Laughingthrush *Trochalopteron formosum*
Atlantic Canary *Serinus canaria*

Monk Parakeet
Myiopsitta monachus
L 29 cm (incl. tail 10 cm)

Atlantic Canary *Serinus canaria*
L 10–14 cm

resembles Serin (p. 499) but longer tail, larger bill; weaker pattern with dark streaks on yellow below.

♂

539

STATUS and LEGISLATION

British and Irish Lists, status and legislation

This table, for the first time in a popular book, gives the official lists of species recorded in Britain and in Ireland, together with a summary of their status and the legislative protection afforded them. The species are listed in taxonomic order, reflecting natural relationships between species and genera. This ordering of species has changed dramatically in recent years with the development of new scientific techniques, such as DNA sequencing, elucidating evolutionary relationships, and further changes are likely. Political response to conservation status is also subject to change, but current EU frameworks provide a logical, evidence-based and robust set of directives that shape national bird and habitat protection laws. The legal situation in the UK (and in England, Wales, Scotland and Northern Ireland where appropriate), and in the Republic of Ireland is outlined here.

LIST CATEGORIES and BoCC STATUS

LIST CATEGORIES

Britain

The British Ornithologists' Union (BOU) (bou.org.uk/british-list) maintains a list of the birds recorded in Britain. There are five broad categories, the first three of which, combined, constitute the official 'British List':

CATEGORY A   Recorded in an apparently natural state at least once since 1 January 1950.

CATEGORY B   Recorded in an apparently natural state at least once between 1 January 1800 and 31 December 1949, but not subsequently.

CATEGORY C   Introduced species with self-sustaining populations. There are six sub-categories: **C1** (naturalized introduced); **C2** (naturalized established); **C3** (naturalized re-established); **C4** (naturalized feral); **C5** (vagrant naturalized (no species currently)); and **C6** (former naturalized).

CATEGORY D (see p. 538)   Species that would otherwise appear in Category A except that there is reasonable doubt that they have ever occurred in a natural state. This is a holding category and is not intended to be a long-term assignment of any species. The species concerned are reviewed regularly with a view to assigning them to either Category A or E.

CATEGORY E   Species recorded as introductions, human-assisted transportees or escapees from captivity, and whose breeding populations (if any) are thought not to be self-sustaining. Species in Category E that have bred in the wild in Britain are designated as E*. Category E species form no part of the British List (unless already included within Categories A, B or C).

Ireland

The Irish Rare Birds Committee (IRBC) (irbc.ie) maintains a separate list of the birds recorded in Ireland. As with Britain, Categories A, B and C constitute the official 'Irish List':

CATEGORIES A, B, D and E – as equivalent BOU categories.

CATEGORY C   Introduced species with self-sustaining populations. There are two sub-categories: **C1** (self-sustaining established feral breeding populations); and **C2** (originated from established naturalized populations outside Ireland).

CATEGORY D (see p. 538)   Four sub-categories:
D1 (species that would otherwise appear in Categories A or B except that there is a reasonable doubt that they have ever occurred in a natural state);
D2 (species that have arrived through ship or other human assistance);
D3 (species that have only ever been found dead on the tideline); and
D4 (species that would otherwise appear in Category C1, except that their feral populations may not be self-supporting).

STATUS and LEGISLATION

Species listed only within either Categories D and E or E* are included in the table and shaded purple . Species that have not been recorded in a country are shaded grey ; birds that could not be assigned to species are coded N/A, shaded pale grey .

At the end of 2019, three species that would be new for the Irish List, and one that would be new for the British List were still under review. They have been included in the table and are coded (A). Figures or dots in brackets indicate that the listing relates to certain subspecies only.

BoCC STATUS

Birds of Conservation Concern (BoCC) codes species as **Red**, **Amber** or **Green** according to conservation status, and is reviewed by leading conservation organizations every five years (Britain in 2015; Ireland in 2013). Species that are Red or Amber listed in Britain and/or Ireland are indicated by red ( ) or amber ( ) shading – all other regularly occurring species are 'green'. In Britain, subspecies have been independently assessed, some being Red or Amber listed in their own right. These are indicated by a red (●) or amber (●) dot respectively; where appropriate, details of the subspecies concerned are given in the relevant species account. In a few instances, subspecies are Green listed, even though the species as a whole is Red or Amber listed; these are indicated with a green dot (●)‡. Details may be found in *British Birds* 108 (December 2015), pp. 708–746 (britishbirds.co.uk/wp-content/uploads/2014/07/BoCC4.pdf).

The criteria for Red and Amber listing are as follows:

RED LIST: Species are categorized as **Red** if they meet one or more of five criteria:
GLOBALLY THREATENED – listed by BirdLife International as Probably Extinct, Critically Endangered, Endangered or Vulnerable (*see IUCN RED LIST below*).
HISTORICAL DECLINE – severe decline in UK/Ireland between 1800 and 1995, without substantial recovery.
BREEDING POPULATION DECLINE – decline in UK/Irish breeding population of more than 50%, over 25 years or since the first BoCC review in 1969 ('longer-term').
NON-BREEDING POPULATION DECLINE – similar severe decline in UK/Irish non-breeding population.
BREEDING RANGE DECLINE – similar severe decline in the UK/Irish range.

AMBER LIST: Species are categorized as **Amber** according to eight criteria:
SPECIES OF EUROPEAN CONSERVATION CONCERN (Endangered world-wide or in an Unfavourable conservation state in Europe).
HISTORICAL DECLINE – RECOVERY – red listed for Historical Decline in a previous review but recent recovery (more than doubled in the last 25 years).
BREEDING POPULATION DECLINE – moderate decline (by more than 25% but less than 50%).
NON-BREEDING POPULATION DECLINE – moderate decline (by more than 25% but less than 50%).
BREEDING RANGE DECLINE – moderate decline (by more than 25% but less than 50%).
RARITY – UK breeding population less than 300 pairs (Irish population less than 100 pairs), or non-breeding population less than 900 individuals.
LOCALISATION – at least 50% of the UK breeding or non-breeding population found in ten or fewer sites.
INTERNATIONAL IMPORTANCE – at least 20% of the European breeding or non-breeding population found in the UK or Ireland.

SPECIES

All species on the official British or Irish Lists (categories A, B or C) are highlighted in the table in **Bold Text**. The names recommended by the British Ornithologists' Union Records Committee (BOURC) (also adopted for the Irish List) are used in this book, as they are best known to most people. This means that diver and skua (rather than loon and jaeger), for example, and simple names such as Avocet, Knot and Swallow (instead of Pied Avocet, Red Knot and Barn Swallow) have been used, in keeping with centuries of popular usage in Britain and Ireland.

‡ **Note**: although only single subspecies of Fulmar, Ptarmigan, Kingfisher and Chough have been recorded in Britain, the BoCC status for these subspecies differs from the overall species-level assessment.

STATUS and LEGISLATION

IUCN RED LIST STATUS [Europe]

BirdLife International (the official International Union for Conservation of Nature (IUCN) Red List authority for birds) determines the global conservation status of birds, including: **EX** (Extinct); **PE** (Possibly Extinct); **CR** (Critically Endangered); **EN** (Endangered); **VU** (Vulnerable) (species categorized as **PE, CR, EN** and **VU** are termed 'Globally Threatened') and **NT** (Near Threatened). All other species are officially categorized as Least Concern (**LC**), although this is not coded in the table in order to highlight the Globally and Near Threatened birds. The 2019 global Red List status and 2015 European Red List status [in square brackets] is given. (NB [**RE**] = Regionally Extinct.)

EU LEG BD Ann (EU Biodiversity Legislation indicating relevant Annex)

Species listed in **Annex 1** or **Annex 2** of the European Union (EU) Wild Birds Directive 2009 are indicated. Annex I of the Directive lists 194 species and subspecies which are: in danger of extinction; vulnerable to specific changes in their habitat; considered rare because of small populations or restricted local distribution or requiring particular attention due to specific habitat requirements. Of these, 117 occur in Britain and Ireland. Annex 2 lists species that can be shot within specified seasons.

LEGAL PROTECTION

Most species of wild bird in Great Britain are afforded a certain level of protection under the Wildlife and Countryside Act 1981 (as amended) (WCA 1981) (exceptions are, for example, poultry and game birds). Although there are slight variations between the various countries (in particular Scotland has a greater suite of offences to protect wild birds), the following is common to England, Scotland and Wales:
(a) it is an offence to kill, injure or take any wild bird;
(b) it is an offence to take, damage or destroy the nest of any wild bird while the nest is in use or being built;
(c) it is an offence to take or destroy the egg of any wild bird.

In England and Wales these three above offences are only triggered if committed "intentionally," whereas in Scotland they may be committed either "intentionally" or "recklessly."

SPECIAL PROTECTION – SPECIAL PROT'N (Sched. 1) (GB and Northern Ireland (NI))

Wild birds listed on Schedule 1 of the WCA 1981 are afforded a higher level of protection in that, for them, it is also an offence (in England, Wales and Scotland) to intentionally or recklessly (a) disturb any wild bird included in Schedule 1 while it is building a nest or is in, or near a nest containing eggs or young; or (b) disturb the dependent young of such a bird. There are further offences in Scotland to protect Schedule 1 birds. In Northern Ireland protection is afforded under Schedule 1 of the Wildlife (Northern Ireland) Order 1985 as amended by The Wildlife and Natural Environment Act (Northern Ireland) 2011, and in the Republic of Ireland under The Wildlife Act 1976 as amended by The Wildlife (Amendment) Act 2000. In Great Britain and Northern Ireland, species on Schedule 1, Part 2 of the relevant Act are afforded special protection during the breeding season but can be killed outside a specified close season. These are shown in the table by a grey-shaded circle (●).

In all UK countries and the Republic of Ireland, the EU Wild Birds Directive 2009 has been adopted and transposed into national law. This Directive gives protection to wild birds and their habitats (and provides for exceptions when wild birds may lawfully be harmed) and also requires classification of Special Protection Areas and other special conservation measures for wild bird species listed in Annex 1 and which are regularly occurring migratory species.

This section has been written as a non-technical summary. Anyone requiring legal advice regarding the protection of birds should consult a qualified legal professional.

STATUS and LEGISLATION | BRITISH and IRISH LISTS

BIODIVERSITY LISTING

Under the UK Biodiversity Action Plan, species and habitats are highlighted for conservation action, and lists have been drawn up for each country. Lists of these habitats and species are published as a requirement of Section 41 (England) and Section 42 (Wales) of the Natural Environment and Rural Communities (NERC) Act 2006, Section 2(4) of the Nature Conservation (Scotland) Act 2004, and Section 3(1) of the Wildlife and Natural Environment Act (Northern Ireland) 2011. They are used to guide decision-makers, such as local and regional authorities, in their duty "to have regard to the conservation of biodiversity in the exercise of their normal functions." A dot indicates that the species is included on the relevant country's Biodiversity List: England (EN); Wales (WA); Scotland (SC) and Northern Ireland (NI). Specially protected species in the Republic of Ireland are detailed in the Wildlife Act 1976 and Wildlife (Amendment) Act 2000. In the Republic of Ireland Biodiversity Action Plans are largely based on counties or local authority areas.

LIST CATEGORIES & BoCC STATUS		KEY TO SPECIAL PROTECTION ● Sched. 1 ◯ Sched. 1, Part 2	IUCN GLOBAL RED LIST STATUS [Europe]	EU LEG BD Ann	SPECIAL PROT'N Sched. 1		BIODIVERSITY LISTING				
Britain (BoCC 2015)	Ireland (BoCC 2013)	SPECIES			GB	NI	NERC EN	WA	SC	Biod. List NI	Page
A, E ●	A	Brent Goose		2			●	●		●	26
A, E*	A, D1	Red-breasted Goose	VU [NT]	1							27
A, C2, E*	A, C1	Canada Goose		2							24
A, C2, E*	A, C1	Barnacle Goose		1					●		28
A, E	A	Cackling (Lesser Canada) Goose									25
D, E*		Ross's Goose									62
A, C2, E*	A, D1	Snow Goose									33
A, C2, C4, E* ●	A, C1	Greylag Goose		2	◯						29
A, E* ●	A	Taiga Bean Goose		2					●		30
A, E*	A	Pink-footed Goose		2							31
A, E ●	A	Tundra Bean Goose		2					●		30
A, E* ●	A	White-fronted Goose		1,2†			●	●	●	●	32
A, E*	A	Lesser White-fronted Goose	VU [EN]	1							33
A, C2	A, C1	Mute Swan		2							19
A, E ●	A	Bewick's Swan	[EN]	1	●	●	●	●	●	●	20
A, E*	A	Whooper Swan		1	●	●			●	●	21
C1, C5, E*		Egyptian Goose									35
A	A	Shelduck									34
B, D, E*	B, D1	Ruddy Shelduck		1							35
D, E*	D1	Wood Duck									61
C1, E*	C1	Mandarin Duck									61
A, E	A, D1	Baikal Teal									67
A	A	Garganey		2	●	●			●	●	45
A, E*	A	Blue-winged Teal									67
A	A	Shoveler		2	◯					●	41
A, C2, E	A	Gadwall		2	◯						42
A, E	D1	Falcated Duck	NT								65
A, E*	A	Wigeon		2	◯						39
A, E	A	American Wigeon									64
A, C2, C4, E* ●	A, C1	Mallard		2							40
A	A	Black Duck									65
A, E	A	Pintail		2	◯	◯				●	43
A ●	A	Teal		2							44
A	A	Green-winged Teal									66
D, E		Marbled Duck	VU [VU]								62
A, C2, E*	A	Red-crested Pochard		2							46

† Greenland White-fronted Goose ssp. *albifrons* on Annex 1;
 White-fronted Goose ssp. *albifrons* on Annex 2.

543

STATUS and LEGISLATION

LIST CATEGORIES & BoCC STATUS		KEY TO SPECIAL PROTECTION ● Sched. 1 ◯ Sched. 1, Part 2	IUCN GLOBAL RED LIST STATUS [Europe]	EU LEG BD Ann	SPECIAL PROT'N Sched. 1		BIODIVERSITY LISTING				
Britain (BoCC 2015)	Ireland (BoCC 2013)	SPECIES			GB	NI	NERC EN	WA	Biod. List SC	NI	Page
A, E		Canvasback									71
A, E	A	Redhead									71
A, E*	A	Pochard	VU [VU]	2		◯			●	●	47
A, E	A	Ferruginous Duck	NT	1							69
A, E	A	Ring-necked Duck									69
A	A	Tufted Duck		2						●	48
A ●	A	Scaup	[VU]	2	●	◯	●		●	●	49
A	A	Lesser Scaup									68
A		Steller's Eider	VU	1							73
A	A	King Eider									72
A ● ●	A	Eider	NT [VU]	2							58
A		Harlequin Duck									74
A	A	Surf Scoter									74
A	A	Velvet Scoter	VU [VU]	2	●						56
A		White-winged Scoter									75
	A	Stejneger's Scoter									75
A	A	Common Scoter		2	●	●	●	●	●	●	57
A	A	Black Scoter	NT								75
A	A	Long-tailed Duck	VU [VU]	2	●						54
A, E	A	Bufflehead									70
A, E* ●	A	Goldeneye		2	◯	◯				●	50
A, E	A	Barrow's Goldeneye	[NT]								73
A	A	Smew		1					●		51
A, E	A, D1	Hooded Merganser									70
A	A	Goosander		2		●					53
A	A	Red-breasted Merganser	[NT]	2							52
C1, E*	C1, C2	Ruddy Duck									60
D, E		White-headed Duck	EN [EN]	1							60
C3, E* ●	B	Capercaillie		1,2	●				●		277
A, E ●		Black Grouse		2			●	●	●		276
A ● ‡		Ptarmigan	[NT]	2							275
A ●	A	Red Grouse	[VU]	2			●	●	●	●	274
C1, E*	D4	Red-legged Partridge		2							272
A, C2, E* ●	A, C1	Grey Partridge		2			●	●	●		273
A, E* ●	A	Quail		2	●	●				●	279
C1, E*	C1	Pheasant		2							278
C1, E*		Golden Pheasant									271
C6, E*		Lady Amherst's Pheasant									271
A	A	Red-throated Diver		1	●	●			●		82
A ●	A	Black-throated Diver		1	●				●	●	83
A	A	Pacific Diver			●						91
A	A	Great Northern Diver	[VU]	1	●				●		84
A	A	White-billed Diver	NT [VU]		●						85
A	A	Wilson's Petrel									105
B		White-faced Storm Petrel	[EN]	1							118
N/A		White-bellied Storm Petrel or Black-bellied Storm Petrel									119
A	A	Black-browed Albatross									114
A		Atlantic Yellow-nosed Albatross	EN								114
A ●	A	Storm Petrel		1		●			●		105

‡ See p. 541.

BRITISH and IRISH LISTS

LIST CATEGORIES & BoCC STATUS		KEY TO SPECIAL PROTECTION ● Sched. 1 ◐ Sched. 1, Part 2	IUCN GLOBAL RED LIST STATUS [Europe]	EU LEG BD Ann	SPECIAL PROT'N Sched. 1		BIODIVERSITY LISTING				Page
Britain (BoCC 2015)	Ireland (BoCC 2013)	SPECIES			GB	NI	NERC EN	WA	Biod. List SC	NI	
N/A	B	Madeiran Storm Petrel or Monteiro's Storm Petrel or Cape Verde Storm Petrel	VU [VU]	1							119
A	A	Swinhoe's Petrel	NT								119
A ●	A	Leach's Petrel	VU	1	●				●		105
A ●‡	A	Fulmar	[EN]								98
N/A	A	Zino's Petrel or Fea's Petrel or Desertas Petrel	EN [EN] NT [NT] VU [VU]	1							116
	At sea	Bermuda Petrel	EN								117
A		Black-capped Petrel	EN								117
A		Scopoli's Shearwater									101
A	A	Cory's Shearwater		1							101
A	A	Sooty Shearwater	NT							●	99
A	A	Great Shearwater									101
A	A	Manx Shearwater				●			●		103
A		Yelkouan Shearwater	VU								103
A	A	Balearic Shearwater	CR [CR]	1			●	●	●	●	103
A	A	Macaronesian (Barolo) Shearwater	[NT]†								103
	A	Bulwer's Petrel									118
A	A	Little Grebe									90
A	A	Pied-billed Grebe									91
A ●	A	Red-necked Grebe							●		87
A	A	Great Crested Grebe									86
A ●	A	Slavonian Grebe	VU [NT]	1	●				●		89
A ●	A	Black-necked Grebe			●	●			●	●	88
D, E	D1	Greater Flamingo		1							539
A	At sea	Red-billed Tropicbird									117
A, E	A	Black Stork		1							265
A, E	A	White Stork		1							265
A, E	A	Glossy Ibis		1							266
A, E ●	A	Spoonbill		1	●						259
A ●	A	Bittern		1	●		●	●	●	●	261
A	A	American Bittern									270
	(A)	Least Bittern									268
A	A	Little Bittern		1	●						267
A, E*	A	Night-heron		1							267
A	A	Green Heron									270
A	A	Squacco Heron		1							268
A		Chinese Pond Heron									269
A, E	A	Cattle Egret									264
A	A	Grey Heron				●					260
A		Great Blue Heron									268
A	A	Purple Heron		1	●						266
A	A	Great White Egret		1							263
	A	Little Blue Heron									269
A		Snowy Egret									269
A	A	Little Egret		1		●					262
D, E		Great White Pelican		1							539
A		Dalmatian Pelican	NT								92

‡ See p. 541.
† Macaronesian (Barolo) Shearwater is considered conspecific with Audubon's Shearwater *Puffinus lherminieri* by BirdLife.

STATUS and LEGISLATION

LIST CATEGORIES & BoCC STATUS		KEY TO SPECIAL PROTECTION ● Sched. 1 ◐ Sched. 1, Part 2	IUCN GLOBAL RED LIST STATUS [Europe]	EU LEG BD Ann	SPECIAL PROT'N Sched. 1		BIODIVERSITY LISTING NERC			Biod. List	
Britain (BoCC 2015)	**Ireland** (BoCC 2013)	SPECIES			GB	NI	EN	WA	SC	NI	Page
A		Ascension Frigatebird	VU								115
A		Magnificent Frigatebird									115
	A	Frigatebird species									115
A	A	**Gannet**									97
A		Red-footed Booby									118
(A)	A, D3	Brown Booby									118
A, E	A	Double-crested Cormorant									92
A ●	A	Shag									81
A ◐	A	Cormorant									80
A, E* ●		Osprey		1	●	●			●		310
B, D, E		Egyptian Vulture	EN [EN]	1					●		322
A	A	Honey-buzzard		1	●				●		311
	B	Griffon Vulture		1							322
A		Short-toed Eagle		1							321
B	B	(Greater) **Spotted Eagle**	VU [EN]	1							321
D, E	D1	Booted Eagle		1							538
A, E	A, D4	**Golden Eagle**		1	●	●			●	●	305
A	A	Sparrowhawk				●					324
A, C3, E*	A	Goshawk			●	●				●	325
A ◐	A	Marsh Harrier		1	●	●			●		315
A ●	A	Hen Harrier	[NT]	1	●	●	●	●	●	●	317
A	A	Northern Harrier			●						320
A	A	Pallid Harrier	NT [NT]	1	●						319
A	A	Montagu's Harrier		1	●						318
A, C3, E*	A, C2, D4	Red Kite	NT [NT]	1	●	●			●		314
A, E	A	Black Kite		1							320
A, C3, E*	A, C2, D4	**White-tailed Eagle**		1	●	●			●	●	304
D, E	A	Bald Eagle									322
A, E	A	Rough-legged Buzzard									313
A, E*	A	Buzzard				●					312
A, E*	B	**Great Bustard**	VU	1							281
A		Macqueen's Bustard	VU [PE]								280
A	B	Little Bustard	NT [VU]	1							280
A	A	Water Rail		2							250
A, E*	A	Corncrake		1	●	●	●	●	●	●	247
A	B	Little Crake		1							252
A	A	Baillon's Crake		1							253
A	A	**Spotted Crake**		1	●				●		251
A	A	Sora Rail									253
A, E		Western (Purple) Swamphen									254
A		Allen's Gallinule									254
A	A	(American) Purple Gallinule									254
A	A	Moorhen									248
A	A	Coot	[NT]	2							249
A	A	American Coot									252
A	B	Sandhill Crane									270
A, E ●	A	Crane		1							258
A ◐	A	Stone-curlew		1	●		●				189
A ◐	A	Oystercatcher	NT [VU]	2							190

BRITISH and IRISH LISTS

Britain (BoCC 2015)	Ireland (BoCC 2013)	SPECIES	IUCN GLOBAL RED LIST STATUS [Europe]	EU LEG BD Ann	SPECIAL PROT'N Sched. 1 GB	NI	BIODIVERSITY LISTING NERC EN	WA	Biod. List SC	NI	Page
A	A	Black-winged Stilt		1	●						193
A	A	Avocet		1	●						192
A	A	Lapwing	NT [VU]	2		●	●	●	●	●	197
A	A	Sociable Lapwing	CR [CR]								229
A		White-tailed Lapwing									229
A	A	Golden Plover		1,2		◐		●	●	●	198
A	A	Pacific Golden Plover									230
A	A	American Golden Plover									230
A	A	Grey Plover		2							199
A ● ●	A	Ringed Plover						●			194
A	A	Semipalmated Plover									232
A	A	Little Ringed Plover			●						195
A	A	Killdeer									231
A	A, E	Kentish Plover		1	●						193
A	A	Lesser Sand Plover									233
A	A	Greater Sand Plover	[VU]								233
A		Caspian Plover	[RE]								233
A	A	Dotterel		1	●	●			●		196
A	A	Upland Sandpiper									240
A ●	A	Whimbrel		2	●	●				●	219
A	A	Hudsonian Whimbrel									219
A		Little Whimbrel									240
B	B	Eskimo Curlew	PE								240
A ●	A	Curlew	NT [VU]	2		●	●	●	●	●	218
A ●	A	Bar-tailed Godwit	NT	1,2				●	●		216
A ● ●	A	Black-tailed Godwit	NT [VU]	2	●	●	●		●	●	217
A	A	Hudsonian Godwit									228
A ●	A	Turnstone									191
A ●	A	Knot	NT	2						●	201
A	A	Ruff		1,2	●	●			●		208
A	A	Broad-billed Sandpiper									236
A	A	Sharp-tailed Sandpiper									238
A	A	Stilt Sandpiper									239
A	A	Curlew Sandpiper	NT [VU]								205
A	A	Temminck's Stint			●				●		206
A	A	Long-toed Stint									236
A	A	Red-necked Stint	NT								235
A	A	Sanderling									200
A ● ●	A	Dunlin				●			●	●	202
A	A	Purple Sandpiper			●				●		204
A	A	Baird's Sandpiper									237
A	A	Little Stint									207
A	A	Least Sandpiper									236
A	A	White-rumped Sandpiper									237
A	A	Buff-breasted Sandpiper	NT								240
A	A	Pectoral Sandpiper									238
A	A	Semipalmated Sandpiper	NT								235
A	A	Western Sandpiper									235

KEY TO SPECIAL PROTECTION
● Sched. 1
◐ Sched. 1, Part 2

STATUS and LEGISLATION

LIST CATEGORIES & BoCC STATUS		KEY TO SPECIAL PROTECTION ● Sched. 1 ◐ Sched. 1, Part 2	IUCN GLOBAL RED LIST STATUS [Europe]	EU LEG BD Ann	SPECIAL PROT'N Sched. 1		BIODIVERSITY LISTING				Page
Britain (BoCC 2015)	Ireland (BoCC 2013)	SPECIES			GB	NI	NERC		Biod. List		
							EN	WA	SC	NI	
A	A	Long-billed Dowitcher									245
A	A	Short-billed Dowitcher									245
A	A	Woodcock		2					●		224
A	A	Jack Snipe		2							223
A	A	Great Snipe	NT	1							241
A ●	A	Snipe		2							222
A	A	Wilson's Snipe									241
A	A	Terek Sandpiper		1							242
A	A	Wilson's Phalarope									226
A	A	Red-necked Phalarope		1	●				●	●	220
A	A	Grey Phalarope									221
A	A	Common Sandpiper									215
A	A	Spotted Sandpiper									242
A	A	Green Sandpiper			●				●		214
A	A	Solitary Sandpiper									243
A		Grey-tailed Tattler	NT								243
A	A	Lesser Yellowlegs									244
A ●	A	Redshank		2		●				●	210
A	A	Marsh Sandpiper									243
A	A	Wood Sandpiper		1	●				●		213
A	A	Spotted Redshank		2							211
A	A	Greenshank		2	●	●					212
A	A	Greater Yellowlegs									244
A	A	Cream-coloured Courser	[NT]	1							228
A	A	Collared Pratincole		1							227
A		Oriental Pratincole									227
A	A	Black-winged Pratincole	NT [VU]								227
A ●	A	Kittiwake	VU [VU]								148
A	A	Ivory Gull	NT								151
A	A	Sabine's Gull									149
A		Slender-billed Gull		1							155
A	A	Bonaparte's Gull									153
A	A	Black-headed Gull		2			●		●	●	146
A	A	Little Gull	[NT]		●						150
A	A	Ross's Gull	[EN]								151
A	A	Laughing Gull									152
A	A	Franklin's Gull									153
A		Audouin's Gull		1							157
A	A	Mediterranean Gull		1	●	●					147
B		Great Black-headed Gull									155
A ●	A	Common Gull		2							144
A	A	Ring-billed Gull									154
A	A	Great Black-backed Gull		2							134
A	A	Glaucous-winged Gull									156
A ●	A	Glaucous Gull									140
A ●	A	Iceland Gull									141
A ● ●	A	Herring Gull	[NT]	2		●	●		●	●	130
A	A	American Herring Gull									158
	A	Vega Gull									159

BRITISH and IRISH LISTS

LIST CATEGORIES & BoCC STATUS		KEY TO SPECIAL PROTECTION ● Sched. 1 ◐ Sched. 1, Part 2	IUCN GLOBAL RED LIST STATUS [Europe]	EU LEG	SPECIAL PROT'N		BIODIVERSITY LISTING				
Britain (BoCC 2015)	Ireland (BoCC 2013)	SPECIES		BD Ann	Sched. 1		NERC		Biod. List		Page
					GB	NI	EN	WA	SC	NI	
A	A	Caspian Gull		2							137
A ●	A	Yellow-legged Gull									136
A	A	Slaty-backed Gull									156
A ● ●	A	Lesser Black-backed Gull		2							132
A	A	Gull-billed Tern		1							169
A	A	Caspian Tern		1							168
A	A, D3	Royal Tern									170
A	A	Lesser Crested Tern									171
A	A	Sandwich Tern		1		●			●		165
A		Cabot's Tern									173
A	A	Elegant Tern	NT								171
A ●	A	Little Tern		1	●	●			●	●	161
A		Least Tern									161
A	A	Aleutian Tern	VU								173
A	D3	Bridled Tern									172
A	A	Sooty Tern									172
A ●	A	Roseate Tern		1	●	●	●	●	●	●	164
A ●	A	Common Tern		1		●			●		162
A	A	Arctic Tern		1		●			●		163
A	A	Forster's Tern									169
A	A	Whiskered Tern		1							168
A	A	White-winged Black Tern									167
A	A	Black Tern		1	●						166
A	A	Great Skua (Bonxie)									179
N/A		South Polar Skua / Brown Skua									179
A	A	Pomarine Skua									177
A	A	Arctic Skua							●	●	176
A	A	Long-tailed Skua									178
A	A	Little Auk									112
A	A	Brünnich's Guillemot									113
A ●	A	Guillemot	[NT]								108
A ● ●	A	Razorbill	NT [NT]								109
B	B	Great Auk	EX								106
A ●	A	Black Guillemot									111
A		Long-billed Murrelet	NT								113
A		Ancient Murrelet									113
A	A	Puffin	VU [EN]			●					110
A		Tufted Puffin									113
A	A	Pallas's Sandgrouse	[EN]								284
A, C4, E*	A	Rock Dove / Feral Pigeon		2							284
A ●	A	Stock Dove		2		●					287
A	A	Woodpigeon		2							286
A ●	A	Turtle Dove	VU [VU]	2		●	●	●		●	289
A		Oriental Turtle Dove									290
A	A	Collared Dove		2							288
A	A	Mourning Dove									290
A	A, D3	Great Spotted Cuckoo									341
A	A	Yellow-billed Cuckoo									537
A	B	Black-billed Cuckoo									537

549

STATUS and LEGISLATION

LIST CATEGORIES & BoCC STATUS		KEY TO SPECIAL PROTECTION ● Sched. 1 ◐ Sched. 1, Part 2	IUCN GLOBAL RED LIST STATUS [Europe]	EU LEG BD Ann	SPECIAL PROT'N Sched. 1		BIODIVERSITY LISTING				
Britain (BoCC 2015)	Ireland (BoCC 2013)	SPECIES			GB	NI	NERC EN	NERC WA	Biod. List SC	Biod. List NI	Page
A ●	A	Cuckoo					●	●	●	●	338
A, E*	A	Barn Owl			●	●			●	●	293
A	A	Scops Owl									299
A, E	A	Snowy Owl	VU	1	●	●					298
A ●		Tawny Owl									294
A		Hawk Owl		1							299
C1, E	A, C2	Little Owl									295
A		Tengmalm's Owl		1							299
A	A	Long-eared Owl				●					297
A ●	A	Short-eared Owl		1		●			●	●	296
A	A	Common Nighthawk									301
B		Red-necked Nightjar									301
A ●	A	Nightjar		1	●	●	●	●	●	●	300
A		Egyptian Nightjar									301
A	A	White-throated Needletail									351
A	A	Chimney Swift	VU								351
A	A	Alpine Swift									350
A ●	A	Swift							●	●	349
A	A	Pallid Swift									350
A		Pacific Swift									351
A	A	Little Swift	[VU]								351
A		White-rumped Swift	[NT]								351
A	A	Roller		1							341
A ●‡	A	Kingfisher	[VU]	1	●	●			●		337
A	A	Belted Kingfisher									537
A		Blue-cheeked Bee-eater									340
A	A	Bee-eater			●						340
A	A	Hoopoe			●						339
A	A	Wryneck			●				●		344
A		Yellow-bellied Sapsucker									537
A ●		Lesser Spotted Woodpecker					●	●			347
A ●	A	Great Spotted Woodpecker									346
	D2	Northern Flicker									539
A	B	Green Woodpecker									345
A	B	Lesser Kestrel		1							334
A ●	A	Kestrel				●		●	●		326
A, E		American Kestrel									334
A	A	Red-footed Falcon	NT [NT]	1							330
A, E		Amur Falcon									335
A		Eleonora's Falcon		1							335
A ● ●	A	Merlin		1	●	●			●		327
A	A	Hobby			●	●			●		328
D, E		Saker Falcon	EN [VU]								332
A, E	A	Gyrfalcon		1	●	●					331
A, E	A	Peregrine		1	●	●			●		329
C1, E*		Ring-necked Parakeet									342
A		Eastern Phoebe									530
A		Acadian Flycatcher									530
A		Alder Flycatcher									530

‡ See p. 541.

BRITISH and IRISH LISTS

LIST CATEGORIES & BoCC STATUS		KEY TO SPECIAL PROTECTION ● Sched. 1 ◐ Sched. 1, Part 2	IUCN GLOBAL RED LIST STATUS [Europe]	EU LEG BD Ann	SPECIAL PROT'N Sched. 1		BIODIVERSITY LISTING				
Britain (BoCC 2015)	Ireland (BoCC 2013)	SPECIES			GB	NI	NERC EN	WA	SC	Biod. List NI	Page
A	A	Eastern Kingbird									530
A	A	Brown Shrike									463
A ●	A	Red-backed Shrike		1	●			●	●		460
A	A	Daurian Shrike									462
A		Turkestan Shrike									462
A		Long-tailed Shrike									464
A	A	Lesser Grey Shrike		1							464
A	A	Great Grey Shrike	[VU]								459
A	A	Woodchat Shrike									461
A		Masked Shrike									464
A		Yellow-throated Vireo									525
A	A	Philadelphia Vireo									525
A	A	Red-eyed Vireo									525
A ●	A	Golden Oriole			●						383
A ◐	A	Jay		2							480
A	A	Magpie		2							481
A		Nutcracker									487
A, E* ●‡	A	Chough		1	●	●		●	●	●	487
A	A	Jackdaw		2							482
	D2	House Crow									539
A	A	Rook		2							485
A	A	Carrion Crow		2							484
A	A	Hooded Crow							●		483
A	A	Raven									486
A, E	A	Waxwing									386
A, E	A	Cedar Waxwing									387
A ◐	A	Coal Tit									471
A ◐		Crested Tit			●						470
A ●	A	Marsh Tit					●	●	●		472
A ●	A	Willow Tit					●	●	●		473
A ◐	A	Blue Tit									468
A ◐	A	Great Tit									469
A		Penduline Tit									477
A	A	Bearded Tit			●				●		466
A	A	Woodlark		1	●		●	●			360
A		White-winged Lark									363
A ● ◐	A	Skylark		2			●	●	●	●	361
A, E		Crested Lark									362
A ◐	A	Shorelark			●						359
A	A	Short-toed Lark		1							362
A		Bimaculated Lark									363
A		Calandra Lark		1							363
A		Black Lark	[CR]								363
A		Lesser Short-toed Lark									362
A	A	Sand Martin				●					354
A		Tree Swallow									356
A	D1	Purple Martin									356
A, E	A	Swallow									353
A		Crag Martin									355

‡ See p.541.

STATUS and LEGISLATION

Britain (BoCC 2015)	Ireland (BoCC 2013)	SPECIES	IUCN GLOBAL RED LIST STATUS [Europe]	EU LEG BD Ann	Sched.1 GB	Sched.1 NI	NERC EN	NERC WA	Biod. List SC	Biod. List NI	Page
A ●	A	House Martin									352
A	A	Red-rumped Swallow									355
A	A	Cliff Swallow									356
A	A	Cetti's Warbler			●						429
A ●	A	Long-tailed Tit									467
A	A	Wood Warbler					●	●	●	●	433
A	A	Western Bonelli's Warbler									448
A		Eastern Bonelli's Warbler									448
A	A	Hume's Warbler									452
A	A	Yellow-browed Warbler									452
A	A	Pallas's Warbler									452
A	A	Radde's Warbler									449
A	A	Dusky Warbler									449
A ● ●	A	Willow Warbler									432
A	A	Chiffchaff									430
A	A	Iberian Chiffchaff									449
A		Eastern Crowned Warbler									451
A		Green Warbler									450
A		Two-barred Greenish Warbler									450
A	A	Greenish Warbler									450
A		Pale-legged Leaf Warbler									451
N/A		Pale-legged Leaf Warbler or Sakhalin Leaf Warbler									451
A	A	Arctic Warbler									451
A	A	Great Reed Warbler									442
A	A	Aquatic Warbler	VU [VU]	1			●	●			442
A	A	Sedge Warbler									426
A	A	Paddyfield Warbler									443
A	A	Blyth's Reed Warbler									441
A	A	Reed Warbler				●			●		427
A	A	Marsh Warbler			●		●				441
A		Thick-billed Warbler									443
A	A	Booted Warbler									447
A	A	Sykes's Warbler									447
A	A	Eastern Olivaceous Warbler									447
A		Olive-tree Warbler		1							446
A	A	Melodious Warbler									445
A	A	Icterine Warbler									445
A	A	Pallas's Grasshopper Warbler									444
A ●	A	Grasshopper Warbler					●	●	●	●	428
A		River Warbler									444
A ●	A	Savi's Warbler			●		●				429
A		Lanceolated Warbler									444
A	A	Fan-tailed Warbler (Zitting Cisticola)									443
A	A	Blackcap									434
A	A	Garden Warbler				●					435
A	A	Barred Warbler		1							453
A	A	Lesser Whitethroat				●					437
A		Western Orphean Warbler									456

BRITISH and IRISH LISTS

LIST CATEGORIES & BoCC STATUS		KEY TO SPECIAL PROTECTION ● Sched. 1 ● Sched. 1, Part 2	IUCN GLOBAL RED LIST STATUS [Europe]	EU LEG BD Ann	SPECIAL PROT'N Sched. 1		BIODIVERSITY LISTING				Page
Britain (BoCC 2015)	Ireland (BoCC 2013)	SPECIES			GB	NI	NERC EN	NERC WA	Biod. List SC	Biod. List NI	
A		Eastern Orphean Warbler									456
A		Asian Desert Warbler		[RE]							453
A	A	Whitethroat									436
A ●	A	Dartford Warbler	NT [NT]	1	●						438
A		Marmora's Warbler		1							453
A		Spectacled Warbler									455
A	A	Subalpine Warbler									454
A		Moltoni's Subalpine Warbler									454
A	A	Sardinian Warbler									457
A		Rüppell's Warbler		1							457
A	A	Firecrest			●						425
A	A	Goldcrest									424
	A	Ruby-crowned Kinglet									525
A ● ●	A	Wren		1†					●†		381
A		Nuthatch									474
A		Red-breasted Nuthatch									477
A		Wallcreeper									477
A	A	Treecreeper									475
A ●		Short-toed Treecreeper			●						476
A	A	Grey Catbird									531
A, E		Northern Mockingbird									531
A		Brown Thrasher									531
D, E		Daurian Starling									539
A	A	Rose-coloured Starling									385
A ● ●	A	Starling		2			●	●	●	●	384
A, E	A	Siberian Thrush									396
A	A	White's Thrush									397
A		Varied Thrush									398
A	(A)	Veery									399
A	A	Grey-cheeked Thrush									399
A	A	Swainson's Thrush									399
A	A	Hermit Thrush									399
A		Wood Thrush	NT								398
A ●	A	Ring Ouzel				●	●	●	●	●	390
A	A	Blackbird		2							391
A		Eyebrowed Thrush									397
A		Black-throated Thrush									396
A		Red-throated Thrush									396
A		Naumann's Thrush									397
A		Dusky Thrush									397
A	A	Fieldfare		2	●					●	394
A ● ●	A	Redwing	NT [NT]	2	●				●	●	395
A ● ●	A	Song Thrush		2			●	●	●	●	392
A ●	A	Mistle Thrush		2							393
A, E	A	American Robin									398
A	A	Rufous-tailed Scrub Robin									414
A ●	A	Spotted Flycatcher				●	●	●	●	●	418
A		Asian Brown Flycatcher									421
A	A	Robin									400

† Wren ssp. *fridariensis* (Fair Isle Wren) is listed on Annex 1;
ssp. *fridariensis* & *hirtensis* (St Kilda Wren) are on Scottish Biodiversity List.

STATUS and LEGISLATION

Britain (BoCC 2015)	Ireland (BoCC 2013)	SPECIES	IUCN Global Red List Status [Europe]	EU LEG BD Ann	Sched.1 GB	Sched.1 NI	NERC EN	NERC WA	SC	Biod. List NI	Page
A		Siberian Blue Robin									413
A		Rufous-tailed Robin									413
A	A	Bluethroat		1	●						412
A	A	Thrush Nightingale									414
A ●	A	Nightingale									401
A		White-throated Robin									415
A		Siberian Rubythroat									413
A, E	A	Red-flanked Bluetail									412
A ●	A	Pied Flycatcher					●		●		419
A	A	Collared Flycatcher		1							421
D		Mugimaki Flycatcher									539
A	A	Red-breasted Flycatcher		1							420
A	(A)	Taiga Flycatcher									420
A ●	A	Black Redstart			●						403
A ●	A	Redstart					●				402
A		Moussier's Redstart									415
A	A	Rock Thrush									416
A, E		Blue Rock Thrush									416
A	A	Whinchat					●				404
A	A	Stonechat									405
A	A	Siberian Stonechat									406
A		Stejneger's Stonechat									406
A	A	Wheatear									408
A	A	Isabelline Wheatear									411
A	A	Desert Wheatear	[NT]								411
A	A	Western Black-eared Wheatear									410
A		Eastern Black-eared Wheatear									410
A	A	Pied Wheatear									411
A	A‡	White-crowned Black Wheatear									415
A ●	A	Dipper									379
A ●	A	House Sparrow					●	●	●	●	490
A		Spanish Sparrow									509
A ●	A	Tree Sparrow					●	●	●	●	491
A		Rock Sparrow									509
A		Alpine Accentor									387
A		Siberian Accentor	[NT]								387
A ● ●	A	Dunnock					●	●	●	●	380
A ● ●	A	Yellow Wagtail					●	●	●	●	374
A	A	Eastern Yellow Wagtail									377
A	A	Citrine Wagtail									377
A ●	A	Grey Wagtail									376
A ●	A	Pied/White Wagtail									372
A	A	Richard's Pipit									370
A		Blyth's Pipit									371
A	A	Tawny Pipit		1							371
A ●	A	Meadow Pipit	NT [NT]								365
A ●	A	Tree Pipit					●	●	●	●	364
A	A	Olive-backed Pipit									369
A	A	Pechora Pipit	[VU]								369

‡ White-crowned Black or Black Wheatear.

BRITISH and IRISH LISTS

LIST CATEGORIES & BoCC STATUS		KEY TO SPECIAL PROTECTION ● Sched. 1 ● Sched. 1, Part 2	IUCN GLOBAL RED LIST STATUS [Europe]	EU LEG BD Ann	SPECIAL PROT'N Sched. 1		BIODIVERSITY LISTING				
Britain (BoCC 2015)	Ireland (BoCC 2013)	SPECIES			GB	NI	NERC EN	WA	SC	Biod. List NI	Page
A	A	Red-throated Pipit									368
A	A	Buff-bellied Pipit									369
A ●	A	Water Pipit									367
A ●	A	Rock Pipit									366
A, E ●	A	Chaffinch									494
A	A	Brambling			●				●		495
A		Evening Grosbeak									534
A ●	A	Hawfinch					●	●	●	●	493
A, E		Pine Grosbeak									508
A ●	A	Bullfinch					●	●	●		492
A, E		Trumpeter Finch		1							509
A	A	Common Rosefinch			●				●		505
A, E ●	A	Greenfinch									497
A ●	A	Twite				●	●	●	●	●	501
A ● ●	A	Linnet					●	●	●	●	500
A ●	A	Common (Mealy) Redpoll									503
A	A	Lesser Redpoll					●	●	●	●	503
A	A	Arctic Redpoll									503
A		Parrot Crossbill			●				●		507
A		Scottish Crossbill		1	●				●		507
A	A	Crossbill			●	●					506
A	A	Two-barred Crossbill			●						508
A ●	A	Goldfinch									496
A		Citril Finch									499
A	A	Serin			●						499
	D1	American Goldfinch									539
A	A	Siskin							●		498
A ●	A	Lapland Bunting			●						511
A ●	A	Snow Bunting			●				●		512
A ●	A	Corn Bunting					●	●	●		517
A ●	A	Yellowhammer					●	●	●	●	514
A	A	Pine Bunting	[VU]								523
A		Rock Bunting									523
A, E	A	Ortolan Bunting		1							522
A		Cretzschmar's Bunting		1							522
A	A	Cirl Bunting			●		●				515
A		Chestnut-eared Bunting									518
A	A	Little Bunting									518
A		Yellow-browed Bunting									521
A	A	Rustic Bunting	VU [VU]								519
A	A	Yellow-breasted Bunting	CR [CR]								520
A		Chestnut Bunting									521
A, E	A	Black-headed Bunting									520
D, E	D1	Red-headed Bunting									538
A, E		Black-faced Bunting									521
A		Pallas's Reed Bunting									519
A ●	A	Reed Bunting					●	●	●	●	516
	A	Red Fox Sparrow									533
A, E		Song Sparrow									533

STATUS and LEGISLATION

LIST CATEGORIES & BoCC STATUS		KEY TO SPECIAL PROTECTION ● Sched. 1 ◌ Sched. 1, Part 2	IUCN GLOBAL RED LIST STATUS [Europe]	EU LEG BD Ann	SPECIAL PROT'N		BIODIVERSITY LISTING				
					Sched. 1		NERC		Biod. List		
Britain (BoCC 2015)	Ireland (BoCC 2013)	SPECIES			GB	NI	EN	WA	SC	NI	Page
A, E	A	White-crowned Sparrow									532
A, E	A	White-throated Sparrow									532
A, E	A	Dark-eyed Junco									535
A		Savannah Sparrow									533
A		Lark Sparrow									533
A		Eastern Towhee									535
D, E		Yellow-headed Blackbird									539
A	A	Bobolink									536
A, E	A	Baltimore Oriole									536
A		Red-winged Blackbird									536
A		Brown-headed Cowbird									536
A	A	Ovenbird									529
A	A	Northern Waterthrush									529
A		Golden-winged Warbler	NT								529
	A	Blue-winged Warbler									529
A	A	Black-and-white Warbler									528
A		Tennessee Warbler									529
A	A	Common Yellowthroat									528
A		Hooded Warbler									528
A, E	A	American Redstart									527
A		Cape May Warbler									526
A, E	A	Northern Parula									527
A, E		Magnolia Warbler									527
A		Bay-breasted Warbler									527
A		Blackburnian Warbler									527
A		Yellow Warbler									528
A		Chestnut-sided Warbler									527
A, E	A	Blackpoll Warbler	NT								526
A	A	Myrtle (Yellow-rumped) Warbler									526
	A	Canada Warbler									529
A	A	Wilson's Warbler									528
A		Summer Tanager									535
A	A	Scarlet Tanager									535
A	A	Rose-breasted Grosbeak									534
A, E	A	Indigo Bunting									534

Acknowledgements and photographic credits

Many people have contributed, directly or indirectly, to the production of this book since its inception almost 15 years ago. Our sincere thanks go to everyone who has influenced the final product. We particularly acknowledge the efforts of enthusiastic birdwatchers across Britain and Ireland who provide much data on the status and distribution of birds, upon which we have drawn heavily.

Chris Batty has been an invaluable and indefatigable consultant whose efforts have already been acknowledged. **Killian Mullarney** has most generously shared his unrivalled knowledge; **Richard Chandler** has kindly solved many conundrums with the waders; and **Dick Forsman**, **Alvaro Jamarillo**, **Paul Mann**, **Tom Stephenson**, **Nils van Duivendijk** and **Dani López Velasco** have offered insightful comments on some key identification issues. Many other contacts, including in particular **Steve Holmes**, **Anne Donnelly** and **Bob Self**, have provided useful comments regarding identification tips and helpful ideas for improving the content. We would like to thank **Joe Hobbs** for his invaluable compilations of Irish bird records, **D. I. M. Wallace** for regular enthusiastic support and encouragement, and to the writers of helpful and positive reviews of the first edition, notably **John Cantelo** and **Andy Stoddart** and **Stuart Winter**.

A special mention goes to **Rachel** and **Anya Still**, **Gill Swash** and **Marcella Hume** for their invaluable contributions behind the scenes, all of which helped to bring this book to fruition, and we would particularly like to thank **Brian Clews** for his commitment and dedication in sourcing hundreds of images, and his keen eye in proof-reading. Thanks, too, go to **Dr. Tim Hounsome** from the environmental consultancy RSK Biocensus and **Jess Chappell** at the RSPB for their assistance with the status and legislation section, and to **Mark Balman** and **Hannah Wheatley** at Birdlife International for their help in preparing the distribution maps. **Robert Kirk**, Publisher, Field Guides & Natural History, at Princeton University Press, has encouraged and helped us throughout this lengthy project.

Although a substantial number of the images in the book were taken by the authors – **Hugh Harrop** (hughharrop.com) (825), **Andy & Gill Swash** (worldwildlifeimages.com) (374) and **David Tipling** (birdphoto.co.uk) (194) – the inevitable gaps in our portfolios meant that achieving the aim of showing images of every distinctive plumage of every species ever recorded in Britain and Ireland would not have been possible without enlisting the help of others. With the generous support of the many photographers who kindly supplied their images, a total of 3,582 photos is featured, including more than 800 that are new since the first edition, representing the work of 279 photographers. Collating these images proved to be a monumental task and we would like to express our gratitude to **Marc Guyt** and **Roy de Haas** at the Agami photo agency in the Netherlands (agami.nl) for their invaluable help in this process.

A number of photographers generously provided access to their entire portfolio of images. Their work is featured extensively throughout the book and their skill is clear to see. All of them spend many hours with a camera, using their technical expertise, extensive local knowledge and understanding of wild birds in pursuit of the perfect picture. We particularly thank **Martin Bennett**, who travels widely in search of birds and is out in the field almost daily studying the wildlife of the New Forest; **Roger and Liz Charlwood** (worldwildlifeimages.com); **Mark Darlaston**, a seabird enthusiast; **Greg and Yvonne Dean** (worldwildlifeimages.com); **David Kjaer** (davidkjaer.com) and **Mike Lane** (nature-photography.co.uk), two prolific and very skilled wildlife photographers; **Michael McKee** (michaelmckee.co.uk), who enjoys photographing his local wildlife but also travels widely in search of rare birds; and **Markus Varesvuo** (facebook.com/markus.varesvuo), an award-winning photographer from Finland whose photographic artistry is highlighted in several books.

CREDITS

The contribution of every photographer is gratefully acknowledged and **each image not taken by one of the authors** is listed in this section, together with the photographer's initials, as follows (images sourced via Agami (agami.nl) are indicated with an ᴬ after the photographer's initials):

Jim Almond (shropshirebirder.co.uk) [JAl]; **Amar-Singh HSS** [A-S HSS]; **John Anderson** (pbase.com/crail_birder) [JAn]; **Dave Appleton** [DA]; **Rafael Armada**/Agami [RAᴬ]; **Aurélien Audevard**/Agami [AAᴬ]; **Jem Babbington** [JBaᴬ]; **Danny Bales** [DBa]; **Robert Balestra** [RBa]; **Keith Barnes** [KBa]; **Sue Barth** [SBar]; **Glenn Bartley**/Agami [GBᴬ]; **Bill Baston**/Agami [BBaᴬ]; **Roy & Marie Battell** (moorhen.me.uk) [R&MB]; **Chris Batty** [CBa]; **Sam Bayley** [SBay]; **Tom Beeke** [TB]; **Ken Behrens** [KBe]; **Boris Belchev** (alcedowildlife.com) [BBe]; **Amir Ben Dov** (gull-research.org) [ABD]; **Martin Bennett** [MB]; **Alex Berryman** [AB]; **Richard Bonser** (rothandb.blogspot.co.uk) [RB]; **Sándor Borzas** [SBo]; **Han Bouwmeester**/Agami [HBᴬ]; **Colin Bradshaw** [CBr]; **Dermot Breen** (dermotbreen.blogspot.co.uk) [DBre]; **Dave Bryan** [DBry]; **John Burnside** [JBu]; **Mark Carmody** (flickr.com/photos/drcarmo) [MCa]; **John K. Cassady** (jkcassady.com) [JKC]; **Graham Catley** (pewit.blogspot.co.uk) [GC]; **Mikael Champion** [MCh]; **Richard Chandler** [RCh]; **Keith Chapman** [KC]; **Roger & Liz Charlwood** (worldwildlifeimages.com) [R&LC]; **Bruce & Joanne Clayton** (butterflyonmyshoulder.ca) [B&JC]; **Trevor Codlin** [TC]; **Pete Coe** [PC]; **David Cooper** [DCoo]; **John Cooper** [JCo]; **Daniel Couch** (flickr.com/photos/25915567@N00) [DCou]; **Richard Crossley** (*Crossley ID Guide Britain and Ireland*) [RCr]; **D. Cuddon** [DCu]; **Stephen Daly** (focusingonwildlife.com/news/author/stephendaly) [SDa]; **Mike Danzenbaker**/Agami [MDanᴬ]; **Mark Darlaston** [MDar]; **Ian Davies**/Agami [IDaᴬ]; **Tony Davison** [TDa]; **Kit Day** (flickr.com/photos/kitdayphotography) [KD]; **Roy de Haas**/Agami [RdHᴬ]; **Raymond De Smet** (pbase.com/raydes) [RDS]; **Greg & Yvonne Dean** (worldwildlifeimages.com) [G&YD]; **Oscar Díez**/Agami [ODᴬ]; **Iosto Doneddu** (flickr.com/photos/38480380@N05) [IDo]; **Adrian Drummond-Hill** [AD-H]; **Kevin Du Rose** [KDR]; **Tony Duckett** [TDu]; **Steve Duffield** [SDu]; **Matt Eade** [ME]; **Dean Eades** (birdmad.com) [DE]; **James Eaton**/Agami [JEᴬ]; **Graham Ekins** (flickr.com/photos/graham_ekins_world_wildlife) [GE]; **Ralph Eldridge** (pbase.com/lightrae) [RE]; **Ivan Ellison** [IE]; **Efi First** [EF]; **Ashley Fisher** [AF]; **Ian Fisher** [IFi]; **Charlie Fleming** (parrotletsuk.typepad.com) [CF]; **Dick Forsman**/Agami [DFᴬ]; **Richard Frèze** [RF]; **Ian Fulton** (pbase.com/ianfulton) [IFu]; **Steve Gantlett** (sgbirdandwildlifephotos.co.uk) [SGan]; **Jacob Garvelink**/Agami [JGᴬ]; **Saverio Gatto**/Agami [SGatᴬ]; **George Gay** [GG]; **Hans Gebuis**/Agami [HGebᴬ]; **Hans Germeraad**/Agami [HGerᴬ]; **Alain Ghignone**/Agami [AGhᴬ]; **Chris Gibbins** (gull-research.org) [CG]; **Doug Gochfeld** (flickr.com/photos/29840397@N08) [DG]; **Lee Gregory** [LG]; **Antonio Gutiérrez** [AGu]; **Pablo Gutiérrez Varga** [PGV]; **Marc Guyt**/Agami [MGᴬ]; **Marlin Harms** [MHa]; **Stanislav Harvančík** [SHa]; **Russell Hayes** (birdmanbirds.blogspot.co.uk) [RHa]; **Jeffrey Hazell** [JH]; **David Hemmings**/Agami [DHᴬ]; **Brian Henderson** [BH]; **Ron Hindhaugh** (flickr.com/photos/16309940@N05) [RHi]; **Michael Daniel Ho** (MichaelDanielHo.com) [MDH]; **Mike Hook** (flickr.com/photos/58239862@N02) [MHo]; **Richard Howard** [RHo]; **Steve Howell** [SHo]; **John L. Irvine** [JLI]; **Jean-Claude Jamoulle** [J-CJ]; **Ayuwat Jearwattanakanok** [AJe]; **Tom Johnson** [TJ]; **Josh Jones**/Agami [JJᴬ]; **Gareth Jones** (pixelbirds.co.uk) [GJo]; **Arto Juvonen**/Agami [AJuᴬ]; **Ronald Kamphuis** [RK]; **Joe Kearney** (flickr.com/photos/122825362@N04) [JKe]; **Dave Key** (wildfowl-photography.co.uk) [DKey]; **David Kjaer** (davidkjaer.com) [DK]; **Steve Kolbe** [SK]; **Maxim Koshkin** [MK]; **Hannu Koskinen** [HK]; **Jainy Kuriakose** [JKu]; **Mike Lane** (nature-photography.co.uk) [ML]; **Paul Lawrence** [PL]; **Vincent Legrand**/Agami [VLᴬ]; **Tony Leukering** (flickr.com/photos/tony_leukering) [TL]; **Wil Leurs**/Agami [WLᴬ]; **David Lindo** (theurbanbirder.com) [DLi]; **Daniel Lopez Velasco**/Agami [DLVᴬ]; **James Lowen** (pbase.com/james_lowen) [JLo]; **Bruce Mactavish** [BMac]; **Michael Malpass** [MMa]; **Phil Mann** (flickr.com/photos/46796989@N02) [PMa]; **Ralph Martin**/Agami [RMᴬ]; **Bence Mate**/Agami [BMᴬ]; **Karel Mauer**/Agami [KMᴬ]; **James McCormick** [JM]; **Michael McKee** (michaelmckee.co.uk) [MMc]; **Arnold Meijer**/Agami [AMᴬ]; **Tim Melling** [TMe]; **David Monticelli**/Agami [DMonᴬ]; **Denzil Morgan** (facebook.com/Denzil-Morgan-Photography-786259851389520) [DMor]; **Pete Morris**/Agami [PMoᴬ]; **Killian Mullarney** [KMu]; **Tomi Muukkonen**/Agami [TMuᴬ]; **Steve Nuttall** [SN]; **Jerry O'Brien** [JO'B]; **Daniele Occhiato**/Agami [DOᴬ]; **Rob Olivier**/Agami [ROᴬ]; **Arie Ouwerkerk**/Agami [AOᴬ]; **Vincent Palomares** (oiseaux.net/photos/vincent.palomares) [VP]; **Jaysukh Parekh "Suman"** [JP"S"]; **Martin D. Parr** [MDP]; **John Pelechaty** (flickr.com/photos/johnpelechaty) [JPele]; **Jari Peltomäki**/Agami [JPeltᴬ]; **Joe Pender** (wwwsapphirepelagics.blogspot.com) [JPen]; **Yoav Perlman**/Agami [YPᴬ]; **Christopher Plummer** (pbase.com/cplummer) [CP]; **Jeff Poklen** [JPo]; **Seppo Pollanen** [SPo]; **Mike Pope** [MP]; **Stuart Price** [SPr]; **Brian Rafferty** (flickr.com/photos/brianrafferty) [BR]; **Markku Rantala**/Agami [MRᴬ]; **George**

CREDITS

Reszeter [GRe]; **Rob Riemer**/Agami [RR^A]; **Ghislain Riou** (oiseaux.net/photos/ghislain.riou/photos.html) [GRi]; **Juan Sagardia Pradera** [JSP]; **Ran Schols**/Agami [RSch^A]; **Reint Jakob Schut**/Agami [RJS^A]; **Ray Scott** [RSco]; **Will Scott** [WS]; **Adam Scott Kennedy** [ASK]; **Glyn Sellors** (glynsellorsphotography.com) [GS]; **Dubi Shapiro**/Agami [DS^A]; **Tom Shevlin** (wildlifesnaps.com) [TSh]; **Pavel Simeonov**/Agami [PS^A]; **Dr. Ajay Kumar Singh** [AKS]; **Brian E. Small**/Agami [BES^A]; **Dave Smallshire** [DSm]; **Walter Soestbergen**/Agami [WS^A]; **Soon Kyoo Choi** [SKC]; **Helge Sorensen**/Agami [HS^A]; **Laurens Steijn**/Agami [LS^A]; **Tom Stevenson** [TSt]; **Richard Stonier** (birdsonline.co.uk) [RSto]; **Brian Sullivan** [BS]; **Tom Tams** [TTam]; **Tim Taylor** (wildimaging.co.uk) [TTay]; **Marc Thibault** [MTh]; **August Thomasson** (augustthomasson.weebly.com) [AT]; **Roger Tidman** [RTi]; **Ralph Todd** [RTo]; **Mark Tomlins** [MTo]; **Purevsuren Tsolmonjav** (flickr.com/photos/wildlife_of_mongolia/with/17053293934) [PT]; **Chris Upson** [CU]; **Arnoud B. van den Berg** [AvdB]; **Bas van den Boogaard**/Agami [BvdB^A]; **Jacques van der Neut** [JvdN^A]; **Harvey van Diek**/Agami [HvD^A]; **Menno van Duijn**/Agami [MvD^A]; **Paul van Hoof** (paulvanhoof.nl) [PvH]; **Chris van Rijswijk**/Agami [CvR^A]; **Mitchell Vanbeekum** [MVan]; **Colin Vanner** [CV]; **Markus Varesvuo** (facebook.com/markus.varesvuo) [MVa]; **Alex Vargas**/Agami [AV^A]; **Aravind Venkatraman** [AVe]; **Martijn Verdoes**/Agami [MVe^A]; **Fred Visscher**/Agami [FV^A]; **Roger Wasley** [RWa]; **Arend Wassink**/Agami [AW^A]; **Mike Watson** (birdquest-tours.com) [MW]; **Ian N. White** (flickr.com/photos/ian_white) [INW]; **Steve Wilce** [SW]; **John Williams** [JW]; **Kristin Wilmers**/Agami [KW^A]; **Wim Wilmers**/Agami [WW^A]; **Peter J. Wilson** [PJW]; **Rob Wilson** (robwilsonphotos.co.uk) [RWi]; **Edwin Winkel**/Agami [EW^A]; **Phil Winter** (flickr.com/photos/philwinter) [PW]; **Michelle & Peter Wong** [M&PW]; **Roger Wyatt** [RWy] and **Steve Young** (birdsonfilm.smugmug.com) [SY].

A number of images have been sourced through the generous terms of the Creative Commons Attribution-ShareAlike 2.0 Generic license. These are indicated by "/CC" after the photographer's name in the list. Other images sourced via the photographic agencies FLPA (flpa-images.co.uk) and Shutterstock (shutterstock.com) are credited in full.

> The following codes are used: M = male; F = female; Juv = juvenile; Imm = immature; 1w = 1st-winter (*etc.*); 1s = 1st-summer (*etc.*); br = breeding; non-br = non-breeding; Ad = adult; sum = summer; win = winter; (st) = standing/perched; (sw) = swimming; (fl) = flying (up = upperwing, un = underwing); (h) = head.

Title page: Hoopoe [DO^A].

INTRODUCTION p5: Blue Tit (wing) [AO^A]; **Fieldfare** (fl-up) [MG^A], (fl-un) & (st) [MVar]. **p10: Geese** (sw) [MB], (fl) [G&YD]; **Ducks** (dabbling) M (fl) [MVar], F (fl) [AO^A]; **Ducks** (diving) (fl) [MG^A], (h [DO^A]; **Cormorants** (sw) [RdH^A]; **Divers** (sw) [RSto]; **Grebes** (sw) [MB], (fl) [RSch^A]; **p11: Spoonbills** (fl) [MVar]; **Cranes** (st) [HB^A]; **Storks** (fl) [DO^A]; **Storm Petrels** [MDar]; **Gulls** (smaller) (st) [MVar], (fl) [RdH^A]; **Terns** (st) [RE]; **Skuas** (fl) [MDar]. **p12: Plovers** (smaller) (fl) [MVar]; **Plovers** (larger) (st) & (fl) [DO^A]; **Stone-curlew** [G&YD]; **Waders** (larger) (st) [MB], (fl) [JPelt^A]; **Curlews/Godwits** (st) [MB]; **Pratincoles** [RSch^A]; **Coursers** [MMc]; **Crakes** [CvR^A]; **Corncrake** [MW]. **p13: Kites** [RSch^A]; **Osprey** [MVar]; **Harriers** [DO^A]; **Buzzards** (st) [HB^A]; **Hawks** (fl) [MVar], (st) [MB]; **Falcons** (st) [RJS^A]; **Cuckoos** (st) [MB]; **Owls** [JPelt^A]; **Nightjars** (st) [MB]; **Swallows** [RSch^A]; **Grouse** [Giedriius/Shutterstock]; **Bustards** [MVar]. **p14: Kingfishers** [DO^A]; **Sandgrouse** [MDan^A‐]; **Oriole** [MG^A]; **Woodpeckers** [MB]; **Wryneck** [MB]; **Crows** [ML]; **Shrikes** [MVar]. **p15: Pipits** [MVar]; **Wagtails** [MB]; **Wren** [MB]; **Starlings** [MB]; **Nuthatches** [G&YD]; **Flycatchers** [MB]; **Sparrows** [MB]; **Finches** [MB]; **Buntings** [DO^A].

WILDFOWL p16: Greylags [MB], **Shelduck** (fl) [JPelt^A]. **p17: Garganey** [DO^A]; **Shoveler** [MDan^A]; **Gadwall** [MB]. **p18: Mallard** F [RM^A]. **p19: Mute Swan** 'Polish' [WL^A]. **p20: Bewick's Swan** 'Whistling' [BES^A]. **p21: Whooper** Ad [DO^A]. **p22: Mute Swan** Imm [MB]; **Whooper Swan** [RdH^A]. **p23: White-fronted Goose** Ad (un) [MVar]; **Bean Goose** (up) [MVar]; **Greylag Goose** (up) [MVar]; **Barnacle Goose** (un) & (up) [MVar]; **Snow Goose** (un) [BES^A], (up) [GB^A]; **Canada Goose** [BES^A]. **p24: Canada Goose** (fl) [G&YD], (skein) [MVar]; **Cackling Goose** (h) [BSm^A]. **p25: Todd's** [BH]; **Richardson's** (sw) [BSm^A]. **p26: Brent Goose** (fl) [RSch^A], Ad [AO^A]. **p27: Red-breasted Goose** (fl-up) [RDS]; **Brent Goose** *nigricans* [AO^A], *bernicla* [MvD^A]. **p30: Bean Goose** (fl) [MVar]; **Taiga Bean Goose** Juv [MG^A]. **p31: Tundra Bean Goose** (fl) [MVar], and **Taiga Bean Goose** (fl) [MVar]. **p32: White-fronted Goose** Greenland [PMo]. **p33: Snow Goose** (fl-up) [GB^A], (fl-un) [BES^A], dark [Dennis W. Donohue/Shutterstock]; **Lesser White-fronted Goose** Ad (st) [MVar], (h) [HGeb^A]. **p34: Shelduck** M (st) [MG^A], (fl-up) [JPelt^A], Juv [DO^A]. **p35: Egyptian Goose** (fl) [RDH^A], (st) [Maciej Olszewski/Shutterstock], Grey (h) [Tristram Brelstaff/CC], Juv (inset) [Charles Sharp/CC]; **Ruddy Shelduck** M [DO^A]. **p36: Mallard** M [MVar], F [AO^A]; **Shoveler** both [BES^A]; **Garganey** both [DO^A]; **Teal** M [DO^A], F [MVar]; **R-b Merganser** F [MVar]; **Goosander** F [MVar]; **Gadwall** M [AB], F [RTi]; **Pochard** M [JPelt^A], F [TMu^A]; **Wigeon** M [RSch^A], F [RTi]; **B-w Teal** both [MDan^A]; **Am Wigeon** F [MDan^A]. **p37: Smew** both [MVar]; **Surf Scoter** [GB^A]; **Velvet Scoter** both [MVar]; **Goldeneye** both [MVar]; **Common Scoter** both [MVar]; **King Eider** 1wM [MVar]; **Eider** 1wM [MvD^A]; **Ferruginous Duck** [JPelt^A]; **Tufted Duck** both [MG^A]; **Scaup** both [MVar]. **p38: Shoveler** (fl) [MVar], (st) [RM^A]; **Mallard** (fl) [Ana Gram/Shutterstock]; **Gadwall** (fl) [MVar]; **Teal** (fl) [RM^A]; **Wigeon** (fl) [MVar]; **Pintail** (fl) [Imran Shah/CC]. **p39: Wigeon** F (Dec) [RSch^A], 1s F (Mar) [DO^A], M (fl) [AO^A], M (Nov–Apr) [RdH^A]. **p40: Mallard** F (fl) [AO^A], M (fl) [MVar]. **p41: Shoveler** M (h) [Steve Byland/Shutterstock]. **p42: Gadwall** (fl) M & F [RTi], (Apr–Sep) [HB^A]. **p43: Pintail** (fl) [JPelt^A], M (h) [JW]. **p44: Teal** pair (st) [HGer^A], F (fl) [MVar]. **p45: Garganey** M (fl) & F (fl) [DO^A]. **p46: Red-crested Pochard** M (fl) [MVar], F (fl) [RM^A], Juv (h) & M (sw) [DO^A], F (sw) [CvR^A]. **p47: Pochard** F (fl) [Maciej

CREDITS

Olszewski/Shutterstock), (sw - top) [DO^], M (fl) [JPelt^], M (h) [RK]. **p48:** Tufted Duck (inset) [WL^], M (fl) [MG^], 1wM [MVar], M (Sep–May) [AO^], F (fl) [MG^]. **p49:** Scaup (flock), M (fl) F (fl) & ImmM [MVar], (Sep–Mar) [AM^]. **p50:** Goldeneye M (fl) & F (fl) [MVar], 1w M (inset) [RM^], 1s M (h) (inset) [DKey]. **p51:** Smew M (fl) & F (fl) [MVar], F (sw) & M (sw) [WS^]. **p52:** R-b Merganser (inset) [AO^]; F (fl) [MVar], F (sw) [DO^]. **p53:** Goosander (inset) [BBe], F (fl), M (fl) [MVar]. **p55:** Long-tailed Duck (flock with scoter) [MVar]. **p56:** Velvet Scoter M (sw) [MMc], (inset) [FV^], others (5) [MVar]. **p57:** Common Scoter all (6) [MVar]. **p58:** Eider 1s M [MVar]. **p59:** Eider Nearctic (h) [DH^]. **p60:** Ruddy Duck F (fl) [MDan^], M (fl), [KBe], M (sw) [MVar]; White-headed Duck F (sw) [ABD]. **p61:** Mandarin F (fl) [MB], F (sw) [Maciej Pisarek/Shutterstock]; M (fl) [MB]; Wood Duck M [MG^]. **p62:** Trumpeter Swan [BES^]; Emperor Goose [Bildagentur Zoonar GmbH/Shutterstock]; Ross's Goose [BES^]; Muscovy Duck [Underworld/Shutterstock]; Cinnamon Teal both [Richard Seeley/Shutterstock]; Marbled Duck [RM^]. **p63:** Mallard × Pintail [TJ], Shoveler × Gadwall [MDan^], Wigeon × American Wigeon [DBa], Tufted Duck × Pochard [TDu], Tufted Duck × Ferruginous Duck [AT], Pochard × Ferruginous Duck [CP], Tufted Duck × Ring-necked Duck [SY]. **p64:** American Wigeon F (fl-up) [MDan^], F (sw - top) [MMc], F (wing) [MDH], F (sw - bottom) & F (fl) [GB^]; Wigeon F (fl) [GB^], F (sw) [DO^]. **p65:** Black Duck × Mallard (inset) [GB^]; Mallard (wing) [DO^], Falcated Duck (flock - inset) [VL^]; M (fl) & F (fl) [M&PW^]; F (sw) [AJe]. **p66:** Teal (wing) [MVar]; Garganey (wing) [DO^]; Blue-winged Teal (wing) [MDan^], (h) [MR^]; Baikal Teal (wing) [TB], (h) [Wang LiQiang/Shutterstock]; Green-winged Teal (fl) both [MDan^], (sw) both [BES^]. **p67:** Blue-winged Teal M (fl) & F (fl) [MDan^], M (sw) & F (sw) [GB^]; Baikal Teal M (fl) & F (fl) [SPr], F (sw) [Wang LiQiang/Shutterstock], M (sw) [VL^]. **p68:** Lesser Scaup M (fl) & F (fl) [GB^]; Scaup (wing) [MVar]; Tufted Duck (fl) [WS^]. **p69** Ring-necked Duck M (fl) [AJL^]; Tufted Duck (wing) [MG^]; Ferruginous Duck M (fl-un) [Weblogia/Shutterstock], (fl-up) [JPelt^]. **p70:** Hooded Merganser M (fl) & F (fl) [MDan^], F (sw) & M (sw) [GB^]; Bufflehead M (fl) & F (fl) [GB^], F (sw) [BES^]. **p71:** Redhead M (fl) [GB^]. **p73:** Goldeneye F (wing) [MVar]; Barrow's Goldeneye M (fl), F (fl) & F (sw) [MVar]. **p74:** Surf Scoter M (h), M (fl) & F (fl) [MDan^]; Harlequin Duck M (fl) [MvD^], M (st) [MMc]. **p75:** White-winged Scoter F (fl) [BES^], M (fl) [EW^]; Stejneger's Scoter M (h) [PT], F (h) [DCoo]; Black Scoter both [GB^]; Velvet Scoter both [MVar]; Common Scoter M [MVar], F [CvR^].

CORMORANTS, DIVERS & GREBES p76: Cormorant (st) [TTay]. **p77:** Red-throated Diver Juv [DO^], non-br [RSto]; Great Crested Grebe (fl) [RSch^], Juv [Maciej Pisarek/Shutterstock], non-br [MB]. **p78:** Black-necked Grebe (fl), [RBa]; Slavonian Grebe (fl) [JPen]; Great Crested Grebe Ad (fl) [RSch^], (sw) [HvD^]; Little Grebe [DO^]. **p79:** Red-throated Diver non-br (fl) [MVar] & (sw) [DO^]; Great Northern Diver non-br (fl) [MHa]; Black-throated Diver (fl-un) & (fl-up) [MVar], non-br (fl) [RSch^], (sw) [AO^]; White-billed Diver br (fl) [MVar], non-br (fl) [PC], (sw) [DSm]; Pacific Diver (fl) [MVe^]. **p80:** Cormorant Ad (h) & (st) [MvD^], non-br [DO^], Imm [ML], (inset) carbo [MDar]. **p81:** Shag Ad non-br [MDar], Juv (st) [KM^]; Cormorant (st) [RdH^]. **p82:** Red-throated Diver Juv/1w [DO^], Ad (fl) [MVar]; Black-throated Diver (fl) [MVar], Ad br [JPelt^], Juv/1w [AO^], Ad non-br [CvR^]. **p84:** Great Northern Diver (fl) [MHa]. **p85:** White-billed Diver (fl) [PC], 1s [MVar], 2w [DSm], Ad br [Bering Land Bridge National Preserve/CC]. **p86:** Great Crested Grebe (fl) [KMa^], Juv [Maciej Pisarek/Shutterstock], non-br (h) [HvD^], br & non-br (sw) [MVar]. **p87:** Red-necked Grebe (fl) [RCr], Ad non-br [DO^], Ad br [MG^]. **p88:** Black-necked Grebe (fl) [RBa], Juv [Bildagentur Zoonar GmbH/Shutterstock], Ad br [RSch^]. **p89:** Slavonian Grebe (fl) [JPen], Juv (h) [MVar], Ad br [DO^], non-br [ABD]. **p90:** Little Grebe Juv (h) [ML], non-br [MVar], br [MB]. **p91:** Pacific Diver (fl) [BES^], non-br [SPr]; Black-throated Diver [CvR^]; Pied-billed Grebe 1w [DO^]. **p92:** Double-crested Cormorant Imm [WL^], Ad [GB^]; Dalmatian Pelican (fl-un) [DO^], (fl-up) [MMc], (st) [DSm].

SEABIRDS p93: Manx Shearwater (fl) [TMu^]. **p94:** Gannet (sw) [MDar], Great Skua [MDar]. **p95:** Sooty Shearwater [DMor]; Manx Shearwater (fl-un) & (fl-up) [MDar], (sw) [MG^]; Storm Petrel [MDar]. **p99:** Sooty Shearwater (fl) top left 4 birds [MDar], (fl-un (bottom)) [MVar]. **p100:** Great Shearwater (fl-un) [MG^]; Scopoli's Shearwater both [DO^]. **p101:** Great Shearwater [DO^]; Cory's Shearwater [DO^]. **p102:** Manx Shearwater (flock) & (fl-up (top)) [MDar], (fl-up (bottom)) [TMu^], (fl-un) [MDan^]; Balearic Shearwater all (3) [MDar]; Macaronesian Shearwater both [MVe^]; Yelkouan Shearwater [DO^]. **p103:** Manx Shearwater [MDar]; Balearic Shearwater [MDar]. **p104:** Storm Petrel (bottom left) [DMon^], others (4) [MDar]; Leach's Petrel (fl-un) [VL^], (fl-up) [SY]; Wilson's Petrel (fl-up) [MG^]. **p106:** Puffin [Mark Caunt/Shutterstock]. **p107:** Black Guillemot non-br [TS]; Little Auk br [G&YD], non-br [TJ]; Razorbill br (fl-up) [MVar], non-br (fl-up) [GRi]. **p110:** Puffin juv (h) & Ad non-br [RE]. **p111:** Black Guillemot Ad non-br (fl) [TSh]. **p112:** Little Auk non-br (fl) [TJ], br (fl) & br (inset) [G&YD]. **p113:** Tufted Puffin (fl) [DMor], (sw) [MVe^]; Ancient Murrelet [MDan^]; Long-billed Murrlet [MMc]. **p114:** Black-browed Albatross Ad (fl-up) [MG^], Imm [MG^]; Atlantic Yellow-nosed Albatross [MG^]. **p115:** Magnificent Frigatebird F [WL^], M [BES^]; Ascension Frigatebird (fl-un) [MG^], (fl-up) [DMor]. **p116:** Desertas Petrel all (3) [MVar]; Zino's Petrel (fl-up) [MG^], (fl-un) & (h) [JSP]. **p117:** Red-billed Tropicbird [WL^]; Bermuda Petrel both [MDan^]; Black-capped Petrel both [MDan^]. **p118:** Red-footed Booby (fl) & (st) [DMon^]; Gannet [DO^]; Brown Booby Juv (fl) [DO^], 1y & 2y [DMon^], 1y (inset) [MMc]; White-faced Storm Petrel both [RB]. **p119:** Swinhoe's Petrel [SHo]; Leach's Petrel [TJ]; Black-bellied Storm (fl-up) [Andrew M Allport/Shutterstock], (fl-un) [MG^].

GULLS & TERNS p120: Black Tern [MDar]. **p121:** Black-headed Gull Ad br (st) & (fl) [MVar]; Little Tern [MVar]. **p122:** Herring Gull 2w [MG^]; Black-headed Gull Juv (fl) [AO^], 1w & 1s (fl) [DO^]. **p123:** Black-headed Gull 2w [DO^], Ad br (fl) [RdH^], Ad br>nb [AM^]. **p124:** Glaucous Gull 3w (fl) [MVar]. **p125:** Lesser B-b Gull (fl) [MDar]; Yellow-legged Gull (fl) [MVar], (st) [RM^]; Caspian Gull (fl) [AO^], (st) [G&YD]. **p126:** Lesser Black-backed Gull [MvD^]; Caspian Gull [RTo]; Yellow-legged Gull [DO^]; American Herring Gull [MDan^]; Thayer's Gull' [MMc]. **p127:** Lesser Black-backed Gull [KMa^]; Yellow-legged Gull [DO^]; Caspian Gull [MMc]; Thayer's Gull [MDan^]; 'Kumlien's Gull' [CvR^]; Slaty-backed Gull [DLV^]; Glaucous-winged Gull [PMo^]. **p128:** Yellow-legged Gull all (3) [DO^]; Herring Gull (fl) [CvR^]; Caspian Gull [CG], (st) [ABD]; Lesser Black-backed Gull (fl) [JKC], [SY]. **p129:** Yellow-legged Gull (fl) [DO^], [AGu]; Caspian Gull [SBc], (st) [CG]; Lesser Black-backed Gull (fl) [MG^]; Great Black-backed Gull (st) [AM^]. **p132:** Lesser Black-backed Gull (fl) 1s [GJo], 2w & 3w [SY], Ad br [MDar].

p133: Lesser Black-backed Gull graellsii [CvR^], intermedius (fl) [RM^], fuscus (fl) [DO^], fuscus (st) [HK], 2w [BMac]. **p134:** Great Black-backed Gull (fl) 1w & 2w [MDar], (h) [CvR^]. **p135:** Great Black-backed Gull 3w [JPo]. **p136:** Yellow-legged Gull Ad (st) [RM^], others (5) [DO^]. **p137:** Caspian Gull (fl) 1w [RTo], 2w [CG], 3w [SBo], Ad (fl) & (st) [AO^]. **p138:** Yellow-l Gull all [DO^],

CREDITS

except tertials [RM^]; **Caspian Gull** (wing) & (fl-side) [RM^], (fl-up) [AM^], (st) [CvR^], (tertials) [KM^]; **p139:** 'Thayer's Gull' Juv/1w [VL^], Ad non-br [DMon^]; **Iceland Gull** 3w [MMc]; **Glaucous Gull** 3w [MVar], Ad non-br [MG^]; **Glaucous-winged Gull** both [MDan^]. **p140: Glaucous Gull** Ad Non-br [MVar], 2w [TC], 3s [VL^]. **p141: Iceland Gull** Juv/1w & 3w [MMc], **Thayer's Gull** [DMon^]. **p142:** 'Thayer's Gull' Ad non-br (fl) [DMon^], (sw) [MDan^], 1w (fl) [VL^], 1w (st) [MDan^]. **p143: Black-h Gull** 1w [DO^]; **Mediterranean Gull** 2w (wing) [MVar], Ad win [JPelt^], 1w [TC]; **Common Gull** Ad non-br [MG^]; **Kittiwake** Ad non-br [MVe^]; **Sabine's Gull** Juv [RJS^], 1s [MDar], Ad non-br [TDu]; **Little Gull** 1w (un) [MHo], Ad non-br [MDar]. **p144: Common Gull** *heinei* [YP]. **p145: Common Gull** Juv (fl) [MVar], Juv (st) [CvR^]. **p146: Black-headed Gull** 1w (fl) [DO^], Ad br (fl) [RdH^], 1s (fl) [MVar]; 1w (st) [DO^], Ad br (st) [MVar]. **p147: Mediterranean Gull** Ad non-br (fl) [SY], Ad br (fl) [MVar], Ad non-br (h) [MVar], 2w [SPo], Juv [CvR^], Ad br (h) [RJS^], 1w (st) [DO^]. **p148: Kittiwake** 1w (fl) [JvdN^], 1s [IDa^], 2w (wing) [MvD^], Ad br (st) [GB^]. **p149: Sabine's Gull** 1s (fl), Ad non-br (fl) & Juv (sw) [MDar], Ad br (fl) [DMor], Juv (fl) [RJS^], Ad br (sw) [GB^], Ad non-br (h) [RCr]. **p150: Little Gull** Ad non-br (fl) [MvD^], 1w (fl-up) [MDan^], 1w (fl-un) [JH]; 2w [KM^], Juv (st) & Ad br (st) [MVar]. **p151: Ross's Gull** 1w (fl) [SY], Ad br (fl) [BMac], 1w (sw) [MMc], Ad non-br (st) [SY]; **Ivory Gull** Ad (fl) [MG^], 1w (fl) [SY]; (st) both [MW]. **p152: Laughing Gull** Ad non-br (fl) [MDar], 1w (fl) [SY]. **p153: Bonaparte's Gull** Ad win (fl) & 1w (fl) [BS], (h) [Bruce MacQueen/Shutterstock]; **Franklin's Gull** (st) [MMc], others (4) [BS]. **p154: Ring-billed Gull** 1w (fl) [VL^]; 1w (fl) [MDan^]. **p155: Great Black-backed Gull** 1w (fl) [MVar], 1w (st) [AO^], Ad or (st) [JPelt^]; **Slender-billed Gull** 1w (fl) [DO^], 1w (fl) [MMc], 1s [DO^]. **p156: Slaty-backed Gull** Ad non-br [MG^], 1w [DCoo], 3w [PMo^]; **Glaucous-winged Gull** Ad non-br [Alan Schmierer/CC], 1w [PMo^], 2w [DLV^]. **p157: Glaucous-winged Gull** both [MDan^]; **Slaty-backed Gull** both [MG^]; **Lesser Black-backed Gull** (wing) [SY]; **Audouin's Gull** 1s (fl-up) & (on ground) [MG^], Juv (inset) [ABD], Ad (st) [DO^]. **p159: American Herring Gull** 3w [KBe], 1w [MDan^]; **Vega Gull** all (3) [PMo^]. **p160: Sandwich Tern** [SY], **Roseate & Black Terns** [MVar], **Caspian Tern** [DO^]. **p161: Little Tern** (fl-hover) [Georgios Alexandris/Shutterstock], (fl-up) [MvD^], Juv (fl) [AO^]; Juv (st) [GS], Ad (st) [TDa]; **Least Tern** (fl-up) [PMo^], Ad (st) [BES^]. **p162: Common Tern** 2s (fl) & Juv (fl) [MDar], Juv (st) [MG^]. **p163: Arctic Tern** 1s (fl) [SN]. **p164: Roseate Tern** Ad (fl-up) [DMon^], Ad (fl-un) [MVar], Juv (fl), Juv (st) & (h) [GS], Ad (st) [MMc], Ad (h) both [SY]. **p165: Sandwich Tern** Ad non-br (fl) [AO^], Juv (fl) & Juv (st) [WL^], Ad br [HB^], (h) [WL^]. **p166: Black Tern** Juv (fl-un) [MVar], Juv (fl-up) [MB], Ad (moult) [MG^], Ad [MDar], Juv (st) [WL^], Ad (AJu^]. **p167: Black Tern** [MG^]; **Whiskered Tern** [MDan^]; **White-winged Black Tern** Juv (fl-up) [GS], Juv (fl-un) [SY], br>non-br [KM^], Juv (st) [RazvanZinica/Shutterstock], Ad br (wing) [RdH^]. **p168: Whiskered Tern** Ad non-br (fl) [LS^], Juv [RMS^], Ad non-br (st) [SGat^]; **Caspian Tern** 1w (fl) [RM^], (h) [R&LC]. **p169: Gull-billed Tern** Ad br (fl) [AO^], non-br (fl) [SGat^], Juv (st) [DO^]; **Sandwich Tern** Ad br (fl) [SY], (h) [MMc]; **Forster's Tern** Ad br (fl) [WL^], Ad non-br (fl) [MDan^], Ad br (h) [BES^], (st) [MMc]; **Common Tern** (tail) [MVar]. **p170: Caspian Tern** [BES^]; **Royal Tern** Ad br (fl) & (st) [BES^], non-br (h) [MMc]; **West African Crested Tern** (fl) [Hugh Lansdown/Shutterstock], non-br (h) [VL^]. **p170: Elegant Tern** (st) [BSm^], (h) [RdH^]; **Lesser Crested Tern** (fl) [AD-H], (st) [KD], (h) [AA^]. **p172: Bridled Tern** (fl) both [TTam], (st) [WS]; **Sooty Tern** all (3) [MMc]. **p173: Aleutian Tern** (fl-un) & (st) [PMo^], (fl-up) [GB^]; **Cabot's Tern** (st) & (h) [WL^]; **Sandwich Tern** Ad non-br (fl) [WL^], (wing) [SY].

SKUAS **p174: Arctic Skua & Arctic Tern** (fl) [MvD^]; **Pomarine Skua** Juv [DBre], 1s [LS^]. **p175: Pomarine Skua** (flock) [MDar], 2s [JPen], Ad br [LS^], Ad non-br [JSP]. **p176: Arctic Skua** (fl) [MDar], Juv [KM^]. **p177: Pomarine Skua** (fl) [LS^], Ad br dark and pale [CvR^], (h) [ML], Juv [AO^]. **p178: Long-tailed Skua** Juv [MMc], dark [JLI]. **p179: Great Skua** Juv (h) [IE], (st) [MvD^]; **South Polar Skua** (fl) [JSP]. **p180: Long-tailed Skua** pale [AO^], Ad br (CvR^]; **Arctic Skua** [AO^], intermediate [MvD^]; **Pomarine Skua** [AO^]; **Great Skua** [IE]. **p181: Long-tailed Skua** pale/'int' (un) & (up) [MDar], 'int'/dark (un) [JPen], 'int'/dark (up) [SY]; **Arctic Skua** (un) [MVar], (up) [SGan]; **Pomarine Skua** all [DBre]; **Great Skua** (up) & (un) [AO^]. **p182: Arctic Skua** pale (3) [MDar]; **Pomarine Skua** (up) & dark [MDan^], (un) [MDar], (side) [LS^].

WADERS **p183: Flock** [DKj], **Sanderling** transitional spring [RCh]. **p184: Curlew Sandpiper** (fl) [JPelt^]; **Little Ringed Plover** (fl) [RSch^]; **Greenshank** (fl) [MVar]; **Common Sandpiper** (st) [AV^]; **Cream-coloured Courser** [Carl Day/Shutterstock]; others (10) [ML]. **p185: Red-necked Phalarope** [MMc], **Green Sandpiper** [Peter Gyure/Shutterstock]; **Ruff** [Michal Kocan/Shutterstock]; **Golden Plover**, **Ringed Plover**, **Dunlin**, **Redshank**, **Bar-tailed Godwit** & **Curlew** all [ML]. **p186: Whimbrel** (up) [Dave Montreuil/Shutterstock], (un) [MVar]; **Curlew** (up) [DO^], (un) [AO^]; **Bar-t Godwit** (up) [DO^]; **Redshank** [JPelt^]; **Spotted Redshank** [DO^]; **Greenshank** [MVar]. **p187: Red-necked Phalarope** [MDan^]; **Temminck's Stint** [DG]; **Little Stint** [MDan^]; **Ruff** [MDan^]; **Knot** [AO^]; **Green Sandpiper** [DO^]; **Woodcock** [HvD^]; **Snipe** [DO^]; **Jack Snipe** [MR^]; **Common Sandpiper** [RDS]. **p188: Avocet**, **Black-winged Stilt**, **Grey Plover** (up), **Little Ringed Plover** & **Dotterel** Juv [DO^]; **Lapwing** (un), **Grey Plover** br & 1w [RM^]; **Golden Plover** juv (up), **Ringed Plover** br & **Dotterel** br [MVar]; **Golden Plover** br [FV^], Juv (un) [AO^]; **Kentish Plover** [IDa^]. **p189: Stone-curlew** (fl) [RDS], M [G&YD], Juv [HS^]. **p193: Black-winged Stilt** Juv/1w [DO^]; **Kentish Plover** br (fl) [IDa^], non-br (fl) & (st) [VL^], M & F [DO^]. **p194: Ringed Plover** Ad (fl) [MVar], *tundrae* [G&YD] non-br (h) [RM^]. **p195: Little Ringed Plover** (fl) [DO^], Juv [MVar], F & M [MB]. **p196: Dotterel** Juv (fl) [DO^], F (fl) [MVar], (flock) [MG^], Juv [MMc]. **p197: Lapwing** Juv [MVar], F non-br [RM^]. **p198: Golden Plover** Juv (fl) [AO^], Ad (fl) & Juv (st) [MVar], 1w [RM^]. **p199: Grey Plover** (flock - inset) [AO^], Juv (fl) & Ad non-br [DO^], Ad (fl) [HS^], Ad br [MVar]. **p200: Sanderling** (fl) [DO^], Ad non-br [RdH^]. **p201: Knot** (fl) [AO^]. **p202: Dunlin** 1w [DO^]. **p203: Dunlin** *arctica* [KMu]. **p204: Purple Sandpiper** Juv [AO^]. **p206: Temminck's Stint** (fl) left [TMu^], (fl) right [DG], Ad br & non-br [RM^], Juv [MDan^]. **p207: Little Stint** (fl) [MDan^], Ad non-br [AO^]. **p208: Ruff** (inset) [MvD^], M non-br [RCh]. **p209: Ruff** (fl), Ad non-br (h), (h - Mar) [MVar]. **p210: Redshank** (inset) [AO^], (fl) [JPelt^], Juv & Ad br [MVar], Ad non-br [DO^]. **p211: Spotted Redshank** (fl) [MDan^], Ad br [MVar], (inset) [DO^]. **p212: Greenshank** (fl) & Juv [MVar], Ad non-br [DO^]. **p213: Wood Sandpiper** (fl-un) [HS^], (fl-up) [RM^], Ad [SGat^]. **p214: Green Sandpiper** (fl) both & Ad non-br [DO^], Juv [MVar]. **p215: Common Sandpiper** (fl-up) [RDS], (fl-un) [MB], Ad non-br [RCh], Juv [AA^], Ad br [DKj]. **p216: Bar-tailed Godwit** (fl) [AO^], Juv [AO^]. **p217: Black-tailed Godwit** *limosa* (fl) [DKj], Juv (fl) & (wing) [RM^], Ad non-br [DKj], Ad F [MVar], Ad M [RSch^]; *islandica* Ad M [MVar]. **p218: Curlew** (fl-un) [DKj], (fl-up) [DO^], Juv (h-facing) [MVar]. **p219: Whimbrel** (fl-un) [AO^], (fl-up) [Dave Montreuil/Shutterstock]; **Hudsonian Whimbrel** (st) [RSto]. **p220: Red-necked Phalarope** Juv (fl) [MDan^], 1w (sw) [Mital Patel/Shutterstock], Juv (sw) [AO^], M br [MMc]. **p221: Grey Phalarope** M br [MVar], F br [MG^]; **Sanderling** [DO^].

561

CREDITS

p222: Snipe (fl-un) [MVar], (fl-up) [RM^]. **p223: Jack Snipe** (fl) both [FV^], in snow [RSch^]. **p224: Woodcock** (fl-up) [HJD^], (fl-un) [RTi]. **p226: Wilson's Phalarope** Juv (fl) [MDan^], F (fl-up) & (fl-un) [USFWS Mountain-Prairie/CC], Juv>1w (st) [BES^], (wing-inset) [MMc]; **Collared Pratincole** [MG^]. **p227: Black-winged Pratincole** Ad (st) [AW^], (fl) both [MDan^], (bill-inset) [DO^]; **Collared Pratincole** Ad (st) [RM^], (fl-up) [RSch^], (bill-inset) [MG^]; **Oriental Pratincole** Ad (st) [HS^], (fl-un) [DO^], (fl) [HB^], [CU], (bill-inset) [John Harrison/CC]. **p228: Hudsonian Godwit** (fl) & 1s M [DMon^], F [MMc]; **Black-t Godwit** [MG^]; **Cream-coloured Courser** (fl) [RDS], (st) [MMc]. **p229: Sociable Lapwing** (fl) [MK], 1w [RA^], Ad (st) [MW]; **White-tailed Lapwing** (fl) [MDan^], (st) [MMc]. **p230: Golden Plover** Ad br [RM^], Juv [MVar]; **American Golden Plover** Ad br [CvR^], Juv [DO^]; **Pacific Golden Plover** Ad br [RSch^], Juv [MVar]. **p231: Golden Plover** (wing) [DO^]; **American Golden Plover** (wing) [IDa^]; **Pacific Golden Plover** (fl-up) [RM^], (fl-un) [MG^] (wing) [MVar]. **p232: Semipalmated Plover** fl [MDan^], Ad [BES^], (st) [DO^]. **p233: Greater Sand Plover** Ad br [DO^], (fl) & nb [RM^], (bill) [SG^]; **Lesser Sand Plover** 'mongolus' Ad br [BvdB^], 'atrifrons' Ad br, (fl), br & (bill) [RM^]; **Caspian Plover** Ad br [MVar], (fl), [MP], 1w [DMon^]. **p234: Temminck's Stint** [MDan^]; **Semipalmated Sandpiper** (wing & scapulars) [DO^]; **Red-necked Stint** (wing & scapulars) [AA^]. **p235: Little Stint** [MDan^]; **Western Sandpiper** (fl) [MDan^]; **Semipalmated Sandpiper** (fl) [HS^]; Ad (May) [IDa^], Juv [DO^]; **Red-necked Stint** (fl) [IDa^]; Ad br [MR^], Juv [AA^]. **p236: Long-toed Stint** [SPr]; **Least Sandpiper** (fl) [VL^]; Ad both [BES^], Juv [Ian Maton/Shutterstock]; **Broad-billed Sandpiper** (fl) [AO^], Juv (h) [Georgios Alexandris/Shutterstock] Ad br [MVar], 1w [MW]. **p237: White-rumped Sandpiper** (fl) [HS^], Ad [MMc]; **Baird's Sandpiper** (fl) [MDan^], Ad [MvD^]; **Pectoral Sandpiper** (fl) [MVar], Juv [DO^]; **Sharp-tailed Sandpiper** Juv [BES^], Ad br [PMo^]. **p239: Great Knot** br (fl) & br (st) [DCoo], non-br (fl) [GJ^], Ad non-br [IDa^], Juv [MDan^]; **Stilt Sandpiper** (fl) [BSu], Juv [MMc], Ad (st) [GB^]. **p240: Buff-breasted Sandpiper** (fl) [TJ], Ad (st) [Asociacion Armonia/CC]; **Upland Sandpiper** (fl) [SBar], Juv [RSto]; **Little Whimbrel** (fl) [PMo^], (st) [BES^]. **p241: Great Snipe** (fl) Juv [MW], (fl) [HvD^]; **Snipe** (wing) [DO^], (fl-un) [MB], (wings raised) [DO^]; **Wilson's Snipe** 1w [Michal Kocan/Shutterstock], (wings raised) [BSu]. **p242: Spotted Sandpiper** (fl) [MVan], Juv & Ad br [GB^]; **Common Sandpiper** (fl) [KMa^], Juv [RM^]; **Terek Sandpiper** (fl) [DF^], Juv [DO^], Ad (h) [AVe]. **p243: Marsh Sandpiper** (fl) [RM^], Ad non-br [AO^], Juv>1w [ABD], Ad br [MVar]; **Greenshank** [MVar]; **Solitary Sandpiper** (fl) [BSu], (st) [MMc]; **Green Sandpiper** (fl) [DO^], (h) [MVar]; **Grey-tailed Tattler** (fl) [A-S HSS], (st) [DMon^]. **p244: Redshank** [AO^]; **Lesser Yellowlegs** (fl) [IDa^], Ad br [BES^], Juv [ML]; **Greater Yellowlegs** (fl) [MDan^], Ad br [BES^], 1w [MMc]. **p245: Long-billed Dowitcher** (fl) [MDan^], non-br [BES^]; **Short-billed Dowitcher** (fl) [MDan^], Juv [Paul Reeves Photography/Shutterstock], Ad br [BSu]; non-br [BES^].

CRAKES & RAILS **p246: Coot** (st) [MB]; **Moorhen** [Abi Warner/Shutterstock]; **Spotted Crake** [MG^]; **Water Rail** [MB]. **p247: Corncrake** (fl) both [HS^], others (3) [DKj]. **p248: Moorhen** (fl) [MG^], (inset) [DCou]. **p249: Coot** (fl) [MVar], (inset) [DKj]. **p250: Water Rail** (fl) [HS^], (inset) & Juv [MVar]. **p251: Spotted Crake** 1w [TTay], Ad [CvR^], Juv (inset) [TMu^]. **p252: Little Crake** Juv [PS^], F [MVar], M [DO^]. **p253: Baillon's Crake** Juv [DO^], Ad [VL^]; **Sora** (tail) & Ad (h) [BES^], 1w [MMc]; **Spotted Crake** (tail) [DO^]. **p254: Allen's Gallinule** Juv>1w [INW], Ad [DMon^]; **Purple Gallinule** [DMon^]; **Western Swamphen** [JAI].

LARGE WATERSIDE BIRDS **p255: Grey Heron** Ad (h) [MvD^]; **Ibis** [MMc]; **Spoonbill** [SGat^]; **White Stork** [DO^], **Grey Heron** [DO^]; **Bittern** [BMat^]. **p256: Little Bittern** F & M [DO^]; **Night-heron** all (3) [DO^]; **Bittern** [DO^]; **Grey Heron** [DO^]; **Purple Heron** Ad [MVar]. **p257: Black Stork** [RdH^]; **Spoonbill** Juv [DO^] Ad [MVar]; **Squacco Heron** [MG^]. **p258: Crane** Ad & Juv [HB^]. **p259: Spoonbill** Juv (fl) [DO^], Ad (fl) [MVar], Ad (st) [MvD^]. **p260: Grey Heron** Ad (h) [MvD^]. **p261: Bittern** (fl) [DO^]. **p262: Little Egret** Juv (fl) [DO^], Juv (h) [DSm], Ad non-br [MG^]. **p263: Great White Egret** non-br [HB^]. **p264: Great White Egret** [RM^]; **Little Egret** [SGat^]; **Cattle Egret** (top panel) [SGat^], (bottom panel) Ad br [MG^]. **p265: White Stork** Juv (fl) [WL^], Ad [DO^]; **Black Stork** Juv (fl) [HB^]. **p266: Glossy Ibis** Imm [MMc]; **Purple Heron** Juv [HB^]. **p267: Little Bittern** all (3) [DO^]; **Night-heron** Juv & 1s [DO^]. **p268: Least Bittern** [BES^]; **Great Blue Heron** [MMc]; **Cattle Egret** (fl) [DO^]; **Squacco Heron** Ad (fl) & Juv (fl-up) [DO^], Juv (fl-un) [RM^], Ad (st) [BBa^], non-br (st) [SGat^]. **p269: Chinese Pond Heron** non-br [John Harrison/CC], Ad br [KBa]; **Snowy Egret** non-br [CvR^], Ad br [BES^]; **Little Egret** Ad br [SGat^]. **p270: Green Heron** Ad [BES^], Juv [MG^]; **American Bittern** [DMon^]; **Bittern** (h) [JPelt^]; **Sandhill Crane** (fl) [HS^], (st) [MW].

'GAMEBIRDS' **p271: Golden Pheasant** M [ML]; **Lady Amherst's Pheasant** M [ML], F [J-CJ]; **Quail** [MVar]. **p272: Red-legged Partridge** Juv [RTi], (fl) [RHi]. **p273: Grey Partridge** (fl-up) [MVar], Juv>1w [IE], M [CvR^], F [RSch^]. **p274: Red Grouse** (fl-up) [BR], M [Giedriius/Shutterstock]. **p275: Ptarmigan** (fl-up) [MVar], F sum & M sum [RTo], M transitional [Dave Pressland/FLPA], M win [Paul Hobson/FLPA], F win (h) [MVar]. **p276: Black Grouse** M (fl) & F (fl-side) [MVar], F (fl) [TMe], M (st) [HB^], F (st) [ML]. **p277: Capercaillie** M (fl) & F (st) [MVar]. **p278: Pheasant** (fl) [Costas Anton Dumitrescu/Shutterstock], F (fl) [Budimir Jevtic/Shutterstock]. **p279: Quail** (fl) [MVar], (inset left) [HvD^], (inset right) [HGeb^], M (st) & F (st) [DO^].

BUSTARDS **p280: Macqueen's Bustard** (fl) [JE^]; **Little Bustard** F (st) [MVar], M (st) [G&YD], M (fl) [AO^]. **p281: Great Bustard** (fl) [MMc], others [MVar].

PIGEONS, DOVES & SANDGOUSE **p283: Feral Pigeon** (up) [MDan^], (un) [MVar]; **Rock Dove** (un) [GG]; **Stock Dove** (up) [RSch^], (un) [MVar]; **Woodpigeon** (up) [RSch^]; **Collared Dove** (un) [RTi]; **Turtle Dove** both [RSch^]; **Rufous Turtle Dove** both [MG^]; **Mourning Dove** [TSh]; **Pallas's Sandgrouse** (fl) both & F [MDan^], M [RM^]. **p285: Feral Pigeon** pied type & rusty/ginger type [hedera.baltica/CC], (fl) [MDan^]; **Rock Dove** [MMc]. **p286: Woodpigeon** (fl) [RSch^]. **p287: Stock Dove** (fl) both [MVar], Juv [MvD^]. **p288: Collared Dove** (fl-up) [MDan^], (fl-un) [RTi], Juv (h) [DO^]. **p289: Turtle Dove** (fl) both [RSch^]. **p290: Rufous Turtle Dove** orientalis [RWy], Juv (h) [DMon^], Ad (h) [PMo^]; **Turtle Dove** Ad (h) [DO^]; **Mourning Dove** Juv [MG^], 1w [MMa].

OWLS & NIGHTJARS **p292: Short-eared Owl** (un) [MB]; **Tawny Owl** (up) [MR^], (un) [MVar]; **Snowy Owl** [MVar]; **Little Owl** [FW]; **Red-necked Nightjar** [SDa]; **Common Nighthawk** [TJ]; **Egyptian Nightjar** [JBu]. **p293: Barn Owl** (st) [BR]. **p294: Tawny Owl** (fl) & rufous [MB], grey [PW]. **p295: Little Owl** (fl-top) [PW], (fl-bottom) [RM^] Juv [G&YD], (inset) [BBa^]. **p296: Short-eared Owl** (fl) [AGh^], (inset) [BBa^], (st) [JPelt^]. **p298: Snowy Owl** (fl) both & M [MVar]. **p299: Hawk Owl** (fl) [MVar]; **Scops Owl** grey [CvR^]. **p300: Nightjar** Ad (st) [MB]. **p301: Common Nighthawk** (fl) [BSm^], (st) [DMon^], **Red-necked Nightjar** (fl) [SDa], (st) [PvH^], **Egyptian Nightjar** (fl) [JBu], (st) [AvdB^].

CREDITS

BIRDS OF PREY p302: Harris's Hawk [Kojihirano/Shutterstock]. **p303**: Osprey [RdH^]. **p304**: White-tailed Eagle Imm (fl) [MW], Juv/1y (h) [MVar]. **p305**: Golden Eagle Ad (st) [MVar], Juv (fl) [MVar], Imm (st) [CvR^]. **p306**: Golden Eagle Imm (un ×2) & (up) [MVar]; White-tailed Eagle Imm (un) [RR^], Imm (up) [MVar]. **p307**: Red Kite Ad (up) & (un) [RSch^]; Black Kite Imm (up) & (un) & Ad (up) [DO^]. **p308**: Honey-buzzard Ad (up) [DO^], Juv (up) [MVar], pale F & pale adult Juvs [DO^], dark M [MMc], dark F [MVar]. **p309**: Buzzard Ad (un) [RdH^], Juv & pale Imm [MVar]; Rough-legged Buzzard F (up) & F (un) & Juv (up) [MVar], Juv (un) [RSch^], M [JPelt^]; Osprey [MVar]. **p310**: Osprey Ad (fl-up) & Ad (fl-un) [MVar], Juv ifl) [DO^], Juv (inset) [SY], Ad [MVar], 1s [VL^]. **p311**: Honey-buzzard Juv (fl) [MVar], others (5) [DO^]. **p312**: Buzzard (hover) [WW^], (fl-up) [SY], Juv (st) [KW^], Ad (fl-un) [RdH^], others (5) [MVar]. **p313**: Rough-legged Buzzard M (fl) [JPelt^], F (fl) [MVar], Juv (un) [RSch^], (hover) [KM^], St (un) [AO^]. **p314**: Red Kite Ad (fl-up) & Ad (fl-un) [RSch^], Juv (st) [HGer^], (un) [MMc]. **p315**: Marsh Harrier Juv (fl) [RTi], F (fl-un), F (st) & M (st) [DO^]. **p316**: Pallid Harrier M (up) [LS^], F (un) [SHa]; Montagu's Harrier M (up) [DO^], Juv (up) [SDa], Juv (up) [JE^], others (3) [MVar]; Hen Harrier M (un) [HGeb^], M (up) [DO^], M (st) [OD^], others (3) [MVar]; Marsh Harrier M (un) [JPelt^], F (un) & (up) [DO^]; Northern Harrier M (st) [Bildagentur Zoonar GmbH/Shutterstock]. **p317**: Hen Harrier M (fl) [SGat^], 2wM (fl) [MB], F (f-up), Ad F (fl) both & Juv (fl) [DO^], F (st) [OD^], M st [MVar]. **p318**: Montagu's Harrier Juv (fl) [SDa], F (fl-up) [DMon^]; M (fl-un) [MB]. **p319**: Hen Harrier (h) [JKu]; Montagu's Harrier (h) [MVar]; Pallid Harrier (h-right) [MR^]; M (fl) [DF^], F (fl-un) [JP"S"], F (fl-up) [MVar], F (fl) [RSch^], F (st) [AJu^], M (st) [R&LC]. **p320**: Black Kite Juv (fl-un) [DO^], (fl-up) [MVar], (st) [MVar]; Northern Harrier M (fl), Juv (fl) & Juv (st) [DO^], (wing) [MMc]; Hen Harrier 2wM [MB], Juv & (wing) [DO^]. **p321**: Short-toed Eagle Ad (fl-left) [DO^], Juv [AM^], Imm (pale) [KDR], Ad (st) [RF]; Buzzard [MVar]; Spotted Eagle (st) [MW], (fl-up) (fl-un) [DO^]. **p322**: Griffon Vulture Ad (st) [G&YD], Imm (fl-un) [MVar]; Egyptian Vulture Ad (st), Imm (st) & Imm (fl-up-right) [DO^]; Bald Eagle (st) [DH^], (fl) [TJ]. **p323**: Sparrowhawk M (side) [MVar], M (un) [MB], M (up) [MVar], F (side) [AO^], F (un) [JPelt^], Juv (up) [AO^], Juv (un) [MVar]; Merlin [MVar]; Goshawk M (un) [DF^], M (side) [RSch^], F (un) [MDar], Juv F (un) & Juv (un-bottom) [MVar], Juv (up) [HS^].

p324: Sparrowhawk Juv 'F' (fl-up) [AO^], 'M' (fl) & Juv F (st) [MVar], F (inset) [RO^], others (4) [MB]. **p325**: Goshawk M (fl-side) [RSch^], M (fl-un) & Juv (fl) [MVar], M (st) & 'F' (st) [WS^], Juv (fl) [HB^]. **p326**: Kestrel M (fl-un) & M (fl-up) [JPelt^], Ad F [RSch^], (st) & M (st) [RJS^]. **p327**: Merlin Juv (fl), F (st) both [AO^], M (st) [MB], F (st) [MVar], others (4) [MVar]. **p328**: Hobby Ad (fl-up) [DKj], Ad (fl-un) [RM^], Juv (fl-up) & Ad (st) [MVar], Juv (fl-un) [DO^]. **p329**: Peregrine Juv (fl-up) [MB], Ad (fl-un) [MVar], Ad (st) both [AO^]. **p330**: Red-footed Falcon 1s (fl-up) [MG^], 1s (fl-un) [RSch^], Juv (fl) [RHa]. **p331**: Gyrfalcon Juv (fl) both & Ad (fl) & Ad (st) [MVar], Imm (white) (fl) [Steve Byland/Shutterstock], Juv (inset) [Ómar Runólfsson/CC], Imm Icelandic (fl) [TMu^]; Peregrine [DO^]. **p332**: Gyrfalcon both [MVar]; Lanner Falcon (fl) [DO^], (st) [RWa]; Saker Falcon (fl) [DO^], (st) [AO^]; Peregrine (st) [AO^]. **p333**: Red-footed Falcon Juv [RHa], 1s M (fl-un) [MG^], 1s M (un) [RSch^]; Peregrine Ad (un) [MB]; Hobby Ad (up) [DKj], Juv (up) [MVar], Juv (un) [DO^]; Kestrel M (up) & M (un) [JPelt^]; Merlin Juv [AO^], others (3) [MVar]. **p334**: Lesser Kestrel 1s M (fl-un) [JSP], 1s M (fl-up) [AA^], M (st) & M (fl-up) [DO^], F (fl-up) [RM^], M (st) & (claw) [SGat^]; Kestrel M (fl-up) [RJS^], M (fl-un), F (f) [RJS^], (claw) [DKj]; American Kestrel M (fl) & F (fl) [DH^], F (fl-un) [BSu], 1w (st) [BSm^]. **p335**: Eleonora's Falcon pale (fl) [VL^] & dark (fl) [MDP], (st) [IDo]; Hobby [MB]; Amur Falcon 1s M (fl) [DBry], Ad M (fl) [RSch^], Ad M (st) [DS^], 1s F (st) [MMc].

'HIGHER LANDBIRDS' p336: Cuckoo & Meadow Pipit [MB]. **p337**: Kingfisher M (st) [DO^], F (st) [PW], F (fl) [DO^]. **p338**: Cuckoo Ad (st) [ML], F (h) [CF], F rufous (inset) [JSP], Juv (inset) [MVar]; Sparrowhawk [MVar]. **p339**: Hoopoe (inset) [MMc], (fl-up) [DO^], (fl-un) [MVar]. **p340**: Bee-eater Ad (fl-up) & 1s (fl) [MVar], Ad (fl-un) & Ad (st) [G&YD], Juv [MDan^]; Blue-cheeked Bee-eater (fl-un) [JPelt^], (fl-up) [DMon^], (st) [MVar]. **p341**: Roller (fl-up) [MVar]; Great Spotted Cuckoo 1s (fl) [DLV^], Juv (fl) [FV^], 1s (st) [JvdN^]. **p342**: Ring-necked Parakeet (flock) [DA], (fl) [KC]; Alexandrine Parakeet [MVar].

WOODPECKERS p343: Green Woodpecker M [MB], Juv (h) [R&LC]; Lesser Spotted & Great Spotted Woodpeckers [MB]. **p344**: Wryneck (st) (Sep) [MB]. **p345**: Green Woodpecker M (MB], M (st) [MB], F (h) [PW], Juv (inset) [R&LC]. **p346**: Great Spotted Woodpecker M (fl) [Victor Tyakht/Shutterstock], M (st) & F (h) [MB], Juv M (h) [R&LC]. **p347**: Lesser Spotted Woodpecker M (st) & (inset) [MB], F [MMc].

AERIAL FEEDERS p350: Pallid Swift all (3) [DO^]; Swift (un) [MVar]; Alpine Swift [RM^]. **p351**: Pacific Swift [RM^]; White-rumped Swift both [ASK]; Little Swift both [MG^]; White-throated Needletail (up) [JJ^], (un) [BSu]; Chimney Swift both [BSu]. **p352**: House Martin Ad (fl-un) [RSch^], Ad (fl-up) & (st) [MVar], (nest) [ML], (group) [JvdN^]. **p353**: Swallow M (fl) [JPelt^], F (fl) [MG^], Juv (fl) [DO^], M (st) [AO^], Juv (inset) [MVar], (nest) [Phototr/Shutterstock]. **p354**: Sand Martin (colony) [RR^], (fl-up) [MVar], (fl-un) [RSch^], Ad (st) [DO^], Juv (st) [RJS^]. **p355**: Red-rumped Swallow (fl-un) [MVar], (fl-up) [MMc], (st) [R&LC], daurica/japonica [IFu]; Swallow [JPelt^]; Crag Martin (fl-up) [MG^]. **p356**: Tree Swallow (fl-un) & Juv (st) [BSu], 1w (fl-Mar) [MDan^], M (st) & (h) [GB^]; Cliff Swallow (fl) both [RA^], (st) [DO^]; Purple Martin (fl-up) [TL], (fl-un) [VL^], (st) [JPe].

LARKS, PIPITS & WAGTAILS p357: Meadow Pipit [MB]; Pied Wagtail [MB]; Yellow Wagtail M (h) [HGeb^], F (h) [TTay], Juv (h) [Paul Hobson/FLPA]. **p358**: Shorelark both [MR^]; Woodlark (fl-un) & (fl-up) [RSch^], (fl-un-side) [MVar]; Skylark (fl-un - tail spread) [DO^], (fl-un - tail closed) [RSch^], (fl-up) [RSch^]; Short-toed Lark (fl) [AF]; Crested Lark (fl-un) [MVar], (fl-side) [MVar]; Lesser Short-toed Lark (fl-un) [MG^], (fl-up) [RHo]; White-winged Lark [HvD^]; Black Lark (fl) [VL^], (fl-up) [MK]; Bimaculated Lark (fl-un) [VP], (fl-up) [DO^]. **p359**: Shorelark (fl-un) [MR^], M (st) [DO^]; 'American Horned Lark' [VL^]. **p360**: Woodlark (fl-up) [JO'B], (fl-un) [RSch^], Ad (on branch) [Menno Schaefer/Shutterstock], Ad (on rock) [DO^], Ad (h) [MVar], Juv [G&YD]. **p361**: Skylark (fl-up) [RSch^], (fl-un) [DO^], (inset) [MVar]. **p362**: Short-toed Lark (fl) [AF], (h) [MMc], Ad (st) (Apr) [R&LC]; Skylark (st) [RSch^]; Crested Lark (fl) [MG^]; Lesser Short-toed Lark (st) [MG^]. **p363**: Calandra Lark (st) [ML]; Bimaculated Lark (fl-un) [VP], (st) [DO^]; Black Lark (f) [VL^], (st) [MDan^]; White-winged Lark (fl) [HvD^], (st) [MDan^]. **p364**: Tree Pipit (fl-un) & (st-Sep) [MVar], (fl-song) [RSch^], (inset) & (claw) [RM^]. **p365**: Meadow Pipit (fl-un) [MG^], (fl-up) & (fl-song) [RSch^], (st-Apr) [HGeb^], (st-Oct) & (st-Jun) [RM^], (inset) [HB^], (claw) [WL^]. **p366**: Rock Pipit (fl) [MVar], littoralis spr [MMc]. **p367**: Water Pipit br & non-br [DO^]; Rock Pipit littoralis (inset) [MMc]. **p368**: Tree Pipit (inset) [DO^]; Meadow Pipit (inset) [RTo]; Red-throated Pipit non-br [AA^], br [MG^]. **p369**: Olive-backed Pipit [MMc]; Water Pipit (fl) [DO^]. **p370**: Richard's Pipit (fl) & (claw) [RM^], Ad [MVar], 1w [RSto]. **p371**: Blyth's Pipit (st) & (claw) [MVar]; Tawny Pipit br & (claw) [DO^], Juv [PJW]. **p372**: Pied Wagtail yarrellii (fl) & (inset wing) [RCh], Ad M [HB^]. **p373**: White Wagtail alba (fl) [DO^], 1w (inset) [MvD^], Ad M [RSch^]; 'Amur Wagtail' [RSch^]; 'Masked Wagtail' [RM^]. **p374**: Yellow Wagtail Juv [Paul Hobson/FLPA],

563

CREDITS

M (inset) [TMe], F [TTay], M (bottom) [RSch^]. **p375:** **Yellow Wagtail** *flavissima* [AA^], 'Channel' [RHa], *thunbergi* [KMa^], *iberiae* [RM^], *cinereocapilla* [DO^], *flava* M [BM^], F [RSch^], (fl) [MVar]. **p376:** **Grey Wagtail** (fl) [RSch^], M non-br (h) & 1w [DO^], M br & F (h) [RM^]. **p377:** **Eastern Yellow Wagtail** M [SKC], 1w [MMc]; **Yellow Wagtail** (claw) [MG^]; **Citrine Wagtail** F [DO^], non-br (h) [AM^], M [RM^].

DIPPERS, ACCENTORS, WRENS, ORIOLES, STARLINGS, WAXWINGS **p378:** **Waxwings**, **Wren** & **Dunnock** [MB], **Golden Oriole** [MG^]. **p379:** **Dipper** Juv [DMor], Ad *hibernicus* [MCa], Ad *cinclus* [MMc]. **p380:** **Dunnock** hebridium [MC^]. **p381:** **Wren** Ad (main) [MB]. **p382:** **Wren** *troglodytes* [MVar], *hirtensis* [JM], *hebridensis* [GC]. **p383:** **Golden Oriole** F/ y M (st) [MVar], others (4) [MG^]. **p384:** **Starling** (fl) both [PMo], Ad non-br [MB]. **p385:** **Rose-coloured Starling** Ad (fl) [LS^, Juv (fl) both [PMo], Ad br (h) [DO^], Ad br (st) [MDan^], Juv (st) [AO^]. **p386:** **Waxwing** (flock) [MB]. **p387:** **Alpine Accentor** [MMc], **Cedar Waxwing** 1w [Kelly Colgan Azar/CC], Ad [Dennis W Donohue/Shutterstock].

THRUSHES & CHATS **p388:** **Song Thrush**, **Nightingale** & **Wheatear** [MB]. **p389:** **Nightingale** Juv [RTi]; **Robin** Juv [MVar]; **Wheatear** Juv [AO^]; **Stonechat** 1w F [DO^]. **p390:** **Ring Ouzel** Juv (inset [DLi], 1w F (inset) [MB], (fl) [MG^], F [SW]. **p391:** **Blackbird** M (fl) [RSch^], F (fl) [MG^]; 1w M (h) [MvD^]. **p391:** **Song Thrush** (fl) [AO^], *hebridensis* [SDu]. **p393:** **Mistle Thrush** (fl-up) [RSch^], (fl-un) [TMu^], Juv [JAn]. **p394:** **Fieldfare** (fl-up) [MG^], (fl-un) [MVar]. **p395:** **Redwing** (fl-up) [AO^], (fl-un) [LA^], *coburni* [RTo]. **p396:** **Black-throated Thrush** M [MMc]; **Red-throated Thrush** [RWi]; **Siberian Thrush** F [MVar], M (h) [RSch^], (fl) [DLV^]. **p397:** **Eyebrowed Thrush** [MVe^]; **Dusky Thrush** 1w M [PMo^], 1w F [JJ^]; **Naumann's Thrush** [Old Apple/Shutterstock]. **p398:** **American Robin** [MMc]; **Varied Thrush** [MVe^]; **Wood Thrush** [VL^]. **p399:** **Swainson's Thrush** (fl) [SK]. **p400:** **Robin** Ad [MB], Juv [MVar], *rubecula* [DO^]. **p401:** **Nightingale** *golzii* [JBa]. **p402:** **Redstart** 1w M [MR^] 1wF [WL^], (fl) [TMu^]. **p403:** **Black Redstart** F [MVar], (fl) [MG^], Eastern (inset) [MMc]. **p404:** **Whinchat** Ad M & F [MVar], 1s M (h) [RM^], (fl) [AKS]. **p405:** **Stonechat** (fl) [DO^], M *rubicola* (inset) [DO^]. **p406:** **Stonechat** (fl) [TMu^]; **Siberian Stonechat** *maurus* (fl) [MR^], (rump) [DO^]; *hemprichii* M [DO^], **Stejneger's Stonechat** [MG^]. **p407:** **Stonechat** (st) [CV], (wing) [DO^]; **Siberian Stonechat** *maurus* (fl) & (wing) [MG^], *hemprichii* 1w M [RB]; **Stejneger's Stonechat** M non-br [DO^], (wing) [MR^], 1w [VL^]. **p408:** **Wheatear** F [DO^], (fl) [MVar]. **p409:** **Wheatear** 1w/F [CvR^]; 'Greenland' Wheatear M spr [TC], 1w/F [DO^]. **p410:** **Western Black-eared Wheatear** (fl) & F [HS^], 1w M [RWi], 1w F [RSto], M (white throat) [MG^]; **Eastern Black-eared Wheatear** 1w M (h) [EW^], F [MVar], M both [DO^]. **p411:** **Isabelline Wheatear** 1w [DO^]; **Wheatear** (fl) [MVar]; **Desert Wheatear** 1w M (h) [DO^], 1w F [MMc]; **Pied Wheatear** 1w M [AM^]. **p412:** **Bluethroat** F [MVar], [G&YD]; **Red-flanked Bluetail** M [MVar]. **p413:** **Siberian Rubythroat** 1w F [IFi]; **Siberian Blue Robin** 1w M [MDan^], M [AV^]. **p414:** **Thrush Nightingale** (st) [AA^], (wing) [MVar]; **Rufous-tailed Scrub Robin** [MVar]. **p415:** **White-throated Robin** both [DO^]; **Moussier's Redstart** F [GE]; **White-crowned Black Wheatear** [DO^]. **p416:** **Rock Thrush** M [G&YD], F [DO^]; **Blue Rock Thrush** M [DMon^], F [DO^].

FLYCATCHERS **p417:** **Alder Flycatcher** M [MMc]. **p418:** **Spotted Flycatcher** Ad (Jun) [MB], Juv [AGh^]. **p419:** **Pied Flycatcher** Ad M [Martin Fowler/Shutterstock], Ad/1s M [DO^]. **p420:** **Taiga Flycatcher** M [RdH^]. **p421:** **Pied Flycatcher** (wing) [MVar].

(OLD WORLD) WARBLERS, CISTICOLAS & CRESTS **p423:** **Grasshopper Warbler** [MVar]; **Melodious Warbler** [RM^]; **Cetti's Warbler** [DO^]; **Fan-tailed Warbler** (fl) [MVar]. **p424:** **Goldcrest** (fl) [MVar]. **p425:** **Firecrest** Juv (h) [SBay]. **p426:** **Sedge Warbler** Juv [DO^]. **p428:** **Grasshopper Warbler** Juv (h) [MMc]. **p429:** **Cetti's Warbler** Ad [MB]; **Savi's Warbler** [HGeb^]. **p430:** **Chiffchaff** Ad [RSch^], (inset-right) [DO^]. **p431:** **Willow Warbler** (inset) [AM]; **Chiffchaff** *collybita* (Apr) & *tristis* (Nov) [DO^], *collybita* (Oct) [CBa]. **p432:** **Willow Warbler** Ad [AM^]. **p433:** **Wood Warbler** Ad (front) [MB], Ad (side) [RSch^]. **p434:** **Blackcap** Juv (h) [IFu], F (h) [DO^], 1w M (h) [Frank Vassen/CC], M [RM^]. **p435:** **Garden Warbler** 1w [DO^]. **p436:** **Whitethroat** F [G&YD], 1w [DO^]. **p437:** **Lesser Whitethroat** *curruca* Ad [DO^], 1w (h) [MB]; *blythi* (left) [CBr], probable *halimodendri* (right) [MMc]. **p438:** **Dartford Warbler** all [MB]. **p439:** **Marsh Warbler** [DCoo]. **p440:** **Reed Warbler** (st) & (wing) [DO^], **Marsh Warbler** (wing) [YP^]; **Paddyfield Warbler** (wing) [AW^]. **p441:** **Marsh Warbler** Ad (Jul) [DCoo]. **p442:** **Aquatic Warbler** Juv [MG^] (h) [HGeb^]; **Great Reed Warbler** [DO^]. **p443:** **Reed Warbler** (fl) [DO^]; **Fan-tailed Warbler** Juv>1w [MVar], Ad [DO^]. **p444:** **River Warbler** [MVar]; **Lanceolated Warbler** both [MMc]; **Grasshopper Warbler** (wing) [MMc]; **Pallas's Grasshopper Warbler** [MMc]. **p445:** **Icterine Warbler** Ad [MVar], (wing) [DO^], **Melodious Warbler** Ad [DO^]. **p446:** **Olive-tree Warbler** Ad [DO^]. **p447:** **Booted Warbler** (h) [MDan^]; **Sykes's Warbler** (h) [DO^], [MDan^]; **Eastern Olivaceous Warbler** (h) & (wing) [DO^]. **p448:** **Western Bonelli's Warbler** Ad [DO^]; **Eastern Bonelli's Warbler** [DO^], 1w [MMc]. **p449:** **Iberian Chiffchaff** [VL^]; **Dusky Warbler** (st) & (h) [AO^]. **p450:** **Greenish Warbler** Ad (inset) [MVar]; **Two-barred Greenish Warbler** [TTam]; **Green Warbler** Ad [DO^]. **p451:** **Eastern Crowned Warbler** [MW]; **Pale-legged Leaf Warbler** [M&PW]; **Sakhalin Leaf Warbler** [DCoo]. **p452:** **Yellow-browed Warbler** (st) [MVar]; **Hume's Warbler** (st) [MTo]. **p453:** **Barred Warbler** [MVar]; **Marmora's Warbler** [MMc]. **p454:** **Moltoni's Subalpine Warbler** M [DO^]. **p455:** **Spectacled Warbler** M & F [DO^], Juv (nset) [YP^]; **Whitethroat** (wing) [DO^], 1w [MB]; **Moltoni's Subalpine Warbler** Juv>1w [DO^]. **p456:** **Western Orphean Warbler** M & Juv (h) [DO^], 1w [MMc]; **Eastern Orphean Warbler** (fl) & 1w [EF]. **p457:** **Sardinian Warbler** all (3) [DO^], **Rüppell's Warbler** F [GRe], M [DO^].

SHRIKES **p458:** **Great Grey Shrike** [MB]; **Red-backed Shrike** Juv [AW^], F [AGh^], M [DO^]. **p459:** **Great Grey Shrike** Ad [MVar], 1w [MB], 'Steppe Grey Shrike' [MMc]. **p460:** **Red-backed Shrike** M (fl) [TMu^], F (fl) [AGh^], M (st) [ML], **p461:** **Woodchat Shrike** (fl) [MVar], Ad F (h) [RR^], 1s M & Ad M [DO^], Juv [John Navajo/Shutterstock], *badius* [TTam]. **p462:** **Daurian Shrike** 'M' [AW^]. **p463:** **Red-backed Shrike** [TMu^], **Daurian Shrike** [RM^], **Turkestan Shrike** [RM^], **Brown Shrike** 1w & (wing) [MMc], Ad [BvdB^]. **p464:** **Lesser Grey Shrike** (fl) [MVar], F [MB], Ad [DO^], Juv [CvR^]; **Long-tailed Shrike** [MG^]; **Masked Shrike** F [AGS].

TITS, NUTHATCHES & 'CREEPERS' **p465:** **Blue Tit** both [MB]; **Long-tailed Tit** [ML]; **Nuthatch** [MB]; **Treecreeper** [MB]. **p466:** **Bearded Tit** Ad M [Bildagentur Zoonar GmbH/Shutterstock], Juv M & Ad F [MVar], Juv F (h) [MvD^]. **p467:** **Long-tailed Tit** (flock) [MB], Juv [PL], *caudatus* [Piotr Krzeslak/Shutterstock]. **p469:** **Great Tit** Juv [MVar], melanistic (inset) [CvR^]. **p470:** **Crested Tit** *cristatus* (inset) [CvR^], *mitratus* (inset) [DO^]. **p471:** **Coal Tit** *hibernicus* (inset) [MC^], *ater* (inset top) [MVar], *ater* (inset bottom) [R&LC]. **p472:** **Marsh Tit** [ML]. **p473:** **Willow Tit** *kleinschmidti* [SY]. **p474:** **Nuthatch** M [G&YD], F [MB]. **p476:** **Short-toed Treecreeper** [RM^]. **p477:** **Wallcreeper** non-br [DO^], (inset) [MVar]; **Penduline Tit** M [MMc], Juv & F [DO^].

CREDITS

CORVIDS p478: Rook (rookery) [SY]. **p479: Hooded Crow** (up), [MG^A], (un) [MVar]; **Carrion Crow** (up) [JL]; **Jay** (up) [MVar]; **Nutcracker** both [MVar]. **p480:** *glandarius* (fl) [MVar], *hibernicus* (inset) [MC^A]. **p481: Magpie** (flock) [PMa]. **p482: Jackdaw** (st) & (fl) [MB]. **p483: Hooded Crow** hybrid [HvD^A]. **p484: Carrion Crow** (st) [ML]. **p486: Raven** (st) [ML]. **p487: Chough** (st) [ML], (fl) [AGS]. **Nutcracker** *caryocatactes* [HB^A], *macrorhynchos* [CvR^A].

SPARROWS & FINCHES p488: Reed Bunting, Brambling & **House Sparrow** [MB]; **Siskin** M [RJS^A]. **p489: Crossbill, Goldfinch, Lesser Redpoll, Hawfinch, Bullfinch** & **Chaffinch** [M.B]; **Greenfinch** [DCu]. **p490: House Sparrow** (fl) [MG^A]. **p491: Tree Sparrow** (fl) [RSch^A], Juv & (inset) [DKj]. **p492: Bullfinch** (fl) [AJu^A], *pyrrhula* [CvR^A]. **p493: Hawfinch** M (st) & F [DO^A], (fl) [MB]. **p494: Chaffinch** (fl-up) [MVar], (fl-un) [RSch^A]; *coelebs* F [MvD^A], M [RJS^A]. **p495: Brambling** (fl) both [MVar], 1w F [MMc]. **p496: Goldfinch** (fl) [JCo]. **p497: Greenfinch** (fl), F & 1w M [DO^A]. **p498: Siskin** M (fl) [MVar], M (st) [DO^A], Juv [WS^A]. **p499: Serin** F & 1w F [MVar], Juv [DO^A]; **Citril Finch** [MMc^.]. **p500: Linnet** (fl) both [EW^A]. **p501: Twite** (fl-up) [RM^A], (fl-un) [EW^A], 'Hebridean' (inset) [SDu]. **p502: Lesser Redpoll** all (3) [MB]. **p504: Redpoll** (fl) [MR^A]; **Lesser Redpoll** 1w [MB]; **Common Redpoll** (tail) [MVar]. **p505: Common Rosefinch** (fl) [MR^A], M & F [DO^A]. **p506: Crossbill** F [CvR^A], M [WS^A]. **p507: Scottish Crossbill** all (3) [DE]; **Parrot Crossbill** [TMe], F [DE], (h) [HS^A]. **p508: Two-barred Crossbill** M [DCoo], **Crossbill** (inset) [ML]. **p509: Spanish Sparrow** F [DO^A]; **Trumpeter Finch** [MMc], **Rock Sparrow** [DO^A].

BUNTINGS p510: Reed Bunting Ad M (Sep–Mar) [DO^A], M br [MB], F 1w & F [HH], F Ad (Sep–Mar) [DO^A], F br [MB]; **Little Bunting** [MMc]. **p511: Lapland Bunting** (fl-up) [MG^A], (fl-un) [RHa], M br [SGat^A], F br [MVar]. **p512: Snow Bunting** *nivalis* F [G&YD], M [MVar], *insulae* F [MVar], M [RTo]. **p513: Snow Bunting** (flock) [MVar], *nivalis* M (Mar) [RO^A]. **p514: Yellowhammer** M br [DO^A], non-br/1w M [MG^A], F br [RdH^A], *caliginosa* M [MB]. **p515: Cirl Bunting** F/1w [DO^A], M non-br (h) [PGV], F [Mike Lane/FLPA]. **p516: Reed Bunting** 1w F (inset), F (Dec), Ad M (Jun) & M non-br (Nov) [DO^A]. **p518: Reed Bunting** M non-br [DO^A], Juv/F [MB]. **p519: Rustic Bunting** M & F [MVar]; **Pallas's Reed Bunting** both [DCoo]. **p520: Black-headed Bunting** F [G&YD], 1w [MMc]; **Yellow-breasted Bunting** M br [RSch^A]. **p521: Yellow-browed Bunting** [RWi], **Black-faced Bunting** 1w F [VL^A], M [MTh]; **Chestnut Bunting** [SGan]. **p522: Ortolan Bunting** M & 1s [DO^A], 1w [AO^A], F (h) [MVar]; **Cretzschmar's Bunting** M [MMc], F [MVar]. **p523: Pine Bunting** M non-br/1w (h) [DO^A], 1w F [VL^A]; **Yellowhammer** [MVar].

VAGRANT LANDBIRDS FROM NORTH AMERICA p525: Red-eyed Vireo [SY]; **Philadelphia Vireo** [VL^A]; **Ruby-crowned Kinglet** [Kelly Colgan Azar/CC]. **p526: Blackpoll Warbler** 1w [MMc]; **Cape May Warbler** M [Lee Kensinger/USFWS/CC]. **p527: Bay-breasted Warbler** [Seabamirum/CC]; **Blackburnian Warbler** [BSu]; **Chestnut-sided Warbler** [G&YD]; **Magnolia Warbler** [MMc]; **American Redstart** [JJ^A]; **Northern Parula** 1w M [DMon^A], 1w F [LG]. **p528: Wilson's Warbler** 1w M [ME], F (h) [USFWS Mountain-Prairie/CC]; **Common Yellowthroat** 1w F [TSt], 1w M (h) [BSu]; **Black-and-white Warbler** 1w F [TSt]. **p529: Canada Warbler** [KD]; **Tennessee Warbler** [Neil Bowman/FLPA]; **Golden-winged Warbler** [DMon^A]; **Blue-winged Warbler** [DO^A]; **Northern Waterthrush** [MMc]; **Ovenbird** [Dennis W Donohue/Shutterstock]. **p530: Eastern Kingbird** [B&JC]; **Eastern Phoebe** [BES^A]; **Alder Flycatcher** [MMc]; **Acadian Flycatcher** [DMon^A]. **p531: Brown Thrasher** [Robert L Kothenbeutel/Shutterstock]; **Northern Mockingbird** [Kelly Colgan Azar/CC]; **Grey Catbird** [MMc]. **p532: White-crowned Sparrow** 1w [BES^A], *gambelli* [DMon^A], *leucophrys* [RA^A]; **White-throated Sparrow** (h) [CBa]. **p533: Red Fox Sparrow** [Steve Byland/Shutterstock]. **p534: Rose-breasted Grosbeak** 1w F [MMc]; **Evening Grosbeak** [MVe^A]; **Indigo Bunting** 1w [DMon^A], M & 1y M (h) [BES^A]. **p535: Eastern Towhee** [Kelly Colgan Azar/CC], **Summer Tanager** [VL^A]; **Scarlet Tanager** 1w M [DMon^A], 1w F [DO^A]. **p536: Baltimore Oriole** [MMc]; **Bobolink** [DO^A]; **Red-winged Blackbird** [VL^A]. **p537: Yellow-bellied Sapsucker** Imm M [MDan^A], Juv [Steven Russell Smith Photos/Shutterstock]; **Belted Kingfisher** M (fl) [MDan^A], M (h) Tim Parker/CC, F [Robert L Kothenbeutel/Shutterstock]; **Black-billed Cuckoo** [MCn]; **Yellow-billed Cuckoo** both [MMc].

BIRDS OF UNCERTAIN ORIGIN AND ESCAPES/INTRODUCTIONS p538: Booted Eagle Juv (both) [DO^A]; **Red-headed Bunting** M [DMon^A], 1w [DCoo]. **p539: Great White Pelican** (fl) [DO^A]; **Northern Flicker** M [VL^A]; **Daurian Starling** [A-S HSS]; **Mugimaki Flycatcher** [AV^A]; **American Goldfinch** [Fyn Kynd/CC]; **Monk Parakeet** [Vladimir Kogan Michael/Shutterstock]; **Atlantic Canary** [R&LC].

All the Illustrations were prepared by Robert Still.

Male Sparrowhawk
by Martin Bennett

Identification and beyond

Where to go next

Top-class professional expertise, voluntary study and monitoring by birdwatching enthusiasts make the birds of Britain and Ireland amongst the most-watched and best-understood in the world. The results can be found in an abundance of books, magazines, journals and online websites, catering for every level of experience and field of interest.

This book draws heavily on many of these resources. We particularly acknowledge the contribution of the **British Ornithologists' Union Records Committee (BOURC)** and **Irish Rare Birds Committee (IRBC)** as the official authorities regarding lists and records, and the **British Birds Rarities Committee** whose authoritative annual reports are irreplaceable. The long-established journals *British Birds* (britishbirds.co.uk) – undoubtedly the 'journal of record' for Britain's birds – and *Irish Birds* publish the annual reports of rare birds and periodic summaries of scarce migrants, as well as a host of other invaluable material on birds' status, biology, taxonomy and identification. More popular birdwatching magazines offering valuable information include *Birdwatch* and *Bird Watching*.

Much information has been obtained from the surveys and studies by the **Royal Society for the Protection of Birds (RSPB)** (rspb.org.uk), **British Trust for Ornithology (BTO)** (bto.org) and **Wildfowl & Wetlands Trust (WWT)** (wwt.org.uk), many using amateur birdwatchers. Their online resources are exhaustive references for any bird book researcher. Organizations such as **Rare Bird Alert** (rarebirdalert.co.uk) and **BirdGuides** (birdguides.com) also offer invaluable services and a fund of information. We have often referred to the sound recordings on **Xeno-Canto** (xeno-canto.org) and the **Cornell Laboratory of Ornithology** site (allaboutbirds.org). For valuable information on ageing and sexing many species, try blascozumeta.com (Javier Blasco-Zumeta and Gerd-Michael Heinze).

There are too many excellent books to mention here, but multi-volume works of huge and lasting value include the classic *Birds of the Western Palearctic* (popularly known as BWP; Oxford University Press, 1977–96) and *Handbook of the Birds of the World* (popularly known as HBW; Lynx Edicions, 1992–2013): both also offer updated and exhaustive online resources. *Identification Guide to Birds in the Hand* by Laurent Demongin (Beauregard-Vendon, 2016) may help answer specific questions, along with *Identification of European Non-passerines* by Jeff Baker (BTO, 2016). For details on bird distribution and habitats, the visionary *BTO Bird Atlas 2007–11* remains indispensable.

STARLINGS and PEREGRINE

IDENTIFICATION AND BEYOND

British Birds: A Pocket Guide

- Written and designed by the *Britain's Birds* team
- Slimmer, smaller, and lighter than *Britain's Birds* – perfect for the pocket
- Not just an edited down version, but a different, complementary book
- Superb for beginners and ideal as a concise guide for the more experienced birder
- Covers the 248 species most likely to be seen, plus another 45 scarce but regular migrants
- Packed with stunning photographs showing the birds in their many variations

ROB HUME, ROBERT STILL, ANDY SWASH, HUGH HARROP & DAVID TIPLING

Descriptions of general identification details for all likely plumages, with **key features highlighted in bold text**

Descriptions of calls and song, focusing on those most useful for identification

Brief notes on food

Notes on special characters shown in flight

Length and wingspan

Hints on how to find and watch each bird

Range map, habitat, status and the months in which species can be expected in Britain and Ireland

"...this is a fantastic piece of work. It continues the spirit of the first book and manages to cram a huge amount of information...this is a must have for new and seasoned birders alike"
— *British Trust for Ornithology*

567

Index

This index includes the English and scientific (*in italics*) names of all the birds in this book.
Bold text highlights main species accounts.
Regular text is used for species and subspecies that are not subject to a full account, and to indicate pages where comparative tables appear.
Italicized figures indicate page(s) on which other photographs appear (including comparison plates).
Blue figures relate to the entry in the status and legislation table.

A

Acanthis cabaret 503
— *flammea* 503
— *hornemanni* 503
Accentor, Alpine 387, 554
—, Siberian 387, 554
Accipiter gentilis 325
— *nisus* 324
Acrocephalus agricola 443
— *arundinaceus* 442
— *dumetorum* 441
— *paludicola* 442
— *palustris* 441
— *schoenobaenus* 426
— *scirpaceus* 427
Actitis hypoleucos 215
— *macularius* 242
Aegithalos caudatus 467
Aegolius funereus 299
Agapornis roseicollis 539
Agelaius phoeniceus 536
Agropsar sturninus 523
Aix galericulata 61
— *sponsa* 61
Alauda arvensis 361
— *leucoptera* 363
Alaudala rufescens 362
Albatross,
  Atlantic Yellow-nosed 114, 544
—, Black-browed 114, 544
Alca torda 109
Alcedo atthis 337
Alectoris chukar 272
— *rufa* 272
Alle alle 112
Alopochen aegyptiaca 35
Anas acuta 43
— *americana* 64
— *carolinensis* 66
— *clypeata* 41
— *crecca* 44
— *discors* 67
— *falcata* 65
— *flavirostris* 539
— *formosa* 67
— *penelope* 39
— *platyrhynchos* 40
— *querquedula* 45

Anas rubripes 65
— *strepera* 42
— *albifrons* 32
— *anser* 29
— *brachyrhynchus* 31
— *caerulescens* 33
— *canagicus* 62
— *cygnoides* 539
— *erythropus* 33
— *fabalis* 30
— *indicus* 16
— *rossii* 16
— *serrirostris* 30
Anthus campestris 371
— *cervinus* 368
— *godlewskii* 371
— *gustavi* 369
— *hodgsoni* 369
— *petrosus* 366
— *pratensis* 365
— *richardi* 370
— *rubescens* 369
— *spinoletta* 367
— *trivialis* 364
Antigone canadensis 270
Apus affinis 351
— *apus* 349
— *caffer* 351
— *melba* 350
— *pacificus* 351
— *pallidus* 350
Aquila chrysaetos 305
— *clanga* 321
Ardea alba 263
— *cinerea* 260
— *herodias* 268
— *purpurea* 266
Ardenna gravis 101
— *grisea* 99
Ardeola bacchus 269
— *ralloides* 268
Arenaria interpres 191
Asio flammeus 296
— *otus* 297
Athene noctua 295
Auk, Great 106, 549
—, Little 107, 112, 549
Avocet 188, 192, 547

Aythya affinis 68
— *americana* 71
— *collaris* 69
— *ferina* 47
— *fuligula* 48
— *marila* 49
Aythya nyroca 53
— *valisineria* 54

B

Bartramia longicauda 240
Bee-eater 340, 550
—, Blue-cheeked 340, 550
Bittern 256, 261, 270, 545
—, American 270, 545
—, Least 268, 545
—, Little 256, 267, 545
Blackbird 391, 553
—, Red-winged 536, 556
—, Yellow-headed 539, 556
Blackcap 434, 472, 552
Bluetail, Red-flanked 412, 554
Bluethroat 412, 554
Bobolink 536, 556
Bombycilla cedrorum 387
— *garrulus* 386
Bonxie 179
Booby, Brown 118, 546
—, Red-footed 118, 546
Botaurus lentiginosus 270
— *stellaris* 261
Brachyramphus perdix 113
Brambling 495, 555
Brant, Black 27
Branta bernicla 26
— *canadensis* 24
— *hutchinsii* 25
— *leucopsis* 28
— *ruficollis* 27
Bubo bubo 291
— *scandiacus* 298
Bubulcus ibis 264
Bucanetes githagineus 509
Bucephala albeola 70
— *clangula* 50
— *islandica* 73
Budgerigar 539
Bufflehead 70, 544
Bullfinch 492, 555

INDEX

Bulweria bulwerii 118
Bunting, Black-faced 521, *555*
—, **Black-headed** 520, *555*
—, **Chestnut** 521, *555*
—, **Chestnut-eared** 518, *555*
—, **Cirl** 515, *555*
—, **Corn** 517, *555*
—, **Cretzschmar's** 522, *555*
—, **Indigo** 534, *556*
—, **Lapland** 511, *555*
—, **Little** 518, *555*
—, **Ortolan** 522, *555*
—, **Pallas's Reed** 519, *555*
—, **Pine** 523, *555*
—, Red-headed 538, *555*
—, **Reed** 510, 516, *518*, *519*, *555*
—, **Rock** 523, *555*
—, **Rustic** 519, *555*
—, **Snow** 512, *555*
—, **Yellow-breasted** 520, *555*
—, **Yellow-browed** 521, *555*
Burhinus oedicnemus 189
Bushchat, Rufous 414
Bustard, Great 281, *546*
—, **Little** 280, *546*
—, **Macqueen's** 280, *546*
Buteo buteo 312
— *lagopus* 313
Butorides virescens 270
Buzzard
.... *303*, *307*, *309*, *312*, *321*, *546*
—, **Honey-** *303*, *308*, *311*, *546*
—, **Rough-legged** *309*, *313*, *546*

C

Cairina moschata 62
Calandrella brachydactyla 362
Calcarius lapponicus 511
Calidris acuminata 238
— *alba* 200
— *alpina* 202
— *bairdii* 237
— *canutus* 201
— *falcinellus* 236
— *ferruginea* 205
— *fuscicollis* 237
— *himantopus* 239
— *maritima* 204
— *mauri* 235
— *melanotos* 238
— *minuta* 207
— *minutilla* 236
— *pugnax* 208
— *pusilla* 235
— *ruficollis* 235
— *subminuta* 236
— *subruficollis* 240
— *temminckii* 206
— *tenuirostris* 239
Calliope calliope 413

Calonectris borealis 101
— *diomedea* 101
Canary, Atlantic *539*
Canvasback 71, *544*
Capercaillie 277, *544*
Caprimulgus aegyptius 301
— *europaeus* 300
— *ruficollis* 301
Cardellina canadensis 529
— *pusilla* 528
Carduelis cabaret 503
— *cannabina* 500
— *carduelis* 496
— *chloris* 497
— *citrinella* 399
— *flammea* 503
— *flavirostris* 501
— *hornemanni* 503
— *spinus* 498
— *tristis* *539*
Carpodacus erythrinus 505
Catbird, Grey 531, *553*
Catharacta skua 179
Catharus fuscescens 399
— *guttatus* 399
— *minimus* 399
— *ustulatus* 399
Cecropis daurica 355
Cepphus grylle 111
Cercotrichas galactotes 414
Certhia brachydactyla 476
— *familiaris* 475
Cettia cetti 429
Chaetura pelagica 351
Chaffinch 494, *555*
Charadrius alexandrinus 193
— *asiaticus* 233
— *dubius* 195
— *hiaticula* 194
— *leschenaultii* 233
— *mongolus* 233
— *morinellus* 196
— *semipalmatus* 232
— *vociferus* 231
Chat, Rufous Bush 414
Chen caerulescens 33
— *canagicus* 62
— *rossii* 62
Chiffchaff 430, *552*
—, **Iberian** 449, *552*
—, Siberian *431*
Chlamydotis macqueenii 280
Chlidonias hybrida 168
— *leucopterus* 167
— *niger* 166
Chloephaga picta *539*
Chloris chloris 497
Chondestes grammacus 533
Chordeiles minor 301

Chough 478, *479*, *487*, *551*
Chroicocephalus genei 155
— *philadelphia* 153
— *ridibundus* 146
Chrysolophus amherstiae 271
— *pictus* 271
Chukar *272*
Ciconia ciconia 265
— *nigra* 265
Cinclus cinclus 379
Circaetus gallicus 321
Circus aeruginosus 315
— *cyaneus* 317
— *hudsonicus* 320
— *macrourus* 319
— *pygargus* 318
Cisticola juncidis 443
Cisticola, Zitting 443, *552*
Clamator glandarius 341
Clanga clanga 321
Clangula hyemalis 54
Coccothraustes coccothraustes 493
Coccyzus americanus 537
— *erythropthalmus* 537
Colaptes auratus *539*
Coloeus monedula 482
Columba livia 284
— *oenas* 287
— *palumbus* 286
Coot 249, *546*
—, **American** 252, *546*
Coracias garrulus 341
Cormorant 78, 80, *92*, *546*
—, **Double-crested** 92, *546*
Corncrake 247, *546*
Corvus corax 486
— *cornix* 483
— *corone* 484
— *frugilegus* 485
— *monedula* 482
— *splendens* *539*
Coturnix coturnix 279
Courser, Cream-coloured
.... 228, *548*
Cowbird, Brown-headed ... 536, *556*
Crake, Baillon's 253, *546*
—, **Corn** 247, *546*
—, **Little** 252, *546*
—, **Spotted** 251, *253*, *546*
Crane *257*, 258, *546*
—, **Sandhill** 270, *546*
Crex crex 247
Crossbill 506, *507*, *508*, *555*
—, **Parrot** 507, *555*
—, **Scottish** 507, *555*
—, **Two-barred** 508, *555*
Crow, Carrion 478, *479*, 484, *551*
—, **Hooded** 478, *479*, 483, *551*
—, **House** *539*, *551*

569

INDEX

Cuckoo 338, 550
—, **Black-billed** 537, 549
—, **Great Spotted** 341, 549
—, **Yellow-billed** 537, 549
Cuculus canorus 338
Curlew 186, 218, 547
—, **Eskimo** 240, 547
—, **Stone-** 189, 546
Cursorius cursor 228
Cyanistes caeruleus 468
Cygnus atratus 62
— *buccinator* 62
— *columbianus* 20
— *cygnus* 21
— *olor* 19

D

Delichon urbicum 352
Dendrocopos major 346
— *minor* 347
Dipper 379, 554
Diver, Black-throated 79, 83, 91, 544
—, **Great Northern** 79, 84, 85, 544
—, **Pacific** 79, 91, 544
—, **Red-throated** 79, 82, 544
—, **White-billed** 79, 85, 544
Dolichonyx oryzivorus 536
Dotterel 188, 196, 547
Dove, Collared 283, 288, 549
—, **Mourning** 283, 290, 549
—, **Oriental Turtle** 283, 290, 549
—, **Rock** 283, 284, 549
—, **Stock** 283, 287, 549
—, **Turtle** 283, 289, 290, 549
Dowitcher, Long-billed 245, 548
—, **Short-billed** 245, 548
Dryobates minor 347
Duck, Black 65, 543
—, **Falcated** 65, 538, 543
—, **Ferruginous** 37, 69, 63, 544
—, **Harlequin** 74, 544
—, **Long-tailed** 37, 54, 544
—, **Mandarin** 61, 543
—, **Marbled** 62, 538, 543
—, **Muscovy** 47
—, **Ring-necked** 69, 63, 544
—, **Ruddy** 60, 544
—, **Tufted** 37, 48, 63, 68, 69, 544
—, **White-headed** 59, 538, 544
—, **Wood** 61, 538, 543
Dumetella carolinensis 531
Dunlin 187, 202, 237, 238, 547
Dunnock 380, 554

E

Eagle-owl, Eurasian 291
Eagle, Bald 322, 538, 546
—, **Booted** 538, 546
—, **Golden** 305, 306, 546

Eagle, Short-toed 321, 546
—, **(Greater) Spotted** 321, 546
—, **White-tailed** 303, 304, 306, 546
Egret, Cattle 257, 264, 268, 545
—, **Great White** 257, 263, 264, 545
—, **Little** 257, 262, 264, 269, 545
—, **Snowy** 269, 545
Egretta caerulea 269
— *garzetta* 262
— *thula* 269
Eider 37, 58, 72, 544
—, **King** 37, 72, 544
—, **Steller's** 72, 73, 544
Emberiza aureola 520
— *bruniceps* 538
— *caesia* 522
— *calandra* 517
— *chrysophrys* 521
— *cia* 523
— *cirlus* 515
— *citrinella* 514
— *fucata* 518
— *hortulana* 522
— *leucocephalos* 523
— *melanocephala* 520
— *pallasi* 519
— *pusilla* 518
— *rustica* 519
— *rutila* 521
— *schoeniclus* 516
— *spodocephala* 521
Empidonax alnorum 530
— *traillii* 530
— *virescens* 530
Eremophila alpestris 359
Erithacus rubecula 400
Erythrina erythrina 505
Eudromias morinellus 196

F

Falco amurensis 335
— *biarmicus* 332
— *cherrug* 332
— *columbarius* 327
— *eleonorae* 335
— *naumanni* 334
— *peregrinus* 329
— *rusticolus* 331
— *sparverius* 334
— *subbuteo* 328
— *tinnunculus* 326
— *vespertinus* 330
Falcon, Amur 335, 550
—, **Eleonora's** 335, 550
—, **Gyr** 331, 332, 550
—, **Lanner** 332
—, **Peregrine** 329, 331–333, 550
—, **Red-footed** 330, 333, 335, 550
—, **Saker** 332, 538, 550
Ficedula albicilla 421

Ficedula albicollis 419
— *hypoleuca* 419
— *mugimaki* 539
— *parva* 420
Fieldfare 394, 553
Finch, Citril 399, 555
—, **Trumpeter** 509, 555
Firecrest 425, 553
Flamingo, Chilean 539
—, **Greater** 539, 545
Flicker, Northern 539, 550
Flycatcher, Acadian 530, 550
—, **Alder** 530, 550
—, **Asian Brown** 421, 553
—, **Collared** 421, 554
—, **Mugimaki** 539, 554
—, **Pied** 419, 421, 554
—, **Red-breasted** 420, 554
—, **Spotted** 418, 421, 553
—, **Taiga** 420, 554
—, **Willow** 530
Fratercula arctica 110
— *cirrhata* 113
Fregata aquila 115
— *magnificens* 115
Fregetta grallaria 119
— *tropica* 119
Frigatebird, Ascension 115, 546
—, **Magnificent** 115, 546
Fringilla coelebs 494
— *montifringilla* 495
Fulica americana 252
— *atra* 249
Fulmar 98, 545
Fulmarus glacialis 98

G

Gadwall 36, 38, 42, 63, 543
Galerida cristata 362
Gallinago delicata 241
— *gallinago* 222
— *media* 241
Gallinula chloropus 248
Gallinule, Allen's 254, 546
—, **(American) Purple** 254, 546
Gannet 97, 546
Garganey 36, 38, 45, 66, 543
Garrulus glandarius 480
Gavia adamsii 85
— *arctica* 83
— *immer* 84
— *pacifica* 91
— *stellata* 82
Gelochelidon nilotica 169
Geokichla sibirica 396
Geothlypis trichas 528
Glareola maldivarum 227
— *nordmanni* 227
— *pratincola* 227
Godwit, Bar-tailed 186, 216, 547

INDEX

Godwit, Black-tailed .. *186*, **217**, 547
—, **Hudsonian** **228**, 547
Goldcrest **424**, 553
Goldeneye *37*, *50*, *73*, 544
—, **Barrow's** *73*, 544
Goldfinch **496**, 555
—, **American** *539*, 555
Goosander *36*, **53**, 544
Goose, Bar-headed *62*
—, **Barnacle** *23*, *28*, 543
—, **Bean** *23*, *30*, *31*, 543
—, **Brent** *23*, *26*, 543
—, **Cackling** *25*, 543
—, **Canada** *23*, *24*, 543
—, **Egyptian** *35*, 543
—, Emperor *62*
—, **Greylag** *23*, *29*, 543
—, **Lesser Canada** *25*
—, **Lesser White-fronted** ... *33*, 543
—, **Pink-footed** *23*, *31*, 543
—, **Red-breasted** *27*, 543
—, **Ross's** *62*, *538*, 543
—, **Snow** *23*, *33*, 543
—, **Swan** *539*
—, **Taiga Bean** *23*, *30*, *31*, 543
—, **Tundra Bean** ... *23*, *30*, *31*, 543
—, **Upland** *539*
—, **White-fronted** ... *23*, *32*, *33*, 543
Goshawk *323*, **325**, 546
Grebe, Black-necked *78*, **88**, 545
—, **Great Crested** *78*, **86**, 545
—, **Little** *78*, **90**, 545
—, **Pied-billed** **91**, 545
—, **Red-necked** *78*, **87**, 545
—, **Slavonian** *78*, **89**, 545
Greenfinch **497**, 555
Greenshank .. *186*, **212**, *243*, *244*, 548
Grosbeak, Evening **534**, 555
—, **Pine** **508**, 555
—, **Rose-breasted** **534**, 556
Grouse, Black **276**, 544
—, **Red** **274**, 544
Grus canadensis *270*
— *grus* *258*
Guillemot *107*, **108**, 549
—, **Black** *107*, **111**, 549
—, **Brünnich's** *107*, **113**, 549
Guineafowl, Helmeted *539*
Gull, American Herring
.... *126*, *127*, **158**, *159*, 548
—, **Audouin's** **157**, 548
—, **Black-headed**
.... *122*–*123*, *143*, **146**, *153*, 548
—, **Bonaparte's** **153**, 548
—, **Caspian** ... *125*–*129*, *137*, *138*, 549
—, **Common** *143*, **144**, *154*, 548
—, **Franklin's** **153**, 548
—, **Glaucous**
.... *124*, *126*, *127*, *139*, **140**, 548

Gull, Glaucous-winged
.... *127*, **156**, 548
—, **Great Black-backed**
.... *125*–*129*, **134**, 548
—, **Great Black-headed** **155**, 548
—, **Herring** *122*–*123*, *125*–*129*,
.... *130*, *138*, *159*, 548
—, **Iceland**
.... *124*, *126*, *127*, *139*, **141**, *142*, 548
—, **Ivory** **151**, 548
—, **Kumlien's** *126*, *127*, *139*, *141*, *142*
—, **Laughing** **152**, 548
—, **Lesser Black-backed**
.... *125*–*129*, **132**, *157*, 549
—, **Little** *143*, **150**, 548
—, **Mediterranean** *143*, **147**, 548
—, **Pallas's** *155*
—, **Ring-billed** **154**, 548
—, **Ross's** **151**, 548
—, **Sabine's** *143*, **149**, 548
—, **Slaty-backed** *127*, **156**, 549
—, **Slender-billed** **155**, 548
—, **Thayer's** .. *126*, *127*, *139*, *141*, *142*
—, **Vega** **159**, 548
—, **Yellow-legged**
.... *125*–*129*, **136**, *138*, 549
Gyps fulvus *322*
Gyrfalcon **331**, *332*, 550

H

Haematopus ostralegus *190*
Haliaeetus albicella *304*
— *leucocephalus* *322*
Harrier, Hen *316*, **317**, *319*, *320*, 546
—, **Marsh** *307*, **315**, *316*, 546
—, **Montagu's**
.... *303*, *316*, **318**, *319*, 546
—, **Northern** *316*, *320*, 546
—, **Pallid** *316*, *319*, 546
Hawfinch **493**, 555
Hawk, Harris's *302*
Helopsaltes certhiola *444*
Heron, Chinese Pond *269*, 545
—, **Great Blue** *268*, 545
—, **Green** *270*, 545
—, **Grey** *256*, **260**, 545
—, **Little Blue** *269*, 545
—, **Night-** **267**, 545
—, **Purple** *256*, **266**, 545
—, **Squacco** *257*, **268**, 545
Hesperiphona vespertina *534*
Hieraaetus pennatus *538*
Himantopus himantopus *193*
Hippolais icterina *445*
— *olivetorum* *446*
— *polyglotta* *445*
Hirundapus caudacutus *351*
Hirundo rustica *353*
Histrionicus histrionicus *74*

Hobby *303*, **328**, *333*, *335*, 550
Honey-buzzard *303*, *308*, **311**, 546
Hoopoe **339**, 550
Houbara, Asian *280*
Hydrobates leucorhoa *105*
— *monorhis* *119*
— *pelagicus* *105*
Hydrocoloeus minutus *150*
Hydroprogne caspia *168*
Hylocichla mustelina *398*

I

Ibis, Glossy *256*, **266**, 545
Ichthyaetus audouinii *157*
— *ichthyaetus* *155*
— *melanocephalus* *147*
Icterus galbula *536*
Iduna aedon *443*
— *caligata* *447*
— *pallida* *447*
— *rama* *447*
Irania gutturalis *415*
Ixobrychus exilis *268*
— *minutus* *267*
Ixoreus naevius *398*

J

Jackdaw *478*, *479*, **482**, 551
Jay *478*, *479*, **480**, 551
Junco hyemalis *535*
Junco, Dark-eyed **535**, 556
Jynx torquilla *344*

K

Kestrel *323*, **326**, *333*, *334*, 550
—, **American** **334**, 550
—, **Lesser** **334**, 550
Killdeer **231**, 547
Kingbird, Eastern **530**, 551
Kingfisher **337**, 550
—, **Belted** **537**, 550
Kinglet, Ruby-crowned **525**, 553
Kite, Black *307*, *320*, 546
—, Black-eared *320*
—, **Red** *303*, *307*, **314**, 546
Kittiwake *143*, **148**, 548
Knot *187*, **201**, 547
—, **Great** **239**, 547

L

Lagopus lagopus *274*
— *muta* *275*
Lanius collurio *460*
— *cristatus* *463*
— *excubitor* *459*
— *isabellinus* *462*
— *minor* *464*
— *nubicus* *464*
— *phoenicuroides* *462*
— *schach* *464*
— *senator* *461*

INDEX

Lapwing *188*, **197**, 547
—, **Sociable** **229**, 547
—, **White-tailed** **229**, 547
Lark, American Horned *359*
—, **Bimaculated** *358*, *363*, 551
—, **Black** *358*, *363*, 551
—, **Calandra** *358*, *363*, 551
—, **Crested** *358*, *362*, 551
—, **Lesser Short-toed** . *358*, *362*, 551
—, **Shore** *358*, *359*, 551
—, **Short-toed** *358*, *362*, 551
—, **Sky** *358*, *361*, *362*, 551
—, **White-winged** *358*, *363*, 551
—, **Wood** *358*, *360*, 551
Larus argentatus 130
— *atricilla* 152
— *audouinii* 157
— *cachinnans* 137
— *canus* 144
— *delawarensis* 154
— *fuscus* 132
— *genei* 155
— *glaucescens* 156
— *glaucoides* 141
— *hyperboreus* 140
— *ichthyaetus* 155
— *marinus* 134
— *melanocephalus* 147
— *michahellis* 136
— *minutus* 150
— *philadelphia* 153
— *pipixcan* 153
— *ridibundus* 146
— *schistisagus* 156
— *smithsonianus* 158
— *vegae* 159
Larvivora cyane 413
— *sibilans* 413
Laughingthrush, Red-winged 539
Leiothlypis peregrina 529
Leucophaeus atricilla 152
— *pipixcan* 153
Limnodromus griseus 245
— *scolopaceus* 245
Limosa haemastica 228
— *lapponica* 216
— *limosa* 217
Linaria cannabina 500
— *flavirostris* 501
Linnet **500**, 555
Locustella certhiola 444
— *fluviatilis* 444
— *lanceolata* 444
— *luscinioides* 429
— *naevia* 428
Lophodytes cucullatus 70
Lophophanes cristatus 470
Lophura nycthemera 539
Lovebird, Rosy-faced 539
Loxia curvirostra 506

Loxia leucoptera 508
— *pytyopsittacus* 507
Loxia scotica 507
Lullula arborea 360
Luscinia luscinia 414
— *megarhynchos* 401
— *svecica* 412
Lymnocryptes minimus 223
Lyrurus tetrix 276

M

Magpie *478*, *479*, **481**, 551
Mallard *36*, *38*, *40*, *63*, **65**, 543
Mareca americana 64
— *falcata* 65
— *penelope* 39
— *strepera* 42
Marmaronetta angustirostris 62
Martin, **Crag** *355*, 551
—, **House** *352*, 552
—, **Purple** *356*, 551
—, **Sand** *354*, 551
Megaceryle alcyon 537
Melanitta americana 75
— *deglandi* 75
— *fusca* 56
— *nigra* 57
— *perspicillata* 74
— *stejnegeri* 75
Melanocorypha bimaculata 363
— *calandra* 363
— *yeltoniensis* 363
Meleagris gallopavo 539
Melopsittacus undulatus 539
Melospiza melodia 533
Merganser, **Hooded** **70**, 544
—, **Red-breasted** *36*, **52**, 544
Mergellus albellus 51
Mergus merganser 53
— *serrator* 52
Merlin *323*, *327*, **333**, 550
Merops apiaster 340
— *persicus* 340
Milvus migrans 320
— *milvus* 314
Mimus polyglottos 531
Mniotilta varia 528
Mockingbird, **Northern** **531**, 553
Molothrus ater 536
Monticola saxatilis 416
— *solitarius* 416
Moorhen **248**, 546
Morus bassanus 97
Motacilla alba 372
— *cinerea* 376
— *citreola* 377
— *flava* 374
— *tschutschensis* 377
Murrelet, **Ancient** **113**, 549
—, **Long-billed** **113**, 549

Muscicapa dauurica 421
— *striata* 418
Myiopsitta monachus 539

N

Needle-tail, **White-throated**
 .... *351*, 550
Neophron percnopterus 322
Netta rufina 46
Night-heron *256*, **267**, 545
Nighthawk, **Common**
 .... *292*, **301**, 550
Nightingale *389*, **401**, *414*, 554
—, **Thrush** **414**, 554
Nightjar *292*, **300**, 550
—, **Egyptian** *292*, **301**, 550
—, **Red-necked** *292*, **301**, 550
Nucifraga caryocatactes 487
Numenius arquata 218
— *borealis* 240
— *hudsonicus* 219
— *minutus* 240
— *phaeopus* 219
Numida meleagris 539
Nutcracker *479*, **487**, 551
Nuthatch **474**, 553
—, **Red-breasted** **477**, 553
Nycticorax nycticorax 267

O

Oceanites oceanicus 105
Oceanodroma castro 119
— *jabejabe* 119
— *leucorhoa* 105
— *monorhis* 119
— *monteiroi* 119
Oenanthe deserti 411
— *hispanica* 410
— *isabellina* 411
— *leucopyga* 415
— *leucura* 415
— *melanoleuca* 410
— *oenanthe* 408
— *pleschanka* 410
Onychoprion aleuticus 173
— *anaethetus* 172
— *fuscatus* 172
Oreothlypis peregrina 529
Oriole, **Baltimore** **536**, 556
—, **Golden** **383**, 551
Oriolus oriolus 383
Osprey *303*, *309*, **310**, 546
Otis tarda 281
Otus scops 299
Ouzel, **Ring** **390**, 553
Ovenbird *527*, **529**, 556
Owl, **Barn** *292*, **293**, 550
—, Eurasian Eagle- *291*
—, **Hawk** **299**, 550
—, **Little** *292*, **295**, 550
—, **Long-eared** *292*, **297**, 550

INDEX

Owl, Scops **299**, 550
—, Short-eared *292, 296,* **550**
—, Snowy *292,* **298,** 550
—, Tawny *292,* **294,** 550
—, Tengmalm's **299**, 550
Oxyura jamaicensis 59
— leucocephala 59
Oystercatcher *188,* **190,** 546

P

Pagophila eburnea **151**
Pandion haliaetus 310
Panurus biarmicus 466
Parabuteo unicinctus *302*
Parakeet, Alexandrine *342*
—, Blue-crowned *539*
—, Monk *539*
—, Ring-necked **342**, 550
Parkesia noveboracensis **529**
Partridge, Chukar *272*
—, Grey **273**, 544
—, Red-legged *272,* **539,** 544
Parula, Northern **527**, 556
Parus ater 471
— caeruleus 468
— cristatus 470
— major 469
— montanus 473
— palustris 472
Passer domesticus 490
— hispaniolensis *509*
— montanus 491
Passerculus sandwichensis **533**
Passerella iliaca **533**
Passerina cyanea **534**
Pastor roseus 385
Pavo cristatus *539*
Peafowl, Indian *539*
Pelagodroma marina 118
Pelecanus crispus 92
— onocrotalus *539*
Pelican, Dalmatian **92**, 545
—, Great White **539**, 545
Perdix perdix 273
Peregrine *329, 331, 332, 333,* **550**
Periparus ater 471
Pernis apivorus 311
Petrel, Bermuda **117**, 545
—, Black-bellied Storm **119**, 544
—, Black-capped **117**, 545
—, Bulwer's **118**, 545
—, Cape Verde Storm **119**, 545
—, Desertas **116**, 545
—, Fea's **116**, 545
—, Leach's **105**, *119,* 545
—, Madeiran Storm **119**, 545
—, Monteiro's Storm **119**, 545
—, Soft-plumaged 116
—, Storm **105**, 544
—, Swinhoe's **119**, 545

Petrel, White-bellied Storm
 .... **119**, 544
—, White-faced Storm **118**, 544
—, Wilson's **105**, 544
—, Zino's **116**, 545
Petrochelidon pyrrhonota 356
Petronia petronia *509*
Phaethon aethereus 117
Phalacrocorax aristotelis 81
— auritus 92
— carbo 80
Phalarope, Grey *187,* **221,** 548
—, Red-necked *187,* **220,** *221,* 548
—, Wilson's **226**, 548
Phalaropus fulicarius **221**
— lobatus **220**
— tricolor **226**
Phasianus colchicus *278*
Pheasant **278**, 544
—, Golden **271**, 544
—, Lady Amherst's **271**, 544
—, Reeves's *539*
—, Silver *539*
Pheucticus ludovicianus **534**
Philomachus pugnax 208
Phoebe, Eastern **530**, 550
Phoenicopterus chilensis *523*
— roseus *523*
Phoenicurus moussieri 415
— ochruros 403
— phoenicurus 402
Phylloscopus bonelli 448
— borealis 451
— borealoides 451
— collybita 430
— coronatus 451
— fuscatus 449
— humei 452
— ibericus 449
— inornatus 452
— nitidus 450
— orientalis 448
— plumbeitarsus 450
— proregulus 452
— schwarzi 449
— sibilatrix 433
— tenellipes 451
— trochiloides 450
— trochilus 432
Pica pica 481
Picus viridis 345
Pigeon, Feral *283,* **284,** 549
—, Wood *283,* **286,** 549
Pinguinus impennis 106
Pinicola enucleator *508*
Pintail *36, 38,* **43,** *63,* 543
Pipilo erythrophthalmus **535**
Pipit, Blyth's *367, 370,* **371,** 554
—, Buff-bellied *367,* **369,** 555

Pipit, Meadow ... **365**, *367, 368,* 554
—, Olive-backed *367,* **369,** 554
—, Pechora *367, 368,* **369,** 554
—, Red-throated *367,* **368,** 555
—, Richard's *367,* **370,** 554
—, Rock **366**, *367, 369,* 555
—, Tawny *367, 370,* **371,** 554
—, Tree **364**, *367, 368, 369,* 554
—, Water *367,* **369,** 555
Piranga olivacea **535**
— rubra **535**
Platalea leucorodia 259
Plectrophenax nivalis *512*
Plegadis falcinellus 266
Plover, American Golden
 .... *230,* **231,** 547
—, Caspian *232,* **233,** 547
—, Golden *188,* **198,** *230, 231,* 547
—, Greater Sand *232,* **233,** 547
—, Grey *188,* **199,** 547
—, Kentish *188,* **193,** *232,* 547
—, Lesser Sand *232,* **233,** 547
—, Little Ringed *188,* **195,** 547
—, Pacific Golden *230,* **231,** 547
—, Ringed
 .... *187, 188,* **194,** *195, 232,* 547
—, Semipalmated *232,* **547**
—, Sociable 229
—, White-tailed 229
Pluvialis apricaria *198*
— dominica 230
— fulva 230
— squatarola *199*
Pochard *36, 47,* **63,** *71,* 544
Pochard, Red-crested **46**, 543
Podiceps auritus 89
— cristatus 86
— grisegena 87
— nigricollis 88
Podilymbus podiceps 91
Poecile montana 473
— palustris 472
Polysticta stelleri 73
Porphyrio alleni *254*
— martinica *254*
— porphyrio *254*
Porzana carolina 253
— parva 252
— porzana 251
— pusilla 253
Pratincole, Black-winged
 .... *226,* **227,** 548
—, Collared *226,* **227,** 548
—, Oriental *226,* **227,** 548
Progne subis 356
Prunella collaris 387
— modularis 380
— montanella 387
Psittacula eupatria *342*

573

INDEX

Psittacula krameri 342
Ptarmigan 275, 544
Pterodroma cahow 117
Pterodroma deserta 116
— *feae* 116
— *hasitata* 117
— *madeira* 116
— *mollis* 116
Ptyonoprogne rupestris 355
Puffin 107, 110, 549
—, **Tufted** 113, 549
Puffinus baroli 103
— *gravis* 101
— *griseus* 99
— *lherminieri* 545
— *mauretanicus* 103
— *puffinus* 103
— *yelkouan* 103
Pyrrhocorax pyrrhocorax 487
Pyrrhula pyrrhula 492

Q
Quail 279, 544

R
Rail, Sora 253, 546
—, **Water** 250, 546
Rallus aquaticus 250
Raven 478, 479, 484, 486, 551
Razorbill 107, 109, 549
Recurvirostra avosetta 192
Redhead 71, 544
Redpoll, Arctic 503–504, 555
—, **Common** 503–504, 555
—, **Lesser** 503–504, 555
—, **Mealy** 503–504, 555
Redshank 186, 210, 244, 548
—, **Spotted** 186, 211, 548
Redstart 389, 402, 554
—, **American** 527, 556
—, **Black** 393, 554
—, **Moussier's** 415, 554
Redwing 395, 553
Reedling, Bearded 466
Regulus calendula 525
— *ignicapilla* 425
— *regulus* 424
Remiz pendulinus 477
Rhodostethia rosea 151
Riparia riparia 354
Rissa tridactyla 148
Robin 389, 400, 553
—, **American** 398, 553
—, **Rufous-tailed** 413, 554
—, **Rufous-tailed Scrub** 414, 553
—, **Siberian Blue** 413, 554
—, **White-throated** 415, 554
Roller 341, 550
Rook 478, 479, 484, 485, 551
Rosefinch, Common 505, 555
Rubythroat, Siberian 413, 554
Ruff 187, 208, 547

S
Sanderling 183, 187, 200, 547
Sandgrouse, Pallas's 284, 549
Sandpiper, Baird's 237, 547
—, **Broad-billed** 236, 547
—, **Buff-breasted** 240, 547
—, **Common** 187, 215, 242, 548
—, **Curlew** 187, 205, 237, 547
—, **Green** 187, 214, 243, 548
—, **Least** 236, 547
—, **Marsh** 243, 548
—, **Pectoral** 238, 547
—, **Purple** 187, 204, 547
—, **Semipalmated** 235, 234, 547
—, **Sharp-tailed** 238, 547
—, **Solitary** 243, 548
—, **Spotted** 242, 548
—, **Stilt** 239, 547
—, **Terek** 242, 548
—, **Upland** 240, 547
—, **Western** 235, 234, 547
—, **White-rumped** 237, 547
—, **Wood** 187, 213, 548
Sandplover, Greater ... 232, 233, 547
—, **Lesser** 232, 233, 547
Sapsucker, Yellow-bellied ... 537, 550
Saxicola maurus 406
— *rubetra* 404
— *rubicola (torquatus)* 405
— *stejnegeri* 406
Sayornis phoebe 530
Scaup 37, 49, 63, 68, 544
Scaup, Lesser 68, 544
Scolopax rusticola 224
Scoter, Black 75, 544
—, **Common** 37, 57, 75, 544
—, **Siberian** 75
—, **Stejneger's** 75, 544
—, **Surf** 37, 74, 544
—, **Velvet** 37, 56, 75, 544
—, **White-winged** 75, 544
Seiurus aurocapilla 529
Serin 399, 555
Serinus canaria 539
— *serinus* 399
Setophaga aestiva 528
— *americana* 527
— *castanea* 527
— *citrina* 528
— *coronata* 526
— *fusca* 527
— *magnolia* 527
— *pensylvanica* 527
— *petechia* 528
— *ruticilla* 527
— *striata* 526
— *tigrina* 526
Shag 78, 81, 92, 546
Shearwater, Audubon's 545
—, **Balearic** 103, 545

Shearwater, Barolo 103
—, **Cory's** 101, 545
—, **Great** 101, 545
—, **Macaronesian** 103, 545
—, **Manx** 103, 545
—, **Scopoli's** 101, 545
—, **Sooty** 99, 545
—, **Yelkouan** 103, 545
Shelduck 34, 36, 543
—, **Ruddy** 35, 543
Shelduck, South African 539
Shorelark 358, 359, 551
Shoveler 36, 38, 41, 63, 543
Shrike, Brown 462, 463, 551
—, **Daurian** 462, 463, 551
—, **Great Grey** 459, 551
—, **Isabelline** 462
—, **Lesser Grey** 464, 551
—, **Long-tailed** 464, 551
—, **Masked** 464, 551
—, **Red-backed**
  .... 458, 460, 462, 463, 551
—, **Red-tailed** 462
—, **Steppe Grey** 459
—, **Turkestan** 462, 463, 551
—, **Woodchat** 461, 551
Sibirionetta formosa 67
Siskin 488, 498, 555
Sitta canadensis 477
— *europaea* 474
Skua, Arctic 176, 180–182, 549
—, **Brown** 179, 549
—, **Great** 179, 180, 181, 549
—, **Long-tailed** 178, 180–182, 549
—, **Pomarine**
  .... 174–175, 177, 180–182, 549
—, **South Polar** 179, 549
Skylark 358, 361, 362, 551
Smew 37, 51, 544
Snipe 187, 222, 223, 241, 548
—, **Great** 241, 548
—, **Jack** 187, 223, 548
—, **Wilson's** 241, 548
Somateria mollissima 58
— *spectabilis* 72
Sora 253, 546
Sparrow, House 490, 509, 554
—, **Lark** 532, 533, 556
—, **Red Fox** 532, 533, 555
—, **Rock** 509, 554
—, **Savannah** 532, 533, 556
—, **Song** 532, 533, 555
—, **Spanish** 509, 554
—, **Tree** 491, 554
—, **White-crowned** 532, 556
—, **White-throated** 532, 556
Sparrowhawk 303, 323, 324, 546
Spatula clypeata 41
— *cyanoptera* 62
— *discors* 67
— *querquedula* 45

INDEX

Sphyrapicus varius **537**
Spinus spinus **498**
— *tristis* *539*
Spoonbill 257, 259, **545**
Starling **384**, 553
—, Daurian *539*, 553
—, **Rose-coloured** **385**, 553
Stercorarius antarcticus **179**
— *longicaudus* **178**
— *maccormicki* **179**
— *parasiticus* **176**
— *pomarinus* **177**
— *skua* **179**
Sterna acuflavida **173**
— *bengalensis* **171**
— *dougallii* **164**
— *elegans* **171**
— *forsteri* **169**
— *hirundo* **162**
— *maxima* **170**
— *paradisaea* **163**
— *sandvicensis* **165**
Sternula albifrons **161**
— *antillarum* **161**
Stilt, Black-winged 188, 193, 547
Stint, Little 187, 207, 234, 235, 547
—, **Long-toed** **236**, 547
—, **Red-necked** 234, 235, 547
Stint, Temminck's
.... 187, 206, 234, 547
Stone-curlew **189**, 546
Stonechat 389, 405, 406, 554
—, Caspian *406*
—, Siberian 406–407, 554
—, Stejneger's 406–407, 554
Stork, Black 257, **265**, 545
—, **White** 257, **265**, 545
Streptopelia decaocto **288**
— *orientalis* **290**
— *turtur* **289**
Strix aluco **294**
Sturnus vulgaris **384**
Sula leucogaster **118**
— *sula* **118**
Surnia ulula **299**
Swallow 353, 355, 551
—, Cliff **356**, 552
—, **Red-rumped** 355, 552
—, **Tree** **356**, 551
Swamphen, Western 254, 546
Swan, Bewick's 20, **22**, 543
—, Black *62*
—, Mute 19, **22**, 543
—, Trumpeter *62*
—, Whistling *20*
—, **Whooper** 20, 21, **22**, 543
Swift 349, 350, 351, 550
—, **Alpine** **350**, 550
—, **Chimney** **351**, 550
—, **Little** **351**, 550

Swift, Needle-tailed **351**
—, Pacific **351**, 550
—, **Pallid** **350**, 550
—, **White-rumped** **351**, 550
Sylvia atricapilla **434**
— *borin* **435**
— *cantillans* **454**
— *communis* **436**
— *conspicillata* **455**
— *crassirostris* **456**
— *curruca* **437**
— *hortensis* **456**
— *melanocephala* **457**
— *nana* **453**
— *nisoria* **453**
— *ruppeli* **457**
— *sarda* **453**
— *subalpina* **454**
— *undata* **438**
Synthliboramphus antiquus **113**
Syrmaticus reevesii *539*
Syrrhaptes paradoxus **284**

T

Tachybaptus ruficollis **90**
Tachycineta bicolor **356**
Tachymarptis melba **350**
Tadorna cana *539*
— *ferruginea* **35**
— *tadorna* **34**
Tanager, Scarlet **535**, 556
—, **Summer** **535**, 556
Tarsiger cyanurus **412**
Tattler, Grey-tailed **243**, 548
Teal 36, 38, **46**, 66, 543
—, **Baikal** 66, **67**, 543
—, **Blue-winged** 36, 66, **67**, 543
—, Cinnamon *62*
—, **Green-winged** 66, 543
Tern, Aleutian **173**, 549
—, **Arctic** 160, **163**, 549
—, **Black** 160, **166**, 167, 549
—, **Bridled** 172, 538, 549
—, **Cabot's** **173**, 549
—, **Caspian** 160, 168, **170**, 549
—, **Common** 160, **162**, 169, 549
—, **Elegant** **171**, 549
—, **Forster's** **169**, 549
—, **Gull-billed** 160, **169**, 549
—, **Least** **161**, 549
—, **Lesser Crested** **171**, 549
—, **Little** 160, **161**, 549
—, **Roseate** 160, **164**, 549
—, **Royal** **170**, 549
—, **Sandwich** 160, 165, 169, **173**, 549
—, **Sooty** 172, 549
—, **West African Crested** *170*
—, **Whiskered** 160, 167, **168**, 549
—, **White-winged Black**
.... 160, **167**, 549

Tetrao tetrix **276**
— *urogallus* **277**
Tetrax tetrax **280**
Thalassarche chlororhynchos **114**
— *melanophris* **114**
Thalasseus acuflavidus **173**
— *albididorsalis* *170*
— *bengalensis* **171**
— *elegans* **171**
— *maximus* *170*
— *sandvicensis* **165**
Thectocercus acuticaudatus *539*
Thrasher, Brown **531**, 553
Thrush, Black-throated **396**, 553
—, **Blue Rock** **416**, 554
—, **Dusky** **397**, 553
—, **Eyebrowed** **397**, 553
—, **Grey-cheeked** **399**, 553
—, **Hermit** **399**, 553
—, **Mistle** **393**, 553
—, **Naumann's** **397**, 553
—, **Red-throated** **396**, 553
—, **Rock** **416**, 554
—, **Siberian** **396**, 553
—, **Song** **392**, 553
—, **Swainson's** **399**, 553
—, **Varied** **398**, 553
—, **White's** **397**, 553
—, **Wood** **398**, 553
Tichodroma muraria **477**
Tit, Bearded **466**, 551
—, **Blue** **468**, 551
—, **Coal** **471**, 551
—, **Crested** **470**, 551
—, **Great** **469**, 551
—, **Long-tailed** **467**, 552
—, **Marsh** 434, **472**, 473, 551
—, **Penduline** **477**, 551
—, **Willow** 472, **473**, 551
Towhee, Eastern **535**, 556
Toxostoma rufum **531**
Treecreeper 475, **476**, 553
—, **Short-toed** **476**, 553
Tringa brevipes **243**
— *erythropus* **211**
— *flavipes* **244**
— *glareola* **213**
— *melanoleuca* **244**
— *nebularia* **212**
— *ochropus* **214**
— *solitaria* **243**
— *stagnatilis* **243**
— *totanus* **210**
Trochalopteron formosum *539*
Troglodytes troglodytes **381**
Tropicbird, Red-billed **117**, 545
Turdus atrogularis **396**
— *eunomus* **397**
— *iliacus* **395**
— *merula* **391**

INDEX

Turdus migratorius 398
— *naumanni* 397
— *obscurus* 397
— *philomelos* 392
— *pilaris* 394
— *ruficollis* 396
— *torquatus* 390
— *viscivorus* 393
Turkey, Wild 539
Turnstone 187, 188, **191**, 547
Twite **501**, 555
Tyrannus tyrannus 530
Tyto alba 293

U

Upupa epops 339
Uria aalge **108**
— *lomvia* **113**

V

Vanellus gregarius 229
— *leucurus* 229
— *vanellus* **197**
Veery **399**, 553
Vermivora chrysoptera 529
— *cyanoptera* 529
Vireo flavifrons 525
— *olivaceus* 525
— *philadelphicus* 525
Vireo, Philadelphia **525**, 551
Vireo, Red-eyed **525**, 551
Vireo, Yellow-throated **525**, 551
Vulture, Egyptian **322**, 546
—, **Griffon** **322**, 546

W

Wagtail, Amur *373*
—, Ashy-headed *375*
—, Black-headed *375*
—, Blue-headed *375*
—, 'Channel' *375*
—, **Citrine** **377**, 554
—, **Eastern Yellow** **377**, 554
—, **Grey** **376**, 554
—, Grey-headed *375*
—, Iberian (Yellow) *375*
—, Masked *373*
—, **Pied** 372, *373*, 554
—, **White** **372**–**373**, 554
—, **Yellow** **374**, *375*, **377**, 554
Wallcreeper **477**, 553
Warbler, Aquatic **442**, 552
—, **Arctic** **442**, 552
—, **Asian Desert** **453**, 553
—, **Barred** **453**, 552
—, **Bay-breasted** **527**, 556
—, **Black-and-white** 527, **528**, 556
—, **Blackburnian** **527**, 556
—, **Blackpoll** **526**, 527, 556

Warbler, Blue-winged
.... 527, **529**, 556
—, **Blyth's Reed** *440*, **441**, 552
—, **Booted** 446, **447**, 552
—, **Canada** 527, **529**, 556
—, **Cape May** **526**, 527, 556
—, **Cetti's** **429**, 552
—, **Chestnut-sided** **527**, 556
—, **Dartford** **438**, 553
—, **Desert** **453**, 553
—, **Dusky** **449**, 552
—, **Eastern Bonelli's** **448**, 552
—, **Eastern Crowned** **451**, 552
—, **Eastern Olivaceous**
.... 446, **447**, 552
—, **Eastern Orphean** **456**, 553
—, **Fan-tailed** **443**, 552
—, **Garden** **435**, 552
—, **Golden-winged** 527, **529**, 556
—, **Grasshopper** **428**, **444**, 552
—, **Great Reed** **442**, 552
—, **Green** **450**, 552
—, **Greenish** **450**, *451*, 552
—, **Hooded** 527, **528**, 556
—, **Hume's** **452**, 552
—, **Icterine** **445**, 552
—, **Lanceolated** **444**, 553
—, **Magnolia** **527**, 556
—, **Marmora's** **453**, 553
—, **Marsh** *440*, **441**, 552
—, **Melodious** **445**, 552
—, **Moltoni's Subalpine**
.... **454**, *455*, 553
—, **Myrtle** **526**, 527, 556
—, **Olive-tree** **446**, 552
—, **Paddyfield** *440*, **443**, 552
—, **Pale-legged Leaf** **451**, 552
—, **Pallas's** **452**, 552
—, **Pallas's Grasshopper** **444**, 552
—, **Radde's** **449**, 552
—, **Reed** 427, *440*, **443**, 552
—, **River** **444**, 552
—, **Rüppell's** **457**, 553
—, **Sakhalin Leaf** **451**, 552
—, **Sardinian** **457**, 553
—, **Savi's** **429**, 552
—, **Sedge** 426, **442**, 552
—, **Spectacled** **455**, 553
—, **Subalpine** **454**, *455*, 553
—, **Sykes's** 446, **447**, 552
—, **Tennessee** 527, **529**, 556
—, **Thick-billed** **443**, 552
—, **Two-barred Greenish** **450**, 552
—, **Western Bonelli's** **448**, 552
—, **Western Orphean** **456**, 553
—, **Willow** **431**, **432**, 552
—, **Wilson's** 527, **528**, 556

Warbler, Wood **433**, 552
—, **Yellow** 527, **528**, 556
—, **Yellow-browed** **452**, 552
—, **Yellow-rumped** **526**, 556
Waterthrush, Northern **529**, 556
Waxwing **386**, 551
—, **Cedar** **387**, 551
Wheatear 389, **408**, *411*, 554
—, Black 415
—, **Desert** **409**, *411*, 554
—, **Eastern Black-eared**
.... **409**, *410*, 554
—, Greenland *409*
—, **Isabelline** **409**, *411*, 554
—, **Pied** **409**, *410*, 554
—, **Western Black-eared**
.... **409**, *410*, 554
—, **White-crowned Black** ... **415**, 554
Whimbrel 186, **219**, 547
—, **Hudsonian** **219**, 547
—, **Little** **240**, 547
Whinchat **404**, 554
Whitethroat **436**, *455*, 553
—, Central Asian Lesser *437*
—, **Lesser** **437**, 552
—, Siberian Lesser *437*
Wigeon 36, **38**, **39**, 63, **64**, 543
—, **American** 36, 63, **64**, 543
Woodcock 187, **224**, 548
Woodlark **358**, 360, 551
Woodpecker, Great Spotted
.... **346**, 550
—, **Green** **345**, 550
—, **Lesser Spotted** **347**, 550
Woodpigeon **283**, 286, 549
Wren **381**–**382**, 553
Wryneck **344**, 550

X

Xanthocephalus xanthocephalus
.... 539
Xema sabini **149**
Xenus cinereus 242

Y

Yellowhammer **514**, *523*, 540
Yellowlegs, Greater **244**, 548
—, **Lesser** **244**, 548
Yellowthroat, Common **528**, 556

Z

Zapornia parva 252
— *pusilla* 253
Zenaida macroura 290
Zonotrichia albicollis 532
Zonotrichia leucophrys 532
Zoothera aurea (dauma) 397

About the authors

This book has been several years in the making: an ambition of **WILD***Guides* only now made possible by advances in digital photography and graphic design.

Rob Hume, freelance writer and editor for 35 years and editor of RSPB publications from 1983 to 2009, was Chairman of the British Birds Rarities Committee, and has led wildlife holidays in the UK, Europe and Africa.

Robert Still, co-founder and publishing director of **WILD***Guides*, is an ecologist and widely travelled naturalist. His design philosophy and exceptional skills in computer graphics have been crucial to the concept, development and production of the **WILD***Guides Britain's Wildlife* series.

Andy Swash has been involved professionally in nature conservation since 1977 and is managing director of **WILD***Guides*. A renowned photographer, he leads photographic tours worldwide, and has devised, co-authored and edited many other books.

Hugh Harrop founded the ecotourism business, Shetland Wildlife, and is one of Shetland's top birders and naturalists. His award-winning photographs have been published throughout Europe and North America.

David Tipling, one of the world's most widely published wildlife photographers, is author or commissioned photographer for many books and writes for leading wildlife and photographic magazines.